# PERFORMANCE OF COMPUTER COMMUNICATION SYSTEMS

# PERFORMANCE OF COMPUTER COMMUNICATION SYSTEMS

## A Model-Based Approach

### BOUDEWIJN R. HAVERKORT
*Rheinisch-Westfälische Technische*
*Hochschule Aachen, Germany*

John Wiley & Sons, Ltd
Chichester • New York • Weinheim • Brisbane • Singapore • Toronto

*Other Wiley Editorial Offices*

New York • Weinheim • Brisbane • Singapore • Toronto

*Library of Congress Cataloguing in Publication Data*

Haverkort, Boudewijn R.
    Performance of computer communication systems : a model-based
approach / Boudewijn R. Haverkort.
        p.   cm.
    Includes bibliographical references and index.
    ISBN 0–471–97228–2  (alk.  paper)
    1. Computer networks—Evaluation.  2. Electronic digital
computers—Evaluation.  3. Queuing theory.  4. Telecommunication
systems—Evaluation.  5. Stochastic processes.  I. Title.
    TK5105.5.H375   1998
004.6—dc21                                                    98–27222
                                                                CIP

*British Library Cataloguing in Publication Data*

A catalogue record for this book is available from the British Library

ISBN 0 471 97228 2

Printed and bound by Antony Rowe Ltd, Eastbourne

In memory of my father
*Johannes Hermannus Hendrikus Haverkort*

# Contents

# V   Simulation                                                      407

# VI   Appendices                                                     439

# Preface

WHEN I began lecturing a course on the performance of communication systems in the electrical engineering department of the University of Twente in the fall of 1990, I had difficulty in finding a suitable textbook for this course. Many books were too much mathematically oriented, others used only a very limited set of evaluation techniques, e.g., only the M|G|1 queue. I therefore decided to use a collection of book chapters, recent survey articles and some research papers, thereby focusing on the performance evaluation of network access mechanisms. During the semester, however, I began to realise that using material from different sources is not the most adequate. To overcome this inadequacy, I started to develop my own course material in the years that followed.

In 1993 I also started lecturing a course on the performance evaluation of computer systems in the computer science department of the University of Twente, traditionally focused on scheduling techniques, queueing networks and multiprogramming models. Trying to organise my teaching more efficiently, I decided to extend my course notes so that they could be used for both classes: an introductory part on stochastic processes and single-server queues, followed by specialisations towards communication networks and computer systems. By mid 1995, the course notes had evolved into a booklet of some 200 pages.

After having moved to the RWTH-Aachen in the fall of 1995, I started two new courses for computer science students, dealing with a superset of the themes I already addressed at the University of Twente. The evolving course notes for these two courses resulted in the book you are now reading.

## Prerequisites

Many performance evaluation textbooks require a rather strong mathematical background of the readers, e.g., by the extensive use of Laplace transforms. In this book, the use of Laplace and $z$-transforms is completely avoided (except for two non-critical issues in Part II); however, it is assumed that the readers are familiar with the basic principles of mathematical analysis, linear algebra, numerical mathematics, and probability theory and statistics (some appendices are included as a refresher). Stochastic processes are treated in this book from first principles; background knowledge in this area is therefore not required.

It should be well understood that this is not a book on queueing theory, nor on stochastic processes, although both will be dealt with. Instead, the aim of the book is to *apply queueing theory and stochastic processes for the evaluation of the performance of computer and communication systems.* In order to address interesting applications, I assume that the readers are familiar with the basic principles of computer architecture [19, 128, 223, 275], operating systems [261, 276, 278] and computer networks [265, 277, 284].

# How to use this book?

The book consists of five main parts, as sketched in Figure 1, which will be introduced below.

**I. Performance modelling with stochastic processes.** Part I starts with a chapter on the aim of model-based performance evaluation. Then, a number of basic performance modelling building blocks are addressed, as well as generally valid rules, such as Little's law in Chapter 2. Chapter 3 then presents background material in the field of stochastic processes, most notably about renewal processes and continuous-time Markov chains.

**II. Single-server queueing models.** In the second part, a wide variety of single-server queueing models is addressed, which can be used to evaluate the performance of system parts, such as network access mechanisms or CPU schedulers. In Chapter 4 we discuss the simplest class of queues, the M|M|1 queues, followed by the slightly more general M|G|1 queues with various types of scheduling in Chapters 5 and 6. We then continue, in Chapter 7, with the analysis of the G|M|1 and G|G|1 queueing models. Although the latter analyses are interesting from a theoretical viewpoint, they are less useful from a practical point of view. We therefore present PH|PH|1 queues, for which efficient matrix-geometric solution techniques exist, in Chapter 8. Finally, we discuss polling models and applications in the area of token-ring communication networks in Chapter 9.

**III. Queueing network models.** In the third part of the book, we study networks of queues. These are especially useful when complex systems consisting of many interacting parts are studied, such as complete computer systems or communication networks. We start, in Chapter 10, with the evaluation of open queueing networks. We address both well-known exact methods (Jackson networks) and approximate methods. In Chapter 11

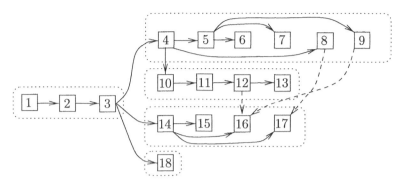

Figure 1: The organisation of the books in 5 parts and 18 chapters

we then continue with the study of load-independent closed queueing networks, including the discussion of computational algorithms such as the convolution method, mean-value analysis and various approximation techniques. These are extended in Chapter 12 to include load-dependent queueing networks in order to handle hierarchical decomposition as a method to cope with model complexity. Finally, in Chapter 13, queueing networks with multiple customer classes and various types of stations are discussed.

**IV. Stochastic Petri net models.** In the fourth part of the book, stochastic Petri nets (SPNs) are discussed as a representative of Markovian techniques to evaluate large performance models. SPNs provide more modelling flexibility than queueing networks, however, most often at the cost of a more expensive solution. We present the basic SPN formalism in Chapter 14, including the computation of invariants and the derivation of the underlying Markov chain. Chapter 15 is then devoted to the numerical solution of large Markov chains, as they arise from SPN models. Both steady-state and transient analysis methods are presented. In Chapter 16 we then present four larger SPN-based performance evaluation case studies. In Chapter 17 we finally address a special class of SPNs that uses the efficient matrix-geometric solution method of Chapter 8.

**V. Simulation.** The fifth part comprises only Chapter 18, in which the basic principles and statistical tools for stochastic discrete-event simulations are discussed.

A final part consisting of **appendices** on probability theory and Laplace transforms completes the book.

In Figure 1 we sketch an overview of the book chapters and their relation ($A \rightarrow B$ expresses that Chapter A is a prerequisite to understand Chapter B; dashed arrows express a similar but less strong relation). Given this ordering, various trajectories can be followed through the book:

- **Single-server queues:** 1–2–3–4–5–6–7–(8)–9;

- **Queueing networks:** 1–2–3–4–10–11–12–13;

- **Stochastic Petri nets:** 1–2–3–14–15–16–(8–17);

- **General introduction:** 1–2–3–4–5–(6)–10–(11–14–16)–18;

- **Advanced course:** (1–2–3–4–5)–6–7–8–9–(10)–11–12–13–(14)–15–16–17;

Regarding the used notation, the following remarks are in place. Normally, mathematical variables are denoted in lower case ($x$ or $\alpha$). Sets are indicated using calligrahic letters ($\mathcal{S}$), except for the sets of natural numbers ($I\!N$) and real numbers ($I\!R$). Vectors are written as underlined lower case ($\underline{v}$ or $\underline{\pi}$) and matrices as boldface upper case ($\mathbf{M}$). Random variables are given in upper case, their realisations as normal mathematical variables, and their estimators have a tilde ($\tilde{X}$ is an estimator for the random variable $X$). Finally, the expectation and variance of a stochastic variable $X$ are denoted as $E[X]$ and $\text{var}[X]$, respectively.

## On the use of tools

Throughout the book many numerical examples are presented. In the simpler cases, these examples have been performed "by hand" or with the computer algebra package MAPLE [129]. The more involved queueing network and stochastic Petri net models have been built and evaluated with the tools SHARPE [250, 249] and SPNP [53], both developed at Duke University. All quasi-birth-death models have been created and evaluated using the tool SPN2MGM [118, 125] developed at the RWTH-Aachen.

To really understand performance evaluation techniques, example modelling studies should be performed, preferably also using modern tools. Many performance evaluation tools can be used free of charge for teaching purposes. Please contact the "tool authors" or the web-site below for more details.

## Get in touch!

For more information on the use of this book, including updates, errata, new exercises, tools and other interesting links, visit the following web-site:

http://www-lvs.informatik.rwth-aachen.de/pccs/

or mail the author at haverkort@informatik.rwth-aachen.de.

# Acknowledgements

I have been working on this book for a long time. Throughout this period, I have had the pleasure to cooperate with many researchers and students, most notably at the University of Twente and the RWTH-Aachen, but also from many other places around the globe, both from industry and academia. All of them have contributed to my understanding of performance evaluation of computer communication systems, for which I am very grateful. I would like to thank a number of people explicitly: Ignas Niemegeers (University of Twente) for his long-time encouragement and the many stimulating discussions; Leonard Franken (KPN Research), Geert Heijenk (Ericsson) and Aad van Moorsel (Bell Laboratories) for the joint work on model-based performance evaluation since the beginning of the 1990's; Bill Henderson (University of Adelaide), John Meyer (University of Michigan), Bill Sanders (University of Illinois) and Kishor Trivedi (Duke University) for being my overseas collaborators and hosts; Henrik Bohnenkamp and Alexander Ost for their support and collaboration since I have been working at the RWTH-Aachen.

Aad van Moorsel and Henrik Bohnenkamp read the complete manuscript; their suggestions and comments improved the book substantially. Many of the presented exercises have been developed in close cooperation with Henrik Bohnenkamp as well. Of course, the final responsibility for any flaws or shortcomings lies with me.

To write a book requires more than just scientific support. The endless encouragement and love of my wife Ellen ter Brugge, my daughter Isabelle and my son Arthur cannot be expressed in words. Without them, there would not have been a "higher aim" to complete this book. My parents, Ans and Henk Haverkort, encouraged me to study ever since I attended school, providing me with the opportunities they never had. Regrettably, my father has not been given time to witness the completion of this book. I dedicate this book to him.

Boudewijn R. Haverkort

Aachen, July 1998

# Part I

# Performance modelling with stochastic processes

# Chapter 1

# Introduction

I̠N this chapter we discuss the aim of and the approach normally followed in performance evaluation of computer and communication systems in Section 1.1. A classification of solution techniques is presented in Section 1.2. The fact that we will need *stochastic* models is motivated in Section 1.3. As a special case of these, we then introduce queueing models in Section 1.4. Finally, in Section 1.5, we discuss the use of software tools for model construction and solution.

## 1.1 Performance evaluation: aim and approach

Performance evaluation aims at forecasting system behaviour in a quantitative way. Whenever new systems are to be built or existing systems have to be reconfigured or adapted, performance evaluation can be employed to predict the impact of architectural or implementation changes on the system performance.

An important aspect of performance evaluation is *performance measurement* or *monitoring*. By monitoring the timing of certain important events in a system, insight can be obtained in which system operations take most time, or which system components are heavily loaded and which are not. Notice that a prerequisite for performance measurement is the availability of a system that can be observed (measured). If such a system is not available, measurement cannot be employed. As can easily be understood, performance measurement will occur much more often in cases where existing systems have to be altered than in cases where new systems have to be designed. Another important aspect of performance measurement is the fact that the system that is studied will have to be changed slightly in order to perform the measurements, i.e., extra code might be required to generate time-stamps and to write event logs. Of course, these alterations themselves affect the system performance. This is especially the case when employing *software monitoring*, i.e., when all the necessary extra functionality for the monitoring process is implemented in software. When employing *hardware monitoring* extra hardware is used to detect certain events, e.g., a computer address bus is monitored to measure the time between certain addresses passing by, thus giving information on the execution time of parts of programs. As a combination of hard- and software monitoring, *hybrid monitoring* can also be employed. In all cases, one sees that system-specific software or hardware is needed, of which the development is very costly.

For the above mentioned cost and availability reasons, performance monitoring can often not be employed. Instead, in those cases, one can use *model-based performance evaluation*. This proceeds as follows. If there is no system available that can be used for performing measurements, we should at least have an unambiguous *system description*. From this system description we can then make an abstract *model*. According to [136]:

> *"a model is a small-scale reproduction or representation of something"*.

In the context of performance evaluation, a model is an abstract description, based on (mathematically) well-defined concepts, of a system in terms of its components and their interactions, as well as its interactions with the environment. The environment part in the model describes how the system is being used, by humans or by other systems. Very often, this part of the model is called the system *workload model*. The process of designing models is called modelling. According to [136]:

> *"modelling is the art of making models"*.

This definition stresses a key issue in model-based performance evaluation, namely the fact that developing models for computer-communication systems is a very challenging task. Indeed, performance modelling requires many engineering skills, but these alone are not enough. There is no such thing as a generally applicable model "cookbook" from which we can learn how to built the right performance models for all types of computer-communication systems. Surely, there are generally applicable guidelines, but these are no more than that. Depending on the situation at hand, a good model (where good needs to be defined) can range from being extremely simple to being utterly complex.

Let us now come to a few of the guidelines in constructing performance models. The choice for a particular model heavily depends on the *performance measure of interest*. The measure of interest should be chosen such that its value answers the questions one has about the system. The measures of interest ar either *user-oriented* (sometimes also called task-oriented) or *system-oriented*. Examples of the former are the (job) response time $(R)$, the throughput of jobs $(X)$, the job waiting time $(W)$ and the job service time $(S)$. In any case, these measures tell something about the performance of system requests (jobs) as issued by system users. As for system-oriented measures, one can think of the number of jobs in the system $(N)$ or in some system queue $(N_q)$, or about the utilisation of system components $(\rho)$. These measures are not so much related to what users perceive as system performance; they merely say something about the internal organisation of the system under study. Very often, system-oriented measures can be related to user-oriented measures, e.g., via Little's law (see Chapter 2). In the course of this book, we will address all these measures in more detail.

Once we have decided to use a particular measure, we have to answer the question how detailed we want to determine it. Do average values suffice, or are variances also of interest, or do we even need complete distributions? This degree of detail clearly has its influence on the model to be developed. As an example of this, for deriving the *average* response time in a multiprogrammed computer system, a different model will be needed than for deriving the probability that the response time is larger than some threshold value. This aspect is related to the required *accuracy* of the measure of interest. If only a rough estimate of a particular measure is required, one might try to keep the model as simple as possible. If a more accurate determination is required, it might be needed to include many system details in the model. It is important to point out at this place the fact that in many circumstances where model-based performance evaluation is employed, there is great uncertainty about many system aspects and parameters. However, for the model to be solvable, one needs exact input. In such cases, it seems to be preferable to make a fairly abstract model with mild assumptions, rather than make a detailed model for which one cannot provide the required input parameters. In any case, the outcome of the model should be interpreted taking into account the accuracy of the input; a model is as good as its input!

Very often, not a single model will be made, but a set of models, one for each design alternative. Also, these models can have parameters that are still unknown or that are subject to uncertainty. The analysis and evaluation phases to follow should be performed for all the model alternatives and parameter values.

Once a model has been *constructed*, it should be analysed. This analysis can proceed by using a variety of *techniques*; we give an overview of the existing solution techniques in the next section. In many practical cases, model construction and analysis should be supported by software *tools*. Real computer and communication systems are generally too complex to be modelled and analysed with just pencil and paper, although this might not be totally true for some quick initial calculations.

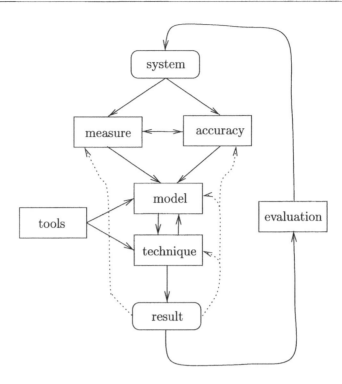

Figure 1.1: The model-based performance evaluation cycle. The dashed arrows denote feedback loops; the normal arrows indicate the procedure order.

The numerical outcome of the model solution should be interpreted with care. First of all, one should ask the question whether the numerical outcomes do provide the answer to the initially posed question. If not, one might need to change to another measure of interest, or one might require a different accuracy. Also, it might be required to use a different solution technique or to change the model slightly. Finally, if the numerical solution does give an answer to the posed question, this answer should be interpreted in terms of the operation of the modelled system. This interpretation, or the whole process that leads to this interpretation, is called *system (performance) evaluation*. The evaluation might point to specific system parts that need further investigation, or might result in a particular design choice. The sketched approach is illustrated in Figure 1.1.

As a final remark, it should be noted that model-based performance evaluation can also be employed in combination with performance monitoring, especially when changes to existing systems are considered. In those cases, one can measure particular events in the system, in order to determine system parameters. These parameters can be input to a fairly detailed system model. Then, using the model, various alternative system configurations can be evaluated, which might lead to conclusions about how the real system needs to be adapted and where investments can best be made. This is, again, often a more cost-effective approach, than just to invest and hope that the system performance improves.

### Example 1.1. Amdahl's law.

Suppose we are interested in determining what the merit of parallelism is for performing a particular task. We know that this task (a program) takes $t$ seconds to execute on a single processor of a particular type, and we like to have answers to the following two questions:

- How long does it take to complete this task on an $n$-processor (of the same type)?

- What is the reached "speed-up"?

To make the above informal questions more concrete, we define two measures:

- $T(n)$, the time it takes to complete the task on an $n$-processor
  (we know $T(1) = t$);

- The speed-up $S(n) = T(1)/T(n)$.

We want to determine these two measures; however, since we do not know much about the task, the processor, etc., we make a very simple model that gives us estimates about what using more processors might bring us. We furthermore like to use the model to determine the performance of massive parallelism $(n \to \infty)$.

The tasks taking $t$ seconds on a single processor can certainly not completely be parallelised. Indeed, it is reasonable to assume that only a fraction $\alpha$ $(0 < \alpha < 1)$ can be parallelised. Therefore, the sequential part of the task, of length $(1 - \alpha)t$, will not be shortened when using multiple processors; the part of length $\alpha t$ will be shortened. Thus we find for $T(n)$:

$$T(n) = (1 - \alpha)t + \alpha \frac{t}{n}.$$

Taking the limit $n \to \infty$, we find that $T(n) \to (1-\alpha)t$, meaning that no matter how many processors we have at our disposal, the task we are interested in will not be completed in less than $(1-\alpha)t$ seconds. This result might be a surprise: we cannot reduce the completion time of tasks to 0 by simply using more processors. A similar observation can be made regarding the speed-up. We find

$$S(n) = \frac{T(1)}{T(n)} = \frac{t}{(1 - \alpha)t + \frac{\alpha t}{n}} = \frac{1}{1 - \frac{n-1}{n}\alpha}.$$

Taking the limit $n \to \infty$, we find $S(n) \to (1 - \alpha)^{-1}$. This result is known as *Amdahl's law* and states that the speed-up gained when using multiple processors is limited by the inverse of the fraction of the task that can only be performed sequentially.

As an example, we consider $\alpha = 90\%$. We then find that the best we can do is to reduce the completion time with a factor 10, i.e., $\lim_{n \to \infty} T(n) = t/10$, and the speed-up is at most $\lim_{n \to \infty} S(n) = 10$. □

## 1.2  Model solution techniques

Regarding the solution techniques that can be employed, two main classes of techniques can be distinguished: analytical and simulative techniques.

If the model at hand fulfills a number of requirements, we can directly calculate important performance measures from the model by using *analytical techniques*. Analytical techniques are of course very convenient, but, as we will see, not many real systems can be modelled in such a way that the requirements are fulfilled. However, we will spend quite some time on deriving and applying analytical techniques. The reasons for this are, among others, that they can give a good insight into the operation of the systems under study at low cost, and that they can be used for "quick engineering" purposes in system design.

Within the class of analytical techniques, a subclassification is often made. First of all, there are the so-called *closed-form* analytical techniques. With these, the performance measure of interest is given as an explicit expression in terms of the model structure and parameters. Such techniques are only available for the simplest models. A broader class of techniques are the *analytic/numerical techniques*, or numerical techniques, for short. With these, we are able to obtain (systems of) equations of which the solution can be obtained by employing techniques known from numerical analysis, e.g., by iterative procedures. Although such numerical techniques do not give us closed-form formulae, we still can obtain exact results from them, of course within the error tolerance of the computer which is used for the numerical calculations.

For the widest class of models that can be imagined, analytical techniques do not exist to obtain model solutions. In these cases we have to resort to *simulation techniques* in order to solve the model, i.e., in order to obtain the measures of interest. With simulation, we mimic the system behaviour, generally by executing an appropriate simulation program. When doing so, we take time stamps, tabulate events, etc. After having simulated for some time, we use the time stamps to derive statistical estimates of the measures of interest.

It is also possible to combine the above modelling approaches. This is called *hybrid modelling.* In such an approach, parts of the model are solved with one technique and the obtained results are used in combination with the other model parts and solved by another technique.

The presented classification of solution techniques is not unique, nor beyond debate. Very often also, the performance models are classified after the techniques that can be used to solve them, i.e., one then speaks of analytical models or of simulation models.

It is difficult to state in general terms which of the three solution techniques is best. Each has its own merits and drawbacks. Analytical techniques tend to be the least expensive and give the modeller deep insight into the main characteristics of the system. Unfortunately, real systems often cannot be adequately modelled by analytically tractable models. Approximate analytical models can be an outcome; however, their validity is often limited to a restricted range of parameters. Numerical techniques, as an intermediate between pure analytical and simulative techniques, can be applied in very many cases. Using simulation, the modeller is tempted to make the models too complex since the model solution technique itself does not bring about any restrictions in the modelling process. This might easily lead to very large and expensive simulation models. As Alan Scherr, IBM's time-sharing pioneer and the first to use analytical techniques for the evaluation of time-sharing computer systems, puts it in [98]:

> "...*blind, imitative simulation models are by and large a waste of time and money. To put it into a more diplomatic way, the return on investment isn't nearly as high as on a simpler, analytic-type model...*",

and

> "...*the danger is that people will be tempted to take the easy way out and use the capacity of the computers as a way of avoiding the hard thinking that often needs to be done*".

Stated differently, (analytical) performance modelling is about "finding those 10% of the system that explains 90% of its behaviour". Throughout this book, we will deal mainly with analytical and numerical modelling techniques.

## 1.3 Stochastic models

As pointed out in Section 1.1, we are generally concerned with models of systems that do not yet exist, of which we do not know all the parameters exactly, and, moreover, of which the usage patterns are not known exactly. Consequently, there is quite some uncertainty in the models to be developed.

Uncertainty in the system parameters is often dealt with by doing parametric analysis, i.e., by solving the model many times for different parameters, or by doing a parametric sensitivity analysis. Both approaches can be used to come up with plots of the system performance, expressed in some measure of interest, against a varying system parameter.

A different type of uncertainty concerns the usage pattern of the system. This is generally denoted as the *workload* imposed on the system. The usage pattern is dependent on many factors, and cannot be described deterministically, i.e., we simply do not know what future system users will require the system to do for them. The only thing we do know are statistics about the usage in the past, or expectations about future behaviour. These uncertainties naturally lead to the use of random variables in the models. These variables then express, in a stochastic way, the uncertainty about the usage patterns.

**Example 1.2. Uncertainty in user behaviour: workload modelling.**
Consider a model of a telephone exchange that is used to compute the long-term probability that an incoming call needs to be rejected because all outgoing lines are busy. A system parameter that might yet be uncertain is the number of outgoing lines. In addition there is uncertainty about at which times (call) arrivals take place and how long calls last. These uncertainties can be described by random variables obeying a chosen interarrival time distribution and call duration distribution.

For a given workload, we can do a parametric analysis on the number of outgoing lines, in order to study the call rejection probability when the telephone exchange is made more powerful (and expensive!). Doing a parametric analysis of the system (with fixed number of outgoing lines) on the mean time between call arrivals, gives insight into the quality of the system, i.e., the call rejection probability, when the workload increases. Changing the distribution of the times between calls or the call duration distribution, but keeping the call rate (one over the mean intercall time) and the number of outgoing lines constant, allows us to study the call rejection probability as a function of the variability in the arrival pattern and the duration of the calls.                                                    □

When making stochastic assumptions we naturally end up with stochastic models. The overall behaviour of the system is then described as a stochastic process in time, i.e., a collection of random variables that change their value in the course of time. The performance measures of interest then need to be expressed as functions of this stochastic process. Depending on the type of the stochastic process and the type of measures requested, this function can be more or less easy to determine.

**Example 1.3. From stochastic model to measure of interest.**
Referring to the previous example, we will see in Chapter 4 that the long-run call rejection probability can be computed in closed form under the assumption that the times between call arrivals and the call duration distributions are negative exponential. Under the same conditions, but if the measure of interest is slightly changed to the call rejection probability *at a certain time instance t*, the numerical solution of a system of linear differential equations is required.                                                                    □

## 1.4   Queueing models

A very important class of stochastic models are queueing models, which we introduce in this section. We discuss the principle of queueing in Section 1.4.1. We then present Kendall's notation to characterise simple queueing stations in Section 1.4.2.

### 1.4.1   The principle of queueing

Queueing models describe queueing phenomena that occur in reality. Queueing can be observed almost everywhere. We know about it from our daily lives: we line up in front of airline check-in counters, in front of coffee machines, at the dentist, at traffic crossings, etc. In all these cases, queueing occurs because the arrival pattern of customers varies in time, and the service characteristics vary from customer to customer. As a general rule of thumb, the more variability is involved, the more we need to queue. Directly associated with queueing is waiting. The longer a queue, the longer one normally has to wait before being served.

Also in technical systems, queueing plays an important role. Although we will focus on computer-communication systems, also in logistic systems and in manufacturing lines, queueing can be observed. It is interesting to note that in all these fields, similar techniques are used to analyse and optimise system operation.

In the area of computer-communication systems, one observes that many system users want to access, every now and then, shared resources. These shared resources vary from printers, to central file or compute servers, or to the access networks for these central facilities. Because the request rates and the requested volumes issued by a large user population vary in time, situations occur when more than one user wants to access a single resource. Waiting for one another is then the only reasonable solution. The alternative to give all users all the resources privately is not a very cost effective solution. Besides

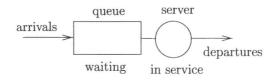

Figure 1.2: The basic model for a scarce resource

that, it would also preclude other advantages of the use of shared resources, such a central support and data sharing.

**Example 1.4. A centralised compute server.**
At a computer centre, jobs from various users (sitting behind their terminals) arrive to be processed at a powerful compute server. Depending on how many other jobs are already being processed, an incoming job is directly served or it has to wait for some time before its predecessors are served. Once in service, the job occupies some part of the system capacity. Let us assume a round-robin scheduling strategy, in which up to some maximum number of jobs are served quasi-simultaneously. When the job processing has completed, the resources that were used (apart from the CPU, some part of virtual memory and disks are mostly involved) are released again and can be used for servicing other jobs. Important to observe is that we deal with a resource with limited capacity, namely the compute server in the computer centre which is to be shared by a large population of customers/terminal users. The population of terminal users is so large that, would they all want to be served simultaneously, the compute server would be overloaded.                                     □

The idea now is to model all types of shared resources as *service providing entities* preceded by *waiting queues*, as depicted in Figure 1.2. Let us try to characterise such a basic *queueing station* at which customers arrive, wait, are served, and finally depart. The following aspects are of importance for the quality of the provided service as perceived by the customers:

- The time between successive arrivals of customers requesting service. These time intervals are often assumed to obey some stochastic regime.

- The customer population. Are we dealing with an infinite or with a finite customer population?

- The amount of waiting room that is available for the customers that cannot directly be served.

- The amount of service a customer requests. This is generally also described by some stochastic variable.

- The number of service providing entities that is available. Are we dealing with a single server or with a multi-server?

- The way in which incoming customers are scheduled to obtain their requested service. Commonly used scheduling principles are:

   - FCFS: First Come, First Served;

   - RR: Round-Robin;

   - PS: Processor Sharing (the limiting case of RR);

   - LCFS(PR): Last Come, First Served, with or without Preemption;

   - IS: Infinite Server;

   - PRIO: Prioritized scheduling.

Once a queueing station has been characterised completely, we can try to evaluate the performance characteristics of such a queueing station.

A remark about the employed terminology should be made here. In general, we speak of either jobs or customers in a queueing station. These two names are used interchangeably. Sometimes, when the application is more computer-network oriented, we also use the term packet.

## 1.4.2    Single queues: the Kendall notation

In order to compactly describe single queueing stations in an unambiguous way, the so-called *Kendall notation* is often used; it consists of 6 identifiers, separated by vertical bars, as follows:

   Arrivals|Services|Servers|Buffersize|Population|Scheduling,

where "Arrivals" characterises the customer arrival process, "Service" the customer service requirements, "Servers" the number of service providing entities, "Buffersize" the maximum number of customers in the queueing station, which includes the customer possibly in the server, "Population" the size of the customer population, and finally, "Scheduling" the employed scheduling strategy. Often, the buffer size and the population are omitted from the description; in that case they are assumed to be infinitely large. The scheduling strategy is also often omitted; in that case, it is assumed to be FCFS. The parameters, especially "Arrivals" and "Services", may assume many different values. We mention some commonly used ones:

- $M$ (Markovian or Memoryless): whenever the interarrival or service times are negative exponentially distributed;

- $G$ (General): whenever the times involved may be arbitrarily distributed;

- $D$ (Deterministic): whenever the times involved are constant;

- $E_r$ ($r$-stage Erlang): whenever the times involved are distributed according to an Erlang-$r$ distribution;

- $H_r$: whenever the times involved are distributed according to an $r$-state hyperexponential distribution.

We will discuss many different types of queueing stations in Part II of the book.

**Example 1.5. Kendall notation.**
When we have an M|G|2|8||LCFS queueing station, we have (negative) exponentially distributed interarrival times, generally distributed service times, 2 service providing entities, maximally 8 customers present, no limitation on the total customer population, and an LCFS scheduling strategy.                                                                 □

**Example 1.6. Queueing in daily life.**
Coin-operated coffee machines can be found in many universities and laboratories. Although their service time, that is, the time for preparing a cup of coffee once a coin has been inserted, is deterministic, some waiting often occurs in front of them. This is typically due to the stochastic nature of the arrival process. A single coffee machine could be described by a G|D|1 queue.

When visiting a doctor, after having made an appointment, one often still has to wait. Although the arrivals of patients can be seen as deterministic if the appointments have been made accurately, long waiting times arise due to the fact that the service times, i.e., the time a doctor talks to or examines patients, is stochastic. This situation could be well described with a D|G|1 queue.

When visiting a doctor without an appointment, that is at the regular "walk-in" consulting hours, things get even worse. In that case, the arrival process of patients is not deterministic any more. The perceived waiting times therefore also increase. This situation could very well be described with a G|G|1 queue. □

Important to note is the fact that sometimes the notation "GI" is used, instead of just "G", to indicate a general arrival process. The added "I" specifically denotes that succeeding arrivals are *independent* of one another; just "G" might allow for dependence between successive arrivals.

## 1.5 Tool support

For complex systems, it is not easy to come up directly with a stochastic model that describes all the relevant aspects of the system in relation to the measure of interest. Instead, we build system models in a stepwise fashion using basic building blocks (submodels). The translation of the thus-constructed model to an underlying stochastic model can often be performed automatically. In this way we "pull up" the modelling activity to a level that is closer to the system designer's point of view than to the mathematician's point of view. Still though, for a proper application of high-level modelling constructs, we need to have knowledge about the underlying mathematics.

Once we have obtained the stochastic model of interest, the derivation of the measure of interest needs to be performed. As already indicated in Section 1.2, the model solution can be more or less intricate, requiring detailed knowledge about simulation or about analytic/numerical techniques.

In both the above cases, i.e., model construction and model solution, tool support is of key importance. We discuss the role of software tools for model construction in Section 1.5.1, and their role in model solution in Section 1.5.2.

### 1.5.1 Model construction

Software tools can be a great help in the construction of large stochastic models. We can distinguish at least two representations of a model. First, there is the *analytical representation* of a model. This is the representation that is directly suitable for a numerical evaluation by one of the techniques mentioned in Section 1.2. Secondly, there is the *modellers representation* of a model. This is a description in a symbolic form oriented towards the specific application, that is the system to be modelled. Clearly, most system designers prefer to use the modellers representation rather than the analytical representation.

The idea of having more than one view of a model, depending on what one wants to do with the model, is central to the *general modelling tool framework* (GMTF) for quantitative systems modelling.

In the GMTF, a hierarchy of descriptive formalisms ranging from $\mathcal{F}_0$ (the lowest level) to $\mathcal{F}_n$ (the highest level) is employed. $\mathcal{F}_0$ yields models that are directly suitable for evaluations of one or another form, by using analytic, numerical or simulation techniques, whereas $\mathcal{F}_n$ is the formalism closest to the application domain. We define $\mathcal{F}_i$-*modelling* as the process of abstracting, simplifying and/or rewriting a system description $\mathcal{S}$ in such a way that it fits the formalism $\mathcal{F}_i$. The result of this process is called an $\mathcal{F}_i$-model $\mathcal{M}_i$ of $\mathcal{S}$. An $\mathcal{F}_i$-model $\mathcal{M}_i$ of $\mathcal{S}$ can be rewritten in another formalism $\mathcal{F}_{i-1}$ (provided $i \geq 1$) yielding an $\mathcal{F}_{i-1}$-model $\mathcal{M}_{i-1}$ of $\mathcal{S}$. This is called $\mathcal{F}_{i-1}$-modelling. The lowest level formalism is $\mathcal{F}_0$ which coincides with the earlier mentioned analytical representation.

When $\mathcal{F}_i$ is the highest-level formalism, most of the user activity in the modelling process will be $\mathcal{F}_i$-modelling. The lower level modelling activities can often be partially or completely automated; the need for tool support is evident.

Once we have a model it should be evaluated. The evaluation of an $\mathcal{F}_0$-model $\mathcal{M}_0$ yields results in the descriptive formalism $\mathcal{R}_0$. To do so, solution techniques like those indicated in Section 1.2 can directly be applied since the formalism $\mathcal{F}_0$ has been chosen to directly suit those techniques. The evaluation of an $\mathcal{F}_0$-model $\mathcal{M}_0$ is called a $\mathcal{V}_0$-*evaluation*. The results presented in the formalism or domain $\mathcal{R}_i$ ($i \geq 0$) can be further processed or enhanced to the higher level $\mathcal{R}_{i+1}$. This is called an $\mathcal{E}_{i+1}$-*enhancement*. Often these enhancements can be done automatically; tool support is again of importance here.

When we have an $\mathcal{F}_j$-model $\mathcal{M}_j$ of a system $\mathcal{S}$ we generally want to evaluate this model and obtain measures that are specified at the same level. That is, we need the results to be given in *domain* $\mathcal{R}_j$. We define a *virtual evaluation* $\mathcal{V}_j$ as the process of subsequently modelling $\mathcal{M}_i$ ($1 \leq i \leq j$) in formalism $\mathcal{F}_{i-1}$, until an $\mathcal{F}_0$-model $\mathcal{M}_0$ is obtained, followed by the $\mathcal{V}_0$-evaluation and the subsequent enhancements $\mathcal{E}_1$ through $\mathcal{E}_j$. Schematically, we have the structure as depicted in Figure 1.3. This structure represents the GMTF. The small boxes represent system models (right hand side) or evaluation results (left hand side). The large box represents the actual mathematical evaluation. The single pointed arrows represent automatic translations of one formalism into another. The double pointed arrows represent the virtual evaluations.

## Example 1.7. A tool based on stochastic Petri nets.

In Chapter 14 we will present stochastic Petri nets (SPNs) as a suitable formalism for many performance models. Various tools have been developed that support this formalism

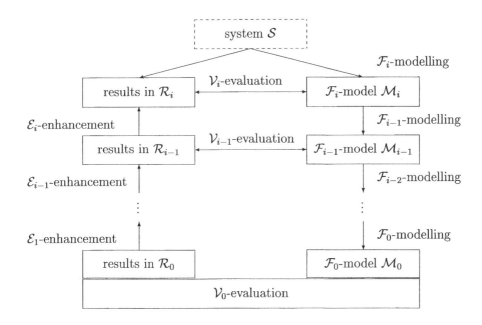

Figure 1.3: The general modelling tool framework

(see the surveys [121, 119]).

When using these tools, the relevant aspects of a system $\mathcal{S}$ have to be captured in the SPN formalism. This is the $\mathcal{F}_1$-modelling activity, yielding an $\mathcal{F}_1$-model $\mathcal{M}_1$ of the system. This modelling activity is performed by a human being.

Model $\mathcal{M}_1$ can be converted to a continuous-time Markov chain (see Chapter 3). This is the $\mathcal{F}_0$-modelling activity, yielding an $\mathcal{F}_0$-model $\mathcal{M}_0$ of the system. Note that this modelling activity can be performed automatically with the algorithm outlined in Chapter 14.

The resulting $\mathcal{M}_0$ model, which is a Markov chain, can be evaluated by a standard numerical technique (see Chapter 15); this is the $\mathcal{V}_0$-evaluation. The results from this evaluation are state probabilities, which fall in the domain $\mathcal{R}_0$. Although interesting as such, the system analyst who does not know that the SPN is solved via an underlying CTMC cannot do anything with these state probabilities. They have to be enhanced to a level which corresponds to the level at which the model was originally made. The calculation of token distributions per place from the state probabilities is an example of an enhancement $\mathcal{E}_1$ to the domain $\mathcal{R}_1$. This enhancement can also be performed automatically. As a conclusion, the tool user only "sees" the virtual evaluation $\mathcal{V}_1$. □

## 1.5.2   Model solution

Once we have obtained a stochastic model, the measure of interest still needs to be derived. Seen in light of the GMTF, one can say that solution techniques are needed to perform the $\mathcal{V}_0$-evaluations, that is, to take the $\mathcal{F}_0$-model $\mathcal{M}_0$ and to "transform it" in results in $\mathcal{R}_0$ which can be more or less intricate. It should be noted also that the transformations from one modelling level to the next level below (and up again as far as the solutions are concerned) should be regarded as part of the solution process. Indeed, as we will see later, these transformations can be more complex and time-consuming than the solution of the lowest-level model once it has been generated.

In a generally applicable performance evaluation tool, one would prefer to have a wide variety of solution techniques available. Depending on the model at hand, e.g., its statistical characteristics or its size, one or another solution technique might be more suitable. It is desirable that the different solution techniques can be fed with models in the same formalism. In that way, different solution techniques can be compared, and, while increasing the complexity of the model by adding details, shifts from more general to more specific solution techniques can be made. It should be understood that the desire to be able to "play around" with different solution techniques is in (mild) conflict with the desire to keep the solution techniques as invisible as possible to the end-users of the tool.

**Example 1.8. Incremental modelling.**
In the early design phases of a system, often imprecise information is known about the durations of certain events. Suppose that one choses to make a queueing network model of such a system design, to evaluate various design alternatives. Since only limited information is available, only fairly abstract models can be made. For such models, a solution based on mean-value analysis might be appropriate (see Chapter 11). When more implementation aspects become clear in the course of the design, more detailed stochastic assumptions can be made, which might overrule the restrictions to perform a mean-value analysis. A simulation approach towards the solution, or an approximate solution might, however, still apply. If these solution techniques are supported, starting from the same model description, a consistent upgrade to the more detailed model can easily be established. Also, it can then be easily investigated whether the more detailed information is indeed of importance for the measure of interest. If not, one can use the "lighter" solution technique.          □

In many performance evaluation techniques some kind of accuracy control is involved. This can be in the form of required confidence interval widths in simulations, in the allowed number of iteration steps in numerical procedures, or in the choice of a truncation point in an infinite series in the case of analytic/numerical techniques. A software tool should provide suitable values for such parameters, so that users unaware of the specific techniques involved are not bothered by these details. However, it should always be possible for the more experienced user to change these values to better ones, given the application at hand. The specification and control of (required and obtained) accuracy remains a difficult task.

## 1.6   Further reading

More information on measurement-based performance evaluation can be found in Jain [145], Hofmann *et al.* [135] and Lange *et al.* [171]. A model-based performance evaluation cycle similar to the one presented here has been presented by Van Moorsel [206]. Amdahl published his now-famous law in 1967 [8], although it is not beyond debate [115]. Queueing models to evaluate system performance have been developed since the beginning of this century; these models and their applications are the main topic of this book. Kendall introduced the short-hand notation for single queueing systems [155]. Scherr describes his time-sharing models already in 1966 [255]. Berson *et al.* [17] and Page *et al.* [227] presented a simpler form of the GMTF. The GMTF was introduced by Haverkort [120]; variants of it, tailored towards specific application areas, can be found in the literature [127, 180, 211, 258]. Interesting general guidelines for the construction of performance evaluation tools have been reported by Beilner [16]. Recent surveys of performance evaluation tools can be found in [126, 125].

## 1.7   Exercises

**1.1. Performance measures.**
The average response times of computer systems A and B are such that $E[R_A] < E[R_B]$.

1. Is system A better than system B for all types of applications?

2. What would be an appropriate performance measure to compare these systems in case they have to fulfill real-time requirements?

3. What would be an appropriate performance measure to compare these systems in case they have to fulfill reliability requirements?

**1.2. Amdahl's law.**
Using the expression for $T(n)$, compute the number of processors $n_\beta$ that is needed to

reduce the task completion time $t$ to $\beta t$ $(0 < \beta < 1)$. What is the range of values that $\beta$ can assume?

**1.3. Queueing in daily life.**
Discuss the models presented in Example 1.6. What are the underlying assumptions?

**1.4. Influence of variability.**
Address the following questions based on your intuition and experience. In later chapters, we will address these questions in more detail.

1. How do you think that increased variability in customer arrival and service patterns does affect the performance of many systems?

2. Is increased variability in service times "worse" for performance than increased variability in interarrival times?

3. What kind of CPU scheduling is often used in operating systems and how do you think it affects the performance of systems?

**1.5. The GMTF.**
Compare the main ideas behind the GMTF with those behind:

1. The use of high-level programming languages and adequate compilers to avoid assembler or machine programming.

2. The possibility to define high-level functions and modules in many programming languages to enhance the programming activity from a solution-algorithm-orientation to a problem-description-orientation.

3. The use of layered communication protocol reference models.

# Chapter 2

# Little's law and the M|M|1 queue

IN Section 2.1 we present Little's law, a very general law that can be applied in many queueing models. Using Little's law, we are able to study the simplest queueing model, the M|M|1 queueing model, in Section 2.2.

## 2.1 Little's law

In this section we will introduce the probably *most general law* in model-based performance evaluation: *Little's law*, named after the author who first proved it [186]. Its generality lies in the fact that it can be applied almost unconditionally to all queueing models and at many levels of abstraction. Its strength furthermore lies in the fact that its form is both intuitively appealing and simple.

In Section 2.1.1 we introduce Little's law and explain it intuitively. A more thorough proof is given in Section 2.1.2.

### 2.1.1 Understanding Little's law

Little's law relates the average number of jobs in a queueing station to the average number of arrivals per time unit and the average time a job spends in a queueing station.

Consider a queueing station as a black box at which on average $\lambda$ jobs per time unit arrive (see Figure 2.1); $\lambda$ is called the *arrival rate* or the *arrival intensity*. When we assume that jobs are served on a first come-first served basis (FCFS), whenever a job arrives at the queueing station, two things might happen. Either the job is immediately served which implies that there are no other jobs in the queueing station, or it has to wait until the jobs already in the queueing station are served before it gets its turn. Notice that we do not

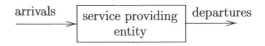

Figure 2.1: Black box view of a job servicing system

assume anything about the distributions of the interarrival and service times; only their means are used! Denote the average time a job spends in the queueing station as $E[R]$ (residence time/ response time), and the average number of jobs in the queueing station as $E[N]$.

Now, suppose that we mark a particular job while observing the queueing station. When the marked job enters the queueing system we take a time stamp $t_i$ ($i$ for "in"). When the marked job comes out of the queueing station, we take a time stamp $t_o$ ($o$ for "out"). The difference $t_o - t_i$ will *on average* be equal to the earlier defined value $E[R]$. However, at the moment the marked job leaves the queueing station, we know that while the job passed through the queueing station, other jobs have arrived. How many? Well, since on average there have elapsed $E[R]$ time units between the arrival and the departure of the marked job, on average $\lambda \times E[R]$ jobs have arrived after the marked job in that period. This number, however, must be equal to the earlied defined value of $E[N]$. This is due to the fact that *every* job can be a marked job, and hence, the product $\lambda E[R]$ always equals the number of jobs left behind in the queueing station by a departing job, i.e., it can be interpreted as the average value of the number of jobs in the system. As a consequence, we have

$$E[N] = \lambda E[R]. \tag{2.1}$$

Notice that we have assumed that all jobs that arrive also leave the system after having received service so that no losses of jobs occur and that the system is not overloaded. In that case, the arrival rate $\lambda$ equals the *throughput* of jobs (denoted $X$). This is normally the case when the system is not overloaded and when there is infinite buffer capacity. In case the system is overloaded or when there are finite buffers, customers will be lost, and only the non-lost customers should be taken into account. In such cases Little's law should read $E[N] = XE[R]$. Due to the fact that losses may occur in some systems, $X$ is not always *a priori* known!

The derivation sketched above can be applied at any desired level of abstraction. Suppose that we open up the black box and look at it as if it were a queue, followed by the actual server (see Figure 2.2). Then we could still apply Little's law; however, we could also apply it on the more detailed level of the queue and the server separately, as we will

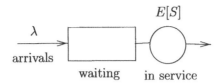

Figure 2.2: The inside view of a job servicing system

explain below.

At the queue on average $\lambda$ jobs arrive per time unit. The time spent in the queue is the waiting time, which on average equals $E[W]$. Applying Little's law, the average number of jobs in the queue, $E[N_q]$, must be equal to the product of the waiting time and the throughput through the server. The latter equals the arrivals at the queue (no jobs are lost in between) and we thus obtain:

$$E[N_q] = \lambda E[W]. \qquad (2.2)$$

When looking solely at the server, we again observe, on average, $\lambda$ job arrivals per time unit, since between the queue and the server no jobs are lost. The average time a job spends in the server, i.e., is being served, is denoted $E[S]$. Then the average number of jobs in the server is given by:

$$E[N_s] = \lambda E[S]. \qquad (2.3)$$

Since we are dealing with a single server, $E[N_s]$ can at most be equal to 1 and must at least equal 0. In fact, $E[N_s]$ not only indicates the average number of jobs in the server but also the average time the server is busy. Therefore, $E[N_s]$ is also called the *utilisation* or *traffic intensity* and denoted as $\rho = X E[S] = \lambda E[S]$ (where the last equality holds when there are no losses).

Returning to our overall queueing system, the average number of jobs in the queueing system must be equal to the sum of the average numbers of jobs in the components of the queueing system, i.e., $E[N] = E[N_q] + E[N_s]$. Applying the earlier derived versions of Little's law, we obtain

$$E[N] = E[N_q] + E[N_s] = \lambda E[W] + \lambda E[S] = \lambda(E[W] + E[S]) = \lambda E[R], \qquad (2.4)$$

which is as expected.

There are some important remarks to be made on the generality and use of Little's law:

- Little's law expresses a simple relationship between the average values of the throughput, the residence times and the number of jobs in the system;

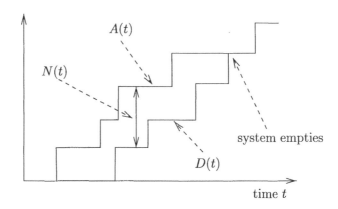

Figure 2.3: Sample evolution of $A(t)$ and $D(t)$

- No assumptions regarding the involved interarrival- and service-time distributions have to be made;

- Little's law is valid independently of the scheduling discipline of a queue as well as of the number of servers;

- As we will see later, with many analysis techniques $E[N]$ can be obtained easily. Using Little's law, measures like $E[R]$ can then be derived;

- Little's law not only applies to single queueing stations, but also to networks of queueing stations.

### 2.1.2   Proof of Little's law

After the proof given by Little in 1961 a wide variety of "simple proofs for $E[N] = \lambda E[R]$" has appeared in the literature. In this section we give a proof of Little's law which indeed is more formal than the intuitive explanation we gave in Section 2.1.1. The presented proof is valid under the assumption that the queueing system empties infinitely often. For a queueing system where the arrival rate of jobs is smaller than the service rate of jobs, this is the case.

As before, we consider the black box view of a queueing system. Without loss of generality we start observing the queueing system at time $t = 0$. Let $A(t)$ denote the number of job arrivals to the queueing system up till time $t$. A similar definition holds for $D(t)$, the number of job departures from the system up to time $t$. Clearly, $D(t) \leq A(t)$.

When we denote with $N(t)$ the number of jobs in the system at time $t$, we have $N(t) = A(t) - D(t)$. In Figure 2.3 we show a possible evolution of $A(t)$ and $D(t)$. We now proceed to define the following four quantities:

- The average arrival rate at the system up to time $t$, denoted $\lambda_t$, simply is the total number of arrivals up to time $t$, i.e., $A(t)$, divided by $t$. Thus, we have $\lambda_t = A(t)/t$, and $\lambda_t \to \lambda$ if $t \to \infty$.

- The total system time of all jobs, $R(t)$, is exactly the area between the two curves of $A(t)$ and $D(t)$, i.e.,

$$R(t) = \int_0^t N(s)ds. \tag{2.5}$$

- The average time a job spends in the system as observed over the period $[0, t)$ is denoted $R_t$. This quantity, however, is equal to the total system time, i.e., $R(t)$, divided by the total number of customers having been present in the system, i.e., $A(t)$. Thus, we have $R_t = R(t)/A(t)$, and $R_t \to E[R]$ if $t \to \infty$.

- If the total system time of all jobs during $[0, t)$ equals $R(t)$ job-seconds, the average number of jobs in the system up to time $t$, denoted $N_t$, equals $R(t)/t$, and $N_t \to E[N]$ if $t \to \infty$.

We now can derive the following relation:

$$N_t = \frac{R(t)}{t} = \frac{A(t)}{A(t)}\frac{R(t)}{t} = \frac{A(t)}{t}\frac{R(t)}{A(t)} = \lambda_t R_t. \tag{2.6}$$

Now, taking the limit as $t \to \infty$, we obtain $E[N] = \lambda E[R]$ since $\lambda_t \to \lambda$, $N_t \to E[N]$ and $R_t \to E[R]$. In case the queue is saturated, the number of jobs queued will grow without bound, hence, the expected response time will not be bounded either.

## 2.2 The simplest queueing model: the M|M|1 queue

In this section we make use of Little's law to evaluate the performance characteristics of the simplest queueing system possible: the M|M|1 queue.

Consider a queueing station where jobs arrive with a negative exponential interarrival time distribution with rate $\lambda$ (mean interarrival time $E[A] = 1/\lambda$). Furthermore, the job service requirements are also negative exponentially distributed with mean $E[S] = 1/\mu$. Such a model typically applies when addressing a telephone exchange: empirical results indeed support the assumptions of negative exponential interarrivals times and service times (call durations).

We first verify whether the utilisation $\rho = \lambda/\mu < 1$, that is, we check whether on average the amount of arriving jobs flowing in per unit of time is smaller than the amount of jobs that the system is able to handle in unit time. If so, the system is stable and we continue our investigations. If not, the system is overloaded and an infinite queue will grow; further analysis will not help us any further.

We are interested in determining the following mean performance measures for this queueing system: the mean queue length $E[N_q]$, the mean number of jobs in the system $E[N]$, the mean waiting time $E[W]$ and the mean response time $E[R]$.

We already know that we can apply Little's law for the complete queueing station as well as for the queue in isolation, yielding:

$$E[N_q] = \lambda E[W], \quad \text{and} \quad E[N] = \lambda E[R]. \tag{2.7}$$

We furthermore know that $E[R] = E[W] + E[S]$. To solve for the above four unknown quantities, we have to have one extra relation. This relation can be derived from the so-called PASTA property (which will be discussed in detail in Chapter 4) which states that jobs arriving according to a Poisson process (a process where the interarrival times are negative exponentially distributed, as we have here (see also Chapter 3)) see the queueing system upon their arrival as if in equilibrium. This means that an arriving job finds, on average, $E[N]$ jobs already in the queueing station upon its arrival, and for which it has to wait before being served. This yields us the following extra equation:

$$E[W] = E[N]E[S]. \tag{2.8}$$

The overall response time of such a customer then consists of two main components: (i) the service time for all customers queued up front; and (ii) its own service time. Thus, we have:

$$E[R] = E[N]E[S] + E[S]. \tag{2.9}$$

We also use the fact here that the service times are negative exponentially distributed since we assume that the remaining service time of the customer in service at the arrival instance of the new customer is the same as a normal service time (we also come back to this issue in Chapter 5). Now, we can use Little's law to write $E[N] = \lambda E[R]$, so that we find:

$$E[R] = \lambda E[R]E[S] + E[S] \quad \Rightarrow \quad E[R](1 - \lambda E[S]) = E[S]. \tag{2.10}$$

Recognising $\rho = \lambda E[S]$ and rearranging terms we find

$$E[R] = \frac{E[S]}{1 - \rho}. \tag{2.11}$$

Using the relations we already had, we then find that

$$E[W] = \frac{\rho E[S]}{1 - \rho}, \quad E[N] = \frac{\rho}{1 - \rho}, \quad \text{and} \quad E[N_q] = \frac{\rho^2}{1 - \rho}. \tag{2.12}$$

There are a number of important conclusions to be drawn from these results. First of all, we observe that the mean performance measures of interest grow infinitely large as $\rho \to 1$. This conforms with our intuition. Secondly, we see that the performance measures of interest do not grow linearly with $\rho$; instead they grow with a factor

$$\frac{1}{1 - \rho} = 1 + \rho + \rho^2 + \rho^3 + \cdots = \sum_{i=0}^{\infty} \rho^i, \tag{2.13}$$

which is called the *stretch factor* since it can be interpreted as the factor with which the mean service time $E[S]$ is stretched (multiplied) to yield the mean response time when a server with total utilisation $\rho$ processes a job with average length $E[S]$.

In Figure 2.4 we present $E[R]$ and $E[W]$ as a function of $\rho$. Note that $E[N] = 1$ for $\rho = 50\%$ (at 50% utilisation, on average, there is one job in the queueing station) and $E[W] = E[S]$ (at 50% utilisation, the mean waiting time equals the mean service time). Consequently, for higher utilisations, the mean response time includes more than 50% of waiting. Also observe that the curves start relatively flat but increase quite sharply once above the 50% boundary. This is typical for most queueing systems and explains why many computer and communication systems exhibit "all of a sudden" bad performance when the load is only moderately increased.

The derivation just given provides us with only the mean values of a number of performance measures of interest. For some applications, this might be enough. However, very often also information on the variance of performance measures is of importance or information on detailed probabilities regarding certain events in the system (e.g., the probability that a buffer contains at least $k$ customers). For these cases a more detailed and intricate analysis of the queueing model is necessary. To derive such information, we need to study the stochastic process underlying the queueing systems. In order to be able to do so we need to study stochastic processes first, which is therefore the topic of Chapter 3.

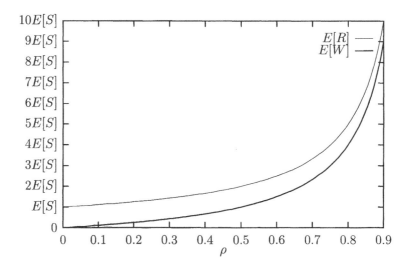

Figure 2.4: The mean waiting time $E[W]$ and the mean response time $E[R]$ (measured in $E[S]$) as a function of $\rho$ for the M|M|1 queueing model

## 2.3 Further reading

Little's law was originally presented in 1961 [186]. Other proofs of Little's results can be found in [81, 150, 193, 269, 270]. The analysis of the M|M|1 queue as presented here is an example of the so-called "method of moments" to derive average performance measures; this method has first been presented by Cobham in 1954 [57, 58]. Paterok *et al.* discuss its suitability for the derivation of higher moments [230]. We will use the method of moments at many occasions in the course of this book.

## 2.4 Exercises

**2.1. Time-sharing computer systems [adapted from [156]].**
Consider a time-sharing computer system that supports $K$ users sitting behind their terminals issuing commands. The time it takes a single user to interpret an answer from the central computer before a new command is issued is called the *think time* and takes, on average, $E[Z]$ seconds. The computer system can process a command in, on average, $E[S]$ seconds. Now assume that there are on average $k$ commands (jobs) being worked upon by the central computer, hence, there are $K - k$ jobs being "processed" by the users; the effective rate at which these users generate new requests for the central computer then

equals $(K - k)/E[Z]$.

1. Express the expected central computer response time $E[R]$ in terms of $K$, $k$ and $E[Z]$ using Little's law applied to the central computer.

2. Let $p_0$ equal the probability that the central computer is empty (all jobs are being worked upon by the users). The throughput of the central computer can then be expressed as $(1 - p_0)/E[S]$. This can be understood as follows. If there would be an infinite supply of jobs, the computer would on average process one every $E[S]$ units of time, yielding a rate of completion of $1/E[S]$. However, with probability $1 - p_0$ there is no job for the computer to work upon, hence its rate of completion is effectively decreased with that factor. Using Little's law for the terminals, express the expected number of customers in the terminals, i.e., $K - k$, as a function of $p_0$, $E[S]$ and $E[Z]$.

3. Show that the combination of the above expressions yields:

$$E[R] = \frac{KE[S]}{1 - p_0} - E[Z].$$

4. Based on the possible values that $p_0$ can assume, derive the following lower bound for $E[R]$ thereby taking into account the fact that $E[R]$ cannot be smaller than $E[S]$:

$$E[R] \geq \max\{KE[S] - E[Z], E[S]\}.$$

We will address this and similar models in more detail in Chapter 4 and in Chapters 11 through 13.

### 2.2. M|M|1 queueing.
How large can the utilisation in an M|M|1 queue be so that the expected response time is at most $n$ times the expected service time?

# Chapter 3

# Stochastic processes

THE aim of this chapter is to provide the necessary background in stochastic processes for practical performance evaluation purposes. We do not aim at completeness in this chapter, nor at mathematical rigour. It is assumed that the reader has basic knowledge about probability theory, as outlined in Appendix A.

We first define stochastic processes and classify them in Section 3.1, after which we discuss a number of different stochastic process classes in more detail. We start with renewal processes in Section 3.2. We follow with the study of discrete-time Markov chains (DTMCs) in Section 3.3, followed by Section 3.4 in which general properties of Markov chains are presented. Then, in Section 3.5, continuous-time Markov chains (CTMCs) are discussed. Section 3.6 then discusses semi-Markov processes. Two special cases of CTMCs, the birth-death process and the Poisson process are discussed in Sections 3.7 and 3.8, respectively. In Section 3.9 we discuss the use of renewal processes as arrival processes; particular emphasis is given to phase-type renewal processes. Finally, in Section 3.10, we summarise the specification and evaluation of the various types of Markov chains.

## 3.1  Overview of stochastic processes

A *stochastic process* is a collection of random variables $\{X(t)|t \in \mathcal{T}\}$, defined on a probability space, and indexed by a parameter $t$ (usually assumed to be time) which can take values in a set $\mathcal{T}$.

The values that $X(t)$ assumes are called *states*. The set of all possible states is called the *state space* and is denoted $\mathcal{I}$. If the state space is discrete, we deal with a *discrete-state stochastic process*, which is called a *chain*. For convenience, it is often assumed that whenever we deal with a chain, the state space $\mathcal{I} = \{0, 1, 2, \cdots\}$. The state space can also

be continuous. We then deal with a *continuous-state stochastic process*. A similar classification can be made regarding the index set $\mathcal{T}$. The set $\mathcal{T}$ can be denumerable, leading
to a *discrete-time stochastic process*, or it can be continuous, leading to a *continuous-time
stochastic process*. In case the set $\mathcal{T}$ is discrete, the stochastic process is often denoted as
$\{N_k | k \in \mathcal{T}\}$. Since we have two possibilities for each of the two sets involved, we end up
with four different types of stochastic processes. Let us give examples of these four:

- **$\mathcal{I}$ and $\mathcal{T}$ discrete.** Consider the number of jobs $N_k$ present in a computer system
  at the moment of the departure of the $k$-th job. Clearly, in a computer system only
  an integer number of jobs can be present, thus $\mathcal{I} = \{0, 1, \cdots\}$. Likewise, only after
  the first job departs, $N_k$ is clearly defined. Thus we have $\mathcal{T} = \{1, 2, \cdots\}$.

- **$\mathcal{I}$ discrete and $\mathcal{T}$ continuous.** Consider the number of jobs $N(t)$ present in the
  computer system at time $t$. Again only integer numbers of jobs can be present, hence
  $\mathcal{I} = \{0, 1, \cdots\}$. We can, however, observe the computer system continuously. This
  implies that $\mathcal{T} = [0, \infty)$.

- **$\mathcal{I}$ continuous and $\mathcal{T}$ discrete.** Let $W_k$ denote the time the $k$-th job has to wait
  until its service starts. Clearly, $k \in \mathcal{T}$ is a discrete index set, whereas $W_k$ can take
  any value in $[0, \infty)$, implying that $\mathcal{I}$ is continuous.

- **$\mathcal{I}$ and $\mathcal{T}$ continuous.** Let $C_t$ denote the total amount of service that needs to
  be done on all jobs present in the computer system at time $t$. Clearly, $t \in \mathcal{T}$ is a
  continuous parameter. Furthermore, $C_t$ can take any value in $[0, \infty)$, implying again
  that $\mathcal{I}$ is continuous.

Apart from those based on the above distinctions, we can also classify stochastic processes
in another way. We will do so below, thereby taking the notation for the case of continuous-
time, continuous-state space stochastic processes. However, the proposed classification is
also applicable for the three other cases.

At some fixed point in time $\tilde{t} \in \mathcal{T}$, the value $X(\tilde{t})$ simply is a random variable describing
the state of the stochastic process. The cumulative density function (CDF) or distribution
(function) of the random variable $X(\tilde{t})$ is called the first-order distribution of the stochastic
process $\{X(t) | t \in \mathcal{T}\}$ and denoted as $F(\tilde{x}, \tilde{t}) = \Pr\{X(\tilde{t}) \leq \tilde{x}\}$. We can generalise this to
the $n$-th order joint distribution of the stochastic process $\{X(t) | t \in \mathcal{T}\}$ as follows:

$$F(\underline{\tilde{x}}, \underline{\tilde{t}}) = \Pr\{X(\tilde{t}_1) \leq \tilde{x}_1, \cdots, X(\tilde{t}_n) \leq \tilde{x}_n\}, \tag{3.1}$$

with $\underline{\tilde{x}} \in \mathcal{I}^n$, and $\underline{\tilde{t}} \in \mathcal{T}^n$.

If all the $n$-th order distributions ($n \in \mathbb{N}^+$) of a stochastic process $\{X(t)|t \in \mathcal{T}\}$ are invariant for time shifts for all possible values of $\tilde{x}$ and $\tilde{t}$, then the stochastic process is said to be *strictly stationary*, i.e., $F(\tilde{x}, \tilde{t}) = F(\tilde{x}, \tilde{t}+\tau)$, where $\tilde{t}+\tau$ is a shorthand notation for the vector $(\tilde{t}_1 + \tau, \cdots, t_n + \tau)$.

We call a stochastic process $\{X(t)|t \in \mathcal{T}\}$ an *independent process* whenever its $n$-th order joint distribution satisfies the following condition:

$$F(\tilde{x}, \tilde{t}) = \prod_{i=1}^{n} F(\tilde{x}_i, \tilde{t}_i) = \prod_{i=1}^{n} \Pr\{X(\tilde{t}_i) \leq \tilde{x}_i\}. \tag{3.2}$$

An example of an independent stochastic process is the *renewal process*. A renewal process $\{X_n|n = 1, 2, \cdots\}$, is a discrete-time stochastic process, where $X_1, X_2, \cdots$ are independent, identically distributed, nonnegative random variables.

A renewal process is a stochastic process in which total independence exists between successive states. In many situations, however, some form of dependence exists between successive states assumed by a stochastic process. The minimum possible dependence is the following: the next state to be assumed by a stochastic process only depends on the current state of the stochastic process, and not on states that were assumed previously. This is called *first-order dependence* or *Markov dependence*, which leads us to the following definition.

A stochastic process $\{X(t)|t \in \mathcal{T}\}$ is called a *Markov process* if for any $t_0 < \cdots < t_n < t_{n+1}$ the distribution of $X(t_{n+1})$, given the values $X(t_0), \cdots, X(t_n)$, only depends on $X(t_n)$, i.e.,

$$\Pr\{X(t_{n+1}) \leq x_{n+1}|X(t_0) = x_0, \cdots, X(t_n) = x_n\} = \Pr\{X(t_{n+1}) \leq x_{n+1}|X(t_n) = x_n\}. \tag{3.3}$$

Equation (3.3) is generally denoted as the *Markov property*. Similar definitions can be given for the discrete-state cases and for discrete-time. Most often, Markov processes used for performance evaluations are invariant to time shifts, that is, for any $s < t$, and $x$, $x_s$, we have

$$\Pr\{X(t) \leq x|X(s) = x_s\} = \Pr\{X(t - s) \leq x|X(0) = x_s\}. \tag{3.4}$$

In these cases we speak of *time-homogeneous Markov processes*. Important to note here is that we stated that the next state only depends on the current state, and *not* on how long we have been already in that state. This means that in a Markov process, the state residence times must be random variables that have a memoryless distribution. As we will see later, this implies that the state residence times in a continuous-time Markov chain need to be exponentially distributed, and in a discrete-time Markov chain need to be geometrically distributed (see also Appendix A).

An extension of Markov processes can be imagined in which the state residence time distributions are not exponential or geometric any more. In that case it is important to know how long we have been in a particular state and we speak of *semi-Markov processes*.

## 3.2 Renewal processes

We define a renewal process to be a discrete-time stochastic process $\{X_n|n = 1, 2, \cdots\}$, where $X_1, X_2, \cdots$ are independent, identically distributed, nonnegative random variables.

Let us now assume that all the random variables $X_i$ are distributed as the random variable $X$ with underlying distribution function $F_X(x)$. Furthermore, let

$$S_k = X_1 + X_2 + \cdots + X_k \tag{3.5}$$

denote the time, from the initial time instance 0 onwards, until the $k$-th occurrence of a renewal $(S_0 = 0)$. Then, $S_k$ has distribution function $F_X^{(k)}(x)$, the $k$-fold convolution of $F_X(x)$, defined as

$$F_X^{(k+1)}(t) = \begin{cases} \mathbf{1}(t \geq 0), & k = 0, \\ \int_0^t F_X^{(k)}(t-s)f_X(s)ds, & k \geq 1, \end{cases} \tag{3.6}$$

with $f_X(s)$ the probability density function of $X$, and $\mathbf{1}(x)$ the indicator function which evaluates to 1 if its argument is true, and to zero otherwise.

Now, let us address the number of renewals during the time interval $[0, t)$. We define the *renewal counting process* $\{N(t)|t \in \mathbb{R}\}$, which counts the number of renewals in the interval $[0, t)$. This stochastic process has a discrete state space, being the natural numbers $\mathbb{N}$, and a continuous time parameter. The probability of having exactly $n$ renewals in a certain time interval, can now be expressed as follows:

$$\begin{aligned} \Pr\{N(t) = n\} &= \Pr\{S_n \leq t < S_{n+1}\} \\ &= \Pr\{S_n \leq t\} - \Pr\{S_{n+1} \leq t\} \\ &= F_X^{(n)}(t) - F_X^{(n+1)}(t). \end{aligned} \tag{3.7}$$

This expression can be understood as follows (see also Figure 3.1). The $n$-th renewal should take place before $t$, yielding the term $\Pr\{S_n \leq t\}$. However, that alone is not enough, the $(n+1)$-th renewal should take place after $t$, so that we have to subtract the probability that the $(n+1)$-th arrival happens before $t$, explaining the second term.

Obtaining the probability distribution for $\{N(t)|t \in \mathbb{R}\}$ is often complex, so that only the expected number of renewals during some time interval, $E[N(t)]$, is computed. This

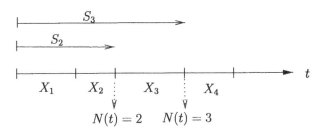

Figure 3.1: A renewal process and the associated counting process

quantity is denoted as $M(t)$ and called the *renewal function*. Using the definition for expectation, we now derive the following:

$$M(t) = E[N(t)] = \sum_{n=0}^{\infty} n \Pr\{N(t) = n\}$$

$$= \sum_{n=0}^{\infty} n F_X^{(n)}(t) - \sum_{n=0}^{\infty} n F_X^{(n+1)}(t)$$

$$= \sum_{n=0}^{\infty} n F_X^{(n)}(t) - \sum_{n=1}^{\infty} (n-1) F_X^{(n)}(t)$$

$$= \sum_{n=1}^{\infty} F_X^{(n)}(t) = F_X^{(1)}(t) + \sum_{n=1}^{\infty} F_X^{(n+1)}(t). \tag{3.8}$$

Considering the fact that $F_X^{(n+1)}(t)$ is the convolution of $F_X^{(n)}(t)$ and $F_X^{(1)}(t) = F_X(t)$ as given in (3.6), we obtain

$$M(t) = F_X(t) + \sum_{n=1}^{\infty} \left( \int_0^t F_X^{(n)}(t-s) f_X(s) ds \right)$$

$$= F_X(t) + \int_0^t \sum_{n=1}^{\infty} \left( F_X^{(n)}(t-s) \right) f_X(s) ds$$

$$= F_X(t) + \int_0^t M(t-s) f_X(s) ds. \tag{3.9}$$

This equation is known as the *fundamental renewal equation*. The derivative of $M(t)$, denoted as $m(t)$, is known as the *renewal density* and can be interpreted as follows. For small values $\epsilon > 0$, $\epsilon \times m(t)$ is the probability that a renewal occurs in the interval $[t, t+\epsilon)$. Taking the derivative of (3.8), we obtain

$$m(t) = \sum_{i=1}^{\infty} f_X^{(n)}(t), \tag{3.10}$$

where $f_X^{(n)}(t)$ is the derivative of $F_X^{(n)}(t)$, and consequently, we obtain the *renewal equation*:

$$m(t) = f_X(t) + \int_0^t m(t-s)f_X(s)ds. \tag{3.11}$$

Renewal processes have a number of nice properties. First of all, under a number of regularity assumptions, it can be shown that the limiting value of $m(t)$ for large $t$ approaches the reciprocal value of $E[X]$:

$$\lim_{t\to\infty} m(t) = \frac{1}{E[X]}. \tag{3.12}$$

This result states that, in the long run, the rate of renewals is inversely related to the mean inter-renewal time. This is an intuitively appealing result. Very often, this limiting value of $m(t)$ is also called the *rate of renewals*, or simply the rate (of the renewal process).

Secondly, a renewal process can be split into a number of less intensive renewal processes. Let $\alpha_i \in (0,1]$ and $\sum_{i=1}^n \alpha_i = 1$ (the $\alpha_i$ form a proper probability density). If we have a renewal process with rate $\lambda$ and squared coefficient of variation of the renewal time distribution $C^2$, we can split it into $n \in I\!N^+$ renewal processes, with rate $\alpha_i\lambda$ and squared coefficient of variation $\alpha_i C^2 + (1 - \alpha_i)$ respectively.

## Example 3.1. Poisson process.

Whenever the times between renewals are exponentially distributed, the renewal process is called a *Poisson process*. A Poisson process has many attractive features which explains part of its extensive use. The other part of the explanation is that for many processes observed in practice, the Poisson process is a very natural representation.

When we have as renewal time distribution $F_X(t) = 1 - e^{-\lambda t}$, $t \geq 0$, we can derive that $M(t) = \lambda t$ and $m(t) = \lambda$. $M(t)$ denotes the expected number of renewals in $[0,t)$ and $m(t)$ denotes the average renewal rate. Finally, notice that the $n$-fold convolution of the interrenewal time distribution has an Erlang-$n$ distribution:

$$F_X^{(n)}(t) = 1 - \left(\sum_{k=0}^{n-1} \frac{(\lambda t)^k}{k!}\right) e^{-\lambda t}. \tag{3.13}$$

This means that the time until exactly $n$ renewals have taken place is Erlang-$n$ distributed. When $n$ increases, the coefficient of variation decreases. This means that the variance that exists in the individual realisations of the renewals, for larger numbers of renewals "averages out".

Finally, as we will also see in Section 3.8, in a Poisson process, the probability density of the number of renewals in an interval $[0,t)$ has a Poisson distribution with parameter $\lambda t$:

$$\Pr\{N(t) = n\} = \frac{(\lambda t)^n}{n!} e^{-\lambda t}. \tag{3.14}$$

This can be understood by considering (3.7) and realizing that $F_X^{(n)}(t)$ is an Erlang-$n$ distribution. In the subtraction (3.7) all the summands cancel against one another, except the one with $k = n$ for $F_X^{(n+1)}(t)$ in (3.13).                                                $\square$

## 3.3   Discrete-time Markov chains

In this section we present in some detail the theory of discrete-time, discrete-state space Markov processes. These types of stochastic processes are generally called *discrete-time Markov chains* (DTMCs).

A DTMC has the usual properties of Markov processes: its future behaviour only depends on its current state and not on states assumed in the past. Without loss of generality we assume that the index set $\mathcal{T} = \{0, 1, 2, \cdots\}$ and that the state space is denoted by $\mathcal{I}$. The Markov property (3.3) has the following form:

$$\Pr\{X_{n+1} = i_{n+1} | X_0 = i_0, \cdots, X_n = i_n\} = \Pr\{X_{n+1} = i_{n+1} | X_n = i_n\}, \tag{3.15}$$

where $i_0, \cdots, i_{n+1} \in \mathcal{I}$. From this definition we see that the future (time instance $n + 1$) depends only on the current status (time instance $n$), and not on the past (time instances $n - 1, \cdots, 0$). Let $p_j(n) = \Pr\{X_n = j\}$ denote the probability of "being" in state $j$ at time $n$. Furthermore, define the conditional probability $p_{j,k}(m, n) = \Pr\{X_n = k | X_m = j\}$, for all $m = 0, \cdots, n$, i.e., the probability of going from state $j$ at time $m$ to state $k$ at time $n$. Since we will only deal with time-homogeneous Markov chains, these so-called *transition probabilities* only depend on the time difference $l = n - m$. We therefore denote them as $p_{j,k}(l) = \Pr\{X_{m+l} = k | X_m = j\}$. These probabilities are called the $l$-step transition probabilities. The 1-step transition probabilities are simple denoted $p_{j,k}$ (the parameter 1 is omitted). The 0-step probabilities are defined as $p_{j,k}(0) = 1$, whenever $j = k$, and 0 elsewhere. The initial distribution $\underline{p}(0)$ of the Markov chain is defined as $\underline{p}(0) = (p_0(0), \cdots, p_{|\mathcal{I}|}(0))$. By iteratively applying the rule for conditional probabilities, it can easily be seen that

$$\Pr\{X_0 = i_0, X_1 = i_1, \cdots, X_n = i_n\} = p_{i_0}(0) p_{i_0, i_1} \cdots p_{i_{n-1}, i_n}. \tag{3.16}$$

This implies that the DTMC is totally described by the initial probabilities and the 1-step probabilities. The 1-step probabilities are easily denoted by a *state-transition probability matrix* $\mathbf{P} = (p_{i,j})$. The matrix $\mathbf{P}$ is a *stochastic matrix* because all its entries $p_{i,j}$ satisfy $0 \leq p_{i,j} \leq 1$, and $\sum_j p_{i,j} = 1$, for all $i$.

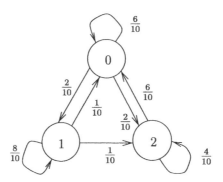

Figure 3.2: State transition diagram for the example DTMC

A DTMC is very conveniently visualised as a labeled directed graph with the elements of $\mathcal{I}$ as vertices. A directed edge with label $p_{i,j}$ exists between vertices $i$ and $j$ whenever $p_{i,j} > 0$. Such representations of Markov chains are often called *state transition diagrams*.

**Example 3.2. Graphical representation of a DTMC.**
In Figure 3.2 we show the state transition diagram for the DTMC with state-transition probability matrix

$$\mathbf{P} = \frac{1}{10} \begin{pmatrix} 6 & 2 & 2 \\ 1 & 8 & 1 \\ 6 & 0 & 4 \end{pmatrix}. \tag{3.17}$$

□

Let us now calculate the 2-step probabilities of a DTMC with state-transition probability matrix $\mathbf{P}$. We have

$$p_{i,j}(2) = \Pr\{X_2 = j | X_0 = i\} = \sum_{k \in \mathcal{I}} \Pr\{X_2 = j, X_1 = k | X_0 = i\}, \tag{3.18}$$

since in going from state $i$ to state $j$ in two steps, any state $k \in \mathcal{I}$ can be visited as intermediate state. Now, due to the rules of conditional probabilities as well as the Markov property, we can write

$$
\begin{aligned}
p_{i,j}(2) &= \sum_{k \in \mathcal{I}} \Pr\{X_2 = j, X_1 = k | X_0 = i\} \\
&= \sum_{k \in \mathcal{I}} \Pr\{X_1 = k | X_0 = i\} \Pr\{X_2 = j | X_1 = k, X_0 = i\} \\
&= \sum_{k \in \mathcal{I}} \Pr\{X_1 = k | X_0 = i\} \Pr\{X_2 = j | X_1 = k\}
\end{aligned}
$$

$$= \sum_{k \in \mathcal{I}} p_{i,k} p_{k,j}. \tag{3.19}$$

In the last equality we recognize the matrix product. We thus have obtained that the 2-step probabilities $p_{i,j}(2)$ are elements of the matrix $\mathbf{P}^2$. The above technique can be applied iteratively, yielding that the $n$-step probabilities $p_{i,j}(n)$ are elements of the matrix $\mathbf{P}^n$. For the 0-step probabilities we can write $\mathbf{I} = \mathbf{P}^0$. The equation that established a relation between the $(m+n)$-step probabilities and the $m$- and $n$-step probabilities is

$$\mathbf{P}^{m+n} = \mathbf{P}^m \mathbf{P}^n, \tag{3.20}$$

which is generally known as the *Chapman-Kolmogorov equation*.

When we want to calculate $p_j(n)$ we can simply condition on the initial probabilities, i.e.,

$$\begin{aligned} p_j(n) = \Pr\{X_n = j\} &= \sum_{i \in \mathcal{I}} \Pr\{X_0 = i\} \Pr\{X_n = j | X_0 = i\} \\ &= \sum_{i \in \mathcal{I}} p_i(0) p_{i,j}(n). \end{aligned} \tag{3.21}$$

Writing this in matrix-vector notation, with $\underline{p}(n) = (p_0(n), p_1(n), \cdots)$, we arrive at

$$\underline{p}(n) = \underline{p}(0) \mathbf{P}^n. \tag{3.22}$$

Recalling that the index $n$ in the above expression can be interpreted as the step-count or the time in the DTMC, (3.22) indeed expresses the time-dependent or transient behaviour of the DTMC.

**Example 3.3. Transient behaviour of a DTMC.**
Let us compute $\underline{p}(n) = \underline{p}(0) \mathbf{P}^n$ for $n = 1, 2, 3, \cdots$ with $\mathbf{P}$ as given in (3.17), and $\underline{p}(0) = (1, 0, 0)$. Clearly, $\underline{p}(1) = \underline{p}(0) \mathbf{P} = (0.6, 0.2, 0.2)$. Then, $\underline{p}(2) = \underline{p}(0) \mathbf{P}^2 = \underline{p}(1) \mathbf{P} = (0.50, 0.28, 0.22)$. We proceed with $\underline{p}(3) = \underline{p}(2) \mathbf{P} = (0.460, 0.324, 0.216)$. We could go on and calculate many more $\underline{p}(n)$ values. What can already be observed is that the successive values for $\underline{p}(n)$ seem to converge somehow, and that the elements of all the vectors $\underline{p}(n)$ always sum to 1. □

It is interesting to note that for many DTMCs (but definitely not all; we will discuss conditions for convergence in the next section) all the rows in $\mathbf{P}^n$ converge to a common limit when $n \to \infty$. For the time being, we assume that such a limit indeed exists and denote it as $\underline{v}$. Define

$$v_j = \lim_{n \to \infty} p_j(n) = \lim_{n \to \infty} \Pr\{X_n = j\} = \lim_{n \to \infty} \sum_{i \in \mathcal{I}} p_i(0) p_{i,j}(n). \tag{3.23}$$

Writing this in matrix-vector notation, we obtain

$$v = \lim_{n\to\infty} p(n) = \lim_{n\to\infty} p(0)\mathbf{P}^n. \tag{3.24}$$

However, we also have

$$v = \lim_{n\to\infty} p(n+1) = \lim_{n\to\infty} p(0)\mathbf{P}^{n+1} = \left(\lim_{n\to\infty} p(0)\mathbf{P}^n\right)\mathbf{P} = v\mathbf{P}. \tag{3.25}$$

We thus have established that whenever the limiting probabilities $v$ exist, they can be obtained by solving the system of linear equations

$$v = v\mathbf{P} \quad \Rightarrow \quad v(\mathbf{I} - \mathbf{P}) = 0, \tag{3.26}$$

with, since $v$ is a probability vector, $\sum_i v_i = 1$, and $0 \le v_i \le 1$. Note that the vector $v$ is the left Eigenvector of $\mathbf{P}$ associated with Eigenvalue 1. The equivalent form on the right, i.e., $v(\mathbf{I} - \mathbf{P}) = 0$, will be discussed in Section 3.5 in relation to CTMCs.

The vector $v$ is called the *stationary* or *steady-state probability vector* of the Markov chain. For the Markov chains we will encounter, a unique limiting distribution will most often exist. Furthermore, in most of the practical cases we will encounter, this steady-state probability vector will be independent of the initial state probabilities.

**Example 3.4. Steady-state probability vector calculation.**
Let us compute $v = v\mathbf{P}$ with $\mathbf{P}$ as in the previous example, and compare it to the partially converged result obtained there. Denoting $v = (v_1, v_2, v_3)$ we have a system of three linear equations:

$$\begin{cases} v_1 = \frac{1}{10}(6v_1 + v_2 + 6v_3), \\ v_2 = \frac{1}{10}(2v_1 + 8v_2), \\ v_3 = \frac{1}{10}(2v_1 + v_2 + 4v_3). \end{cases} \tag{3.27}$$

Multiplying all equations by 10 and collecting terms yields

$$\begin{cases} 4v_1 = v_2 + 6v_3, \\ 2v_2 = 2v_1, \\ 6v_3 = 2v_1 + v_2. \end{cases} \tag{3.28}$$

From the middle equation we obtain $v_1 = v_2$. Substituting this in the other two equations reveals that $v_3 = v_1/2$. Using the fact that $v_1 + v_2 + v_3 = 1$ then gives us $v = (\frac{4}{10}, \frac{4}{10}, \frac{2}{10})$. Note that the observed convergence in the previous example goes indeed in the direction of $v$. □

The steady-state probabilities can be interpreted in two ways. One way is to see them as the long-run proportion of time the DTMC "spends" in the respective states. The other way is to regard them as the probabilities that the DTMC would be in a particular state if one would take a snapshot after a very long time. It is important to note that for large values of $n$ state changes do still take place in the DTMC.

Let us finally address the state residence time distributions in DTMCs. We have seen that the matrix $\mathbf{P}$ describes the 1-step state transition probabilities. If, at some time instance $n$, the state of the DTMC is $i$, then, at time instance $n + 1$, the state will still be $i$ with probability $p_{i,i}$, but the state will be $j \neq i$ with probability $1 - p_{i,i} = \sum_{j \neq i} p_{i,j}$. For time instance $n + 1$ a similar reasoning holds, so that the probability of residing still in state $i$ (given residence there at time instance $n$ and $n + 1$) equals $p_{i,i}^2$. Taking this further, the probability to reside in state $i$ for exactly $m$ consecutive time steps equals $(1 - p_{i,i})p_{i,i}^{m-1}$, that is, there are $m - 1$ steps in which the possibility (staying in $i$) with probability $p_{i,i}$ is taken, and one final step with probability $1 - p_{i,i}$ where indeed a step towards another state $j \neq i$ is taken. Interpreting leaving state $i$ as a success and staying in state $i$ as a failure (one fails to leave) we see that the state residence times in a DTMC obey a geometric distribution. The expected number of steps of residence in state $i$ then equals $1/(1 - p_{i,i})$ and the variance of the number of residence steps in state $i$ then equals $p_{i,i}/(1 - p_{i,i})^2$.

The fact that the state residence times in a DTMC are geometrical distributions need not be a surprise. When discussing the Markov property, we have stated that only the actual state, at some time instance, is of importance in determining the future, and not the residence time in that state. The geometric distribution is the only discrete distribution exhibiting this memoryless property.

## 3.4 Convergence properties of Markov chains

As indicated in the previous section many DTMCs exhibit convergence properties, but certainly not all. In this section we will discuss, in a very compact way, a number of properties of DTMCs that help us in deciding whether a DTMC has a unique steady-state distribution or not. In a similar way such properties can also be established for CTMCs (see Section 3.5).

Let us start with a classification of the states in a DTMC. A state $j$ is said to be *accessible* from state $i$ if, for some value $n$, $p_{i,j}(n) > 0$, which means that there is a step number for which there is a nonzero probability of going from state $i$ to $j$. For such a pair of states, we write $i \rightarrow j$. If $i \rightarrow j$ and $j \rightarrow i$, then $i$ and $j$ are said to be *communicating* states, denoted $i \sim j$. Clearly, the communicating relation ($\sim$) is:

- transitive: if $i \sim j$ and $j \sim k$ then $i \sim k$;

- symmetric: by its definition in terms of $\rightarrow$, $i \sim j$ is equivalent to $j \sim i$;

- reflexive: for $n = 0$, we have $p_{i,i}(0) = 1$, so that $i \rightarrow i$ and therefore $i \sim i$.

Consequently, $\sim$ is an *equivalence relation* which partitions the state space in communicating classes. If all the states of a Markov chain belong to the same communicating class, the Markov chain is said to be *irreducible*. If not, the Markov chain is called *reducible*.

The *period $d_i \in I\!N$* of state $i$ is defined as the greatest common divisor of those values $n$ for which $p_{i,i}(n) \geq 0$. When $d_i = 1$, state $i$ is said to be aperiodic, in which case, at every time step there is a non-zero probability of residing in state $i$. It has been proven that within a communicating class all states have the same period. Therefore, one can also speak of periodic and aperiodic communicating classes, or, in case of an irreducible Markov chain, of an *aperiodic* or *periodic Markov chain* (consisting of just one communicating class).

A state $i$ is said to be *absorbing* when $\lim_{n\to\infty} p_{i,i}(n) = 1$. When there is only one absorbing state, the Markov chain will, with certainty, reach that state for some value of $n$. A state is said to be *transient* or *non-recurrent* if there is a nonzero probability that the Markov chain will not return to that state again. If this is not the case, the state is said to be recurrent. For *recurrent* states, we can address the time between successive visits. Let $f_{i,j}(n)$ denote the probability that exactly $n$ steps after leaving state $i$, state $j$ is visited for the first time. Consequently, $f_{i,i}(n)$ is the probability that the Markov chain takes exactly $n$ steps between two successive visits to state $i$. The probability to end up in state $j \neq i$ when started in state $i$, can now be expressed as

$$f_{i,j} = \sum_{n=1}^{\infty} f_{i,j}(n). \tag{3.29}$$

From this definition, it follows that if $f_{i,i} = 1$, then state $i$ is recurrent. If state $i$ is nonrecurrent then $f_{i,i} < 1$. In the case $f_{i,i} = 1$ we can make a further classification based upon the mean recurrence time of state $i$:

$$m_i = \sum_{n=1}^{\infty} n f_{i,i}(n). \tag{3.30}$$

A recurrent state $i$ is said to be *positive recurrent* (or recurrent non-null) if the mean recurrence time $m_i$ is finite. If $m_i$ is infinite, state $i$ is said to be *null recurrent*.

Having defined the above properties, the following theorem expresses when a DTMC has a (unique) steady-state probability distribution.

**Theorem 3.1. Steady-state probability distributions in a DTMC.**

In an irreducible and aperiodic DTMC with positive recurrent states:

- the limiting distribution $\underline{v} = \lim_{n\to\infty} p_j(n) = \lim_{n\to\infty} p_{i,j}(n)$ does exist;

- $\underline{v}$ is independent of the initial probability distribution $\underline{p}(0)$;

- $\underline{v}$ is the unique stationary probability distribution (the steady-state probability vector).

$\square$

In most of the performance models we will encounter, the Markov chains will be of the last type. When we do not state so explicitly, we assume that we deal with irreducible and aperiodic DTMCs with positive recurrent states. When we are dealing with continuous-time Markov chains, similar conditions apply.

## 3.5 Continuous-time Markov chains

In this section we present in some detail the theory of continuous-time Markov chains (CTMCs). We first discuss how CTMCs can be constructed by enhancing DTMCs with state residence time distributions in Section 3.5.1. We then present the evaluation of the steady-state and transient behaviour of CTMCs in Section 3.5.2; this section also includes examples.

### 3.5.1 From DTMC to CTMC

As before, we assume without loss of generality that the state space is denoted $\mathcal{I} = \{0, 1, 2, \cdots\}$. In DTMCs we have only been addressing abstract time steps up till now. No "physical" time has been associated with these steps. With CTMCs we interpret the index as real time, i.e., we denote $\mathcal{T} = [0, \infty)$, where $t = 0$ is the time point at which the CTMC starts, and is in its initial state.

The easiest way to introduce CTMCs is to develop them from DTMCs. We do so by associating with every state $i$ a state residence time distribution. Since for CTMCs the general Markov property must be valid, we do not have complete freedom to choose any state residence time distribution. Recalling the Markov property, we must have, for all non-negative $t_0 < t_1 < \cdots < t_{n+1}$ and $x_0, x_1, \cdots, x_{n+1}$:

$$\Pr\{X(t_{n+1}) = x_{n+1} | X(t_0) = x_0, \cdots, X(t_n) = x_n\} = \Pr\{X(t_{n+1}) = x_{n+1} | X(t_n) = x_n\}.$$
(3.31)

As can be observed, the probability distribution for the $(n + 1)$-th state residence time only depends on the current ($n$-th) state *and not* on the time the chain has already resided in the current state, nor on states assumed in the past. This implies that a memoryless continuous distribution is needed to describe the state residence times. Since there is only one memoryless continuous distribution, we have little choice here. Indeed, as will be shown later, the state residence times in CTMCs are exponentially distributed. Thus, we can associate with every state $i$ in the CTMC a parameter $\mu_i$ describing the rate of the exponential distribution, that is, we have as residence distribution in state $i$:

$$F_i(t) = 1 - e^{-\mu_i t}, \ t \geq 0.$$
(3.32)

The vector $\underline{\mu} = (\cdots, \mu_i, \cdots)$ thus describes the state residence time distributions in the CTMC. We can still use the state transition probability matrix $\mathbf{P}$ to describe the state transition behaviour. The initial probabilities remain $\underline{p}(0)$. The operation of the CTMC can now be interpreted as follows. When entering state $i$, the CTMC will "stay" in $i$ for a random amount of time, distributed according to the state residence distribution $F_i(t)$. After this delay, a state change to state $j$ will take place with probability $p_{i,j}$; to ease understanding at this point, assume that $p_{i,i} = 0$ for all $i$.

Instead of associating with every state just one negative exponentially distributed delay, it is also possible to associate as many delays with a state as there are transition possibilities. We therefore define the matrix $\mathbf{Q}$ with $q_{i,j} = \mu_i p_{i,j}$, in case $i \neq j$, and $q_{i,i} = -\sum_{j \neq i} q_{i,j} = -\mu_i$ (in some publications the diagonal entries $q_{i,i}$ are denoted as $-q_i$ with $q_i = \sum_{j \neq i} q_{i,j}$). Notice that since we assume that $p_{i,i} = 0$, we have $q_{i,i} = -\mu_i$. Using this notation allows for the following interpretation. When entering state $i$, it is investigated which states $j$ can be reached from $i$, namely those $j \neq i$ for which $q_{i,j} > 0$. Then, for each of these possibilities, a random variable is thought to be drawn, according to the (negative exponential) distributions $F_{i \rightarrow j}(t) = 1 - e^{-q_{i,j} t}$; these distributions model the delay perceived in state $i$ when going from $i$ to $j$. One of the "drawn" delays will be the smallest, meaning that the transition corresponding to that delay will take the smallest amount of time, and hence will take place. The possible transitions starting from state $i$ can be interpreted as if in a race condition: the faster one wins.

Why is this interpretation also correct? The answer lies in the special properties of the employed negative exponential distributions. Let us first address the state residence times.

Being in state $i$, the time it takes to reach state $j$ is exponentially distributed with rate $q_{i,j}$. When there is more than one possible successor state, the next state will be such that the residence time in state $i$ is minimised (race condition). However, the minimum value of a number of exponentially distributed random variables with rates $q_{i,j}$ ($j \neq i$) is again an exponentially distributed random variable, with as rate the sum $\sum_{j \neq i} q_{i,j}$ of the original rates. This is exactly equal to the rate $\mu_i$ of the residence time in state $i$.

A second point to verify is whether the state transition behaviour is still the same. In general, if we have $n$ negative exponentially distributed random variables $X_k$ (with rates $l_k$), then $X_i$ will be the minimum of them with probability $l_i / \sum_k l_k$. In our case, we have a number of competing delays when starting from state $i$, which are all negative exponentially distributed random variables (with rates $q_{i,j}$). The shortest one will then lead to state $j$ with probability

$$\frac{q_{i,j}}{\sum_{k \neq i} q_{i,k}} = \frac{p_{i,j} \mu_i}{\mu_i} = p_{i,j}, \tag{3.33}$$

which shows the equivalence of the transition probabilities in both interpretations.

Let us now discuss the case where $p_{i,i} > 0$, that is, the case where, after having resided in state $i$ for an exponentially distributed period of time (with rate $\mu_i$), there is a positive probability of staying in $i$ for another period. In particular, we have seen in Section 3.3 that the state residence distributions in a DTMC obey a geometric distribution (measured in "visits"), with mean $1/(1 - p_{i,i})$ for state $i$. Hence, if we decide that the expected state residence *time* in the CTMC constructed from the DTMC is $1/\mu_i$, the time spent in state $i$ *per visit* should on average be $(1 - p_{i,i})/\mu_i$. Hence, the rate of the negative exponential distribution associated with that state should equal $\mu_i/(1 - p_{i,i})$. Using this rate in the above procedure we find that we have to assign the following transition rates for $j \neq i$:

$$q_{i,j} = \frac{\mu_i p_{i,j}}{1 - p_{i,i}} = \mu_i \frac{p_{i,j}}{1 - p_{i,i}} = \mu_i \Pr\{\text{jump } i \to j | \text{jump away from } i\}, \quad j \neq i, \tag{3.34}$$

that is, we have renormalised the probabilities $p_{i,j}$ ($j \neq i$) such that they make up a proper distribution. To conclude, if we want to associate a negative exponential residence time with rate $\mu_i$ to state $i$, we can do so by just normalising the probabilities $p_{i,j}$ ($j \neq i$) appropriately.

## 3.5.2 Evaluating the steady-state and transient behaviour

As DTMCs, CTMCs can be depicted conveniently using state transition diagrams. These state transition diagrams are labelled directed graphs, with the states of the CTMC represented by the vertices. An edge between vertices $i$ and $j$ ($i \neq j$) exists whenever $q_{i,j} > 0$. The edges in the graph are labelled with the corresponding rates.

Formally, a CTMC can be described by an *(infinitesimal) generator matrix* $\mathbf{Q} = (q_{i,j})$ and initial state probabilities $\underline{p}(0)$. Denoting the system state at time $t \in \mathcal{T}$ as $X(t) \in \mathcal{I}$, we have, for $h \to 0$:

$$\Pr\{X(t+h) = j | X(t) = i\} = q_{i,j}h + o(h), \quad i \neq j, \tag{3.35}$$

where $o(h)$ is a term that goes to zero faster than $h$, i.e., $\lim_{t \to 0} o(h)/h = 0$. This result follows from the fact that the state residence times are negative exponentially distributed. The value $q_{i,j}$ ($i \neq j$) is the rate at which the current state $i$ changes to state $j$. Denote with $p_i(t)$ the probability that the state at time $t$ equals $i$: $p_i(t) = \Pr\{X(t) = i\}$. Given $p_i(t)$, we can compute the evolution of the Markov chain in the very near future $[t, t+h)$, as follows:

$$
\begin{aligned}
p_i(t+h) &= p_i(t) \Pr\{\text{do not depart from } i\} + \sum_{j \neq i} p_j(t) \Pr\{\text{go from } j \text{ to } i\} \\
&= p_i(t) \left(1 - \sum_{j \neq i} q_{i,j}h\right) + \left(\sum_{j \neq i} p_j(t) q_{j,i}\right) h + o(h).
\end{aligned}
\tag{3.36}
$$

Now, using the earlier defined notation $q_{i,i} = -\sum_{j \neq i} q_{i,j}$, we have

$$p_i(t+h) = p_i(t) + \left(\sum_{j \in \mathcal{I}} q_{j,i} p_j(t)\right) h + o(h). \tag{3.37}$$

Rearranging terms, dividing by $h$ and taking the limit $h \to 0$, we obtain

$$p_i'(t) = \lim_{h \to 0} \frac{p_i(t+h) - p_i(t)}{h} = \sum_{j \in \mathcal{I}} q_{j,i} p_j(t), \tag{3.38}$$

which in matrix notation has the following form:

$$\underline{p}'(t) = \underline{p}(t)\mathbf{Q}, \tag{3.39}$$

where $\underline{p}(t) = (\cdots, p_i(t), \cdots)$ and where the initial probability vector $\underline{p}(0)$ is given. We thus have obtained that the time-dependent or *transient state probabilities* in a CTMC are described by a system of linear differential equations, which can be solved using a Taylor series expansion as follows:

$$\underline{p}(t) = \underline{p}(0)e^{\mathbf{Q}t} = \underline{p}(0) \left(\sum_{i=0}^{\infty} \frac{(\mathbf{Q}t)^i}{i!}\right). \tag{3.40}$$

As we will see in Chapter 15, this solution for $\underline{p}(t)$ is not the most appropriate to use. Other methods will be shown to be more efficient and accurate.

In many cases, however, the *transient behaviour* $\underline{p}(t)$ of the Markov chain is more than we really need. For performance evaluation purposes we are often already satisfied when we are able to compute the long-term or *steady-state probabilities* $p_i = \lim_{t \to \infty} p_i(t)$. When we assume that a steady-state distribution exists, this implies that the above limit exists, and thus that $\lim_{t \to \infty} p'_i(t) = 0$. Consequently, for obtaining the steady-state probabilities we only need to solve the system of linear equations:

$$\underline{p}\mathbf{Q} = \underline{0}, \quad \sum_{i \in \mathcal{I}} p_i = 1. \tag{3.41}$$

The right part is added to ensure that the obtained solution is indeed a probability vector; the left part alone has infinitely many solutions, which upon normalisation all yield the same probability vector.

It is important to note here that the equation $\underline{p}\mathbf{Q} = \underline{0}$ is of the same form as the equation $\underline{v} = \underline{v}\mathbf{P}$ we have seen for DTMCs. Since this equation can be rewritten as $\underline{v}(\mathbf{P} - \mathbf{I}) = \underline{0}$, the matrix $(\mathbf{P} - \mathbf{I})$ can be interpreted as a generator matrix. It conforms the format discussed above: all non-diagonal entries are non-negative and the diagonal entries equal the (negated) sums of the off-diagonal elements in the same row.

Given a CTMC described by $\mathbf{Q}$ and $\underline{p}(0)$, it is also possible to solve the steady-state probabilities via an associated DTMC. We therefore construct a state-transition probability matrix $\mathbf{P}$ with $p_{i,j} = q_{i,j}/|q_{i,i}|$ $(i \neq j)$ and with diagonal elements $p_{i,i} = 0$. The resulting DTMC is called the embedded Markov chain corresponding to the CTMC. The probabilities $p_{i,j}$ represent the branching probabilities, given that a transition out of state $i$ occurs in the CTMC. For this CTMC we solve the steady-state probability vector $\underline{v}$ via $\underline{v}\mathbf{P} = \underline{v}$; $v_i$ now represents the probability that state $i$ is visited, irrespective of the length of staying in this state. To include the latter aspect, we have to renormalise the probabilities $v_i$ with the mean times spent in each state according to the CTMC definition. In the CTMC, the mean residence time in state $i$ is $1/q_i$, so that the steady-state probabilities for the CTMC become:

$$p_i = \frac{v_i/q_i}{\sum_j v_j/q_j}, \quad \text{for all } i. \tag{3.42}$$

**Example 3.5. Evaluation of a 2-state CTMC.**
Consider a computer system that can either be completely operational or not at all. The time it is operational is exponentially distributed with mean $1/\lambda$. The time it is not operational is also exponentially distributed, with mean $1/\mu$. Signifying the operational

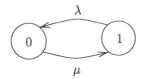

Figure 3.3: A simple 2-state CTMC

state as state "1", and the down state as state "0", we can model this system as a 2-state CTMC with generator matrix $\mathbf{Q}$ as follows:

$$\mathbf{Q} = \begin{pmatrix} -\mu & \mu \\ \lambda & -\lambda \end{pmatrix}. \tag{3.43}$$

Furthermore, it is assumed that the system is initially fully operational so that $\underline{p}(0) = (0, 1)$. In Figure 3.3 we show the corresponding state transition diagram. Note that the numbers with the edges are now rates and not probabilities.

Solving (3.41) yields the following steady-state probability vector:

$$\underline{p} = \left( \frac{\lambda}{\lambda + \mu}, \frac{\mu}{\lambda + \mu} \right). \tag{3.44}$$

This probability vector can also be computed via the embedded DTMC which is given as:

$$\mathbf{P} = \begin{pmatrix} 0 & 1 \\ 1 & 0 \end{pmatrix}. \tag{3.45}$$

Solving for $\underline{v}$ yields us $\underline{v} = (\frac{1}{2}, \frac{1}{2})$, indicating that both states are visited equally often. However, these visits are not equally long. Incorporating the mean state residence times, being respectively $1/\mu$ and $1/\lambda$, yields

$$\underline{p} = \left( \frac{\frac{1}{2}\frac{1}{\mu}}{\frac{1}{2}\left(\frac{1}{\mu}+\frac{1}{\lambda}\right)}, \frac{\frac{1}{2}\frac{1}{\lambda}}{\frac{1}{2}\left(\frac{1}{\mu}+\frac{1}{\lambda}\right)} \right) = \left( \frac{\lambda}{\lambda + \mu}, \frac{\mu}{\lambda + \mu} \right), \tag{3.46}$$

which is the solution we have seen before.

We can also study the transient behaviour of the CTMC. We then have to solve the corresponding system of linear differential equations. Although this is difficult in general, for this specific example we can obtain the solution explicitly. From

$$\underline{p}(t) = \underline{p}(0)e^{\mathbf{Q}t}, \tag{3.47}$$

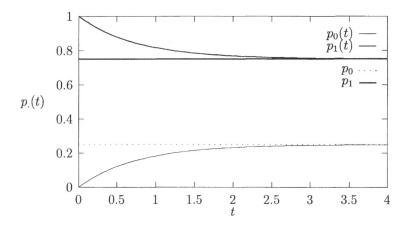

Figure 3.4: Steady-state and transient behaviour of a 2-state CTMC

we derive

$$
\begin{aligned}
p_0(t) &= \frac{\lambda}{\lambda+\mu} - \frac{\lambda}{\lambda+\mu}e^{-(\lambda+\mu)t}, \\
p_1(t) &= \frac{\mu}{\lambda+\mu} + \frac{\lambda}{\lambda+\mu}e^{-(\lambda+\mu)t}.
\end{aligned}
\tag{3.48}
$$

Notice that $p_0(t) + p_1(t) = 1$ (for all $t$) and that the limit of the transient solutions for $t \to \infty$ indeed equals the steady-state probability vectors derived before. In Figure 3.4 we show the transient and steady-state behaviour of the 2-state CTMC for $3\lambda = \mu = 1$. □

## Example 3.6. Availability evaluation of a fault-tolerant system.

Consider a fault-tolerant computer system consisting of three computing nodes and a single voting node. The three computing nodes generate results after which the voter decides upon the correct value (by selecting the answer that is given by at least two computing nodes). Such a fault-tolerant computing system is also known as a triple-modular redundant system (TMR). The failure rate of a computing node is $\lambda$ and of the voter $\nu$ failures per hour (fph). The expected repair time of a computing node is $1/\mu$ and of the voter is $1/\delta$ hours. If the voter fails, the whole system is supposed to have failed and after a repair (with rate $\delta$) the system is assumed to start "as new". The system is assumed to be operational when at least two computing nodes and the voter are functioning correctly.

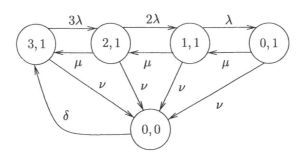

Figure 3.5: CTMC for the TMR system

To model the availability of this system as a CTMC, we first have to define the state space: $\mathcal{I} = \{(3,1), (2,1), (1,1), (0,1), (0,0)\}$, where state $(i,j)$ specifies that $i$ computing nodes are operational as well as $j$ voters. Note that the circumstance of the computing nodes does not play a role any more as soon as the voter goes down; after a repair in this down state the whole system will be fully operational, irrespective of the past state. Using the above description, the state-transition diagram can be drawn easily, as given in Figure 3.5. The corresponding generator matrix is given as:

$$Q = \begin{pmatrix} -(3\lambda + \nu) & 3\lambda & 0 & 0 & \nu \\ \mu & -(\mu + 2\lambda + \nu) & 2\lambda & 0 & \nu \\ 0 & \mu & -(\mu + \lambda + \nu) & \lambda & \nu \\ 0 & 0 & \mu & -(\mu + \nu) & \nu \\ \delta & 0 & 0 & 0 & -\delta \end{pmatrix}. \tag{3.49}$$

We assume that the system is fully operational at $t = 0$. The following numerical parameters are given: $\lambda = 0.01$ fph, $\nu = 0.001$ fph, $\mu = 1.0$ repairs per hour (rph) and $\delta = 0,2$ rph.

We can now compute the steady-state probabilities by solving the linear system $\underline{p}Q = \underline{0}$ under the condition that $\sum_i p_i = 1$, which yields the following values:

| $(i,j)$ | $(3,1)$ | $(2,1)$ | $(1,1)$ | $(0,1)$ | $(0,0)$ |
|---|---|---|---|---|---|
| $P_{i,j}$ | $9.6551 \times 10^{-1}$ | $2.8936 \times 10^{-2}$ | $5.7813 \times 10^{-4}$ | $5.7755 \times 10^{-6}$ | $4.9751 \times 10^{-3}$ |

The probability that the system is operational can thus be computed as 0.99444. Although this number looks very good (it is very close to 100%) for a non-stop transaction processing facility, it would still mean an expected down-time of 48.7 hours a year $((1 - 0.99444) \times 24 \times 365)$.

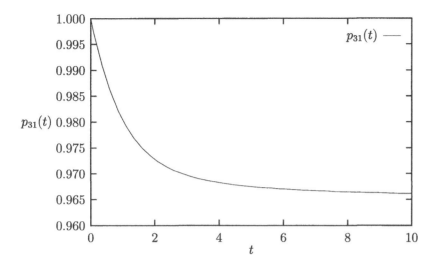

Figure 3.6: Transient probabilities for the TMR system (1)

We can also address the transient behaviour of this small CTMC by numerically solving the differential equations for $\underline{p}(t)$ with a technique known as uniformisation (see Chapter 15). In Figure 3.6 we show the probability $p_{3,1}(t)$ for the first 10 hours of system operation. As can be observed, the transient probability reaches the steady-state probability relatively fast. A similar observation can be made for the other transient probabilities in Figure 3.7 (note the logarithmic scale of the vertical axis).                                   □

## 3.6   Semi-Markov chains

It is possible to associate other than exponential distributions with the states in a Markov chain. In *semi-Markov chains* (SMCs) the rate of the transition from state $i$ to state $j$ may depend on the time already spent in state $i$ (since the last entrance) but not on states visited before entering state $i$ nor on any previous residence times. Thus, we deal with a time-dependent probability matrix $\mathbf{K}(t)$ known as the *kernel of the SMC*, where an entry $k_{i,j}(t)$ equals the probability that, after having entered state $i$, it takes at most $t$ time units to switch to state $j$ (given that no transition to any other state takes place).

We can now define two important intermediate quantities. First, we define $p_{i,j} = \lim_{t\to\infty} k_{i,j}(t)$ which expresses the probability that once state $i$ has been entered, the next state will be $j$. Furthermore, we define $F_i(t) = \sum_j k_{i,j}(t)$. As before, $F_i(t)$ is the residence

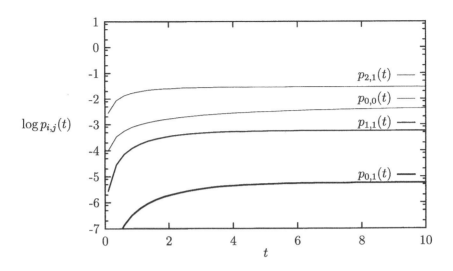

Figure 3.7: Transient probabilities for the TMR system (2)

time distribution for state $i$ (per visit to state $i$). Using these two definitions we can describe the operation of an SMC as follows. Once state $i$ has been entered, the residence time in that state will be a random variable with distribution $F_i(t)$ (and density $f_i(t)$). After this period, the state changes to $j$ with probability $p_{i,j}$.

To obtain the steady-state probabilities for an SMC, we can follow the same method as has been presented to solve the steady-state probabilities for CTMCs using DTMCs. Indeed, at the moments of state changes, the SMC behaves exactly as a DTMC. Therefore, we can compute the steady-state probabilities for the DTMC with $\mathbf{P} = (p_{i,j})$, denoted here as $\underline{v}$. Now, we have to compute the average state residence times $f_i$ for all states $i$ in the SMC. We do this directly from the state residence time distributions:

$$f_i = \int_0^\infty t f_i(t) dt. \tag{3.50}$$

We then obtain the steady-state probabilities in the SMC by taking these residence times into account, as follows:

$$p_i = \frac{v_i f_i}{\sum_j v_j f_j}, \quad \text{for all } i. \tag{3.51}$$

## 3.7   The birth-death process

A special case of the CTMCs discussed in Section 3.5 is the *birth-death process*. Since such processes have many applications in queueing theory (see also Chapter 4) we introduce them here. A birth-death process on state space $\mathcal{I} = \{0, 1, 2, \cdots\}$ is a CTMC in which from any state $i \in \mathbb{N}^+$ only transitions to the neighbouring states $i - 1$ and $i + 1$ are allowed. From state 0, the only allowed transition is to state 1. When interpreting the current state $i \in \mathbb{N}$ as the current population in a system, a *birth* occurs with rate $\lambda_i > 0$, resulting in state $i + 1$. On the other hand, from state $i \in \mathbb{N}^+$ a *death* occurs with rate $\mu_i > 0$, resulting in state $i - 1$. This type of CTMC is characterised by a tridiagonal generator matrix $\mathbf{Q}$ as follows:

$$\mathbf{Q} = \begin{pmatrix} -\lambda_0 & \lambda_0 & 0 & \cdots & \cdots & \cdots & \cdots \\ \mu_1 & -(\lambda_1 + \mu_1) & \lambda_1 & 0 & \cdots & \cdots & \cdots \\ 0 & \mu_2 & -(\lambda_2 + \mu_2) & \lambda_2 & 0 & \cdots & \cdots \\ \vdots & \vdots & \vdots & \vdots & \vdots & \vdots & \ddots \end{pmatrix}. \tag{3.52}$$

Birth-death models do not necessarily have an infinite state space. a finite state space $\mathcal{I} = \{0, 1, 2, \cdots, n\}$ is also possible. The interpretation of state $n$ is then such that no births can occur in this state. We will see in Chapter 4 that birth-death models are very well suited for the analysis of elementary queueing stations. Moreover, due to the tridiagonal structure of $\mathbf{Q}$ the solution of the system of linear equations (3.41) can in many cases be given explicitly.

## 3.8   The Poisson process

Consider a birth-death model on an infinite state space $\mathcal{I} = \{0, 1, 2, \cdots\}$ with two special properties:

1. All the birth-rates are equal to one another, i.e., $\lambda_i = \lambda$, $i = 0, 1, 2, \cdots$; $\lambda$ is called the intensity or rate of the Poisson process;

2. All the death-rates are equal to 0, i.e., $\mu_i = 0$, $i = 1, 2, 3, \cdots$.

We deal here with a pure birth model with constant birth-rate. The state probability $p_i(t) = \Pr\{N(t) = i\}$ can be obtained by solving the differential equation $\underline{p}'(t) = \underline{p}(t)\mathbf{Q}$

with

$$
\mathbf{Q} = \begin{pmatrix}
-\lambda & \lambda & 0 & \cdots & \cdots & \cdots & \cdots \\
0 & -\lambda & \lambda & 0 & \cdots & \cdots & \cdots \\
0 & 0 & -\lambda & \lambda & 0 & \cdots & \cdots \\
\vdots & \vdots & \vdots & \vdots & \vdots & \vdots & \ddots
\end{pmatrix}.
\tag{3.53}
$$

It can be shown (see also the exercises) that

$$
p_i(t) = \Pr\{N(t) = i\} = \frac{(\lambda t)^i}{i!} e^{-\lambda t}, \quad t \geq 0, \quad i \in \mathbb{N}.
\tag{3.54}
$$

Consequently, $N(t)$ is distributed according to a Poisson distribution with parameter $\lambda t$ (also $E[N(t)] = \sigma^2_{N(t)} = \lambda t$). Notice that $N(t)$ is exactly equal to the number of births in $[0, t)$, and thus the state of the CTMC indicates the count of births. The time between state changes is exponentially distributed with rate $\lambda$.

There are two other properties of the Poisson process of importance in practical modelling studies (in Figure 3.8 we visualise these two properties):

- *Merging of independent Poisson streams*: $n$ independent Poisson streams with intensities $\lambda_1$ through $\lambda_n$ can be merged to form a single Poisson stream with intensity $\lambda_1 + \cdots + \lambda_n$.

- *Splitting of a Poisson stream*: A Poisson stream with intensity $\lambda$ can be split into $n > 1$ Poisson streams with intensities $\alpha_1 \lambda$ through $\alpha_n \lambda$, with $\alpha_1, \cdots, \alpha_n \geq 0$, and $\sum_{i=1}^{n} \alpha_i = 1$.

Notice that the merging property does not hold for all renewal processes; the splitting property, however, does.

Another important property of Poisson processes is the PASTA property; it will be discussed in Section 4.3. Finally, recall that we have discussed two ways to arrive at a Poisson process: (i) as a special renewal process with negative exponential renewal time distributions, and (ii) as a special birth-death process with constant birth-rate and zero death-rate.

## 3.9   Renewal processes as arrival processes

Stochastic processes describing the arrival streams of jobs at a queueing station are often assumed to be renewal processes. This implies that the times between successive arrivals are assumed to be independently and identically distributed. Via the choice of the renewal

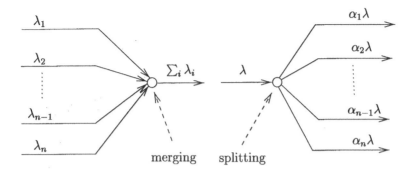

Figure 3.8: Merging and splitting of Poisson streams

time distribution, a wide variety of arrival processes can be constructed. For instance, the network traffic generated by a fixed bit-rate voice source will be very deterministic, e.g., with a rate of 8000 packets/second, and with the packets equidistantly spaced in time. On the other hand, the data traffic generated over a network by a general computer user will have a high variance: periods of long inactivity, e.g., for local word processing, will be followed by high activity periods, e.g., for the sending and receiving of files or programs to/from a file server. Consequently, the variance of the interrenewal time distribution will be high.

As we have seen before, the Poisson process is a very special case of a renewal process. One can, of course, use many distributions other than the exponential for the interrenewal times. A class of distributions that is very well suited for this purpose is the class of phase-type distributions (PH-distributions). The resulting PH-renewal processes have the nice property that they fall within the range of Markovian models, thus allowing for many analysis techniques (see also Chapter 8).

We present some background on PH-distributions in Section 3.9.1 and continue with the description of a number of special PH-renewal processes in Section 3.9.2.

## 3.9.1 Phase-type distributions

PH-distributions are an important class of distributions that can be seen as generalisations of the exponential distribution. In Figure 3.9 we depict the exponential distribution as an absorbing CTMC with two states. The initial probability distribution $p(0) = (1, 0)$, and the time until absorption (in state 1) has an exponential distribution with rate $\lambda$. When we now generalise the single state (state 0) of this CTMC into a number of states, but maintain

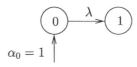

$\alpha_0 = 1$

Figure 3.9: The exponential distribution as a phase-type distribution

the property that the CTMC is absorbing in a single state, we obtain a PH-distribution. The time until absorption consists of a number of phases, each of exponentially distributed length. The initial probability distribution is denoted $\underline{\alpha}$ (as far as the non-absorbing states are concerned).

To generalise this, consider a CTMC on the state space $\mathcal{I} = \{1, \cdots, m, m+1\}$, with generator matrix

$$\mathbf{Q} = \begin{pmatrix} \mathbf{T} & \underline{T}^0 \\ \underline{0} & 0 \end{pmatrix}, \tag{3.55}$$

where $\mathbf{T}$ is an $m \times m$ matrix with $t_{i,i} < 0$ $(i = 1, \cdots, m)$, $t_{i,j} \geq 0$ $(i \neq j)$ and $\underline{T}^0$ is a column vector with nonnegative elements. The row sums of $\mathbf{Q}$ equal zero, i.e., $\mathbf{T}\underline{1} + \underline{T}^0 = \underline{0}$. Notice that $\mathbf{T}$ by itself is not a proper generator matrix. The initial probability vector is given as $(\underline{\alpha}, \alpha_{m+1})$ with $\underline{\alpha}\underline{1} + \alpha_{m+1} = 1$. Furthermore, the states $1, \cdots, m$ are transient, and consequently, state $m+1$ is the one and only absorbing state, regardless of the initial probability vector. In Figure 3.10 we visualise this.

The probability distribution $F(x)$ of the time until absorption in state $m+1$ is then given as [217]:

$$F(x) = 1 - \underline{\alpha}e^{\mathbf{T}x}\underline{1}, \quad x \geq 0. \tag{3.56}$$

We now can define a distribution $F(x)$ on $[0, \infty)$ to be of phase type, if and only if it is the distribution of the time to absorption in a CTMC as defined above. The pair $(\underline{\alpha}, \mathbf{T})$ is called *a representation of $F(x)$*. Note that since $\mathbf{Q}$ is a generator matrix of which the row sums equal 0, the elements of $\underline{T}^0$ can be computed from $\mathbf{T}$. Then, the following properties hold:

- the distribution $F(x)$ has a jump of $\alpha_{m+1}$ at $x = 0$ and its density on $(0, \infty)$ equals

$$f(x) = F'(x) = \underline{\alpha}e^{\mathbf{T}x}\underline{T}^0.$$

- the moments $E[X^i]$ of $F(x)$ are finite and given by

$$E[X^i] = (-1)^i i! (\underline{\alpha}\mathbf{T}^{-i}\underline{1}), \quad i = 0, 1, \cdots. \tag{3.57}$$

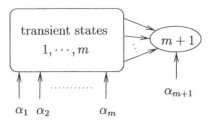

Figure 3.10: Schematic view of a PH distribution

Examples of PH-distributions are the earlier mentioned exponential distribution, the Erlang-$k$ distribution, and the hyper- and hypoexponential distribution. Note that these well-known PH distributions are all represented by acyclic CTMCs. The definition above, however, also allows for the use of non-acyclic CTMCs.

Important to note is the fact that the first moment of a PH-distribution exactly expresses the *mean time to absorption* in an absorbing CTMC. Using (3.57) for that specific case, we obtain:

$$E[X] = -\underline{\alpha}\mathbf{T}^{-1}\underline{1}. \tag{3.58}$$

Note that the last multiplication (with $\underline{1}$) is just included to sum the elements in the row-vector $-\underline{\alpha}\mathbf{T}^{-1}$. We thus can also write:

$$E[X] = \sum_{i=1}^{m} x_i = \underline{x} \cdot \underline{1}, \quad \text{with} \quad \underline{x} = -\underline{\alpha}\mathbf{T}^{-1}, \tag{3.59}$$

where $\underline{x} = (x_1, \cdots, x_m)$ is a vector in which $x_i$ denotes the mean time spent in state $i$ before absorption. Instead of explicitly computing $\mathbf{T}^{-1}$ and performing a vector-matrix multiplication, it is often smarter to solve the linear system

$$\underline{x}\mathbf{T} = -\underline{\alpha}, \tag{3.60}$$

to obtain $\underline{x}$ and compute $E[X] = \sum_i x_i$. In a similar way we can compute the $j$-th moment $E[X^j] = \sum_i x_i^{(j)}$ where the vector $\underline{x}^{(j)}$ follows from

$$\underline{x}^{(j)}\mathbf{T}^j = (-1)^j j!\underline{\alpha}. \tag{3.61}$$

Suppose we have already computed $\underline{x}^{(j)}$ and want to compute $\underline{x}^{(j+1)}$, we then proceed as follows:

$$\underline{x}^{(j+1)}\mathbf{T}^{j+1} = (-1)^{j+1}(j+1)!\underline{\alpha} \tag{3.62}$$

Multiplying both sides of this equation with $\mathbf{T}^{-j}$ we obtain

$$
\begin{aligned}
\underline{x}^{(j+1)}\mathbf{T} &= (-1)^{j+1}(j+1)!\underline{\alpha}\mathbf{T}^{-j} \\
&= -(j+1)\underbrace{(-1)^{j}(j)!\underline{\alpha}\mathbf{T}^{-j}}_{\underline{x}^{(j)}} = -(j+1)\underline{x}^{(j)}, \qquad (3.63)
\end{aligned}
$$

that is, we have obtained a linear system of equations that expresses $\underline{x}^{(j+1)}$ in terms of $\underline{x}^{(j)}$. If we solve this linear system of equations with a direct method such as LU-decomposition (see Chapter 15) we only have to decompose $\mathbf{T}$ once and we can compute successive vectors $\underline{x}^{(j)}$ using back-substitutions only. However, if $\mathbf{T}$ is large and we only require the first few moments, then an iterative solution might be the fastest way to proceed.

## 3.9.2   Phase-type renewal processes

In this section we discuss a number of PH-renewal processes that have practical significance.

### The $E_k$-renewal process

The Erlang-$k$ distribution is a phase-type distribution consisting of a series of $k$ exponential phases, followed by a single absorbing state. An Erlang-$k$ distribution results when the sum of $k$ independent and identically distributed exponential random variables is taken. The squared coefficient of variation of the Erlang-$k$ distribution is $1/k$. Consequently, for large $k$, it approaches a deterministic arrival pattern. Erlang-$k$ interarrival time distributions are often used to approximate true deterministic arrivals patterns (which cannot be incorporated in Markov models).

Instead of Erlang-$k$ interarrival times, one can also define hypo-exponentially distributed interarrival times; they are the sum of a number of independent exponentially distributed random variables which need not be identically distributed. Hypo-exponentially distributed interarrival times also have a squared coefficient of variation at most equal to 1. It can be shown though, that no hypo-exponential distribution with $k$ phases yields a coefficient of variation smaller than $1/k$, i.e., the Erlang-$k$ distribution is the PH-distribution with the smallest coefficient of variation, for given $k$.

### The $H_k$-renewal process

Where the Erlang-$k$ distribution is a series of exponential phases, the hyperexponential distribution can be interpreted as a probabilistic choice between $k$ exponential distributions (see Figure 3.11). As this probabilistic choice introduces extra randomness, one can imagine

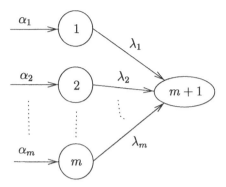

Figure 3.11: The hyperexponential distribution as a phase-type distribution

that for the $H_k$-renewal process the squared coefficient of variation is at least equal to 1. When modelling "bursty" traffic sources, this therefore seems to be a good choice.

Often, a two-phase hyperexponential distribution is used. The $H_2$-distribution has three free parameters, $\alpha$, $\lambda_1$ and $\lambda_2$, so that

$$F_{H_2}(t) = 1 - \alpha e^{-\lambda_1 t} - (1 - \alpha)e^{-\lambda_2 t}, \quad t \geq 0. \tag{3.64}$$

Fitting such a distribution on the first and second moment (or coefficient of variation) derived via measurements, leaves one free parameter. Therefore, often the $H_2$ distribution with balanced means is taken. The balanced means property can be expressed mathematically as $\alpha/\lambda_1 = (1 - \alpha)/\lambda_2$. This extra equation can then be used to fit the interarrival time distribution.

Suppose that measurements have revealed that the first moment of the interarrival times in a job stream can be estimated as $\hat{X}$, and that the squared coefficient of variation can be estimated as $\hat{C}_X^2$, then the parameters of the $H_2$ distribution can be expressed as follows:

$$\alpha = \frac{1}{2} + \frac{1}{2}\sqrt{\frac{\hat{C}_X^2 - 1}{\hat{C}_X^2 + 1}}, \quad \lambda_1 = \frac{2\alpha}{\hat{X}}, \quad \lambda_2 = \frac{2(1 - \alpha)}{\hat{X}}. \tag{3.65}$$

**The Cox-renewal process**

A well-known class of PH-distributions is formed by the Cox distributions. They can be regarded as a generalisation of the Erlang distributions. A Cox distribution consists of $n$ exponential phases, with possibly different rates $\lambda_1$ through $\lambda_n$. Before each phase, it is decided whether the next phase is entered (with probability $1 - \gamma_i$) or not (with

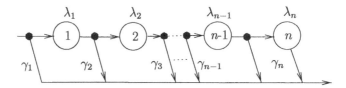

Figure 3.12: The Cox distributions as a mixed DTMC/CTMC state transition diagram

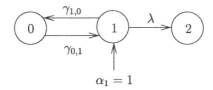

Figure 3.13: The interrenewal distribution of the IPP as a phase-type distribution

probability $\gamma_i$). The Cox distribution is visualised in Figure 3.12 where the small black diamonds indicate the probabilistic choices to be made before each exponential phase. With a proper choice of parameters, coefficients of variation both smaller and larger than 1 can be dealt with.

### The interrupted Poisson process

In many telecommunication systems, the arrival stream of packets can be viewed as a Poisson stream, however, switched on and off randomly. The on-period then corresponds to an active period of a source, the off-period to a passive period of a source. The on- and off-periods are determined by the characteristics of the source. As an example of this, one can think of the stream of digitised voice packets that is originating from a telephone user: periods of speaking are interchanged with periods of silence. These two period durations determine the on- and off-time distributions. When on, the rate of digitised voice packets determines the rate of a Poisson process. When off, no arrivals are generated. The on/off-process is also called an interrupted Poisson process (IPP).

In Figure 3.13 we depict the interrenewal distribution of the IPP as a PH-distribution. Starting state is, deterministically, state 1, representing the on-state. In that state, a renewal period can end, i.e., an arrival can take place, via the transition with rate $\lambda$ to the absorbing state. However, instead of an arrival, also the active period can end, according to the transition with rate $\gamma_{1,0}$ to state 0, the off-state. After an exponentially distributed off-period, with rate $\gamma_{0,1}$ the on-state is entered again. The generator matrix of this absorbing CTMC is given as

$$\mathbf{Q}_{\text{IPP}} = \begin{pmatrix} -\gamma_{0,1} & \gamma_{0,1} & 0 \\ \gamma_{1,0} & -(\gamma_{1,0} + \lambda) & \lambda \\ 0 & 0 & 0 \end{pmatrix}, \tag{3.66}$$

and the initial probability vector $\underline{\alpha} = (0,1)$. Note that due to the choice of $\underline{\alpha}$, we have established that after a packet arrival (an absorption) the PH distribution starts anew in state 1 (a renewal) so that the arrival process remains in a burst. From $\mathbf{Q}_{\text{IPP}}$, we have

$$\mathbf{T} = \begin{pmatrix} -\gamma_{01} & \gamma_{01} \\ \gamma_{10} & -(\gamma_{10} + \lambda) \end{pmatrix}, \tag{3.67}$$

so that we can easily derive moments, using (3.57):

$$\begin{aligned} E[X] &= (-1)^1 1! (0,1) \cdot \mathbf{T}^{-1} \cdot \underline{1} \\ &= -\frac{1}{\gamma_{0,1}\lambda}(0,1) \cdot \begin{pmatrix} -(\gamma_{1,0} + \lambda) & -\gamma_{0,1} \\ -\gamma_{1,0} & -\gamma_{0,1} \end{pmatrix} \cdot \underline{1} \\ &= \frac{1}{\lambda}\left(1 + \frac{\gamma_{1,0}}{\gamma_{0,1}}\right). \end{aligned} \tag{3.68}$$

Note that the inverse of a $2 \times 2$ matrix can be expressed directly:

$$\mathbf{A} = \begin{pmatrix} a & b \\ c & d \end{pmatrix} \implies \mathbf{A}^{-1} = \frac{1}{\det(\mathbf{A})}\begin{pmatrix} d & -b \\ -c & a \end{pmatrix},$$

where $\det(\mathbf{A}) = ad - cb$ is the determinant of matrix $\mathbf{A}$.

The first moment $E[X]$ of an IPP can also be obtained using an alternative calculation as follows. When one enters the initial state of an IPP, i.e., state 1 in Figure 3.13, the average time until absorption $E[X]$ consists of a number of phases. With probability 1, there is residence in state 1, with average length $1/(\lambda + \gamma_{1,0})$. Then, with probability $\gamma_{1,0}/(\lambda + \gamma_{1,0})$, a state change to state 0 takes place, adding to the average time to absorption $1/\gamma_{0,1}$, the average state residence time in state 0, plus, after returning to state 1 again, another $E[X]$. In other words, when entering state 1 for the second time, it is as if one enters there for the first time. In equational form, this can be written as

$$E[X] = \frac{1}{\lambda + \gamma_{1,0}} + \frac{\gamma_{1,0}}{\lambda + \gamma_{1,0}}\left(\frac{1}{\gamma_{0,1}} + E[X]\right). \tag{3.69}$$

Collecting terms, this can be written as

$$E[X] = \frac{1}{\lambda}\left(1 + \frac{\gamma_{1,0}}{\gamma_{0,1}}\right), \tag{3.70}$$

which is the result we have seen before.

## 3.10   Summary of Markov chains

To finish this chapter, we present in Table 3.1 an overview of the three classes of Markov chains we have discussed.

As can be observed from this table, to obtain the steady-state behaviour of Markov chains (DTMCs, CTMCs and SMCs) we need to solve systems of linear equations. How can this best be done? To answer this question, we first have to answer whether the Markov chain under study, and thus the corresponding system of linear equations, exhibits a special structure. This is for instance the case when we are addressing a Markov chain that actually is a birth-death process (where the generator matrix has a tri-diagonal structure). If such a special structure does exist, we can often exploit it, yielding explicit expressions for the steady-state probabilities, even when the number of states is infinitely large. Examples of such cases will be discussed in Chapter 4 where we discuss birth-death models, in Chapter 8 where we discuss quasi-birth-death models, and in Chapters 10 through 13 where we discuss queueing network models.

When the Markov chain under study does not exhibit a nice structure but is finite, we can still obtain the steady-state probabilities by solving the system of linear equations with numerical means (known from linear algebra). For small Markov chains, say, with up to 5 states, we might be able to perform the computations "by hand". For larger models, with up to 100 or even 1000 states, we might employ so-called direct techniques such as Gaussian elimination of LU-decomposition. For even larger models, with possibly tens or hundreds of thousands of states, we have to employ iterative techniques such as Gauss-Seidel iterations or the successive over-relaxation technique. We will come back to these techniques in Chapter 15.

As can also be observed from Table 3.1, to evaluate the transient behaviour of DTMCs just requires matrix-vector multiplications. To evaluate the transient behaviour of CTMCs we have to solve a system of linear differential equations. For CTMCs with an infinite state space, the transient behaviour can only be obtained in very special cases which go beyond the scope of this book. For finite CTMCs, explicit expressions (closed-form solutions) for the transient behaviour can be obtained, e.g., when the CTMC is acyclic. For general CTMCs, however, we have to solve the system of differential equations numerically, either via standard techniques such as Runge-Kutta methods, or via a technique specially developed for CTMCs, known as uniformisation. We will also discuss these techniques in Chapter 15.

|                        | DTMC                       | CTMC                                      | SMC                          |
| ---------------------- | -------------------------- | ----------------------------------------- | ---------------------------- |
| initial probabilities  | $\underline{p}(0)$         | $\underline{p}(0)$                        | $\underline{p}(0)$           |
| transitions            | $\mathbf{P} = [p_{i,j}]$   | $\mathbf{Q} = [q_{i,j}]$                  | $\mathbf{P} = [p_{i,j}]$     |
| interpretation         | probabilities              | rates                                     | probabilities                |
| state residence        | steps, mean $1/p_{i,i}$    | implicit in rates, mean $1/q_{i,i}$       | $F_i(t)$, mean $h_i$         |
| times                  | (geometric number)         | (negative exponential)                    | (any distribution)           |
| steady-state           | $\underline{v}\mathbf{P} = \underline{v}$ | $\underline{p}\mathbf{Q} = \underline{0}$ | $\underline{v}\mathbf{P} = \underline{v},\ \sum_i v_i = 1$ |
| distribution           | $\sum_i v_i = 1$           | $\sum_i p_i = 1$                          | $p_i = v_i h_i / \sum_j v_j h_j$ |
| transient              | $\underline{p}(n) = \underline{p}(0)\mathbf{P}^n$ | $\underline{p}'(t) = \underline{p}(t)\mathbf{Q}$ | not addressed       |
| distribution           | $= \underline{p}(n-1)\mathbf{P}$ | given $\underline{p}(0)$            |                              |

Table 3.1: Tabular overview of three classes of Markov chains

## 3.11   Further reading

More information on stochastic processes, in much more detail than we have presented here, can be found in many mathematics textbooks. We mention Kemeny and Snell [154], Feller [87], Howard [138, 139], Çinlar [55], Wolff [290] and Ross [247]. Phase-type distributions have extensively been treated by Neuts [217]. Cox introduced the Coxian distributions [69]. Many books on performance evaluation also contain chapters on stochastic processes.

## 3.12   Exercises

### 3.1. Poisson and renewal processes.

We consider a collection of overhead projectors. The life-time of a light-bulb in the $i$-th overhead projector is given by the stochastic variable $L_i$. All variables $L_i$ obey a negative exponential distribution with mean 1000 hours. A university teaching term lasts 16 weeks of 5 days of 8 hours each, hence 640 hours.

1. Assume that an overhead projector has a built-in spare light-bulb. Compute the probability that an overhead projector becomes useless during a term.

2. Assume now that a projector does not have its own spare light-bulb. Instead, the warden who is in charge of the 5 overhead projectors in the computer science building is keeping spare light-bulbs. How many spare light-bulbs should he have at his disposal to assure that the probability that an overhead projector becomes unusable during a term is below 10%?

### 3.2. Alternating renewal processes.

An extension of the renewal process is the *alternating renewal process* in which the inter-event times are distributed alternatingly according to two distributions: $X_{2i}$ is distributed as $U$ with given distribution $F_U$ and $X_{2i+1}$ is distributed as $D$ with given distribution $F_D$ ($i \in \mathbb{N}$). This type of process is often used to model the operational lifetime of a component which switches between "up" and "down" periods.

Define the length of the $i$-th cycle as $C_i = X_{2i} + X_{2i+1}$ and assume that $U$ and $D$ both are negative exponentially distributed with rates $1/10$ and $2/3$ respectively.

1. Compute the mean up-, down-, and cycle-time.

2. Give the distribution of the length of a cycle.

3. Compute the percentage of time the renewal process resides in an "up"-period, given a very long observation interval ($t \to \infty$); this quantity is often called the steady-state availability $A$.

4. Give the probability of having exactly $n$ cycles in an interval $[0, t)$.

### 3.3. Exponential distribution.

Derive expressions for the distribution, the density and the first two moments of an exponential distribution, thereby using the more generally applicable results for PH-distributions.

### 3.4. A small CTMC.

Given is a CTMC with generator matrix

$$
Q = \begin{pmatrix}
-4 & 1 & 3 & 0 \\
0 & -2 & 2 & 0 \\
0 & 0 & -1 & 1 \\
3 & 0 & 0 & -3
\end{pmatrix}.
$$

Draw the state-transition diagram of this CTMC and compute the steady-state probabilities (i) directly from the CTMC specification, and (ii) via the embedded DTMC.

### 3.5. Multiprocessor interference [adapted from [280]].

Consider a shared-memory multiprocessor system consisting of $n$ processors and $m$ memory modules all connected to an interconnection network (which we do not address any further). We make the following assumptions:

- all memory modules can be addressed independently from one another and in parallel;

- every memory access takes a fixed amount of time (the same for all modules);

- every memory module can serve one request per time unit;

- every processor has at most one outstanding request for a single memory module;

- as soon as a memory request has been answered, a processor immediately issues a new request for memory module $i$ with probability $q_i$ where $\sum_i q_i = 1$ (the values $q_i$ are independent of the processor index (uniform memory access assumption)).

Consider the case where $n = m = 2$.

1. Construct a DTMC (with three states) that describes the access pattern of the processors over the memory modules; use as state description a tuple $(n_1, n_2)$ where $n_i$ is the number of processors accessing memory module $i$; clearly, $n_1 + n_2 = n$.

2. Compute the steady-state probability of having no memory-access conflicts and the probability of having memory-access conflict at memory module $i$.

3. Compute the mean number of requests, denoted $E[B]$ for bandwidth, the memory handles per unit of time.

4. Compute the maximum value $E[B]$ can attain as a function of $q_1$ and $q_2$.

**3.6. Two-component availability model.**
A component of a system can either be up or down. The component has an exponentially distributed lifetime with mean $1/\lambda$; the repair of a component takes an exponentially distributed amount of time with mean $1/\mu$.

1. Describe the state of a component as a simple CTMC.

2. Compute the steady-state probabilities $p_i$ for the component to be operational or not (this probability is often called the availability).

3. Consider the case where we have two identical components (each with their own repair facility). Describe the states of these two components as a CTMC.

4. Compute the steady-state probabilities $p_{i,j}$ of the two components together and show that $p_{i,j} = p_i p_j$ where $p_i$ (and $p_j$) have been computed above.

5. How would the availability of just a single repair facility for both the components affect the steady-state probabilities $p_{i,j}$? First reason about the expected changes in availability and then explicitly compute the probability that both components are operational (using a three-state CTMC).

## 3.7. Poisson distribution and Poisson processes.

Show that the expected number of arrivals in $[0, t)$ in a pure birth process has a Poisson distribution by explicitly solving the linear system of differential equations $\underline{p}'(t) = \underline{p}(t)\mathbf{Q}$.

## 3.8. Cox distributions.

Show that any Cox distribution can be represented as a PH-distribution. Show that the Erlang- and the hypo-exponential distributions are special cases of the Cox distribution.

## 3.9. Higher moments of the IPP.

Derive, using the moments-property of PH-distributions, the second moment of an IPP, as well as its variance and squared coefficient of variation.

# Part II

# Single-server queueing models

# Chapter 4

# M|M|1 queueing models

IN the previous chapter we have already presented birth-death processes as an important class of CTMCs. In this chapter, we will see that a birth-death model can be used perfectly for analysing various types of elementary queueing stations. Furthermore, by the special structure of the birth-death process, the steady-state probability vector $\underline{p}$ can be expressed explicitly in terms of the model parameters, thus making these models attractive to use.

In Section 4.1 we consider the solution of the most fundamental birth-death model: an M|M|1 queueing model with variable service and arrival rates. In principle, all other queueing models discussed in this chapter are then derived from this model. In Section 4.2 we deal with a (single server) queueing model with constant arrival and service rates. We then discuss the important PASTA property for queues with Poisson arrivals in Section 4.3; it is used in the derivation of many interesting performance measures. The response time distribution in such a queueing model is addressed in Section 4.4. We then address multi-server queueing stations in Section 4.5, and infinite-server queueing stations in Section 4.6. A comparison of a number of queueing stations with equal capacity but different structure is presented in Section 4.7. We address the issue of limited buffering space and the associated losses of jobs in Section 4.8 for single servers and in Section 4.9 for multi-server stations. In Section 4.10 we address a queueing model in which the total number of customers is limited. We finally present a mean-value based computational procedure for such a model in Section 4.11.

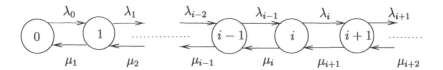

Figure 4.1: State transition diagram for the most general M|M|1 model

## 4.1   General solution of the M|M|1 queue

Consider a single-server queueing station at which jobs arrive. As discussed already in
Chapter 3, we can see these arrivals as births. Similarly, the departure of a job at the end
of its service (or transmission) can be regarded as a death. We now make the following
assumptions regarding the time durations that are involved:

- the time between successive arrivals is exponentially distributed with mean $1/\lambda_i$
  whenever there are $i$ jobs in the queueing station, i.e., we have a Poisson arrival
  process with *state dependent rates* $\lambda_i$;

- the time it takes to serve a job when there are $i$ jobs present obeys a negative
  exponential distribution with mean $1/\mu_i$.

We can now describe the overall behaviour of this queueing station with a very simple
CTMC on the state space $\mathcal{I} = \{0, 1, 2, \cdots\}$. From every state $i \in I\!N$ a transition with rate
$\lambda_i$ exists to state $i + 1$, corresponding to an arrival of a job. From every state $i \in I\!N^+$
a transition with rate $\mu_i$ exists to state $i - 1$, corresponding to a departure of a job. In
Figure 4.1 we depict the state transition diagram. The corresponding generator matrix
then has the following form:

$$\mathbf{Q} = \begin{pmatrix} -\lambda_0 & \lambda_0 & 0 & \cdots & \cdots & \cdots & \cdots \\ \mu_1 & -(\lambda_1 + \mu_1) & \lambda_1 & 0 & \cdots & \cdots & \cdots \\ 0 & \mu_2 & -(\lambda_2 + \mu_2) & \lambda_2 & 0 & \cdots & \cdots \\ \vdots & \vdots & \vdots & \vdots & \vdots & \vdots & \ddots \end{pmatrix}. \tag{4.1}$$

We can now use (3.41) for solving the steady-state probabilities $p_i$, $i = 0, 1, \cdots$, that is,
we solve $p\mathbf{Q} = \underline{0}$ under the normalisation condition. Instead of using (3.41), we can also
infer the appropriate equations directly from the state transition diagram by assuming
"probability flow balance". Since we assume that the system will reach some equilibrium,
finally, the probability flow (or flux) into each state must equal the probability flow out of

each state, where the probability flow out of a state equals the state probability multiplied with the outgoing rates. This interpretation also explains why (3.41) are often called the *global balance equations* (GBEs). Thus, we have:

$$\text{For state } 0 \quad : \quad p_0\lambda_0 = p_1\mu_1, \tag{4.2}$$

$$\text{For states } i = 1, 2, \cdots \quad : \quad p_i(\lambda_i + \mu_i) = p_{i-1}\lambda_{i-1} + p_{i+1}\mu_{i+1}. \tag{4.3}$$

Of course, since the probability of being in any of all possible states equals 1, we have the normalisation equation:

$$\sum_{i=0}^{\infty} p_i = 1. \tag{4.4}$$

Having obtained the global balance equations we have to solve them. Only in very special cases do these equations allow for an explicit solution of the state probabilities $p_i$ in terms of the system parameters. An important aspect here is that it is in general difficult to say *a priori* whether there exists such an explicit solution or not. However, here we deal with such a special case. From (4.2) we have:

$$p_1 = \frac{\lambda_0}{\mu_1} p_0. \tag{4.5}$$

Substituting this in (4.3) for the case $i = 1$ we obtain:

$$p_1(\lambda_1 + \mu_1) = p_0\lambda_0 + p_2\mu_2, \tag{4.6}$$

which, after using (4.5), yields:

$$p_2 = \frac{\lambda_0\lambda_1}{\mu_1\mu_2} p_0. \tag{4.7}$$

Examining (4.7) gives us the idea that the general solution takes the form:

$$p_i = \frac{\lambda_0\lambda_1 \cdots \lambda_{i-1}}{\mu_1\mu_2 \cdots \mu_i} p_0 = p_0 \prod_{k=0}^{i-1} \frac{\lambda_k}{\mu_{k+1}}, \quad i = 1, 2, \cdots \tag{4.8}$$

Substitution of (4.8) in (4.2)–(4.3) immediately confirms this. We can use (4.8) to express all the state probabilities in terms of $p_0$. We finally obtain $p_0$ by considering the normalisation equation (4.4):

$$\sum_{i=0}^{\infty} p_i = \sum_{i=0}^{\infty} p_0 \prod_{k=0}^{i-1} \frac{\lambda_k}{\mu_{k+1}} = p_0 \left(1 + \sum_{i=1}^{\infty} \prod_{k=0}^{i-1} \frac{\lambda_k}{\mu_{k+1}}\right) = 1, \tag{4.9}$$

from which we derive:

$$p_0 = \frac{1}{1 + \sum_{i=1}^{\infty} \prod_{k=0}^{i-1} \frac{\lambda_k}{\mu_{k+1}}}. \tag{4.10}$$

Of course, $p_0$ is only positive when the infinite sum has a finite limit. If the latter is the case, the queue is said to be stable. In the more specific models that follow, we can state this stability criterion more exactly and in a way that is more easy to validate.

An important remark here is the following. It has been pointed out that the flow balance holds for any single state. However, the flow balance argument holds for any connected group of states as well. Sometimes, the resulting system of equations is easier to solve when smartly chosen groups of states are addressed. We will address this in more detail when such a situation arises.

A third way to solve the steady-state probabilities of this birth-death Markov chain is the following. From the GBE for state 0 we see that the probability flows from and to state 0 must be equal. Because this is the case in the GBE for state 1, the terms $p_0 \lambda_0$ and $p_1 \mu_1$ cancel so that we obtain $p_1 \lambda_1 = p_2 \mu_2$. This can be done repeatedly, resulting in the following system of equations:

$$p_i \lambda_i = p_{i+1} \mu_{i+1}, \quad i \in \mathbb{N}, \tag{4.11}$$

again under the normalisation condition. These balance equations are called the *local balance equations* (LBEs) and are often easier to solve than the GBEs. The LBEs are obtained by setting equal the probability flow into a particular state due to the arrival of a job with the probability flow out of that state due to the departure of that same job. Important to note is the fact that not for all CTMCs do LBEs hold. Only for a special class of queueing models is this the case (for more details we refer to [74]).

Finally, note that since we are dealing with a queueing station with an infinite buffer, no jobs will be lost. Define the overall arrival rate $\lambda = \sum_{i=0}^{\infty} p_i \lambda_i$ and the overall service rate $\mu = \sum_{i=0}^{\infty} p_i \mu_i$. As long as $\rho = \lambda/\mu < 1$ the queueing station is stable and the throughput $X$ will be equal to the overall arrival rate $\lambda$.

Other measures of interest are the expected number of jobs in the queueing station and in the queue, respectively defined as:

$$E[N] = \sum_{i=0}^{\infty} i p_i, \quad \text{and} \quad E[N_q] = \sum_{i=1}^{\infty} (i-1) p_i, \tag{4.12}$$

from which, via Little's law and $X = \lambda$, the expected response time $E[R] = E[N]/\lambda$ and the expected waiting time $E[W] = E[N_q]/\lambda = E[R] - E[S]$ can be derived. Also more detailed measures such as the probability of having at least $k$ jobs in the queueing system can easily be computed as $B(k) = \sum_{i=k}^{\infty} p_i$.

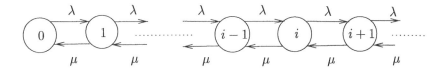

Figure 4.2: State transition diagram of the constant-rate M|M|1 model

## 4.2 The M|M|1 queue with constant rates

The simplest possible form of the general model discussed in Section 4.1 is the one in which all the arrival rates are the same, i.e., $\lambda_i = \lambda$, $i = 0, 1, 2, \cdots$, and in which all the service rates are the same, i.e., $\mu_i = \mu$, $i = 1, 2, 3, \cdots$. Figure 4.2 shows the state transition diagram. Note that the arrival process is a Poisson process. Substituting the model parameters in the general result (4.8) we obtain

$$p_i = p_0 \left(\frac{\lambda}{\mu}\right)^i, \; i = 0, 1, 2, \cdots. \tag{4.13}$$

If we define $\rho = \lambda/\mu$, we can compute $p_0$ using the normalisation equation:

$$\sum_{i=0}^{\infty} p_i = p_0 \sum_{i=0}^{\infty} \rho^i = \frac{p_0}{1 - \rho} = 1, \tag{4.14}$$

where we use the well-known solution of the geometric series under the assumption that $\rho < 1$ (see also Appendix B). We thus find $p_0 = 1 - \rho$ whenever $\rho < 1$ or $\lambda < \mu$. This existence condition is intuitively appealing since it states that a solution exists whenever the average number of arrivals per unit of time is smaller than the average number of services per unit of time. In summary, we find for the steady-state probabilities in the M|M|1 queue:

$$p_i = (1 - \rho)\rho^i, \; i = 0, 1, 2, \cdots. \tag{4.15}$$

We observe that these steady-state probabilities are geometrically distributed with base $\rho$. Moreover, since $p_0 = 1 - \rho$, we have $\rho = 1 - p_0 = \sum_{i=1}^{\infty} p_i$. So, $\rho$ equals the sum of the probabilities of the states in which at least one job is present, or, in other words, the sum of the probabilities of states in which there is work to do. This equality explains why $\rho$ is often called the *utilisation*. By the fact that all jobs that enter the queueing station also leave the queueing station, we can directly state that the throughput $X = \lambda$, so that we can also express $\rho = XE[S]$.

Having obtained the steady-state probabilities, we can easily calculate other quantities of interest such as $E[N]$, the average number of jobs in the queueing station (see also

Appendix B.2):

$$
\begin{aligned}
E[N] &= \sum_{i=0}^{\infty} i p_i = (1 - \rho) \sum_{i=0}^{\infty} i \rho^i = (1 - \rho) \rho \sum_{i=0}^{\infty} i \rho^{i-1} \\
&= (1 - \rho) \rho \frac{d}{d\rho} \left( \frac{1}{1 - \rho} \right) = \frac{\rho}{1 - \rho}.
\end{aligned}
\tag{4.16}
$$

Note that we have again used the result for the geometric series and that we have changed the order of summation and differentiation. Although the latter is not allowed at all times, in the cases where we do so, it is. We can continue to apply Little's result to obtain the average time $E[R]$ spent in the queueing station:

$$
E[R] = E[N]/\lambda = \frac{1/\mu}{1 - \rho} = \frac{E[S]}{1 - \rho} = \frac{1}{\mu - \lambda}.
\tag{4.17}
$$

What we see here is that the time spent in the station basically equals the average service time ($E[S]$); however, it is "stretched" by the factor $1/(1 - \rho)$ due to the fact that there are other jobs in need of service as well. Note that we have already seen these results in Chapter 2. Now we can, however, also derive more detailed results as follows.

A measure of interest might be the variance $\sigma_N^2$ of the number of packets in the station. This measure can be derived as the expectation of $(i - E[N])^2$ under the probability distribution $p$:

$$
\sigma_N^2 = \sum_{i=0}^{\infty} (i - E[N])^2 p_i = \frac{\rho}{(1 - \rho)^2}.
\tag{4.18}
$$

The probability $B(k)$ of having at least $k$ packets in the queueing station is also of interest, for instance when dimensioning buffers. We have

$$
B(k) = \sum_{i=k}^{\infty} p_i = \sum_{i=k}^{\infty} (1 - \rho) \rho^i = \rho^k (1 - \rho) \sum_{i=0}^{\infty} \rho^i = \rho^k.
\tag{4.19}
$$

We observe that the probability $B(k)$ of having $k$ or more jobs in the station is decreasing exponentially with $k$. Very often, the value $B(k)$ is called a *blocking probability*. This name, however, might easily lead to confusion since no losses actually occur.

## 4.3   The PASTA property

A well-known and often applied result of queueing theory is the PASTA property (*Poisson Arrivals See Time Averages*; see also [291]):

**Theorem 4.1. PASTA property.**

The distribution of jobs in a queueing station at the moment a new job of a Poisson arrival process arrives is the same as the long-run or steady-state job distribution. □

We have already used the PASTA property in Chapter 2 where we derived first moments for the performance measures of interest of an M|M|1 queue. There we used that an arriving customer "sees" the queue at which it arrives "as if in equilibrium".

Although the PASTA property is intuitively appealing, it is certainly not true for all arrival processes. Consider as an example a D|D|1 queueing station where every second a job arrives which requires 0.6 seconds to be served. Clearly, since $\rho = \lambda E[S] = 0.6$ this queueing station is stable. However, whenever a job arrives it will find the station completely empty with probability 1, although in the long run the queue-empty probability will only be $1 - \rho = 0.4$.

The proof of the PASTA property is relatively simple, as outlined below. Let us consider a queueing system in which the number of customers present is represented by a stochastic process $(X_t, t \geq 0)$. Furthermore, define the event "there was (at least) one arrival at this queueing station in the interval $(t - h, t]$". Since the arrivals as such form a homogeneous Poisson process, the probability of this event equals the probability that there is an arrival in the interval $(0, h]$ which equals $\Pr\{N(h) \geq 1\}$, where $N(t)$ is the counting process defined in Chapter 3. For non-Poisson processes, this "shift to the origin" would not be valid. Since the interarrival times are memoryless, the thus defined probability is independent of the past history of the arrival process and of the state of the queueing station: $\Pr\{N(h) \geq 1 | X_{t-h} = i\} = \Pr\{N(h) \geq 1\}$ so that $\Pr\{N(h) \geq 1 \cup X_{t-h} = i\} = \Pr\{N(h) \geq 1\} \Pr\{X_{t-h} = i\}$. From this, we can conclude that also

$$\Pr\{X_{t-h} = i | N(h) \geq 1\} = \Pr\{X_{t-h} = i\}. \tag{4.20}$$

If we now take the limit $h \to 0$, the left-hand side of this equality simply expresses the probability that an arrival at time-instance $t$ arrives at a queue with $i$ customers in it. This probability then equals the probability that the queue at time $t$ has $i$ customers in it, independent from any arrival, hence, the steady-state probability of having $i$ customers in the queue. As a conclusion, we see that a Poisson arrival acts as a *random observer* and sees the queue as if in equilibrium.

Important to note is that we have used the memoryless property of the interarrival times here. Indeed, it is only for the Poisson process that this property holds, simply since there is no memoryless interarrival time distribution other than the negative exponential one used in the Poisson process. The discrete-time analogue of the PASTA property is the BASTA property where in every time-slot an arrival takes place (or not) with a fixed probability $p$ (or $1 - p$). This means that in every slot the decision on an arrival is taken by an independent Bernoulli trial so that the times between arrivals have a geometrically distributed length. The latter might be no surprise since the geometric distribution is the only discrete-time memoryless distribution.

## 4.4  Response time distribution in the M|M|1 queue

In Section 4.2 we have computed the steady-state probability distribution of the number of customers in an M|M|1 queueing station. From this distribution, we were able to derive the mean response time (via Little's law). In many modelling studies, obtaining such mean performance measures is enough to answer the dimensioning questions at hand. However, in some applications it is required to have knowledge of the complete response time distribution, e.g., when modelling real-time systems for which the probability of missing deadlines should be investigated. In general, obtaining complete response or waiting time distributions is a difficult task; however, for the M|M|1 queue it remains relatively simple, as we will see below.

When a job arrives at an M|M|1 queue, it will find there, due to the PASTA property, $n$ jobs with probability $p_n = (1 - \rho)\rho^n$. As the exponential distribution is memoryless, the remaining processing time of a job in service again has an exponential distribution. Therefore, the response time distribution of a job arriving at an M|M|1 queue which is already occupied by $n$ other jobs has an Erlang-$(n + 1)$ distribution, that is, the sum of $n$ exponentially distributed service times, plus its own service time.

From Appendix A we know that the Erlang-$k$ $(E_k)$ distribution with rate $\mu$ per stage has the following form:

$$F_{E_k}(t) = 1 - e^{-\mu t} \sum_{i=0}^{k-1} \frac{(\mu t)^i}{i!}. \tag{4.21}$$

Using this result, we can calculate the response time distribution by unconditioning: the complete response time distribution is the weighted sum of response time distributions when there are $n$ jobs present upon arrival, added over all possible $n$:

$$
\begin{aligned}
F_R(t) = \Pr\{R \le t\} &= \sum_{n=0}^{\infty} p_n \Pr\{R \le t | n \text{ packets upon arrival}\} \\
&= \sum_{n=0}^{\infty} p_n F_{E_{n+1}}(t) = \sum_{n=0}^{\infty} (1 - \rho)\rho^n F_{E_{n+1}}(t)
\end{aligned}
$$

$$\begin{aligned}
&= 1 - e^{-\mu t} \sum_{n=0}^{\infty} (1-\rho)\rho^n \sum_{i=0}^{n} \frac{(\mu t)^i}{i!} \\
&= 1 - e^{-\mu t} \sum_{i=0}^{\infty} (1-\rho)\frac{(\mu t)^i}{i!} \sum_{n=i}^{\infty} \rho^n = 1 - e^{-\mu t} \sum_{i=0}^{\infty} \frac{(\mu t)^i}{i!}\rho^i \\
&= 1 - e^{-\mu t} \sum_{i=0}^{\infty} \frac{(\mu \rho t)^i}{i!} = 1 - e^{-\mu t} e^{\mu \rho t} \\
&= 1 - e^{-\mu(1-\rho)t} = 1 - e^{-(\mu-\lambda)t}.
\end{aligned} \tag{4.22}$$

Surprisingly, the response time is exponentially distributed, now with parameter $(\mu - \lambda)$. We can directly conclude from this that the average response time equals $E[R] = 1/(\mu-\lambda)$ as we have seen before.

Response time distributions can often be used to give system users guarantees of the form "with probability $p$ the response time will be less than $F_R^{-1}(p)$ seconds". Especially for time-critical applications such response time guarantees are often more useful than the average response time.

**Example 4.1. Response time distributions at varying $\rho$.**
Consider an M|M|1 queue with $\mu = 1$ and where $\lambda$ is either 0.2, 0.5 or 0.8. For these cases, the response time distribution is given in Figure 4.3. As can be observed, the higher $\rho$, the smaller $\Pr\{R \le t\}$, i.e., the higher the probability that the response time exceeds a certain threshold $(\Pr\{R > t\} = 1 - \Pr\{R \le t\})$.                □

## 4.5  The M|M|m multi-server queue

In the previous sections we have discussed models of systems in which there is only a single server. Now consider a system in which a number of service providing units can work independently on a number of jobs. Examples of such systems are (homogeneous) multiprocessor systems or telecommunications systems (telephone switches) with multiple outgoing lines.

The multi-server aspect can easily be incorporated in the general birth-death model we developed before. We assume constant arrival rates, such that $\lambda_i = \lambda$ for all $i = 0, 1, \cdots$, but the number of active servers depends on the number of jobs present, as follows:

$$\mu_i = \begin{cases} i\mu, & i = 0, 1, \cdots, m, \\ m\mu, & i = m+1, m+2, \cdots. \end{cases} \tag{4.23}$$

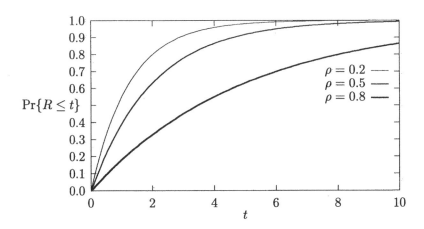

Figure 4.3: Response time distributions in an M|M|1 queue for $\mu = 1$ and various $\lambda$'s

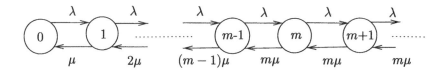

Figure 4.4: State transition diagram for the M|M|m model

This definition says that as long as there are less than $m$ jobs present, the effective service rate equals that number times the per-server service rate, and when at least $m$ jobs are present, the effective service rate equals $m\mu$. In Figure 4.4 we show the corresponding state transition diagram.

When we define $\rho = \lambda/m\mu$, the stability condition for this model can again be expressed as $\rho < 1$; $\rho$ can also be interpreted as the utilisation of each individual server. The expected number of busy servers equals $m\rho = \lambda/\mu$. When the station is not overloaded the throughput $X = \lambda$. When the station is highly loaded, it will operate at maximum speed, i.e., with rate $m\mu$. Under these assumptions, we can compute the following steady-state probabilities from the global balance equations:

$$p_i = p_0 \frac{(m\rho)^i}{i!}, \quad i = 0, \cdots, m - 1, \tag{4.24}$$

and

$$p_i = p_0 \frac{(m\rho)^m}{m!} \frac{(m\rho)^{i-m}}{m^{i-m}}, \quad i = m, m+1, \cdots, \tag{4.25}$$

where $p_0$ follows from the normalisation as follows:

$$p_0 = \left( \sum_{j=0}^{m-1} \frac{(m\rho)^j}{j!} + \frac{(m\rho)^m}{(1-\rho)m!} \right)^{-1}. \tag{4.26}$$

Using these steady-state probabilities we can compute $E[N]$ as follows:

$$E[N] = \sum_{i=0}^{\infty} i p_i = \cdots = m\rho + \rho \frac{(m\rho)^m}{m!} \frac{p_0}{(1-\rho)^2}. \tag{4.27}$$

An arriving job will have to wait before its service start when all the $m$ servers are busy upon its arrival. Due to the PASTA property this probability can be expressed as the sum over all state probabilities for which there are at least $m$ jobs present as follows:

$$\Pr\{\text{waiting}\} = \sum_{i=m}^{\infty} p_0 \frac{(m\rho)^i}{m! \frac{m^i}{m^m}} = p_0 \frac{m^m}{m!} \sum_{i=m}^{\infty} \rho^i = p_0 \frac{(m\rho)^m}{m!} \frac{1}{1-\rho}. \tag{4.28}$$

By explicitly including (4.26) for $p_0$, we obtain *Erlang's C formula*:

$$C(m, \rho) = \frac{\frac{(m\rho)^m}{m!} \frac{1}{1-\rho}}{\sum_{j=0}^{m-1} \frac{(m\rho)^j}{j!} + \frac{(m\rho)^m}{(1-\rho)m!}}. \tag{4.29}$$

## 4.6 The M|M|∞ infinite-server queue

As an extreme form of a multi-server system, consider now a system which increases its capacity whenever more jobs are to be served. Stated differently, the effective service rate increases linearly with the number of jobs present: $\mu_i = i\mu$, for $i = 1, 2, \cdots$. Combining this with an arrival process with fixed rate, i.e., $\lambda_i = \lambda$, for $i = 0, 1, \cdots$, and using (4.8) we can immediately derive that

$$p_i = p_0 \prod_{k=0}^{i-1} \frac{\lambda}{(k+1)\mu} = p_0 \frac{\rho^i}{i!}, \quad i = 1, 2, \cdots, \tag{4.30}$$

with $\rho = \lambda/\mu$ as usual. In Figure 4.5 we show the corresponding state transition diagram. Using the normalisation equation (4.4) we find that

$$p_0 = \frac{1}{1 + \sum_{i=1}^{\infty} \left(\frac{\lambda}{\mu}\right)^i \frac{1}{i!}} = \frac{1}{\sum_{i=0}^{\infty} \frac{\rho^i}{i!}} = \frac{1}{e^\rho} = e^{-\lambda/\mu}. \tag{4.31}$$

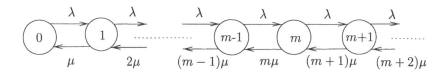

Figure 4.5: State transition diagram for the infinite-server model

Now, we can compute $E[N]$ as

$$
\begin{aligned}
E[N] &= \sum_{i=0}^{\infty} i p_i = e^{-\rho} \sum_{i=0}^{\infty} i \frac{\rho^i}{i!} = e^{-\rho} \sum_{i=1}^{\infty} i \frac{\rho^i}{i!} \\
&= e^{-\rho} \rho \sum_{i=1}^{\infty} \frac{\rho^{i-1}}{(i-1)!} = e^{-\rho} \rho e^{\rho} = \rho,
\end{aligned}
\tag{4.32}
$$

which can easily be explained. Since all arriving jobs are immediately served, the queue will always be empty, i.e., $E[N] = E[N_q] + E[N_s] = 0 + E[N_s] = \rho$. The average time spent in the queueing system simply equals the average service time $1/\mu$.

Infinite servers are often used for modelling the behaviour system user. For instance, the delay that computer jobs perceive when a user has to give a command from a terminal can be modelled by an infinite-server. There is no queueing of jobs at the terminal (every user has its terminal and there is only one job per user/terminal), but submitting a command takes time. Consequently, there is only a service delay (the "think time"). Infinite-server queueing stations are also used when fixed delays in communication links have to be modelled. For that reason, infinite-servers are sometimes also called delay servers.

## 4.7 Job allocation in heterogeneous multi-processors

When investments for computer systems have to be made, very often the question arises what is most effective to buy: a single fast multi-user computer, or a number of smaller single-user computers. We can formalise this question now, using some of the models we have just presented, albeit in a fairly abstract way.

The three abstract system models are given in Figure 4.6. In case (1) we consider a single fast processing device with service rate $K\mu$ (all users share a single but fast computer). In the second case we consider $K$ smaller computers, each with capacity $\mu$. In doing so, we can either deal with a single queue with $K$ servers (all users share a number of smaller computers; case (2a)), each of speed $\mu$, or with $K$ totally separate computers

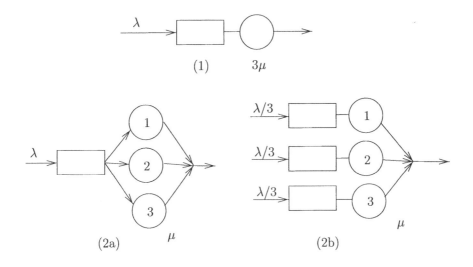

Figure 4.6: Three equal-capacity systems $(K = 3)$

among which we divide the workload (each user has its own machinery; case (2b)). What is the most profitable in terms of the average response time $E[R]$, provided that jobs arrive as a Poisson process with rate $\lambda$ and that the service times are exponentially distributed with mean $E[S]$? For this example, we define $\rho = \lambda/\mu$.

In case (1) we deal with an M|M|1 queue with arrival rate $\lambda$ and service rate $K\mu$. The actual average service time then equals $E[S]/K$ and the actual utilisation equals $\lambda E[S]/K = \rho/K$. The average response time then equals

$$E[R_1] = \frac{E[S]/K}{1 - \rho/K} = \frac{E[S]}{K - \rho}. \tag{4.33}$$

In case (2a) we deal with an M|M|K queue with job arrival rate $\lambda$ and job service rate $\mu$. We calculate $E[R_2]$ using (4.27), thereby taking into account the used definition of $\rho$ in this example, and Little's law as follows:

$$E[R_2] = E[N_2]/\lambda = E[S] + \frac{E[S]}{K} \frac{\rho^K}{K!} \frac{p_0}{(1 - \rho/K)^2}, \tag{4.34}$$

with $p_0$ as defined in (4.26), and with $m = K$. In case (2b), we deal with $K$ M|M|1 queues in parallel, each with arrival rate $\lambda/K$ and service rate $\mu$. The average service time equals $E[S]$ but the utilisation per queue is only $\lambda/K \times E[S] = \rho/K$. Therefore, we have

$$E[R_3] = \frac{E[S]}{1 - \rho/K} = K \frac{E[S]}{K - \rho} = K E[R_1]. \tag{4.35}$$

It now follows that

$$E[R_1] < E[R_2] < E[R_3]. \tag{4.36}$$

This can also be intuitively explained. Case (2b) is worse than case (2a) because in case (2b) some of the servers might be idle while others are working. These busy servers might even have jobs queued which is not possible in case (2a). Case (2a) in turn, is worse than case (1) because if there are $L < K$ jobs in the system, the system in case (2) only operates at effective speed $L\mu$ whereas in case (1) the speed of operation always is $K\mu$. If there are $K$ or more jobs in the system, cases (1) and (2a) are equivalent. Despite this fact, case (1) is best in general. In general, we observe that pooling of jobs and systems is the most efficient, apart from possibly introduced overheads.

Now suppose that we have to divide a Poisson stream, with rate $\lambda$, of arriving jobs, of length $S$, to two processors, one with capacity $K_1$ and one with capacity $K_2$. How should we choose the probabilities $\alpha_1$ and $\alpha_2$, with $\lambda_i = \alpha_i\lambda$ and $\alpha_1 + \alpha_2 = 1$, such that the average job response time is minimised?

For the average job response time we have $E[R] = \alpha_1 E[R_1] + \alpha_2 E[R_2]$. First of all, we know that

$$E[R_i] = \frac{E[S_i]}{1 - \rho_i}, \quad E[S_i] = E[S]/K_i, \quad \rho_i = \lambda_i E[S_i], \quad i = 1, 2. \tag{4.37}$$

Writing $E[R] = \alpha_1 E[R_1] + (1 - \alpha_1)E[R_2]$ and substituting $\alpha_2 = 1 - \alpha_1$ whenever possible, we obtain an expression for $E[R]$ as a function of $\alpha_1$:

$$E[R(\alpha_1)] = \alpha_1 \frac{E[S]/K_1}{1 - \alpha_1\lambda E[S]/K_1} + (1 - \alpha_1)\frac{E[S]/K_2}{1 - (1 - \alpha_1)\lambda E[S]/K_1}. \tag{4.38}$$

Taking the derivative of this expression with respect to $\alpha_1$ and collecting terms, we obtain

$$\frac{dE[R(\alpha_1)]}{d\alpha_1} = \frac{E[S]/K_1}{(1 - \rho_1)^2} - \frac{E[S]/K_2}{(1 - \rho_2)^2}. \tag{4.39}$$

Now, to optimise $E[R(\alpha_1)]$ we set $dE[R(\alpha_1)]/d\alpha_1 = 0$ which yields

$$\frac{dE[R(\alpha_1)]}{d\alpha_1} = 0 \Leftrightarrow \frac{(1 - \rho_1)^2}{(1 - \rho_2)^2} = \frac{K_2}{K_1} \Leftrightarrow \frac{(1 - \rho_1)}{(1 - \rho_2)} = \frac{\sqrt{K_2}}{\sqrt{K_1}}. \tag{4.40}$$

We observe that the quotient of the squared idle fractions for queues 1 and 2 should equal the quotient of $K_2$ and $K_1$! Thus, the queue with the highest capacity should have the smallest idle fraction. Stated differently, the faster queue should be more heavily loaded to optimise $E[R]$. From the quotient of the idle fractions, we can straightforwardly calculate $\alpha_1$ and $\alpha_2$.

**Example 4.2. Calculating $\alpha_1$ and $\alpha_2$.**

As an example, consider the case where $\lambda = 4$ and $E[S] = 1$ and where server 2 is four times as fast as server 1, i.e., $K_1 = 1$ and $K_2 = 4$. Following the above computations will yield $\alpha_1 = 1/6$ and $\alpha_2 = 5/6$, yielding $\rho_1 = 4/6$ and $\rho_2 = 5/6$. Clearly, the faster server is more heavily loaded! This implies that load balancing on the basis of (average) utilisations is not always the best choice. The expected queue lengths at the queues can be computed as $E[N_1] = 2$ and $E[N_2] = 5$. Note that the faster server will have a larger average queue length. This implies that load-balancing on the basis of (average) queue lengths without taking into account server speeds is not a good idea either! □

## 4.8 The M|M|1|m single-server queue with bounded buffer

In the models we have addressed so far, the buffer capacity has always been infinitely large. In practice the buffer capacity of a system is limited. In some performance evaluation studies it is important to reflect this fact in the model. In this section we therefore address an M|M|1 system where the total number of jobs in the queueing station is limited by $m$. Jobs arriving whenever there are already $m$ present in the queueing station are not accepted; they are simply lost. From the viewpoint of the queueing station, the situation is as follows. Whenever there are $m$ jobs in the station, no new arrivals can occur. It is as if the Poisson arrival stream has been switched off in these cases. The serving of jobs, however, always happens with the same speed. Consequently, we have:

$$\lambda_i = \begin{cases} \lambda, & i = 0, 1, \cdots, m - 1, \\ 0, & i = m, m + 1, \cdots, \end{cases} \quad \text{and} \quad \mu_i = \begin{cases} \mu, & i = 1, \cdots, m, \\ 0, & i = m + 1, m + 2, \cdots. \end{cases} \tag{4.41}$$

The corresponding state transition diagram is given in Figure 4.7. It is interesting to notice that this model is always stable; when $\lambda > \mu$ jobs will queue, but only up till a total of $m$. The jobs that arrive after the queue has been filled completely are simply discarded. Turning to the solution of this model, we have from (4.8) that

$$p_i = p_0 \prod_{k=0}^{i-1} \frac{\lambda}{\mu} = p_0 \left(\frac{\lambda}{\mu}\right)^i = p_0 \rho^i, \quad i = 1, \cdots, m, \tag{4.42}$$

where $\rho$ equals the ratio $\lambda/\mu$. Notice that this ratio does not represent the utilisation any more. We can solve for $p_0$ by using the normalisation equation (4.4):

$$p_0 = \left(\sum_{i=0}^{m} \rho^i\right)^{-1} = \left(\frac{1 - \rho^{m+1}}{1 - \rho}\right)^{-1} = \frac{1 - \rho}{1 - \rho^{m+1}}, \tag{4.43}$$

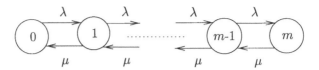

Figure 4.7: State transition diagram for an M|M|1|m loss system

where we used the result for the finite geometric series (see Appendix B). Substituting (4.43) in (4.42), we obtain the following steady-state probabilities:

$$p_i = \frac{1-\rho}{1-\rho^{m+1}}\rho^i, \quad i = 0, 1, \cdots, m. \tag{4.44}$$

In queueing stations with finite buffer capacity, arriving jobs can be lost. Due to the PASTA property the probability that an arriving job will be lost equals $p_m$. Therefore, the throughput of such a queueing station is not automatically equal to the job arrival rate. For the case considered here, we can derive that the throughput $X$ only equals $\lambda$ (the arrival rate) whenever the queue is not yet completely filled: whenever the state upon arrival of a new packet is not equal to $m$, so that we have $X = \lambda(1 - p_m)$. On the other hand, as long as the queue is not empty, which is the case with probability $1 - p_0$, the server serves jobs with rate $\mu$. Therefore, the throughput is also equal to $X = \mu(1 - p_0)$. The utilisation now equals $X E[S]$ or $1 - p_0$.

**Example 4.3. The throughput of the M|M|1|5 queue.**
In an M|M|1|5 queue, the probability that an arriving job will be lost equals $p_5$. We therefore have: $X = \lambda(1 - p_5)$ but also $X = \mu(1 - p_0)$ so that:

$$X = \mu(1 - p_0) = \lambda(1 - p_5) = \lambda\left(\frac{1-\rho^5}{1-\rho^6}\right). \tag{4.45}$$

□

**Example 4.4. Losses and overflow.**
Due to the fact that the M|M|1|m has finite buffering capacity, losses occur. The probability that an arriving customer is lost is expressed by $p_m$. In Table 4.1 we show $p_m$ as a function of $m$, for three values of $\rho = \lambda/\mu$. As can be observed, the loss probability remains to be substantial for higher utilisations, even when the buffer capacity becomes larger.           □

| $m$ | $\rho = 0.2$ | $\rho = 0.6$ | $\rho = 0.9$ |
|---|---|---|---|
| 0 | 1.0000 | 1.0000 | 1.0000 |
| 1 | 0.1667 | 0.3750 | 0.4737 |
| 2 | 0.0322 | 0.1837 | 0.2989 |
| 3 | 0.0064 | 0.0993 | 0.2120 |
| 4 | 0.0013 | 0.0562 | 0.1602 |
| 5 | 0.0003 | 0.0326 | 0.1260 |
| 6 | 0.0000 | 0.0192 | 0.1019 |
| 7 | 0.0000 | 0.0114 | 0.0840 |
| 8 | 0.0000 | 0.0068 | 0.0703 |
| 9 | 0.0000 | 0.0041 | 0.0595 |
| 10 | 0.0000 | 0.0024 | 0.0508 |

Table 4.1: Blocking probabilities $p_m$ in the M|M|1|m queue

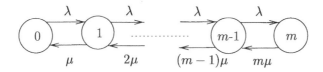

Figure 4.8: State transition diagram for the M|M|m|m model

## 4.9 The M|M|m|m multi-server queue without buffer

Finite buffers and multi-server behaviour can also be combined. A particularly important class of models arises where the number of servers equals the number of jobs that can be dealt with; in principle no buffering takes place in such models. Whenever an arriving job does not find a free server, it is lost. This typically occurs in (older) telephone switches where the number of outgoing lines equals the maximum number of customers that can be coped with. In case all $m$ lines are busy, no further queueing can occur and the request is not accepted, nor is it queued (the user simply hears the busy-tone). In Figure 4.8 we show the corresponding state transition diagram.

We can see this model again as a special case of the general birth-death model, now with the following parameters:

$$\lambda_i = \lambda, \quad i = 0, 1, \cdots, m-1, \quad \text{and} \quad \mu_i = i\mu, \quad i = 1, 2, \cdots, m. \tag{4.46}$$

Solving (4.8) and setting again $\rho = \lambda/\mu$, we obtain

$$p_i = p_0 \frac{\rho^i}{i!}, \quad i = 0, 1, \cdots, m, \tag{4.47}$$

where $p_0$ follows from the normalisation:

$$p_0 = \left( \sum_{j=0}^{m} \frac{\rho^j}{j!} \right)^{-1}. \tag{4.48}$$

The probability $p_m$ signifies the probability that all servers are in use. Due to the PASTA property, this probability equals the long term probability that an arriving packet is lost. The formula for $p_m$ was first established by Erlang in 1917 and is therefore often referred to as *Erlang's loss formula* or *Erlang's B formula* and denoted as $B(m, \lambda/\mu) = B(m, \rho)$:

$$p_m = B(m, \rho) = \frac{\rho^m/m!}{\sum_{j=0}^{m} \rho^j/j!} \tag{4.49}$$

## 4.10   The M|M|1||K queue or the terminal model

We finally address a queueing station in an environment where the total number of jobs is limited. This occurs in numerous situations, e.g., in a computer network system in which a finite set of users may all issue one request at a time to a network file server. Only after an answer has been received from the file server, may a new request be issued by each user. Thus, there can never be more jobs (modelling requests) in the queueing station (modelling the server) than there are users.

We can interpret the M|M|1||K queueing model as follows. There are $K$ system users sitting behind their terminals. These users issue requests for service after an exponentially distributed think time $Z$ with mean $E[Z] = 1/\lambda$. The more users there are in the thinking state, the higher the effective completion rate of thinkers is, that is, the effective arrival rate at the system is proportional to the number of thinkers. Stated differently, the users can be modelled as an infinite server, where each user has its own server. Once jobs have been submitted, the users wait for the answer. The system completes jobs with mean time $E[S] = 1/\mu$.

To formalise this model, we proceed as follows. When there are $i$ jobs in the queueing station, there will be $K - i$ potential other jobs. We thinks of these jobs as being part of some "environment" of the queueing station. Furthermore, the arrival rate of jobs is proportional to the number of jobs in this environment, i.e., proportional to $K - i$. This means that we have:

$$\lambda_i = \lambda(K - i), \ i = 0, \cdots, K - 1, \quad \text{and} \quad \mu_i = \mu, \ i = 0, 1, \cdots, K. \tag{4.50}$$

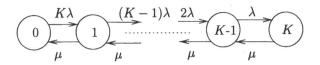

Figure 4.9: State transition diagram for the M|M|1||K model

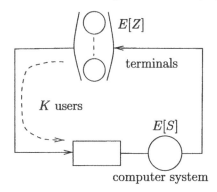

Figure 4.10: Simple terminal model

Notice that this queueing station can never be overloaded. When all the jobs are in the queueing station, no new jobs will arrive, so the queue will not grow infinitely large. In Figure 4.9 the state transition diagram is depicted. Again, we can use (4.8) to obtain the following expression for $p_i$:

$$p_i = p_0 \prod_{k=0}^{i-1} \frac{\lambda(K-k)}{\mu} = p_0 \prod_{k=0}^{i-1} \rho(K-k) = p_0 \rho^i \prod_{k=0}^{i-1}(K-k), \quad i = 0, 1, \cdots, K. \quad (4.51)$$

Using the normalisation equation we find that

$$p_0 = \left( \sum_{i=0}^{K} \left( \frac{\lambda}{\mu} \right)^i \frac{K!}{(K-i)!} \right)^{-1}. \quad (4.52)$$

In Figure 4.10 we sketch this so-called *terminal model*. It is an example of a *closed queueing network* with a population of $K$ customers circling between the terminals and the processing system; note the special representation we use to signify infinite server nodes. One can think of closed queueing models as models in which a departing customer at one station will result immediately in the arrival of that customer at one of the other queueing stations in the model. We will discuss queueing network models at length in Chapter 10 through 13.

## 4.11   Mean values for the terminal model

Using the birth-death model developed in Section 4.10 we can compute the steady-state probabilities $p$ and from those we can compute average performance measures such as $E[N]$ in a similar way to that done before. However, if we are only interested in average performance values and not in the precise queue-length distribution $p$, there is a simpler method available. This method, known as *mean-value analysis*, can be applied in many cases for more general queueing networks; we will come back to it in Chapter 11 through 13. Here we develop the method for this special case only.

Let us first address the average response times at the terminals ($E[R_t]$) and at the system ($E[R_s(K)]$). In an infinite-server queueing station, every job has its own server, so no queueing or waiting occurs. Therefore: $E[R_t] = E[Z]$, independently of the number of customers $K$ actually present. For the processing system, however, the average response time depends on the number of customers $K$. To compute $E[R_s(K)]$, we first have to introduce the average cycle time as $E[C(K)] = E[R_t] + E[R_s(K)] = E[Z] + E[R_s(K)]$. $E[C(K)]$ expresses the mean time it takes for a customer to go once through the cycle "think-serve". The throughput $X(K)$ (again note the dependence on $K$) can now be expressed as $K/E[C(K)]$, that is, as the product of the frequency with which jobs cycle and the number of jobs (notice that $X(K)$ is *not* equal to $1/E[Z]$). Combining the above two results, we obtain

$$X(K) = \frac{K}{E[C(K)]} = \frac{K}{E[Z] + E[R_s(K)]},\qquad(4.53)$$

from which we derive the *response time law*:

$$E[R_s(K)] = \frac{K}{X(K)} - E[Z].\qquad(4.54)$$

Using Little's law for the system, we have $E[N_s(K)] = X(K)E[R_s(K)]$. Using Little's law for the terminals, we have $E[N_t(K)] = X(K)E[R_t]$. Using $X(K) = K/E[C(K)]$ in the two instances of Little's law, we can eliminate $X(K)$, as follows:

$$E[N_s(K)] = \frac{E[R_s(K)]}{E[C(K)]}K, \quad \text{and} \quad E[N_t(K)] = \frac{E[Z]}{E[C(K)]}K.\qquad(4.55)$$

As can be observed, the $K$ customers spread themselves over the two nodes in the model with ratios proportional to the average time spend at the nodes divided by the time spend on an average cycle.

Although the above equations give some insight, they still do not yield us answers. For that purpose we need to know the throughput $X(K)$ which equals the product of the server-busy probability and the service rate of the system: $X(K) = (1 - p_0)\mu = (1 - p_0)/E[S]$.

We can evaluate this throughput by using the result of Section 4.10, thereby again noting that if we change $K$, $p_0$ will change as well (we therefore write $p_0$ as a function of $K$ below). In summary, we have

$$E[R_s(K)] = \frac{KE[S]}{(1 - p_0(K))} - E[Z].\tag{4.56}$$

Instead of computing $p_0(K)$ explicitly, let us first address two asymptotic results. For large values of $K$, the idle fraction is very small so that the denominator $1 - p_0(K)$ will approach 1. For large $K$ we therefore have $E[R_s(K)] \approx KE[S] - E[Z]$. For $K = 1$, the server-busy probability ($\rho(1)$, the utilisation in case of 1 job) simply equals $E[S]/(E[S] + E[Z])$ (the average time the job spends in the server divided by the time for an average cycle). This is due to the fact that $E[R_s(1)] = E[S]$ since queueing will not occur.

The above two limiting cases can be regarded as asymptotes for the actual curve of $E[R_s(K)]$. Their crossing point, that is, the value for $K^*$ such that $E[S] = K^*E[S] - E[Z]$, is called the *saturation point* and computed as follows:

$$E[R_s(1)] = E[R_s(\infty)] \quad \Rightarrow \quad K^* = \frac{E[S] + E[Z]}{E[S]}.\tag{4.57}$$

Notice that $K^* = 1/\rho(1)$. When the think and service times would have been constants rather than random variables, $K^*$ would have been the maximum number of users that could have been served before any queueing would occur in the system. Having more than $K^*$ customers present would for sure imply that at some place in the model queueing would occur. Since the involved service times are not constants but random variables the actual values for the response time at the system ($E[R_s(K)]$) are of course larger than the asymptotes and queueing will already occur for values of $K$ smaller than $K^*$. In Figure 4.11 $E[R_s(K)]$ is depicted as a function of $K$ for the parameter values of the example to be discussed below. The asymptotes are also indicated.

For the precise calculation of $E[R_s(K)]$ we still need to know the value of $p_0(K)$. Although we can compute this value by using the summation as in Section 4.10 there is a smarter way to go. We can calculate $E[R_s(K)]$ recursively from $E[R_s(K - 1)]$. To understand this, we need a result, which we will discuss in more detail in Chapters 11 and 12, known as the *arrival theorem* which was proven in the late 1970s.

### Theorem 4.2. Arrival theorem.

A customer in a closed queueing network arriving at a queue, will see this queue in equilibrium (with average filling), however, for the case in which there is one customer less in the queueing network. $\qquad\square$

According to this theorem, the average response time at the system can be expressed as
follows:

$$E[R_s(K)] = E[N_s(K-1)]E[S] + E[S].\tag{4.58}$$

The first term represents the average waiting time because of jobs already queued (or in
service) upon arrival, whereas the second term is the average service time of the job just
arriving. Now, using (4.55) we can write

$$E[N_s(K-1)] = \frac{E[R_s(K-1)]}{E[C(K-1)]}(K-1),\tag{4.59}$$

so that

$$E[R_s(K)] = \left(\frac{E[R_s(K-1)]}{E[R_s(K-1)] + E[Z]}(K-1)\right)E[S] + E[S].\tag{4.60}$$

To begin this recursion, we use $E[R_s(1)] = E[S]$.

**Example 4.5. An MVA of the terminal model.**
Consider a terminal model as described throughout this section in which $E[S] = 2$ and
$E[Z] = 10$. The saturation point can easily be calculated as

$$K^* = \frac{E[S] + E[Z]}{E[S]} = \frac{2+10}{2} = 6.\tag{4.61}$$

The asymptotes of $E[R_s(K)]$ are respectively given as $E[R_s(K = 1)] = E[S] = 2$ and
$E[R_s(K \to \infty)] = KE[S] - E[Z] = 2K - 10$. Using the MVA recursion we can now
compute $E[R_s(K)]$, for $K = 1, \cdots, 12$. Notice that we can also express $\rho(K)$ and $X(K)$
directly in terms of $E[R_s(K)]$ as follows:

$$\rho(K) = \frac{KE[S]}{E[R_s(K)] + E[Z]} \quad \text{and} \quad X(K) = \frac{K}{E[R_s(K)] + E[Z]}.\tag{4.62}$$

In Table 4.2 we present the values for $E[R_s(K)]$, $\rho(K)$ and $X(K)$. In Figure 4.11 we show
the average response time curve and its asymptotes (lower bounds). In Figure 4.12 we
show the throughput curve, again with its asymptotes (upper bounds). Note that in both
cases the asymptotes are very easy to compute and that their crossing points lie in both
cases at $K^*$. It is clearly visible that adding more customers (adding more terminal users)
does increase the response times; however, it does *not* significantly increase the throughput
after a particular point.                                                                    □

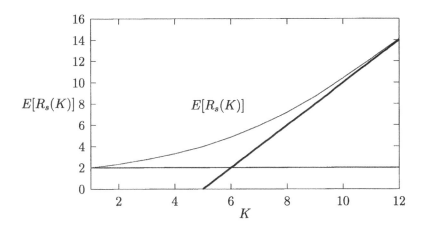

Figure 4.11: $E[R_s(K)]$ and its two lower bounds as a function of $K$

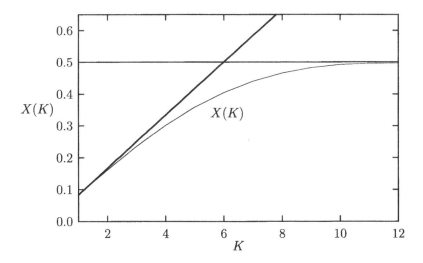

Figure 4.12: $X(K)$ and its two upper bounds as a function of $K$

| $K$ | $E[R_s(K)]$ | $\rho(K)$ | $X(K)$ | $K$ | $E[R_s(K)]$ | $\rho(K)$ | $X(K)$ |
|---|---|---|---|---|---|---|---|
| 1 | 2.00 | 0.167 | 0.084 | 7 | 5.92 | 0.880 | 0.440 |
| 2 | 2.33 | 0.324 | 0.162 | 8 | 7.21 | 0.930 | 0.465 |
| 3 | 2.76 | 0.470 | 0.235 | 9 | 8.70 | 0.963 | 0.482 |
| 4 | 3.30 | 0.602 | 0.301 | 10 | 10.37 | 0.982 | 0.492 |
| 5 | 3.98 | 0.715 | 0.358 | 11 | 12.18 | 0.992 | 0.496 |
| 6 | 4.85 | 0.808 | 0.404 | 12 | 14.08 | 0.997 | 0.497 |

Table 4.2: $E[R_s(K)]$, $\rho(K)$ and $X(K)$ for $K = 1, \cdots, 12$

## 4.12  Further reading

Further information on birth-death processes and their application to simple queueing models can be found in many performance evaluation books. Early work related to birth-death processes and blocking probabilities is due to Erlang [84]. Background information on the existence of local balance equations and their relation to the global balance equations can be found in the books by Kelly [153] and Van Dijk [74]. The PASTA property has been described by Wolff [291]. The arrival theorem and the associated mean-value analysis will be discussed in more detail in Chapters 11 through 12; seminal papers in this area have been published by Reiser and Lavenberg [245, 243].

## 4.13  Exercises

**4.1. Calculation of $B(k)$.**
Compute the minimum number of jobs $k$ such that for an M|M|1 queue with $\rho = 0.8$ the value $B(k) < 10^{-6}$.

**4.2. Waiting time distribution.**
The waiting time distribution in the M|M|1 queue can be derived in a similar way as the response time distribution. First notice that with probability $p_0$ the waiting time equals 0 and that with probability $p_k$ ($k = 1, 2, \cdots$) the waiting time has an Erlang-$k$ distribution. Show that

$$F_W(t) = \Pr\{W \le t\} = p_0 + \sum_{k=1}^{\infty} p_k F_{E_k}(t) = 1 - \rho e^{-(\mu - \lambda)t} = 1 - \rho e^{-\mu(1-\rho)t}.$$

### 4.3. Variance in the M|M|1 queue.
Show that the variance of the number of customers in an M|M|1 queue indeed corresponds to (4.18).

### 4.4. Multi-server queueing stations.
For the multiserver M|M|m queue introduced in Section 4.5 show that:

1. the solutions for $p_i$ reduce to those for the M|M|1 queue when $m = 1$,

2. the expressions for $p_i$ do indeed fulfill the global balance equations,

3. $E[N]$ can indeed be computed using (4.27).

### 4.5. Comparing average response times when $K = 2$.
Show that inequality (4.36) holds for $K = 2$.

### 4.6. The M|M|1 queue with server breakdowns.
Consider an M|M|1 queue in which the server has an exponentially distributed life-time with mean $1/l$. Once failed, the server is repaired; such a repair takes an exponentially distributed amount of time, with mean $1/r$. Customer arrivals form a Poisson process with rate $\lambda$ and services last a negative exponentially distributed time with mean $1/\mu$. For the time being, assume that the arrival process is stopped as soon as the server breaks down.

1. Draw the state-transition diagram for this extended M|M|1 queue.

2. Derive the global balance equations for this CTMC.

3. Derive a formula for $E[N]$ (be inspired by the normal M|M|1 queue).

4. Derive a formula for $\sigma_N^2$.

5. Now assume that arrivals continue to occur, even if the server has broken down. How does this change the state-transition diagram and the global balance equations? What is the stability condition in this situation?

### 4.7. Capacity and arrival rate increase.
How does the average response time in an M|M|1 queue change, when both the arrival rate $\lambda$ and the service rate $\mu$ are increased by a multiplicative factor $\alpha$, i.e., when $\rho$ remains the same?

**4.8. Erlang's B formula.**

Calculate $B(m, \lambda/\mu)$ for $m = 5$, 10, 15, 25 and 100 and $\lambda/\mu = 0.1, \cdots, 0.9$.

**4.9. Multi-server queues.**

Prove (4.26) and (4.27) using (4.24) and (4.25).

**4.10. MVA and the terminal model.**

Consider a terminal model with $K$ customers, $E[Z] = 15$ and $E[S] = 3$.

1. Compute the saturation point $K^*$.

2. Compute the asymptotes for the system response time $E[R_s(K)]$ and draw them in a graph.

3. Compute the asymptotes for the system throughput $X(K)$ and draw them in a graph.

4. Compute the exact values of $X(K)$ and $E[R_s(K)]$, for $K = 1, \cdots, 12$, using MVA.

5. Propose an MVA-based scheme to compute $p_0(K)$ from $\rho(K)$. Do not directly compute $p_0(K)$ via (4.52)!

# Chapter 5

# M|G|1-FCFS queueing models

IN the previous chapter we have discussed a number of Markovian queueing models and shown various applications of them. In practice, however, there are systems for which the negative exponential service times that were assumed in these models are not realistic. There exist, however, also single server models that require less strict assumptions regarding the used service time distributions. Examples are the M|G|1 model, the G|G|1 model and the G|PH|1 model. The analysis of these models is more complicated than that of the simple birth-death models encountered in Chapter 4.

In this chapter we focus on the M|G|1 queueing model. This model is rather generally applicable in environments where multiple users (a large population of potential customers) are using a scarce resource, such as a transmission line or a central server, for generally distributed periods of time.

This chapter is organised as follows. In Section 5.1 we present the well-known results for various mean performance measures of interest for the M|G|1 queue. We pay special attention to the impact of the general service time distribution. The M|G|1 result can be proven in an intuitive fashion; we do so in Section 5.2. A rigorous proof based on a embedded Markov chain is then presented in Section 5.3. In Section 5.4 we discuss an extension of the M|G|1 model in which batches of jobs arrive simultaneously. Finally, in Section 5.5, we discuss M|G|1 queueing models with server breakdowns.

## 5.1 The M|G|1 result

Consider a single server queueing station with unlimited buffering capacity and unlimited customer population. Jobs arriving at the queueing station form a Poisson process with rate $\lambda$. The service requirement of a job is a random variable $S$, distributed according to the distribution function $B(s)$, i.e., $B(s) = \Pr\{S \leq s\}$. $S$ has expectation $E[S]$ (first moment) and second moment $E[S^2]$.

Again we use the notation $E[N]$ for the average number of jobs in the queueing system, $E[N_q]$ for the average number of customers in the queue, and $E[N_s]$ for the average number of customers in the server. Applying Little's law for the server alone we have: $\rho = E[N_s] = \lambda E[S]$ and we assume $\rho < 1$ for stability. The derivation of $E[N_q]$ is somewhat more complicated. At this stage we will only present and discuss the result. Proofs will be postponed to later sections.

For the average number of jobs in the queue of an M|G|1 queueing station the following expression has been derived:

$$E[N_q] = \frac{\lambda^2 E[S^2]}{2(1-\rho)}. \tag{5.1}$$

Applying Little's law ($E[W] = E[N_q]/\lambda$), we obtain

$$E[W] = \frac{\lambda E[S^2]}{2(1-\rho)}. \tag{5.2}$$

These two equations only address the queueing part of the overall queueing station. By including the service, we arrive at the following expressions:

$$E[N] = \lambda E[S] + \frac{\lambda^2 E[S^2]}{2(1-\rho)}, \tag{5.3}$$

$$E[R] = E[S] + \frac{\lambda E[S^2]}{2(1-\rho)}. \tag{5.4}$$

The M|G|1 result is presented mostly in one of the four forms above. The form (5.3) is often referred to as the *Pollaczek-Khintchine* (or PK-) formula. Let us discuss this equation in more detail now.

Looking at the PK-formula we observe that $E[N]$ depends on the first *and second* moment of the service time distribution. What does this imply? From the first two moments of a distribution its variance can be obtained as $\sigma_S^2 = E[(S - E[S])^2] = E[S^2] - E[S]^2$. We thus see that a higher variance implies a higher average number of jobs in the system. From a queueing point of view, exhibiting no variance in the service times ($E[S^2] = E[S]^2$) is optimal. This is a very general observation: the more variability exists in the system, the worse the performance. With worse performance we of course mean longer queues, longer waiting times etc.

**Example 5.1. Influence of variance.**
Consider two almost equivalent queueing stations. In the first one the service requirement

is 1, deterministically, i.e., $E[S_1] = 1$ and $E[S_1^2] = 1$ so that $\text{var}[S_1] = 0$. In the second the service requirement is also 1 on average, but the actual values are either 0.5 or 1.5 (with probability 0.5 each), i.e., $E[S_2] = 1$ and $E[S_2^2] = 0.5(0.5)^2 + 0.5(1.5)^2 = 1.25$, so that $\text{var}[S_2] = 0.25$. Consequently, in the second system, the average waiting times will be 25% higher than in the first system, although the average work requirements are the same! □

**Example 5.2. Infinite variance.**
Consider a queueing station at which jobs arrive as a Poisson process with rate $\lambda = 0.4$. The service requirement $S$ has a probability density function $f_S(s) = 2/s^3$, whenever $s \geq 1$, and $f_S(s) = 0$, whenever $s < 1$. Calculating the average service time, we obtain

$$E[S] = \int_0^\infty s f_S(s)ds = \int_1^\infty 2s^{-2}ds = \left(-2s^{-1}\right)_{s=1}^{s=\infty} = 2 \text{ (seconds)}.$$

Clearly, since $\rho = \lambda E[S] = 0.8 < 1$ the queueing station is stable. However, when calculating the second moment of the service time distribution, we obtain

$$E[S^2] = \int_1^\infty s^2 f_S(s)ds = \int_1^\infty 2s^{-1}ds = (2\ln s)_{s=1}^{s=\infty} = \infty.$$

Application of the PK formula thus reveals that $E[N] = \infty$, even though the queue is not overloaded! □

It is important to note that *not* the total M|G|1 queueing or waiting time behaviour is given by the first two moments of the service time distribution, but only the averages. The effect that the performance becomes worse when the variance of the service time distribution increases becomes clear nicely when we use the squared coefficient of variation in our formulae. The squared coefficient of variation of a stochastic variable $X$, that is, $C_X^2 = \sigma_X^2/E[X]^2$, expresses the variance of a random variable relative to its (squared) mean. Using this notation the PK-formula can be rewritten as:

$$E[N] = \lambda E[S] + \frac{(\lambda E[S])^2(1 + C_S^2)}{2(1 - \rho)} = \rho + \frac{\rho^2(1 + C_S^2)}{2(1 - \rho)}. \tag{5.5}$$

We observe that $E[N]$ increases linearly with $C_S^2$. For $E[W]$ we obtain a similar equation:

$$E[W] = \frac{\lambda E[S]^2(1 + C_S^2)}{2(1 - \rho)} = \frac{\rho E[S](1 + C_S^2)}{2(1 - \rho)}. \tag{5.6}$$

Before we end this section with two examples, we make a few remarks about the applicability of the PK-formula:

1. The arrival and service processes must be independent of each other.

2. The server should be *work conserving*, meaning that the server may never be idle whenever there are jobs to be served.

3. The scheduling discipline is not allowed to base job scheduling on *a priori* knowledge about the service times, e.g., shortest-job-next scheduling is not allowed. Disciplines that are allowed are e.g., FCFS or LCFS.

4. The scheduling discipline should be non-preemptive, i.e., jobs being served may not be interrupted.

### Example 5.3. A simple communication channel.

Consider a buffered 10 kbps (kilo bit per second) communication channel, over which two types of packets have to be transmitted. The overall stream of packets constitutes a Poisson process with arrival rate $\lambda = 40$ packets per second (p/s). Of the arriving packets, a fraction $\alpha_1 = 0.2$ is short; the remaining packets, a fraction $\alpha_2 = 0.8$ is long. Short packets have an average length $E[S_1] = 10$ bits, whereas long packets are on average $E[S_2] = 200$ bits. Both packet lengths are exponentially distributed. We are interested in the average waiting time for and the average number of packets in the communication channel.

This system can be modelled as an M|G|1 queueing station at which packets arrive as a Poisson stream with intensity 40 p/s. The fact that we have two types of packets which are of different lengths, can be coped with by choosing an appropriate service time distribution. The appropriate distribution in this case is the hyperexponential distribution with 2 stages (see also Appendix A). The hyperexponential density function with $r$ stages has the following form: $f(x) = \sum_{i=1}^{r} \alpha_i \mu_i e^{-\mu_i x}$, where $1/\mu_i$ is the time it takes to transmit a packet of class $i$, and $\sum_{i=1}^{r} \alpha_i = 1$. The average value then equals $\sum_{i=1}^{r} \alpha_i/\mu_i$, and the variance $2\sum_{i=1}^{r} \alpha_i/\mu_i^2 - (\sum_{i=1}^{r} \alpha_i/\mu_i)^2$.

Let us first calculate the $\mu_i$ by taking into account the packet sizes and the channel transmission speed. $\mu_1 = 10$ kbps/10 bits/packet $= 1000$ p/s. In a similar way we obtain $\mu_2 = 10^4/200 = 50$ p/s. For the utilisation we find $\rho = \sum_{i=1}^{2} \lambda \alpha_i/\mu_i = 0.648$. Applying the formula for the service time variance, we obtain $\sigma_S^2 = 0.3164$ msec, whereas $E[S^2] = 6.404 \times 10^{-4}$. Substituting these results in the M|G|1 result for $E[W]$ and $E[N]$ we obtain:

$$E[W] = 40\frac{6.404 \times 10^{-4}}{2(1 - 0.648)} = 36.39 \text{ msec.} \tag{5.7}$$

Applying Little's law we obtain $E[N] = \rho + \lambda E[W] = 2.1034$ packets.

If we would have modelled this system as an M|M|1 queue with $\lambda = 40$ and $E[S] = 0.0162$, we would have obtained $E[W] = 19.82$ msec, and $E[N] = 1.841$ packets. Here we clearly see the importance of using the correct model. □

**Example 5.4. Comparing M|M|1, M|E₂|1, M|H₂|1, and M|D|1.**
We now proceed with comparing four queueing stations: an M|M|1, an M|E₂|1, an M|H₂|1 and an M|D|1. These models only differ by their service requirement *distribution*. We assume that the mean value of the distributions is the same and equal to 1. In the M|H₂|1 case we assume that $\alpha_1 = \alpha_2 = 0.5$ and that $\mu_1 = 2.0$ and $\mu_2 = 2/3$. The performance metric we will use as a comparison is the average number of jobs in the queueing station.

Let us first derive the coefficients of variation of the four service time distributions involved. For the deterministic distribution we have $C_D^2 = 0$. For the exponential distribution $C_M^2 = 1$, for the 2-stage Erlang distribution $C_{E_2}^2 = 1/2$ and for the 2-stage hyperexponential distribution we have $C_{H_2}^2 = 1.5$. Substituting this in (5.6) we obtain:

$$E[W_M] = \frac{\rho E[S](1+1)}{2(1-\rho)} = \frac{\rho}{1-\rho},$$

$$E[W_D] = \frac{\rho E[S](1+0)}{2(1-\rho)} = \frac{\rho E[S]}{2(1-\rho)} = \frac{1}{2}E[W_M],$$

$$E[W_{E_2}] = \frac{\rho E[S](1+0.5)}{2(1-\rho)} = \frac{3}{4}E[W_M],$$

$$E[W_{H_2}] = \frac{\rho E[S](1+1.5)}{2(1-\rho)} = \frac{5}{4}E[W_M].$$

We observe that in the case of deterministic service times, the waiting times reduce 50% in comparison to the exponential case. A reduction to 75% can be observed for the Erlang-2 case, whereas an increase to 125% can be observed for the hyperexponential case. In Figure 5.1 we show the curves for the average waiting times $E[W]$ (for the deterministic, the hyperexponential and the exponential service time distribution) as a function of the utilisation $\rho$. □

## 5.2 An intuitive proof of the M|G|1 result

In this section we will give an intuitive proof of the M|G|1 result as discussed in the previous section. For this intuitive proof we will use the *PASTA property* discussed in Section 4.3.

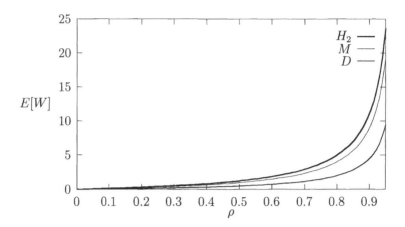

Figure 5.1: Comparison of the M|H$_2$|1, the M|M|1 and the M|D|1 queueing systems (top to bottom): the average waiting time $E[W]$ as a function of the utilisation $\rho$

Furthermore, we will need information about the so-called *residual lifetime* of a stochastic variable. We will discuss this issue in Section 5.2.1 before we prove the M|G|1 result in Section 5.2.2.

## 5.2.1   Residual lifetime

Consider a Poisson arrival process. The time between successive arrivals is exponentially distributed. From the memoryless property that holds for these exponentially distributed interarrival times we know that when we observe this Poisson process at any point in time, the time from that observation until the next arrival is again exponentially distributed. This is in fact a very peculiar property which, as we will see later, has some interesting implications which have puzzled probability engineers a long time.

Let us now try to derive the residual lifetime distribution of a more general renewal process. Assume that we deal with a renewal process where the interevent times $X$ are distributed with (positive) density function $f_X(x)$. If we observe this process at some random time instance, we denote the time until the next event as $Y$, the so-called residual lifetime or the *forward recurrence time*. The time from the observation instance to the previous event is denoted $T$ and called the *backward recurrence time*. We denote the length of the interval in which the observation takes place, i.e., the "intercepted" interval, with a

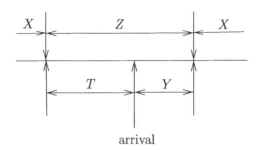

$X$: interevent time<br>$Z$: intercepted interval length<br>$T$: backward recurrence time<br>$Y$: forward recurrence time

Figure 5.2: Stochastic variables involved in the derivation of the residual lifetime

stochastic variable $Z$. Note that $Z$ does *not* have the same distribution as $X$, although one is tempted to think so at first sight. Since longer intervals have higher probability to be intercepted, a shift of probability mass from lower to higher values can be observed when comparing the density functions of $X$ and $Z$. In Figure 5.2 we show the various stochastic variables.

It is reasonable to assume that the probability that the random observation falls in an interval with length $z$ is proportional to the length of $z$ and to the relative occurrence probability of such an interval, which equals $f_X(z)dz$. We thus have that $f_Z(z)dz = Czf_X(z)dz$, where $C$ is a constant which assures that $f_Z(z)$ is indeed a proper density function. Taking the integral from 0 to infinity should yield 1, i.e.,

$$\int_0^\infty f_Z(z)dz = \int_0^\infty Czf_X(z)dz = CE[X] = 1, \tag{5.8}$$

so that we must conclude that $C = 1/E[X]$ and

$$f_Z(z) = \frac{zf_X(z)}{E[X]}. \tag{5.9}$$

Now that we have an expression for $f_Z(z)$, we will derive an expression for $f_{Y|Z}(y)$, the probability density of $Y$, given a particular $Z$. Together with $f_Z(z)$ we can then derive $f_Y(y)$ by unconditioning.

Assume that we have "intercepted" an interval with length $z$. Given such an interval, the only reasonable assumption we can make is that the actual random observation point occurs in this interval according to a uniform distribution. Consequently, we have

$$f_{Y|Z}(y|z) = \begin{cases} 1/z, & 0 < y \le z \\ 0, & \text{elsewhere.} \end{cases} \tag{5.10}$$

Now, applying the law of conditional probability, we obtain:

$$
\begin{aligned}
f_{Z,Y}(z,y) &= f_Z(z)f_{Y|Z}(y|z) \\
&= \frac{zf_X(z)}{E[X]}\frac{1}{z} \\
&= \frac{f_X(z)}{E[X]}, \quad 0 < y \le z < \infty.
\end{aligned}
\tag{5.11}
$$

In order to obtain $f_Y(y)$ we now have to integrate over all possible $z$:

$$
f_Y(y) = \int_{z=y}^{\infty} f_{Z,Y}(z,y)dz = \int_{z=y}^{\infty} \frac{f_X(z)}{E[X]}dz = \frac{1 - F_X(y)}{E[X]}.
\tag{5.12}
$$

We thus have obtained the density function of $Y$, the forward recurrence time. A similar expression can, by similar arguments, be derived for the backward recurrence time $T$. Applying this result now for deriving $E[Y]$ we obtain:

$$
\begin{aligned}
E[Y] &= \int_0^{\infty} yf_Y(y)dy \\
&= \frac{1}{E[X]}\int_0^{\infty} y(1 - F_X(y))dy \\
&= \frac{1}{E[X]}\left( \left(\frac{1}{2}y^2(1 - F_X(y))\right)_{y=0}^{y=\infty} + \int_0^{\infty} \frac{1}{2}y^2 f_X(y)dy \right) \\
&= \frac{1}{2E[X]}\int_0^{\infty} y^2 f_X(y)dy \\
&= \frac{E[X^2]}{2E[X]},
\end{aligned}
\tag{5.13}
$$

by using partial integration ($\int uv' = uv - \int u'v$). In the same way, we have

$$
E[T] = E[X^2]/2E[X].
\tag{5.14}
$$

It is important to observe that the expected forward/backward recurrence time is *not* equal to half the expected lifetime!

### Example 5.5. Exponentially distributed periods $X$.

Let us now apply these results to the case where $X$ is exponentially distributed with rate $\lambda$. Calculating

$$
f_Y(y) = \frac{1 - F_X(y)}{E[X]} = \frac{1 - (1 - e^{-\lambda y})}{1/\lambda} = \lambda e^{-\lambda y} = f_X(y),
\tag{5.15}
$$

reveals that the residual lifetime is distributed similarly to the overall lifetime. This is exactly the memoryless property of the exponential distribution. A similar derivation can be made for the backward recurrence time. The expected residual lifetime equals

$$E[Y] = \frac{E[X^2]}{2E[X]} = \frac{2/\lambda^2}{2/\lambda} = 1/\lambda. \qquad (5.16)$$

Similarly, we have $E[T] = 1/\lambda$. Now, since $E[Z] = E[T] + E[Y] = 2/\lambda$, we see that $E[Z] \neq E[X]$. This inequality is also known as the *waiting time paradox*. It can be understood by imagining that long intervals $X$ have more probability to be "hit" by a random observer. This implies that in $Z$ the longer intervals from $X$ are more strongly represented. □

**Example 5.6. Deterministic periods $X$.**
In case the random intervals $X$ are not really random but have deterministic length, we have $E[X^2] = E[X]^2$. In that case, the forward recurrence time equals $E[X^2]/2E[X]$ which reduces to $E[X]/2$. We find that the, maybe intuitively appealing, value for the forward recurrence time, namely half the normal time, is only correct when the time periods themselves are of deterministic length. □

**Example 5.7. Waiting on a bus.**
Consider the case where at a bus stop a bus arrives according to the schedule at $x$.00, $x$.20 and $x$.40, i.e., three times an hour at equidistance points per hour. If one would go to the bus stop at random time-instances, one is tempted to think that one would have to wait on average 10 minutes for the next bus to come. This is, however, not correct. Although the "inter-bus" times $B$ are planned to be exactly 20 minutes, in practice they are not, hence, the variance in the inter-bus times is positive, and so $E[B^2] > E[B]^2$. The correct expected waiting time for the bus is $E[B^2]/2E[B]$, which is larger than $E[B]/2$. When the "inter-bus" times are deterministic, the expected waiting time is 10 minutes. □

## 5.2.2 Intuitive proof

Combining the results of the previous section with the PASTA property, we are in a position to intuitively prove the PK-result. We are interested in the average response time $E[R]$ a job perceives in an M|G|1 queueing station. Jobs arrive as a Poisson stream with rate $\lambda$. The service time per job is a random variable $S$ with first and second moment $E[S]$ and

$E[S^2]$ respectively. For the derivation, which is similar to the derivation for the M|M|1 queue presented in Chapter 2, we assume an FCFS scheduling discipline.

At the moment a new job arrives, it will find, due to the PASTA property, $E[N]$ jobs already in the system. Of these jobs, on average $\rho = \lambda E[S]$ will reside in the server, and consequently, on average $E[N_q] = E[N] - \rho$ jobs will reside in the queue. The average response time $E[R]$ for the arriving job can then be seen as the sum of three parts:

- $E[R_1]$: the residual service time of the job in service, if any at all;

- $E[R_2]$: the service time for the jobs queued in front of the newly arriving packet;

- $E[R_3]$: the service time of the new job itself.

The term $E[R_1]$ equals the product of the probability that there is a packet in service and the mean residual service time, i.e., $E[R_1] = \rho E[S^2]/2E[S]$. The $E[N] - \rho$ jobs in the queue in total require on average $E[R_2] = (E[N] - \rho)E[S]$ time to be served. The packet itself requires $E[R_3] = E[S]$ amount of service. Noting that due to Little's law $E[N] = \lambda E[R]$, we have:

$$
\begin{aligned}
E[R] &= E[R_1] + E[R_2] + E[R_3] \\
&= \rho \frac{E[S^2]}{2E[S]} + (\lambda E[R] - \rho)E[S] + E[S] \\
\Rightarrow (1 - \rho)E[R] &= \rho \frac{E[S^2]}{2E[S]} + E[S](1 - \rho) \\
\Rightarrow E[R] &= E[S] + \frac{\lambda E[S^2]}{2(1 - \rho)}.
\end{aligned}
\tag{5.17}
$$

This is the result that we have seen before and concludes our proof. This intuitively appealing form of proof, based on mean-values, is also known as "the method of moments". We will see examples of it in later chapters as well.

## 5.3   A formal proof of the M|G|1 result

One of the difficulties in analysing the M|G|1 queue is the fact that the state of the queue is not simply given by the number of jobs in the queue as was the case with the M|M|1 model. Because of the fact that the service time distribution is not memoryless any more, the time a particular job has already been served has to be represented in the state of the queueing station. Consequently, we deal with a stochastic process with a state variable that takes values in the two-dimensional mixed discrete-continuous set $\mathbb{N} \times \mathbb{R}$. There is, however, a particular set of time values, for which the already expired service time of the job in service is known, and always the same: the instances of time immediately after the departure of a job and before the new job starts being served. At these time instances, the so-called *departure instances*, the already expired service time equals 0. Consequently, a correct and sufficient state description at departure instances is the number of jobs in the queueing station. In the following we will first derive a result for the average number of jobs in the queueing system at departure instances. After that we will reflect on the general applicability of this formula.

We will first find an expression for the expected number of customers left behind by a departing customer. Let $n_i$ denote the number of jobs left behind in the queue by the $i$-th job. During the service of the $i$-th job, $a_i$ new jobs arrive. We first express $n_{i+1}$ in terms of $n_i$ and $a_i$. In case $n_i > 0$, the number of jobs left behind by the $(i+1)$-th job equals the number left behind by the $i$-th job minus 1 (the $(i+1)$-th job itself), plus the number of jobs arrived during the servicing of the $(i+1)$-th job. Consequently, we have $n_{i+1} = n_i + a_{i+1} - 1$. When $n_i = 0$, the number of jobs left behind by the $(i+1)$-th job simply is the number of arrivals during its service: $n_{i+1} = a_{i+1}$. Introducing the indicator-function $\mathbf{1}(x)$ which equals 1, if $x > 0$, and 0 elsewhere, we have:

$$n_{i+1} = n_i + a_{i+1} - \mathbf{1}(n_i). \tag{5.18}$$

Now, taking expectations on both sides in this equation we obtain

$$E[n_{i+1}] = E[n_i] + E[a_{i+1}] - E[\mathbf{1}(n_i)], \tag{5.19}$$

where we assume that the expectations exist. Now, realizing that in equilibrium the average number of jobs left behind by the $i$-th and the $(i+1)$-th job must be equal, we have $E[n_{i+1}] = E[n_i] = E[n]$. Noting that we deal with Poisson arrivals, $E[a_i]$ will also be independent from $i$, i.e., $E[a] = E[a_i]$. By a similar argument, we also have $E[\mathbf{1}(n_i)] = E[\mathbf{1}(n)]$. Substituting this in (5.19) yields

$$E[a] = E[\mathbf{1}(n)]. \tag{5.20}$$

Note that $E[a]$, the average number of arrivals per average amount of service time, equals $\rho = \lambda E[S]$. We can also derive this differently (more intricate in this case, but it serves as a step-up to the derivation of $E[a^2]$ later): the average number of Poisson arrivals in an interval of length $t$ is $\lambda t$ (the first moment of a Poisson distribution with parameter $\lambda t$). Deconditioning on the length of the service time, we obtain

$$E[a] = \lambda \int_0^\infty sb(s)ds = \lambda E[S] = \rho. \tag{5.21}$$

Although we now have an expression for $E[1(n)]$, we still do not have the desired result. To come further to the desired measure, $E[n]$, we employ a trick: we square both sides of (5.18):

$$n_{i+1}^2 = n_i^2 + (1(n_i))^2 + a_{i+1}^2 - 2n_i 1(n_i) - 21(n_i)a_{i+1} + 2n_i a_{i+1}. \tag{5.22}$$

First observe that $(1(x))^2 = 1(x)$ and $x1(x) = x$ in case $x \geq 0$. Now, taking expectations on both sides and again using the earlier discussed "$i$-independence" we obtain

$$E[n^2] = E[n^2] + E[1(n)] + E[a^2] - 2E[n] - 2E[a1(n)] + 2E[na]. \tag{5.23}$$

First observe that the two $E[n^2]$ terms cancel. Furthermore, since arrivals are independent of the state of the queue, we have $E[na] = E[n]E[a]$ and $E[a1(n)] = E[a]E[1(n)] = E[a]^2$ (by (5.20)). Rewriting (5.23) then results in

$$2E[n] = E[a] + E[a^2] - 2E[a]^2 + 2E[n]E[a]. \tag{5.24}$$

Bringing the $E[n]$-terms together on the left-hand-side, we obtain

$$2E[n](1 - E[a]) = E[a] + E[a^2] - 2E[a]^2 = 2E[a](1 - E[a]) + E[a^2] - E[a]. \tag{5.25}$$

Dividing both sides by $2(1 - E[a])$ yields

$$E[n] = E[a] + \frac{E[a^2] - E[a]}{2(1 - E[a])}. \tag{5.26}$$

We already know that $E[a] = \rho$, so the only unknown still is $E[a^2]$. Given that the service period lasts $t$ seconds, the number of arrivals during this service period has a Poisson distribution with parameter $\lambda t$. The second moment of this distribution equals $(\lambda t)^2 + \lambda t$. Consequently, we have $E[a^2|\text{service time is } t] = (\lambda t)^2 + \lambda t$. Deconditioning on the service time, we obtain

$$\begin{aligned} E[a^2] &= \int_0^\infty ((\lambda s)^2 + \lambda s)b(s)ds \\ &= \lambda^2 \int_0^\infty s^2 b(s)ds + \lambda \int_0^\infty sb(s)ds = \lambda^2 E[S^2] + \lambda E[S]. \end{aligned} \tag{5.27}$$

Using this result, we derive

$$E[n] = \rho + \frac{(\lambda^2 E[S^2] + \lambda E[S]) - \lambda E[S]}{2(1 - \rho)} = \lambda E[S] + \frac{\lambda^2 E[S^2]}{2(1 - \rho)}. \tag{5.28}$$

This is the result that we have seen before, e.g., in (5.3), except for the fact that we now have an expression for $E[n]$, the average number of jobs in the queueing station upon departure instances, whereas (5.3) gives an expression for $E[N]$, the average number of jobs in the queueing station at *any* time instance. Now we have to make use of the following theorem, which we state without proof (for a proof, we refer to [160, Section 5.3, p.176]).

**Theorem 5.1. Departure instances are arrival instances.**

In a queueing system in which customers arrive and depart one at a time, the distribution of the number of customers left behind at a departure instance is equal to the distribution of the number of customers found upon arrival instance.                                                                        □

Using this theorem and knowing that for the M|G|1 queue (due to the PASTA property) the distribution of the number of customers found at arrival instances equals the customer distribution at arbitrary time instances, we have established $E[n] = E[N]$.

## 5.4  The M|G|1 model with batch arrivals

In many communication systems, packets that have to be transmitted come from a higher protocol entity in which a user-originated packet has been split into a number of mini-packets that fit the packet size used at lower levels in the protocol stack. Since the splitting of a packet in mini-packets proceeds normally very fast, it is as if a number of mini-packets (a batch) arrive at the same time (or within a very short time period).

We can model this kind of system by assuming so-called *batch* or *bulk arrivals*. We assume that we have a Poisson arrival process of batches of mini-packets with intensity $\lambda$. An arriving batch consists of a random amount $H$ of mini-packets, characterised by the discrete probabilities $h_k$, $k = 1, 2, \cdots$. The expected number of mini-packets in a batch is

$$E[H] = \sum_{k=1}^{\infty} k h_k, \tag{5.29}$$

and the *second factorial moment* equals

$$E[H^2] - E[H] = E[H(H-1)] = \sum_{k=1}^{\infty} k(k-1)h_k. \tag{5.30}$$

Each mini-packet requires a random amount of service $S$ with first and second moment $E[S]$ and $E[S^2]$ respectively. We thus have $\rho = \lambda E[H]E[S]$. Without proof, we state the average mini-packet waiting time $E[W]$:

$$E[W] = \frac{\lambda E[H]E[S^2]}{2(1-\rho)} + \frac{E[H(H-1)]E[S]}{2E[H](1-\rho)}. \tag{5.31}$$

The first term indeed is the average mini-packet waiting time in a normal M|G|1 model as if packets arrived with average size $E[H]E[S]$ and second moment $E[H]E[S^2]$. The second term accounts for the extra waiting time experienced by packets that are not the first in the batch.

The M|G|1 model with batch arrivals is often denoted as M$^{[H]}$|G|1, where the $H$ denotes the batch-size distribution.

### Example 5.8. Fixed mini-packet size.

Consider a distributed computing application that generates exponentially distributed application packets with length $A$, with $E[A] = 1/\mu$ bytes. The underlying network can only accept mini-packets (frames) with fixed length $\nu$ bytes. The overall stream of application packets forms a Poisson process with rate $\lambda$. The network transmission speed is $\tau$ bytes per second.

Let us compute the average mini-packet waiting time $E[W]$, given that $\lambda = 75$ packets per second, $E[A] = 1$ Kbyte, $\nu = 50$ bytes and $\tau = 100$ Kbytes per second.

We first compute the density of the number of mini-packets $H$, i.e., the probabilities $h_k$, $k = 1, 2, \cdots$, that an application packet is split in $k$ mini-packets. An application packet of length $a$ will be split in $k$ mini-packets whenever $(k-1)\nu < a \le k\nu$. Consequently, we have

$$
\begin{aligned}
h_k &= \int_{(k-1)\nu}^{k\nu} f_A(a)da = F_A(k\nu) - F_A((k-1)\nu) \\
&= (1 - e^{-\mu k\nu}) - (1 - e^{-\mu(k-1)\nu}) = e^{-\mu(k-1)\nu}(1 - e^{-\mu\nu}) \\
&= (e^{-\mu\nu})^{k-1}(1 - e^{-\mu\nu}) = (1 - \Omega)^{k-1}\Omega, \ k = 1, 2, \cdots.
\end{aligned}
\tag{5.32}
$$

We thus find that $H$ is geometrically distributed with parameter $\Omega = 1 - e^{-\mu\nu}$. We know that (see also Appendix A) $E[H] = 1/\Omega$. Then note that $\mathrm{var}[H] = (1 - \Omega)/\Omega^2$ so that $E[H^2] = \mathrm{var}[H] + (E[H])^2 = (2 - \Omega)/\Omega^2$. Consequently,

$$
E[H(H-1)] = E[H^2] - E[H] = \frac{2 - \Omega}{\Omega^2} - \frac{1}{\Omega} = \frac{2(1 - \Omega)}{\Omega^2}.
\tag{5.33}
$$

Substituting these results in (5.31), and noting that we have deterministic mini-packet service times so that $E[S^2] = E[S]^2$, we obtain

$$
E[W] = \frac{\lambda E[S]^2}{2(1 - \rho)\Omega} + \frac{(1 - \Omega)E[S]}{(1 - \rho)\Omega}.
\tag{5.34}
$$

Let us now use the above given numerical values. We first calculate $\Omega = 1 - e^{-\nu\mu} = 1 - e^{-50/1000} = 0.049$. Consequently, the average number of mini-packets an application is split into equals $E[H] = 1/\Omega = 20.504$. Furthermore, the first moment of the mini-packet service time $E[S] = 50/100000 = 0.5$ msec, and $\rho = \lambda E[H]E[S] = 0.769$. We thus obtain

$$
\begin{aligned}
E[W] &= \frac{\lambda E[S]^2}{2(1-\rho)\Omega} + \frac{(1-\Omega)E[S]}{(1-\rho)\Omega} \\
&= \frac{75(5 \times 10^{-4})^2}{2(1-0.769)0.049} + \frac{(1-0.049)5 \times 10^{-4}}{(1-0.769)0.049} = 43 \text{ msec.} \quad (5.35)
\end{aligned}
$$

Interesting to note is that when there is no splitting, that is, when the application packets can be transmitted directly, we would have obtained

$$
E[W] = \frac{\lambda E[S_A^2]}{2(1-\lambda E[S_A])} = \frac{150 \times 10^{-4}}{2(1-75 \times 10^{-2})} = 30 \text{ msec,} \quad (5.36)
$$

where $E[S_A]$ and $E[S_A^2]$ are the first and second moment of the application packet lengths measured in seconds. Observe that the batch arrivals cause an increase in waiting time of 13 msec (around 43%)! □

## 5.5 M|G|1 queueing systems with server breakdowns

In many computer-communication applications one can observe temporary unavailability of resources. One can think of the breakdown of a server, the unavailability of a server due to maintenance, or the unavailability of a server for a particular customer class due to the fact that the server is occupied by another customer class. One also often speaks about server vacation models in this context, simply because from a customer point-of-view, the server is taking a vacation and cannot serve customers for some time.

There are many aspects that characterise queueing models with breakdowns. Apart from the "normal" characteristics of a queueing system, there are various characteristics concerning the vacations the server takes:

- The length of the server vacation, that is, its distribution and its dependence on, e.g., the state of the queue.

- The time-instances at which server vacations start. Do they start during a normal service, thus implying a preemption of the job in service, or can they only take place when the server is idle or when the server changes from one customer to the next?

- The scheduling of server vacations. Are vacations starting randomly, after some fixed number of (job) services or after some fixed time period?

- The resume policy of the server. Is a new vacation started if after a vacation the server finds the queue empty, or is the server just becoming idle in these cases?

Depending on the application that one studies, one can decide for one or another model. As an example, maintenance work is preferably done during idle periods of a system. When modelling a system including its maintenance, the maintenance activities could be modelled as server vacations which can only start when there are no jobs to be served. Depending on the maintenance strategy, a maintenance activity may be started after a fixed number of services or after a fixed time interval, whichever comes first (compare a car maintenance schedule: e.g., every 20000 km or once a year, whichever comes first).

Without going into too much detail regarding derivations, we will present M|G|1 queueing systems with server breakdowns and single arrivals in Section 5.5.1 and with server breakdowns and batch arrivals in Section 5.5.2.

## 5.5.1   Single arrivals

We first consider a variant of the M|G|1 model in which the server takes a vacation of random length whenever the system becomes empty. Upon returning from a vacation, the server starts working again when there are jobs queued, until the station empties again. Whenever, upon return from a vacation, the server finds the queue empty, it takes another vacation. This model is called *an M|G|1 model with exhaustive service and multiple vacations.*

Assume that jobs arrive as a Poisson stream with intensity $\lambda$, and that job lengths have a distribution characterised by the first two moments $E[S]$ and $E[S^2]$. As usual, $\rho = \lambda E[S]$. A vacation has a duration $V$ and is characterised by its first two moments $E[V]$ and $E[V^2]$.

Let us use the method of moments to derive the average waiting time. The average waiting time $E[W]$ consists of three parts. The first part is the average remaining vacation time, given that a vacation is going on at the instance of arrival. The latter is the case with probability $1 - \rho$, the probability that there is no work to be done. The second and third part are similar to the corresponding parts in the normal M|G|1 queue: $\rho$ times the average residual service time for the job being served and $E[N_q] = E[N] - \rho$ times the average service times of the jobs queued in front of the arriving job. Consequently, we have

$$E[W] = (1 - \rho)\frac{E[V^2]}{2E[V]} + \rho\frac{E[S^2]}{2E[S]} + E[N_q]E[S]. \tag{5.37}$$

By using Little's law to rewrite $E[N_q] = \lambda E[W]$ and rearranging terms, we obtain

$$E[W] = \frac{E[V^2]}{2E[V]} + \frac{\lambda E[S^2]}{2(1-\rho)}.$$ (5.38)

We observe that the expected waiting time $E[W]$ of a packet in this system simply equals the sum of the residual vacation duration, $E[V^2]/2E[V]$, and the waiting time as perceived in a normal M|G|1 model. This result is not surprising. *All* jobs being served in fact receive service as in a normal M|G|1 queue, however, delayed by the expected remaining vacation time (of the last vacation).

A slight change to the above model is the case where at most one vacation is taken: *an M|G|1 model with exhaustive service and a single vacation.* Whenever the server returns from a vacation and finds the system empty, it simply becomes idle, waiting on the next arrival. For $E[W]$ we then have the following slightly more complex result:

$$E[W] = \frac{\lambda E[V^2]}{2(f_V^*(\lambda) + \lambda E[V])} + \frac{\lambda E[S^2]}{2(1-\rho)},$$ (5.39)

where we recognize the normal M|G|1 waiting time, plus a term accounting for the server vacation. In this term, $f_V^*(\lambda)$ is the Laplace transform of the density function of $V$, evaluated at $s = \lambda$ (see also Appendix B):

$$f_V^*(s = \lambda) = \left( \int_0^\infty e^{-st} f_V(t) dt \right)_{s=\lambda}.$$ (5.40)

For the above evaluation we thus require knowledge of $f_V^*(s)$ and, hence, of the distribution of $V$. What can be observed though, is the fact that the single vacation model yields a smaller expected waiting time than the multiple vacation model since the additive term $f_V^*(\lambda)$ in the left denominator is always positive, thus yielding a smaller contribution to the waiting time.

## 5.5.2 Batch arrivals

We can easily generalise the M|G|1 model with server breakdowns to one with batch arrivals, as discussed in Section 5.4. We have a Poisson arrival process of batches with rate $\lambda$. An arriving batch of random size $H$ consists of $k = 1, 2, \cdots$ mini-packets with probabilities $h_k$, $k = 1, 2, \cdots$. The expected number of mini-packets in a batch is $E[H]$; the second factorial moment is $E[H(H-1)]$. Each mini-packet requires a random amount of service with first and second moment $E[S]$ and $E[S^2]$, respectively. Recalling that $\rho = \lambda E[H]E[S]$, we have for the average message waiting time $E[W]$ the following result:

$$E[W] = \frac{E[V^2]}{2E[V]} + \frac{\lambda E[H]E[S^2]}{2(1-\rho)} + \frac{E[H(H-1)]E[S]}{2E[H](1-\rho)},$$ (5.41)

where the first term indeed is the residual vacation time and the latter two terms represent the earlier presented average message waiting time in an $M^{[H]}|G|1$ model without vacations.

## 5.6  Further reading

The M|G|1 queue is treated in most textbooks on computer performance evaluation. The earliest results on the M|G|1 queue have been derived by Pollaczek [235]. Early work on the embedded Markov chain approach has been performed by Palm [228] and Kendall [155]. Background on queues with server breakdowns can be found in the survey of Doshi [76]. Many variants of the M|G|1 queue are treated in depth in the book by Takagi [274].

## 5.7  Exercises

**5.1. The M|G|1 queue.**
In a university computer center three types of jobs are distinguished (with their relative occurrence): student jobs (30%), faculty jobs (50%) and administrative jobs (20%). Jobs of these three classes have negative exponential lengths with mean values 10, 30 and 20 milliseconds, respectively.

1. Compute the first and second moment of the job service time.

2. At which overall job arrival rate does the system become overloaded?

3. Express $E[W]$ as a function of the overall arrival rate $\lambda$ and draw a graph of $E[W]$ against $\lambda$.

4. What value does the arrival rate reach, when the expected waiting time is at most equal to two times the expected service time? How big is the utilisation in that case?

**5.2. Modelling of a disk system.**
We consider a (simplified) single disk system. The disk has $t$ tracks and $s$ sectors per track. We assume that seek operations can be performed with constant speed $v$ tracks per second. The number of disk rotations per second is $r$. A single sector (containing $b$ bytes) corresponds to the smallest unit of transfer (a block). We consider the case where disk requests (for single blocks) arrive as a Poisson process with rate $\lambda$ and assume that requests are uniformly distributed over the disk; successive requests are independent of one another. The service time of a single request then consists of the rotational latency, the seek time and the block transfer time.

1. Find expressions for the first and second moment of the rotational latency.

2. Find expressions for the first and second moment of the seek time.

3. Find expressions for the first and second moment of the block transfer time.

4. Give an expression for the expected response time for a disk request.

5. How would the analysis change when a single disk request consists of $i$ blocks with probability $b_i$ ($i = 1, \cdots, s$) under the assumption that these blocks are stored consecutively.

The issue of disk modelling is discussed in detail in [248].

### 5.3. M|G|1 queues with batch arrivals.

Consider a M|G|1 queue with batch arrivals. The arrival process (of batches) has rate $\lambda$. Every batch consists of $H$ mini-jobs (mini-packets), with $h_k = \frac{1}{5}$, for $k = 1, \cdots, 5$. We furthermore have: $E[S] = 0.03$ deterministically.

1. Compute the mean batch size $E[H]$.

2. Compute the second factorial moment $E[H(H-1)]$.

3. How large can $\lambda$ be before the system becomes unstable?

4. Compute $E[W]$ in case $\rho = 0.9$.

5. Now, *suppose* we are not aware of the results for the M|G|1 queue with batch arrivals. Instead, to approximate the fact that arrivals take place in batches, we accelerate the arrival process with a factor $E[H]$ and treat the resulting system as a normal M|G|1 queueing model. How large is $E[W]$ in this case?

6. To improve upon the approximation derived in the previous exercise, we now assume that arrivals of batches do take place, but we "encode" the batch size in the service times, i.e., we assume that a service lasts $\frac{3}{100}k$ when the arrival consists of $k$ mini-packets (which is the case with probability $h_k$, $k = 1, \cdots, 5$). Compute $E[S]$ and $E[S^2]$ and evaluate the expected waiting time $E[W]$ using the normal M|G|1 result.

# Chapter 6

# M|G|1 queueing models with various scheduling disciplines

$I$N this chapter we continue the study of M|G|1 queueing models. In particular, we will study the influence of various new scheduling disciplines, in comparison to the FCFS scheduling we have addressed in Chapter 5. We address non-preemptive priority scheduling in Section 6.1 and preemptive priority scheduling in Section 6.2. A limiting case of the non-preemptive priority scheduling is shortest job next scheduling, which is discussed in Section 6.3. Then, in Section 6.4 we discuss the round robin scheduling strategy and, in Section 6.5, its limiting case, processor sharing scheduling. Finally, we discuss scheduling disciplines based on the already elapsed service time of jobs in Section 6.6.

## 6.1 Non-preemptive priority scheduling

Up till now we have assumed that all the jobs that need to be served have the same priority. In practice, this is often not the case. In communication systems, as an example, short packets that contain control information might have priority over the generally longer user packets. Another case where priorities are needed is in integrated services communication systems which transmit real-time data such as voice or video samples next to time-insensitive data. Also in computer system scheduling multiple priority classes do make sense, e.g., to distinguish between interactive jobs and computation-intensive batch jobs. To illustrate the need for priority scheduling, let us consider the following example.

**Example 6.1. A computer center without priorities.**
Consider a computer center where jobs enter as a Poisson process with rate $\lambda$. Of the

| $\lambda$ | $\rho$ | $E[W]$ |
|---|---|---|
| 1 | 0.1540 | 0.0222 |
| 2 | 0.3080 | 0.0542 |
| 3 | 0.4620 | 0.1046 |
| 4 | 0.6160 | 0.1953 |
| 5 | 0.7700 | 0.4076 |
| 6 | 0.9240 | 1.4803 |

Table 6.1: Mean waiting times $E[W]$ (in seconds) in a non-priority computing center

incoming jobs, a fraction $\alpha_i = 40\%$ comprises inter-active jobs with fixed length of 10 msec, and a fraction of $\alpha_b = 60\%$ comprises batch jobs with a fixed length of 250 msec. We can compute the expected service time $E[S] = 0.4 \times 10 + 0.6 \times 250 = 154$ msec. We thus find that the system becomes unstable at $\lambda = 1/0.154 \approx 6.6$ job arrivals per second. For the second moment we find $E[S^2] = 0.4 \times 0.01^2 + 0.6 \times 0.250^2 = 0.0375$ seconds$^2$. Using the standard M|G|1 result, we can compute the expected waiting times for increasing load, as indicated in Table 6.1

What can be observed is that even for small utilisations the average waiting time $E[W]$ is significantly larger than the time required to serve interactive jobs. This is an undesirable situation which can be overcome by introducing (higher) priority for the interactive jobs.

□

An important characteristic of priority strategies is whether they are preemptive or not:

- In *preemptive priority strategies* a job in service is stopped being served as soon as a higher-priority job arrives. In that case, first the higher-priority job is served, after which the service of the lower-priority job that was originally being serviced is resumed or restarted. Preemptive scheduling strategies thus order the jobs in the queue, including the one in service.

- In *non-preemptive priority strategies*, a job in service is always first finished before a new job is put into service. Non-preemptive priority strategies only order the jobs in the queue. Apart from the introduced overhead, preemptive priority strategies are better for the higher-priority jobs than non-preemptive ones. On the other hand, non-preemptive strategies are generally easier to implement and cause less overhead.

In this section we focus on non-preemptive priority scheduling, whereas Section 6.2 is devoted to preemptive priority scheduling.

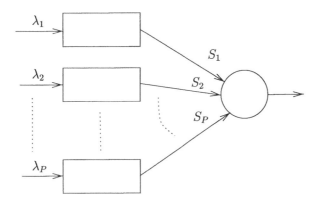

Figure 6.1: M|G|1 model with $P$ priority classes

Let us now consider a model of a single server system in which arriving jobs can be classified in $P$ priority classes, numbered 1 through $P$. We assume that class 1 has the highest and class $P$ the lowest priority. Jobs of class $r = 1, \cdots, P$, arrive at the queueing station according to a Poisson process with rate $\lambda_r$. The average service requirement for class $r$ jobs is $E[S_r] = 1/\mu_r$. The second moment of the service requirements for class $r$ jobs is $E[S_r^2]$. In Figure 6.1 we show the M|G|1 model with multiple priorities. Note that we have drawn multiple queues for convenience only; one could also consider a single queue in which the customers are ordered on the basis of their priority.

We will now derive a relation between the average waiting time $E[W_r]$ of a class $r$ job and the average waiting times of jobs of higher priority classes $1, \cdots, r-1$.

A job of class $r$ arriving at the queueing station has to wait before it can be served. Its waiting time $W_r$ consists of three components:

- The remaining service time of the job in service, if any;

- The time it costs to serve all the jobs of priority classes $k = 1, \cdots, r$, i.e., of all higher and equal priority jobs, that are present in the system upon the arrival of the class $r$ job;

- The time it costs to serve jobs of higher priority classes, i.e., jobs of classes $k = 1, \cdots, r-1$, that arrive during the waiting period of the class $r$ job.

In an equation, this takes the following form:

$$W_r = T_P + \sum_{k=1}^{r} T_k' + \sum_{k=1}^{r-1} T_k'', \tag{6.1}$$

where $W_r$ is the waiting time of class $r$ jobs, $T_P$ the remaining service time of the job in service, $T'_k$ the time it costs to serve all the class $k$ customers that are present upon the arrival of the class $r$ customer (note the summation index that ranges from 1 to $r$), and $T''_k$ the time it costs to serve all the class $k$ customers that arrive during $W_r$ and that need to be served before the class $r$ customer (note the summation index that ranges from 1 to $r - 1$). Taking expectations on both sides we obtain:

$$E[W_r] = E[T_P] + \sum_{k=1}^{r} E[T'_k] + \sum_{k=1}^{r-1} E[T''_k]. \tag{6.2}$$

We will now derive expressions for the three terms on the right hand side of this equation:

- The remaining service time of the job in service clearly depends on the class of the job that is in service. A job of class $r$ is in service with probability $\rho_r$, where $\rho_r = \lambda_r E[S_r]$, the utilisation caused by class $r$ jobs. The remaining processing time of a class $r$ job equals $E[S_r^2]/2E[S_r]$. In total, we thus obtain:

$$E[T_P] = \sum_{k=1}^{P} \rho_k \frac{E[S_k^2]}{2E[S_k]} = \frac{1}{2} \sum_{k=1}^{P} \lambda_k E[S_k^2]. \tag{6.3}$$

- The term $E[T'_k]$ is determined by the number of jobs per class in the queueing station upon the arrival of the new class $r$ job. Due to the PASTA property and Little's law we know that on average there are $E[N_{q,k}] = \lambda_k E[W_k]$ class $k$ jobs upon arrival in the queue. Since they require on average $1/\mu_k$ amount of service each, we have $E[T'_k] = E[N_{q,k}]/\mu_k = \lambda_k E[W_k]/\mu_k = \rho_k E[W_k]$.

- Finally, we have to calculate $E[T''_k]$. During the $E[W_r]$ time units the class $r$ job has to wait, on average $\lambda_k E[W_r]$ jobs of class $k$ arrive, each requiring $1/\mu_k$ service. Thus, we have $E[T''_k] = \lambda_k E[W_r]/\mu_k = \rho_k E[W_r]$.

Substituting these results in (6.2), we obtain

$$
\begin{aligned}
E[W_r] &= \sum_{k=1}^{P} \frac{\lambda_k}{2} E[S_k^2] + \sum_{k=1}^{r} \rho_k E[W_k] + \sum_{k=1}^{r-1} \rho_k E[W_r] \\
&= \sum_{k=1}^{P} \frac{\lambda_k}{2} E[S_k^2] + \sum_{k=1}^{r-1} \rho_k E[W_k] + \sum_{k=1}^{r} \rho_k E[W_r] \\
&= \sum_{k=1}^{P} \frac{\lambda_k}{2} E[S_k^2] + \sum_{k=1}^{r-1} \rho_k E[W_k] + E[W_r] \left( \sum_{k=1}^{r} \rho_k \right).
\end{aligned} \tag{6.4}
$$

Bringing the $E[W_r]$-terms to the left, we obtain

$$E[W_r](1 - \sum_{k=1}^{r} \rho_k) = \sum_{k=1}^{P} \frac{\lambda_k}{2} E[S_k^2] + \sum_{k=1}^{r-1} \rho_k E[W_k]. \tag{6.5}$$

Defining $\sigma_r = \sum_{k=1}^{r} \rho_k$ (with $\sigma_0 = 0$) and dividing by $(1 - \sigma_r)$ we obtain:

$$E[W_r] = \frac{\sum_{k=1}^{P} \frac{\lambda_k}{2} E[S_k^2] + \sum_{k=1}^{r-1} \rho_k E[W_k]}{1 - \sigma_r}. \tag{6.6}$$

We thus have established a relation that expresses $E[W_r]$ in terms of $E[W_{r-1}]$ through $E[W_1]$. Taking the case $r = 1$ we obtain:

$$E[W_1] = \frac{E[T_P]}{(1 - \sigma_1)} = \frac{E[T_P]}{1 - \rho_1} = \frac{\sum_{k=1}^{P} \lambda_k E[S_k^2]}{2(1 - \rho_1)}. \tag{6.7}$$

Notice the similarity of this expression with the normal M|G|1 waiting time formula. If $P = 1$, the above expression even reduces to the PK result we have seen before. For the case $r = 2$ we obtain

$$E[W_2] = \frac{E[T_P] + \rho_1 E[W_1]}{(1 - \sigma_2)} = \cdots = \frac{E[T_P]}{(1 - \sigma_2)(1 - \sigma_1)}. \tag{6.8}$$

Continuing this process we will recognize the following relation:

$$E[W_r] = \frac{E[T_P]}{(1 - \sigma_r)(1 - \sigma_{r-1})}, \tag{6.9}$$

with $E[T_P] = \sum_{k=1}^{P} \lambda_k E[S_k^2]/2$. This result is known as Cobham's formula [57, 58]. Notice that we can express the average response time for class $r$ as

$$E[R_r] = E[S_r] + \frac{E[T_P]}{(1 - \sigma_r)(1 - \sigma_{r-1})}. \tag{6.10}$$

**Example 6.2. A computer center with two priority classes.**
To illustrate the impact of the use of priorities, let us readdress the computer center that serves two types of customers. Instead of merging the two classes we now give priority to the shorter interactive jobs. In Table 6.2 we show the results. For ease in comparison we also include the non-priority results. We observe that the average waiting time for interactive jobs is only slightly longer than the remaining service time of the job in service (shown in the rightmost column of the table). As can be seen, the performance improvement for interactive jobs is tremendous, at almost no performance penalty for the batch jobs. □

| $\lambda$ | $\rho$ | $E[W]$ | $\lambda_i$ | $\rho_i$ | $\lambda_b$ | $\rho_b$ | $E[W_i]$ | $E[W_b]$ | $E[T_P]$ |
|---|---|---|---|---|---|---|---|---|---|
| 1 | 0.1540 | 0.0222 | 0.4 | 0.004 | 0.6 | 0.15 | 0.0188 | 0.0222 | 0.0188 |
| 2 | 0.3080 | 0.0542 | 0.8 | 0.008 | 1.2 | 0.30 | 0.0378 | 0.0547 | 0.0375 |
| 3 | 0.4620 | 0.1046 | 1.2 | 0.012 | 1.8 | 0.45 | 0.0570 | 0.1059 | 0.0563 |
| 4 | 0.6160 | 0.1953 | 1.6 | 0.016 | 2.4 | 0.60 | 0.0763 | 0.1987 | 0.0750 |
| 5 | 0.7700 | 0.4076 | 2.0 | 0.020 | 3.0 | 0.75 | 0.0958 | 0.4164 | 0.0938 |
| 6 | 0.9240 | 1.4803 | 2.4 | 0.024 | 3.6 | 0.90 | 0.1154 | 1.5183 | 0.1126 |

Table 6.2: The waiting times in a computer center with job priorities

The non-preemptive priority scheduling strategy in fact does nothing more than change the *ordering* of service of arriving jobs. The amount of work to be done by the queueing station remains the same. Note that we assume that the overhead for "implementing" the priorities is negligible. One might therefore expect that some kind of law exists that expresses that whenever one gives one class of jobs a higher priority, that other classes of jobs suffer from this.

Indeed, such *conservation law* does exist. This law expresses that the sum of the average waiting times per class, weighted by their utilisations, remains the same, independent of the priority assignment to the various classes. This law, often denoted as *Kleinrock's conservation law* [160] has the following form:

$$\sum_{r=1}^{P} \rho_r E[W_r] = \rho E[W], \tag{6.11}$$

where $\rho = \sum_{r=1}^{P} \rho_r$, and $E[W]$ is the average waiting time when there are no priority classes. $E[W]$ can thus be derived by the normal M|G|1 result. Substituting $\rho_r = \lambda_r/\mu_r$ (Little's law for the server only) and $E[W_r] = E[N_{q,r}]/\lambda_r$ (Little's law for the queue only) we obtain

$$\rho E[W] = \sum_{r=1}^{P} \rho_r E[W_r] = \sum_{r=1}^{P} \frac{\lambda_r}{\mu_r} \frac{E[N_{q,r}]}{\lambda_r} = \sum_{r=1}^{P} E[N_{q,r}] E[S_r]. \tag{6.12}$$

The right-hand side of this equation expresses a quantity that is often called the *amount of work in the system*, that is, the sum over all priority classes of the number of queued jobs multiplied by their average service requirements.

**Example 6.3. The conservation law for the computer center with job priorities.**
As an example of the conservation law reconsider the computer center with job priorities. From Table 6.1 we read that for $\lambda = 5$, the amount of work in the system equals 0.314. Computing $\rho_i E[W_i] + \rho_b E[W_b]$ from Table 6.2 yields the same result. □

## 6.2 Preemptive priority scheduling

In non-preemptive priority scheduling, a high-priority job might have to wait for a low-priority job already in service when the former arrives. To circumvent this, we might allow for the *preemption* of low-priority jobs by arriving high-priority jobs. In a time-sharing computer system such a scheduling mechanism can be implemented very well; in a communication system such a scheduling mechanism can be applied at the mini-packet level.

A job that has been preempted can be handled in various ways when the processor restarts working on it. Most efficient is to resume the work from the point where the preemption took place. This is called the *preemptive resume* (PRS) strategy. Instead of resuming the work, the job can also be restarted. Two possibilities exists in this case, at least from a modelling point of view. One can either repeat exactly the same job, or one can repeat a job with a service time redrawn from the service time distribution. The former variant is known as the *preemptive repeat identical* (PRI) strategy and is what happens most often in reality. The latter strategy is known as *preemptive repeat different* (PRD). As the PRS-strategy excludes the possibility of work being redone, it seems to be the most efficient. That the PRD-strategy is more efficient than the PRI-strategy can be seen as follows. First observe that the probability of a job being preempted increases when the job increases in length. If such a job is then later repeated identically, it will again be long, and the probability that it is preempted remains relatively high. If on the other hand a different job drawn from the same distribution is repeated, there is a fair probability that it will be shorter than the "original" (long) one. It will thus finish faster and will be preempted with a smaller probability.

We now focus on the PRS-strategy. For jobs of the highest priority class (class 1) the workload imposed by the lower priority classes does not matter at all. Therefore, $E[W_1]$ can simply be derived via the PK-formula for class 1:

$$E[W_1] = \frac{\lambda_1 E[S_1^2]}{2(1 - \rho_1)} = \frac{\lambda_1 E[S_1^2]}{2(1 - \sigma_1)}. \tag{6.13}$$

For jobs of class $r = 2, \cdots, P$, the situation is slightly different. These jobs first of all have to wait for the remaining service time of the job in service if it is of class $r$ or higher priority, i.e., of one of the classes $1, \cdots, r$. The expected value of this quantity equals

$$E[T_r] = \sum_{k=1}^{r} \rho_k \frac{E[S_k^2]}{2E[S_k]}. \tag{6.14}$$

Notice the difference with the non-preemptive case here. There, the arriving job always has to wait for the completion of the job in service, regardless of its class, that is, we always deal with a remaining processing time $E[T_P]$.

Then, similar to the non-preemptive case, the job has to wait for the completion of jobs of classes 1 through $r$ that are already waiting when it arrives. Following the same derivation as in the non-preemptive case, we obtain that the average waiting time for a job of class $r$ before it is put into service (denoted as $W_r^*$) equals

$$E[W_r^*] = \frac{E[T_r]}{(1 - \sigma_r)(1 - \sigma_{r-1})}. \tag{6.15}$$

However, there is one element that we did not yet take into account, namely the fact that once a class $r$ job is in service, it can be preempted by higher-priority jobs, so that extra waiting time is introduced. The amount of work that flows in during the service of the class $r$ job and that needs to be handled first equals, on average, $\sigma_{r-1}E[S_r]$, i.e., the utilisation of high-priority job class multiplied by the service duration of the class $r$ job. However, also when serving this extra work, additional work might flow in: a quantity equal to $\sigma_{r-1}^2 E[S_r]$. Taking this reasoning further reveals that the effective time to complete the service of the single class $r$ job takes

$$E[S_r](1 + \sigma_{r-1} + \sigma_{r-1}^2 + \sigma_{r-1}^3 + \cdots) = \frac{E[S_r]}{1 - \sigma_{r-1}}. \tag{6.16}$$

Since the actual average service time still is $E[S_r]$, extra waiting time due to preemptions, of length

$$\frac{E[S_r]}{1 - \sigma_{r-1}} - E[S_r] = \frac{\sigma_{r-1}E[S_r]}{1 - \sigma_{r-1}} \tag{6.17}$$

is introduced, so that the average waiting time for a class $r$ customer finally becomes

$$E[W_r] = \frac{\sigma_{r-1}}{1 - \sigma_{r-1}}E[S_r] + \frac{E[T_r]}{(1 - \sigma_r)(1 - \sigma_{r-1})}. \tag{6.18}$$

Defining $\sigma_0 = 0$, this equation is also valid for class 1. For the average response time for class $r$ we derive:

$$E[R_r] = \frac{E[S_r]}{1 - \sigma_{r-1}} + \frac{E[T_r]}{(1 - \sigma_r)(1 - \sigma_{r-1})}. \tag{6.19}$$

Notice that in comparison with the non-preemptive case the average service time $E[S_r]$ for class $r$ jobs is stretched by a factor $(1 - \sigma_{r-1})^{-1}$, and $E[T_P]$ has been changed to $E[T_r]$.

### Example 6.4. Preemptive priorities in the computer center.
We can further improve on the performance (mean waiting time) for the interactive jobs by giving them preemptive priority over the batch jobs. In Table 6.3 we show the expected

| | | non-preemptive | | preemptive | |
|---|---|---|---|---|---|
| $\lambda$ | $\rho$ | $E[W_i]$ | $E[W_b]$ | $E[W_i]$ | $E[W_b]$ |
| 1 | 0.1540 | 0.0188 | 0.0222 | 0.00002 | 0.0233 |
| 2 | 0.3080 | 0.0378 | 0.0547 | 0.00004 | 0.0567 |
| 3 | 0.4620 | 0.0570 | 0.1059 | 0.00006 | 0.1090 |
| 4 | 0.6160 | 0.0763 | 0.1987 | 0.00008 | 0.2028 |
| 5 | 0.7700 | 0.0958 | 0.4164 | 0.00010 | 0.4215 |
| 6 | 0.9240 | 0.1154 | 1.5183 | 0.00012 | 1.5244 |

Table 6.3: The waiting times (in seconds) in a computer center with non-preemptive and preemptive priorities

waiting times for the two job classes. For ease of comparison, we have also included the expected waiting times in the non-preemptive priority case. As can be seen, the waiting time for the interactive jobs almost vanishes; only when another interactive job is still in service does an arriving one have to wait (the probability that no such arrivals take place equals $e^{-\rho_i}$ which is very close to 1). The batch jobs do suffer from this improvement only to a very limited extent.                                                                    □

## 6.3  Shortest job next scheduling

Given that the required service times for jobs are known in advance, which is sometimes the case when transmitting packets in a communication system or when submitting "standard jobs" to a computer system, one might want to give priority to small jobs. This leads to what is known as *shortest job next* (SJN) scheduling. In fact, SJN scheduling is a form of priority scheduling in which shorter jobs get priority over longer jobs, i.e., the length of the job is the priority criterion. Therefore, a derivation similar to the one presented in Section 6.1 is possible; however, we now deal with a continuous priority-criterion, thereby assuming that job service times or job transmission times take values in some continuous domain. Again, we assume that the priority mechanism works in a non-preemptive way.

Let us assume that jobs arrive to the queue as a Poisson process with rate $\lambda$ and with service requirement $S$. $S$ is a random variable with probability density $f_S(t)$. We say that a job has "priority $t$" whenever $t \leq S < t + dt$ and $dt \to 0$. All jobs with priority $t$ together form a Poisson process with intensity

$$\lambda_t = \lambda \Pr\{t \leq S < t + dt\} = \lambda f_s(t)dt. \tag{6.20}$$

The jobs with priority $t$ together constitute a job class with utilisation

$$\rho_t = \lambda_t t = \lambda t f_s(t)dt, \tag{6.21}$$

as the (average) service requirement of class $t$ jobs is $t$ units of time.

Analogous to $\sigma_r$ for the priority scheduling mechanism discussed in Section 6.1, we define $\beta_t$ to be the cumulative utilisation of jobs of priority $t$ and higher. Note that a higher priority corresponds to a lower value of $t$. Consequently, we have

$$\beta_t = \int_0^t \lambda s f_S(s)ds. \tag{6.22}$$

As a result, $\beta_\infty = \lambda \int_0^\infty s f_S(s)ds = \lambda E[S] = \rho$, the total utilisation.

In the derivation in Section 6.1 the average remaining processing time $E[T_P]$ of a job in service, given $P$ different priority classes, played an important role. This quantity can now be calculated as the summation over all priority classes of the product of the probability to find a class $t$ customer in service and its average remaining processing time; we denote this quantity as $E[T_\infty]$. First note that a class $t$ customer is in service with probability density value $\rho_t$. Then note that a class $t$ customer has a fixed service time of $t$ seconds, so that the average remaining processing time equals $t/2$. Consequently, we have

$$\begin{aligned}
E[T_\infty] &= \int_0^\infty \rho_t \frac{t}{2}dt = \int_0^\infty \lambda t f_s(t)\frac{t}{2}dt = \int_0^\infty \frac{\lambda}{2}t^2 f_s(t)dt \\
&= \frac{1}{2}\lambda E[S^2] = \frac{\rho E[S^2]}{2E[S]} = \rho E[Y],
\end{aligned} \tag{6.23}$$

where $Y$ is the residual service time. The conditional average waiting time for a class $t$ customer, denoted $E[W_t]$, now simply equals the average remaining processing time, divided by $(1 - \beta_t)$ and $(1 - \beta_{t-h})$ $(h \to 0)$, in a similar way as in (6.9). In this case, however, $\beta_t$ and $\beta_{t-h}$ are the same since $h \to 0$, so that we obtain:

$$E[W_t] = \frac{E[T_\infty]}{(1 - \beta_t)^2} = \frac{\lambda E[S^2]}{2(1 - \beta_t)^2}. \tag{6.24}$$

This result is known as *Phipp's formula* [233]. This conditional waiting time can be used to calculate the *unconditional* waiting time as follows:

$$E[W] = \int_0^\infty E[W_t]f_S(t)dt. \tag{6.25}$$

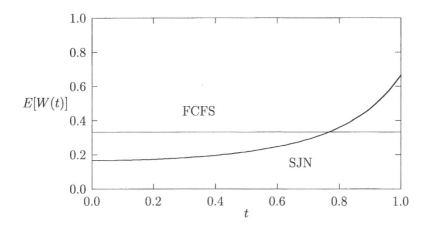

Figure 6.2: Comparing SJN and FCFS scheduling for the M|U|1 queue

As in the discrete case, also in the continuous case there exists a conservation law. It takes a form completely analogously to the form seen before:

$$\int_0^\infty \rho_t E[W_t] = \int_0^\infty \lambda t f_S(t) E[W_t] dt = \frac{\rho E[T_\infty]}{1-\rho} = \rho E[W_{FCFS}].$$  (6.26)

**Example 6.5. FCFS and SJN scheduling in a M|U|1 queue.**
Let us now compare the average waiting time of two M|U|1 queues: one with FCFS scheduling and one with SJN scheduling. Let the service times be uniformly distributed in $[0,1]$ and let us assume that $\lambda = 1.0$. Consequently, $\rho = \lambda E[S] = 1/2$. Furthermore, we have $E[S^2] = 1/3$. Using $f_S(t)$ we can easily calculate $\beta_t$ as follows:

$$\beta_t = \int_0^t \lambda x f_S(x) dx = \int_0^t x dx = \frac{1}{2} t^2, \quad 0 \le t \le 1.$$  (6.27)

For the FCFS scheduling case, we can simply apply the PK-formula which yields

$$E[W_{FCFS}] = \frac{\lambda E[S^2]}{2(1-\rho)} = \frac{1}{3}.$$  (6.28)

For the SJN scheduling we find

$$E[W_t] = \frac{\lambda E[S^2]}{2(1-\beta_t)^2} = \frac{1/3}{2(1-\frac{1}{2}t^2)^2} = \frac{1}{6(1-\frac{1}{2}t^2)^2}, \quad 0 \le t \le 1.$$  (6.29)

In Figure 6.2 we show the two curves for the (conditional) average waiting times. As can be observed, SJN is advantageous for short jobs; the price to be paid is the longer expected waiting time for long jobs.

It is also possible to calculate the unconditional waiting time for SJN scheduling, simply by unconditioning $E[W_t]$, according to (6.25):

$$E[W_{SJN}] = \int_0^1 E[W_t] f_S(t) dt \tag{6.30}$$

$$= \left( \frac{\text{arctanh}(t/\sqrt{2})}{6\sqrt{2}} - \frac{t}{6(t^2 - 2)} \right)_{t=0}^{t=1} = 0.2705 \tag{6.31}$$

As can be seen, the unconditional average waiting time for SJN scheduling is smaller than for FCFS scheduling (note that we have used a formula manipulation package to establish the last equality). □

A disadvantage of SJN scheduling is that the required service times have to be known in advance. As an example of a system where this is the case, consider a communication system in which packets are queued for transmission. The service times (the packet transmission times) are then readily known, in which case SJN scheduling can be fruitfully employed. In general purpose computer systems, however, such knowledge will not be available. Indications of job durations provided by the system users are generally very unreliable and therefore not a solid basis for a scheduling discipline. One way to overcome this problem is to quit (and later restart) jobs that last longer than the durations indicated by the users. This prevents the users being overly optimistic about their job lengths; estimating too tightly will result in necessary reruns of jobs and even higher effective response times.

## 6.4 Round robin scheduling

Although SJN scheduling improves the performance of short jobs, there is still a non-zero probability that long jobs are taken into service. In fact, in any stable system, all jobs finally receive service. An unlucky short job can therefore experience a long delay if the job in service happens to be a rather long one. In such a case the preemption of the long job will help the small job significantly, whereas the long job will not be delayed that much, relative to its own long service time.

A very special preemptive scheduling discipline is *round robin* (RR) scheduling. With RR scheduling all the customers in the queue receive service on a turn-by-turn basis. Per turn, the customers receive a maximum quantum or time-slice of $Q$ time-units of service. If the customer completes during such a short service period, it leaves the system. Otherwise, it rejoins the queue at the end. Clearly, RR is only possible when it makes sense to work on jobs little by little. In time-shared or multi-programmed computer systems this is possible (and normally practiced): after having received an amount of CPU time, the status of a job can be saved. At a later stage the work on that job can be resumed. For communication networks a similar scheme can also be employed: large application-packets from various sources are then split into mini-packets (segmentation). These can then be transmitted on a turn by turn basis, e.g., in a cyclic way. The result is a multiplexing scheme at the mini-packet level.

Below, we outline the derivation of the response time $E[R_k]$ for customers requiring $k$ quanta, as given in [59]. We assume that the actual service time of a customer is an integer number of the quantum $Q$ and that the probability that a customer requires $i$ quanta is geometrically distributed with parameter $\sigma$:

$$g_i = \Pr\{\text{customer length} = iQ\} = (1-\sigma)\sigma^{i-1}, \quad i = 1, 2, \cdots. \tag{6.32}$$

For the first and second moment of the service time distribution, we then find:

$$E[S] = \sum_{i=0}^{\infty} (iQ)g_i = \frac{Q}{1-\sigma}, \tag{6.33}$$

and

$$E[S^2] = \sum_{i=0}^{\infty} (iQ)^2 g_i = \frac{1+\sigma}{(1-\sigma)^2} Q^2. \tag{6.34}$$

The analysis then proceeds to compute

$$E[R_k] = \sum_{i=0}^{\infty} p_i E[R_k|i], \tag{6.35}$$

where $p_i$ is the steady-state probability of having $i$ customers in the queue (at arrival instances), and $E[R_k|i]$ is the expected waiting time for a job requiring $k$ quanta of service when upon its arrival $i$ jobs are already queued. A recursive expression for $E[R_k|i]$ is then derived which, using the summation (6.35) reduces to a recursive expression for $E[R_k]$ which can be solved to a direct expression (as we have seen for priority queues). For a customer requiring only a single quantum of service ($k = 1$), we immediately see

$$E[R_1] = \rho\frac{Q}{2} + E[N_q]Q + Q. \tag{6.36}$$

The first term is the remaining time for the service quantum currently given to the customer in service, if any at all (this explains the factor $\rho$); the second term is the waiting time for all the quanta of service given to the customers queued in front of the arriving customer; the third term is the quantum for the arriving customer itself. Note that $\rho$ is defined as $\lambda E[S] = \lambda Q/(1-\sigma)$ here. Furthermore, $E[N_q]$ is computed using the normal M|G|1 result, however, with the first and second moment of the service time as given above:

$$E[N_q] = \frac{(1+\sigma)\rho^2}{2(1-\rho)}.$$
(6.37)

Knowing $E[R_1]$, we can compute $E[R_k]$ as follows (without derivation):

$$E[R_k] = E[R_1] + \frac{(k-1)Q}{1-\rho} + Q\left(\lambda E[R_1] + \sigma E[N] - \frac{\rho}{1-\rho}\right)\frac{1-\alpha^{k-1}}{1-\alpha}, \quad k = 1, 2, \cdots,$$
(6.38)

where $\alpha = \lambda Q + \sigma$.

## 6.5   Processor sharing scheduling

Let us now focus on the case that the quantum $Q$ in the RR scheduling case of Section 6.4 approaches zero. However, we adjust $\sigma$ so that $E[S] = Q/(1-\sigma)$ is kept constant. In doing so, the number of required quanta per job goes to infinity. Under the assumption that the switching between processes does not take any time, we obtain what is called *processor sharing* (PS) scheduling. In PS scheduling all the jobs in the queue are processed quasi-simultaneously. When there are $n$ jobs in the queue, every job receives a fraction $1/n$ of the total processing capacity.

We assume that a job of general length requires $t$ seconds to complete, so that it requires $k = t/Q$ quanta. Substituting this value of $k$ in (6.38) and keeping $\rho$ (and thus $E[S]$) fixed, we find the conditional expected response time of a job with length $t$:

$$E[R_{PS}(t)] = \frac{t}{1-\rho},$$
(6.39)

that is, the time spent in the queueing system is linearly dependent on the service requirement. A job's actual service time $t$ is stretched by a factor $(1-\rho)^{-1}$ to its *perceived average response time*. Note that this property holds without the need to have *a priori* knowledge about the job length. This also illustrates why the PS and the RR scheduling mechanism are attractive to use in multiprogrammed computer systems. However, note that the limiting case PS cannot be implemented efficiently; if the quanta are too small, too much time will be spent at context switches. Therefore, in practice the RR discipline is implemented.

Although there are no waiting customers in a processor sharing system, we can still compute the difference between the average response and service time. Thus, the (virtual) average waiting time for PS scheduling for customers of length $t$ becomes:

$$E[W_{PS}(t)] = E[R_{PS}(t)] - t = \frac{\rho t}{1 - \rho}. \tag{6.40}$$

The unconditional average waiting time then becomes:

$$E[W_{PS}] = \int_0^\infty E[W_{PS}(t)]f_S(t)dt = \int_0^\infty \frac{\rho t}{1 - \rho}f_S(t)dt = \frac{\rho E[S]}{1 - \rho} = \frac{\lambda E[S]^2}{1 - \rho}. \tag{6.41}$$

We observe that this result is the same as for the M|M|1 queue! This, again, is remarkable. The use of the PS scheduling implies that the second moment of the service time distribution does not play a role any more. One explanation for this is that since all jobs are processed simultaneously in the PS case, a source of variance is removed from the queue (short jobs do not suffer specifically from long jobs). Less variance normally implies better performance, in this case a performance equal to the M|M|1 queue. On the other hand, if we deal with deterministic service times, a source of variance is introduced: the processing of a job now is dependent on how many other jobs there are in the queue, which was not the case with FCFS scheduling. In this case, therefore, the performance becomes worse. To make this more concrete, we can compare the PK-result (for FCFS scheduling) with $E[W_{PS}]$. We see that

$$E[W_{FCFS}] > E[W_{PS}] \Rightarrow E[S^2] > 2E[S]^2 \Rightarrow C_S^2 = \frac{E[S^2] - E[S]^2}{E[S]^2} > 1. \tag{6.42}$$

Concluding, when $C_S^2 > 1$, PS is better than FCFS scheduling, otherwise FCFS is better. When $C_S^2 = 1$, we deal with exponential service times and PS and FCFS result in the same *mean* waiting time.

## 6.6 Scheduling based on elapsed processing time

Although PS scheduling and its practical counterpart RR scheduling exhibit very attractive behaviour, there are circumstances in which one does want to decrease (or increase) the service-intensity for jobs that already have received a large amount of service or that still need a large amount of service. We briefly touch upon three of such disciplines in this section.

The *shortest-elapsed processing time* (SEPT) scheduling discipline uses the elapsed processing time (EPT) of a job as priority criterion; the lower the SEPT, the higher the job priority. Since SEPT scheduling disciplines do not require the actual processing time $a$ *priori* they are more easy to implement than SJN scheduling. Typically, SEPT scheduling is organised using an RR mechanism with multiple queues. Upon arrival, jobs enter the queue with highest priority. After having received a quantum of service, they are either finished, or rejoin a queue of one priority level less, until they are finally finished. Notice that the number of queues is not known in advance. It has been derived that the expected response time of a job of length $t$ can be computed as follows:

$$E[R_{SEPT}(t)] = \frac{\frac{\lambda}{2}E[S^2]}{(1 - \beta_t - \lambda t(1 - F_S(t)))^2} + \frac{t}{1 - \beta_t - \lambda t(1 - F_S(t))}, \tag{6.43}$$

where $\beta_t = \lambda \int_0^t t f_S(t) dt$ is the utilisation due to customers with a length of at most $t$ seconds, as we have encountered before in the derivation of the SJN scheduling.

A slightly different approach is taken in the *shortest-remaining processing time* (SRPT) scheduling discipline. This variant of SJN scheduling takes exactly that customer into service (with preemption, if necessary) which requires the smallest amount of time to be completed. Of course, as with SJN scheduling, the service requirements of the jobs have to be known in advance. It has been derived that

$$E[R_{SRPT}(t)] = \frac{\lambda \int_0^t s^2 dF_S(s) + \lambda t^2(1 - F_S(t))}{2(1 - \beta_t)^2} + \int_0^t \frac{dx}{(1 - \beta_x)}. \tag{6.44}$$

Finally, we mention scheduling based on the so-called *response ratio* of a job, which is defined as

$$\frac{\text{expected response time}}{\text{expected service time}}.$$

By scheduling on the basis of this ratio (which is maintained and updated for all jobs in their process record) where a higher ratio means a higher priority, all jobs will perceive in the end a similar ratio. Notice that such a scheduling method can only be implemented using a round robin mechanism of some form. Brinch Hansen derives the following approximation for the expected waiting times for jobs of length $t$ in such a system:

$$E[W_{HRN}(t)] = \begin{cases} E[\tilde{T}] + \frac{t\rho^2}{2(1-\rho)}, & t \leq 2E[\tilde{T}]/\rho, \\ \frac{E[\tilde{T}]}{(1-\rho)(1-\rho+\frac{2E[\tilde{T}]}{t})}, & t > 2E[\tilde{T}]/\rho, \end{cases} \tag{6.45}$$

where $E[\tilde{T}] = \lambda E[S^2]/2$. Simulations have been conducted to validate the accuracy of this approximation.

## 6.7   Further reading

Many books on performance evaluation address the M|G|1 queue only in combination with
FCFS and priority scheduling. The more advanced scheduling mechanisms are not treated
so often.  Since the M|G|1 models discussed in this chapter find their application most
directly in the context of operating systems and processor scheduling, more information
on these queues can be found in the earlier books on operating systems, most notably in
Coffmann and Denning [59] and Brinch Hansen [29]. Many more recent books on operating
systems do not address scheduling and queueing effects in so much detail.

The non-preemptive priority model was first developed by Cobham [57] and the shortest-
job next model by Phipps [233]. Early work on round robin scheduling and processor sharing was reported by Coffmann, Kleinrock and Muntz [60, 61, 159, 161]. The SEPT and
SRPT scheduling disciplines have been studied by Schrage [256] and Miller and Schrage
[201]. The HRN scheduling mechanism has been studied by Brinch Hansen [29].

## 6.8   Exercises

**6.1. The M|G|1 queue with three priority classes.**
Reconsider Exercise 5.1, but now assign different non-preemptive priorities to the three
customer classes. Compute the expected waiting times per class when the priority ordering
is (from highest to lowest):

1. faculty–student–administrative;

2. faculty–administrative–student;

3. student–faculty–administrative.

**6.2. M|G|1 with 2 priority classes.**
Readdress the computer center example with interactive and batch jobs given in this chapter.

1. Compute the expected waiting times for the two job classes when priority is given to
   the batch jobs and check the validity of the conservation law.

2. Compute the expected waiting times for the two classes when preemptive priority is
   given to the batch jobs.

### 6.3. SJN versus FCFS scheduling.

Compare FCFS and SJN scheduling for an M|M|1 queue. Take $\lambda = 1$ and $E[S] = 0.8$ and find expressions for $\beta_t$, $E[W_t]$ and $E[W_{FCFS}]$.

### 6.4. FCFS versus PS scheduling.

Compare FCFS and PS scheduling for an M|G|1 queue with $E[S] = 0.8$ and $\mathrm{var}[S] \in [0, 2]$. Draw graphs of $E[W]$ against $\mathrm{var}[S]$ for both queueing models thereby varying $\lambda = 0.25, 0.5$ and 0.75.

### 6.5. A voice/data multiplexer.

Consider a multiplexer that has to merge one data stream and one real-time voice stream. The server speed is assumed to be 3642 packets per second, which totals to 1.544 Mbps with packets of 53 bytes; note that the size of a packet conforms to the size of an ATM cell [225, 251].

   The data load forms a Poisson process and accounts for 40% of the multiplexer capacity, i.e., $\lambda_d = 1456$ packet/sec (p/s). The voice load is increased from 1 to 13 calls where every call brings an extra $\lambda_v = 150$ p/s, also as a Poisson process. Packets have a deterministic length.

1. Compute the first and second moment of the packet transmission time.

2. Express the overall arrival rate and utilisation as a function of the number of active calls $k$.

3. Taking no priorities into account, compute the average response time $E[R(k)]$ for both voice and data packets, given $k$ active voice calls.

4. Giving priority to the delay sensitive voice packets, compute the average response time for voice packets $E[R_v(k)]$ and the average response time for data packets $E[R_d(k)]$, given $k$ voice calls.

5. Would a preemption mechanism increase the performance of the data stream *dramatically?*

# Chapter 7

# G|M|1-FCFS and G|G|1-FCFS queueing models

IN Chapters 5 and 6 we have addressed queues with generally distributed service time distributions, but still with Poisson arrivals. In this chapter we focus on queues with more general interarrival time distributions. In Section 7.1 we address the G|M|1 queue, the important "counterpart" of the M|G|1 queue. Then, in Section 7.2, we present an exact result for the G|G|1 queue. Since this result is more of theoretical than of any practical interest, we conclude in Section 7.3 with a well-known approximate result for the G|G|1 queue.

It should be noted that most of the exact results presented in this chapter are less easy to apply in practical performance evaluation. For a particular subclass of G|G|1 queueing models, namely those where the interarrival and service times are of phase-type, easy-applicable computational techniques have been developed, known as matrix-geometric techniques. These techniques will be studied in Chapter 8.

## 7.1 The G|M|1 queue

For the analysis of the G|M|1 queue, one encounters similar problems as for the analysis of the M|G|1 queue. As before, the state of the G|M|1 queue consist of two parts, a continuous and a discrete part, since the state is given by the number of customers in the system and the time since the last arrival. Unfortunately, the intuitively appealing method of moments followed for the M|G|1 queue, based on average values, the PASTA property and knowledge about the residual service time cannot be used in this case because the PASTA property does not hold. Instead, we will simply state a number of important results and discuss their meaning in detail.

We first have to define some notation. The interarrival time distribution is denoted $F_A(t)$, and has as first moment $E[A] = 1/\lambda$ and as second moment $E[A^2]$. The service time distribution $F_S(t) = 1 - e^{-\mu t}$, $t \geq 0$, $E[S] = 1/\mu$, $E[S^2] = 2/\mu^2$ and $C_S^2 = 1$.

As we will see below, we need knowledge about the full interarrival time distribution and density; the latter is denoted $f_A(t)$ and has Laplace transform $f_A^*(s)$:

$$f_A^*(s) = \int_0^\infty e^{-st} f_A(t) dt. \tag{7.1}$$

The Laplace transforms of many interarrival time densities are easy to derive; some of them are listed in Appendix B.

For the G|M|1 queue, an embedded Markov chain approach can be employed, similar to the one discussed in Section 5.3 for the M|G|1 queue. A general two-dimensional Markov chain can then be defined: $((N(t), V(t)), t \geq 0)$, where $N(t) \in I\!N$ denotes the number of customers in the queueing station and $V(t) \in I\!R$ denotes the time since the last arrival; we have to keep track of this time since the interarrival times are not memoryless anymore. Suitable embedding moments are now arrival instances, since then $V(t) = 0$. Taking this further will reveal that the probability that an arriving job finds $i$ jobs in the queueing system is of the form

$$r_i = (1 - \sigma)\sigma^i, \quad i = 0, 1, \cdots, \tag{7.2}$$

with $0 < \sigma < 1$. Surprisingly, this is a geometric distribution, just as in the M|M|1 case. Notice, however, that the base of this geometric distribution is not $\rho$ but $\sigma$, which is defined as the probability that the system is perceived not empty by an arriving customer. This agrees with the fact that $r_0 = 1 - \sigma$, and thus we also have that $\sigma = 1 - r_0 = \sum_{i>0} r_i$. Notice that in general $\sigma \neq \rho$; only in case of Poisson arrivals are these two quantities the same, thus reflecting the PASTA property. As a result of this, for general arrival processes, the probability that an arriving customer finds the queue non-empty differs from $\rho$. The long-term probability that the queue is not empty, however, remains equal to $\rho$.

Knowing the probabilities $r_i$, we can compute the expected waiting time for a customer as

$$E[W] = \sum_{i=0}^\infty r_i i E[S], \tag{7.3}$$

by noting that for a customer arriving at a station with $i$ customers in it, which happens with probability $r_i$, $i$ services of average length $E[S]$ have to be performed before the arriving customer is being served. Notice that we use the memoryless property of the service time distribution here. Continuing our computation, we find:

$$
\begin{aligned}
E[W] &= \sum_{i=0}^{\infty} r_i i E[S] = \sum_{i=0}^{\infty} (1-\sigma)\sigma^i i E[S] = \sigma E[S](1-\sigma)\sum_{i=0}^{\infty} i\sigma^{i-1} \\
&= \sigma E[S](1-\sigma) \sum_{i=0}^{\infty} \frac{d}{d\sigma}(\sigma^i) = \sigma E[S](1-\sigma)\frac{d}{d\sigma}\left(\sum_{i=0}^{\infty}\sigma_i\right) \\
&= \sigma E[S](1-\sigma)\frac{d}{d\sigma}\left(\frac{1}{1-\sigma}\right) = \frac{\sigma E[S]}{1-\sigma}. 
\end{aligned}
\tag{7.4}
$$

This is again a remarkable result since it has exactly the same form as the M|M|1 result for the expected waiting time, however, with $\rho$ replaced by $\sigma$. Hence, we can view the G|M|1 queue as an M|M|1 queue in which $\rho$ is replaced by $\sigma$ through some transformation. Without proof we now state that $\sigma$ can be derived from the following nonlinear equation involving the Laplace transform of the interarrival time density:

$$
\sigma = f_A^*(\mu - \mu\sigma) = f_A^*(\mu(1-\sigma)).
\tag{7.5}
$$

This fixed-point equation can be understood as the transformation of $\rho$ in $\sigma$. Unfortunately, (7.5) can most often not be solved explicitly. We therefore usually have to employ the following (straightforward) fixed-point iteration. Pick a first guess for $\sigma$, denoted $\sigma^{(1)}$. It can be proven that $0 < \sigma < 1$ as long as $\rho = \lambda E[S] < 1$, so a first guess could be $\sigma^{(1)} = \rho$. Then, we compute $\sigma^{(2)} = f_A^*(\mu(1-\sigma^{(1)}))$, and so on, until we find a $\sigma^{(k)}$ such that (7.5) is sufficiently well satisfied. Notice that $\sigma = 1$ is always a solution of (7.5), however, this solution is not valid as it would not result in a proper density $r_i$.

**Example 7.1. Poisson arrivals.**
In case we have Poisson arrivals, $f_A(t) = \lambda e^{-\lambda t}$, and the above results should reduce to results we already know for the M|M|1 queue. We find as Laplace transform

$$
f_A^*(s) = \int_0^{\infty} e^{-st}\lambda e^{-\lambda t}dt = \left(-\frac{\lambda}{s+\lambda}e^{-(s+\lambda)t}\right)\Big|_{t=0}^{t=\infty} = \frac{\lambda}{s+\lambda},
\tag{7.6}
$$

so that (7.5) becomes:

$$
\sigma = \frac{\lambda}{\mu(1-\sigma)+\lambda} \Rightarrow (\sigma-1)(\mu\sigma-\lambda) = 0.
\tag{7.7}
$$

The solution $\sigma = 1$ is not valid; it would not result in a proper density for $r_i$. Therefore, the result is $\sigma = \lambda/\mu$, which equals our expectation since for the M|M|1 queue, the queue length distribution at arrival instances equals the steady-state queue length distribution.

□

## Example 7.2. The D|M|1 queue.

For the D|M|1 queue, we have $F_A(t) = 1(t \geq 1/\lambda)$, that is, arrivals take place exactly every $1/\lambda$ time units. The density $f_A(t)$ is a Dirac impulse at $t = 1/\lambda$ (see Appendix B). As Laplace transform we find $f_A^*(s) = e^{-s/\lambda}$, so that we have to obtain $\sigma$ from

$$\sigma = e^{-\mu(1-\sigma)/\lambda} = e^{-\frac{1-\sigma}{\rho}}. \tag{7.8}$$

This nonlinear equation cannot be solved explicitly, so that we have to resort to the fixed-point iteration scheme.

As a numerical example, consider the case where $E[S] = 1.0$ and where $\lambda$ increases from 0.05 to 0.95, i.e., $\rho$ increases from 5% to 95%. In Table 7.1 we compare the results for the D|M|1 queue with those of the M|M|1 queue. As performance measure of interest, we have chosen the average waiting time. As can be observed, the deterministic arrivals have a positive effect on the performance since $E[W]$ is smaller in the deterministic arrivals case.

Also observe that $\sigma$ approaches $\rho$ as $\rho$ increases. As $\sigma$ has taken over the role of $\rho$ in the expression for the mean waiting time, we see that for small utilisations (when $\sigma$ is much smaller than $\rho$) the waiting time is much lower than in the corresponding M|M|1 case. For larger utilisations the effect of having deterministic arrivals instead of Poisson arrivals becomes *relatively* less important.

To conclude this example, we can state that with respect to man waiting times the D|M|1 queue can be seen as an M|M|1 queue with reduced utilisation $\sigma$ where $\sigma$ follows from (7.8).      □

Since we have knowledge about the number of customers seen by an arriving customer, we can express the waiting time distribution for such an arriving customer as well. If $n$ customers are present upon its arrival, there are $n$ services to be performed, before the arriving customer is taken into service. Since all the services are of exponentially distributed length, the arriving customer perceives an Erlang-$n$ waiting time distribution (denoted $F_{E_n}(t)$) with probability $r_n$. This is similar to what we have already seen in Chapter 4, where we computed the response time distribution for the M|M|1 queue. Summing over all possible numbers of customers present at arrivals, and weighting with the appropriate occurrence probabilities, we find

$$\Pr\{W \leq t\} = \sum_{n=0}^{\infty} r_n F_{E_n}(t) = \sum_{n=0}^{\infty} (1-\sigma)\sigma^n F_{E_n}(t)$$

$$= (1-\sigma) \sum_{n=0}^{\infty} \sigma^n \left(1 - e^{-\mu t} \sum_{i=0}^{n-1} \frac{(\mu t)^i}{i!}\right)$$

| $\rho$ | $\sigma$ | D|M|1 | M|M|1 |
|---|---|---|---|
| 0.05 | $2.06 \times 10^{-9}$ | $2.06 \times 10^{-9}$ | $5.26 \times 10^{-2}$ |
| 0.15 | $1.28 \times 10^{-3}$ | $1.29 \times 10^{-3}$ | $1.77 \times 10^{-1}$ |
| 0.25 | $1.98 \times 10^{-2}$ | $2.02 \times 10^{-2}$ | $3.33 \times 10^{-1}$ |
| 0.35 | $7.02 \times 10^{-2}$ | $7.55 \times 10^{-2}$ | $5.39 \times 10^{-1}$ |
| 0.45 | $1.52 \times 10^{-1}$ | $1.79 \times 10^{-1}$ | $8.18 \times 10^{-1}$ |
| 0.55 | $2.61 \times 10^{-1}$ | $3.83 \times 10^{-1}$ | 1.22 |
| 0.65 | $3.93 \times 10^{-1}$ | $6.48 \times 10^{-1}$ | 1.86 |
| 0.75 | $5.46 \times 10^{-1}$ | 1.20 | 3.00 |
| 0.85 | $7.16 \times 10^{-1}$ | 2.52 | 5.67 |
| 0.95 | $9.01 \times 10^{-1}$ | 9.17 | $1.90 \times 10^{1}$ |

Table 7.1: Comparing the expected waiting time $E[W]$ of a D|M|1 queue with an M|M|1 queue

$$
\begin{aligned}
&= (1-\sigma) \sum_{n=0}^{\infty} \sigma^n - (1-\sigma) \sum_{n=0}^{\infty} \sigma^n e^{-\mu t} \sum_{i=0}^{n-1} \frac{(\mu t)^i}{i!} \\
&= 1 - (1-\sigma) e^{-\mu t} \sum_{i=0}^{\infty} \sum_{n=i+1}^{\infty} \sigma^n \frac{(\mu t)^i}{i!} \\
&= 1 - (1-\sigma) e^{-\mu t} \sum_{i=0}^{\infty} \frac{(\mu t)^i}{i!} \sum_{n=i+1}^{\infty} \sigma^n \\
&= 1 - (1-\sigma) e^{-\mu t} \sum_{i=0}^{\infty} \frac{(\mu t)^i}{i!} \frac{\sigma^{i+1}}{1-\sigma} \\
&= 1 - \sigma e^{-\mu t} \sum_{i=0}^{\infty} \frac{(\mu \sigma t)^i}{i!} \\
&= 1 - \sigma e^{-\mu(1-\sigma)t}, \quad t \geq 0.
\end{aligned}
\tag{7.9}
$$

In a similar way, we find for the response time distribution:

$$
\Pr\{R \leq t\} = 1 - e^{-\mu(1-\sigma)t}, \quad t \geq 0.
\tag{7.10}
$$

Both these results are again similar to those obtained previously for the M|M|1 queue (see Section 4.4); the only difference is that $\sigma$ takes over the role of $\rho$.

From the waiting time density $f_W(t) = \sigma \mu (1 - \sigma) e^{-\mu(1-\sigma)t}$, we can also derive the average waiting time as we have seen before.

**Example 7.3. The Hypo-2|M|1 queue.**
In the Hypo-2|M|1 queue services take an exponentially distributed time (here, we take

$E[S] = 1/\mu = 1$). The interarrival times can be considered to consist of two exponential phases; only after an exponentially distributed time with rate $\lambda_1$ and an exponentially distributed time with rate $\lambda_2$ an arrival takes place (here we assume that $\lambda_1 = 2$ and $\lambda_2 = 1$). Thus, the mean interarrival time $E[A] = 1/2 + 1/1 = 1.5$ and the utilisation $\rho = 2/3$. From Appendix A we know that

$$f_A(t) = \frac{\lambda_1 \lambda_2}{\lambda_1 - \lambda_2}(e^{-\lambda_2 t} - e^{-\lambda_1 t}), \quad t \geq 0. \tag{7.11}$$

For the Laplace transform we find (with $\lambda_1 = 2$ and $\lambda_2 = 1$):

$$f_A^*(s) = \frac{\lambda_1}{(\lambda_1 + s)}\frac{\lambda_2}{(\lambda_2 + s)} = \frac{2}{(s+2)(s+1)}. \tag{7.12}$$

The fixed-point equation becomes:

$$\frac{2}{(1 - \sigma + 2)(1 - \sigma + 1)} = \sigma \quad \Rightarrow \quad \sigma^3 - 5\sigma^2 + 6\sigma - 2 = 0. \tag{7.13}$$

This third-order polynomial can be solved easily by noting that $\sigma = 1$ must be a solution to it (check this!) so that we can divide it by $(\sigma - 1)$ yielding

$$\sigma^2 - 4\sigma + 2 = 0. \tag{7.14}$$

This quadratic equation has solutions $\sigma = 2 \pm \sqrt{2}$. Since we are looking for a solution in the range $(0, 1)$, the only valid solution we find is $\sigma = 2 - \sqrt{2} \approx 0.586$. Note that $\sigma < \rho \approx 0.667$. Thus, we find $E[W] = (2 - \sqrt{2})/(\sqrt{2} - 1) = 1.42$. The waiting time distribution has the form

$$F_W(t) = 1 - (2 - \sqrt{2})e^{-(\sqrt{2}-1)t}, \quad t \geq 0, \tag{7.15}$$

and is depicted in Figure 7.1. Notice the "jump" at $t = 0$; it corresponds to the fact that there is a non-zero probability of not having to wait at all.                                    □

**Example 7.4. Waiting time distribution in the $E_k|M|1$ queue.**
We will now study the influence of the variance of the arrival process for a single server queue with memoryless services. We assume $E[S] = 1/\mu = 1$ and $\rho = \lambda$. For an Erlang-$k$ interarrival time distribution with rate parameter $k\lambda$, the mean interarrival time equals $E[A] = k/k\lambda = 1/\lambda$ and the Laplace transform equals

$$f_A^*(s) = \left(\frac{k\lambda}{s + k\lambda}\right)^k. \tag{7.16}$$

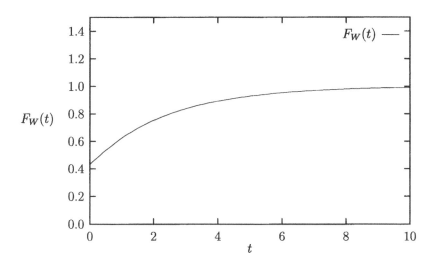

Figure 7.1: The waiting time distribution in a Hypo-2|M|1 queue ($\rho = 0.667$)

The fixed-point iteration to solve becomes

$$\sigma = \left( \frac{k\rho}{1 - \sigma + k\rho} \right)^k. \tag{7.17}$$

In Figure 7.2 we show the value of $\sigma$ as a function of $\rho$ for various values of $k$. As can be observed, we always have $\sigma \leq \rho$. Moreover, the larger $k$, the more $\sigma$ deviates from $\rho$. Hence, for a given utilisation $\rho$ in the $E_k$|M|1 queue, a larger $k$ implies a smaller utilisation $\sigma$ in the M|M|1 queue. Clearly, increasing $k$ removes variance from the model and thus improves the performance. □

## 7.2 The G|G|1 queue

For the G|G|1 queue, explicit results for mean performance measures are even more difficult to obtain. The main difficulty lies in the complex state space of the stochastic process underlying this queueing system which, apart from the discrete number of customers present, also consists of continuous components for both the remaining service time and the remaining interarrival time. Even an embedding approach as has been followed for the M|G|1 and the G|M|1 queue is therefore not possible anymore. Still though, an important general result known as Lindley's integral equation can be obtained quite easily; its practical applicability is, however, limited.

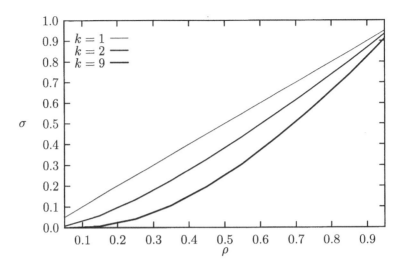

Figure 7.2: Values of $\sigma$ as a function of $\rho$ for $k = 1, 2, 9$ (top to bottom) in the $E_k|M|1$ queue

As before, we assume that we deal with independent and identically distributed inter-arrival and service times, with distributions (and densities) $F_A(t)$ $(f_A(t))$ and $F_S(t)$ $(f_S(t))$, respectively. Moments and (squared) coefficients of variation are denoted as usual.

Let us now try to express the waiting time perceived by the $(n + 1)$-th customer in terms of the waiting time of the $n$-th customer. For that purpose, let $\tau_n$ denote the arrival time for the $n$-th customer, $S_n$ the service time and $W_n$ the waiting time perceived by the $n$-th customer. Furthermore, we can define $A_n = \tau_n - \tau_{n-1}$, so that $A_n$ is the interarrival time between the $n$-th and the $(n - 1)$-th arrival. Notice that the random variables $S_n$ and $A_n$ are in fact independent of $n$; they are only governed by the interarrival and service time distributions. We have to distinguish two cases now (see also Figure 7.3):

(a) the $(n + 1)$-th customer finds a busy system: the sum of the service and waiting time of the $n$-th customer is more than the time between the arrival of the $n$-th and $(n + 1)$-th customer, and we have

$$W_{n+1} = W_n + S_n - A_{n+1}, \quad \text{if} \quad W_n + S_n \geq A_{n+1};$$

(b) the $(n + 1)$-th customer finds an empty system: the sum of the service and waiting time of the $n$-th customer is less than the time between the arrival of the $n$-th and

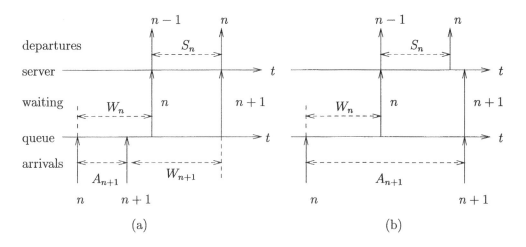

Figure 7.3: Two cases for the evolution of a G|G|1 system: (a) system non-empty upon an arrival, and (b) system empty upon an arrival

$(n+1)$-th customer, and we have

$$W_{n+1} = 0, \quad \text{if } W_n + S_n \leq A_{n+1}.$$

The equations for these two cases describe the evolution of the G|G|1 system. By introducing a new random variable $U_n = S_n - A_{n+1}$, we can rewrite them as

$$W_{n+1} = \max\{W_n + U_n, 0\} = \begin{cases} W_n + U_n, & W_n + U_n \geq 0, \\ 0, & W_n + U_n \leq 0. \end{cases} \tag{7.18}$$

The random variable $U_n$ measures the difference in interarrival and service time of the $n$-th and $(n+1)$-th customer. For stability of the G|G|1 queue, it should have an expectation smaller than 0, meaning that, on average, the interarrival time is larger than the service time. If we know the distribution of $U_n$, we can calculate the distribution of $W_n$. To start, we have to compute

$$\Pr\{U_n \leq u\} = \Pr\{S_n - A_{n+1} \leq u\}. \tag{7.19}$$

Since $u$ can be both negative and positive, we have to distinguish between these two cases. In Figure 7.4 we show the two possible cases. On the $x$- and $y$-axis we have drawn $S$ and $A$ (since our arguments are valid for all $n$, we can drop the subscript $n$). If $u \geq 0$, the area that signifies the events "$S - A \leq u$" is the shaded area in Figure 7.4(a) over which we have to integrate. If $u \leq 0$ we have to integrate over the shaded area in Figure 7.4(b). Since

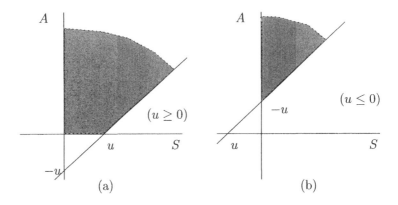

Figure 7.4: The two cases to be distinguished when computing $F_U(u)$

$A$ and $S$ are independent random variables, we have $f_{A,S}(a,s) = f_A(a)f_S(s)$. In summary, we have

$$\Pr\{U \le u\} = \begin{cases} \int_0^u \int_0^\infty f_S(s)f_A(a)da\,ds + \int_u^\infty \int_{s-u}^\infty f_S(s)f_A(a)da\,ds, & u \ge 0, \\ \int_0^\infty \int_{s+u}^\infty f_S(s)f_A(a)da\,ds, & u \le 0. \end{cases} \tag{7.20}$$

Note that in case $u \ge 0$, the first integral reduces to $F_S(u)$.

Now that we have obtained the distribution of $U$, we can derive the waiting time distribution $F_{W_n}(t)$. Clearly, we have $F_{W_n}(t) = 0$, for $t \le 0$. For $t > 0$, we have from (7.18):

$$\begin{aligned} F_{W_{n+1}}(t) &= \Pr\{W_{n+1} \le t\} = \Pr\{W_n + U_n \le t\} \\ &= \int_0^\infty \Pr\{U_n \le t - w | W_n = w\}dF_{W_n}(w), \end{aligned} \tag{7.21}$$

where we have conditioned on $W_n$ taking a specific value $w$, which happens to be the case with probability density $dF_{W_n}(w)$. We omit the subscripts $n$; this can be done under the assumption that the system is stable, i.e., $\rho < 1$, in which case, in steady state, all customers experience the same waiting time distribution. Because the random variables $U = S - A$ and $W$ are independent, we can rewrite the above conditional probability as follows:

$$F_W(t) = \int_0^\infty \Pr\{U \le t - w\}dF_W(w) = \int_0^\infty F_U(t - w)dF_W(w). \tag{7.22}$$

Combining the above two results, we obtain *Lindley's integral equation*:

$$F_W(t) = \begin{cases} \int_0^\infty F_U(t-w)dF_W(w), & t \ge 0, \\ 0, & t < 0. \end{cases} \tag{7.23}$$

Lindley's integral equation is a fundamental result for the G|G|1 queue. As this equation is implicit in $F_W(t)$, we still do not have an explicit expression for $F_W(t)$ or for $E[W]$. Unfortunately, such expressions are not readily available. They require the solution of (7.23) which is a complicated task. Various approaches have been proposed for that purpose, however, they all require fairly advanced mathematics and go beyond the scope of this book.

## 7.3   Approximate results for the G|G|1 queue

To do practical performance evaluations for G|G|1 queues various approximate results have been derived. It would go beyond the scope of this chapter to give a complete overview of all these approximations. Instead we restrict ourselves to a prominent approximation proposed by Krämer and Langenbach-Belz [164]. Adhering to the same notation as before, we have:

$$E[W] \approx (C_A^2 + C_S^2)\frac{\lambda(E[S])^2}{2(1-\rho)}g(\rho, C_A^2, C_S^2), \tag{7.24}$$

where

$$g(\rho, C_A^2, C_S^2) = \begin{cases} \exp\left(-\frac{2(1-\rho)(1-C_A^2)^2}{3\rho(C_A^2+C_S^2)}\right), & C_A^2 < 1, \\ 1, & C_A^2 \geq 1. \end{cases} \tag{7.25}$$

Notice that this result reduces to the exact result for the M|M|1 and the M|G|1 queue.

**Example 7.5. The Hypo-2|M|1 queue revisited.**
We now use the KLB-approximation to compute $E[W]$ for the Hypo-2|M|1 queue we addressed before. Since we deal with exponential services, we have $C_S^2 = 1$. We can compute the variance of the hypo-exponential distribution as the sum of the variances of its exponential phases. We find $\sigma_A^2 = \frac{5}{4}$ and we thus have $C_A^2 = \frac{5}{4}/(\frac{3}{2})^2 = \frac{5}{9} = 0.556$. We then compute $g(0.667, 0.556, 1.000) = 0.959$. Using this in (7.24) we find $E[W] \approx 1.492$ which is only 5% off the exact value we have derived before. □

## 7.4   Further reading

In contrast to M|G|1 queues, the theory of queues of G|M|1 and G|G|1 type is not often addressed in manuscripts on performance evaluation of computer and communication systems. A notable exception is Kleinrock [160, Chapters 6 and 8], on which most of this chapter is based; note that Kleinrock treats the G|G|1 queue as "advanced material". A very thorough overview of single server queues of a wide variety, including the ones addressed in this chapter, can be found in the book by Cohen [62]. Lindley published his integral equation already in 1952 [185]! Kendall published the embedded Markov chain approach for the G|M|1 queue in 1951 [155]. Many approximation schemes do exist for G|M|1 and M|G|1 queues; we only addressed the KLB-approximation [164].

## 7.5  Exercises

**7.1. The $H_2|M|1$ queue.**
For hyperexponential interarrival times, the Laplace transform of the interarrival density is given as:

$$f_A^*(s) = \frac{p\lambda_1}{\lambda_1 + s} + \frac{(1-p)\lambda_2}{\lambda_2 + s}. \tag{7.26}$$

Take $E[S] = 1$, and evaluate $\sigma$ for increasing values of $1/E[A] = \lambda = p\lambda_1 + (1-p)\lambda_2$, and for various values of $p$ and $\lambda_i$. How does $\sigma$ relate to $\rho$ when $C_{H_2}^2 > 1$. Compare the exact value for $E[W]$ with the Krämer and Langenbach-Belz approximation.

**7.2. The IPP|M|1 queue.**
Derive the fixed-point equation for $\sigma$ in case of IPP-arrivals (see Chapter 4).

**7.3. Comparison with the D|M|1 queue.**
Derive the average waiting time for the D|M|1 queue with the Krämer and Langenbach-Belz approximation and compare it with the exact results in case $E[S] = 1$, for $\lambda = 0.05, 0.10, \cdots, 0.95$.

**7.4. $F_U(u)$ for the M|M|1 queue (adapted from [160, Example 8.2]).**
Show that for the M|M|1 queue (with usual parameters $\lambda$ and $\mu$) $F_U(u)$ can be computed as:

$$F_U(u) = \begin{cases} 1 - \frac{\lambda}{\lambda+\mu}e^{-\mu u}, & u \geq 0, \\ \frac{\mu}{\mu+\lambda}e^{\lambda u}, & u \leq 0. \end{cases}$$

# Chapter 8

# PH|PH|1 queueing models

IN this chapter we address the class of PH|PH|1 queues. These queues can be seen as special cases of G|G|1 queues; however, due to the specific distributions involved, efficient numerical algorithms known as matrix-geometric methods can be applied for their solution.

The aim of this chapter is not to present all the known material on PH|PH|1 queues and their matrix-geometric solution. Instead, our aim is to show the usefulness of matrix-geometric methods, to provide insight into their operation, and to show that PH|PH|1 models, together with their efficient solution techniques, are a good alternative to G|G|1 queueing models.

This chapter is further organised as follows. In Section 8.1 we readdress the analysis of the M|M|1 queue in a "matrix-geometric way". This is used as an introduction to the matrix-geometric analysis of the PH|PH|1 queue in Section 8.2. Numerical algorithms that play an important role in the matrix-geometric technique are discussed in Section 8.3. We then discuss a few special cases in Section 8.4. In Section 8.5 we discuss the caudal curve which plays an interesting role when studying the "tail behaviour" of queues. We finally comment on additional queueing models that still allow for a matrix-geometric solution in Section 8.6.

## 8.1  The M|M|1 queue

Consider an M|M|1 queueing model with arrival rate $\lambda$ and service rate $\mu$. The Markov chain underlying this queueing model is a simple birth-death process where the state variable denotes the total number of packets in the queueing station. Since the state variable is a scalar, such a process is sometimes called a *scalar state process*. The generator matrix

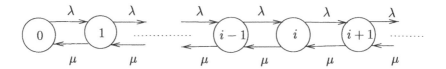

Figure 8.1: The state-transition diagram for the M|M|1 queue

$\mathbf{Q}$ of the CTMC underlying the M|M|1 queue has the following form:

$$
\mathbf{Q} = \left(
\begin{array}{c|ccccc}
-\lambda & \lambda & 0 & \cdots & \cdots & \cdots \\
\mu & -(\lambda+\mu) & \lambda & 0 & \cdots & \cdots \\
0 & \mu & -(\lambda+\mu) & \lambda & 0 & \cdots \\
\vdots & 0 & \mu & -(\lambda+\mu) & \lambda & \cdots \\
\vdots & \vdots & \vdots & \vdots & \vdots & \ddots
\end{array}
\right). \tag{8.1}
$$

Observe that, apart from the first column, all the columns are basically the same, except that "they are shifted down one row". We call the first column a *boundary column* and the other ones *repeating columns*. Notice that the repeating structure can also be observed nicely in the state-transition diagram of the CTMC underlying the M|M|1 queue, as given in Figure 8.1. The balance equations for states $i = 1, 2, \cdots$, have the following form:

$$
p_i(\lambda + \mu) = p_{i-1}\lambda + p_{i+1}\mu. \tag{8.2}
$$

Now, let us assume that the steady-state probability for state $i$ only depends on the probability $p_{i-1}$ and the rates between states $i$ and $i - 1$. As those rates are constants, we *guess* that there is a constant $\rho$, of yet unknown value, which defines that $p_i = \rho p_{i-1}$, for $i = 1, 2, \cdots$, or equivalently, $p_i = \rho^i p_0$, for $i = 1, 2, \cdots$. Substituting this in the global balance equation for the repeating portion of the CTMC ($i = 1, 2, \cdots$):

$$
p_0\rho^i(\lambda + \mu) = p_0\rho^{i-1}\lambda + p_0\rho^{i+1}\mu. \tag{8.3}
$$

Since all steady-state probabilities depend via the multiplicative factor $\rho$ on $p_0$, we have to assume that $\rho > 0$, otherwise all $p_i$ would be equal to 0. In doing so, we may divide the above equation by $\rho^{i-1}$, so that we obtain

$$
p_0\rho(\lambda + \mu) = p_0\lambda + p_0\rho^2\mu \;\Rightarrow\; p_0(\mu\rho^2 - (\lambda+\mu)\rho + \lambda) = 0. \tag{8.4}
$$

The latter is true when either $p_0 = 0$ which does not make sense because in that case all the $p_i = 0$, or when the quadratic equation in $\rho$ evaluates to 0. This is true for two values of $\rho$: $\rho = \lambda/\mu$ or $\rho = 1$. The latter solution cannot be accepted due to the fact that a proper normalisation of all the probabilities requires $\rho < 1$, otherwise $\sum_i p_i \neq 1$. We thus conclude that $\rho = \lambda/\mu$. Using this result, we can solve the "boundary" of the global balance equations as follows. We have

$$p_0 \lambda = p_1 \mu \implies p_0 \lambda = \rho \mu p_0 = p_0 \lambda. \tag{8.5}$$

This equality is always true and does not yield us the value of $p_0$. We therefore use the normalisation equation:

$$\sum_{i=0}^{\infty} p_i = 1 \Rightarrow p_0 \sum_{i=0}^{\infty} \rho^i = \frac{p_0}{1-\rho} = 1, \tag{8.6}$$

provided that $\rho < 1$. We therefore conclude that $p_0 = 1 - \rho$, and, consequently, $p_i = (1-\rho)\rho^i$, $i \in I\!N$. This result is of course well-known; however, the method by which we derived it here differs from the methods we used earlier.

We need the fact that $\rho < 1$ in order for the geometric sum to be finite. The requirement $\rho < 1$ also exactly expresses a stability requirement for the queue: on average, the rate of incoming jobs must be smaller than the rate at which jobs can be served. In the state-transition diagram, this property can be interpreted as follows: the rate to the next higher state must be smaller than the rate to the next lower state.

Once the steady-state probabilities $p_i$ $(i = 0, 1, \cdots)$ are known, we can derive various performance metrics, such as:

- the average number of jobs in the queue: $E[N] = \sum_{i=0}^{\infty} i p_i = \frac{\rho}{1-\rho}$;

- the average response time (via Little's law): $E[R] = \frac{E[N]}{\lambda} = \frac{E[S]}{1-\rho}$, with the average service time $E[S] = 1/\mu$;

- the probability of at least $k$ jobs in the queue: $B(k) = \sum_{i=k}^{\infty} p_i = \rho^k$.

In summary, to evaluate the M|M|1 queue, we have gone through 4 steps:

1. Guessing a solution based on the repetitive CTMC structure;

2. Substituting this solution in the repeating part of the global balance equations to derive the multiplicative constant $\rho$;

3. Computing the solution of the "boundary probabilities" by solving the corresponding part of the global balance equations, thereby using the normalisation equation and the result from Step 2;

4. Computing performance measures of interest.

In the next section we will use this 4-step approach to evaluate more complex queueing systems.

## 8.2 The PH|PH|1 queue

In Section 8.2.1 we present a structured description of the CTMC underlying a PH|PH|1 queue. In Section 8.2.2 we then proceed with the matrix-geometric solution. Stability issues are discussed in Section 8.2.3 and explicit expressions for performance measures of interest are discussed in Section 8.2.4.

### 8.2.1 A structured description of the CTMC

Now, consider the PH|PH|1 queue, the generalisation of the M|M|1 queue in which both the service and the interarrival times have a phase-type distribution (see also Chapter 3 and Appendix A). In this case, the state of the underlying CTMC is not totally described by the number of jobs in the queueing system. Part of the state description now is the phase of the arrival process, and the phase of the job in service, if any. Consequently, the state is a vector of three elements. The underlying Markov chain is therefore referred to as a *vector state process*.

Suppose that the representation of the arrival process is given by $(\underline{\alpha}, \mathbf{T})$, where $\mathbf{T}$ is an $m_a \times m_a$ matrix, and that the representation of the service process is given by $(\underline{\beta}, \mathbf{S})$, where $\mathbf{S}$ is an $m_s \times m_s$ matrix. Ordered lexicographically, the states of the Markov chain underlying this PH|PH|1 queueing system are of the form $(n, a, s)$ where $n$ is the number of jobs in the queue, $a \in \{1, \cdots, m_a\}$ is the phase of the arrival process, and $s \in \{1, \cdots, m_s\}$ is the phase of the service process:

$$\mathcal{I} = \{(0,1,1), (0,2,1), \cdots, (0, m_a, 1), (1,1,1), \cdots, (1,1,m_s), (1,2,1), \cdots, (1,2,m_s),$$
$$\cdots, (1, m_a, 1), \cdots, (1, m_a, m_s), \cdots, (2, m_a, m_s), \cdots, (\infty, m_a, m_s)\}.$$

All the states that have the same number of jobs in the queue are said to belong to one *level*. For example, level $i$, $i = 1, 2, \cdots$, corresponds to the set of states

$$\{(i,1,1), \cdots, (i,1,m_s), (i,2,1), \cdots, (i,2,m_s), \cdots, (i, m_a, 1), \cdots, (i, m_a, m_s)\}.$$

Level 0 consists of the states $\{(0,1,1), (0,2,1), \cdots, (0, m_a, 1)\}$. Apart from some irregularities at the boundary, the matrix $\mathbf{Q}$ shows great similarity with the generator matrices we have seen for birth-death queueing models. In particular, we observe that $\mathbf{Q}$ is block-tridiagonal. The upper-diagonal blocks describe the transitions from a certain level to the next higher level: they correspond to arrivals. The lower-diagonal blocks describe the transitions from a certain level to the next lower level: they correspond to service completions. The diagonal blocks describe transitions internal to a level causing arrivals nor departures, that is, they correspond to phase changes in the arrival or service process. Viewing the levels as "super states" the matrix $\mathbf{Q}$ in fact describes a birth-death process on them. For this reason vector state processes are most often called *quasi-birth-death models* (QBDs).

Returning to the specific case at hand, the generator matrix $\mathbf{Q}$ of the underlying Markov chain has the following structure:

$$
\mathbf{Q} = \begin{pmatrix}
\mathbf{B}_{00} & \mathbf{B}_{01} & 0 & 0 & \cdots \\
\mathbf{B}_{10} & \mathbf{A}_1 & \mathbf{A}_0 & 0 & \cdots \\
0 & \mathbf{A}_2 & \mathbf{A}_1 & \mathbf{A}_0 & \cdots \\
0 & 0 & \mathbf{A}_2 & \mathbf{A}_1 & \cdots \\
\vdots & \vdots & \vdots & \vdots & \ddots
\end{pmatrix}. \tag{8.7}
$$

The square matrices $\mathbf{A}_i$ are of size $m_a m_s \times m_a m_s$ and have the following form:

$$
\begin{aligned}
\mathbf{A}_0 &= \underline{T}^0 \underline{\alpha} \otimes \mathbf{I}, \\
\mathbf{A}_1 &= (\mathbf{T} \otimes \mathbf{I}) + (\mathbf{I} \otimes \mathbf{S}), \\
\mathbf{A}_2 &= \mathbf{I} \otimes \underline{S}^0 \underline{\beta},
\end{aligned} \tag{8.8}
$$

where the binary operator $\otimes$ is used to represent the tensor or Kronecker product of two matrices (see Appendix B). The matrix $\mathbf{A}_0$ describes the transitions to the next higher level and includes the component $\underline{T}^0$ which indicates the rate at which the arrival process completes. The factor $\underline{\alpha}$ accounts for the possible change in phase in the next arrival interval directly starting afterwards. Similarly, $\mathbf{A}_2$ describes the rate at which services complete (factor $\underline{S}^0$) multiplied by the vector $\underline{\beta}$ in order to account for the starting phase of the next service epoch. The matrix $\mathbf{A}_1$ describes changes in arrival or service process phase within a single level. The matrices $\mathbf{B}_{ij}$ are all differently dimensioned and have the following form:

$$
\begin{aligned}
\mathbf{B}_{00} &= \mathbf{T} \ (\text{size } m_a \times m_a), \\
\mathbf{B}_{01} &= \underline{T}^0 \underline{\alpha} \otimes \underline{\beta} \ (\text{size } m_a \times m_a m_s), \\
\mathbf{B}_{10} &= \mathbf{I} \otimes \underline{S}^0 \ (\text{size } m_a m_s \times m_a).
\end{aligned} \tag{8.9}
$$

Matrix $\mathbf{B}_{00}$ describes state changes internal to level 0; because there is no job in the queue at level 0, only changes in the arrival process need to be kept track of, which explains its equality to **T**. Matrix **B**$_{01}$ has a similar structure to **A**$_0$; however, as it represents the arrival of the first job after the system has been empty for some time, it needs an extra factor taking into account the phase at which the next service is started, which explains the factor $\underline{\beta}$. Similarly, **B**$_{10}$ much resembles **A**$_2$; however, as this matrix represents transitions to the empty system, no new service epochs can start, so that a factor $\underline{\beta}$ is missing.

## Example 8.1. The $E_2|H_2|1$ queue (I).

Consider a queueing model with a single server and with Erlang-2 interarrival times and hyper-exponentially distributed service times. Notice that this model is a special case of the G|G|1 queue, which we cannot solve. We use the following PH-type representation of a 2-stage Erlang distribution:

$$\mathbf{T} = \begin{pmatrix} -2\lambda & 2\lambda \\ 0 & -2\lambda \end{pmatrix}, \quad \underline{T}^0 = \begin{pmatrix} 0 \\ 2\lambda \end{pmatrix} \text{ and } \underline{\alpha} = (1,0), \tag{8.10}$$

that is, we have two exponential phases which are visited one after another. If both phases have been passed, an arrival takes place and the next interarrival period begins (a renewal process). We take the following representation of a 2-stage hyper-exponential service time distribution:

$$\mathbf{S} = \begin{pmatrix} -\mu_1 & 0 \\ 0 & -\mu_2 \end{pmatrix}, \quad \underline{S}^0 = \begin{pmatrix} \mu_1 \\ \mu_2 \end{pmatrix}, \text{ and } \underline{\beta} = \left(\frac{1}{4}, \frac{3}{4}\right), \tag{8.11}$$

that is, with probability $1/4$ phase 1 is taken, with mean length $1/\mu_1$ and with probability $3/4$ phase 2 is taken, with mean length $1/\mu_2$.

The CTMC describing this queueing model is a QBD process where the number of states per level is 4 ($2 \times 2$; two phase possibilities for the service as well as for the arrival process). When the system is empty, only the arrival process can be in one of its two states, hence, the first level (level 0) only has two states. The state transition diagram is depicted in Figure 8.2. As can be observed, transitions related to services always point to states one level lower. Notice that at the end of a service period, the next service period is started; the probabilities $\underline{\beta}$ are used for that purpose by multiplying them with the service rates $\mu_i$. The first phase in the arrival process always leads to a state transition within a level; the completion of the second phase in the arrival process leads to a next higher level. Notice that only at the arrival of the first customer (transition from level 0 to level 1) the service time distribution is chosen (with probability $\beta_i$ take rate $\mu_i$). For arrivals at a non-empty queue the choice of the service time distribution is postponed until the next customer has completed its service.

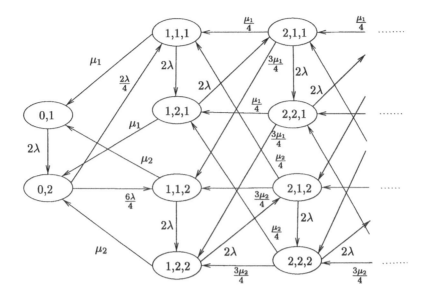

Figure 8.2: State transition diagram for the QBD underlying the $E_2|H_2|1$ queue

From Figure 8.2 the generator matrix for this queueing system can readily be obtained. Instead, one could also apply the definitions of the block matrices to arrive at:

$$\mathbf{B}_{00} = \mathbf{T} = \begin{pmatrix} -2\lambda & 2\lambda \\ 0 & -2\lambda \end{pmatrix}, \quad \mathbf{B}_{01} = \underline{T}^0 \underline{\alpha} \otimes \underline{\beta} = \frac{1}{4} \begin{pmatrix} 0 & 0 & 0 & 0 \\ 2\lambda & 6\lambda & 0 & 0 \end{pmatrix},$$

$$\mathbf{B}_{10} = \mathbf{I} \otimes \underline{S}^0 = \begin{pmatrix} \mu_1 & 0 \\ \mu_2 & 0 \\ 0 & \mu_1 \\ 0 & \mu_2 \end{pmatrix}, \quad \mathbf{A}_0 = \underline{T}^0 \underline{\alpha} \otimes \mathbf{I} = \begin{pmatrix} 0 & 0 & 0 & 0 \\ 0 & 0 & 0 & 0 \\ 2\lambda & 0 & 0 & 0 \\ 0 & 2\lambda & 0 & 0 \end{pmatrix},$$

$$\mathbf{A}_1 = \begin{pmatrix} -(\mu_1 + 2\lambda) & 0 & 2\lambda & 0 \\ 0 & -(\mu_2 + 2\lambda) & 0 & 2\lambda \\ 0 & 0 & -(\mu_1 + 2\lambda) & 0 \\ 0 & 0 & 0 & -(\mu_2 + 2\lambda) \end{pmatrix},$$

and
$$\mathbf{A}_2 = \mathbf{I} \otimes \underline{S}^0 \underline{\beta} = \frac{1}{4} \begin{pmatrix} \mu_1 & 3\mu_1 & 0 & 0 \\ \mu_2 & 3\mu_2 & 0 & 0 \\ 0 & 0 & \mu_1 & 3\mu_1 \\ 0 & 0 & \mu_2 & 3\mu_2 \end{pmatrix}. \tag{8.12}$$

□

## 8.2.2   Matrix-geometric solution

We now proceed to solve the CTMC for its steady-state probabilities in a way that closely resembles the approach followed for the M|M|1 queue. First, let $\underline{z}_i$ denote the vector of lexicographically ordered steady-state probabilities of states in level $i$. Then, for $i = 1, 2, \cdots$, we have

$$\underline{z}_i = \left(p_{(i,1,1)}, \cdots, p_{(i,1,m_s)}, p_{(i,2,1)}, \cdots, p_{(i,2,m_s)}, \cdots, p_{(i,m_a,1)}, \cdots, p_{(i,m_a,m_s)}\right). \tag{8.13}$$

The arguments that led to the simple geometric form for the steady-state probabilities in an M|M|1 queue apply again here; however, we now have to take levels of states as neighbours between which probability flows. That is, the probability of residence in level $i$ $(\underline{z}_i)$ depends only on the probability of residence in level $i - 1$ $(\underline{z}_{i-1})$, for those levels $i$ which are already in the repeating portion of the CTMC, i.e., for $i = 2, 3, \cdots$. Since the rates between neighbouring levels of states are constants, we hope that the relation we are aiming at can be expressed as a multiplicative constant between $\underline{z}_i$ and $\underline{z}_{i-1}$. Note, however, that since we are dealing with vectors now, this constant needs to be a square matrix $\mathbf{R}$ of size $m_a m_s \times m_a m_s$. If we *assume* that

$$\underline{z}_i = \underline{z}_{i-1}\mathbf{R}, \tag{8.14}$$

it follows that the steady-state probability vectors $\underline{z}_i$ must have the form

$$\underline{z}_i = \underline{z}_1\mathbf{R}^{i-1}, \quad i = 1, 2, \cdots. \tag{8.15}$$

Notice that we "go back in the recursion" to level 1 here, and not to level 0 as in the M|M|1 case. This difference is due to the fact that in the M|M|1 case we had only one boundary level, whereas we have two here. The length of the vectors $\underline{z}_i$, $i = 1, 2, \cdots$, is $m_a m_s$. As in the M|M|1 case for $\rho$, the square matrix $\mathbf{R}$ of size $m_a m_s \times m_a m_s$ follows from a quadratic equation obtained by substituting the assumed geometric form in the repeating portion of the global balance equation:

$$\underline{p}\mathbf{Q} = \underline{0} \Rightarrow [\cdots, \underline{z}_i, \underline{z}_{i+1}, \underline{z}_{i+2}, \cdots]\mathbf{Q} = \mathbf{0} \Rightarrow \underline{z}_i\mathbf{A}_0 + \underline{z}_{i+1}\mathbf{A}_1 + \underline{z}_{i+2}\mathbf{A}_2 = \underline{0}, \tag{8.16}$$

which, after rewriting the vectors $\underline{z}_i$ in terms of $\underline{z}_1$ yields

$$\underline{z}_1\left(\mathbf{R}^2\mathbf{A}_2 + \mathbf{R}^1\mathbf{A}_1 + \mathbf{R}^0\mathbf{A}_0\right) = \underline{0}. \tag{8.17}$$

This equation can only be true when either $\underline{z}_1 = \underline{0}$, or when the quadratic equation within parentheses equals $\mathbf{0}$. For the same reasons as mentioned when discussing the M|M|1 queue, the latter must be the case, and the matrix $\mathbf{R}$ thus follows from the following matrix quadratic equation:

$$\mathbf{R}^2 \mathbf{A}_2 + \mathbf{R}^1 \mathbf{A}_1 + \mathbf{R}^0 \mathbf{A}_0 = \mathbf{0}. \tag{8.18}$$

We discuss the actual computation of $\mathbf{R}$ from this quadratic equation in Section 8.3; for the time being we assume that we can do so.

To start the recursive relation (8.15) the following boundary equations must be solved to obtain $\underline{z}_0$ and $\underline{z}_1$:

$$(\underline{z}_0, \underline{z}_1) \cdot \begin{pmatrix} \mathbf{B}_{00} \\ \mathbf{B}_{10} \end{pmatrix} = \underline{0}, \quad \text{and} \quad (\underline{z}_0, \underline{z}_1, \underline{z}_2) \cdot \begin{pmatrix} \mathbf{B}_{01} \\ \mathbf{A}_1 \\ \mathbf{A}_2 \end{pmatrix} = \underline{0}. \tag{8.19}$$

By the fact that $\underline{z}_2 \mathbf{A}_2 = (\underline{z}_1 \mathbf{R}) \mathbf{A}_2$ we can rewrite the right-hand equation as

$$(\underline{z}_0, \underline{z}_1) \cdot \begin{pmatrix} \mathbf{B}_{01} \\ \mathbf{A}_1 + \mathbf{R} \mathbf{A}_2 \end{pmatrix} = \underline{0}, \tag{8.20}$$

so that we obtain the following boundary equations:

$$(\underline{z}_0, \underline{z}_1) \cdot \begin{pmatrix} \mathbf{B}_{00} & \mathbf{B}_{01} \\ \mathbf{B}_{10} & \mathbf{A}_1 + \mathbf{R} \mathbf{A}_2 \end{pmatrix} = (\underline{0}, \underline{0}). \tag{8.21}$$

As can be observed, the length of $\underline{z}_0 = (p_{(0,1,0)}, \cdots, p_{(0,m_a,0)})$ is $m_a$. Also, since (8.21) is not of full rank, the normalisation equation has to be used to arrive at a unique solution:

$$\sum_{i=0}^{\infty} \underline{z}_i \underline{1} = \underline{z}_0 \underline{1} + \sum_{i=1}^{\infty} \underline{z}_i \underline{1} = \underline{z}_0 \underline{1} + \underline{z}_1 \left( \sum_{i=0}^{\infty} \mathbf{R}^i \right) \underline{1} = \underline{z}_0 \underline{1} + \underline{z}_1 (\mathbf{I} - \mathbf{R})^{-1} \underline{1} = 1. \tag{8.22}$$

This equation might be integrated in (8.21) to yield one system of linear equations although this might not be most attractive to do from a numerical point of view (see Chapter 15).

## 8.2.3   Stability issues

Let us now return to the question under which conditions (8.18) can indeed be solved and lead to a unique matrix $\mathbf{R}$.

First recall from the M|M|1 queue that such a queue is stable as long as $\lambda < \mu$. Translated to the state-transition diagram, this inequality can be interpreted as follows. As long as the "drift" to higher level states is smaller than the "drift" to lower level states, the system is stable: $\lambda < \mu \Rightarrow \rho = \lambda/\mu < 1$ and a steady-state solution exists.

A similar reasoning can be followed when we deal with QBDs. Let us denote $\mathbf{A} = \mathbf{A}_0 + \mathbf{A}_1 + \mathbf{A}_2$; this matrix can be interpreted as a Markov generator matrix which describes the transition behaviour within a level. Transitions between levels, normally described by matrices $\mathbf{A}_0$ and $\mathbf{A}_2$, are simply "looped back" to their originating level. Now, define the vector $\underline{\pi}$ to be the steady-state probability vector belonging to the CTMC with generator matrix $\mathbf{A}$. $\underline{\pi}$ follows from $\underline{\pi}\mathbf{A} = \underline{0}$ under the normalising condition $\sum_i \pi_i = 1$. Thus, given presence in some repeating level $j$, the probability of being in the $i$-th state of that level, i.e., in state $(j, i)$, equals $\pi_i$. Given this probability, the total "drift" to a next higher level can be expressed as $\sum_i \pi_i \sum_l A_{(i,l)}^{(0)}$, where $A_{(i,l)}^{(0)}$ is the $(i, l)$-th element of matrix $\mathbf{A}_0$. Similarly, the drift to the next lower level can be expressed as $\sum_i \pi_i \sum_l A_{(i,l)}^{(2)}$. Notice that in both these expressions, the rates to the next higher (lower) level are weighted by their relative occurrence. Now, as long as the drift to next higher levels, i.e., $\sum_i \pi_i \sum_l A_{(i,l)}^{(0)}$, is smaller than the drift to a next lower level, i.e., $\sum_i \pi_i \sum_l A_{(i,l)}^{(2)}$, we have a stable system. In matrix notation, the required inequality for stability then becomes:

$$\pi\mathbf{A}_0\underline{1} < \pi\mathbf{A}_2\underline{1}. \tag{8.23}$$

Once the matrices $\mathbf{A}_i$ have been derived, this inequality can easily be verified.

### 8.2.4   Performance measures

Once the matrix $\mathbf{R}$ and the boundary vectors $\underline{z}_0$ and $\underline{z}_1$ have been obtained, various interesting performance metrics can be derived:

- Arrival and service process characteristics:

    - the average interarrival time $E[A] = -\underline{\alpha}\mathbf{T}^{-1}\underline{1}$; we define $\lambda = 1/E[A]$;
    - the average service time $E[S] = -\underline{\beta}\mathbf{S}^{-1}\underline{1}$; we define $\mu = 1/E[S]$.

- Average performance measures:

    - the utilisation $E[N_s] = \rho = \lambda/\mu$;
    - the average number of jobs in the queue and server:

$$
\begin{aligned}
E[N] &= \sum_{i=1}^{\infty} i\underline{z}_i\underline{1} = \underline{z}_1\left(\sum_{i=1}^{\infty} i\mathbf{R}^{i-1}\right)\underline{1} \\
&= \underline{z}_1\left(\sum_{i=1}^{\infty} \frac{d}{d\mathbf{R}}\mathbf{R}^i\right)\underline{1} = \underline{z}_1\frac{d}{d\mathbf{R}}\left(\sum_{i=1}^{\infty}\mathbf{R}^i\right)\underline{1} \\
&= \underline{z}_1\frac{d}{d\mathbf{R}}\left((\mathbf{I} - \mathbf{R})^{-1} - \mathbf{I}\right)\underline{1} = \underline{z}_1(\mathbf{I} - \mathbf{R})^{-2}\underline{1}; \tag{8.24}
\end{aligned}
$$

- the average number of jobs in the queue $E[N_q] = E[N] - \rho$;

- the average response time $E[R] = E[N]/\lambda$;

- the average waiting time $E[W] = E[N_q]/\lambda$.

- Detailed performance measures:

  - the probability $z_i$ of having $i$ jobs in the queue: $z_i = \underline{z}_i \underline{1}$;

  - the probability $B_k$ of having at least $k$ jobs in the queue, which for $k \geq 1$ can be written as:

$$
\begin{aligned}
B(k) &= \sum_{i=k}^{\infty} z_i \cdot \underline{1} = \underline{z}_1 \left( \sum_{i=k}^{\infty} \mathbf{R}^{i-1} \right) \underline{1} \\
&= \underline{z}_1 \mathbf{R}^{k-1} \left( \sum_{i=0}^{\infty} \mathbf{R}^i \right) \underline{1} = \underline{z}_1 \mathbf{R}^{k-1} (\mathbf{I} - \mathbf{R})^{-1} \underline{1}. \quad (8.25)
\end{aligned}
$$

For all these measures, the similarity with the corresponding measures for the M|M|1 queue is striking.

## 8.3    Numerical aspects

In order to really compute steady-state probabilities we have to solve for the matrix $\mathbf{R}$ as well as for the (normalised) boundary equations. We discuss the numerical solution of the boundary equations in Section 8.3.1. Only in special cases can $\mathbf{R}$ be computed explicitly (see Section 8.4). Normally, $\mathbf{R}$ is computed iteratively. We present a simple and straightforward substitution algorithm in Section 8.3.2, after which we present the recently developed logarithmic reduction algorithm in Section 8.3.3.

### 8.3.1    Solving the boundary equations

The calculation of the boundary probability vectors from the (normalised) system of linear equations can be done using the standard techniques for solving linear systems of equations, as will be described in Chapter 15. As the number of boundary equations is normally not too large, direct approaches such as Gaussian elimination are in general well-suited. Notice that we need to compute $\mathbf{R}$ before we can solve the linear system of boundary equations (8.21).

## 8.3.2   A successive substitution algorithm

From the quadratic matrix equation

$$\mathbf{F}(\mathbf{R}) = \mathbf{R}^2\mathbf{A}_2 + \mathbf{R}^1\mathbf{A}_1 + \mathbf{R}^0\mathbf{A}_0 = \mathbf{0}, \tag{8.26}$$

we can derive

$$\mathbf{R} = -(\mathbf{A}_0 + \mathbf{R}^2\mathbf{A}_2)\mathbf{A}_1^{-1}. \tag{8.27}$$

Now, taking as a first guess $\mathbf{R}(0) = \mathbf{0}$, we obtain the next guess $\mathbf{R}(1) = -\mathbf{A}_0\mathbf{A}_1^{-1}$. We obtain successive better approximations of $\mathbf{R}$ as follows:

$$\mathbf{R}(k+1) = -(\mathbf{A}_0 + \mathbf{R}^2(k)\mathbf{A}_2)\mathbf{A}_1^{-1}, \quad k = 1, 2, \cdots. \tag{8.28}$$

The iteration is stopped when $\|\mathbf{F}(\mathbf{R})\| < \epsilon$. It has been shown that the sequence $\{\mathbf{R}(k), k = 0, 1, \cdots\}$ is entry-wise nondecreasing, and that it converges monotonically to the matrix $\mathbf{R}$.

The following remark is of importance when implementing this method in an efficient way. First notice that $\mathbf{R}(1)$ is defined as $-\mathbf{A}_0\mathbf{A}_1^{-1}$. In many cases we will see only a few non-zero entries in the vectors $\underline{\alpha}$ and $\underline{T}^0$. Since $\mathbf{A}_0 = (\underline{T}^0 \cdot \underline{\alpha}) \otimes \mathbf{I}$ (it describes arrivals to the queue) we see that rows containing just 0's in $\mathbf{A}_0$ will yield similar zero-rows in $\mathbf{R}$. Further iteration steps do not change this situation for the matrix $\mathbf{R}$. Therefore, the matrix $\mathbf{R}$ will often have many rows completely zero. This fact can be exploited in the multiplications by simply skipping rows which contain only zero entries.

For each iteration step, 3 matrix-multiplications have to be made. If $\mathbf{R}$ is of size $N \times N$, then we require $O(3N^3)$ operations per iteration step. The number of iteration steps heavily depends on the utilisation of the queue under study.

**Example 8.2. The $E_2|H_2|1$ queue (II).**
Consider again the $E_2|H_2|1$ queue in which we assume the following numerical values: $\lambda = 8$, $\mu_1 = 20$ and $\mu_2 = 10$. Due to this choice, $\rho = 0.7$. The matrix $\mathbf{R}$ is calculated with the above simple algorithm, with precision $10^{-8}$ in 72 steps and equals:

$$\mathbf{R} = \begin{pmatrix} 0.0000 & 0.0000 & 0.0000 & 0.0000 \\ 0.0000 & 0.0000 & 0.0000 & 0.0000 \\ 0.4678 & 0.0970 & 0.2229 & 0.1217 \\ 0.0415 & 0.7879 & 0.0521 & 0.6247 \end{pmatrix}. \tag{8.29}$$

First notice that the matrix $\mathbf{R}$ has two non-zero rows; these correspond to those situations in which arrivals can take place (at each level). There are 4 states per level, but in only two

| $2\lambda$ | $\rho$ | $E[N_q]$ | SS | LR |
|---|---|---|---|---|
| 2 | 0.0875 | 0.0023 | 6 | 3 |
| 4 | 0.1750 | 0.0160 | 11 | 4 |
| 6 | 0.2625 | 0.0492 | 15 | 4 |
| 8 | 0.3500 | 0.1122 | 21 | 4 |
| 10 | 0.4375 | 0.2200 | 28 | 5 |
| 12 | 0.5250 | 0.3985 | 38 | 5 |
| 14 | 0.6125 | 0.6963 | 52 | 5 |
| 16 | 0.7000 | 1.2186 | 72 | 6 |
| 18 | 0.7875 | 2.2432 | *100* | 6 |
| 20 | 0.8750 | 4.8242 | *100* | 7 |
| 22 | 0.9581 | 17.5829 | *100* | 9 |

Table 8.1: Analysis results for the $E_2|H_2|1$ queue

of them can arrivals take place, namely in those states where the Erlang-2 arrival process is in its second phase.

To compute the boundary probabilities, we have to solve (8.21) under the normalising condition (8.22). We find $\underline{z}_0 = (0.1089, 0.1911)$ from which we quickly verify that $\rho = 1 - \underline{z}_0\underline{1} = 0.70$.

In Table 8.1 we show some more analysis results. We vary $\lambda$ from 1 through 11. Note the increase in the average queue length with increasing utilisation. We tabulated the required number of steps in the successive substitution procedure to compute $\mathbf{R}$ (column SS). Note that when $\rho$ increases the iterative solution of $\mathbf{R}$ slows down tremendously; since we stopped the iterative procedure after 100 steps, the last three rows do not represent accurate results.                                                                                  □

We finally note that a number of more efficient methods (based on successive substitutions) have been developed than the one presented here. These methods rely on the computation of the intermediate matrices $\mathbf{G}$ and $\mathbf{U}$, which will be introduced and related to $\mathbf{R}$ in the next section. However, since these algorithms are also outperformed by the recently developed logarithmic reduction algorithm, we do not discuss them any further here; for further details, refer to [172, 188].

### 8.3.3   The logarithmic reduction algorithm

Recently, Latouche and Ramaswami developed the logarithmic reduction (LR) algorithm to compute $\mathbf{R}$ [173]. It is regarded as the most efficient to date. The algorithm is based on the following three matrix-quadratic equations (here given in the case of a discrete-time QBD):

$$
\begin{aligned}
\mathbf{G} &= \mathbf{A}_2 + \mathbf{A}_1\mathbf{G} + \mathbf{A}_0\mathbf{G}^2, \\
\mathbf{R} &= \mathbf{A}_0 + \mathbf{R}\mathbf{A}_1 + \mathbf{R}^2\mathbf{A}_2, \\
\mathbf{U} &= \mathbf{A}_1 + \mathbf{A}_0(\mathbf{I} - \mathbf{U})^{-1}\mathbf{A}_2.
\end{aligned}
\tag{8.30}
$$

The three unknown matrices (all of size $N \times N$) have the following interpretation:

- the element $g_{i,j}$ of the matrix $\mathbf{G}$ is the probability that, starting from state $(1, i)$, the QBD process eventually visits level 0 in state $(0, j)$;

- the element $u_{i,j}$ of the matrix $\mathbf{U}$ is the *taboo probability* that, starting from state $(1, i)$, the QBD eventually returns to level 1 by visiting state $(1, j)$, under taboo of level 0, that is, without visiting level 0 in between;

- the element $r_{i,j}$ of the matrix $\mathbf{R}$ can be interpreted as the expected number of visits into state $(1, j)$, starting from state $(0, i)$, until the first return to level 0.

Once one of these matrices is known, the other ones can be readily computed. For instance, having computed $\mathbf{G}$, we can derive $\mathbf{U} = \mathbf{A}_1 + \mathbf{A}_0\mathbf{G}$, and $\mathbf{R} = -\mathbf{A}_0\mathbf{U}^{-1}$.

When the QBD is recurrent, the matrix $\mathbf{G}$ is stochastic. We can therefore iteratively compute successive estimates for $\mathbf{G}$, denoted as $\mathbf{G}(k)$, $k = 1, 2, \cdots$, until the row sums equal (almost) 1, that is, until $||\underline{1} - \mathbf{G}\underline{1}|| < \epsilon$, where $\epsilon$ is a prespecified accuracy criterion. We have: $\lim_{k \to \infty} \mathbf{G}(k) = \mathbf{G}$.

The $(i, j)$-th element of $\mathbf{G}(k)$, denoted as $g_{i,j}(k)$, now has the following interpretation [173]: $g_{i,j}(k)$ is the probability that, starting from state $(1, i)$, the QBD visits level 0 in state $(0, j)$, under taboo of levels $k + 1$ and beyond. Clearly, to compute $\mathbf{G}$ accurately, we should make $k$ large, so that even very long queue lengths are allowed for (so that effectively the taboo is not there). The algorithms developed in the past all compute successive matrices $\mathbf{G}(k)$ by increasing $k$ one-at-a-time. Especially for queueing models with high utilisation, large queue lengths occur quite often, thus requiring many iteration steps (as witnessed by Table 8.1). In contrast, the new LR algorithm doubles the value of $k$ in every step, thus reaching a far smaller effective taboo, given a fixed number of iteration steps. In practice,

1.   $\mathbf{B}_0 := -\mathbf{A}_1^{-1}\mathbf{A}_0; \ \mathbf{B}_2 := -\mathbf{A}_1^{-1}\mathbf{A}_2$
2.   $\mathbf{G} := \mathbf{B}_2; \ \mathbf{T} := \mathbf{B}_0$
3.   while $\|\underline{1} - \mathbf{G}\underline{1}\| > \epsilon$ do
4.        $\mathbf{D} := \mathbf{B}_0\mathbf{B}_2 + \mathbf{B}_2\mathbf{B}_0$
5.        $\mathbf{B}_0 := (\mathbf{I} - \mathbf{D})^{-1}\mathbf{B}_0^2$
6.        $\mathbf{B}_2 := (\mathbf{I} - \mathbf{D})^{-1}\mathbf{B}_2^2$
7.        $\mathbf{G} := \mathbf{G} + \mathbf{T}\mathbf{B}_2$
8.        $\mathbf{T} := \mathbf{T}\mathbf{B}_0$
9.   od
10.  $\mathbf{U} := \mathbf{A}_1 + \mathbf{A}_0\mathbf{G}$
11.  $\mathbf{R} := -\mathbf{A}_0\mathbf{U}^{-1}$

Figure 8.3: The logarithmic-reduction algorithm for continuous-time QBDs

20 iteration steps suffice most of the time, thus allowing the QBD to have upsurges to levels as high as $2^{20}$ (about 1 million).

Without going into the detailed derivations, we now present the basic equations to compute $\mathbf{G}$ (note that we treat the case of a continuous-time QBD here; in [172, 173, 268], the discrete-time variant is presented):

$$G = -\sum_{k=0}^{\infty} \underbrace{\left( \prod_{i=0}^{k-1} \mathbf{B}_0(i) \right)}_{\mathbf{T}(k)} \mathbf{B}_2(k), \tag{8.31}$$

with

$$\mathbf{B}_0(0) = -\mathbf{A}_1\mathbf{A}_0, \ \text{and} \ \mathbf{B}_2(0) = -\mathbf{A}_1\mathbf{A}_2, \tag{8.32}$$

and

$$\mathbf{B}_i(k+1) = (\mathbf{I} - \underbrace{(\mathbf{B}_0(k)\mathbf{B}_2(k) + \mathbf{B}_2(k)\mathbf{B}_0(k))}_{\mathbf{D}(k)})^{-1}\mathbf{B}_i^2(k), \ \ i = 0, 2. \tag{8.33}$$

The corresponding algorithm is given in Figure 8.3. The first line represent the initialisation according to (8.32), and in the second line $\mathbf{G}$ is set equal to the first term in (8.31); note that when $k = 0$, $\mathbf{T}(0) = \mathbf{I}$ so that $\mathbf{G} = \mathbf{B}_2$. Then, until $\mathbf{G}$ truly is a stochastic matrix, successive terms for $\mathbf{D}(k)$ and the matrices $\mathbf{B}_i(k)$ are computed in lines 4–6, according to (8.33). In line 7 the current term is added to $\mathbf{G}$ and in line 8 the new value for $\mathbf{T}(k)$ is computed. When the iteration ends, $\mathbf{U}$ and $\mathbf{R}$ are finally computed.

Regarding the complexity of the LR algorithm, it can be shown that the number of operations per iteration step equals $O(\frac{25}{3}N^3)$. This is about eight times more than in the case of the successive substitution method. However, the strength of the LR algorithm lies in the fact that it does need far less iterations; roughly speaking, when the successive substitution method requires $k_\epsilon$ iteration steps to reach an accuracy $\epsilon$, then the LR-algorithm requires only $O(\log_2 k_\epsilon)$ steps. Recently, a slightly faster iteration step has been proposed by Wagner et al. [282]; their algorithm requires $O(\frac{19}{3}n^3)$ per iteration steps and the same number of steps as the LR algorithm.

### Example 8.3. The $E_2|H_2|1$ queue (III).

In the last column of Table 8.1 we show the number of steps required by the LR algorithm to reach the same accuracy as the SS algorithm. The increase in performance is indeed tremendous. The number of steps still increases for increasing $\rho$, however, only very slowly. Needing more than 20 iterations to compute $\mathbf{R}$ has been an exception in the case studies we have performed so far.                                                                  □

### Example 8.4. The $IPP|E_k|1$ queue (I).

To model the bursty nature of many arrival processes we can use an IPP which has two states: "off" (0) and "on" (1) (see also Section 3.9.1). The transition rate from state $i$ to state $j$ equals $\gamma_{i,j}$. In state $i$, jobs are generated as a Poisson process with rate $\lambda_i$. Such an IPP is completely described by the matrix $\mathbf{T}$:

$$\mathbf{T} = \begin{pmatrix} -\gamma_{0,1} & \gamma_{0,1} \\ \gamma_{1,0} & -(\gamma_{1,0}+\lambda) \end{pmatrix}, \tag{8.34}$$

and the vector $(\underline{\alpha}, \alpha_A) = (0,1,0)$. Note that due to the choice of $\underline{\alpha}$, we have established that after an arrival (an absorption) the PH distribution stays in state 1 so that the arrival process remains in a burst. An important parameter for an IPP is the *burstiness b*. It is defined as the ratio between the arrival rate in a burst and the overall average arrival rate:

$$b = \frac{\text{arrival rate in a burst}}{\text{overall average arrival rate}} = \frac{\lambda}{\lambda\gamma_{0,1}/(\gamma_{0,1}+\gamma_{1,0})} = \frac{\gamma_{0,1}+\gamma_{1,0}}{\gamma_{0,1}}. \tag{8.35}$$

We will first study the influence of the burstiness of the IPP on the average number of customers queued while keeping the utilisation constant. This allows us to investigate quantitatively the influence of $b$ on the performance. At the same time, we vary the number of Erlang phases $k$ in the service time distribution from 1 to 10. We address four different burstiness levels: $b = 1$, 2.75, 5.5 and 11; we kept $\gamma_{0,1} = 10$ and varied $\gamma_{1,0}$ from

| | $E[N_q]$ for given $b$ | | | |
|---|---|---|---|---|
| $k$ | $b = 1$ | $b = 2.75$ | $b = 5.5$ | $b = 11$ |
| 1 | 0.375 | 1.759 | 2.859 | 3.496 |
| 2 | 0.284 | 1.595 | 2.741 | 3.394 |
| 3 | 0.253 | 1.537 | 2.702 | 3.361 |
| 4 | 0.237 | 1.508 | 2.682 | 3.344 |
| 5 | 0.227 | 1.489 | 2.670 | 3.334 |
| 6 | 0.221 | 1.477 | 2.662 | 3.328 |
| 7 | 0.216 | 1.468 | 2.657 | 3.323 |
| 8 | 0.213 | 1.462 | 2.652 | 3.320 |
| 9 | 0.210 | 1.457 | 2.649 | 3.317 |
| 10 | 0.208 | 1.452 | 2.646 | 3.315 |

Table 8.2: The average queue length $E[N_q]$ in the IPP$|E_k|1$ queue, for increasing number of phases $k$ and different burstiness factors ($\rho = 0.4545$)

17.5 via 45 to 100 in the latter three cases. We want to keep the utilisation equal to 45.45% in all cases and we therefore adjusted $\lambda$ to 45.45, 125, 250 and 500 respectively; the service rate $\mu = 100$. Notice that the case $b = 1$ corresponds to the case where the IPP has been replaced by a normal Poisson arrival process (or an IPP with $\gamma_{1,0} = 0$).

The results are depicted in Table 8.2. We observe that for all burstiness levels the average number of queued customers decreases as the service times become more deterministic, i.e., as $k$ increases. Notice, however, that the relative decrease becomes less pronounced for higher values of $b$. This implies that for (very) bursty sources, the service time distribution (or its second moment) plays a less important role, as far as the average performance variables are concerned. Looking at the arrival rates, we see that for the larger burstiness values, the queue is overloaded when the arrival process is active; this causes the enormous increase in average number of customers queued for larger values of $b$ (and so, via Little's law, in the average waiting time).

In Figure 8.4 we show the effect of increasing the number of Erlang stages in the service time distribution from 1 to 50. The figure shows the expected queue length when the arrival process has $b = 11$ and utilisation 72.73%. Notice that altering $k$ to a value around 5 already makes the services very deterministic. Adding more phases does not change the performance measure of interest very much any more; it does change the number of states per level. The number of rows and columns in **R** equals $2k$. □

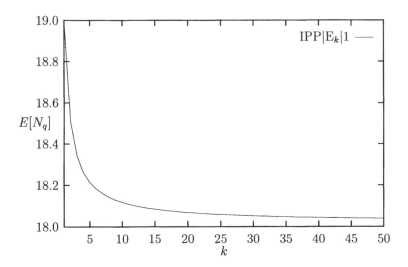

Figure 8.4: $E[N_q]$ for the IPP|$E_k$|1 queue as a function of the number of phases $k$ in the Erlang service time distribution

## 8.4   A few special cases

We address a few often recurring special cases of the general theory we have addressed so far. These, and a few other cases can also be found in [217, Section 3.2]. We discuss the M|PH|1 queue in Section 8.4.1 because it allows for an explicit computation of $\mathbf{R}$. We then discuss the PH|M|$m$ multi-server queue in Section 8.4.2.

### 8.4.1   The M|PH|1 queue: an explicit expression for R

Consider an M|PH|1 queue in which the Poisson arrival rate equals $\lambda$ and in which the service time distribution has representation $(\underline{\beta}, \mathbf{S})$ of order $m_s$. We assume that the queue is stable, i.e., $\rho = \lambda E[S] = -\lambda \underline{\beta} \mathbf{S}^{-1} \underline{1} < 1$. The CTMC describing this queueing system has states $\mathcal{I} = \{0\} \cup \{(i, j) | i \in \mathbb{N}^+, j = 1, \cdots, m_s\}$. State 0 signifies the empty state and state $(i, j)$ is the state with $i$ customers and the service process in phase $j$. The generator matrix $\mathbf{Q}$ is then given as:

$$\mathbf{Q} = \begin{pmatrix} -\lambda & \lambda\underline{\beta} & \underline{0} & \underline{0} & \cdots \\ \underline{S}^0 & \mathbf{S} - \lambda\mathbf{I} & \lambda\mathbf{I} & \mathbf{0} & \cdots \\ \underline{0} & \mathbf{S}^0\underline{\beta} & \mathbf{S} - \lambda\mathbf{I} & \lambda\mathbf{I} & \cdots \\ \underline{0} & \mathbf{0} & \mathbf{S}^0\underline{\beta} & \mathbf{S} - \lambda\mathbf{I} & \cdots \\ \underline{0} & \mathbf{0} & \mathbf{0} & \mathbf{S}^0\underline{\beta} & \cdots \\ \vdots & \vdots & \vdots & \vdots & \ddots \end{pmatrix}. \tag{8.36}$$

The steady-state probability vector $\underline{z} = (z_0, \underline{z}_1, \underline{z}_2, \cdots)$ is then given as

$$z_i = \begin{cases} 1 - \rho, & i = 0, \\ (1 - \rho)\underline{\beta}\mathbf{R}^i, & i = 1, 2, \cdots, \end{cases} \tag{8.37}$$

where the matrix $\mathbf{R}$ is given as

$$\mathbf{R} = \lambda(\lambda\mathbf{I} - \lambda\tilde{\mathbf{B}} - \mathbf{S})^{-1}, \tag{8.38}$$

with $\tilde{\mathbf{B}} = \underline{1} \cdot \underline{\beta}$. It is worthwhile for the reader to investigate the validity of the above result for the case of an exponential service time distribution.

## 8.4.2 The PH|M|m queue

As the next special case we consider an $M$-server queueing system with exponentially distributed service times and a general PH-renewal process as arrival process. Although for this queueing system no explicit expression for $\mathbf{R}$ exists, we include it here since it can be regarded as a computationally attractive special case of the GI|M|m queueing system.

We assume that the interarrival distribution has a PH-representation $(\mathbf{T}, \underline{\alpha})$ and that we deal with an exponentially distributed service time with mean $1/\mu$. The generator matrix describing the corresponding QBD is then given as (only non-zero blocks are shown):

$$\mathbf{Q} = \begin{pmatrix} \mathbf{T} & \underline{T}^0\underline{\alpha} & \cdots & \cdots & & & & & \\ \mu\mathbf{I} & \mathbf{T} - \mu\mathbf{I} & \underline{T}^0\underline{\alpha} & \cdots & & & & & \\ & 2\mu\mathbf{I} & \mathbf{T} - 2\mu\mathbf{I} & \underline{T}^0\underline{\alpha} & & & & & \\ \vdots & \vdots & \ddots & \ddots & \ddots & & \vdots & \vdots & \vdots \\ & & & & \ddots & \mathbf{T} - (m-1)\mu\mathbf{I} & \underline{T}^0\underline{\alpha} & & \\ & & & & \ddots & m\mu\mathbf{I} & \mathbf{T} - m\mu\mathbf{I} & \underline{T}^0\underline{\alpha} & \\ & & & & \ddots & & m\mu\mathbf{I} & \mathbf{T} - m\mu\mathbf{I} & \\ \vdots & \vdots & \vdots & \vdots & \vdots & & \vdots & \ddots & \ddots \end{pmatrix}. \tag{8.39}$$

All submatrices have their size equal to the size of $\mathbf{T}$: $m \times m$. The difference with the PH|PH|1 queue, is that we now have $m$ boundary columns, instead of only 2. Therefore, the geometric regime in the steady-state probability vectors per level now starts from level $m$ onwards:

$$\underline{z}_i = \underline{z}_m \mathbf{R}^{i-m}, \quad i = m, m+1, \cdots, \tag{8.40}$$

where the matrix $\mathbf{R}$ again is the minimal nonnegative solution of the matrix quadratic equation

$$\mathbf{R}^2 \mathbf{A}_2 + \mathbf{R}\mathbf{A}_1 + \mathbf{A}_0 = \mathbf{0}, \tag{8.41}$$

where

$$\mathbf{A}_2 = m\mu\mathbf{I}, \, \mathbf{A}_1 = \mathbf{T} - m\mu\mathbf{I}, \, \text{and } \mathbf{A}_0 = \underline{T}^0 \cdot \underline{\alpha}. \tag{8.42}$$

The first $m$ (boundary) probability vectors, $\underline{z}_0$ through $\underline{z}_{m-1}$, follow from the boundary equations:

$$\begin{cases} \underline{z}_0 \mathbf{T} + \mu \underline{z}_1 = \underline{0}, \\ \underline{z}_{i-1}\underline{T}^0\underline{\alpha} + \underline{z}_i(\mathbf{T} - i\mu\mathbf{I}) + (i+1)\mu\underline{z}_{i+1} = \underline{0}, \quad i = 1, \cdots, m-2, \\ \underline{z}_{m-2}\underline{T}^0\underline{\alpha} + \underline{z}_{m-1}(\mathbf{T} - (m-1)\mu\mathbf{I} + m\mu\mathbf{R}) = \underline{0}. \end{cases} \tag{8.43}$$

This system of linear equations is not of full rank, so we need the normalisation equation to reach a unique solution:

$$\begin{aligned} \sum_{i=0}^{\infty} \underline{z}_i \underline{1} &= \left( \sum_{i=0}^{m-2} \underline{z}_i \underline{1} \right) + \left( \sum_{i=m-1}^{\infty} \underline{z}_i \underline{1} \right) \\ &= \sum_{i=0}^{m-2} \underline{z}_i \underline{1} + \underline{z}_{m-1}(\mathbf{I} - \mathbf{R})^{-1}\underline{1} = 1. \end{aligned} \tag{8.44}$$

## 8.5   The caudal curve

A specially interesting result that can be obtained from the matrix $\mathbf{R}$ is the so-called *caudal curve*, which is the graph of the largest Eigenvalue of $\mathbf{R}$, denoted $\eta$, as a function of the utilisation $\rho$. The name caudal curve stems from the Latin *cauda*, meaning tail, a name that will become clear shortly. It has been shown that

$$\lim_{i \to \infty} \frac{\underline{z}_{i+1}\underline{1}}{\underline{z}_i\underline{1}} = \lim_{i \to \infty} \frac{\underline{z}_1 \mathbf{R}^i \underline{1}}{\underline{z}_1 \mathbf{R}^{i-1}\underline{1}} = \eta. \tag{8.45}$$

This means that for large $i$ the ratio of the relative amount of time spent at level $i+1$ compared to that at level $i$ is approximately equal to $\eta$. A similar result holds for any two corresponding elements of the probability vectors $\underline{z}_i$ and $\underline{z}_{i+1}$. Recalling that a level corresponds to the set of states for which the number of customers in the queue is the same, it is clear that (8.45) expresses the rate of decay of (the tail of) the queue length distribution. In a similar way, the equality

$$\Pr\{N_q > k\} = h\eta^k + o(\eta^k), \quad \text{for } k \to \infty, \tag{8.46}$$

holds, with $h$ a nonnegative constant. So, we observe that $\eta$ "rules" the rate of decrease of the steady-state queue length distribution. Knowledge of $\eta$ thus gives us insight into the tail of the queues.

Only for very few queueing systems can the caudal curve be obtained with little effort. For M|M|c queueing systems, we have $\mathbf{R} = (\rho)$, so that $\eta(\rho) = \rho$. We could regard an M|M|c queueing system as a reference queueing system.

For $E_r|E_r|1$ queueing systems, it can be derived that $\eta(\rho) = \rho^r$, which implies that $\eta(\rho) \leq \rho$. Intuitively, one might have expected the latter inequality. Erlang-$r$ distributions have a smaller coefficient of variation than exponential distributions. Less variance often implies better performance (smaller waiting times and smaller queues). Thus, $\eta$ can be expected to be smaller than $\rho$ because then there will be less probability mass for states representing longer queue lengths.

In a similar way, for an $H_2|M|1$ queueing system, the explicit solution for the caudal curve reveals that $\eta(\rho) \geq \rho$. By a suitable parameter choice for the 2-phase hyperexponential distribution, the caudal curve will increase very steeply to close to 1 in the interval $[0, h')$, and then increase very slowly to 1 in the interval $[h', 1]$, for small $h' > 0$ (see also [218]). Again, this is intuitively appealing since the hyperexponential distribution is known to introduce more randomness in the system, which often implies worse performance (longer queues and longer waiting times). A value of $\eta$ larger than $\rho$ will cause a shift in the queue length distribution towards states representing longer queues.

For more general queueing systems than those mentioned, the caudal curve $\eta(\rho)$ can best be computed numerically from $\mathbf{R}$. A practical method for that purpose is the Power method; it will be discussed after the following examples.

## Example 8.5. The $E_2|H_2|1$ queue (IV).
We present the values of the largest Eigenvalue $\eta$ of $\mathbf{R}$ as a function of $\rho$ in Table 8.3. As can be observed, for all utilisations, we have $\eta < \rho$. This means that the $E_2|H_2|1$ queue is a very "friendly" system, in the sense that it has a smaller tendency than the M|M|1 queue to build up long queues. □

## Example 8.6. The IPP$|E_k|1$ queue (II).
When we address the caudal curve of the IPP$|E_k|1$ queue, we find that despite the rather

| $2\lambda$ | $\rho$ | $\eta$ | $2\lambda$ | $\rho$ | $\eta$ | $2\lambda$ | $\rho$ | $\eta$ |
|---|---|---|---|---|---|---|---|---|
| 1 | 0.044 | 0.00836 | 2 | 0.088 | 0.02882 | 3 | 0.131 | 0.05705 |
| 4 | 0.175 | 0.09057 | 5 | 0.219 | 0.12788 | 6 | 0.263 | 0.16800 |
| 7 | 0.306 | 0.21018 | 8 | 0.350 | 0.25406 | 9 | 0.394 | 0.29928 |
| 10 | 0.436 | 0.34560 | 11 | 0.481 | 0.38288 | 12 | 0.525 | 0.44097 |
| 13 | 0.569 | 0.48979 | 14 | 0.613 | 0.53927 | 15 | 0.656 | 0.58936 |
| 16 | 0.700 | 0.64000 | 17 | 0.744 | 0.69117 | 18 | 0.786 | 0.74282 |
| 19 | 0.831 | 0.79495 | 20 | 0.875 | 0.84752 | 21 | 0.919 | 0.90051 |

Table 8.3: The values of $\eta$ against $\rho$ for the $E_2|H_2|1$ queue

deterministic arrivals, the value of $\eta$ is always at least as large as that of $\rho$. This implies that in this queue, there is a clear tendency towards states with more customers queued. As an example, when $b = 11$ and $k = 10$, we find $\eta = 0.9613$ in case $\rho = 0.7273$. Note that in both the examples the arrival process dominates the service process regarding the influence on the caudal curve.                                                                                                □

Let us now return to the actual computation of the caudal curve. The Eigenvalues of $\mathbf{R}$ are defined as those values $\lambda$ for which $\mathbf{R}\underline{x} = \lambda\underline{x}$ for any $\underline{x}$. To find them all, we have to find those values of $\lambda$ for which the determinant of $(\mathbf{R} - \lambda\mathbf{I})$ equals zero. When doing so, we have to solve the so-called characteristic polynomial, which is of the same order as the number of rows (and columns) in $\mathbf{R}$. If we have computed them all, we can select the largest one.

Instead of computing all the Eigenvalues, we can also compute the largest one only, via a numerical procedure known as the *Power method*. This method can be described as follows. We choose an initial row-vector $\underline{y}^0$ and successively compute

$$\underline{y}^{(k+1)} = \mathbf{R}\underline{y}^{(k-1)}. \qquad (8.47)$$

Suppose that the matrix $\mathbf{R}$ has $N$ Eigenvalues which can be ordered as follows: $|\eta| = |\eta_1| \geq |\eta_2| \geq \cdots \geq |\eta_N|$. We furthermore introduce an initial approximation vector $\underline{y}^{(0)}$ which can be written as a linear combination of the Eigenvectors $\underline{\nu}_i$ corresponding to $\eta_i$ $(i = 1, \cdots, N)$:

$$\underline{y}^{(0)} = \sum_{i=1}^{N} x_i \underline{\nu}_i. \qquad (8.48)$$

After $k$ iterations in the Power method, the resulting vector can be described as:

$$\underline{y}^{(k)} = \mathbf{R}^k \underline{y}^{(0)} = \sum_{i=1}^{N} x_i \eta_i^k \underline{\nu}_i = \eta_1^k \left( x_1 \underline{\nu}_1 + \sum_{i=2}^{N} x_i \left( \frac{\eta_i}{\eta_1} \right)^k \underline{\nu}_i \right). \tag{8.49}$$

The smaller the ratios $|\eta_i/\eta_1|$ $(i = 2, \cdots, N)$, the faster the summation on the right-hand side will turn to zero. For large $k$, what remains is the following approximation:

$$\underline{y}^{(k)} \approx \eta^k x_i \underline{\nu}_i, \tag{8.50}$$

so that the most-dominant Eigenvalue of $\mathbf{R}$ can be computed as the ratio of the $j$-th element in two successive vectors $\underline{y}^{(\cdot)}$:

$$\eta = \lim_{k \to \infty} \frac{y_j^{(k+1)}}{y_j^{(k)}}. \tag{8.51}$$

In practice, the iteration is continued until two successive approximations of $\eta$ differ less than some predefined value $\epsilon > 0$. Since $0 < \eta < 1$, the computation of $\underline{y}^{(k)}$ might lead to loss of accuracy if $k$ is large. To avoid this, the successive vectors $\underline{y}^{(k)}$ are often renormalised during the iteration process as follows:

$$\underline{y}^{(k+1)} = \frac{1}{l_{k-1}} \mathbf{R} \underline{y}^{(k-1)}, \tag{8.52}$$

where $l_{k-1} = \min_j \{ y_j^{(k-1)} \}$. This does not change the result since in the quotient that computes $\eta$ these factors cancel.

## 8.6 Other models with matrix-geometric solution

The queues of PH|PH|1 type we have addressed so far are not the only queueing models that can be solved using matrix-geometric methods. In this section we will briefly address other queueing models for which similar methods as those presented here can be applied.

First of all, we can use the QBD structure when we are dealing with queues of PH|PH|1 type, in a more general context. The QBD structure still exists when the arrival and service process are no longer renewal processes but they are still Markovian. This can best be understood by addressing an arrival process with multiple active modes; in each mode the (Poisson) arrival process may have a different rate. Mode changes in the arrival process can coincide with arrivals, but can also be dependent on another Markov chain, i.e., we deal with a Poisson process of which the rate is modulated by an independent Markov chain. At the service side, we can have a similar situation; we then often speak of a multi-mode server. General QBD models are very important in studying the performance aspects of communication systems subject to complex arrival streams and to systems with server breakdowns and repairs. However, their specification at the level of the block matrices constituting the Markov chain is cumbersome. Instead, one should use higher-level mechanisms to construct these models; we will see an example of such an approach in Chapter 17.

In the QBD models we have addressed in this chapter the state space has been unbounded in one direction. In other words, we have addressed system models with an infinite buffer. QBD models on a finite state space can be studied with similar means. For the M|PH|1 and the PH|M|1 queue, the matrix **R** that needs to be computed is in fact the same as the one that is computed in the unbounded case; the only difference lies in another normalisation equation. For general QBDs on a finite state space, we have to deal with two different boundaries of the state space (one corresponding to the empty system and one corresponding to the completely filled system). This most naturally leads to two second-order matrix equations that need to be solved, as well as two sets of boundary equations. The state probabilities $z_i$ can then be computed as the sum of two geometric terms.

A remark should be made here about another powerful solution method for queueing models with a QBD structure known as the *spectral expansion method*. Using this method, the global balance equations for the states in the repeating part of the CTMC are interpreted as a matrix-vector difference equation of second order. To solve this difference equation, a characteristic matrix polynomial has to be solved. Using an Eigenvalue analysis, the probability vectors for each level can be written as a sum of weighted Eigenvectors; the coefficients in the sum are given by powers of the Eigenvalues. Recent comparisons with the logarithmic reduction algorithm show favourable performance for the spectral expansion method in most cases [119].

Finally, queues of type G|M|1 and M|G|1 can be handled using matrix-geometric techniques. Studying these queues at arrival and departure instances, the embedded Markov chains have an upper and lower triangular form, respectively. In practice, this means that we have to deal with matrices $\mathbf{A}_i$ ($i \in \mathbb{N}$) in the repeating part of the Markov chain. This then leads to the following non-linear equation that needs to be solved (for the M|G|1 case):

$$\mathbf{R} = \sum_{i=0}^{\infty} \mathbf{R}^i \mathbf{A}_i. \tag{8.53}$$

Special variants of the successive substitution and logarithmic reduction algorithm then have to be used to compute $\mathbf{R}$. The solution of the boundary probabilities and the probability vectors $\underline{z}_i$ remain as we have seen.

## 8.7    Further reading

Despite their great applicability and their numerically attractiveness, only a few books on model-based performance evaluation of computer-communication systems address matrix-geometric methods, all very concisely; most notably are [117, 152, 156, 216]. The tutorial paper by Nelson provides a good introduction [215]. Background information can be found in the books by Neuts [217, 219] and in many mathematical journals; a seminal paper has been written by Evans [85]. Matrix-geometric analyses of queues subject to complex arrival processes, such as Markov-modulated arrival processes, can be found in [89, 187]. Surveys on algorithms to solve for the matrix $\mathbf{R}$ can be found in [172, 188]. The logarithmic-reduction algorithm has been published by Latouche and Ramaswami [173]. Information on the caudal curve can be found in [218]. The spectral expansion method has been advocated by Daigle and Lucantoni [71] and Mitrani *et al.* [203]; a comparison with the logarithmic reduction method has been performed by Haverkort and Ost [119]. Finite QBD models have been discussed by various authors as well. Gün and Makowski [114], Bocharov and Naoumov [24] and Wagner *et al.* [282] present a matrix-geometric solution. Chakka and Mitrani use the spectral expansion method also for these models [39] whereas Ye and Li recently proposed a new (and fast) folding algorithm [293].

## 8.8    Exercises

**8.1. The $E_k|M|1$ queue.**
For the $E_k|M|1$ queue with $k > 1$:

1. Draw the state-transition diagram.

2. Find the matrices $\mathbf{A}_i$.

3. Given the specific form of the matrices $\mathbf{A}_i$, what will be the form of $\mathbf{R}$?

4. For $k = 2$, $\lambda = 10$ (rate per arrival phase), $\mu = 10$ (service rate) and compute $E[N]$ for this queueing model. Compare your results with those obtained via the Laplace-transform approach for the $G|M|1$ queue (see Chapter 7).

## 8.2. The IPP|M|1 queue.

Consider an IPP|M|1 queue with arrival rate $\lambda$, service rate $\mu$ and on- and off-rates $\gamma_{0,1}$ and $\gamma_{1,0}$.

1. Draw the state transition diagram.

2. Recognise the block matrices $\mathbf{A}_i$ and $\mathbf{B}_{ij}$.

3. Compute the matrix $\mathbf{R}$ for suitable numerical values of the model parameters.

4. Recognise the boundary blocks $\mathbf{B}_{ij}$ and solve the boundary equations.

## 8.3. An M|M|1 queue with slow-starting server.

Consider an M|M|1 queueing system in which the server only starts working when at least $T = 3$ customers are queued. Once it is serving customers, it continues to do so until the queue is empty. The job arrival rate $\lambda = 2$ and the service rate $\mu = 3$.

1. Define the state space $\mathcal{I}$ of the QBD underlying this model.

2. Draw the state-transition diagram.

3. Recognise the QBD structure and the block matrices $\mathbf{A}_i$ and $\mathbf{B}_{ij}$.

4. Compute $\mathbf{R}$. Does the value of $\mathbf{R}$ surprise you?

5. Compute the boundary probabilities.

6. Show that $E[N] = 3$ in this slow-starting M|M|1 queue. For a normal M|M|1 queue, i.e., with $T = 1$, we would find that $E[N] = 2$. Explain the difference.

## 8.4. Two queues in series.

Consider a system that can be modelled as a tandem of two queues. At queue 1 jobs arrive as a Poisson process with rate $\lambda$ and are served with rate $\mu_1$. After service at queue 1, jobs are transferred to queue 2. The service rate of queue 2 is $\mu_2$. The number of customers that can be held in queue 2 is limited to $K$ (in queue 1 this number is not limited). Whenever queue 2 is completely filled, the service process in queue 1 is stopped, in order to avoid a customer ready at queue 1 being unable to move into queue 2. This form of blocking at queue 1, due to a full successor queue is known as communication blocking. The model sketched so far can be regarded as a QBD.

1. Define the state space $\mathcal{I}$.

2. Draw the state-transition diagram.

3. Define the block matrices $\mathbf{A}_i$ and $\mathbf{B}_{ij}$.

### 8.5. Exponential polling systems with 2 stations.

Consider a two-station polling model (see also Chapter 9) with arrival, service and switch-over rates $\lambda_i$, $\mu_i$ and $\delta_i$ respectively ($i = 1, 2$). The service strategy is exhaustive in both stations. Furthermore, the queue at station 1 has infinite capacity, the queue at station 2 is bounded to $K$ customers.

1. Define the state space $\mathcal{I}$ of this Markovian polling model.

2. Draw the state-transition diagram for $K = 1$.

3. Indicate how a matrix-geometric solution can be performed (define the matrices $\mathbf{A}_i$ and $\mathbf{B}_{ij}$).

4. Indicate the changes in the model and matrices when both stations are served according to the 1-limited strategy.

# Chapter 9

# Polling models

T HE principle of polling is well-known in many branches of computer science applications. In early timed-sharing computers, terminals were polled in order to investigate
whether they had any processing to be done. These days, intelligent workstations access
file or computing servers via a shared communication medium that grants access using a
polling scheme. Also in other fields, e.g., manufacturing, logistics and maintenance, the
principle of polling is often encountered.

When trying to analyse systems that operate along some polling scheme, so-called
polling models are needed. In this chapter we provide a concise overview of the theory and
application of polling models. Although we do provide some mathematical derivations,
our main aim is to show how relatively simple models can be used, albeit sometimes
approximately, for the analysis of fairly complex systems.

This chapter is further organised as follows. In Section 9.1 we characterise polling
models and introduce notation and terminology. In Section 9.2 we address some important
general results for polling models. Symmetric and asymmetric count-based polling models
are addressed in Section 9.3 and 9.4 respectively. Using these models, the IBM token
ring system is analysed in Section 9.5. Time-based polling models, both symmetric and
asymmetric, are finally discussed in Section 9.6.

## 9.1 Characterisation of polling models

In polling models, there is a single server which visits (polls) a number of queues in some
predefined order. Customers arrive at the queues following some arrival process. Upon
visiting a particular queue, queued customers are being served according to some scheduling
strategy. After that, the server leaves the queue and visits the next queue. Going from

one queue to another takes some time which is generally called the switch-over time.

In the above description a number of issues have deliberately been left unspecified. It is these issues that, once specified, characterise the polling model. In particular, the visit ordering of the server to the queues and the strategy being used to decide how long a particular queue receives service before the server leaves, characterise the model. These issues will be addressed in Section 9.1.2 and 9.1.3 respectively after some preliminary notation and terminology has been introduced in Section 9.1.1.

### 9.1.1   Basic terminology

We will assume that we deal with a polling model with $N$ stations, modelled by queues $Q_1$ through $Q_N$. We use queue indices $i, j \in \{1, \cdots, N\}$. At queue $i$ customers arrive according to a Poisson process with rate $\lambda_i$. The mean and second moment of the service requirement of customers arriving at queue $i$ is $E[S_i]$ and $E[S_i^2]$ respectively. The total offered load is given by $\rho = \sum_{i=1}^{N} \rho_i$, with $\rho_i = \lambda_i E[S_i]$. The mean and variance of the time needed by the server to switch from queue $i$ to queue $j$ are denoted $\delta_{i,j}$ and $\delta_{i,j}^{(2)}$ respectively.

When the queues are assumed to be unbounded, under stability conditions, the throughput of each queue equals the arrival rate of customers at each queue. The main performance measure of interest is then the customer waiting time for queue $i$, i.e., $W_i$. Most analytic models only provide insight into the average waiting time $E[W_i]$. When the queues are bounded, the throughput and blocking probability at the stations are also of interest; we will come back to finite-buffer polling models in Chapter 16.

### 9.1.2   The visit order

We distinguish three different visit orders: a cyclic ordering, a Markovian ordering and an ordering via a polling table.

- **Cyclic polling.** In a cyclic visiting scheme, after having served queue $i$, the server continues to poll station $i \oplus 1$ where $\oplus$ is the modulo-$N$ addition operator such that $N \oplus 1 = 1$. As a consequence of this deterministic visit ordering only "neighbouring" switch-over times and variances are possibly non-zero, i.e., $\delta_{i,j} = \delta_{i,j}^{(2)} = 0$ whenever $j \neq i \oplus 1$. For ease of notation we set $\delta_i = \delta_{i,i\oplus 1}$ and $\delta_i^{(2)} = \delta_{i,i\oplus 1}^{(2)}$. The mean and variance of the total switch-over time, defined as the total time spent switching during a cycle in which all stations are visited once, are given by $\Delta = \sum_{i=1}^{N} \delta_i$ and $\Delta^{(2)} = \sum_{i=1}^{N} \delta_i^{(2)}$ respectively. In Figure 9.1 we show a polling model with cyclic visit ordering.

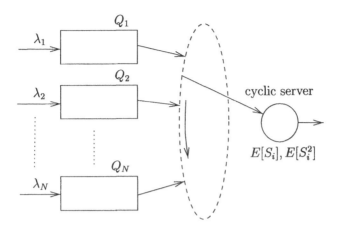

Figure 9.1: Basic polling model with cyclic visit ordering

Due to the fact that most, and especially the earlier, results on polling models assumed the cyclic visit order, polling models are often called cyclic server models. This, however, is a slight abuse of terminology: the class of polling models is larger, as discussed below.

- **Markovian polling.** In a Markovian polling scheme, after having polled queue $i$, the server switches to poll queue $j$ with probability $p_{i,j}$. Since the probabilities $p_{i,j}$ are independent of the state of the polling model this form of polling is called Markovian polling. The probabilities are gathered in an $N \times N$ matrix $\mathbf{P}$. The mean and variance of the total switch-over time are now defined as $\Delta = \sum_{i=1}^{N} \sum_{j=1}^{N} p_{i,j} \delta_{i,j}$ and $\Delta^{(2)} = \sum_{i=1}^{N} \sum_{j=1}^{N} p_{i,j} \delta_{i,j}^{(2)}$ respectively.

  Notice that the degenerate case of Markovian polling in which $p_{i,i\oplus1} = 1$ and $p_{i,j} = 0$ $(j \neq i \oplus 1)$ is equivalent to a polling model with a cyclic visit ordering.

- **Tabular polling.** Finally, an ordering via a polling table $T = (T_1, T_2, \cdots, T_M)$ establishes a cyclic visit ordering of the server along the queues; however, these cycles may contain multiple visits to the same queue. The server starts with visiting queue $Q_{T_1}$, then goes to $Q_{T_2}$, etc. After having visited $Q_{T_M}$ the server visits $Q_{T_1}$ again and a new cycle starts.

  Typically, when the polling process is controlled in a centralised way, a polling table is used, e.g., when station 1 actively controls the system, we have $T = (1, 2, 1, 3, 1, 4, \cdots, 1, N - 1, 1, N)$. Also the scan-polling order can be observed quite frequently:

$T = (1, 2, 3, \cdots, N-1, N, N, N-1, N-2, \cdots, 2, 1)$, e.g., when the queues model disk tracks that are visited by a moving disk head.

The mean and variance of the total switch-over time are now defined as $\Delta = \sum_{k=1}^{M} \delta_{T_k, T_{k\oplus 1}}$ and $\Delta^{(2)} = \sum_{k=1}^{M} \delta^{(2)}_{T_k, T_{k\oplus 1}}$ respectively. Note that the $\oplus$-operator is now defined on $\{1, \cdots, M\}$.

Whenever $T = (1, 2, \cdots, N)$, i.e., $M = N$, a polling model with polling table $T$ is equivalent to a polling model with a cyclic visit ordering.

## 9.1.3   The scheduling strategy

The scheduling strategy defines how long or how many customers are served by the server once it visits a particular queue. Two main streams in scheduling strategies can be distinguished: count-based scheduling and time-based scheduling.

**Count-based scheduling.** With count-based scheduling the maximum amount of service that is granted during one visit of the server at a particular queue is based on the *number of customers* served in the polling period. Among the well-known scheduling disciplines are the following (for a more complete survey, see [286, Chapter 1]):

- **Exhaustive (E):** the server continuously serves a queue until it is empty;

- **Gated (G):** the server only serves those customers that were already in the queue at the time the service started (the polling instant);

- **$k$-limited ($k$-L):** each queue is served until it is emptied, or until $k$ customers have been served, whichever occurs first. The case where $k = 1$ is often mentioned separately as it results in simpler models;

- **Decrementing or semi-exhaustive (D):** when the server finds at least one customer at the queue it starts serving the queue until there is one customer less in the queue than at the polling instant;

- **Bernoulli (B):** when the server finds at least one customer in the queue it serves that customer; with probability $b_i \in (0, 1]$ an extra customer is served, after which, again with probability $b_i$ another one is served, etc.;

- **Binomial (Bi):** when the server finds $k_i$ customers in queue $i$ at the polling instant, the number of customers served in the current service period is binomially distributed with parameters $k_i$ and $b_i \in (0, 1]$.

All of the above strategies are local, i.e., they are determined per queue. One can also imagine global count-based strategies. For instance, the global-gated strategy marks all jobs present at the beginning of a polling cycle. During that cycle all of those jobs are served exhaustively. Jobs arriving during the current cycle are saved for the next cycle.

**Time-based scheduling.** With time-based scheduling the maximum amount of service that is granted during one visit of the server at a particular queue is based on the *time already spent* at that queue. Two basic variants exist:

- **Local time-based:** the server continues to serve a particular queue until either all customers have been served or until some local timer, which has been started at the polling instant, expires;

- **Global time-based:** the server continues to serve a particular queue until either all customers have been served or until some global timer, which might have been started when the server last left the queue, expires.

In fact, the first mechanism can be found in the IBM token ring (IEEE P802.5) [35] whereas the second one can be found in FDDI [35, 277, 284].

## 9.2  Cyclic polling: cycle time and conservation law

In this section we restrict ourselves to polling models with a cyclic visit order and a mixture of count-based scheduling strategies (exhaustive, 1-limited, gated and/or decrementing).
    The mean cycle time $E[C]$ is defined as the average time between two successive polling instants at a particular queue. $E[C]$ is independent of $i$, also for asymmetric systems. This can easily be shown using the following conservation argument. Assuming that the service discipline is exhaustive, one cycle consists, on average, of the servicing of all jobs plus the total switch-over time. The latter component equals $\Delta = \sum_i \delta_i$. In one cycle all the jobs that arrive at station $i$, i.e., $\lambda_i E[C]$ jobs, have to be served. This requires, for the $i$-th station $\lambda_i E[C] E[S_i]$ time units. Thus we have:

$$E[C] = \sum_{i=1}^{N} \delta_i + \sum_{i=1}^{N} \lambda_i E[C] E[S_i] = \Delta + E[C]\rho \Rightarrow E[C] = \frac{\Delta}{1 - \rho}. \tag{9.1}$$

This result is also valid when the service discipline is other than exhaustive. The average service period $E[P_i]$ for queue $i$ can be derived as

$$E[P_i] = \lambda_i E[C] E[S_i] = \frac{\rho_i \Delta}{1 - \rho}. \tag{9.2}$$

This equation follows from the fact that for stability reasons, on average, everything that arrives in one cycle at station $i$, must be servable in one cycle. For the average time between the departure of the server from station $i$ and the next arrival at station $i$, the so-called *inter-visit time* $I_i$, we have

$$E[I_i] = E[C] - E[P_i] = \frac{(1 - \rho_i)\Delta}{1 - \rho}. \tag{9.3}$$

Important to note is that upon the arrival of a job at station $i$, the average time until the server reaches that station is *not* $E[I_i]/2$. This is due to the fact that $I_i$ is a random variable, and we thus have an example of the waiting time paradox. The average time until the next server visit therefore equals the residual inter-visit time $E[I_i^2]/2E[I_i]$. Notice that, in general, an explicit expression for $E[I_i^2]$ is not available.

The (cyclic) polling models we address are generally *not work conserving*, that is, there are situations in which there is work to be done (the queues are non empty) but in which the server does no real work since it is switching from one queue to another. When the switching times are zero, the polling model would have been work conserving and *Kleinrock's conservation law* would apply ([160]; see also Chapters 5 and 6 on M|G|1 queues):

$$\sum_{i=1}^{N} \rho_i E[W_i] = \rho \frac{\sum_{i=1}^{N} \lambda_i E[S_i^2]}{2(1 - \rho)}. \tag{9.4}$$

Because $\rho_i E[W_i] = \lambda_i E[S_i] \times E[N_{q,i}]/\lambda_i = E[N_{q,i}]E[S_i]$, the left-hand side of (9.4) is often called the amount of work in the system. Independent of how the queues are visited, this amount always equals the steady-state amount of work in a model in which the service order is FCFS (the right-hand side of (9.4)). If we have only one station ($N = 1$) and zero switch-over times, we obtain a normal (work conserving) M|G|1 queue, and the right-hand side of (9.4) is just the expected waiting time in the M|G|1 model. When we have only one station with exhaustive service but now with positive switch-over times, we obtain a queue with multiple server vacations.

When the model is not work conserving, that is, when the switch-over times are positive, Kleinrock's conservation law does not hold anymore. It has, however, been shown by Boxma *et al.* [28, 27, 112] that a so-called *pseudo-conservation law* still does hold. This pseudo-conservation law is based on the principle of work decomposition:

$$\hat{V} = V + Y, \tag{9.5}$$

where $\hat{V}$ is a random variable indicating the steady-state amount of work in the model with positive switch-over times, $V$ is a random variable indicating the steady-state amount of work in the model when the switch-over times are set to 0, and $Y$ is a random variable indicating the steady-state amount of work in the model at an arbitrary switch-over instance. The principle of work decomposition is valid for cyclic polling models as well as for polling models with Markovian routing or a polling table. $V$ is totally independent of the scheduling discipline, whereas $Y$ and therefore $\hat{V}$ are dependent on the scheduling. Intuitively, one expects $Y$ and $\hat{V}$ to decrease if the switch-over times decrease, if the visit order becomes more efficient or if the scheduling becomes "more exhaustive". In particular, for polling models with non-zero switch-over times (with cyclic, tabular or Markovian visit ordering) a pseudo-conservation law of the following form applies:

$$E[\hat{V}] = \sum_{i=1}^{N} \rho_i E[W_i] = \rho \frac{\sum_{i=1}^{N} \lambda_i E[S_i^2]}{2(1-\rho)} + E[Y]. \tag{9.6}$$

When we are dealing with a cyclic polling order, one has:

$$\sum_{i \in E,G} \frac{\rho_i}{\rho} E[W_i] + \sum_{i \in L} \frac{\rho_i}{\rho} \left(1 - \frac{\lambda_i \Delta}{1-\rho}\right) E[W_i] + \sum_{i \in D} \frac{\rho_i}{\rho} \left(1 - \frac{\lambda_i(1-\rho_i)\Delta}{1-\rho}\right) E[W_i] =$$
$$= \frac{\sum_{i=1}^{N} \lambda_i E[S_i^2]}{2(1-\rho)} + \frac{\Delta^{(2)}}{2\Delta} + \frac{\Delta(\rho - \sum_{i=1}^{N} \rho_i^2)}{2\rho(1-\rho)} + \frac{\Delta \sum_{i \in G,L} \rho_i^2}{\rho(1-\rho)} - \frac{\Delta \sum_{i \in D} \rho_i \lambda_i^2 E[S_i^2]}{2\rho(1-\rho)}, \tag{9.7}$$

where $E$, $G$, $L$, and $D$ are the index sets of the queues with an exhaustive, a gated, a 1-limited and a decrementing scheduling discipline, respectively. Clearly, the pseudo-conservation law expresses that the sum of the waiting times at the queues, weighted by their relative utilisations (for $E$ and $G$ directly and with more complex factors for $L$ and $D$) equals a constant.

The pseudo-conservation law does not give explicit expressions for the individual mean waiting times since it is only one equation with as many unknowns as there are stations. Nevertheless, it does provide insight into system operation and in the efficiency of scheduling strategies. Also, it can be used as a basis for approximations or to verify simulation results (see below).

It is interesting to study the stability conditions for cyclic server models. For cyclic server models with an exhaustive or a gated service discipline a necessary and sufficient condition is $\rho < 1$. For models with a 1-limited service strategy, a necessary condition can be derived as follows. The mean number of customers arriving at station $i$ per cycle equals $\lambda_i E[C]$. This number must be smaller than 1, as there is only 1 customer served per cycle. Using the fact that $E[C] = \Delta/(1-\rho)$, the necessary stability condition equals $\rho + \lambda_i \Delta < 1$, for all $i$. For models with a decrementing scheduling strategy a necessary stability condition of the form $\rho + \lambda_i(1-\rho_i)\Delta < 1$, for all $i$, can be derived.

**Example 9.1. A 2-station asymmetric polling model (I).**

Consider an asymmetric polling model with 2 stations: station 1 has exhaustive scheduling and station 2 1-limited scheduling. Furthermore, the following parameters apply: $E[S_i] = 0.4$, $E[S_i^2] = 0.32$, $\lambda_i = 1$, $\delta_i = 0.05$ and $\delta_i^{(2)} = 0$ for $i = 1, 2$. Clearly, the stability conditions are satisfied so finite average waiting times do exist for both stations. We are not in the position to compute $E[W_1]$ and $E[W_2]$ directly; however, we can apply the pseudo-conservation law, yielding the following relation between $E[W_1]$ and $E[W_2]$:

$$E[W_1] + \frac{1}{2}E[W_2] = 3.7. \tag{9.8}$$

This linear relation can be drawn in the $E[W_1]$–$E[W_2]$ plane; the exact solutions for $E[W_1]$ and $E[W_2]$ have to lie on this line.                                                          □

## 9.3   Count-based symmetric cyclic polling models

When we address models in which all the scheduling disciplines and parameters are station independent, we can obtain closed-form results for the average waiting times by using the pseudo-conservation law, since in a fully symmetric system all the average waiting times are equal to one another so that we are left with only one unknown in (9.7). We will not use this approach here, since it does not provide us much insight into the actual system operation. Instead, we will derive the expected waiting time in a fully symmetric exhaustive scheduling polling model in an operational way, following the lines of the proofs for the expected waiting times in the M|G|1 and related queues as presented in Chapters 5 and 6.

For an exhaustive count-based symmetric polling model, the expected waiting time for an arriving customer can be thought to consist of 4 components:

$$E[W] = E[W_1] + E[W_2] + E[W_3] + E[W_4], \tag{9.9}$$

where the 4 components can be understood as follows:

1. An arriving customer will, due to the PASTA property, find another customer (at some queue) in service with probability $\rho$. The remaining service time of this customer equals $E[S^2]/2E[S]$.

2. Similarly, with probability $1 - \rho$ an arriving customer will find the server switching from one queue to another. The remaining switch-over time equals $\delta^2/2\delta$ (notice that $\delta^{(2)}$ denotes the variance in switch-over times, whereas $\delta^2$ denotes the second moment of the switch-over time here).

3. An arriving job arrives at any queue with equal probability, so on average $(N-1)/2$ switch-overs, each of expected length $\delta$, are needed for the server to arrive at the particular queue (since the number of queues $N$ is a constant, the waiting time paradox does not apply).

4. Finally, upon arrival of a customer, the steady-state amount of work in the system equals $NE[N_q]E[S]$. In equilibrium, this amount of work should be handled before the randomly arriving customer is served.

Adding these 4 components, we have:

$$E[W] = (1-\rho)\frac{\delta^2}{2\delta} + \frac{N-1}{2}\delta + \rho\frac{E[S^2]}{2E[S]} + NE[N_q]E[S].\tag{9.10}$$

Using Little's law to rewrite $E[N_q] = \lambda E[W]$, we obtain

$$(1-\rho)E[W] = (1-\rho)\frac{\delta^2}{2\delta} + \frac{N-1}{2}\delta + \rho\frac{E[S^2]}{2E[S]}$$

$$\Rightarrow E[W] = \frac{\delta^2}{2\delta} + \frac{N-1}{2(1-\rho)}\delta + N\lambda E[S]\frac{E[S^2]}{2(1-\rho)E[S]}.\tag{9.11}$$

We can rewrite the first two additive terms as follows:

$$\frac{\delta^2}{2\delta} + \frac{N-1}{2(1-\rho)}\delta = \frac{\delta^{(2)}}{2\delta} + \frac{(N-\rho)\delta}{2(1-\rho)},\tag{9.12}$$

so that we have

$$E[W_E] = \frac{\delta^{(2)}}{2\delta} + \frac{N\lambda E[S^2] + \delta(N-\rho)}{2(1-\rho)}.\tag{9.13}$$

The subscript 'E' is added to indicate that the formula is valid for exhaustive scheduling. Along the above lines, one can also derive the mean waiting time when all scheduling strategies are of gated type:

$$E[W_G] = \frac{\delta^{(2)}}{2\delta} + \frac{N\lambda E[S^2] + \delta(N+\rho)}{2(1-\rho)}.\tag{9.14}$$

For the 1-limited scheduling discipline we have:

$$E[W_L] = \frac{\delta^{(2)}}{2\delta} + \frac{N\lambda E[S^2] + \delta(N+\rho) + N\lambda\delta^{(2)}}{2(1-\rho-N\lambda\delta)}.\tag{9.15}$$

Finally, for the decrementing scheduling discipline we have:

$$E[W_D] = \frac{\delta^{(2)}}{2\delta} + \frac{N\lambda E[S^2](1-\lambda\delta) + (N-\rho)(\delta+\lambda\delta^{(2)})}{2(1-\rho-\lambda\delta(N-\rho))}.\tag{9.16}$$

| $\rho$ | $E[W_E]$ | $E[W_G]$ | $E[W_L]$ | $E[W_D]$ | $\rho$ | $E[W_E]$ | $E[W_G]$ | $E[W_L]$ | $E[W_D]$ |
|------|--------|--------|--------|--------|------|--------|--------|--------|--------|
| 0.05 | 0.6000 | 0.6053 | 0.6085 | 0.6031 | 0.55 | 1.711 | 1.833 | 2.089 | 1.931 |
| 0.15 | 0.7176 | 0.7353 | 0.7485 | 0.7302 | 0.65 | 2.314 | 2.500 | 3.070 | 2.793 |
| 0.25 | 0.8667 | 0.9000 | 0.9310 | 0.8953 | 0.75 | 3.400 | 3.700 | 5.286 | 4.690 |
| 0.35 | 1.062 | 1.115 | 1.179 | 1.119 | 0.85 | 5.933 | 6.500 | 15.00 | 12.27 |
| 0.45 | 1.327 | 1.409 | 1.535 | 1.428 | 0.95 | 18.60 | 20.50 | - | - |

Table 9.1: $E[W]$ in symmetric polling models with exhaustive, gated, 1-limited, and decrementing scheduling

From these explicit formulae, the earlier derived stability conditions can also easily be seen; they correspond to those traffic conditions where the right-hand denominator becomes zero. From these expressions, it can also be observed that

$$E[W_E] \leq E[W_G] \leq E[W_L], \quad \text{and} \quad E[W_E] \leq E[W_D] \leq E[W_L], \tag{9.17}$$

and

$$E[W_G] > E[W_D] \quad \text{(at low load)}, \quad \text{and} \quad E[W_G] < E[W_D] \quad \text{(at high load)}. \tag{9.18}$$

**Example 9.2. Symmetric polling models: influence of scheduling.**
In Table 9.1 we have tabulated the average waiting times for symmetric polling models with exhaustive, gated, 1-limited, and decrementing scheduling strategies for increasing utilisation (established by increasing the arrival rate). The other parameters are: $N = 10$, $\delta = 0.1$, $\delta^{(2)} = 0.01$, $E[S] = 1.0$, and $E[S^2] = 1.0$. The above inequalities can easily be observed. Also notice that for $\rho = 0.95$, the 1-limited and decrementing systems are already overloaded. □

The fact that the exhaustive scheduling discipline is the most efficient can easily be understood. It simply does not spoil its time for switching purposes when there is still work to do, i.e., when the queue it is serving still is not empty. The gated and decrementing discipline, however, sometimes take time to switch when there are still customers in the current queue. This counts even more for the 1-limited case where every service is effectively lengthened with the succeeding switch-over time. The fact that the amount of switching overhead per customer is smallest with an exhaustive scheduling strategy does not necessarily imply that it is also the best. From a fairness point of view, the other disciplines might be considered better since they prevent one station from totally hogging the system.

**Example 9.3. A 2-station asymmetric polling model (II).**
Reconsider the asymmetric polling model addressed before. Since station 2 uses a 1-limited scheduling strategy, station 1 profits from this as it receives more opportunities to serve customers. In fact, $E[W_1]$ should be smaller in the mixed scheduling case than when both stations would have exhaustive scheduling. In this latter symmetric case, however, we can exactly compute the average waiting times: $E[W_{1,2}] = 1.75$. So, in the asymmetric case station 1 is expected to perform better, i.e., $E[W_1] \leq 1.75$. This implies, by the pseudo-conservation law derived for this example, that in the asymmetric case station 2 will suffer more, i.e., $E[W_2] \geq 3.9$.

We can improve on the above bounds by considering the case where the arrival rate of station 2 is set to zero. In that case, the model reduces to an M|G|1 queue with exhaustive service and multiple vacations (as seen from station 1) because at station 2 no jobs arrive. Thus, after the queue in station 1 empties, the server switches to queue 2 and directly back to queue 1. This switching can be interpreted as a vacation with average length 0.1 (two switches of length 0.05). The variance of the switching (vacation) time is 0, so that we can compute $E[W_1]$ using (5.38) as follows:

$$E[W_1] = \frac{E[V^2]}{2E[V]} + \frac{\lambda E[S^2]}{2(1-\rho)} = \frac{0.1}{2} + \frac{0.32}{2(1-0.4)} = 0.317. \tag{9.19}$$

We thus have: $0.317 \leq E[W_1] \leq 1.75$ and, using the pseudo-conservation law again, $3.9 \leq E[W_2] \leq 6.766$. □

# 9.4 Count-based asymmetric cyclic polling models

The analysis of asymmetric cyclic server models is much more complicated than the analysis of symmetric models. We will present the exact analysis of an asymmetric cyclic polling model with exhaustive service in Section 9.4.1 followed by a number of approximate results derived by using the pseudo-conservation law in Section 9.4.2.

## 9.4.1 Exhaustive service: exact analysis

In the exhaustive asymmetric case the average waiting time $E[W_i]$ perceived at station $i$ has the following form (see also (5.38) for the M|G|1 queue with server vacations in

Chapter 5):

$$E[W_{E,i}] = \frac{E[I_i^2]}{2E[I_i]} + \frac{\lambda_i E[S_i^2]}{2(1 - \rho_i)}, \tag{9.20}$$

where we recognise as the first term the residual inter-visit time, i.e., the average time it costs for the server to arrive at the station. The second term is simply the M|G|1 waiting time applied for station $i$ only. Since the scheduling discipline is exhaustive, once the server is at station $i$, we can analyse station $i$ in isolation as if it were an M|G|1 queue. The second term can readily be computed. $E[I_i]$ directly follows from (9.3). The only problem we have in evaluating $E[W_{E,i}]$ is the determination of $E[I_i^2]$; it has been derived by Ferguson and Aminetzah [88] as:

$$E[I_i^2] = E[I_i]^2 + \delta_{i-1}^{(2)} + \frac{1 - \rho_i}{\rho} \sum_{j \neq i} r_{i,j}, \tag{9.21}$$

where the coefficients $r_{i,j}$ $(i, j = 1, \cdots, N)$ follow from a system of $N^2$ linear equations:

$$r_{i,j} = \begin{cases} \frac{\rho_i}{1-\rho_i} \left( \sum_{m=i+1}^{N} r_{j,m} + \sum_{m=1}^{j-1} r_{j,m} + \sum_{m=j}^{i-1} r_{m,j} \right), & j < i, \\ \frac{\rho_i}{1-\rho_i} \left( \sum_{m=i+1}^{j-1} r_{j,m} + \sum_{m=j}^{N} r_{m,j} + \sum_{m=1}^{i-1} r_{m,j} \right), & j > i, \\ \frac{\delta_{i-1}^{(2)}}{(1-\rho_i)^2} + \frac{\lambda_i E[S_i^2] E[I_i]}{(1-\rho_i)^3} + \frac{\rho_i}{1-\rho_i} \cdot \sum_{j \neq i} r_{i,j}, & j = i. \end{cases} \tag{9.22}$$

A similar solution exists for gated systems. For $k$-limited and decrementing systems such solution schemes do not exist. For these cases, one has to resort to approximate solutions.

## 9.4.2   Some approximate results

For most asymmetric system models, exact results do not (yet) exist. For these cases, there is a wide variety of approximate results, some of which we will present here. The pseudo-conservation law plays an important role in the construction of these approximations, by the use of the following three-step approach:

1. The expected waiting time for queue $i$, $E[W_i]$, is expressed in terms of the expected residual cycle time $E[\tilde{R}_i] = E[I_i^2]/2E[I_i]$ (for the congestion due to traffic at other queues) and some local parameters (for the congestion at queue $i$, e.g., in the form of an M|G|1 result). As a result, $E[W_i]$ is expressed as a function of known parameters and the unknown parameter $E[\tilde{R}_i]$, similar to (9.20).

2. It is then *assumed* that the residual inter-visit times are equal for all the stations, i.e., $E[\tilde{R}_i] = E[\tilde{R}]$, for all $i$. This assumption has been shown to be less accurate when the system becomes more asymmetric and when the variance of the switch-over

times increases. The resulting expressions for $E[W_i]$ are substituted in the pseudo-conservation law in which, due to the assumption just made, only one unknown remains, being $E[\tilde{R}]$. This yields an explicit expression for $E[\tilde{R}]$.

3. The results of Steps 1 and 2 are combined to obtain explicit expressions for all the $E[W_i]$.

Using this approach, for a mixture of exhaustive and gated scheduling disciplines, the following result has been derived by Everitt [86]:

$$E[W_{E,G,i}] \approx (1 \pm \rho_i)\frac{\Delta}{2(1-\rho)}\left(1 + \frac{\rho}{\sum_{j=1}^{N}\rho_j(1\pm\rho_j)}\left(\frac{(1-\rho)\Delta^{(2)}}{\Delta^2} + \frac{\sum_{j=1}^{N}\lambda_j E[S_j^2]}{\Delta}\right)\right).$$
(9.23)

For the gated scheduling discipline the $+$ sign should be taken, whereas for the exhaustive scheduling discipline the $-$ sign holds.

Similarly, for an asymmetric 1-limited model, the following approximation has been derived by Boxma and Meister [28]:

$$
\begin{aligned}
E[W_{L,i}] &\approx \frac{1-\rho+\rho_i}{1-\rho-\lambda_i\Delta} \times \frac{1-\rho}{(1-\rho)\rho+\sum_{i=1}^{N}\rho_i^2} \\
&\times \left(\frac{\rho\Delta^{(2)}}{2\Delta} + \frac{\rho}{2(1-\rho)}\sum_{i=1}^{N}\lambda_i E[S_i^2] + \frac{\Delta}{2(1-\rho)}\sum_{i=1}^{N}\rho_i(1+\rho_i)\right).
\end{aligned}
$$
(9.24)

An iterative and more accurate solution procedure for asymmetric 1-limited models has been proposed by Groenendijk [112, Section 7.2.3].

For models in which a mixture of exhaustive, gated, and 1-limited scheduling disciplines exists, the following approximation has been proposed by Groenendijk [111]. First set

$$E[W_{E,i}] = (1-\rho_i)E[\tilde{R}], \quad E[W_{G,i}] = (1+\rho_i)E[\tilde{R}], \quad E[W_{L,i}] = \frac{1-\rho+\rho_i}{1-\rho-\lambda_i\Delta}E[\tilde{R}], \quad (9.25)$$

where $E[\tilde{R}]$ approximates the mean, scheduling dependent, residual cycle time. Substituting this result in the pseudo-conservation law yields:

$$E[\tilde{R}] \approx \frac{\frac{\rho\sum_{j=1}^{N}\lambda_j E[S_j^2]}{2(1-\rho)} + \frac{\rho\Delta^{(2)}}{2\Delta} + \frac{\Delta(\rho-\sum_{j=1}^{N}\rho_j^2)}{2(1-\rho)} + \frac{\Delta\sum_{j\in G,L}\rho_j^2}{1-\rho}}{\sum_{j\in E}\rho_j(1-\rho_j) + \sum_{j\in G}\rho_j(1+\rho_j) + \sum_{j\in L}\rho_j\frac{1-\rho+\rho_j}{1-\rho}}.$$
(9.26)

**Example 9.4. A 2-station asymmetric polling model (III).**

Reconsider the asymmetric polling model addressed before. Using the above approximation we calculate $E[\tilde{R}] \approx 1.028$ and consequently $E[W_1] \approx 0.617$ and $E[W_2] \approx 6.167$. As can be observed, these values not only lie on the line described by the pseudo-conservation law but also within the bounds we established before. □

Finally, for $k$-limited systems, Fuhrmann has derived the following bound for the symmetric case [101]:

$$E[W_{k-\mathrm{lim}}] + E[S] \leq \frac{1-\rho}{1 - \rho - \lambda \Delta/k} \left( E[W_E] + E[S] \right). \tag{9.27}$$

This bound is so tight that it can be used as an approximation. Note that the equal sign holds if either $k = 1$ (1-limited) or $k = \infty$ (exhaustive). For asymmetric $k_i$-limited systems, Fuhrmann and Wang have also provided an approximation based on the pseudo-conservation law [100].

## 9.5    Performance evaluation of the IBM token ring

In this section we discuss the use of count-based cyclic server models for the analysis of timed-token ring systems such as the IBM token ring. We briefly touch upon the IBM token ring access mechanism in Section 9.5.1. Then we discuss an approximation of this timed-token access mechanism by means of (approximate) $k$-limited cyclic server models in Section 9.5.2, and discuss the influence of the token holding time on the system performance in Section 9.5.3. The methods presented here have been developed by Groenendijk in his Ph.D thesis [112, Chapter 8].

### 9.5.1    Timed-token access mechanisms

In this section a brief operational explanation is given of the timed-token network access mechanism as used in the IBM token ring. We do not address the priority mechanism. For more details, we refer to the survey paper by Bux [35].

In a token ring system a number of stations, denoted $Q_1$ through $Q_N$, are connected to a ring shaped medium. On this medium, a special pattern of bits circulates, the *token*. There are two types of tokens: *busy tokens* and *free tokens*. A busy token is always followed by an actual data packet. At the beginning of the data packet is the *header* which contains, among others, a field of bits reserved for the indication of the destination address (the *address field*).

Whenever a token passes a particular station $Q_i$, there are two possibilities. When the passing token is of the busy type, $Q_i$ checks whether the address field matches its own address. If so, it starts copying the trailing data packet(s) in its input buffer. If the address field does not match the station's address, $Q_i$ simply lets the busy token and the trailing packet pass.

When a free token passes the station, there are again two possibilities. If $Q_i$ has no data packets to send, it just does nothing to the token: it simply passes it to the next downstream station which will take a certain switch-over time. If $Q_i$ has data packets to send, it grabs the empty token, changes it to a busy token and puts it on the ring again, directly followed by the data packets it wants to send, of course preceded by the correct header.

At the moment $Q_i$ starts transmitting data packets on the ring, it also starts its (local) token holding timer (THT), which operates as a count-down timer with initial value $tht_i$. Now, $Q_i$ continues to send until either all its data packets have been transmitted or the THT expires, whichever comes first. After finishing the transmission of data packets, by one of the two above reasons, the station issues a new free token.

Important to note is that the expiration of the THT is non-preemptive. This means that once the THT expires, $Q_i$ is still allowed to finish the transmission of the data packet that is in progress. Because data packets have a maximum length, one can calculate the maximum time a station will hold the token.

Upon receipt of a data packet by a station, there are two ways to go. The receiving station might change the busy token in a free token (so-called *destination release*) or it forwards the token to the sending station, which then releases a free token (*source release*). Note that destination release is more efficient, although it might incur unfairness between stations as a truly cyclic polling order is not guaranteed.

## 9.5.2 Approximating the timed-token access mechanism

We cannot directly model the above timed-token ring access mechanism in terms of count-based polling models. However, we can approximate it by a cyclic (asymmetric) polling model with a $k$-limited scheduling strategy as follows.

Consider a timed-token ring system, in which for station $i$ the token holding time is $tht_i$ and the average packet transmission time is $E[S_i]$. $E[S_i]$ and $E[S_i^2]$ should reflect the transmission time of the packet, plus possibly the propagation delay on the medium or even the total round-trip delay, depending on which token scheme is used [35].

Whenever $tht_i$ is much smaller than $E[S_i]$, in most cases no more than 1 packet will be transmitted per visit to station $i$. This situation can conveniently be modelled as a 1-limited scheduling discipline.

If, on the other hand $tht_i$ is much larger than $E[S_i]$, in most cases all queued packets

| | simulation | | 1-limited | | 2-limited | |
|---|---|---|---|---|---|---|
| $\rho$ | $E[W_1]$ | $E[W_{2,3}]$ | $E[W_1]$ | $E[W_{2,3}]$ | $E[W_1]$ | $E[W_{2,3}]$ |
| 0.3 | 0.421 | 0.347 | 0.525 | 0.370 | 0.420 | 0.322 |
| 0.5 | 1.12 | 0.747 | 1.51 | 0.775 | 1.12 | 0.670 |
| 0.8 | 10.6 | 2.33 | 55.7 | 2.31 | 9.67 | 2.23 |
| 0.3 | 0.442 | 0.399 | 0.506 | 0.444 | 0.317 | 0.558 |
| 0.5 | 1.20 | 0.989 | 1.38 | 1.16 | 0.861 | 1.38 |
| 0.8 | 7.52 | 5.60 | 10.72 | 8.30 | 6.91 | 6.22 |

Table 9.2: Comparison of the expected waiting time for a timed token protocol; simulation results and approximate results using $k$-limited cyclic server models (results from [112])

at station $i$ will be served. This can be modelled as an exhaustive scheduling discipline.

Clearly, interesting modelling problems arise whenever $tht_i \approx E[S_i]$. Noting that, on average, $tht_i/E[S_i]$ packets "fit" in a single service period at station $i$, a $k$-limited scheduling strategy seems reasonable to assume, with

$$k = \text{round}\left(1 + \frac{tht_i}{E[S_i]}\right). \qquad (9.28)$$

The addition of 1 comes from the fact that the timer expiration is non-preemptive.

**Example 9.5. A 3-station, timed-token ring system (adapted from [112]).**
Consider a timed-token ring system with only three stations. For comparison purposes, the average waiting times $E[W_i]$ have been derived in two ways: (1) by simulation, using the timed-token mechanism in all its details, and (2) by using cyclic server models with a 1-limited and a 2-limited scheduling strategy.

The value of the token holding time in station $i$ is equal to the average packet service duration, i.e., $tht_i = E[S_i]$. The switch-over times $\delta_i$ are assumed to be 0.1, deterministically, i.e., $\delta_i^{(2)} = 0$. All packet lengths are assumed to be exponentially distributed. According to (9.28), we should use a 2-limited scheduling discipline when these parameters apply $(k = 2)$.

In the upper half of Table 9.2 we present the results for $\lambda_1 = 0.6$, $\lambda_2 = \lambda_3 = 0.2$, and $E[S_1] = E[S_2] = E[S_3]$. In the lower half of Table 9.2 we present the results for $\lambda_1 = \lambda_2 = \lambda_3 = 1/3$, and $E[S_1] = 3E[S_2] = 3E[S_3]$. The results for the 1-limited cyclic server models have been obtained by the Boxma and Meister approximation (9.24) for small utilisation $(\rho = 0.3)$ and by an improved approximation for the higher utilisations

[112]. The results for the 2-limited case have been derived with the Fuhrmann and Wang approximation [100]. The results reveal that especially for higher loads ($\rho = 0.8$) the 1-limited approximation overestimates the waiting time, especially for the station with the higher arrival rate. This is due to the fact that when at a polling instant a queue is not empty (which is normally the case when $\rho$ is high), then in the timed token protocol at least one packet will be transmitted whereas in the 1-limited case at most one packet is transmitted. This causes more switching overhead and consequently higher waiting times. Also notice that the approximations for the system with different arrival intensities (upper half of Table 9.2) are more accurate than the approximations for the systems with different service intensities (lower half of Table 9.2).                                         □

**Example 9.6. Stability condition.**
Observing Table 9.2, we see a very high value for $E[W_1]$ in the 1-limited case. This is not surprising if we consider the stability condition for 1-limited models: we should have $\rho + \lambda_i \Delta < 1$. Although $\rho = 0.8$ does not directly suggest that the model is extremely heavily loaded, the per-station stability condition $\rho + \lambda_1 \Delta = 0.8 + 0.6 \times 0.3 = 0.98$ actually does indicate that it is operating close to saturation.                                         □

## 9.5.3   The influence of the token holding timer

One of the problems in the management of token ring systems is the setting of the token holding times for the stations. Dependent on the overall loading of the system and the relative loading of the connected stations, one or another choice might yield a better performance or might be more or less unfair. One of the things which we expect from (9.28) is that large THTs coincide with the exhaustive scheduling discipline, i.e., a $k$-limited discipline with $k \to \infty$, whereas very small THTs coincide with a 1-limited scheduling strategy.

**Example 9.7. The symmetric case (adapted from [112]).**
Consider a symmetric cyclic server system with only two connected stations. The following parameters are chosen ($i = 1, 2$): $\lambda_i = \lambda = 0.5$, $E[S_i] = E[S] = 0.5$ where the distribution is assumed to be negative exponential. The switch-overs equal $\delta_i = \delta = 0.1$ deterministically.

   We derive that $\rho = N\lambda E[S] = 0.5$. Assuming that $tht_i = tht$, we have a totally symmetric system. If we choose $tht$ very small, the system will behave as a 1-limited cyclic server system, so that according to (9.15) we have:

$$tht \to 0 \Rightarrow \text{ 1-limited } \Rightarrow E[W_L] = 0.938. \tag{9.29}$$

Conversely, taking *tht* very large, we end up with an exhaustive cyclic server system, with the following solution (according to (9.13)):

$$tht \to \infty \Rightarrow \text{ exhaustive } \Rightarrow E[W_E] = 0.650. \tag{9.30}$$

By the symmetric nature of the model one would now expect that $E[W_E] \leq E[W_{\mathrm{tht}}] \leq E[W_L]$. Simulations of a model including the timed-token mechanism have indeed confirmed this [112]. □

**Example 9.8. The asymmetric case (adapted from [112]).**
Now, consider an *asymmetric* cyclic server system with only two connected stations. The following parameters are chosen ($i = 1, 2$): $E[S_i] = E[S] = 0.5$ where the distribution is assumed to be negative exponential. The switch-overs again equal $\delta_i = \delta = 0.1$ deterministically. The arrival rates, however, differ for the two stations: $\lambda_1 = 0.7$ and $\lambda_2 = 0.3$.

We derive that $\rho = \sum_i \lambda_i E[S_i] = 0.5$. Once again, we choose both THTs to be the same. If we choose *tht* very small, the system will behave as an asymmetric 1-limited cyclic server system which can be solved approximately. We thus have, following (9.24):

$$tht \to 0 \Rightarrow \text{ 1-limited } \Rightarrow \begin{cases} E[W_{L,1}] \approx 1.133, \\ E[W_{L,2}] \approx 0.709. \end{cases} \tag{9.31}$$

An exact result, only available for a **2**-station asymmetric 1-limited cyclic polling model derived by Groenendijk [112, Chapter 6] provides

$$tht \to 0 \Rightarrow \text{ 1-limited } \Rightarrow \begin{cases} E[W_{L,1}] = 1.152, \\ E[W_{L,2}] = 0.671. \end{cases} \tag{9.32}$$

Conversely, taking *tht* very large, we end up with an asymmetric exhaustive cyclic server system, for which the following exact solution can be obtained (see (9.21)–(9.22)):

$$tht \to \infty \Rightarrow \text{ exhaustive } \Rightarrow \begin{cases} E[W_{E,1}] = 0.585, \\ E[W_{E,2}] = 0.792. \end{cases} \tag{9.33}$$

Interesting to observe here is that for a small THT, station 1 does worse than station 2, whereas for a large THT, station 1 does better than station 2. By the asymmetric nature of the model it is now *not correct* to assume that $E[W_{E,i}] \leq E[W_{\mathrm{tht},i}] \leq E[W_{L,i}]$. An increase in the THT now makes the access mechanism more efficient, but also more unfair. Especially the large value for THT might not be acceptable for station 2. We will come back to this issue in Section 16.2 where we discuss SPN-based polling models. □

## 9.6   Local and global time-based polling models

As has become clear from Section 9.5 many real systems do not operate with the mathematically attractive count-based scheduling strategies. Instead they use scheduling strategies based on the elapsed service time already spent at the queues. Although it often makes sense to use count-based scheduling strategies for bounding purposes, it would be good to have closed-from results available for time-based scheduling strategies as well. To the best of my knowledge, only the work of Tangemann proceeds in this direction [279].

The model addressed by Tangemann is a cyclic polling model where the scheduling strategy is either locally or globally timed. Let $\mathcal{L}$ be the set of nodes having a locally timed scheduling strategy and let $\mathcal{G}$ be the set of nodes having a globally timed scheduling strategy. In the first case, there is a limit $T_i^l$ on the time the server may stay at station $i$ during one visit. In the second case, there is a limit $T_i^g$ on the sum of the time the server may stay at station $i$ in one visit and the length of the previous cycle. These two scheduling strategies correspond to the operation of the access mechanisms of the IBM token ring and FDDI [246, 277, 284] respectively. Since both access mechanisms allow for so-called overrun of the timers, i.e., a packet being transmitted when the timer expires will be completed, the above timers include an additive factor accounting for the allowance of overrun. This factor equals the expected remaining service time, i.e., $E[S_i^2]/2E[S_i]$. If an access mechanism is studied which does not allow for overrun, the above timers should not include such a component.

The stability conditions are derived as follows. For the overall model we must have $\rho < 1$. For the individual queues, however, some extra restrictions apply. In the locally timed case, the expected amount of work flowing into queue $i$ must be less than the timer threshold $T_i^l$, i.e., $\lambda_i E[S_i]E[C] < T_i^l$ or, by the fact that $E[C] = \Delta/1 - \rho$,

$$\rho + \rho_i \frac{\Delta}{T_i^l} < 1. \tag{9.34}$$

Notice that in case $T_i^l = E[S_i]$, this condition reduces to the stability condition for the 1-limited system. For globally timed models, the amount of work flowing into queue $i$ during one cycle, i.e., $\lambda_i E[S_i]E[C]$, must be less than the threshold $T_i^g$ minus the length of the previous cycle. This results in the condition

$$\rho + (1 + \rho_i)\frac{\Delta}{T_i^g} \leq 1. \tag{9.35}$$

Tangemann now proceeds by deriving approximate solutions for the mean unfinished work $E[U_i^*]$ at queue $i$, that is, the expected amount of work left behind in queue $i$ when the

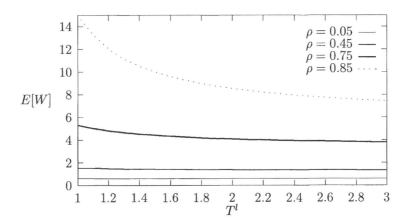

Figure 9.2: The influence of $T^l$ in a symmetric locally-timed polling model

server leaves there (the $*$ denotes either a 'g' or an 'l'). The pseudo-conservation law can be written as

$$\sum_{i=1}^{N} \rho_i E[W_i^*] = \sum_{i=1}^{N} \rho_i E[W_{E,i}] + \sum_{i=1}^{N} \rho_i E[U_i^*], \qquad (9.36)$$

where $E[W_i^*]$ is the exact average waiting time in the globally and locally timed stations and where $E[W_{E,i}]$ is the expected waiting time in the queues when all the scheduling strategies would have been of exhaustive type. Using an approximation for $E[U_i^*]$, Tangemann derives the following approximate pseudo-conservation law for time-based cyclic polling models:

$$\sum_{i \in \mathcal{L}} \rho_i E[W_i^l] \left( 1 - \frac{\rho_i E[C]}{T_i^l} \right) + \sum_{i \in \mathcal{G}} \rho_i E[W_i^g] \left( 1 - \frac{(\rho_i + \rho) E[C]}{(T_i^g - \Delta)} \right)$$

$$\approx \sum_{i=1}^{N} \rho_i E[W_{E,i}] + \sum_{i \in \mathcal{L}} \frac{\rho_i E[S_i] E[C]}{T_i^l} \left( \rho_i - (1 - \rho_i) \frac{\lambda_i E[C]}{2} \left( 1 - \frac{E[S_i]}{T_i^l} \right) \right)$$

$$+ \sum_{i \in \mathcal{G}} \frac{(\rho + \rho_i) E[S_i] E[C]}{(T_i^g - \Delta)} \left( \rho_i - (1 - \rho_i) \frac{\lambda_i E[C]}{2} \left( 1 - \frac{E[S_i]}{T_i^g - \Delta} \right) \right), \qquad (9.37)$$

where

$$\sum_{i=1}^{N} \rho_i E[W_{E,i}] = \rho \frac{\sum_{i=1}^{N} \lambda_i E[S_i^2]}{2(1 - \rho)} + \rho \frac{\Delta^{(2)}}{2\Delta} + \frac{\Delta(\rho - \sum_{i=1}^{N} \rho_i^2)}{2(1 - \rho)}, \qquad (9.38)$$

and where $E[C] = \Delta/(1 - \rho)$ is the mean cycle length. For symmetric systems, the approximate pseudo-conservation law can directly be used for deriving expected waiting times since it will then only contain one unknown. For locally-timed scheduling we can derive

$$E[W_\mathcal{L}] = \frac{(1-\rho)E[W_E] + \frac{\Delta E[S]}{T^l}\left(\frac{\rho}{N} - \frac{(1-\rho/N)\lambda E[C]}{2}\left(1 - \frac{E[S]}{T^l}\right)\right)}{1 - \rho - \frac{\rho\Delta}{NT^l}},$$ (9.39)

where $E[W_E]$ is as in (9.13). For globally timed scheduling we can derive

$$E[W_\mathcal{G}] = \frac{(1-\rho)E[W_E] + \frac{(N+1)\Delta E[S]}{T^g-\Delta}\left(\frac{\rho}{N} - \frac{(1-\rho/N)\lambda E[C]}{2}\left(1 - \frac{E[S]}{T^g-\Delta}\right)\right)}{1 - \rho - \frac{(N+1)\rho\Delta}{N(T^g-\Delta)}}.$$ (9.40)

For asymmetric systems, an approximation procedure as in Section 9.4.2 can be followed. The average waiting time in each queue is expressed in terms of known parameters and the expected remaining cycle time, which is then assumed to be station independent. Taking into account the stability conditions and the limiting case $T^* \to \infty$, the following two results have been derived:

$$E[W_i]_\mathcal{L} = \frac{1 - \rho_i\left(1 - \frac{E[S_i]}{T_i^l}\frac{2-\rho}{1-\rho}\right)}{1 - \frac{\rho_i E[C]}{T_i^l}}$$

$$\times \frac{\sum_{i=1}^N \rho_i E[W_{E,i}] + \sum_{i=1}^N \frac{\rho_i E[S_i]E[C]}{T_i^l}\left(\rho_i - (1-\rho_i)\frac{\lambda_i E[C]}{2}\left(1 - \frac{E[S_i]}{T_i^l}\right)\right)}{\sum_{i=1}^N \rho_i\left(1 - \rho_i\left(1 - \frac{E[S_i]}{T_i^l}\frac{2-\rho}{1-\rho}\right)\right)},$$ (9.41)

and

$$E[W_i]_\mathcal{G} = \frac{1 - \rho_i\left(1 - \frac{E[S_i]}{(T_i^g-\Delta)}\frac{2-\rho}{1-\rho}\right)}{1 - \frac{(\rho_i+\rho)E[C]}{(T_i^g-\Delta)}}$$

$$\times \frac{\sum_{i=1}^N \rho_i E[W_{E,i}] + \sum_{i=1}^N \frac{(\rho_i+\rho)E[S_i]E[C]}{(T_i^g-\Delta)}\left(\rho_i - (1-\rho_i)\frac{\lambda_i E[C]}{2}\left(1 - \frac{E[S_i]}{(T_i^g-\Delta)}\right)\right)}{\sum_{i=1}^N \rho_i\left(1 - \rho_i\left(1 - \frac{E[S_i]}{(T_i^g-\Delta)}\frac{2-\rho}{1-\rho}\right)\right)},$$ (9.42)

where $\sum_i \rho_i E[W_{E,i}]$ is defined in (9.38).

**Example 9.9. The influence of $T^l$.**
Consider the symmetric polling model with 10 stations we have addressed before: $N = 10$, $\delta = 0.1$, $\delta^{(2)} = 0.01$, $E[S] = 1.0$, and $E[S^2] = 1.0$. In Figure 9.2 we depict the expected waiting time as a function of $T^l$ based on the approximation (9.39) for $\rho = 0.05, 0.45, 0.75$ and 0.85. Comparing these results with those calculated in Table 9.1, we observe that for

$T^l = 1$ the values rougly agree with those calculated for the 1-limited scheduling strategy and that the results for $T^l = 3$ rougly agree with those calculated for the exhaustive scheduling strategy.                                                                                        □

**Example 9.10. Limiting cases for large values of $T^*$.**
The above approximate results are correct for large values of the timers. In the two symmetric cases, taking the limit $T^* \to \infty$ reduces the expressions to the average waiting time in symmetric exhaustive models as given in (9.13), which seems intuitively correct. Similarly, in the asymmetric case, taking $T^* \to \infty$ reduces the expressions to the approximate result for the average waiting times for exhaustive models (9.25).                      □

## 9.7   Further reading

Polling models have been the subject of research for many years now. Early papers in this field were written in the 1970s, e.g., by Avi-Itzhak *et al.*[9], Cooper and Murray [67, 66], Eisenberg [82, 83], Kühn [167], Konheim and Meister [163] and Bux and Truong [36]. Surprisingly though, polling models are treated in only a few textbooks on performance evaluation, see e.g., [152, 156]. Over the last 10 to 15 years the number of research papers on polling models has increased tremendously; Takagi reports about 250 publications in the period 1986–1990 only [272, 273]! The book on polling models by Takagi [271] focusses on mathematical issues, whereas the survey by Levy and Sidi puts more emphasis on applications [181]. The Ph.D. theses by Groenendijk [112] and Weststrate [286] also provide excellent reading on the topic. Recently, Blanc published interesting work on the power method with application to polling models [21, 20]. The Ph.D. thesis of Tangemann treats time-based scheduling in polling models in great detail [279]. Background on the IBM token-ring can be found in [35]. FDDI is described in [246]. The issue of timer-setting in token ring networks is discussed by Jain in more detail [146]. Johnson and Sevcik discuss stability and cycle time issues for FDDI in detail [151, 259]. We will come back to the evaluation of polling models in Chapter 16 where we discuss applications of stochastic Petri nets.

## 9.8   Exercises

**9.1. Symmetric polling systems.**
Use the pseudo-conservation law to compute the expected waiting time when all the stations

have either gated, 1-limited or decrementing service ordering.

### 9.2. Priority and polling systems.
Consider a 2-station polling model where, at each station, jobs arrive as a Poisson process with rate $\lambda = 5$ and have fixed duration $E[S] = 75$ msec. Furthermore, the switch-over times $\delta$ are fixed and small. This model can be interpreted as a model of a priority queueing system when station 1 has exhaustive scheduling (highest priority) and station 2 has 1-limited scheduling (lowest priority). The switch-over time now models the overhead incurred by the switching between priority classes.

1. Approximate $E[W_1]$ and $E[W_2]$ as a function of $\Delta$.

2. Compute $E[W_1]$ and $E[W_2]$ using a suitable priority model from Chapter 6, thereby neglecting the switching overhead.

3. What happens when we take the limit $\Delta \to 0$ in the result of 1?

### 9.3. Polling models with matrix-geometric solution.
Consider a 2-station polling model with exhaustive service with the following parameters. Arrivals form a Poisson process with rate $\lambda_i$ and services are negative exponentially distributed with rate $\mu_i$. The switch-overs take a negative exponentially distributed amount of time with rate $\delta_i$. Furthermore, the queue in station 1 has unlimited capacity but the queue in station 2 has a limited capacity of $K$.

1. Define the state space $\mathcal{I}$ of this Markovian polling model.

2. Draw the state-transition diagram of this quasi-birth-death model for $K = 2$.

3. Discuss how such a model can be solved, thereby explicitly stating the block matrices $\mathbf{A}_i$ and $\mathbf{B}_{i,j}$.

# Part III

# Queueing network models

# Chapter 10

# Open queueing networks

IN the previous chapters we have addressed single queueing stations. In practice, many systems consist of multiple, fairly independent service providing entities, each with their own queue. Jobs in such systems "travel" from queueing station to queueing station in order to complete. Instances of these so-called *queueing networks* can be observed at many places: in computer systems where a number of users are trying to get things done by a set of processors and peripherals, or in communication systems where packets travel via independent links and intermediate routers from source to destination. In fact, in Chapter 4 we already saw an example of a queueing network: the simple terminal model in which many system users attended a central processing system and their terminals in a cyclic manner. In this chapter we will elaborate in particular on the class of *open* queueing network models, i.e., queueing networks in which the number of customers is not *a priori* limited.

We first introduce basic terminology in Section 10.1 after which we discuss the class of feed-forward queueing networks in Section 10.2. This discussion provides us with a good insight into the analysis of more general open queueing networks, such as Jackson networks in Section 10.3. Although Jackson queueing networks can be applied in many cases, there are situations in which the model class supported does not suffice, in particular when arrival streams are not Poisson and service times are not exponentially distributed. Therefore, we present in Section 10.4 an approximation procedure for large open queueing networks with characteristics that go well beyond the class of Jackson networks. We finally address the evaluation of packet-switched telecommunication networks as an application study in Section 10.5.

## 10.1  Basic terminology

Queueing networks (QNs) consist of a number of interconnected queueing stations, which we will number $1, \cdots, M$. Individual queueing stations or *nodes*, are independent of one another. They are, however, connected to each other so that the input stream of customers of one node is formed by the superposition of the output streams of one or more other nodes. We assume that there is a never-empty source from which customers originate and arrive at the QN, and into which they disappear after having received their service.

A more formal way to describe QNs is as a directed graph of which the nodes are the queueing stations and the vertices the routes along which customers may be routed from node to node. The vertices may be labelled with routing probabilities or arrival rates. When dealing with open QNs, the source (and sink) is generally denoted as a special node, mostly numbered 0 (we will do so as well).

A well-known example of an open QN model is a model of a (public) telecommunication infrastructure where calls are generated by a very large group of potential system users. We will address such a model in Section 10.5.

## 10.2  Feed-forward queueing networks

In this section we discuss *feed-forward queueing networks* (FFQNs). In such networks the queues can be ordered in such a way that whenever customers flow from queue $i$ to queue $j$, this implies that $i < j$, i.e., these QNs are *acyclic*. Note that due to this property FFQNs must be open. We focus on the case where the individual queueing stations are of M|M|1 type, but will indicate generalisations to multi-server queueing stations.

In order to increase the understandability we present the evaluation of FFQNs in three steps. We first discuss the M|M|1 queue as the simplest case of an FFQN in Section 10.2.1. We then discuss series of M|M|1 queues in Section 10.2.2 and finally come to the most general form of FFQNs in Section 10.2.3.

### 10.2.1  The M|M|1 queue

Consider a simple M|M|1 queue with arrival rate $\lambda$ and service rate $\mu$. Given that the queue operates in a stable fashion, i.e., $\rho = \lambda/\mu < 1$, we know from Chapter 4 that the steady-state probability of having $i$ customers in the queue is given by

$$p_i = \Pr\{N = i\} = (1 - \rho)\rho^i, \ i \in I\!N. \tag{10.1}$$

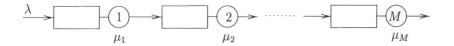

Figure 10.1: Series connection of $M$ queues

The correctness of this result can be verified by substituting it in the global balance equations of the underlying CTMC. From $p$ all kinds of interesting performance measures can be obtained. Notice that we have implicitly defined the state space $\mathcal{I}$ of the underlying CTMC to be equal to $\mathbb{N}$.

## 10.2.2  Series of M|M|1 queues

Now consider the case where we deal with $M$ queues in series. The external arrival rate to queue 1 equals $\lambda$ and the service rate of queue $i$ equals $\mu_i$. For stability we require that all $\rho_i = \lambda/\mu_i < 1$. If there are queues for which $\rho_j \geq 1$, these queues build up an infinitely large waiting line and the average response time of the series of queues goes to infinity as well. The queue with the largest value of $\rho_j$ is said to be the *bottleneck node* (or weakest link) of the QN. In Figure 10.1 we show a series QN.

Since there are no departures from the QN, nor arrivals to the QN in between any two queues, the arrival rate at any queue $i$ equals $\lambda$. Furthermore, a departure at queue $i$ $(i = 1, \cdots, M - 1)$ results in an arrival at queue $i + 1$. In Figure 10.2 we show the state-transition diagram of the CTMC underlying a series QN with $M = 2$. Notice that the state space $\mathcal{I} = \mathbb{N}^2$. Every state $(i, j) \in \mathcal{I}$ signifies the situation with $i$ customers in queue 1 and $j$ customers in queue 2. The sum of $i$ and $j$ is the total number of customers in the series QN. As can be observed form Figure 10.2, a "column of states" represent states with the same overall number of customers present in the QN. Recognising that there are basically 4 different types of states, it is easy to write down the GBEs for this CTMC:

$$
\begin{aligned}
\text{state } (0,0) \quad &: \quad p_{0,0}\lambda = p_{0,1}\mu_2, \\
\text{states } (i,0), \ i \in \mathbb{N}^+ \quad &: \quad p_{i,0}(\lambda + \mu_1) = p_{i-1,0}\lambda + p_{i,1}\mu_2, \\
\text{states } (0,j), \ j \in \mathbb{N}^+ \quad &: \quad p_{0,j}(\lambda + \mu_2) = p_{1,j-1}\mu_1 + p_{0,j+1}\mu_2, \\
\text{states } (i,j), \ i,j \in \mathbb{N}^+ \quad &: \quad p_{i,j}(\lambda + \mu_1 + \mu_2) = p_{i-1,j}\lambda + p_{i+1,j-1}\mu_1 + p_{i,j+1}\mu_2, \\
\text{normalisation} \quad &: \quad \sum_{i=0}^{\infty}\sum_{j=0}^{\infty} p_{i,j} = 1. \qquad\qquad (10.2)
\end{aligned}
$$

Solving these GBEs seems a problem at first sight; however, their regular structure and

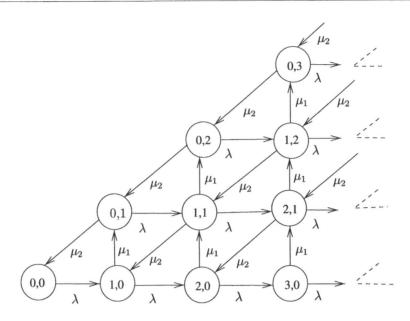

Figure 10.2: CTMC underlying two M|M|1 queues in series

the fact that we already know the answer when $M = 1$ might lead us to try whether

$$p_{i,j} = (1 - \rho_1)\rho_1^i \times (1 - \rho_2)\rho_2^j \tag{10.3}$$

is the correct solution. That this is indeed the case, we leave as an exercise to the reader. Now we will spend some more time on interpreting this result. In a series QN it seems that the overall customer probability distribution can be obtained as a product over the per-queue customer probability distributions. It is therefore that series QNs (and many more QNs we will encounter later) are often called *product-form queueing networks* (PFQNs). For series QNs the product-form property is easy to show. In fact, all the customer streams in a series QN are Poisson streams. This fact has been proven by Burke and is known as:

**Theorem 10.1. Burke's theorem.**
The departure process from a stable single server M|M|1 queue with arrival and service rates $\lambda$ and $\mu$ respectively, is a Poisson process with rate $\lambda$.             □

That Burke's theorem is indeed valid, can easily be seen. Consider an M|M|1 queue as sketched. As long as the queue is non-empty, customers will depart with the inter-departure time distribution being the same as the service time distribution. If upon a departure the queue empties, one has to wait for the next arrival, which takes a negative exponentially distributed length (with rate $\lambda$), plus the successive service period. So, when leaving behind an empty queue, the time until the next departure has a hypo-exponential distribution with 2 phases, with rates $\lambda$ and $\mu$ (see Appendix A). The probability that upon departure instances the queue is non-empty equals $\rho$, so that we can compute the inter-departure time distribution $F_D(t)$ as follows:

$$F_D(t) = \rho(1 - e^{-\mu t}) + (1 - \rho)\left(1 - \frac{\mu}{\mu - \lambda}e^{-\lambda t} + \frac{\lambda}{\mu - \lambda}e^{-\mu t}\right), \tag{10.4}$$

which reduces to $F_D(t) = 1 - e^{-\lambda t} = F_A(t)$.

In fact, Burke's theorem also applies to M|M|$m$ queues, in which case the output process of every server is a Poisson process with rate $\lambda$. However, it is easy to see that for an M|M|1 queue with feedback, the resulting outgoing job stream is not a Poisson stream any more. In fact, also the total stream of jobs entering such a queue is no Poisson stream. The superposition of the external arrival stream and the jobs fed back after having received service is not a Poisson process since the superpositioned Poisson streams are no longer independent.

Given the steady-state probability distribution for series of queues, we can address average performance measures for the individual queues. Here also the results for an individual M|M|1 queue simply apply. As an example, the average number of customers in queue 2 is derived as

$$\begin{aligned}
E[N_2] &= \sum_{i=0}^{\infty}\sum_{j=0}^{\infty} j p_{i,j} = \sum_{i=0}^{\infty}\sum_{j=0}^{\infty}(1 - \rho_1)\rho_1^i \times j(1 - \rho_2)\rho_2^j \\
&= \left((1 - \rho_1)\sum_{i=0}^{\infty}\rho_1^i\right)\left((1 - \rho_2)\sum_{j=0}^{\infty}j\rho_2^j\right) \\
&= \frac{\rho_2}{1 - \rho_2}.
\end{aligned} \tag{10.5}$$

Finally, we generalise the above results to a series of $M$ queueing stations (given all $\rho_i < 1$). Denoting with $N_i$ the number of customers in queue $i$, the vector valued random variable $\underline{N} = (N_1, \cdots, N_M)$ represents the state of the series QN. Consequently, we have state space $\mathcal{I} = \mathbb{N}^M$ and find the following steady-state probabilities:

$$\begin{aligned}
\Pr\{\underline{N} = \underline{n}\} &= \prod_{i=1}^{M}(1 - \rho_i)\rho_i^{n_i} \\
&= \left(\prod_{i=1}^{M}(1 - \rho_i)\right)\left(\prod_{i=1}^{M}\rho_i^{n_i}\right) = \frac{1}{G}\prod_{i=1}^{M}\rho_i^{n_i},
\end{aligned} \tag{10.6}$$

where $G$ is called the normalising constant, i.e.,

$$G = \left( \prod_{i=1}^{M} (1 - \rho_i) \right)^{-1}, \tag{10.7}$$

which assures that the sum of all probabilities $\sum_{\underline{n} \in \mathcal{I}} \Pr\{\underline{N} = \underline{n}\} = 1$.

### 10.2.3 Feed-forward queueing networks

In this section we address general FFQNs, i.e., acyclic QNs, not necessarily in series. All the queues themselves are M|M|1 queues. Denote the environment with "0" and let the overall arrival process from the environment be a Poisson process with rate $\lambda_0$. Let $r_{i,j}$ be the (user-specified) probability that a customer leaving queue $i$ goes to queue $j$. By definition, we have $r_{i,j} = 0$ whenever $j \leq i$. The probabilities $r_{0,i}$ indicate how the arrivals are spread over the individual queues and the probabilities $r_{i,0}$ represent departures from the QN.

The overall flow of jobs through queue $j$ now equals the sum of what comes in from the environment and what comes from other queues upon service completion, i.e.,

$$\lambda_j = \lambda_0 r_{0,j} + \sum_{i<j} \lambda_i r_{i,j}, \quad j = 1, \cdots, M. \tag{10.8}$$

These equations are called the *(first-order) traffic equations*. Their number equals the number of queues in the QN. As FFQNs are acyclic we can solve the traffic equations successively:

$$\lambda_0 \rightarrow \lambda_1 \rightarrow \lambda_2 \rightarrow \cdots \rightarrow \lambda_M. \tag{10.9}$$

Now, if all the $\rho_i = \lambda_i/\mu_i < 1$, the QN is said to be stable. If that is the case, the overall steady-state probability distribution of the QN can again be seen as the product of the per-queue steady-state probability distributions. Again, the queues can be regarded as independent from each other. Using the same notation as above, the steady-state probabilities are given as:

$$\begin{aligned}
\Pr\{\underline{N} = \underline{n}\} &= \Pr\{\bigwedge_{i=1}^{M} N_i = n_i\} \\
&= \prod_{i=1}^{M} \Pr\{N_i = n_i\} = \prod_{i=1}^{M} (1 - \rho_i)\rho^{n_i} = \frac{1}{G} \prod_{i=1}^{M} \rho_i^{n_i}.
\end{aligned} \tag{10.10}$$

The factor $1/G$ is independent of $\underline{N}$ and can again be regarded as a normalisation constant for the probabilities to sum up to 1.

When we deal with multiple server FFQNs, a similar results hold. Only the normalisation constant changes according to the results derived in Chapter 4 for M|M|$m$ queues. In any case, Burke's theorem applies so that in FFQNs all the job streams are Poisson streams.

## 10.3 Jackson queueing networks

Jackson QNs (JQNs) are an extension of FFQNs in the sense that the "feed-forward restriction" is removed, i.e., jobs may be routed to queues they attended before. The job streams between the various queues now are not Poisson streams because they are composed out of dependent streams. Surprisingly enough, however, the queue-wise decomposition of the QN can still be applied! Despite the fact that the job streams are not Poisson, the steady-state probabilities for the QN take a form as if they are! This also implies that we still have a nice product-form solution for the steady-state probabilities. The only difference with the FFQN is now given by the traffic equations:

$$\lambda_j = \lambda_0 r_{0,j} + \sum_{i=1}^{M} \lambda_i r_{i,j}, \quad j = 1, \cdots, M. \tag{10.11}$$

These cannot be solved successively any more, so that we either have to use a Gaussian elimination procedure or an iterative technique (see Chapter 15). Once the values $\lambda_i$ are known we can establish the stability of the QN by verifying whether $\rho_i = \lambda_i/\mu_i < 1$ for all $i$. If this is indeed the case, we have the following solution for the steady-state customer probability distribution:

$$\Pr\{\underline{N} = \underline{n}\} = \prod_{i=1}^{M}(1 - \rho_i)\rho_i^{n_i} = \frac{1}{G}\prod_{i=1}^{M}\rho_i^{n_i}, \tag{10.12}$$

with $G = \left(\prod_{i=1}^{M}(1 - \rho_i)\right)^{-1}$. Again, the state space of the underlying CTMC equals $\mathcal{I} = \mathbb{N}^M$.

As we will see in the application in Section 10.5, we do not always have to specify the routing probabilities. In many cases, it is more natural to specify routes through the queueing network and to compute the values $\lambda_j$ directly from them. Furthermore, under the restriction that all queues are stable, the throughputs $X_i$ are equal to the arrival rates $\lambda_i$, for all queues.

When changing from single-server queues to multiple-server queues, the presented product-from result still holds. The only difference lies in the steady-state probability

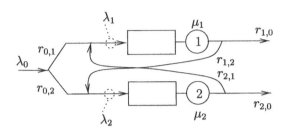

Figure 10.3: A simple Jackson QN

distributions for the multiple-server queueing stations (all according to the results given in Section 4.5). The first-order traffic equations remain unchanged.

### Example 10.1. A simple Jackson queueing network.

Consider the simple 2-station Jackson QN given in Figure 10.3. We denote the external arrival rate at queue $i$ as $\lambda_0 r_{0,i}$; the overall arrival rate at queue $i$ is $\lambda_i$. Services in queue $i$ take place with rate $\mu_i$ and after service, the customer leaves the QN with probability $r_{i,0}$ or goes to the other queue with probability $r_{i,3-i} = 1 - r_{i,0}$. The corresponding state-transition diagram is given in Figure 10.4. From the state transition diagram we can conclude the following GBEs:

$$p_{0,0}\lambda_0 = p_{0,1}\mu_2 r_{2,0} + p_{1,0}\mu_1 r_{1,0},$$

$$p_{i,0}(\lambda_0 + \mu_1) = p_{i-1,0}\lambda_0 r_{0,1} + p_{i+1,0}\mu_1 r_{1,0} + p_{i,1}\mu_2 r_{2,0} + p_{i-1,1}\mu_2 r_{2,1}, \quad i \in \mathbb{N}^+,$$

$$p_{0,j}(\lambda_0 + \mu_2) = p_{0,j-1}\lambda_0 r_{0,2} + p_{0,j+1}\mu_2 r_{2,0} + p_{1,j}\mu_1 r_{1,0} + p_{1,j-1}\mu_1 r_{1,2}, \quad j \in \mathbb{N}^+,$$

$$p_{i,j}(\lambda_0 + \mu_1 + \mu_2) = p_{i,j-1}\lambda_0 r_{0,2} + p_{i+1,j-1}\mu_1 r_{1,2} + p_{i+1,j}\mu_1 r_{1,0}$$
$$+ p_{i,j+1}\mu_2 r_{2,0} + p_{i-1,j-1}\mu_2 r_{2,1} + p_{i-1,j}\lambda_0 r_{0,1}, \quad i,j \in \mathbb{N}^+. \quad (10.13)$$

To verify whether the general solution given satisfies these GBEs (including the normalisation equation) we have to solve the traffic equations first. The overall traffic arriving at queue $i$ can be computed as:

$$\lambda_i = \lambda_0 r_{0,1} + \lambda_{3-i} r_{3-i,i}, \quad i = 1, 2. \quad (10.14)$$

From these equations we find:

$$\lambda_1 = \frac{\lambda_0 r_{0,1} + \lambda_0 r_{0,2} r_{2,1}}{1 - r_{1,2} r_{2,1}}, \quad \text{and} \quad \lambda_2 = \frac{\lambda_0 r_{0,2} + \lambda_0 r_{0,1} r_{1,2}}{1 - r_{1,2} r_{2,1}}. \quad (10.15)$$

Notice the easy interpretation of these expressions: the overall traffic that flows into queue 1 equals that what flows in from the environment, plus that which flows in after it has

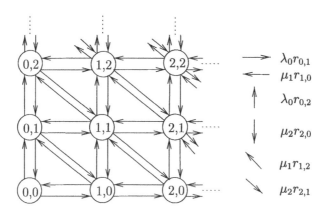

Figure 10.4: State transition diagram for the simple Jackson QN

been at queue 2. However, since customers may cycle through the queues more than once, this sum has to be "stretched" by a factor $(1 - r_{1,2}r_{2,1})^{-1}$.

The stability conditions are $\rho_i = \lambda_i/\mu_i < 1$. Using these $\rho_i$-values, the result for Jackson QNs can be verified by substituting it in the above GBEs. We will start with the case $i = j = 0$. We have:

$$(1 - \rho_1)(1 - \rho_2)\lambda_0 = (1 - \rho_1)(1 - \rho_2)\rho_2\mu_2 r_{0,2} + (1 - \rho_1)\rho_1(1 - \rho_2)\mu_1 r_{1,0}. \tag{10.16}$$

Dividing by $(1 - \rho_1)(1 - \rho_2)$ and using the fact that $\rho_i\mu_i = \lambda_i$, we obtain:

$$\lambda_0 = \lambda_1 r_{1,0} + \lambda_2 r_{2,0}. \tag{10.17}$$

This equality must hold, since it expresses that whatever flows into the QN, i.e., $\lambda_0$, equals that which flows out of both queues together. Moreover, if we substitute (10.15), and write $r_{i,0} = 1 - r_{i,3-i}$, this equality becomes trivial. We leave the validation of the other GBEs as an exercise to the reader.                                                                     □

## 10.4   The QNA method

In many modelling applications, the restriction to Poisson arrival processes and negative exponential service times in combination with FCFS scheduling cannot be justified. As an example, think of a model for a multimedia communication system in which arrivals of fixed-length packets (containing digitized voice or video) have either a very bursty or a very deterministic nature. For such systems, Jackson queueing networks might not be the most appropriate modelling tool. Instead, a modelling method known as the Queueing Network Analyzer (QNA) might be applied in such cases.

The QNA method, as developed by Kühn and later extended by Whitt, allows for quick analyses of large open queueing networks with fixed routing probabilities and FCFS scheduling. Its most important characteristic, though, is that it treats queueing networks in which the arrival processes need not be Poisson, and the service-time distribution need not be exponential. With QNA all arrival processes are assumed to be renewal processes characterised by their first two moments, i.e., successive arrivals are still independent of one another. Similarly, all service time distributions are characterised by the first two moments; in particular, constant services times can be dealt with, albeit approximately. Besides that, the QNA method also allows for the merging and splitting of customers, as well as for multiple customer classes. In its simplest form, it reduces to an exact analysis of Jackson queueing networks as we have seen in Section 10.3.

With QNA the computational complexity is linearly dependent on the number of queueing stations. Once the traffic equations have been solved, all queueing stations can be studied individually. This advantage, however, comes not without costs; the decomposition of the overall queueing network into a number of individual queueing stations is approximate. We will discuss how good this approximation is.

This section is further organised as follows. The considered queueing network class is introduced in section 10.4.1. The computational method is discussed in Section 10.4.2 and a summary of the involved approximation steps is given in Section 10.4.3.

### 10.4.1   The QNA queueing network class

A queueing network to be solved with QNA consists of $M$ nodes or queueing stations. Customers travel between nodes according to fixed routing probabilities $r_{i,j}$, $i, j = 0, 1, \cdots, M$ ($i$ and $j$ not both equal to 0). There is one special node, the environment (indexed 0) from which external arrivals and to which departures take place.

A special property of QNA is that it allows for customer creation (splitting) and combination (merging) so as to represent the segmentation and reassembly process in communication networks or the fork/join-operation in parallel processing. The combination or creation capability is indicated with every station. For each queueing station $i$, the following parameters have to be defined:

- the arrivals from the environment, characterised by the first and second moment, i.e., by the arrival rate $\lambda_{0,i}$ and the squared coefficient of variation $C_{A;0,i}^2$;

- the number of servers $m_i$;

- the service time distribution, characterised by the first and second moment, i.e., by the average service time $E[S_i] = 1/\mu_i$ and the squared coefficient of variation $C^2_{S;i}$;

- the routing probabilities $r_{i,j}$;

- the customer creation or combination factor $\gamma_i$, with

$$
\gamma_i \in
\begin{cases}
(0,1), & \text{for combination stations,} \\
1, & \text{for ordinary stations,} \\
(1,\infty), & \text{for creation stations.}
\end{cases}
\tag{10.18}
$$

For all the queues, it is assumed that the scheduling strategy is FCFS and that the buffer is infinitely large.

## 10.4.2 The QNA method

The general approach in the QNA method consists of four steps:

1. **Input.** Description of the QN in terms of the defining parameters as given in Section 10.4.1;

2. **Flows.** Determination of the customer flows inside the network which includes the generation and the solution of the traffic equations, both for the first moment (similar to that seen in Section 10.3), and for the second moment (to be discussed below);

3. **Per-node results.** The computation of the results for the individual queues, given the first and second moment of the service time distribution, and the first and second moment of the interarrival time distribution, using exact and approximate results for the M|G|m, the G|M|m and the G|G|m queue;

4. **Network-wide results.** Calculation of the network-wide performance results, i.e., the throughput, the customer departure rate, mean and variance of the sojourn time and number of customers, per queue and for the overall network.

These steps are treated in more detail in the following subsections.

## Input

Although the QNA method allows for multiple customer classes, we restrict ourselves here to the single-class case. In the papers on QNA a multiple class queueing network is transformed to a single class queueing network by aggregating customer classes.

Once all the parameters for the single class queueing network have been specified, it might be the case that some values $r_{i,i} > 0$, i.e., some queues have immediate feedback. Although this is allowed as such, the approximations used in QNA are more accurate when such immediate feedback is eliminated. The idea here is to regard the multiple visits of the immediately fed-back customer as one larger visit, and to compensate for this later in the computations. With immediate feedback probability $r_{i,i}$, the expected number of successive visits to node $i$ equals $(1 - r_{i,i})^{-1}$, so that we alter the model for node $i$ as follows:

$$
\begin{aligned}
E[S_i] &\leftarrow \frac{E[S_i]}{1 - r_{i,i}}, \\
C^2_{S;i} &\leftarrow r_{i,i} + (1 - r_{i,i})C^2_{S;i}, \\
r_{i,j} &\leftarrow \frac{r_{i,j}}{1 - r_{i,i}}, \quad j \neq i, \\
r_{i,i} &\leftarrow 0.
\end{aligned}
\tag{10.19}
$$

When computing the performance measure per node, we have to correct for these changes.

## Flows: first-order traffic equations

In this step the customer flows between nodes should be obtained. We first concentrate on the mean traffic flow, i.e., the arrival rates $\lambda_i$ to all the nodes. The first-order traffic equations are well-known and given by

$$
\lambda_j = \lambda_{0,j} + \sum_{i=1}^{M} \lambda_i \gamma_i r_{i,j}, \quad j = 1, \cdots, M,
\tag{10.20}
$$

that is, the arrival rate at node $j$ is just the sum of the external arrival rate at that node, and the departure rates $\lambda_i$ of every node $\lambda_i$, weighted by the customer creation factor $\gamma_i$ and the appropriate routing probabilities $r_{i,j}$.

There are basically three operations that affect the traffic through the QN and which are illustrated in Figure 10.5:

 (a) the probabilistic splitting of a renewal stream, induced by the constant routing probabilities which take place after customer completion at a queueing station;

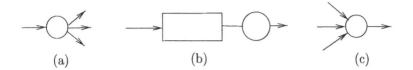

Figure 10.5: The basic operations (a) splitting, (b) superpositioning and (c) servicing that affect the traffic streams

(b) the service process at a particular queueing station;

(c) the superpositioning of renewal streams before entering a particular queueing station.

The fact that the first-order traffic equations are so easily established comes from the fact that the superpositioning of renewal streams as well as the probabilistic splitting of renewal streams can be expressed as additions and multiplications of rates. Also, the service process at a queueing station does not affect the average flows.

The first-order traffic equations form a non-homogeneous system of linear equations, which can easily be solved with such techniques as Gaussian elimination or Gauss-Seidel iterations.

Now that the arrival rates to the queues have been found, it is possible to calculate the utilisation $\rho_i = \lambda_i / m_i \mu_i$ at node $i$. If $\rho_i \geq 1$ for some $i$, that queueing station is overloaded. If all the $\rho_i < 1$, the queueing network is stable and the analysis can be taken further.

**Flows: second-order traffic equations**

To determine the second moment of the traffic flows we use the so-called second-order traffic equations. The three operations that affect the traffic characteristics are superpositioning and probabilistic splitting of renewal streams, and the service process. We therefore focus on these three factors and the way they influence the second-order characteristics of the arrival processes.

(a) **Splitting.** The probabilistic splitting of renewal processes can be expressed exactly. As we have seen in Chapter 3, if a renewal stream with rate $\lambda$ and squared coefficient of variation $C^2$ is split by independent probabilities $\alpha_i$, $i = 1, \cdots, n$, then the outgoing processes are again renewal processes, with rates $\lambda_i = \alpha_i \lambda$ and with squared coefficient of variation $C_i^2 = \alpha_i C^2 + (1 - \alpha_i)$. If, however, at node $i$ customer creation or combination takes place with value $\gamma_i$, then $C^2$ is scaled by a factor $\gamma_i$ as well, i.e., $C_i^2 = \alpha_i \gamma_i C^2 + (1 - \alpha_i)$. It should be noted that this scaling is an approximation.

**(b) Servicing.** The service process also has its influence on the departure process. If the service process has a very high variability, it increases the variability of the outgoing stream, or on the other hand, a more deterministic service process decreases the variability of the outgoing stream (in comparison with the variability of the incoming stream).

Apart from the service time variability, the utilisation of the server is also of importance, and therefore the average service time, i.e.,

- when the utilisation is low, the outgoing stream will more closely resemble the characteristics of the incoming stream;

- if the utilisation is high, there will almost always be customers present so that the departure process is almost completely determined by the service process.

In QNA , an adaptation of Marshall's result for $C_D^2$, the variability of the departure process in the GI|G|1 queue, is used. Marshall's result states that

$$C_D^2 = C_A^2 + 2\rho^2 C_S^2 - 2\rho(1-\rho)\frac{E[W]}{E[S]}. \qquad (10.21)$$

Since $E[W]$ is not known for the GI|G|1 queue, the Krämer and Langenbach-Beltz approximation (7.24) is used, under the assumption that $C_A^2 \geq 1$:

$$E[W] = (C_A^2 + C_S^2)\frac{\rho E[S]}{2(1-\rho)}. \qquad (10.22)$$

Recall that this approximation is exact in the M|G|1 and the M|M|1 case. Combining these two results, we obtain

$$C_D^2 = \rho^2 C_S^2 + (1-\rho^2)C_A^2. \qquad (10.23)$$

We observe that the coefficient of variation of the service process is weighted with $\rho^2$ and the coefficient of variation of the arrival process is weighted with $(1-\rho^2)$ to add up to the coefficient of variation of the departure process.

For multiple server queues, i.e., GI|G|m queues, this result has been extended to

$$\begin{aligned} C_D^2 &= 1 + (1-\rho^2)(C_A^2 - 1)\frac{\rho^2}{\sqrt{m}}(C_S^2 - 1) \\ &= \frac{\rho^2}{\sqrt{m}}C_S^2 + (1-\rho^2)C_A^2 + \rho^2(1 - \frac{1}{\sqrt{m}}). \end{aligned} \qquad (10.24)$$

This result reduces to the earlier result for $m = 1$, and yields $C_D^2 = 1$ for the M|M|m and the M|G|$\infty$ queue, as it should.

Practical experience has revealed that although low-variance service processes can decrease the variability of the departure process, this decrease is often less than predicted by (10.24). Therefore, instead of taking $C_S^2$, in the QNA approach $\max\{C_S^2, 0.2\}$ is proposed.

(c) **Superpositioning.** Finally, we turn our attention to the superpositioning of renewal streams. Consider the case where we have to superposition a number of renewal streams with rates $\lambda_i$ and coefficients of variation $C_i^2$. A first approximation for the coefficient of variation of the merged stream would be

$$C_\alpha^2 = \sum_i \left( \frac{\lambda_i}{\sum_k \lambda_k} \right) C_i^2, \tag{10.25}$$

which is a weighted sum of the coefficients of variation of the merged streams. Experimental work, however, showed that the actual $C^2$ is better given by

$$C^2 = wC_\alpha^2 + (1 - w)C_\beta^2, \tag{10.26}$$

where a good choice for $C_\beta^2$ is $C_\beta^2 = 1$. The weighting factor $w$ $(0 < w < 1)$ is derived as

$$w = \frac{1}{1 + 4(1 - \rho)^2(v - 1)}, \tag{10.27}$$

with

$$v = \left( \sum_i \left( \frac{\lambda_i}{\sum_k \lambda_k} \right)^2 \right)^{-1}. \tag{10.28}$$

It should be noted that these last three equations are based on experience and extensive simulations, rather than on theory.

Combining the results for superpositioning, splitting and the service of customer flows, we obtain the following system of *second-order traffic equations*:

$$C_{A,j}^2 = a_j + \sum_{i=1}^M C_{A,i}^2 b_{i,j}, \ j = 1, \cdots, M, \tag{10.29}$$

where $a_j$ and $b_{i,j}$ are constants which follow from the above considerations:

$$a_j = 1 + w_j((p_{0,j}C_{A;0,j}^2 - 1) + \sum_{i=1}^M p_{i,j}((1 - r_{i,j}) + \gamma_i r_{i,j}\rho_i^2 x_i)), \tag{10.30}$$

and

$$b_{i,j} = w_j p_{i,j} r_{i,j} \gamma_i (1 - \rho_i^2),$$  (10.31)

with $p_{i,j}$ the proportion of arrivals to $j$ that came from $i$:

$$p_{i,j} = \frac{\lambda_i \gamma_i r_{i,j}}{\lambda_j},$$  (10.32)

and

$$x_i = 1 + \frac{\max\{C_{S,i}^2, 0.2\} - 1}{\sqrt{m_i}},$$

$$w_j = \frac{1}{1 + 4(1 - \rho_j)^2 (v_j - 1)},$$

$$v_j = \frac{1}{\sum_{i=0}^{M} p_{i,j}^2}.$$  (10.33)

Consequently, (10.29) comprises a non-homogeneous system which can be easily solved using such techniques as Gaussian elimination or Gauss-Seidel iterations (see also Chapter 15).

**Example 10.2. Second-order traffic equations: simple case.**
To obtain more insight into the QNA approximation, consider the case where $w = 1$ in (10.26), i.e., where the first approximation for the superpositioning of renewal streams is used. The total coefficient of variation of the stream arriving at node $j$ is then just the weighted sum of the incoming streams:

$$C_{A,j}^2 = p_{0,j} C_{A;0,j}^2 + \sum_{i=1}^{M} p_{i,j} C_{D;i,j}^2,$$  (10.34)

where $C_{D;i,j}^2$ is the coefficient of variation of the stream that left node $i$ and is directed to node $j$ and $C_{A;0,j}^2$ is the coefficient of variation of the external arrival stream. The weighting factors $p_{i,j}$ are derived such that they express the relative weight of stream $i$ in the total arrival stream at node $j$, i.e., if $\lambda_{i,j} = \lambda_i \gamma_i r_{i,j}$, then $p_{i,j} = \lambda_{i,j}/\lambda_j$. The stream from $i$ to $j$ is the result of the splitting or merging of the stream that has been multiplied by $\gamma_i$ after it left node $i$:

$$C_{D;i,j}^2 = r_{i,j} \gamma_i C_{D;i}^2 + (1 - r_{i,j}),$$  (10.35)

where $C_{D;i}^2$ is the coefficient of variation of the stream that left server $i$, but before the splitting or merging took place. But this stream is the result of an incoming stream at node $i$ and the service process there:

$$C_{D;i}^2 = \frac{\rho_i^2}{\sqrt{m_i}} C_{S;i}^2 + (1 - \rho_i^2) C_{A,i}^2 + \rho_i^2 (1 - \frac{1}{\sqrt{m_i}}).$$  (10.36)

Using these two results, we can rewrite (10.34), in a number of steps, to

$$
\begin{aligned}
C_{A;j}^2 &= p_{0;j} C_{A;0,j}^2 + \sum_{i=1}^{M} p_{i,j}(1 - r_{i,j}) + \sum_{i=1}^{M} \gamma_i p_{i,j} r_{i,j} \frac{\rho_i^2}{\sqrt{m_i}} C_{S;i}^2 \\
&\quad + \sum_{i=1}^{M} p_{i,j} r_{i,j} \gamma_i \rho_i^2 \left(1 - \frac{1}{\sqrt{m_i}}\right) + \sum_{i=1}^{M} p_{i,j} r_{i,j} \gamma_i (1 - \rho_i^2) C_{A;i}^2 \\
&= a_j + \sum_{i=1}^{M} b_{i,j} C_{A;i}^2,
\end{aligned}
\tag{10.37}
$$

with $a_j$ and $b_{i,j}$ as defined before. Notice that the only difference that remains is that the above equation uses $C_{S;i}^2$ directly, whereas the more general result presented before uses $\max\{C_{S;i}^2, 0.2\}$. As this adaptation was based on experience rather than on a mathematical argument, this is no surprise.                                                          □

### Performance measures at the nodes

Now that we have decomposed the queueing network into separate service facilities of GI|G|m type characterised by the first two moments of the interarrival time and the service time distribution, we can analyse them in isolation. We first focus on the single server case, i.e., $m = 1$, and then on the multi-server case.

An important performance measure is the mean waiting time $E[W]$ for which the Krämer and Langenbach-Belz approximation (7.24) is used:

$$
E[W] \approx (C_A^2 + C_S^2) \frac{\rho E[S]}{2(1 - \rho)} g(\rho, C_A^2, C_S^2),
\tag{10.38}
$$

where

$$
g(\rho, C_A^2, C_S^2) = \begin{cases} \exp\left(-\frac{2(1-\rho)(1-C_A^2)^2}{3\rho(C_A^2 + C_S^2)}\right), & C_A^2 < 1, \\ 1, & C_A^2 \geq 1. \end{cases}
\tag{10.39}
$$

The mean of the number of customers in the queueing station, $E[N]$, can easily be found employing Little's law:

$$
E[N] = \rho + \lambda E[W].
\tag{10.40}
$$

The probability of delay, i.e., $\sigma = \Pr\{W > 0\}$, is also based on the Krämer and Langenbach-Belz approximation as follows

$$
\sigma \approx \rho + (C_A^2 - 1)\rho(1 - \rho)h(\rho, C_A^2, C_S^2),
\tag{10.41}
$$

with

$$h(\rho, C_A^2, C_S^2) = \begin{cases} \frac{1+C_A^2+\rho C_S^2}{1+\rho(C_S^2-1)+\rho^2(4C_A^2+C_S^2)}, & C_A^2 \leq 1, \\ \frac{4\rho}{C_A^2+\rho^2(4C_A^2+C_S^2)}, & C_A^2 \geq 1. \end{cases} \qquad (10.42)$$

Notice that in case of an M|G|1 queue (10.41) reduces to $\sigma = \rho$, which is correct since in that case the Poisson arrivals see the average utilisation of the queue (due to the PASTA property). The squared coefficient of variation of the waiting time, i.e., $C_W^2$, is approximated as follows (see [288, (50)–(53)]):

$$C_W^2 \approx \frac{1}{\sigma}\left(2\rho + \frac{4(1-\rho)(2C_S^2 + \max\{C_S^2, 1\})}{3(C_S^2+1)} - \sigma\right). \qquad (10.43)$$

From this result, the squared coefficient of variation of the number of customers in the facility, i.e., $C_N^2$ is derived as:

$$C_N^2 = (E[N] + \rho^2 C_S^2 + \lambda^2 \text{var}[W]) \frac{\frac{(1-\rho+\sigma)}{\max\{1-\sigma+\rho, 10^{-6}\}}}{\max\{E[N]^2, 10^{-6}\}}. \qquad (10.44)$$

Also here various approximations and results based on experience have been used.

In the case of multiserver nodes, only a few approximate measures can be computed, by modifying the exact results for the M|M|$m$ queue. The multiserver results are therefore less accurate. As an example of such an approximate result, the average waiting time in a GI|G|$m$ node is obtained as

$$E[W]_{\text{GI|G|m}} = \left(\frac{C_A^2 + C_S^2}{2}\right) E[W]_{\text{M|M|m}}, \qquad (10.45)$$

where $E[W]_{\text{M|M|m}}$ is the average waiting time in an M|M|$m$ queue with the same arrival and service rates. For M|G|$m$ queues, this approach is known to perform well. More advanced methods can of course be included here.

Finally, notice that for those queues for which we have eliminated the immediate feedback in the input-phase, we have to adjust the obtained performance measures as follows:

$$\lambda_i \leftarrow \frac{\lambda_i}{1 - r_{i,i}},$$
$$E[S_i] \leftarrow (1 - r_{i,i})E[S_i],$$
$$C_{S;i}^2 \leftarrow \frac{C_{S;i}^2 - r_{i,i}}{1 - r_{i,i}},$$
$$E[W_i] \leftarrow (1 - r_{i,i})E[W_i]. \qquad (10.46)$$

For higher moments of $N$ and $W$, more complex back-transformations are necessary [288].

### Network-wide performance measures

In the last step the performance results of the separate queueing facilities have to be combined to final network-wide performance results. The throughput is defined in QNA as the total external arrival rate:

$$\lambda_0 = \lambda_{0,1} + \cdots + \lambda_{0,M}. \tag{10.47}$$

When no customers are combined or created at the nodes, the departure rate from the network will be equal to the throughput. Otherwise the departure rate can differ from the throughput. In general, the departure rate from the network is given as:

$$\lambda_d = \sum_{i=1}^{M} \lambda_i \gamma_i \left( 1 - \sum_{j=1}^{M} r_{i,j} \right). \tag{10.48}$$

The mean number of customers in the network is given by

$$E[N] = E[N_1] + \cdots + E[N_M]. \tag{10.49}$$

Neglecting the fact that the nodes are dependent, the variance of the number of customers can be approximated as:

$$\text{var}[N] = \text{var}[N_1] + \cdots + \text{var}[N_M]. \tag{10.50}$$

The response time is calculated from the perspective of an aggregate customer. A customer enters queue $i$ with probability $\lambda_{0,i}/\lambda_0$. The expected number of visits to node $i$, the so-called visit-count $V_i$ (see Chapter 11), is

$$V_i = \lambda_i/\lambda_0. \tag{10.51}$$

The mean time an arbitrary customer spends in node $i$ during its total time in the network (for all its visits to node $i$) therefore equals

$$E[\hat{R}_i] = V_i(E[S_i] + E[W_i]). \tag{10.52}$$

Note that the response time for an arbitrary customer to pass through queue $i$ *once*, simply equals $E[S_i] + E[W_i]$. The expected total response time for an arbitrary customer to pass through the network then equals

$$E[\hat{R}] = \sum_{i=1}^{M} E[\hat{R}_i]. \tag{10.53}$$

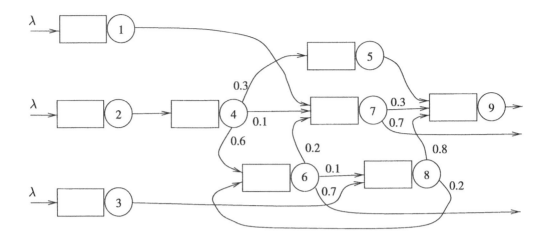

Figure 10.6: The nine-node example queueing network

|          | $C_A^2 = 0.5, C_S^2 = 0.5$ | | | $C_A^2 = 6.0, C_S^2 = 0.5$ | | | $C_A^2 = 6.0, C_S^2 = 4.0$ | | |
|----------|-------|-------|------|-------|-------|-------|-------|-------|-------|
|          | QNA   | SIM   | RE   | QNA   | SIM   | RE    | QNA   | SIM   | RE    |
| $E[W_{1;3}]$ | 0.533 | 0.497 | 7.2  | 3.972 | 3.220 | 23.4  | 6.111 | 6.228 | -1.9  |
| $E[W_4]$ | 3.008 | 2.931 | 2.6  | 9.189 | 10.97 | -16.2 | 21.00 | 22.92 | -8.4  |
| $E[W_5]$ | 1.377 | 1.301 | 5.8  | 1.596 | 1.559 | 2.4   | 6.005 | 6.591 | -9.7  |
| $E[W_6]$ | 1.091 | 0.985 | 10.8 | 1.372 | 1.282 | 7.0   | 5.257 | 5.956 | -11.7 |
| $E[W_7]$ | 1.830 | 1.695 | 7.9  | 5.604 | 6.026 | -7.5  | 12.29 | 13.31 | -7.7  |
| $E[W_8]$ | 0.820 | 0.758 | 8.2  | 3.273 | 2.685 | 21.9  | 6.719 | 7.597 | -11.6 |
| $E[W_9]$ | 20.22 | 18.40 | 9.9  | 34.51 | 70.25 | -50.9 | 113.1 | 100.2 | 12.9  |

Table 10.1: The expected waiting times for the nine-node example queueing network

**Example 10.3. Kühn's nine-node queueing network.**

We take a queueing network similar to the one discussed in [166, Section 4.2.3] and [287, Section VI]. It is a nine-node queueing network as depicted in Figure 10.6. Customers arrive via a renewal process at nodes 1–3, each with arrival intensity $\lambda = 0.55$. All node service times are, on average, equal to 1, except for node 5, at which the mean service time equals 2. Three cases are addressed, with different coefficients of variation for the arrival and service processes. For every case, all the arrival processes have identical coefficients of variation, and so have the service times.

The results are presented in Table 10.1. For the three different cases we present the expected waiting time at each node (notice that nodes 1–3 have the same expected waiting time), both derived with QNA and with simulation (SIM). The relative error (RE) is defined as RE= $100\% \times$ (QNA −SIM)/SIM. In the first case, QNA gives acceptable results. In the second case, QNA provides less good results, except for queues 5–7. This is most probably due to the rather extreme coefficient of variation of the arrival process. In the last case, the results are a little better again. It is interesting to see that the QNA result for the queues "in the middle" of the queueing network are often better than those for queues "on the border". As QNA is based on a number of approximations, it is difficult to track down the exact source of the errors.  □

## 10.4.3   Summary of approximations

It is important to realise that the QNA method is not exact but is based on a number of approximations. The results obtained with QNA therefore always have to be interpreted carefully. Below we mention which approximations are made in the QNA approach:

1. Performance measures for the network as a whole are obtained by assuming that the nodes are stochastically independent given the approximate flow parameters;

2. It is assumed that traffic streams are renewal processes that can be characterised adequately by the first two moments of the interrenewal time;

3. A GI|G|$m$ approximation for the performance at a node is used which is only exact for the M|M|1 or the M|G|1 queue;

4. Several equations are not based on an exact mathematical derivation, but on approximate results, sometimes obtained after extensive simulations.

To avoid the third approximate step, one can consider the use of PH|PH|$m$ queues, for which an exact matrix-geometric solution exists. For networks with queues in series and where some of the queues include customer creation, the arrival processes at intermediate nodes are no renewal processes. In fact, such arrivals are better described as batch arrivals, as we have seen in relation to the M|G|1 queue. Under some circumstances, it is therefore better to use batch queueing models for the intermediate nodes.

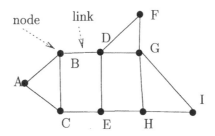

Figure 10.7: An example telecommunication network with $\hat{M}_l$ links connecting $\hat{M}_n$ nodes

# 10.5   Telecommunication network modelling

In this section we present a typical application of open queueing network models: the evaluation of possibly large packet-switched telecommunication networks. We begin with a system description of such a telecommunication network in Section 10.5.1. We then proceed with the first modelling approach, based on Jackson networks, in Section 10.5.2. We refine our evaluation method by switching from networks of M|M|1 queues to networks of M|G|1 queues in Section 10.5.3. We finish this section by illustrating the use of QNA for the evaluation of telecommunication networks in Section 10.5.4.

## 10.5.1   System description

Consider a packet-switched telecommunication network consisting of $\hat{M}_n$ nodes connected by $\hat{M}_l$ links. The topology of the network might take any form, i.e., we do not restrict ourselves to ring- or star-shaped networks. Most often, we will see meshed structures, as depicted in Figure 10.7, with switching nodes A, B, $\cdots$, I. In what follows, we assume that all the links, as depicted in the figure, are bidirectional but may have different capacity in each direction (notice that this includes the case of having uni-directional links). The nodes are capable of buffering incoming traffic and transmitting it on any of the outgoing links. For this reason, these networks are also often called store-and-forward networks. Examples of such networks are the ARPANET and the Internet [161, 277, 284].

The nodes in the network model should not necessarily be understood as end-nodes in the network; they can best be understood as concentrators for a large user group. As an example of this, the nodes could be university computer centers and the network could span a complete country. All computer users within a certain university would then be able to communicate with all other users at all other universities via the central nodes for their respective universities. We denote the aggregate stream of traffic originating in

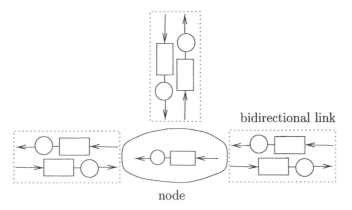

Figure 10.8: The queueing network equivalent of a switching node and its associated bi-directional links

node $i$ destined for node $j$ as $\gamma_{i,j}$ (in packets per second) and assume that it is a Poisson process; normally $\gamma_{i,i} = 0$. Since the traffic originating at one node is the aggregate traffic of many users connected directly to this node, this assumption seems reasonable. The overall aggregate network traffic, measured in packets per second, is denoted

$$\gamma = \sum_{i=1}^{\hat{M}_n} \sum_{j=1}^{\hat{M}_n} \gamma_{i,j}. \tag{10.54}$$

The complete traffic to be transported by the network is often summarised in a square traffic matrix $\mathbf{\Gamma}$ with entries $\gamma_{i,j}$.

Let us now have a look at a possible queueing network model for such a telecommunication network. We take an abstract point of view and assume that a switching node can be modelled as a single-server queue. Furthermore, we assume that each unidirectional link has to be modelled as a separate queueing station as well. The queueing-network equivalent of a switching node such as B, C, E or H in Figure 10.7 and its three associated bidirectional links is illustrated in Figure 10.8. In doing so, we end up with a queueing network with $M_n = \hat{M}_n$ queueing stations representing the nodes and $M_l = 2\hat{M}_l$ queueing stations representing the links.

Let us now come to the characteristics of the queueing stations. For every switching node $i$ we assume that the scheduling order is FCFS and that the service rate $\mu_i$ (in switching operations per second) is known. For now, we do not dwell on the actual switching time distribution. For the queueing stations representing the links, the situation is more complicated. Every link $l$ is assumed to have a certain capacity $c_l$ (in bits per second). Now consider a packet generated at node $i$ and destined for node $j$; its length is drawn from a particular packet length distribution. On its way, the packet passes through a number of links and switching nodes. Since the packet length does not change on its way, we observe that the service times over the links are in fact not independent. In the queueing network models we have introduced so far, however, the service time at every node is assumed to be independent of the service times at all the other nodes. Thus, when we try to model the actual packet flow through the network realistically, we end up with a queueing network model that we cannot solve. However, it seems reasonable to assume that in the overall network, packets from many source-destination pairs will be transmitted in an interleaved fashion. This source of randomness then justifies the assumption that the packet length *itself* is a random variable with fixed mean, that is regenerated at every queue. In a sense, we assume that the queues operate independently from one another. This assumption has become known as *Kleinrock's independence assumption* and has been validated as accurate using extensive simulations.

We assume that all the packets originating at any of the nodes have the same mean length and obey the same packet length distribution $F_B(b)$ (in bits) with mean value $1/\mu$ (bits per packet). A packet of $b$ bits length will then take $b/c_i$ seconds to be transmitted over link $i$. The number of packets that can be transmitted over link $i$ is $\mu c_i$ (packets per second).

Now that we have established the characteristics of the queueing network nodes, we have to compute the workload per node. We do so by readdressing the traffic matrix $\Gamma$ and the actual routes through the network. Let $\mathcal{R}(i, j)$ be the set of links visited by packets routed from $i$ to $j$ and let $\mathcal{N}(i, j)$ be the set of switching nodes in the route from $i$ to $j$. We assume that these sets are uniquely defined and that they are static. We do not address the question how these sets, i.e., the actual routes through the network, are obtained or established. We then can compute the arrival rate of packets to a link $l$ as

$$\lambda_l = \sum_{\{(i,j)|l\in\mathcal{R}(i,j)\}} \gamma_{i,j}, \tag{10.55}$$

and the arrival rate to switching node $n$ as

$$\lambda_n = \sum_{\{(i,j)|n\in\mathcal{N}(i,j)\}} \gamma_{i,j}. \tag{10.56}$$

Given these arrival rates, we can validate the stability of the system by verifying whether the utilisations $\rho_l = \lambda_l/\mu c_l$ and $\rho_n = \lambda_n/\mu_n$ are all smaller than 1. We can then compute the expected response time for packets from $i$ to $j$ (often denoted as the expected delay) as the sum over the response times at all the links and nodes visited along the way:

$$E[R(i,j)] = \sum_{l \in \mathcal{R}(i,j)} E[R_l] + \sum_{n \in \mathcal{N}(i,j)} E[R_n],$$

$$= \sum_{l \in \mathcal{R}(i,j)} (E[W_l] + E[S_l] + P_l) + \sum_{n \in \mathcal{N}(i,j)} (E[W_n] + E[S_n]), \quad (10.57)$$

where we have split the response times per link and node in waiting and service time per link and node, for reasons to become clear below. For links, we furthermore have added the term $P_l$ which is the propagation delay for link $l$. It depends on the actual size of the network and on the technology employed whether $P_l$ does play a role in the response time for a link or not. In networks with links of moderate capacity and small geographical size, the service time, i.e., the transmission time, normally dominates the propagation time; in these cases $P_l$ is often neglected. In high-speed wide-area networks, on the other hand, $P_l$ can play an important role and can even be larger than $E[S_l]$.

The overall average network response time can be expressed as the expected response time on a route from node $i$ to $j$, weighted by its relative importance with respect to the overall traffic carried, i.e.,

$$E[R] = \sum_{i=1}^{M_n} \sum_{j=1}^{M_n} \frac{\gamma_{i,j}}{\gamma} E[R(i,j)]. \quad (10.58)$$

Notice that we do not specify the routing probabilities $r_{i,j}$ directly. Instead, we specify routes. Given the information on the routes, we can of course compute the long-term probability that an incoming packet in a switching node needs to be transmitted over a particular outgoing link, but we do not need these probabilities as such.

## 10.5.2 Evaluation using Jackson queueing networks

We can evaluate a packet-switched communication network as sketched in the previous section easily using a Jackson queueing network. Note, however, that we have already made a number of assumptions in the sketched modelling trajectory in order to make this possible.

The queueing network model of the communication network is completely specified by the link and switching node parameters ($c_i$ and $\mu_i$), the traffic matrix $\Gamma$, the mean packet length $1/\mu$ and the routing information (the sets $\mathcal{R}(i,j)$ and $\mathcal{N}(i,j)$). Extra assumptions we have to make here are that the packet length and the switching time are negative exponentially distributed random variables.

Having made these assumptions, we can compute the per-link expected delay as:

$$E[R_l] = \frac{1}{\mu c_l - \lambda_l} = \frac{\rho_l E[S_l]}{1 - \rho_l} + E[S_l], \quad (10.59)$$

where the first term represents the expected waiting time and the second term $E[S_l] = 1/\mu c_l$ is the expected service time (see Chapter 4). Note that we have left out the propagation delay over link $l$. Similarly, the expected per-node delay at node $n$ is:

$$E[R_n] = \frac{\rho_n E[S_n]}{1 - \rho_n} + E[S_n], \qquad (10.60)$$

with $E[S_n] = 1/\mu_n$.

We can adapt this model slightly when we consider the expected delay in the communication network for a specific class of packets, e.g., user-oriented packets. The overall traffic mix will consist of user packets and control packets. Since control packets are generally shorter than user packets, the overall expected packet length will be smaller than the expected user packet length. For the per-link delay, we then can compute the expected waiting time using the overall expected packet length, but the service time for user-packets is then changed to the specific value for the user packets. For the switching nodes, we do not change anything.

In our treatment so far we have restricted ourselves to the computation of mean performance measures. Of course, using Jackson networks, we can also compute specific customer distributions for the model, as indicated in Section 10.3.

## 10.5.3   Evaluation using networks of M|G|1 queues

There are a number of restrictions in the use of Jackson queueing networks to evaluate communication networks that might be overcome when switching to networks of M|G|1 queues. First of all, such queueing networks allow us to use other than exponential service times (in the switching nodes) and packet length distributions. Secondly, the use of different packet lengths (in mean or distribution) would be possible. However, these advantages do not come without cost. The computational procedure we will outline below is slightly more complicated than the one sketched before and it is no longer exact.

Let us first address the case with fixed-length packets, since many networks do operate with them. As we have seen in Chapter 5 the expected waiting time in a queueing station with deterministic service times as opposed to negative exponentially distributed service times, reduces by a factor 2. Hence, the only thing we change in the computations is the M|M|1 based term for $E[R_l]$ with the corresponding term for the M|G|1 queue. A similar procedure can be followed for the expected response times at the switching nodes. First note that this approach can also be followed when distributions other than deterministic are required. Secondly, notice that we are making an approximation here. The fact that we can analyse a network of queues by assessing one queue at a time is a typical characteristic of Jackson queueing networks (its product-form result) that does, in fact, not apply to networks of M|G|1 queues. Still though, simulation studies have confirmed that in most cases this approximate approach yields results that are reasonably accurate.

We can take this even further by assuming that the packets from node $i$ to $j$, which form a Poisson process with rate $\gamma_{i,j}$, have fixed length $1/\mu_{i,j}$. A random packet arriving at link $l$ then has the following mean and second moment (of transmission time):

$$E[S_l] = \sum_{(i,j),l \in \mathcal{R}(i,j)} \frac{\gamma_{i,j}}{\lambda_l} \frac{1}{c_l \mu_{i,j}}, \quad \text{and} \quad E[S_l^2] = \sum_{(i,j),l \in \mathcal{R}(i,j)} \frac{\gamma_{i,j}}{\lambda_l} \frac{1}{(c_l \mu_{i,j})^2}. \tag{10.61}$$

We finally comment on the use of even other M|G|1 queues as models for the links and switching nodes. We already addressed the possibility that in the network two types of packets are communicated: control packets and user packets. By addressing these streams of packets separately, one can use M|G|1 models with priority scheduling to further enhance the performance of the control packets. Any of the other M|G|1 queueing models presented in Chapter 6 might be used for modelling the nodes and links in a more appropriate way. It should be noted, however, that these approaches are all approximate and thus should be practiced with care.

## 10.5.4   Evaluation using QNA

In the previous section we have addressed a number of extensions to Jackson queueing networks that lead to approximate performance measures. A large number of these extensions have already been captured in the QNA approach. Given a telecommunication network as we have defined in Section 10.5.1, with QNA the performance evaluation would take the following form.

The traffic matrix $\Gamma$ would be used to compute the values $\lambda_l$ and $\lambda_n$, and also to compute the routing probabilities $r_{i,j}$. The second-order traffic equations are then used to compute the second moment of the packet streams between links and nodes. Notice that the traffic originating at node $i$ and destined for node $j$ does not need to be a Poisson process any more. Furthermore, the packet length between each pair of end-nodes may be different. As we have indicated in Section 10.5.3, in many cases the packet length per source-destination pair is deterministic. We can then easily compute the first two moments of the transmission or service time distribution at each of the links and nodes. The number of servers per node $m_i$ can still be varied; the packet splitting and reassembly option can also be used.

When the above has been given, the complete QNA input is known and the computational procedure as sketched in Section 10.4 can be performed.

## 10.6    Further reading

Seminal work on open queueing networks was done by Jackson in the 1950s [143, 144]. Later, his work has been extended and combined with other queueing network results (see Chapter 12). Burke presented the result on the flow out of a M|M|1 queue as early as 1956 [34].

The work on the QNA method was initiated by Kühn [166] and has later been extended by Whitt [288, 287]. Important steps in the QNA method are given by the Krämer and Langenbach-Beltz approximation [164] and by Marschall's result [191]. Haverkort recently improved on the approximation for the individual node performance by using matrix-geometric methods under the restriction of having phase-type renewal arrival streams and phase-type service time distributions. Under the same restrictions, he also extended the model class to the case where the nodes have finite capacity so that customer losses can occur [122, 123].

Kleinrock has done pioneering work in the application of Jackson queueing networks (and various variants) to computer networking problems. In [161], Chapters 5 and 6 are devoted to the analysis of the early ARPANET in which a similar (but less detailed) modelling approach is presented to that given here.

## 10.7    Exercises

**10.1. Feed-forward queueing networks.**
Show that the suggested solution for the series QN in Section 10.2.2 indeed fulfills the given GBEs (case $M = 2$). Also show that a similar result applies for general $M$.

**10.2. Jackson networks.**
Show that the suggested solution for the Jackson network in Example 10.1 indeed fulfills the given global balance equations.

**10.3. A central server QN.**
Consider the central server QN given in Figure 10.9. Jobs arrive at the CPU (the central server) with rate $\lambda$ as a Poisson process. After service at the CPU, they either leave the system (with probability $r_{1,0}$) or they move to one of the $M - 1$ I/O-devices (with probability $r_{1,j}, j = 2, \cdots, M$). After service at the I/O-device of choice, the jobs return to the central server. All service times are assumed to be negative exponentially distributed.

We here address the case with $M = 3$, i.e., we have 2 I/O subsystems. Furthermore,

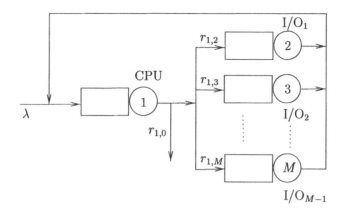

Figure 10.9: A central server QN

it is given that $E[S_1] = 2$ and $E[S_j] = 1.2$ $(j = 2, 3)$, $\lambda = 1/7$ and the non-zero routing probabilities are $r_{1,0} = 0.3$, $r_{1,2} = 0.6$ and $r_{1,3} = 0.1$.

1. Draw the CTMC underlying this JQN.

2. Write down the GBEs and show that Jackson's solution for these equations is indeed valid.

3. Compute the mean queue lengths at the stations.

4. Compute the mean time a (random) customer spends in this system.

**10.4. QNA without customer creation and combination.**
Derive the simplified QNA traffic equations when no customer creation nor combination takes place, i.e., all $\gamma_i = 1$ and $w = 1$.

**10.5. QNA without multiserver queues.**
Further reduce the simplified QNA traffic equations when all queues are served by single servers, i.e., all $m_i = 1$.

**10.6. A simple QNA application.**
Consider a QN with $M = 2$ queues and the following numerical parameters. For the arrival streams we have: $\lambda_{0,1} = 2$ with $C^2_{A;0,1} = 2$ and $\lambda_{0,2} = 3$ with $C^2_{A;0,2} = 3$. For the service time distributions we have: $E[S_1] = 0.1$ with $C_{S;1} = 3$ and $E[S_2] = 0.05$ with $C_{S;2} = 0.5$. Furthermore, the following routing probabilities are given: $r_{1,2} = 1$, $r_{2,1} = 0.5$

and $r_{2,0} = 0.5$. Finally, there is no splitting and combining ($\gamma_i = 1$) and the queues have a single server ($m_i = 1$).

1. Derive and solve the first-order traffic equations.

2. derive and solve the second-order traffic equations.

3. Compute $E[W_i]$ and $E[N_i]$.

4. Assume that the squared coefficients of variation are all equal to 1. Now, compute $E[W_i]$ and $E[N_i]$ using Jackson queueing networks, and compare the results.

# Chapter 11

# Closed queueing networks

$I$N Chapter 10 we addressed queueing networks with, in principle, an unbounded number of customers. In this chapter we will focus on the class of queueing networks with a fixed number of customers. The simplest case of this class is represented by the so-called Gordon-Newell queueing networks; they are presented in Section 11.1. As we will see, although the state space of the underlying Markov chain is finite, the solution of the steady-state probabilities is not at all straightforward (in comparison to Jackson networks). A recursive scheme to calculate the steady-state probabilities in Gordon-Newell queueing networks is presented in Section 11.2. In order to ease the computation of average performance measures, we discuss the mean value analysis (MVA) approach to evaluate GNQNs in Section 11.3. Since this approach still is computationally quite expensive for larger QNs or QNs with many customers, we present MVA-based bounding techniques for such queueing networks in Section 11.4. We then discuss an approximate iterative technique to evaluate GNQNs in Section 11.5. We conclude the chapter with an application study in Section 11.6.

## 11.1 Gordon-Newell queueing networks

Gordon-Newell QNs (GNQNs), named after their inventors, are representatives for a class of closed Markovian QNs (all services have negative exponential service times). Again we deal with $M$ M|M|1 queues which are connected to each other according to the earlier encountered routing probabilities $r_{i,j}$. The average service time at queue $i$ equals $E[S_i] = 1/\mu_i$. Let the total and fixed number of customers in such a QN be denoted $K$, so that we deal with a CTMC on state space

$$\mathcal{I}(M, K) = \{\underline{n} \subset \mathbb{N}^M | n_1 + \cdots + n_M = K\}.$$

To stress the dependence of the performance measures on both the number of queues and the number of customers present, we will often include both $M$ and $K$ as (functional) parameters of the measures of interest.

As we have seen before, the involved customer streams between the queues are not necessarily Poisson but this type of QN still allows for a product-form solution as we will see later. Let us start with solving the traffic equations:

$$X_j(K) = \sum_{i=1}^{M} X_i(K)r_{i,j}, \tag{11.1}$$

where $X_j(K)$ denotes the throughput through node $j$, given the presence of $K$ customers in the QN. This system of equations, however, is of rank $M - 1$. We can only calculate the values of $X_j$ relative to some other $X_i$ $(i \neq j)$, and therefore we introduce relative throughputs as follows. We define $X_i(K) = V_i X_1(K)$, where the so-called *visit count* or *visit ratio* $V_i$ expresses the throughput of node $i$ relative to that of node 1; clearly $V_1 = 1$. These $V_i$-values can also be interpreted as follows: whenever node 1 is visited once $(V_1 = 1)$, node $i$ is visited, on average, $V_i$ times. Stated differently, if we call the period between two successive departures from queue 1 a *passage*, then $V_i$ expresses the number of visits to node $i$ during such a passage. Using the visit counts as just defined, we can restate the traffic equations as follows:

$$V_j = \sum_{i=1}^{M} V_i r_{i,j} = V_1 + \sum_{i=2}^{M} V_i r_{i,j} = 1 + \sum_{i=2}^{M} V_i r_{i,j}. \tag{11.2}$$

This system of linear equations has a unique solution. Once we have computed the visit counts, we can calculate the *service demands per passage* as $D_i = V_i E[S_i]$ for all $i$. So, $D_i$ expresses the amount of service a customer requires (on average) from node $i$ during a single passage. The queue with the highest service demand per passage clearly is the bottleneck in the system. Here, $D_i$ takes over the role of $\rho_i$ in open queueing networks.

Notice that in many applications, the visit-ratios are given as part of the QN specification, rather than the routing probabilities. Of course, the latter can be computed from the former; however, as we will see below, this is not really necessary. We only need the visit-ratios to compute the performance measures of interest.

Furthermore, notice that the values for $D_i$ might be larger than 1; this does not imply that the system is unstable in these cases. We simply changed the time basis from the percentage of time server $i$ is busy (expressed by $\rho_i$) to the amount of service server $i$ has to handle per passage (expressed by $D_i$). Moreover, a closed QN is never unstable, i.e., it will never build up unbounded queues: it is self-regulatory because the maximal filling of any queue is bounded by the number of customers present $(K)$.

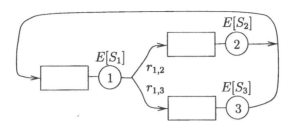

Figure 11.1: A small three-node GNQN

Let us now address the state space of a GNQN. Clearly, if we have $M$ queues, the state space must be a finite subset of $I\!N^M$. In particular, we have

$$\mathcal{I}(M, K) = \{\underline{n} \in I\!N^M | n_1 + \cdots + n_M = K\}. \tag{11.3}$$

We define the vector $\underline{N} = (N_1, \cdots, N_M)$ in which $N_i$ is the random variable denoting the number of customers in node $i$. Note that the random variables $N_i$ are not independent from one another any more (this was the case in Jackson networks). It has been shown by Gordon and Newell that the steady-state distribution of the number of customers over the $M$ nodes is still given by a product-form:

$$\Pr\{\underline{N} = \underline{n}\} = \frac{1}{G(M, K)} \prod_{i=1}^{M} D_i^{n_i}, \tag{11.4}$$

where the normalising constant (or normalisation constant) is defined as

$$G(M, K) = \sum_{\underline{n} \in \mathcal{I}(M,K)} \prod_{i=1}^{M} D_i^{n_i}. \tag{11.5}$$

It is the constant $G(M, K)$, depending on $M$ and $K$, that takes care of the normalisation so that we indeed deal with a proper probability distribution. Only once we know the normalising constant are we able to calculate the throughputs and other interesting performance measures for the QN and its individual queues. This makes the analysis of GNQNs more difficult than that of JQNs, despite the fact that we have changed an infinitely large state space to a finite one.

### Example 11.1. A three-node GNQN (I).

Consider a GNQN with only three stations, numbered 1 through 3. It is given that $E[S_1] = 1$, $E[S_2] = 2$ and $E[S_3] = 3$. Furthermore, we take $r_{1,2} = 0.4$, $r_{1,3} = 0.6$, $r_{2,1} = r_{3,1} = 1$.

The other routing probabilities are zero. The number of jobs circulating equals $K = 3$. This GNQN is depicted in Figure 11.1.

We first calculate the visit ratios. As usual, we take station 1 as a reference station, i.e., $V_1 = 1$, so that $V_2 = 0.4$ and $V_3 = 0.6$ (in a different type of specification, these visit-counts would be directly given). The service demands equal: $D_1 = 1$, $D_2 = 2(0.4) = 0.8$ and $D_3 = 1.8$. Station 3 has the highest service demand and therefore forms the bottleneck.

Let us now try to write down the state space of the CTMC underlying this GNQN. It comprises the set $\mathcal{I}(3,3) = \{(n_1, n_2, n_3) \in \mathbb{N}^3 | n_1 + n_2 + n_3 = 3\}$ which is small enough to state explicitly:

$$\begin{aligned} \mathcal{I}(3,3) = \ & \{(3,0,0), (0,3,0), (0,0,3), (1,2,0), (1,0,2), \\ & (0,1,2), (2,1,0), (2,0,1), (0,2,1), (1,1,1)\}. \end{aligned} \tag{11.6}$$

As can be observed, $|\mathcal{I}(3,3)| = 10$. Applying the definition of $G(M, K)$, we calculate

$$G(3,3) = \sum_{\underline{n} \in \mathcal{I}(3,3)} D_1^{n_1} D_2^{n_2} D_3^{n_3} = 19.008. \tag{11.7}$$

The probability of residing in state $(1,1,1)$ now, for instance, equals

$$\Pr\{\underline{N} = (1,1,1)\} = \frac{D_1 D_2 D_3}{G(3,3)} = \frac{1.44}{19.008} = 0.0758. \tag{11.8}$$

The probability that station 1 is empty can be calculated as

$$\Pr\{n_1 = 0\} = \frac{0.8^3 + 1.8^3 + 0.8(1.8^2) + 0.8^2(1.8)}{19.008} = \frac{10.0880}{19.008} = 0.5307. \tag{11.9}$$

Consequently, we have $\rho_1(3) = 1 - 0.5307 = 0.4693$, and $X_1(3) = \rho_1 \mu_1 = 0.4693$. Note that we stress the dependence on the number of customers present by including this number between parentheses. From this, the other throughputs can be derived using the calculated visit counts. The average filling of e.g., station 1 can be derived as

$$\begin{aligned} E[N_1(3)] &= \frac{1(D_1 D_2^2 + D_1 D_3^2 + D_1 D_2 D_3) + 2(D_1^2 D_2 + D_1^2 D_3) + 3D_1^3}{19.008} \\ &= \frac{13.520}{19.008} = 0.7113. \end{aligned} \tag{11.10}$$

Then, the expected response time when there are 3 customers present, denoted $E[R_1(3)]$, can be calculated using Little's law as

$$E[R_1(3)] = \frac{E[N_1(3)]}{X_1(3)} = \frac{0.7113}{0.4693} = 1.516. \tag{11.11}$$

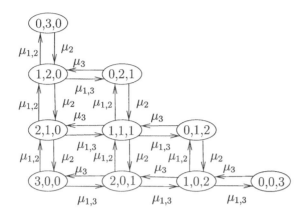

Figure 11.2: The CTMC underlying the three-node GNQN

In a similar way, we can compute for node 2: $\Pr\{n_2 = 0\} = 0.6246$, $\rho_2(3) = 0.3754$, $X_2(3) = 0.1877$, $E[N_2(3)] = 0.5236$ and $E[R_2(3)] = E[N_2(3)]/X_2(3) = E[N_2(3)]/V_2X_1(3) = 2.789$. For node 3, the corresponding values are 0.8447, 0.2816, 1.765 and 6.2683 respectively. Note the large utilisation and average queue length and response time at node 3 (the bottleneck station).                                                                                   □

Notice that it is also possible to solve directly the CTMC underlying the GNQN from the previous example. The only thing one has to do for that is to solve the global balance equations that follow directly from the state-transition diagram that can be drawn for the QN; it is depicted in Figure 11.2, where a state identifier is a triple $(i, j, k)$ indicating the number of customers in the three nodes and where $\mu_{1,2} = \mu_1 r_{1,2}$ and $\mu_{1,3} = \mu_1 r_{1,3}$. In general, the derivation of the CTMC is a straightforward task; however, due to its generally large size, it is not so easy in practice. In this example, the number of states is only 10, but it increases quickly with increasing numbers of customers. To be precise, in a GNQN with $M$ nodes and $K$ customers, the number of states equals

$$|\mathcal{I}(M, K)| = \binom{M + K - 1}{M - 1}. \tag{11.12}$$

This can be understood as follows. The $K$ customers are to be spread over $M$ nodes. We can understand this as the task to put $M - 1$ dividing lines between the $K$ lined-up customers, i.e., we have a line of $K + M - 1$ objects, of which $K$ represent customers and $M - 1$ represent boundaries between queues. The number of ways in which we can assign $M - 1$ of the objects to be of type "boundary" is exactly the number of combinations of $M - 1$ out of $K + M - 1$. For the three-node example at hand we find $|\mathcal{I}(3, K)| = \frac{1}{2}(K^2 + 3K + 2)$, a quadratic expression in the number of customers present. For larger customer populations, the construction of the underlying CTMC therefore is not practically feasible, nor is the explicit computation of the normalising constant as a sum over all the elements of $\mathcal{I}(M, K)$. Fortunately, there are more efficient ways to compute the normalising constant; we will discuss such methods in the following sections. Before doing so, however, we present an important result to obtain, in a very easy way, bounds on the performance of a system.

It is important to realise that in a GNQN all queues are stable. The worst thing that can happen is that almost all customers spend most of their time waiting at a particular queue. We denote the queueing station with the largest service demand as the system bottleneck; its index is denoted $b$. Since $\rho_i(K) = X(K)V_iE[S_i] < 1$ for all $i$, we can immediately derive the following throughput bound:

$$X(K) < \frac{1}{\max_i D_i} = \frac{1}{D_b}, \quad \text{for all } K, \tag{11.13}$$

that is, the bottleneck station determines the maximum throughput. If we increase $K$, the utilisation of station $b$ will approach 1:

$$\lim_{K \to \infty} \rho_b(K) = 1, \quad \text{and} \quad \lim_{K \to \infty} X(K) = \frac{1}{D_b}. \tag{11.14}$$

By this fact, the utilisations of other stations will also be bounded. We have

$$\lim_{K \to \infty} \rho_i(K) = \lim_{K \to \infty} V_iE[S_i]\lambda(K) = \frac{D_i}{D_b} \leq 1, \quad \text{for all } i. \tag{11.15}$$

Thus, when $K$ increases, the utilisation of station $i$ will converge to a fixed, station-specific value, the utilisation limit $D_i/D_b$. It is very important to realise that not all the limiting utilisations are equal to 1. Some stations cannot be used to their full capacity because another station is fully loaded. This result also implies that when a bottleneck in a system is exchanged by an $x$-times faster component it does not follow that the overall speed of the system is increased by the same factor. Indeed, the old bottleneck may have been removed, but another one might have appeared. We will illustrate these concepts with two examples.

**Example 11.2. A three-node GNQN (II).**
We come back to the previous three-node GNQN. There we observed the following three

service demands: $D_1 = 1, D_2 = 0.8, D_3 = 1.8$. Since $D_3$ is the largest service demand, node 3 is the bottleneck in the model ($b = 3$). This implies that

$$\lim_{K \to \infty} \lambda(K) = \frac{1}{D_3} = 0.5556. \tag{11.16}$$

Furthermore, we find that

$$\begin{align}
\lim_{K \to \infty} \rho_1(K) &= \frac{D_1}{D_3} = \frac{1}{1.8} = 0.5556, \\
\lim_{K \to \infty} \rho_2(K) &= \frac{D_2}{D_3} = \frac{0.8}{1.8} = 0.4444, \\
\lim_{K \to \infty} \rho_3(K) &= \frac{D_3}{D_3} = 1. \tag{11.17}
\end{align}$$

We observe that nodes 2 and 3 can only be used up to 55% and 44% of their capacity! □

### Example 11.3. Bottleneck removal.

Consider a simple computer system that can be modelled conveniently with a two-node GNQN. Analysis of the system parameters reveals that the service demands to be used in the GNQN have the following values: $D_1 = 4.0$ and $D_2 = 5.0$. Clearly, node 2 is the bottleneck as its service demand is the largest. The throughput of the system is therefore bounded by $1/D_2 = 0.2$. By doubling the speed of node 2, we obtain the following situation: $D'_1 = 4.0$ and $D'_2 = 2.5$. The bottleneck has been removed but another one has appeared: station 1. In the new system, the throughput is bounded by $1/D'_1 = 0.25$. Although this is an increase by 25%, it is not an increase by a factor 2 (200%) which might have been expected by the doubling of the speed of the bottleneck node. □

## 11.2 The convolution algorithm

In the GNQNs presented in the previous section, the determination of the normalising constant turned out to be a computationally intensive task, especially for larger queueing networks and large numbers of customers, since then the employed summation (11.5) encompasses very many elements. This is made worse by the fact that the summands are often very small or very large, depending on the values of the $D_i$ and the particular value of $\underline{n}$ one is accounting for (one can often avoid summands that become either too small or too large by an appropriate rescaling of the $D_i$-values). In general though, it will be very difficult to limit round-off errors so it is better to avoid direct summation.

Fortunately, a very fast and stable algorithm for the computation of $G(M, K)$ does exist and is known as the *convolution algorithm*; it was first presented by Buzen in the early 1970s. Let us start with the definition of $G(M, K)$:

$$G(M, K) = \sum_{\underline{n} \in \mathcal{I}(M,K)} \prod_{i=1}^{M} D_i^{n_i}. \tag{11.18}$$

We now split this sum into two parts, one part accounting for all the states with $n_M = 0$ and one part accounting for all the states with $n_M > 0$:

$$\begin{aligned}
G(M, K) &= \sum_{\substack{\underline{n} \in \mathcal{I}(M,K) \\ n_M = 0}} \prod_{i=1}^{M} D_i^{n_i} + \sum_{\substack{\underline{n} \in \mathcal{I}(M,K) \\ n_M > 0}} \prod_{i=1}^{M} D_i^{n_i} \\
&= \sum_{\underline{n} \in \mathcal{I}(M-1,K)} \prod_{i=1}^{M-1} D_i^{n_i} + D_M \sum_{\underline{n} \in \mathcal{I}(M,K-1)} \prod_{i=1}^{M} D_i^{n_i}. \tag{11.19}
\end{aligned}$$

Since the first term sums over all states such that there are $K$ customers to distribute over $M - 1$ queues (queue $M$ is empty) it represents exactly $G(M - 1, K)$. Similarly, in the second term one sums over all states such that there are $K - 1$ customers to distribute over the $M$ queues, as we are already sure that one of the $K$ customers resides in queue $M$, hence we have a term $D_M G(M, K - 1)$. Consequently, we find:

$$G(M, K) = G(M - 1, K) + D_M G(M, K - 1). \tag{11.20}$$

This equation allows us to express the normalising constant $G(M, K)$ in terms of normalising constants with one customer and with one queue less, i.e., we have a recursive expression for $G(M, K)$. To start this recursion we need boundary values. These can be derived as follows. When there is only 1 queue, by definition, $G(1, k) = D_1^k$, for all $k \in \mathbb{N}$. Also, by the fact that there is only one way of distributing 0 customers over $M$ queues, we have $G(m, 0) = 1$, for all $m$.

A straightforward recursive solution can now be used to compute $G(M, K)$. However, this does not lead to an efficient computation since many intermediate results will be computed multiple times, as illustrated by the following double application of (11.20):

$$\begin{aligned}
G(M, K) &= G(M - 1, K) + D_M G(M, K - 1), \\
&= G(M - 2, K) + D_{M-1} G(M - 1, K - 1) \\
&\quad + D_M G(M - 1, K - 1) + D_M D_{M-1} G(M, K - 2). \tag{11.21}
\end{aligned}$$

Instead, (11.20) can be implemented efficiently in an iterative way, as illustrated in Table 11.1. The boundary values are easily set. The other values for $G(m, k)$ can now be

| $k$ | $G(1,k)$ | $G(2,k)$ | $\cdots$ | $G(m-1,k)$ | $G(m,k)$ | $\cdots$ | $G(M,k)$ |
|---|---|---|---|---|---|---|---|
| 0 | 1 | 1 | $\cdots$ | 1 | 1 | $\cdots$ | 1 |
| 1 | $D_1$ | | | | | | |
| 2 | $D_1^2$ | | | | | | |
| 3 | $D_1^3$ | | | | | | |
| $\vdots$ | $\vdots$ | | | $\downarrow$ | $\downarrow$ | | |
| $k-1$ | $D_1^{k-1}$ | | $\to$ | $G(m-1,k-1) \to$ | $G(m,k-1) \to$ | | |
| | | | | $\downarrow \cdot D_{m-1}$ | $\downarrow \cdot D_m$ | | |
| $k$ | $D_1^k$ | | $\to$ | $G(m-1,k) \to$ | $G(m,k) \to$ | | |
| $\vdots$ | $\vdots$ | | | $\downarrow$ | $\downarrow$ | | $\downarrow \cdot D_M$ |
| $K$ | $D_1^K$ | | | | | $\to$ | $G(M,K)$ |

Table 11.1: The calculation of $G(M,K)$ with Buzen's convolution algorithm

calculated in a column-wise fashion, left to right, top to bottom. In its most efficient form, the iterative approach to compute $G(M,K)$ only requires $M-1$ columns to compute, each of which requires $K$ additions and $K$ multiplications. Hence, we have a complexity $O(MK)$ which is far less than the direct summation approach employed earlier. Furthermore, if only the end value $G(M,K)$ is required, only a single column of intermediate values needs to be stored. New columns replace older columns as the computation proceeds. Thus, we need only $O(K)$ storage for this algorithm.

Once we have computed the normalising constant $G(M,K)$ we can very easily calculate interesting performance measures. For instance, to evaluate the probability of having at least $n_i$ customers in queue $i$, we have

$$\Pr\{N_i \geq n_i\} = \sum_{\substack{\underline{n} \in \mathcal{I}(M,K) \\ N_i \geq n_i}} \frac{1}{G(M,K)} \prod_{j=1}^{M} D_j^{n_j}$$

$$= D_i^{n_i} \left( \sum_{\underline{n} \in \mathcal{I}(M,K-n_i)} \frac{1}{G(M,K)} \prod_{j=1}^{M} D_j^{n_j} \right) = D_i^{n_i} \frac{G(M,K-n_i)}{G(M,K)}. \quad (11.22)$$

Using this result, we find for the utilisation of queue $i$:

$$\rho_i = \Pr\{N_i \geq 1\} = D_i \frac{G(M,K-1)}{G(M,K)}. \quad (11.23)$$

Using the fact that $\rho_i = X_i(K)E[S_i] = X(K)V_iE[S_i] = X(K)D_i$, we find:

$$X(K) = \frac{G(M,K-1)}{G(M,K)}. \quad (11.24)$$

Thus, the throughput for the reference station simply equals the quotient of the last two computed normalising constants. To compute the probability of having exactly $n_i$ customers in node $i$, we proceed as follows:

$$
\begin{aligned}
\Pr\{N_i = n_i\} &= \sum_{\substack{\underline{n} \in \mathcal{I}(M,K) \\ N_i = n_i}} \frac{1}{G(M,K)} \prod_{i=1}^{M} D_i^{n_i} \\
&= D_i^{n_i} \sum_{\underline{n} \in \mathcal{I}(M,K)} \frac{1}{G(M,K)} \prod_{j=1}^{i-1} D_j^{n_j} \prod_{j=i+1}^{M} D_j^{n_j}.
\end{aligned}
\tag{11.25}
$$

As can be observed, the sum in the last expression resembles the normalising constant in a GNQN in which one queue (namely $i$) and $n_i$ customers are removed. However, it would be wrong to "recognize" this sum as $G(M - 1, K - n_i)$ since we have removed the $i$-th station, and not the $M$-th station; the column $G(M - 1, \cdot)$ corresponds to a GNQN in which station $M$ has been removed. However, if we, for the time being, assume that $i = M$, we obtain the following:

$$
\begin{aligned}
\Pr\{N_M = n_M\} &= D_M^{n_M} \sum_{\underline{n} \in \mathcal{I}(M,K)} \frac{1}{G(M,K)} \prod_{j=1}^{M-1} D_j^{n_j} \\
&= D_M^{n_M} \frac{G(M - 1, K - n_M)}{G(M,K)}.
\end{aligned}
\tag{11.26}
$$

In this expression we see two normalising constants appearing, one corresponding to column $M - 1$ and one corresponding to column $M$. It is this dependence on *two* columns that makes the ordering of the stations in the convolution scheme important.

We will now derive an alternate expression for $\Pr\{N_M = n_M\}$ in which only normalising constants of the form $G(M, \cdot)$ appear, so that the ordering of the stations, as sketched above, does not pose a problem any more. These expressions are then valid for all stations. We first rewrite (11.20) as

$$
G(M - 1, K) = G(M, K) - D_M G(M, K - 1),
\tag{11.27}
$$

and substitute it in (11.26) and set the number of customers equal to $K - n_i$; we then obtain

$$
\Pr\{N_M = n_M\} = \frac{D_M^{n_M}}{G(M,K)} \left( G(M, K - n_M) - D_M G(M, K - n_M - 1) \right).
\tag{11.28}
$$

In this expression, however, we see only normalising constants appearing that belong to the $M$-th column in the tabular computational scheme. Since the last column must always

be same, independently of the ordering of the stations, this expression is not only valid for
the $M$-th station, but for all stations, so that we have:

$$\Pr\{N_i = n_i\} = \frac{D_i^{n_i}}{G(M,K)} \left( G(M, K - n_i) - D_i G(M, K - n_i - 1) \right). \tag{11.29}$$

Another advantage of expressions only using the normalising constant of the form $G(M, \cdot)$
is that they are all available at the end of the computation. The columns $G(M-i, \cdot)$ might
have been overwritten during the computations to save storage.

For calculating average queue fillings the situation is a little bit more complicated,
however, still reasonable. We have

$$E[N_i(K)] = \sum_{k=1}^{K} k \Pr\{N_i = k\} = \sum_{k=1}^{K} \Pr\{N_i \geq k\} = \sum_{k=1}^{K} D_i^k \frac{G(M, K - k)}{G(M, K)}. \tag{11.30}$$

From these results we can, by applying Little's law, derive the expected response time
$E[R_i(K)]$ for queue $i$ as follows:

$$E[R_i(K)] = \frac{E[N_i(K)]}{X_i(K)} = \frac{E[N_i(K)]}{V_i X(K)} = \frac{\sum_{k=1}^{K} D_i^k G(M, K - k)}{V_i G(M, K - 1)}. \tag{11.31}$$

### Example 11.4. A three-node GNQN (III).

Consider the GNQN with 3 nodes we have addressed before, and of which we do know
the visits counts and the service demands: $V_1 = 1, V_2 = 0.4, V_3 = 0.6$ and $D_1 = 1.0, D_2 = 0.8, D_3 = 1.8$, respectively. The procedure to calculate $G(M, K)$ is now performed by
stepwisely filling the following table:

| $k$ | $G(1, k)$ | $G(2, k)$ | $G(3, k)$ |
|---|---|---|---|
| 0 | 1.0 | 1.0 | 1.0 |
| 1 | 1.0 | 1.8 | 3.6 |
| 2 | 1.0 | 2.44 | 8.92 |
| 3 | 1.0 | 2.952 | 19.008 |

Using the result that $X(K) = G(M, K - 1)/G(M, K)$, we have $X(1) = 1/3.6 = 0.278$,
$X(2) = 3.6/8.92 = 0.404$ and $X(3) = 8.92/19.008 = 0.469$. Using these values, we can
calculate the utilisations: $\rho_i(3) = X(3)D_i$. For instance, we have $\rho_2(3) = 0.469 \times 0.8 = 0.3752$. For calculating the average number of customers in node 2, we use

$$E[N_2(3)] = \sum_{k=1}^{3} D_2^k \frac{G(M, K - k)}{G(M, K)} = \frac{(0.8 \times 8.92) + (0.8^2 \times 3.6) + (0.8^3 \times 1.0)}{19.008} = 0.5236.$$

$$\tag{11.32}$$

| $k$ | $\rho_1(k)$ | $\rho_2(k)$ | $\rho_3(k)$ | $E[N_1(k)]$ | $E[N_2(k)]$ | $E[N_3(k)]$ | $E[R_1(k)]$ | $E[R_2(k)]$ | $E[R_3(k)]$ |
|---|---|---|---|---|---|---|---|---|---|
| 1 | 0.278 | 0.222 | 0.500 | 0.278 | 0.222 | 0.500 | 1.000 | 2.000 | 3.000 |
| 2 | 0.404 | 0.323 | 0.726 | 0.516 | 0.395 | 1.090 | 1.278 | 2.445 | 4.500 |
| 3 | 0.469 | 0.375 | 0.845 | 0.711 | 0.524 | 1.765 | 1.516 | 2.791 | 6.268 |

Table 11.2: Performance results for the small GNQN derived with the convolution method

From this, we derive

$$E[R_2(3)] = \frac{E[N_2(3)]}{X_2(3)} = \frac{E[N_2(3)]}{V_2 X(3)} = \frac{0.5236}{0.4 \times 0.469} = 2.7909. \tag{11.33}$$

Other performance measures can be derived similarly and are presented in Table 11.2. □

In the computations presented so far we have computed the expected response time at nodes *per visit*; we have taken the viewpoint of an arbitrary customer and computed its expected residence time at a particular node. Very often in the analysis of GNQNs, the expected response time *per passage* is also computed. This is nothing more than the usual expected response time weighted by the number of times the particular node is visited in a passage. We denote the expected response time per passage at node $i$ as $E[\hat{R}_i(K)]$ and have:

$$E[\hat{R}_i(K)] = V_i E[R_i(K)]. \tag{11.34}$$

$E[\hat{R}_i(K)]$ simply denotes the expected amount of time a customer spends in node $i$ during an average passage through the network. Consequently, if node $i$ is visited more than once per passage $(V_i > 1)$, the residence times of all these visits to node $i$ are added. Similarly, if node $i$ is only visited in a fraction of passages $(V_i < 1)$ the average time a customer spends at node $i$ is weighted accordingly. In a similar way, the overall expected response time per passage is defined as

$$E[\hat{R}(K)] = \sum_{i=1}^{M} E[\hat{R}_i(K)] = \sum_{i=1}^{M} V_i E[R_i(K)], \tag{11.35}$$

and expresses the expected amount of time it takes a customer to pass once through the queueing network. Given $E[\hat{R}(K)]$, the frequency at which a single customer attends the reference node (usually node 1) is then $1/E[\hat{R}(K)]$. Since there are $K$ customers cycling through the QN the throughput through the reference node must be:

$$X(K) = \frac{K}{E[\hat{R}(K)]}. \tag{11.36}$$

We will use this result in the mean-value analysis to be presented in Section 11.3.

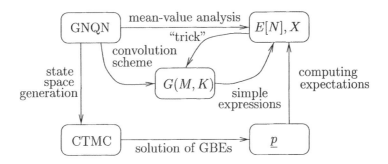

Figure 11.3: The role of CTMCs and MVA in the solution of QN models

A final remark regarding the convolution approach follows here. We have presented it for GNQN where all the queues are M|M|1 queues. However, various extensions do exist, most notably to the case where the individual nodes have service rates that depend on their queue length. In particular, the infinite-server queue belongs to this class of nodes. We will come back to these extensions of the convolution algorithm in Chapter 12.

## 11.3   Mean-value analysis

In the analysis of the GNQNs discussed so far, we have used intermediate quantities such as normalising constants (in the case of the convolution algorithm) or steady-state probabilities (in the case of a direct computation at the CTMC level) to compute user-oriented measures of interest such as average response times or utilisations at the nodes of the QN. This is illustrated in Figure 11.3. Although this approach as such is correct, there may be instances in which it is inefficient or computationally unattractive. This happens when one is really only interested in average performance measures. Then we do not need the steady-state probabilities nor the normalising constants, but resort to an approach known as *mean-value analysis* (MVA) which was developed by Reiser and Lavenberg in the late 1970s. With MVA, the average performance measures of interest are directly calculated at the level of the QN without resorting to an underlying CTMC and without using normalising constants. The advantage of such an approach is that the quantities that are employed in the computations have a "physical" interpretation in terms of the GNQN and hence the computations can be better understood and verified for correctness. Note that in Chapter 4 we have already encountered a special case of the MVA approach in the discussion of the terminal model. Here we will generalise that approach.

A key role in MVA is played by the so-called *arrival theorem* for closed queueing networks, which was derived independently in the late 1970s by Lavenberg and Reiser [174] and Sevcik and Mitrani [260]; we refer to these publications for the (involved) proof of this theorem.

**Theorem 11.1. Arrival theorem.**

In a closed queueing network the steady-state probability distribution of customers at the moment a customer moves from one queue to another, equals the (usual) steady-state probability distribution of customers in that queueing network without the moving customer.                                                                   □

A direct consequence of the arrival theorem is that a customer moving from queue $i$ to queue $j$ in a QN with $K$ customers, will find, upon its arrival at queue $j$, on average $E[N_j(K-1)]$ customers in queue $j$. Assuming that customers are served in FCFS order, we can use this result to establish a recursive relation between the average performance measures in a GNQN with $K$ customers and a GNQN with $K-1$ customers as follows. The average waiting time of a customer arriving at queue $i$, given an overall customer population $K$, equals the number of customers present upon arrival, multiplied by their average service time. According to the arrival theorem, this can be expressed as:

$$E[W_i(K)] = E[N_i(K-1)]E[S_i]. \tag{11.37}$$

The average response time (per visit) then equals the average waiting time plus the average service time:

$$E[R_i(K)] = (E[N_i(K-1)]+1)E[S_i]. \tag{11.38}$$

Multiplying this with the visit ratio $V_i$, we obtain the average response time per passage:

$$E[\hat{R}_i(K)] = (E[N_i(K-1)]+1)E[S_i]V_i = (E[N_i(K-1)]+1)D_i. \tag{11.39}$$

Using Little's law, we know

$$E[N_i(K)] = X_i(K)E[R_i(K)] = X(K)V_iE[R_i(K)]) = X(K)E[\hat{R}_i(K)], \tag{11.40}$$

or, if we sum over all stations,

$$\sum_{i=1}^{M} E[N_i(K)] = X(K)\sum_{i=1}^{M} E[\hat{R}_i(K)] = X(K)E[\hat{R}(K)] = K. \tag{11.41}$$

From this equation, we have

$$X(K) = \frac{K}{E[\hat{R}(K)]}, \tag{11.42}$$

as we have seen before, and which can be substituted in Little's law applied to a single node:

$$
\begin{aligned}
E[N_i(K)] &= X_i(K)E[R_i(K)] = X(K)(V_iE[R_i(K)]) \\
&= \frac{K}{E[\hat{R}(K)]}E[\hat{R}_i(K)] = K\frac{E[R_i(K)]}{E[R(K)]}. \tag{11.43}
\end{aligned}
$$

This result is intuitively appealing since it expresses that the average number of customers at queue $i$ equals the fraction of time that each customer passage, the customers resides in queue $i$ during a passage, i.e., $E[\hat{R}_i(K)]/E[\hat{R}(K)]$, times the total number of customers $K$. Using (11.39) and (11.43), we can recursively compute average performance measures for increasing values of $K$. Knowing $E[R(K)]$, we can use (11.42) to calculate $X(K)$. Finally, we can compute $\rho_i(K) = X(K)V_iE[S_i]$. The start in the recursion is formed by the case $K = 1$, for which $E[\hat{R}_i(1)] = D_i$, for all $i$.

**Example 11.5. A three-node GNQN (IV).**
We readdress the example of the previous sections, but this time apply the MVA approach to solve for the average performance measures. For $K = 1$, we have

$$
\begin{cases}
E[\hat{R}_1(1)] &= (E[N_1(0)] + 1)D_1 = D_1 = 1.0 \\
E[\hat{R}_2(1)] &= (E[N_2(0)] + 1)D_2 = D_2 = 0.8 \\
E[\hat{R}_3(1)] &= (E[N_3(0)] + 1)D_3 = D_3 = 1.8
\end{cases} \tag{11.44}
$$

From this, we derive $E[\hat{R}(1)] = \sum_{i=1}^{3} E[R_i(1)] = 3.6$ and so $X(1) = 1/E[\hat{R}(1)] = 0.278$. Using $E[N_i(1)] = X(1)E[\hat{R}_i(1)]$ we have $E[N_1(1)] = 0.278$, $E[N_2(1)] = 0.222$ and $E[N_3(1)] = 0.500$. We also have immediately $\rho_1(1) = D_1X(1) = 0.278$, $\rho_2(1) = 0.222$ and $\rho_3(1) = 0.500$. For $K = 2$, we have

$$
\begin{cases}
E[\hat{R}_1(2)] &= (E[N_1(1)] + 1)D_1 = 1.278D_1 = 1.278 \\
E[\hat{R}_2(2)] &= (E[N_2(1)] + 1)D_2 = 1.222D_2 = 0.978 \\
E[\hat{R}_3(2)] &= (E[N_3(1)] + 1)D_3 = 1.500D_3 = 2.700
\end{cases} \tag{11.45}
$$

From this, we derive $E[\hat{R}(2)] = \sum_{i=1}^{3} E[\hat{R}_i(2)] = 4.956$ and so $X(2) = 2/E[\hat{R}(2)] = 0.404$. Using $E[N_i(2)] = X(2)E[\hat{R}_i(2)]$ we have $E[N_1(2)] = 0.516$, $E[N_2(2)] = 0.395$ and $E[N_3(2)] = 1.091$. We also have immediately $\rho_1(2) = D_1X(2) = 0.404$, $\rho_2(2) = 0.323$ and $\rho_3(2) = 0.726$.

We leave it as an exercise for the reader to derive the results for the case $K = 3$ and compare them with the results derived with Buzen's convolution scheme.                        □

When the scheduling discipline at a particular queue is of infinite server type (IS), we can still employ the simple MVA approach as presented here. For more general cases of *load-dependency* a more intricate form is needed (to be addressed in Chapter 12). The only thing that changes in the infinite-server case is that for the stations $j$ with IS semantics, equation (11.39) changes: there is no waiting so the response time always equals the service time, i.e., we have

$$\text{for IS nodes}: \ E[R_j(K)] = E[S_j], \quad \text{or} \quad E[\hat{R}_j(K)] = D_j. \tag{11.46}$$

As can be observed, the case of IS nodes makes the computations even simpler!

Regarding the complexity of the MVA approach the following remarks can be made. We have to compute the response times at the nodes for a customer population increasing to $K$. Given a certain customer population, for every station one has to perform one addition, one multiplication and one division. Consequently, the complexity is of order $O(KM)$. In principle, once results for $K$ have been computed, the results for $K-1$ do not need to be stored any longer. Therefore, one needs at most $O(M)$ storage for the MVA approach.

Although the MVA approach might seem slightly more computationally intensive, its advantage clearly is that one computes with mean values that can be understood in terms of the system being modelled. Since these mean values are usually not as large as normalising constants tend to be, computational problems relating to round-off and loss of accuracy are less likely to occur. Furthermore, while computing performance measures for a particular GNQN with $K$ customers, the results for the same GNQN with less customers present are computed as well. This is very useful when performing parametric studies on the number of customers.

After an MVA has been performed, it might turn out that at a particular station the average response time is very high and one might be interested in obtaining more detailed performance measures for that station, e.g., the probability of having more than a certain number of customers in that station. Such measures cannot be obtained with an MVA, but they can be obtained using the convolution method. The question then is: should we redo all the work and perform a convolution solution from the start, or can we reuse the MVA results? Fortunately, the latter is the case, i.e., we can use the MVA results to calculate normalising constant! From Section 11.2 we recall that

$$X(K) = \frac{G(M, K-1)}{G(M, K)} \ \Rightarrow \ G(M, K) = \frac{G(M, K-1)}{X(K)}. \tag{11.47}$$

Since we have calculated the values of $X(k)$ for $k = 1, \cdots, K$, using the MVA, we can calculate $G(M, 1) = 1/X(1)$, then calculate $G(M, 2) = G(M, 1)/X(2)$, etc. This approach is shown in Figure 11.3 by the arc labelled "trick". Using the thus calculated normalising constants we can proceed to calculate more detailed performance measures as shown in Section 11.1.

**Example 11.6. A three-node GNQN (V).**
Using MVA we have computed the following values for the throughputs at increasing customer populations: $X(1) = 0.278$, $X(2) = 0.404$ and $X(3) = 0.469$. Consequently, as indicated above, we have

$$
\begin{aligned}
G(M, 1) &= \frac{1}{X(1)} = \frac{1}{0.278} = 3.600, \\
G(M, 2) &= \frac{G(M, 1)}{X(2)} = \frac{3.6}{0.404} = 8.920, \\
G(M, 3) &= \frac{G(M, 2)}{X(3)} = \frac{8.92}{0.469} = 19.008.
\end{aligned}
\tag{11.48}
$$

As can be observed, these normalising constants correspond with those calculated via Buzen's algorithm. For the computations as presented here, it is of key importance to maintain a large number of significant digits; typically, using ordinary floating point numbers, such as those of the 64-bit IEEE 754 floating point number standard, does not suffice when evaluating large GNQNs!                                                              □

## 11.4  Mean-value analysis-based approximations

The larger the number of customers $K$ in a GNQN, the longer the MVA recursion scheme takes. To overcome this, a number of approximation and bounding techniques have been proposed; we discuss three of them here. We start with asymptotic bounds in Section 11.4.1; we have already seen these in a less general context in Chapter 4. The well-known Bard-Schweitzer approximation is presented in Section 11.4.2 and an approximation based on balanced networks is discussed in Section 11.4.3.

### 11.4.1  Asymptotic bounds

We have already encountered asymptotic bounds in a less general context in Chapter 4 when discussing the terminal model, as well as in Section 11.1, when discussing throughput bounds. Here we present these bounds in a more general context.

Consider a GNQN in which all but one of the nodes are normal FCFS nodes. There is one node of infinite-server type which is assumed to be visited once during a passage (note that this does not form a major restriction since the visit-counts $V_i$ can be scaled at will). Denote its expected service time as $E[Z]$ and the service demands at the other nodes as $D_i = V_i E[S_i]$. Furthermore, let $D_+ = \max_i\{D_i\}$ and $D_\Sigma = \sum_i D_i$.

We first address the case where the number of customers is the smallest possible: $K = 1$. In that case, the time for the single customer to pass once through the queueing network can be expressed as $E[\hat{R}(1)] = E[Z] + D_\Sigma$, simply because there will be no queueing. From this, we can directly conclude that the expected response time for $K \geq 1$ will always be at least equal to the value when $K = 1$:

$$E[\hat{R}(K)] \geq E[Z] + D_\Sigma. \tag{11.49}$$

When there is only a single customer present, the throughput equals $1/\hat{R}(1)$. We assume that the throughput will increase when more customers are entering the network (this assumption implies that we do not take into account various forms of overhead or inefficiencies). However, as more customers are entering the network, queueing effects will start to play a role. Hence, the throughput with $K$ customers will not be as good as $K$ times the throughput with a single customer only:

$$X(K) \leq \frac{K}{E[Z] + D_\Sigma}. \tag{11.50}$$

Although the above bounds are also valid for large $K$ they can be made much tighter in that case. Since we know that for large $K$ the bottleneck device does have a utilisation approaching 1, we know that for $K \to \infty$ the following must hold: $X(K)D_+ \to 1$, so that $X(K) \to 1/D_+$ or

$$X(K) \leq \frac{1}{D_+}. \tag{11.51}$$

Using Little's law for the queueing network as a whole we find $K = X(K)E[\hat{R}(K)]$, or, when taking $K \to \infty$:

$$E[\hat{R}(K)] = \frac{K}{X(K)} \leq KD_+. \tag{11.52}$$

In conclusion we have found the following bounds:

$$
\begin{aligned}
X(K) &\leq \min\left\{\frac{K}{E[Z] + D_\Sigma}, \frac{1}{D_+}\right\}, \\
E[\hat{R}(K)] &\geq \max\{E[Z] + D_\Sigma, KD_+\}.
\end{aligned} \tag{11.53}
$$

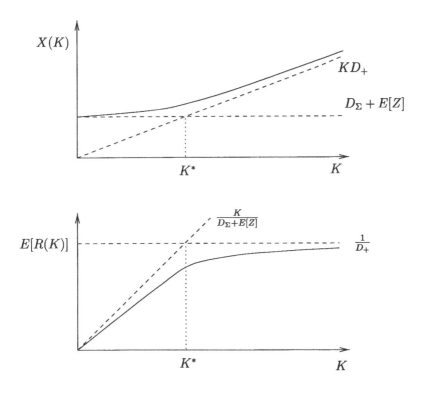

Figure 11.4: Asymptotic bounds for a closed queueing network (dashed lines: asymptotes; solid lines: true values (estimated))

These bounds are illustrated in Figure 11.4. The crossing point $K^*$ of the two asymptotes is called the *saturation point* and is given by

$$K^* = \frac{D_\Sigma + E[Z]}{D_+}. \tag{11.54}$$

The integer part of $K^*$ can be interpreted as the maximum number of customers that could be accommodated without any queueing when all the service times are of deterministic length. Stated differently, if the number of customers is larger than $K^*$ we are sure that queueing effects in the network contribute to the response times.

## 11.4.2  The Bard-Schweitzer approximation

A simple approximation for GNQNs with large customer population was proposed by Bard and Schweitzer in the late 1970s. When the number of customers in the GNQN is large, it might be reasonable to assume that

$$E[N_i(K-1)] \approx \frac{K-1}{K} E[N_i(K)], \qquad (11.55)$$

that is, the decrease in customer number is divided equally over all queues. Substituting this in the basic MVA equation (11.39), we obtain

$$E[\hat{R}_i(K)] = \begin{cases} (\frac{K-1}{K} E[N_i(K)] + 1)D_i, & \text{FCFS nodes}, \\ D_i, & \text{IS nodes}. \end{cases} \qquad (11.56)$$

We can use this equation to compute an estimate for $E[\hat{R}_i(K)]$ given an estimate for $E[N_i(K)]$. As a first guess, typically the uniform distribution of all $K$ customers over the $M$ nodes is taken, i.e., $E[N_i(K)] \approx K/M$. Then, (11.56) can be used to obtain a more exact estimate for $E[\hat{R}_i(K)]$, after which (11.43) is used to compute a more accurate approximation of $E[N_i(K)]$. This process is continued until convergence is reached. It is important to note that convergence should be tested on all the measures of interest. If the interest is in mean response times at the nodes, the iteration should be stopped when two successive estimates for *that* measure are sufficiently close to one another. At that point, it is possible that the estimates for the mean queue lengths or throughput are not as good.

The Bard-Schweitzer approximation scheme often works very well in practice, however, its accuracy depends on the model and parameters at hand. Notice that an iteration step in the approximation is as expensive as a normal MVA iteration step; thus, the approximation scheme is computationally only attractive when the expected number of iterations is smaller than the number of customers in the GNQN.

**Example 11.7. A three-node GNQN (VI).**
Let us address the simple three-node GNQN again, but now with $K = 60$. Using the Bard-Schweitzer iterative scheme as given above, we find the performance measures as given in Table 11.3 for increasing number of iterations (the number of iterations is seen in the column headed #). As can be observed, with only few iterations, the approximation scheme approaches the correct values relatively well.                                                          □


## 11.4.3   Balanced networks

A class of GNQN that can very easily be solved using MVA is the class of *balanced networks*. A GNQN is said to be balanced whenever $D_i = D$, for all $i$; in other words, in a balanced QN all the nodes have the same service demand. If this is the case, the performance

| # | $E[R_1(60)]$ | $E[R_2(60)]$ | $E[R_3(60)]$ | $E[N_1(60)]$ | $E[N_2(60)]$ | $E[N_3(60)]$ |
|---|---|---|---|---|---|---|
| 1 | 21.0000 | 42.0000 | 63.0000 | 16.6667 | 13.3333 | 30.0000 |
| 2 | 17.6667 | 28.6667 | 93.0000 | 12.4804 | 8.1005 | 39.4192 |
| 3 | 13.4804 | 18.2009 | 121.2575 | 8.6491 | 4.6711 | 46.6798 |
| 4 | 9.6491 | 11.3423 | 143.0393 | 5.7889 | 2.7219 | 51.4892 |
| 5 | 6.7889 | 7.4438 | 157.4676 | 3.9074 | 1.7137 | 54.3789 |
| 6 | 4.9074 | 5.4274 | 166.1366 | 2.7580 | 1.2201 | 56.0219 |
| 7 | 3.7580 | 4.4402 | 171.0657 | 2.0844 | 0.9851 | 56.9304 |
| 8 | 3.0844 | 3.9703 | 173.7913 | 1.6987 | 0.8746 | 57.4267 |
| 9 | 2.6987 | 3.7492 | 175.2802 | 1.4805 | 0.8227 | 57.6967 |
| 10 | 2.4805 | 3.6455 | 176.0902 | 1.3580 | 0.7983 | 57.8436 |
| 11 | 2.3580 | 3.5967 | 176.5309 | 1.2895 | 0.7868 | 57.9237 |
| 12 | 2.2895 | 3.5735 | 176.7711 | 1.2513 | 0.7812 | 57.9674 |
| $\vdots$ | $\vdots$ | $\vdots$ | $\vdots$ | $\vdots$ | $\vdots$ | $\vdots$ |
| 20 | 2.2041 | 3.5520 | 177.0597 | 1.2038 | 0.7760 | 58.0203 |
| MVA | 2.2500 | 3.6000 | 173.8500 | 1.2500 | 0.8000 | 57.9500 |

Table 11.3: Bard-Schweitzer approximation for the three-node GNQN when $K = 60$

measures will be the same for all queues. As a consequence of this, the $K$ customers are divided equally over the $M$ queues, i.e., $E[N_i(K)] = K/M$, for all $i$.

The expected response times (per passage) are then also the same for all stations. Using the basic MVA relation (11.39) and substituting $E[N_i(K - 1)] = (K - 1)/M$, we find:

$$E[\hat{R}_i(K)] = \left(\frac{K - 1}{M} + 1\right) D = \frac{K + M - 1}{M} D. \tag{11.57}$$

The overall expected response time per passage $E[\hat{R}(K)] = (K + M - 1)D$. For the throughput and utilisations we obtain:

$$X(K) = \frac{K}{E[\hat{R}(K)]} = \frac{K}{D(K + M - 1)} \quad \text{and} \quad \rho_i(K) = X(K)D = \frac{K}{K + M - 1}. \tag{11.58}$$

In practice almost no system can be modelled as a balanced GNQN. However, we can use a balanced QN to obtain bounds for the throughput and average response times in non-balanced GNQNs as follows. Define:

$$D_+ = \max_i\{D_i\}, \quad D_- = \min_i\{D_i\}, \quad \text{and} \quad D_\Sigma = \sum_i D_i. \tag{11.59}$$

These values correspond to the smallest, the largest and the sum of the service demands. The throughput $X(K)$ in the unbalanced GNQN will be smaller than the throughput in a completely balanced GNQN with service demands set to $D_-$, but higher than in a completely balanced GNQN with service demands set to $D_+$. Consequently,

$$\frac{K}{D_+(K + M - 1)} \le X(K) \le \frac{K}{D_-(K + M - 1)}. \tag{11.60}$$

From this inequality, we can also derive bounds for the response times:

$$(K + M - 1)D_- \le E[\hat{R}(K)] \le (K + M - 1)D_+. \tag{11.61}$$

The above bounds can be made a little bit tighter by realising that the performance is best when the overall service demand $D_\Sigma$ is divided equally over the $M$ stations, i.e., when $D_i = \overline{D} = D_\Sigma/M$. Also, the throughput is bounded by $1/D_+$. These considerations lead to the following throughput upperbound:

$$X(K) \le \min\left\{\frac{K}{\overline{D}(K + M - 1)}, \frac{1}{D_+}\right\} = \min\left\{\frac{K}{\overline{D}(K - 1) + D_\Sigma}, \frac{1}{D_+}\right\}. \tag{11.62}$$

The worst performance appears when the network is most unbalanced, keeping in mind that the largest service demand is $D_+$. We then have $\lfloor D_\Sigma/D_+ \rfloor$ stations with service demand $D_+$ and $M - \lfloor D_\Sigma/D_+ \rfloor$ stations with service demand zero. From this, we derive the following lower bound:

$$X(K) \ge \frac{K}{(K + \lfloor \frac{D_\Sigma}{D_+} \rfloor - 1)D_+} = \frac{K}{D_+(K - 1) + D_\Sigma}. \tag{11.63}$$

From these two inequalities we can easily derive the following bound for the expected response time per passage:

$$\max\left\{D_\Sigma + \overline{D}(K - 1), KD_+\right\} \le E[\hat{R}(K)] \le D_\Sigma + D_+(K - 1). \tag{11.64}$$

### Example 11.8. A three-node GNQN (VII).

Let us consider the three-node GNQN again with $M = K = 3$ and $D_1 = 1, D_2 = 0.8$ and $D_3 = 1.8$. For the simple bounds we derive the following:

$$0.333 \le X(3) \le 0.750, \quad \text{and} \quad 4.000 \le E[\hat{R}(3)] \le 9.000.$$

As can be observed, these bounds are not too tight; the exact values are: $X(3) = 0.469$ and $E[R(3)] = 6.393$. When we employ the tighter bounding scheme we find, however, much better bounds:

$$0.417 \le X(3) \le 0.500, \quad \text{and} \quad 6.000 \le E[\hat{R}(3)] \le 7.200.$$

The error is about 10%. The bounds obtained in this way improve when the differences in the involved service demands $D_i$ are smaller. $\square$

When the queueing network to be bounded does not only contain FCFS nodes but also nodes of infinite-server type, the bounds presented above cannot be used. Instead, a special treatment has to be given to the infinite-server nodes. Below, we will consider bounds for the performance measures in a GNQN in which there is only one infinite-server node with think time $E[Z]$. Since we will use the think time directly in the bounds below, we have to make sure that the visit count $V_i$ for the infinite-server station is 1; this can be achieved by simply renormalising them as such. The values $D_-$, $D_+$, $\overline{D}$ and $D_\Sigma$ are defined as before, however, taking into account the renormalised visit counts. Without proof, we state that in such a QN the expected response time given $K$ customers present, i.e., $E[\hat{R}(K)]$, lies in the following interval:

$$\left[\max\left\{KD_+ - E[Z], D_\Sigma + (K-1)\overline{D}\frac{D_\Sigma}{D_\Sigma + E[Z]}\right\}, D_\Sigma + (K-1)D_+\frac{(K-1)D_\Sigma}{(K-1)D_\Sigma + E[Z]}\right].$$
(11.65)

Notice that these bounds are to be interpreted as the bounds for the system to respond to a request from the infinite-server station (normally, the modelled terminals), i.e., the think time itself is *not* included in the response time bound. Similarly, we find that the throughput of the infinite-server station (the station with $V_i = 1$) when there are $K$ customers present, i.e., $X(K)$ lies in the following interval:

$$\left[\frac{K}{E[Z] + D_\Sigma + (K-1)D_+\frac{(K-1)D_\Sigma}{(K-1)D_\Sigma + E[Z]}}, \min\left\{\frac{1}{D_+}, \frac{K}{E[Z] + D_\Sigma + (K-1)\overline{D}\frac{D_\Sigma}{D_\Sigma + E[Z]}}\right\}\right].$$
(11.66)

Note that when there are no infinite-server stations, setting $E[Z] = 0$ in these bounds will yield the bounds for a model without infinite-server station, as we have seen before. A four-page proof of these bounds can be found in [145, Section 34.4]. We will show the usefulness of the bounds in Section 11.6.

## 11.5 An approximate solution method

As pointed out in the previous sections, exact solution methods for GNQNs suffer from the fact that the computational requirements increase rapidly with increasing numbers of customers and nodes. Also, a normally quite efficient method such as MVA becomes less attractive when multi-server queues or nodes with load-dependent service rates are introduced (see Chapter 13 for details). In order to circumvent these difficulties, we present a generally applicable approximate approach that has been developed by Bolch *et al.* [26]; since his approach is based on finding the zero of a function, it is sometimes referred to as the "functional approach".

We define the class of queueing networks that can be handled in Section 11.5.1. Then, we discuss the basic solution approach in Section 11.5.2. A numerical solution procedure is presented in Section 11.5.3, and Section 11.5.4 addresses a few extensions.

### 11.5.1  Queueing network definition

To start with, we consider a GNQN with $M$ nodes and $K$ customers and assume that, for every node, the visit ratios $V_i$ and the service rates $\mu_i$ ($E[S_i] = 1/\mu_i$) are known. Then, we assume that every node in the queueing network is of one of the four following types:

- 1. M|M|$m$-FCFS;
  2. M|G|1-PS;
  3. M|G|$\infty$-IS;
  4. M|G|1-LCFSPR.

These four node types coincide with the four node types allowed in BCMP queueing networks which we will present in Chapter 13.

### 11.5.2  Basic approach

Central to the approximation procedure is the observation that in open, load-independent queueing stations, the mean number of customers is an increasing function of the throughput (or the utilisation). For instance, in the M|M|1-case we have

$$E[N_i] = f_i(X_i) = \frac{X_i E[S_i]}{1 - \lambda_i E[S_i]} = \frac{\rho_i}{1 - \rho_i}. \tag{11.67}$$

For (load-dependent) queueing stations in closed queueing networks, this functional relation might be slightly different, but we will assume that such a function $f_i$ exists and is non-decreasing. For a type 3 station, it is known that $f_i(X_i) = X_i/\mu_i$. Observe that $f_i(0) = 0$ and that $f_i$ is only defined for $X_i \in [0, m_i\mu_i)$, i.e., for cases in which the node is not saturated.

Now, suppose that we know the functions $f_i$ for all the queueing stations in the network. Let $N_i(K)$ be a random variable that denotes the number of customers in station $i$, given there are in total $K$ customers present. Clearly, by the fact that the total number of customers is fixed, we have

$$N_1(K) + N_2(K) + \cdots + N_M(K) = K. \tag{11.68}$$

Taking expectations on both sides, we obtain

$$E[N_1(K)] + E[N_2(K)] + \cdots + E[N_M(K)] = K, \tag{11.69}$$

which, by using the functions $f_i$ and the fact that $X_i(K) = X(K)V_i$, can be rewritten as

$$\sum_{i=1}^{M} E[N_i(K)] = \sum_{i=1}^{M} f_i(X_i(K)) = \sum_{i=1}^{M} f_i(X(K)V_i) = K. \tag{11.70}$$

This equation basically states that the sum of the average number of customers in all stations must equal the total number of customers. If we know the functions $f_i$, the non-linear equation (11.70) in $X(K)$ can be solved numerically. Let us now first focus on the determination of the functions $f_i$ before we discuss the numerical solution of (11.70) in Section 11.5.3.

For ease in notation, we use $\rho_i = X_i/(m_i\mu_i)$. One problem in the determination of the functions $f_i$ is that they should be valid in the finite-customer domain. Normal functional relationships, e.g., those derived from M|M|1 analysis, are valid for open QNs, hence for infinite customer populations.

We first address the type 1 queueing stations with $m = 1$. For the infinite-buffer single-server case, we know from M|M|1 analysis that (11.67) holds. Observe that $\lim_{\rho_i \to 1} E[N_i] = \infty$ in this case. However, if we introduce a correction factor $(K-1)/K$ in the denominator, we obtain

$$E[N_i] = \frac{\rho_i}{1 - \frac{K-1}{K}\rho_i}. \tag{11.71}$$

This equation has a limiting value of $K$ when $\rho_i \to 1$, which is intuitively appealing: when the utilisation approaches 100%, all $K$ customers will reside in this node. Due to the insensitivity property in BCMP queueing networks (see Chapter 13) this result can also be used for nodes of type 2 (PS) and type 4 (LCFSPR). Note that the above result can also be derived from the Bard-Schweitzer approximation discussed in Section 11.4.2, in particular, by rewriting (11.56).

When we deal with an M|M|$m_i$-FCFS station, we have to adapt the result so as to account for the multiserver behaviour. Maintaining the same line of thinking, we obtain:

$$E[N_i] = m_i\rho_i + p_m(\rho_i) \times \frac{\rho_i}{1 - \frac{K-m_i-1}{K-m_i}\rho_i}. \tag{11.72}$$

The first additive term gives the number of customers in service, whereas the latter gives the number of customers queued, since $p_m(\rho_i)$ is the probability that there are customers queued. From analyses similar to those performed in Chapter 4, we can derive that

$$p_m(\rho) = \frac{\frac{(m\rho)^m}{m!(1-\rho)}}{\sum_{j=0}^{m-1} \frac{(m\rho)^m}{j!} + \frac{(m\rho)^m}{m!(1-\rho)}}, \tag{11.73}$$

which can be approximated as

$$p_m(\rho) = \begin{cases} \rho^{(m+1)/2}, & \rho \le 0.7, \\ \frac{1}{2}(\rho^m + \rho), & \rho \ge 0.7. \end{cases} \qquad (11.74)$$

Again notice the behaviour of $E[N_i]$ when $\rho_i \to 1$: the first additive term will equal $m_i$; the probability $p_m(\rho)$ approaches 1, and the second term will therefore approach $K - m_i$, so that for the overall number of customers we have: $E[N_i] \to K$. Finally, for type 3 stations, i.e., IS stations, we have the exact relation

$$E[N_i] = X_i/\mu_i. \qquad (11.75)$$

## 11.5.3   Numerical solution

Now that we have obtained the individual functions $f_i$ for the allowed types of nodes in the queueing network we have to solve (11.70). Denoting the left-hand side of this equation as $F(X(K))$, we have to solve $F(X(K)) = K$. Since the additive parts of $F(X(K))$ are all increasing, $F(X(K))$ does so as well. By the fact that $f_i(0) = 0$, for all $i$, and the fact that $f_i$ is increasing, $X(K)$ must be non-negative. Also, because

$$\rho_i(K) = \frac{X(K)V_i}{m_i\mu_i} \le 1,$$

we have

$$X(K) \le \frac{m_i\mu_i}{V_i}, \text{ for all } i,$$

i.e., we require

$$X(K) \le \min_i \left\{ \frac{m_i\mu_i}{V_i} \right\}.$$

To solve $F(X(K)) = K$, we start with two guesses: we set $l = 0$ (low) and $h = \min_i\{\frac{m_i\mu_i}{V_i}\}$ (high) so that $F(l) \le K$ and $F(h) \ge K$. Then, we compute $\overline{m} = (l + h)/2$ (middle) and evaluate $F(m)$. If $F(m) < K$, we set $l \leftarrow m$; otherwise, if $F(m) > K$ we set $h \leftarrow m$. We repeat this procedure until we have found that value $m$ such that $F(m) = K \pm \epsilon$, where $\epsilon$ is some preset accuracy level. The approach is illustrated in Figure 11.5; we basically determine a zero of the function $F(X(K)) - K$ by interval splitting. Of course, other methods such as Newton's method might be employed for this purpose as well.

Once $X(K)$ has been determined, one can easily compute other performance measures of interest. For $i = 1, \cdots, M$, one has $X_i(K) = X(K)V_i$, $\rho_i(K) = X_i(K)/m_i\mu_i$, $E[N_i(K)] = f_i(X_i(K))$, $E[N_{q,i}(K)] = E[N_i(K)] - \rho_i(K)$, $E[R_i(K)] = f_i(X_i(K))/X_i(K)$ and $E[W_i(K)] = E[N_{q,i}(K)]/X_i(K)$.

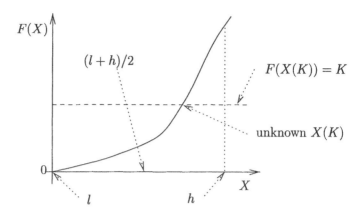

Figure 11.5: Interval splitting to determine $F(X(K)) = K$

It can be seen that although the non-linear equation increases in size (complexity) when the number of stations $M$ increases, it does not increase in complexity when either $K$ increases or the number of servers $m_i$ becomes larger than 1. This is an important advantage of this solution technique.

**Example 11.9. The three-node GNQN (VIII).**
Applying this method to our small three-node GNQN, we find

$$E[N_i(K;X)] = \frac{XD_i}{1 - \frac{K-1}{K}XD_i}$$

so that we have to solve, for $K = 3$:

$$\frac{X}{1 - \frac{2}{3}X} + \frac{8X}{10(1 - \frac{8}{15}X)} + \frac{18X}{10(1 - \frac{6}{5}X)} = 3.$$

Using a numerical method as sketched above, we find $X = 0.460$ which differs by only 2% from the exact value 0.4693 we found earlier. We find also: $E[N_1(3)] = 0.664$, $E[N_2(3)] = 0.488$ and $E[N_3(3)] = 1.848$. Here the differences with the exact values are less than 7%.
□

**Example 11.10. A four-node BCMP queueing network (adapted from [26]).**
Consider a queueing network with $M = 4$ nodes and $K = 10$ customers. The station parameters are given in Table 11.4. Since the example network is of BCMP type, a direct MVA can also be employed. In Table 11.5 we present the results for both the MVA and

| $i$ | $V_i$ | $\mu_i$ | $m_i$ |
|---|---|---|---|
| 1 | 1.0 | 1.9 | 4 |
| 2 | 0.4 | 0.9 | $\infty$ |
| 3 | 0.4 | 5.0 | 1 |
| 4 | 0.2 | 1.5 | 1 |

Table 11.4: Parameters of the four-node queueing network

| | MVA | | | | approximation | | | |
|---|---|---|---|---|---|---|---|---|
| $i$ | $X_i$ | $\rho_i$ | $E[N_i]$ | $E[R_i]$ | $X_i$ | $\rho_i$ | $E[N_i]$ | $E[R_i]$ |
| 1 | 6.021 | 0.792 | 3.990 | 0.662 | 5.764 | 0.758 | 4.156 | 0.721 |
| 2 | 2.408 | 0.267 | 3.676 | 1.111 | 2.305 | 0.256 | 2.561 | 1.111 |
| 3 | 2.408 | 0.481 | 0.856 | 0.355 | 2.305 | 0.461 | 0.788 | 0.314 |
| 4 | 1.204 | 0.802 | 2.476 | 2.056 | 1.152 | 0.768 | 2.492 | 2.162 |

Table 11.5: MVA and approximate results for the four-node queueing network

the approximate analysis. As can be observed, the results match within about 10–15%. This seems to be reasonable, given the difference in computational effort required to get the solution.                                                                □

## 11.5.4 Extension to other queueing stations

Given the approach, we can easily extend it to include other nodes as long as we are able to find functions $E[N_i(K)] = f_i(X_i(K))$. One such function can for instance be found for the M|G|m-FCFS queueing station:

$$E[N_i(K)] = m_i\rho_i + \alpha p_m(\rho_i) \times \frac{\rho_i}{1 - \frac{K-m_i-\alpha}{K-m_i}\rho_i}, \qquad (11.76)$$

where $p_m(\rho)$ is defined as before, and where

$$\alpha = \frac{1}{2}(1 + C_S^2), \qquad (11.77)$$

where $C_S^2$ is the squared coefficient of variation of the service time distribution. This type of queueing station does not fall into the category of BCMP queueing networks any more. Notice that for $\alpha = 1$, i.e., for negative exponentially distributed service times, the above

| $i$ | $V_i$ | $\mu_i$ | $m_i$ | $C_S^2$ |
|---|---|---|---|---|
| 1 | 1.00 | 0.20 | 4 | 0.30 |
| 2 | 1.13 | 0.08 | 7 | 2.40 |
| 3 | 0.33 | 0.80 | 1 | 1.00 |
| 4 | 0.33 | 0.12 | 10 | 3.90 |
| 5 | 0.67 | 0.05 | $\infty$ | 1.00 |

Table 11.6: Parameters of the five-node non-BCMP queueing network

| | simulation | | | | approximation | | | |
|---|---|---|---|---|---|---|---|---|
| $i$ | $X_i$ | $\rho_i$ | $E[N_i]$ | $E[R_i]$ | $X_i$ | $\rho_i$ | $E[N_i]$ | $E[R_i]$ |
| 1 | 0.339 | 0.424 | 2.045 | 6.038 | 0.322 | 0.402 | 1.649 | 5.115 |
| 2 | 0.382 | 0.682 | 5.848 | 15.328 | 0.364 | 0.650 | 5.437 | 14.927 |
| 3 | 0.112 | 0.140 | 0.184 | 1.643 | 0.106 | 0.132 | 0.152 | 1.434 |
| 4 | 1.127 | 0.939 | 17.465 | 15.502 | 1.073 | 1.073 | 18.415 | 17.155 |
| 5 | 0.228 | 0.152 | 4.399 | 19.330 | 0.215 | 0.215 | 4.319 | 20.000 |

Table 11.7: Approximate and simulation results for the five-node non-BCMP network

result reduces to the earlier presented result for the M|M|$m_i$ queue. Also note that when $\rho_i(K) \to 1$, then $E[N_i(K)] \to K$. Finally, for G|G|$m_i$ queues we can use $\alpha' = \frac{1}{2}(C_A^2 + C_S^2)$, instead of $\alpha$ in the equation above (see the Krämer and Langenbach-Belz approximation (7.24)).

**Example 11.11. A five-node non-BCMP queueing network (adapted from [26]).**
Consider a non-BCMP queueing network with $M = 5$ stations and $K = 30$ customers. The station parameters are given in Table 11.6. Notice the extra column which denotes the coefficient of variation of the service time distribution. Since the example network is not of BCMP type, MVA cannot be employed. In Table 11.5 we present the results for both the approximate analysis and a simulation. Confidence intervals are within 5% of the mean values. As can be observed, the results match within 5–10%. This seems to be reasonable, given the difference in computational effort required to find the solution. □

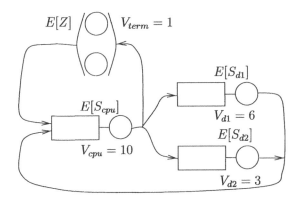

Figure 11.6: A simple queueing network model of a central server system

## 11.6 Application study

We consider a modelling study of a central server system; the structure of this model has been adapted from [249, Section 10.2.1]. The system and model are presented in Section 11.6.1. A first performance evaluation, using MVA and a bounding technique, is presented in Section 11.6.2. Suggestions for performance improvements are studied in Section 11.6.3.

### 11.6.1 System description and basic model

We consider a central server system consisting of a CPU and two disk systems. A number of terminals (users) is connected to this system. Requests from the users are processed by the CPU. The CPU needs to access the disks during its processing after which a response is given back to the users. Users think, on average, 10 seconds between receiving an answer from the system and submitting a new request: $E[Z] = 10$ (seconds). A single burst of CPU processing on a job takes $E[S_{cpu}] = 0.02$ (seconds). Similarly, the two disks require $E[S_{d1}] = 0.03$ and $E[S_{d2}] = 0.05$ (seconds) to perform requests issued to them. An average user request requires 10 CPU bursts, 6 disk accesses at disk 1, and 3 at disk 2, so that we have: $V_{term} = 1$, $V_{cpu} = 10$, $V_{d1} = 6$ and $V_{d2} = 3$. In Figure 11.6 we show the corresponding queueing network model. We denote the numerical parameter set presented thus far as configuration C1.

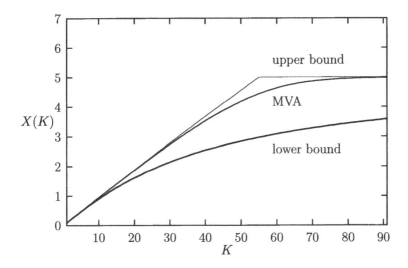

Figure 11.7: The actual throughput $X(K)$ (middle curve) and lower and upper bounds for increasing $K$ in the central server model (configuration C1)

## 11.6.2 Evaluation with MVA and other techniques

On the basis of the service demands and the visit-counts, we can directly establish which system component is the bottleneck and compute the maximum throughput reachable. We compute $D_{cpu} = 0.2$, $D_{d1} = 0.18$ and $D_{d2} = 0.15$. The terminals cannot form a bottleneck. Clearly, the CPU is the most heavily used component and we can directly compute that $X(K) \to 5$ for $K \to \infty$. Furthermore, we note that for $K \to \infty$: $\rho_{cpu}(K) \to 1$, $\rho_{d1}(K) \to 0.9$ and $\rho_{d2}(K) \to 0.75$.

In Figure 11.7 we show the bounds on the throughput as well as the exact values (computed using MVA) for $K$ increasing from 1 to 91. Similarly, we show the expected response time as perceived by the terminal users in Figure 11.8. It can be seen that the actual $X(K)$ is very close to the computed upper bound, whereas the actual $E[\hat{R}(K)]$ is very close to the computed lower bound. If the system had had more balanced service demands, and if $E[Z]$ had been closer to any of the other service demands, the computed bounds would have been tighter.

We finally compare the exact and the approximate throughput computed using the method of Section 11.5 as a function of $K$ in Figure 11.9. It can be seen that over the full spectrum of $K$, the method performs very well

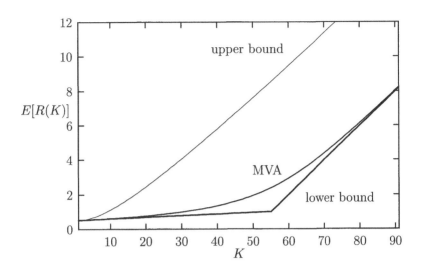

Figure 11.8: The actual expected response time $E[R(K)]$ (middle curve) and lower and upper bounds for increasing $K$ in the central server model (configuration C1)

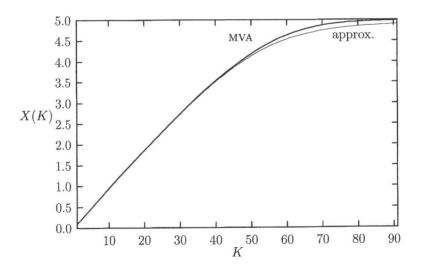

Figure 11.9: Comparison of the exact and the approximate throughput (computed with the method of Section 10.5) as a function of $K$ (configuration C1)

### 11.6.3    Suggestions for performance improvements

After having studied the performance of the central server system in configuration C1, we try to evaluate some system changes. We will first investigate what the impact is of improvement of the CPU, the bottleneck in C1. We therefore evaluate the central server model with a two times faster CPU; we denote this changed configuration by C2. In C2, $D_{cpu}$ has decreased from 0.2 to 0.1, thus making disk D1 the bottleneck. We immediately can see that the new throughput is bounded from above by $1/0.18 = 5.56$.

To improve further on the system performance, we have to increase the speed of the disk subsystem. Although disk D1 is the bottleneck in the system, it might not be wise to increase its speed; since disk D1 is already a rather fast disk, an increase of its speed will most probably be expensive. Instead, we improve upon the speed of disk D2, by doubling its speed. However, that alone would not be a good investment since not many requests are handled by disk D2. To take care of a larger share of disk requests, we have to change the partitioning of the file system such that $V_{d1} = 4$ and $V_{d2} = 5$, that is, we let the fastest disk do most of the work. We denote these latter changes as configuration C3. In this final configuration, we have disk D2 as bottleneck and the throughput is bounded from above by $1/0.125 = 8$.

In Figure 11.10 we show the throughput as a function of the number of users, for the three configurations. The increase in throughput when going from C1 via C2 to C3 is clear. With C3, we can support even more than 100 users before the throughput curve starts to flatten. Similar observations can be made from Figure 11.11; the better the configuration, the flatter the response time curve.

## 11.7    Further reading

Seminal work on closed queueing networks has been done by Gordon and Newell [106]. Buzen first introduced the convolution method [37] and Reiser, Kobayashi and Lavenberg developed the mean-value analysis approach [244, 241, 245, 243] which is based on the use of the arrival theorem [174, 260]. Reiser also discusses the application of closed queueing networks for the modelling of window flow control mechanisms [242]. The special issue of *ACM Computing Surveys* (September 1978) on queueing network models of computer system performance contains a number of very interesting papers from the early days of computer performance evaluation [12, 38, 44, 72, 107, 212, 292].

Approximation schemes for large GNQNs have been developed by Bard and Schweitzer [13, 257]. An extension of it is the so-called Linearizer approach developed by Chandy and

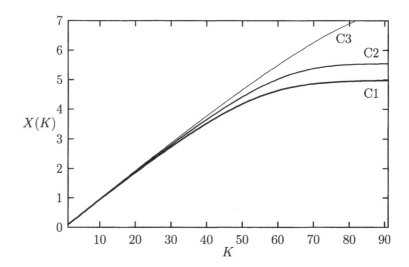

Figure 11.10: The throughput $X(K)$ for increasing $K$ for the three configurations

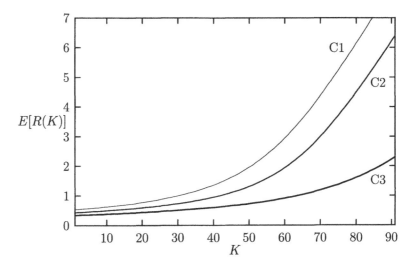

Figure 11.11: The expected response time $E[R(K)]$ for increasing $K$ for the three configurations

Neuse [43]. Zahorjan *et al.* describe the bounds based on balanced networks [294]; they can also be found in [177]. Jain also also discusses the bounds on GNQN with infinite-server stations at length [145, Chapter 33 and 34]. Extensions to bound hierarchies have been developed by Eager and Sevcik [77, 78]. King also discusses many approximate methods in his book [156, Chapter 12]. Bolch *et al.* introduced the approximation approach presented in Section 11.5 [26].

## 11.8 Exercises

### 11.1. Approximate M|M|1 result.
Derive the M|M|1 result that is used in the "functional approach" of Bolch *et al.* in Section 11.5, starting from the Bard-Schweitzer approximation (11.56).

### 11.2. Convolution in GNQNs.
Consider a GNQN with three nodes ($M = 3$). The mean service times at the nodes are given as: $E[S_1] = 20$ msec, $E[S_2] = 100$ msec and $E[S_3] = 50$ msec. For the routing probabilities we have: $r_{1,1} = 0.1$, $r_{1,2} = 0.2$, $r_{1,3} = 0.7$, $r_{2,1} = r_{3,1} = 1.0$; all other routing probabilities equal 0.

1. Compute the visit counts $V_i$.

2. Compute the average service demands $D_i$.

3. Compute the normalising constant when $K = 3$, i.e., $G(3,3)$ with the convolution method.

4. Compute, using the convolution scheme, for all stations $i$: $X_i(K)$, $E[N_i(K)]$ and $E[R_i(K)]$.

### 11.3. MVA in GNQN.
We readdress the GNQN of the previous exercise.

1. Compute, using the MVA scheme, for all stations $i$: $X_i(K)$, $E[N_i(K)]$ and $E[R_i(K)]$.

2. Compute the normalising constants $G(3,k)$, $k = 1, 2, 3$, using the results from MVA.

3. For $K = 1, \cdots, 6$, find bounds for the throughput $X(K)$ using balanced queueing networks.

4. For $K = 1, \cdots, 6$, find better bounds for the throughput $X(K)$ using balanced queueing networks.

5. For $K = 1, \cdots, 6$, use the Bard-Schweitzer approximation to compute $X(K)$ and compare the results with the above bounds and the exact values.

6. For $K = 1, \cdots, 6$, use the functional approach of Bolch *et al.* to compute $X(K)$ and compare the results with the above bounds and the exact values.

**11.4. Normalising constants.**
Consider a GNQN with $M > 2$ queues and $K \geq M$ customers.

1. Find an expression in terms of $D_i$'s and normalising constants for the probability that node 1 contains exactly 1 customer and node 2 exactly 2, i.e., find an expression for $\Pr\{n_1 = 1, n_2 = 2\}$.

2. Assume that $K = M$. Find an explicit expression for $\Pr\{n_i = 1, i = 1, \cdots, M\}$.

3. Assume that $E[S_i] = i$ and $V_i = D/i$. Give an explicit expression for $G(M, K)$ for $M > 2$ and $K \geq M$.

4. Show that under the assumptions of 3, the following holds:
$$X(K) = \frac{K}{(M + K - 1)D}.$$

**11.5. Approximation schemes.**
Consider a GNQN with $M = 4$ and the following service rates: $\mu_1 = \mu_2 = 200$, $\mu_3 = 100$ and $\mu_4 = 50$. Furthermore, the routing probabilities are given in the following matrix:
$$\frac{1}{10} \begin{pmatrix} 0 & 1 & 7 & 2 \\ 6 & 0 & 4 & 0 \\ 6 & 4 & 0 & 0 \\ 0 & 0 & 0 & 10 \end{pmatrix}.$$

1. Compute the visit counts $V_i$ and the average service demands $D_i$.

2. Compute $E[R_i(K)]$, $E[N_i(K)]$ and $X(K)$ for $K = 60$ using the Bard-Schweitzer approximation.

3. Compute $E[R_i(K)]$, $E[N_i(K)]$ and $X(K)$ for $K = 60$ using Bolch's functional approach.

# Chapter 12

# Hierarchical queueing networks

IN the previous chapter it has become clear that the evaluation of large closed queueing networks can be quite unattractive from a computational point of view; this was also the reason for addressing approximation schemes and bounding methods. In this chapter we go a different way to attack large queueing network models: hierarchical modelling and evaluation. We address a modelling and evaluation approach where large submodels are solved in isolation and where the results of such an isolated evaluation are used in other models. To be able to do so, however, we need load-dependent queueing stations, that is, queueing nodes in which the service rate depends on the number of customers present. In Section 12.1 we introduce load-dependent servers and show the corresponding product-form results for closed queueing networks including such servers. We then continue with the extension of the convolution algorithm to include load-dependent service stations in Section 12.2 and discuss two important special cases, namely infinite-server systems and multi-server systems, in Section 12.3. In Section 12.4 we extend the mean-value analysis method to the load-dependent case. We then outline an exact hierarchical decomposition approach using load-dependent service centers in Section 12.5. The hierarchical decomposition method can also be used in an approximate fashion; an example of that is discussed in Section 12.6, where we study memory management issues in time-sharing computer systems.

## 12.1 Load-dependent servers

Up till now we have assumed that the service rate at the nodes in a queueing network is constant and independent of the state of the queue or the state of the queueing network. It is, however, also possible to deal with *load-dependent* service rates (or load-dependent servers). In fact we have already encountered two special cases of load-dependent servers in Chapter 4:

- multiple server stations in which the service rate grows linearly with the number of customers present until there are more customers in the stations than there are servers;

- infinite server stations in which the service rate grows linearly (without bound) with the number of customers present.

Observe that in both these cases the load-dependency is "local" to a single queueing station: the service rate in a certain station only depends on the number of customers in *that* station. One can also imagine similar dependencies *among* queueing stations. Although they can have practical significance, we do not address them here because their analysis is more difficult; in general such dependencies spoil the product-form properties of a queueing network so that mean-value and convolution solution approaches cannot be employed any more. When using stochastic Petri nets, however, such dependencies can be modelled with relative ease, albeit at the cost of a more expensive solution (see Chapter 14).

Having load-dependent service rates, it becomes difficult to specify the service time distribution of a single job since this distribution depends on the number of customers present during the service process. It is therefore easier to specify the service rate of node $i$ as a function of the number of customers present: $\mu_i(n_i)$. The value $E[S_i(n_i)] = 1/\mu_i(n_i)$ can then be interpreted as the average time between service completions at station $i$, given that during the whole service period there are exactly $n_i$ customers present. In principle, $\mu_i(n_i)$ can be any non-negative function of $n_i$.

The load-independent case and the above two special cases can easily be expressed in the above formalism:

- load-independent nodes: $\mu_i(n_i) = \mu_i$, for all $n_i$;

- infinite server nodes (delay centers): $\mu_i(n_i) = n_i\mu_i$, for all $n_i$;

- $K$-server nodes: $\mu_i(n_i) = \min\{n_i\mu_i, K\mu_i\}$ (see also Chapter 4).

Load-dependency as introduced above does not change the product-form structure of queueing networks of the Jackson (JQN) and Gordon-Newell (GNQN) type introduced in Chapters 10 and 11. Having $M$ queueing stations and population $K$ we still have a product-form solution for the steady-state probabilities:

$$\Pr\{\underline{N} = \underline{n}\} = \frac{1}{G(M, K)} \prod_{i=1}^{M} p_i(n_i), \tag{12.1}$$

with

$$p_i(n_i) = \prod_{j=1}^{n_i} \rho_i(j) \quad (\text{JQN}), \quad \text{or} \quad p_i(n_i) = \prod_{j=1}^{n_i} D_i(j) \quad (\text{GNQN}), \qquad (12.2)$$

and the normalising constant defined as usual. Comparing this with (10.12) for JQNs, we observe that the $n_i$-th power of $\rho_i$ has been replaced by the product $\prod_j \rho_i(j)$ in the load-dependent case. Similarly, comparing this with (11.4) for GNQNs, we observe that the $n_i$-th power of $D_i$ has been replaced by the product $\prod_j D_i(j)$ in the load-dependent case. In both cases, the above result reduces to the simpler expressions for the load-independent case whenever $\mu_i(n_i) = \mu_i$, for all $i$.

Before we proceed with the analysis of QN including load-dependent service stations, we give two examples of such stations.

### Example 12.1. Non-ideal multi-processing.

Consider a $K$-processor system where, due to multiprocessing-overhead, not the full capacity of all the processors can be used. To be more precise, whenever there is only one customer present, this customer can be served in a single processor at full speed, i.e., $\mu(1) = \mu$. However, if two customers are present, each will be processed in a separate processor with speed $\mu(1 - \epsilon)$, where $\epsilon$ is the fraction of the processing capacity "lost" due to overhead, i.e., we have $\mu(2) = 2\mu(1 - \epsilon)$. This continues until the number of jobs present equals $K$, i.e., $\mu(k) = k\mu(1 - \epsilon)$, $k \leq K$. For $k > K$, we have $\mu(k) = K\mu(1 - \epsilon)$. Clearly, the service rate of this multi-server system is load-dependent. □

### Example 12.2. Modelling of CSMA/CD networks.

For the modelling of CSMA/CD network access mechanisms like Ethernet [194, 277, 284], the queueing analysis methods we have discussed so far do not suffice (we cannot model the carrier sensing, the collisions and the binary-exponential backoff period in all their details, to name a few examples). Instead of modelling the exact system operation in all its details, we can also try to incorporate in a model just their net effect. In particular, measurement studies have revealed that the effective throughput at the network boundary in CSMA/CD systems strongly depends on the length of the network, the used packet length and the number of users simultaneously trying to use the network. In modelling studies, one therefore may include these three aspects in an expression for the effective capacity that a CSMA/CD network offers, as follows. If the number of customers increases, more collisions will occur. If a collision occurs, it will take longer to be resolved when the network length is larger due to the longer propagation time. A good approximation of the network efficiency $F(n)$ when $n$ users are trying to access the network is therefore given by:

$$E(n) = \frac{E[S]}{E[S] + C(n)t_R},\tag{12.3}$$

where $E[S]$ is the average packet length, $t_R$ equals the round-trip delay, and $C(n)$ is the expected number of collisions before a successful transmission. This expression can be understood as follows. If there are no other users, $C(n) = 0$ and the efficiency is equal to 1. On the contrary, if there are $n$ customers trying to use the network, this will cause on average $C(n)$ collisions before a successful transmission takes place. A collision takes $t_R$ time to be resolved, because the information that there has been a collision has to be passed through the whole network. Thus, to send one packet of (average) length requires $C(n)t_R$ collision resolution time plus the actual packet transmission time $E[S]$. Of these $E[S] + C(n)t_R$, only the transmission time for $E[S]$ is effectively used, yielding the above expression.

What can immediately be seen is that longer CSMA/CD networks are less efficient since collisions take longer to be resolved. Rewriting $E(n)$ slightly we obtain

$$E(n) = \frac{1}{1 + \frac{C(n)t_R}{E[S]}},\tag{12.4}$$

which reveals that having longer packets is better for the efficiency since in that case, the time spent on collision resolution relative to the amount of information sent decreases. With a few extra assumptions, it has been shown that a good expression for the expected number of collisions with $n$ active users is [177]:

$$C(n) = \frac{1 - A(n)}{A(n)}, \text{ with } A(n) = \left(1 - \frac{1}{n}\right)^{n-1}.\tag{12.5}$$

As $n \to \infty$, $A(n) \to 1/e$ and $C(n) \to e - 1$.

We can use the above efficiency $E(n)$ in a simple load-dependent queueing model of a CSMA/CD network in which the service rate $\mu(n) = \mu E(n)$, where $\mu$ is the transmission rate. Comparison of this simple model with measurements on Ethernet show that this model does reasonably well [25].

As a final remark, note that the presentation above follows [177]. In [277] a similar derivation is given, however, with some differences. Since the model in [177] follows the measurement results presented in [25] more accurately than the model in [277], we stick to the former model.                                                                                   □

## 12.2 The convolution algorithm

We now proceed to the solution of closed queueing networks with load-dependent servers using the convolution scheme. Consider a GNQN consisting of $M$ M|M|1 stations with $K$ customers. As before, the routing probabilities are denoted $r_{i,j}$ and the state space $\mathcal{I}(M, K)$. The traffic equations are solved as usual, yielding the visit counts $V_i$. Since we allow for load-dependent service rates now, we have to define $\mu_i(j)$, the service rate at station $i$, given that station $i$ is currently being visited by $j$ customers. We define the service demand (per passage) of station $i$ given that there are $j$ customers present as $D_i(j) = V_i/\mu_i(j)$. For the steady-state customer distribution, we now have the following expression:

$$\Pr\{\underline{N} = \underline{n}\} = \frac{1}{G(M, K)} \prod_{i=1}^{M} p_i(n_i), \text{ with } p_i(n_i) = \prod_{j=1}^{n_i} D_i(j). \tag{12.6}$$

As we have seen before, the latter product replaces the $n_i$-th power of $D_i$ we have seen in the load-independent case. A direct calculation of the state probabilities and the normalising constant therefore does not change so much; however, a more practical way to calculate performance measures of interest is via a recursive algorithm. This recursive solution of $G(M, K)$ does change by the introduction of load-dependency, as we now need to take care of all different populations in each station. In particular, we have:

$$G(M, K) = \sum_{\underline{n} \in \mathcal{I}(M,K)} \prod_{i=1}^{M} \prod_{j=1}^{n_i} D_i(j). \tag{12.7}$$

We now split the single sum into $K + 1$ smaller sums, each accounting for a particular population at station $M$, which then ranges from 0 to $K$:

$$
\begin{aligned}
G(M, K) &= \sum_{k=0}^{K} \sum_{\substack{\underline{n} \in \mathcal{I}(M,K) \\ n_M = k}} \prod_{i=1}^{M} \prod_{j=1}^{n_i} D_i(j) \\
&= \sum_{k=0}^{K} \sum_{\substack{\underline{n} \in \mathcal{I}(M,K) \\ n_M = k}} \left( \prod_{i=1}^{M-1} \prod_{j=1}^{n_i} D_i(j) \right) \prod_{l=1}^{n_M = k} D_M(l) \\
&= \sum_{k=0}^{K} \left( \prod_{l=1}^{k} D_M(l) \right) \sum_{\underline{n} \in \mathcal{I}(M-1,K-k)} \prod_{i=1}^{M-1} \prod_{j=1}^{n_i} D_i(j). \tag{12.8}
\end{aligned}
$$

In the first term, we recognize $p_M(k)$, the (unnormalised) probability of having $k$ customers in queue $M$, and in the second term we recognize the normalising constant with 1 station (namely, the $M$-th) and $k$ customers less. Hence, we can write:

$$G(M, K) = \sum_{k=0}^{K} p_M(k) G(M - 1, K - k). \tag{12.9}$$

| $k$ | $G(1,k)$ | $G(2,k)$ | $\cdots$ | $G(m-1,k)$ | $G(m,k)$ | $\cdots$ | $G(M,k)$ |
|---|---|---|---|---|---|---|---|
| 0 | 1 | 1 | $\cdots$ | $1 \cdot p_m(k)+$ | 1 | $\cdots$ | 1 |
| 1 | $p_1(1)$ | | | $\vdots$ | | | |
| $\vdots$ | $\vdots$ | | | $\vdots$ | | | |
| $k-1$ | $p_1(k-1)$ | | $\cdots$ | $G(m-1,k-1) \cdot p_m(1)+$ | $G(m,k-1)$ | $\cdots$ | |
| $k$ | $p_1(k)$ | | $\cdots$ | $G(m-1,k) \cdot p_m(0) \Rightarrow$ | $\mathbf{G(m,k)}$ | $\cdots$ | $G(M,k)$ |
| $\vdots$ | $\vdots$ | | | | | | $\vdots$ |
| | | | | | | | $G(M,K-1)$ |
| $K$ | $p_1(K)$ | | | | | $\cdots$ | $G(M,K)$ |

Figure 12.1: The calculation of $G(M,K)$ with Buzen's convolution algorithm

This summation explains the name convolution method: the normalising constant $G(M,K)$ is computed as the convolution of the sequences $p_M(0), \cdots, p_M(K)$ and $G(M-1,K), \cdots$, $G(M-1,0)$. As initial values for the recursion, we have $G(m,0) = 1$, for $m = 1, \cdots, M$ (there is only one way to divide 0 customers over $m$ nodes), and $G(1,k) = p_1(k) = \prod_{k=1}^{M} D_1(k)$, for $k = 1, \cdots, K$.

Although this recursion scheme is slightly more involved than the load-independent case, we can easily represent it in a two-dimensional scheme as before (see Figure 12.1). We can still work through the scheme column-wise, however, we need to remember the complete left-neighbouring column for the calculation of the entries in the current column. We therefore need to store one column more than in the load-independent case; the memory requirements are therefore of order $O(2K)$. If all the nodes are load-dependent, we need to store the precomputed values $D_i(j)$ which costs $O(MK)$. In summary, the memory requirements are of order $O(MK)$. The time complexity can be bounded as follows. To compute the $k$-th entry in a column, we have to add $k$ products. Since $k$ can at most be equal to $K$, we need at most $O(K)$ operations per element in the table. Since the table contains $MK$ elements, the overall computational complexity is $O(MK^2)$.

To compute $\Pr\{N_i = n_i\}$ we now proceed in a similar way as for load-independent nodes. As we have seen there, it turns out to be convenient to first address the case $i = M$:

$$\Pr\{N_M = n_M\} = \sum_{\substack{n \in \mathcal{I}(M,K) \\ N_M = n_M}} \frac{1}{G(M,K)} \prod_{i=1}^{M} p_i(n_i)$$

$$\begin{aligned}
&= p_M(n_M) \sum_{\underline{n} \in \mathcal{I}(M-1, K-n_M)} \frac{1}{G(M,K)} \prod_{i=1}^{M-1} p_i(n_i) \\
&= p_M(n_M) \frac{G(M-1, K-n_M)}{G(M,K)}.
\end{aligned} \tag{12.10}$$

As we have seen before, this expression contains normalising constants of columns $M$ and $M-1$; hence, the ordering of columns (stations) is important. In the load-independent case we were in the position to write $G(M-1, K-n_M)$ as the difference of two normalising constants of the form $G(M, \cdot)$ by using the simple recursion (11.20). Due to the convolution-based expression in the load-dependent case (12.9) we cannot do so now, so we cannot generalise the above expression for all stations $i$. If we want to compute this measure for more than one station, the only thing we can do is to repeat the convolution scheme with all of the stations of interest appearing once as station $M$. Notice that the nodes for which no such detailed measures are necessary can be numbered from 1 onwards and the part of the convolution for these nodes does not have to be repeated. Using the above result, the utilisation of station $M$ can be calculated as

$$\rho_M(K) = 1 - \Pr\{n_M = 0\} = 1 - \frac{G(M-1, K)}{G(M,K)}. \tag{12.11}$$

For the calculation of the throughput $X(K)$ we need the following result, which is valid for all $i = 1, \cdots, M$:

$$\begin{aligned}
p_i(j)\mu_i(j) &= \prod_{l=1}^{j} D_i(l) \cdot \mu_i(j) = \prod_{l=1}^{j-1} D_i(l) \cdot D_i(j)\mu_i(j) \\
&= p_i(j-1)V_i,
\end{aligned} \tag{12.12}$$

because $D_i(j) = V_i/\mu_i(j)$. For the throughput of station $M$ we now find:

$$\begin{aligned}
X_M(K) &= \sum_{k=1}^{K} \Pr\{N_M = k\}\mu_M(k) = \sum_{k=1}^{K} p_M(k)\frac{G(M-1, K-k)}{G(M,K)}\mu_M(k) \\
&= \frac{V_M}{G(M,K)} \sum_{k=1}^{K} p_M(k-1)G(M-1, K-k) \\
&= \frac{V_M}{G(M,K)} \sum_{k=0}^{K-1} p_M(k)G(M-1, K-1-k) \\
&= V_M \frac{G(M, K-1)}{G(M,K)}.
\end{aligned} \tag{12.13}$$

Here we are fortunate to find again an expression based on only the $M$-th column in the computational scheme, and hence it is valid not only for station $M$, but for all stations:

$$X_i(K) = V_i \frac{G(M, K-1)}{G(M,K)}. \tag{12.14}$$

As we have seen in the load-independent case, the throughput through the reference node (with visit-count 1) is the quotient of the last two normalising constants; all other node throughputs depend on that value via their visit ratio $V_i$. For the average population of station $M$ we find

$$E[N_M(K)] = \sum_{k=1}^{K} k \Pr\{N_M = k\} = \sum_{k=1}^{K} p_M(k) \frac{G(M-1, K-k)}{G(M, K)}. \tag{12.15}$$

Notice that this expression is again only valid for station $M$. If one would be interested in $E[N_i(K)]$ ($i \neq M$), the convolution algorithm should be run with a different ordering of stations so that station $i$ is the last one to be added.

We finally comment on the difficulty in computing $\Pr\{N_M \geq n_M\}$ in the load-dependent case. Similar to the load-independent case, we can express this probability as follows:

$$\Pr\{N_M \geq n_M\} = \sum_{\substack{n \in \mathcal{I}(M,K) \\ N_M \geq n_M}} \frac{1}{G(M, K)} \prod_{i=1}^{M} p_i(n_i)$$

$$= \frac{1}{G(M, K)} \prod_{j=1}^{n_M} D_M(j) \sum_{\substack{n \in \\ \mathcal{I}(M, K-n_M)}} \prod_{i=1}^{M-1} p_i(n_i) \prod_{l=n_M+1}^{n'_M} D_M(l). \tag{12.16}$$

We observe that we cannot reduce the remaining sum to a well-known normalising constant, since the terms $D_M(l)$ over which the product for station $M$ is taken ($l$ ranges from the smallest number larger than $n_M$, i.e., $n_M + 1$, to the actual number ($n'_M$) of customers in station $M$) are different from the terms $D_M(l')$ that would appear in the expression for the normalising constant $G(M, K - n_M)$ ($l'$ would then range from 0 to $K - n_M$). This subtle observation shows the increased complexity of computing performance measures in queueing networks with load-dependent servers.

## 12.3  Special cases of the convolution algorithm

There are two special cases when using the convolution algorithm for GNQN with load-dependent service rates: the case of having multiple servers per queue (Section 12.3.1) and the case of having an infinite server station (Section 12.3.2).

### 12.3.1  Convolution with multi-server queueing stations

Consider the case where we deal with a GNQN with $M$ stations as we have seen before, however, the number of identical servers at station $i$ is $m_i$. The service rate at station $i$

then is:

$$\mu_i(j) = \begin{cases} j\mu_i, & j < m_i \\ m_i\mu_i, & j \geq m_i. \end{cases} \tag{12.17}$$

Consequently, the steady-state distribution of the number of customers in such a queueing network, given in total $K$ customers, equals:

$$\Pr\{\underline{N} = \underline{n}\} = \frac{1}{G(M,K)} \prod_{i=1}^{M} \frac{D_i^{n_i}}{\alpha_i(n_i)}, \tag{12.18}$$

where $D_i = X_i/\mu_i$ and

$$\alpha_i(n_i) = \begin{cases} n_i!, & n_i < m_i, \\ m_i!m_i^{n_i-m_i}, & n_i \geq m_i. \end{cases} \tag{12.19}$$

The normalising constant is defined as usual to sum all the terms to one. It can be shown that the following recursion holds for the normalising constant:

$$G(M,K) = \sum_{k=0}^{K} \frac{D_i^k}{\alpha_i(k)} G(M-1, K-k), \tag{12.20}$$

with as initial conditions $G(m, 0) = 1$, for $m = 1, \cdots, M$, and $G(1, k) = D_1^k/\alpha_1(k)$, for $k = 0, \cdots, K$.

The recursion given here is only to be used for nodes that are indeed multi-servers. For those columns in the tabular computational scheme that correspond to load-independent single server nodes, the simpler load-independent recursion can be used.

## 12.3.2   Convolution with an infinite-server station

A special case arises when we address a GNQN with a single infinite-server station. In principle, an infinite-server station in a GNQN with $K$ customers can be regarded as a $K$-server station. It is reasonable to assume that there is only one such station in the queueing network (if there are more they can be merged into a single one). Without loss of generality we assume this node is numbered one. Then, the only thing we need to do is to change the initialisation to the tabular computational scheme as follows.

The steady-state distribution of the number of customers in such a queueing network, given in total $K$ customers, equals

$$\Pr\{\underline{N} = \underline{n}\} = \frac{1}{G(M,K)} \frac{D_1^{n_1}}{n_1!} \prod_{i=2}^{M} D_i^{n_i}. \tag{12.21}$$

The normalising constant is defined as usual to obtain probabilities that sum to one. The following recursion then holds for the normalising constant:

$$G(M, K) = G(M - 1, K) + D_M G(M, K - 1), \qquad (12.22)$$

with as initial conditions $G(m, 0) = 1$, for $m = 1, \cdots, M$, and $G(1, k) = D_1^k / k!$, for $k = 0, \cdots, K$. The only "irregularity" in the queueing network is brought into the computational scheme directly at the initialisation; the rest of the computations do not change.

## 12.4   Mean-value analysis

In Chapter 11 we have developed an MVA recursion for the load-independent case and for the special load-dependent case of the infinite servers. In this section we develop an MVA recursion scheme for general load-dependency.

As before, the throughput $X(K)$ is simply expressed as the fraction of the number of customers $K$ present and the overall response time per passage:

$$X(K) = \frac{K}{\sum_{i=1}^{M} E[\hat{R}_i(K)]}. \qquad (12.23)$$

In order to calculate the value of $E[\hat{R}_i(K)]$ we again use the arrival theorem for closed queueing networks. However, since the service times depend on the exact number of customers in the queue, the average number $E[N_i(K)]$ in the queue does not provide us with enough information for the calculation of $E[\hat{R}_i(K)]$. Instead, we need to know the probability $\pi_i(j|k)$ for $j$ customers to be present at queue $i$, given overall network population $k$. Let us for the time being assume we know these probabilities.

In a more detailed version, the arrival theorem for closed queueing networks states that an arriving customer at queue $i$ will find $j$ $(j = 0, \cdots, K - 1)$ customers already in that queue with probability $\pi_i(j|k - 1)$, i.e., with the steady-state probability of having $j$ customers in queue $i$, given in total one customer less in the queueing network. Since $E[\hat{R}_i(K)]$ includes the service of the arriving customer, we have $j$ services with average demand $D_i(j)$ with probability $\pi(j - 1|K - 1)$, and thus:

$$E[\hat{R}_i(K)] = \sum_{j=1}^{K} j \pi_i(j - 1|K - 1) D_i(j). \qquad (12.24)$$

As before, we have $E[\hat{R}(K)] = \sum_{i=1}^{M} E[\hat{R}_i(K)]$ and $X(K) = K / E[\hat{R}(K)]$, $X_i(K) = V_i X(K)$, and the average population at station $i$ can be can be computed using Little's law or can be expressed as:

$$E[N_i(K)] = \sum_{j=0}^{K} j\pi_i(j|K). \tag{12.25}$$

Anyway, the only unknowns to be solved are the probabilities $\pi_i(j|k)$. We will develop a recursion scheme for the $\pi_i(j|k)$ below.

### Example 12.3. Readdressing the load-independent case.

Before we present the solution of the probabilities $\pi_i(j|k)$ it might be instructive to address the case when $D_i(j) = D_i$, for all $j$, that is, for the case that we again deal with the load-independent case. We have:

$$
\begin{aligned}
E[\hat{R}_i(K)] &= \sum_{j=1}^{K} j\pi_i(j-1|K-1)D_i \\
&= D_i\left(\pi_i(0|K-1) + 2\pi_i(1|K-1) + \cdots + K\pi_i(K-1|K-1)\right) \\
&= D_i\left(\pi_i(0|K-1) + \pi_i(1|K-1) + \pi_i(2|K-1) + \cdots + \pi_i(K-1|K-1)\right) \\
&\quad + D_i\left(\pi_i(1|K-1) + 2\pi_i(2|K-1) + \cdots + (K-1)\pi_i(K-1|K-1)\right) \\
&= D_i\left(\sum_{j=0}^{K-1} \pi_i(j|K-1)\right) + D_i\left(\sum_{j=0}^{K-1} j\pi_i(j|K-1)\right) \\
&= D_i + D_i E[N_i(K-1)] \\
&= (E[N_i(K-1)] + 1)D_i, \tag{12.26}
\end{aligned}
$$

which indeed conforms to the load-independent case we have seen before. □

Let us now come to the actual computation of $\pi_i(j|k)$. First, notice that $\pi_i(0|0) = 1$ since with probability 1 there are no customers at queue $i$ when there are none in the network at all. Secondly, we have

$$\pi_i(0|K) = 1 - \sum_{j=1}^{K} \pi_i(j|K), \tag{12.27}$$

since $\sum_{j=0}^{K} \pi_i(j|K) = 1$. Notice that this subtraction can be a source of round-off errors. We then use (12.10) as follows:

$$
\begin{aligned}
\pi_i(j|K) = \Pr\{N_i(K) = j\} &= p_i(j)\frac{G(M-1, K-j)}{G(M,K)} \\
&= \prod_{l=1}^{j} D_i(l)\frac{G(M-1, K-j)}{G(M,K)} \\
&= \left(\prod_{l=1}^{j-1} D_i(l)\right) D_i(j)\frac{G(M-1, K-j)}{G(M,K)}
\end{aligned}
$$

$$= \left( p_i(j-1)\frac{G(M-1, K-j)}{G(M, K-1)} \right) \left( \frac{G(M, K-1)}{G(M, K)} \right) D_i(j)$$

$$= \pi_i(j-1|K-1) \left( \frac{X_i(K)}{V_i} \right) D_i(j)$$

$$= \pi_i(j-1|K-1)\frac{X_i(K)}{\mu_i(j)}. \qquad (12.28)$$

As can be observed, we have found a way to express $\pi_i(j|K)$ in terms of $\pi_i(j-1|K-1)$ so that the MVA recursion scheme for load-dependent GNQNs is complete.

It is possible to combine the MVA presented here with those for load-independent and infinite-server nodes. To summarize, the following MVA computational scheme can be used to evaluate closed queueing networks with FCFS, IS and load-dependent nodes for increasing customer number $k = 1, \cdots, K$, and for all nodes $i$:

1. Initialise $k = 1$, $E[N_i(0)] = 0$, and $\pi_i(0|0) = 1$;

2. Compute $E[\hat{R}_i(k)]$ as follows:

   - $E[\hat{R}_i(k)] = (E[N_i(k-1)] + 1)D_i$, if node $i$ is of type FCFS;
   - $E[\hat{R}_i(k)] = D_i$, if node $i$ is of IS type;
   - $E[\hat{R}_i(k)] = \sum_{j=1}^{k} j\pi_i(j-1|k-1)D_i(j)$, if node $i$ is load-dependent, thereby using the probabilities $\pi_i(\cdot|k-1)$;

3. Compute $E[\hat{R}(k)] = \sum_i E[\hat{R}_i(k)]$;

4. Compute $X(k) = k/E[\hat{R}(k)]$ and $X_i(k) = V_i X(k)$;

5. For the load-dependent nodes, compute the values $\pi_i(\cdot|k)$ using (12.27) and (12.28);

6. Increase $k$ with 1 and continue with 2, until $k = K$ is reached.

Regarding the cost of this version of MVA, the following remarks are in place. Since we iterate over $K$ customers and $M$ stations, the computational cost is directly proportional to the product $MK$. However, to compute $E[\hat{R}_i(K)]$ we need to compute the $K$ probabilities $\pi_i(j|K-1)$ which involves another $K$ operations. In total, the computational cost is $O(MK^2)$. Regarding memory costs, we have to store the extra information for the probabilities $\pi_i(j|K)$ which is (at most) $K$ times more than we used to store, hence, we have $O(MK)$ memory costs.

## 12.5   Exact hierarchical decomposition

Load-dependent servers are especially useful in *hierarchical model decomposition*, which not only saves computation time, but also keeps the modelling process structured and allows for reuse of subsystem models. In this section, we restrict ourselves to the case where hierarchical model decomposition can be applied exactly. We describe hierarchical model decomposition informally in Section 12.5.1, after which we formalize it in Section 12.5.2.

### 12.5.1   Informal description of the decomposition method

Consider the case where one has to model a large computer or communication system involving many queueing stations ($M$) and customers ($K$). We have seen that the required computational effort is at least proportional to the product $MK$ (in the load-independent case), so that we might try to decrease either $K$ or $M$. Therefore, instead of constructing a monolithic model and analysing that, we proceed to analyse subsystems first. The results of these detailed analyses, each with a smaller number of nodes, are "summarized" in a load-dependent server modelling the behaviour of the subsystem, which can subsequently be used in a higher-level model of the whole system (again with a smaller number of nodes). The hierarchical decomposition approach as sketched here is also often referred to as *Norton's approach* by its similarity with the well-known decomposition approach in electrical circuit analysis. By the fact that a subsystem model, possibly consisting of multiple queueing stations, is replaced by a single load-dependent queueing station, this queueing station is often referred to as a *flow-equivalent service center* (FESC) or as an *aggregate service center*. The former name indicates that the load-dependency is chosen such that the single station acts in such a way that its customer flow is equivalent to that of the original queueing network.

Let us illustrate this approach for dealing with a GNQN with $M$ stations numbered $1, \cdots, M^*, M^* + 1, \cdots, M$ and $K$ customers. Stations 1 through $M^*$ are the nodes to be aggregated in a single FESC. Stations $M^*+1, \cdots, M$ are the queueing stations that will not be affected; sometimes these are called the high-level nodes. Note that the node numbering scheme does not affect generality. Furthermore, we assume that the queueing network is structured in such a way that there is only a single customer stream from the high-level model stations to the stations to be aggregated and back. This is visualized in Figure 12.2; we come back to the interpretation of the probabilities $\alpha$ and $\beta$ later.

Since the total number of customers in the GNQN equals $K$, the number of customers in the stations to be aggregated varies between 0 and $K$ as well. Given a certain population in

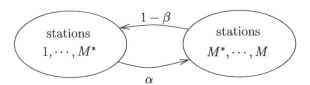

Figure 12.2: High-level view of a GNQN that is to be decomposed

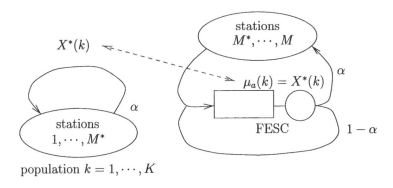

Figure 12.3: Decomposition approach using a FESC

the group of stations to be aggregated, the high-level stations perceive a fixed average delay for customers passing through the stations to be aggregated, namely the average response time (per passage!) for this subnetwork with $k$ customers in it (denoted $E[\hat{R}^*(k)]$). From this, we can compute the perceived rate $X^*(k) = k/E[\hat{R}^*(k)]$ at which customers are served in the subnetwork. We compute $X^*(k)$ by studying the subnetwork in isolation by connecting the in- and out-going flows to the high-level model. That is, the outgoing branch (labelled with probability $\alpha$) is looped back to the queueing station at which the flow labelled $1 - \beta$ ends. The throughput along this shorted circuit can then be used as service rate for the aggregated subnetwork (the FESC) that can be embedded in the high-level nodes, as visualized in Figure 12.3. Notice that we have added an immediate feedback loop around the FESC (with probability $1 - \alpha$); this is to ensure that the visit counts in the original non-decomposed GNQN of the non-aggregated stations, relative to the visit-count of the FESC, remain the same. In many textbooks on queueing networks this immediate feedback loop is not explicitly mentioned.

Note that since the overall network is a GNQN, the subnetwork is so as well. Therefore, one can employ MVA or the convolution approach to solve it. Since an MVA is recursive in the number of customers in the network, with one MVA for the maximum population $K$, the throughputs for smaller populations are computed as well.

When we need to aggregate a subnetwork which is to be embedded in a yet unknown high-level model, we face the problem that there is no given bound on the population in the subnetwork. One then often assumes that the subnetwork population is bounded by some $\tilde{k}$ and computes the throughputs $X^*(1), \cdots, X^*(\tilde{k})$. Whenever in the high-level model evaluation the situation occurs that the number of customers in the FESC is larger than $\tilde{k}$, one assumes $X^*(k) \approx X^*(\tilde{k})$. If $\tilde{k}$ is taken large enough, this yields reasonably accurate results in most practical cases.

## 12.5.2 Formal derivation of the decomposition method

Let us now formalize the hierarchical decomposition approach and show its correctness by using results from the convolution method with load-dependent stations. To keep the notation and terminology simple, we assume that all stations are load-independent and have visit-counts $V_i$, mean service times $E[S_i]$ and service demands $D_i$. The nodes 1 through $M^*$ are to be aggregated in a single FESC (we use the subscript "a" to refer to this aggregate station).

If we study the queueing stations 1 through $M^*$ in isolation (in the above sketched short-circuited way) the service demands for these stations do not alter. Hence, we can perform a standard convolution to obtain the normalising constants $G(M^*, 0) = 1, G(M^*, 1), G(M^*, 2), \cdots, G(M^*, K)$, using the computational scheme depicted in Figure 11.1 (we basically compute the first $M^*$ columns in this scheme). According to (11.24), we then know that the throughput through this queueing network, given $k$ customers are present, is given by

$$X^*(k) = \frac{G(M^*, k-1)}{G(M^*, k)}, \quad k = 1, \cdots, K. \tag{12.29}$$

Notice that $X^*(k)$ is the throughput through a station in the subnetwork that is being aggregated for which $V_i = 1$. When $V_i \neq 1$, the actual throughput through station $i$ in the subnetwork is $V_i X(k)$. To keep the notation simple, we assume that $V_1 = 1$ and that the short-circuit originates and ends at station 1, that is, customers from the high-level model enter and leave the subnetwork at station 1. We find that the throughput through the short-circuit equals $X^*(k)(1 - \sum_{j=2}^{M^*} V_j)$. For reasons to become clear below, we now construct a load-dependent queueing station with service rate $\mu_a(k) = X^*(k)$.

We now consider the high-level model with the embedded FESC, i.e., we consider the new station indexed "a" and the stations $M^*$ through $M$. To evaluate this GNQN, we

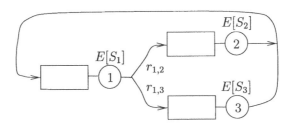

Figure 12.4: A small three-node GNQN

can use a convolution scheme for load-dependent servers. As first column in the tabular computation scheme we take the aggregated station. We know from Table 12.1 that the first column is given as

$$p_a(k) = \prod_{j=1}^{k} D_a(j) = \prod_{j=1}^{k} \frac{1}{\mu_a(j)}. \tag{12.30}$$

Now, by our choice $\mu_a(k) = X^*(k)$, we find that $p_a(0) = 1$ (as it should), but also $p_a(1) = 1/\mu_a(1) = G(M^*, 1)$ by (11.24). In a similar way, we find

$$
\begin{aligned}
p_a(k) &= \frac{1}{\mu_a(1)} \frac{1}{\mu_a(2)} \cdots \frac{1}{\mu_a(k)} \\
&= \frac{G(M^*, 1)}{G(M^*, 0)} \frac{G(M^*, 2)}{G(M^*, 1)} \cdots \frac{G(M^*, k)}{G(M^*, k-1)} \\
&= G(M^*, k).
\end{aligned}
\tag{12.31}
$$

The service rates $\mu_a(k)$ have apparently been chosen such that the original column of normalising constants for the subnetwork to be aggregated is exactly reproduced. We can now continue with adding more columns to the convolution table, namely the columns corresponding to stations $M^* + 1$ through $M^*$. In other words, stations 1 through $M^*$ have been summarized in a single station yielding the same "behaviour" in the sense of the computational method used. For this approach to work correctly, the visit-count to the aggregate should be the same in the overall and in the decomposed model.

### Example 12.4. A three-node GNQN.

We reconsider the small GNQN we have used throughout Chapter 11 to illustrate algorithms. For ease of reference, we depict this GNQN again in Figure 12.4 and restate the model parameters: $V_1 = 1$, $V_2 = 0.4$, $V_3 = 0.6$, and $E[S_i] = i$, so that $D_1 = 1$, $D_2 = 0.8$ and $D_3 = 1.8$. We are now intending to aggregate station 2 and 3 into a single load-dependent queueing station. Note that when adhering to the above introduced notation, we should

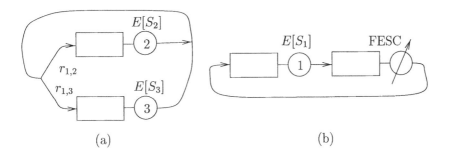

Figure 12.5: Aggregating the three-node GNQN

renumber the nodes as follows: $(1, 2, 3) \rightarrow (2, 3, 1)$, so that we can aggregate the new nodes 1 and 2 into an aggregate "a"; however, to avoid confusion, we will adhere to the node numbering scheme of Figure 12.4.

Short-circuiting nodes 2 and 3 will yield the simple GNQN as depicted in Figure 12.5(a); note that the visit counts remain the same. After we have computed the service rates for the FESC, we have to evaluate the GNQN as given in Figure 12.5(b). Note that there is no need to have an immediate feedback loop around the FESC with probability $1 - \alpha$, since the probability to make more than a single pass through the subnetwork to be aggregated equals $0$ $(\alpha = 1 \rightarrow 1 - \alpha = 0)$.

Let us now start the computations. We find for the subnetwork to be aggregated the following normalising constants:

| $k$ | $G(2, k)$ | $G(3, k)$ |
|---|---|---|
| 0 | 1.0 | 1.0 |
| 1 | 0.8 | 2.6 |
| 2 | 0.64 | 5.32 |
| 3 | 0.512 | 10.088 |

The throughput through the subnetwork, given $k$ customers present, and hence the service rates for the FESC can then be computed as the usual ratios of normalising constants:

| $k$ | 1 | 2 | 3 |
|---|---|---|---|
| $\mu_a(k)$ | 0.385 | 0.489 | 0.527 |

We now continue to embed the FESC in the overall network. We therefore have to compute the normalising constant for the queueing network given in Figure 12.5(b). As first column, we take the column computed for the aggregated subnetwork, as follows:

| $k$ | $G(a,k)$ | $G(1,k)$ |
|---|---|---|
| 0 | 1.0 | 1.0 |
| 1 | 2.6 | 3.6 |
| 2 | 5.32 | 8.92 |
| 3 | 10.088 | 19.008 |

The second column is then computed by standard convolution (load-independent), using the service demand $D_1 = 1$ for station 1. As can be observed, this column is the same as the column of normalising constants we have computed before (in Chapter 11) without aggregation. □

Having computed the normalising constants for the GNQN including the FESC, we can compute other performance measures of interest in the usual way. The big advantage of aggregating model parts is to cope with model complexity. Subsystems that appear in a number of models, e.g., a disk subsystem model as part of a number of models of various computer architecture alternatives, only need to be analysed once and can then be used in its aggregate form.

We have demonstrated the hierarchical decomposition method here, using the convolution scheme. Needless to say the MVA scheme can also be used for this purpose. The subnetwork to be aggregated is then evaluated using MVA for all possible populations $K$ and the relevant throughputs are computed. These are then used as service rates in a load-dependent queueing station. The MVA variant for queueing networks with load-dependent stations is then used to evaluate the overall network.

The result presented here has been proven by Chandy, Herzog and Woo in the mid-1970s (it is sometimes referred to as the CHW-Theorem). To be more precise, the following theorem holds.

**Theorem 12.1. Hierarchical decomposition.**

   In any GNQN, a group of queueing stations can be replaced by a single load-dependent server with suitably chosen service rates, without changing the queue length distribution at the nodes. □

**Example 12.5. Central server model.**

Hierarchical decomposition works very well for queueing network models of central server systems, as addressed in Section 11.6. A typical decomposition approach would then be to simply aggregate the CPU and the two disks into a single load-dependent service station. What remains of the overall model are two queues, one with infinite-server semantics (the terminals) and one with general load-dependent behaviour (the system).                    □

# 12.6    Approximate hierarchical decomposition

Although hierarchical model decomposition is a very useful technique for GNQNs, its use also lies in the analysis of queueing networks which do not conform to the class of GNQNs. In such a case the decomposition is not exact any more; however, in many practical situations, the approximations obtained with it are reasonably good. Without going into too much detail, we state that the approximation becomes better whenever the customers in the subnetwork to be aggregated are less affected by what happens in the high-level model. This is most notably the case when the services in the submodel complete at much higher rates than in the high-level model and the customers stay relatively long in the aggregate. In such cases, between any two interactions of the high-level model and the submodel to be aggregated, many activities take place in the submodel. We say then that there are time-scale differences between the two model parts.

As a representative example of a case in which approximate hierarchical decomposition works well, we consider a model of a multiprogramming computer system. A simple case, not taking into account paging effects, is addressed in Section 12.6.1 whereas Section 12.6.2 deals with a model including paging effects.

## 12.6.1    Multiprogrammed computer system models

Consider a model of a multiprogramming computer system as given in Figure 12.6. $K$ terminals are connected to a computer system consisting of a CPU and two IO-systems. Due to the limited memory size of the computer, not all jobs can be processed at the same time (think of the CPU as a processor with PS or RR scheduling). There is a so-called *multiprogramming limit $J < K$*. Jobs issued from the terminals are taken into service as long as the number of jobs currently being processed is smaller than $J$, otherwise they are queued in a *swap-in queue*.

In a way, the swap-in queue could be regarded as a load-dependent server in which the service rate depends on the population at the CPU and the IO-systems; the service rate is infinite as long as the latter population is smaller than $J$, and zero otherwise. As indicated in Section 12.1 such non-local load-dependency cannot be analysed using queueing network

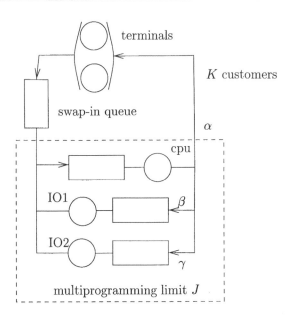

Figure 12.6: Central server model with $K$ terminals and multiprogramming limit $J < K$

models (as we will see later, this model can easily be solved using stochastic Petri nets if the number of customers $K$ is not too large). We therefore employ an approximate model decomposition. We solve the "dashed" submodel in Figure 12.6 in isolation for possible populations ranging from 1 through $J$ in order to obtain $X^*(1), \cdots, X^*(J)$, as depicted in Figure 12.7(a). We then solve the high-level model with a load-dependent FESC as a substitute for the system with multiprogramming limit, as depicted in Figure 12.7(b). The effect that only $J$ customers are allowed to enter the subnetwork will be reflected in the approximate model by taking $X^*(k) = X^*(J)$, whenever $k > J$.

Note that based on the above considerations, the approximation will become better when the probability $\alpha$ decreases (the interactions between the high-level and the low-level model takes place less frequently) or when the CPU and IO service times decrease as opposed to the terminal think time.

We consider the same numerical parameters as we have considered in case C1 in Section 11.6, i.e., the mean service times are $E[S_{cpu}] = 20$ msec, $E[S_{IO1}] = 30$ msec, and $E[S_{IO2}] = 50$ msec, and the visit counts are given as $V_{term} = 1$, $V_{cpu} = 10$, $V_{IO1} = 6$ and $V_{IO2} = 3$. The multiprogramming limit is set to $J = 20$. Solving the short-circuited model,

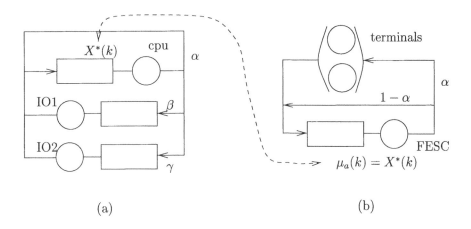

(a)                                                    (b)

Figure 12.7: Decomposition of the model with multiprogramming limit

yields the following throughputs (we show only a few of the computed values):

| $j$ | 1 | 6 | 11 | 16 | $\geq 20$ |
|---|---|---|---|---|---|
| $X^*(j)$ | 1.8868 | 3.9907 | 4.6471 | 4.8239 | 4.8934 |

We can use these throughputs in the analysis of the overall model of Figure 12.7(b). First note that the swap-in queue is no longer present in the model. Its effect is still present in the model by the use of the specific values for the rates of the FESC. Also notice the direct feedback loop around the FESC (with probability $\alpha$); it is included to obtain the proper visit counts in the model (see also Section 12.5.1).

Without presenting the detailed recursion, the approximate terminal throughput $\tilde{X}(K)$ is presented in Table 12.1 as a function of the number of users $K$. Next to the throughput results from the decomposition analysis, we present the exact throughputs $X(K)$ obtained via a numerical analysis of the underlying CTMC, thereby using the stochastic Petri net formalism as will be presented in Chapter 14. As can be observed, the results agree very well. This is due to the large time-scale differences in the two models; the rates involved differ by three orders of magnitude! To indicate that we have gained a lot by the decomposition approach, we show the number of states in the CTMC model as well; as will become clear later, we have to solve a linear system of equations of that size to compute the solution. Surely, the hierarchical decomposition method is much cheaper to pursue.

A few remarks can be made regarding the employed model. We did not distinguish between different jobs and therefore assumed that the memory requirements of all jobs are the same. Furthermore, we assumed that when terminal requests enter the system, the

| $K$ | $\tilde{X}(K)$ | $X(K)$ | states |
|---|---|---|---|
| 1 | 0.0950 | 0.0945 | 4 |
| 5 | 0.4731 | 0.4731 | 56 |
| 11 | 1.0343 | 1.0343 | 364 |
| 16 | 1.4948 | 1.4948 | 969 |
| 21 | 1.9468 | 1.9468 | 2002 |
| 26 | 2.3875 | 2.3875 | 3157 |
| 31 | 2.8133 | 2.8133 | 4312 |
| 36 | 3.2191 | 3.2191 | 5467 |
| 41 | 3.5981 | 3.5980 | 6622 |
| 46 | 3.9419 | 3.9416 | 7777 |
| 51 | 4.2409 | 4.2397 | 8932 |
| 56 | 4.4861 | 4.4830 | 10087 |

Table 12.1: Comparing the throughputs obtained via a decomposition $(\tilde{X}(K))$ and a numerical $(X(K))$ solution approach for the multiprogramming system model for increasing number of customers $K$

jobs already present are not affected. This is not the case in practice. More often than not, allowing new customers to start their execution influences the amount of memory that is granted to the customers already there. Either these customers will be able to use less memory or they will perceive extra delays due to increased paging activity.

## 12.6.2 Studying paging effects

In multiprogramming computer systems the number of jobs being processed simultaneously is limited by the multiprogramming limit $J$. When there are more requests for job processing, jobs are queued in the swap-in queue. We assumed that only jobs being processed by the terminals are swapped out. This, however, is only part of the truth. When the processing of a job requires a lengthy I/O operation, this job may be swapped out as long as the I/O device can autonomously work on the job. To speedup the swapping process (in which large process images might have to be stored) use is made of fast I/O devices, or of I/O devices that are relatively close to the system's main memory (local disks) as opposed to remote disks that need to be accessed for normal user I/O. Apart from the above swapping phenomena, virtual memory and paging play an important role. In virtual memory systems, every job can have a virtual work space larger than the physical memory of the

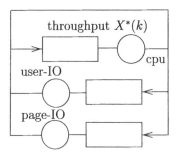

Figure 12.8: A decomposed GNQN of the multiprogramming system with user and page I/O devices

system. Only those parts or pages of the job that are needed are loaded in main memory; the other pages are stored in a secondary storage device, normally disk. Depending on the characteristics of the individual jobs, more or less pages are needed by a job to progress efficiently. Whenever a running job needs to access a page that is not yet in main memory a page fault occurs. The page fault results in a page I/O request to get the missing page from secondary storage and to place it in main memory, thereby most often replacing the least recently used page, either from the same job or from all jobs being processed.

The number of pages needed by a job over a time interval of length $t$ is called the job's working set $w(t)$. $w(t)$ is increasing with $t$, however, its derivative $w'(t)$ goes to zero for increasing $t$ since there is a maximum number of pages that the job needs to complete (the total memory requirement is limited). If the number of jobs that is simultaneously accepted by the system increases, possibly up to the multiprogramming limit $J$, less main memory per job is available to store the job's working set. Hence, the higher the number of jobs in the system, the higher the page-fault rate. As a consequence of this, the probability that job processing has to be interrupted by a page I/O device access increases with increasing numbers of jobs. As can be understood, this decreases the perceived speed of the system.

Now, we will discuss the above sketched phenomenon once more, illustrated with a simple queueing model. Consider a QN model of a multiprogramming computer system, similar to the one depicted in Figure 12.2; however, there is one so-called user-I/O device and one dedicated page-I/O device. Due to the multiprogramming limit $J$, we have to apply a decomposition to solve the submodel with $j = 1, \cdots, J$ customers in it. This short-circuited submodel is shown in Figure 12.8.

Whenever the service demands at the queues are constant, for increasing multiprogramming limit $j = 1, \cdots, J$, the throughput $X^*(j)$ will be limited by the highest service

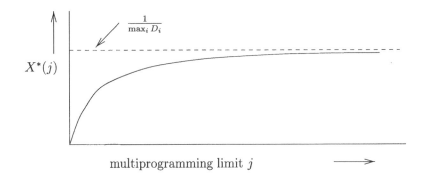

Figure 12.9: The throughput $X^*(j)$ approaches its bound for increasing $j$, with fixed paging load

demand:

$$X^*(j) \leq \frac{1}{\max_i\{D_i\}}. \tag{12.32}$$

The result of this is that with increasing $j$, $X^*(j)$ approaches its maximum value, as illustrated in Figure 12.9. However, when the multiprogramming limit increases, the amount of main memory per admitted job decreases. Since this results in more page faults, it seems reasonable to assume that the routing probability from the CPU to the page-I/O device increases; therefore the visit ratio $V_{\text{page}}(j)$ will increase relative to the other visit ratios (we explicitly indicate the dependence of the visit ratios on the multiprogramming limit $j$). We take the CPU as a reference, i.e., $V_{\text{cpu}}(j) = 1$, and assume that the system initially is *CPU bound* which means that for small $j$ the CPU has the largest service demand. When increasing $j$, by the increase of $V_{\text{page}}(j)$, $D_{\text{page}}(j)$ becomes the largest service demand so that under larger load the system becomes *page-IO bound*. In the latter case, it is possible that the throughput $X^*(j) = 1/\max_i\{D_i(j)\}$ decreases for increasing $j$. The effect that by increasing the multiprogramming limit the performance of a system deteriorates is known as *thrashing*, and is illustrated in Figure 12.10. When the multiprogramming degree is taken too small the system is under-utilized and the throughput is too small, but when the multiprogramming limit is taken too high, the system performs badly due to too much page-I/O overhead.

To evaluate a multiprogramming computer system, including paging effects, as sketched above, we can use an evaluation similar to the approximate hierarchical decomposition we have seen before. We can aggregate the complete computer system model, excluding the terminals, in a single FESC. As in the previous case, we need to evaluate the submodel to be

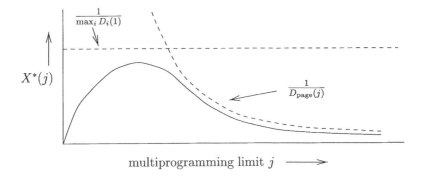

Figure 12.10: The throughput $X^*(j)$ decreases for larger multiprogramming limits $j$; the thrashing effect

aggregated for all possible populations; however, we now have to take into account different routing probabilities (or visit counts) for different multiprogramming limits to reflect the fact that for higher values of the multiprogramming limit, the visit count for the paging device becomes larger. Since we cannot cope in our models with routing probabilities that change depending on the population of a model part, we have to assume that the routing probabilities are fixed. We assume them to be equal to the case when the maximum number of jobs is present, even if less customers are being processed (interpreted in the context of the modelled system, this implies that for a given multiprogramming limit, each process obtains a fixed number of pages, whether it uses these or not, and whether the other pages are free or not). In summary, we have to use the following computational scheme:

1. For $j = 1, \cdots, J$ compute the visit ratios $V_i(j)$ from the traffic equations;

2. For a given value of $j$, use $D_i$ and $V_i(j)$ to compute $X^*(j)$ using an MVA or convolution scheme;

3. Construct a FESC with $\mu_a(j) = X^*(j)$ as computed above; for $l > J$ we set $\mu_a(l) = X^*(J)$.

Important to observe is that we need multiple MVAs (or convolutions) to compute the service rates for the FESC. The problem we now face is that of embedding the above FESC in the overall model. As we have seen in Section 12.5.1, when embedding the FESC in the overall model, we need to route jobs departing from the FESC directly back to it, with probability $1 - \alpha$. However, when we change the population $j$, in the submodel to be aggregated the visit count for the paging device changes. Although the other visit counts remain the same, this changes the routing probabilities in the model. Thus, for every population $j$, $\alpha$ has been different. Hence, there is no unique way to construct the overall aggregated model. Thus, at this point the only thing we can do is to study $X(k)$ of the aggregate in itself. In Chapter 14 we will use stochastic Petri net models to solve the unresolved modelling problem.

**Example 12.6. Increased paging device load.**
Consider a multiprogramming computer system as we have addressed before with the following numerical parameters: $E[S_{cpu}] = 20$ msec, $E[S_{page}] = 40$ msec, $E[S_{user}] = 50$ msec, the multiprogramming limit $J = 20$ and $\alpha(j) = 0.3 - j/80$ and $\beta(j) = 0.6 + j/80$ and $\gamma(j) = 0.3$, for $j = 1, \cdots, J$.

For increasing $j$, the service demands $D_i(j)$ can be computed from the traffic equations and the service times. We find (in msec):

$$D_{cpu}(j) = 20, \quad D_{page}(j) = 16 + j/2, \quad D_{user}(j) = 15, \tag{12.33}$$

so that, according to the bounds presented in Section 11.4.1:

$$X^*(j) \leq \begin{cases} 50, & j \leq 8, \\ \frac{1000}{16+j/2}, & j \geq 8. \end{cases} \tag{12.34}$$

Using multiple MVA evaluations, the aggregate throughputs $X_a(j)$ are depicted in Figure 12.11; the discussed thrashing effect is clearly visible. Notice how tight the upper bound is for larger $j$, e.g., for $j = 20$ we find $X^*(20) \leq 38.46$ whereas the exact value equals $X^*(20) = 38.38$. In order to increase the system performance, admitting more customers is not a good idea. In fact, one should try to keep the number of admitted customers below the value of $j$ for which $X_a(j)$ is not yet decreasing (here, a multiprogramming limit of 10 would have been a good choice). A suggestion for a performance improvement would be to either increase the speed of the paging device (decreasing $E[S_{page}]$), or to increase the size of the main memory so that less page faults occur (decreasing $V_{page}(j)$); both will decrease $D_{page}(j)$ and therefore increase $X_a(k)$. □

## 12.7  Further reading

The hierarchical decomposition approach has been developed by Chandy, Herzog and Woo in the mid-seventies [42, 41]. It should be noted that the FESC approach can be applied iteratively: an FESC can be embedded in a model which in turn is aggregated in an FESC.

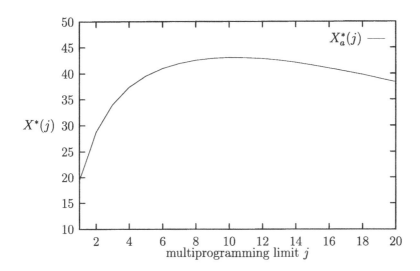

Figure 12.11: The aggregate throughput $X^*(j)$ as a function of the multiprogramming limit $j$

For each aggregation phase, the most suitable computational method can be chosen. In fact, when different computational methods are chosen (including possibly also simulation) to obtain the FESC, one often speaks of hybrid modelling. In the book by Lazowska *et al.* these issues are treated in more detail [177].

The convolution method for QN with load-dependent stations has first been presented by Buzen [37]. The MVA for this case has been presented by Reiser and Lavenberg [245, 243]. Interesting work on multiprogrammed central server systems, including paging effects and working sets can be found in the book of Trivedi (a simple model similar to the one discussed here) [280] and the book by Coffmann and Denning (a complete discussion of memory management issues) [59].

## 12.8   Exercises

### 12.1. Load-independent convolution.
Show that when $D_i(j) = D_i$, for all $i, j$, the convolution recursion for the load-dependent case (12.9) indeed reduces to the one for the load-independent case (11.20).

### 12.2. I/O-subsystems.
A typical system component in many computer systems is the I/O-subsystem, consisting

of a number of parallel independent disks. Suppose we have $n_{I/O}$ of these parallel disks and that a disk request is handled by disk $i$ with probability $\alpha_i$ and takes $1/\mu_i$ seconds to complete $(i = 1, \cdots, n_{I/O})$.

1. Discuss how an I/O-subsystem as described above can be aggregated into a single FESC.

2. Simplify the results of 1, when $\alpha_i = 1/n_{I/O}$ and $\mu_i = \mu$.

3. Simplify the results of 1, when $V_i = \alpha_i E[S_i] = V$.

**12.3. A three-node GNQN.**
Reconsider the three-node GNQN for $K = 3$.

1. Aggregate nodes 1 and 2 and construct an appropriate FESC.

2. Embed this aggregate in the overall network, i.e., combine it with node 3.

3. Solve the resulting two-node GNQN (with one load-dependent node) with both MVA and the convolution method.

# Chapter 13

# BCMP queueing networks

IN this chapter we present a number of results for a yet richer class of (mixed) open and closed queueing networks, the so-called BCMP queueing networks. The seminal paper on this class of queueing networks, published by Baskett, Chandy, Muntz and Palacios in 1975, is probably the most referenced paper in the performance evaluation literature. We present the BCMP result in Section 13.1, and then we discuss a number of computational algorithms in Section 13.2. It is important to note that we do not strive for completeness in this chapter; we merely selected a few computational algorithms to show their similarity to the algorithms discussed so far and to comment on their computational complexity.

## 13.1 Queueing network class and solution

The best-known class of (mixed) open and closed queueing networks with product-form solution has been published by Baskett, Chandy, Muntz and Palacios in 1975 [14]. We first present this class of queueing models in Section 13.1.1, after which we discuss the steady-state probability distribution of customers in Section 13.1.2.

### 13.1.1 Model class

A BCMP queueing network consists of $M$ queueing stations (or nodes). Customers belong to one of $R$ *classes*. For each class, routing probabilities through the network must be specified. A class can either be open or closed and jobs are allowed to change classes when changing from queue to queue. The queueing stations can be of 4 types:

1. In **FCFS nodes**, jobs are served in a first come, first served fashion. Although FCFS nodes may be visited by jobs of multiple classes, the service time distributions

of all classes need to be the same and must be negative exponential, albeit possibly load-dependent. This latter option can be used to model multiple server stations or FESCs.

2. In **PS nodes**, jobs are served in a processor sharing fashion. All jobs are processed simultaneously with an equal share of the capacity. Jobs of different classes may have different service requirements and the service rates (per class) may depend on the queue length at the node. Service time distributions must be of Coxian type, although only the first moment does play a role in the computations.

3. In **IS** or **delay nodes**, an infinite number of servers is available. All jobs will be served by "their own" server (sometimes this is called the server-per-job strategy). Jobs of different classes may have different service requirements and the service rates (per class) may depend on the queue length at the node. Service time distributions must be of Coxian type; only the first moment needs to be specified.

4. In **LCFSPR nodes**, jobs are served on a last come first served basis with preemption. Further restrictions are the same as for the PS and IS case.

In the literature, these nodes types are also often referred to as type 1, type 2, type 3 and type 4 nodes.

When leaving node $i$, a job of class $r$ will go to node $j$ as a class $s$ job with probability $r_{i,r;j,s}$. Jobs leave the network with probability $r_{i,r;0}$. Depending on which routing possibilities are present, the pairs (node, class) can be partitioned into so-called *routing chains*. In many practical cases, class changes do not occur and a class is then directly connected to a particular route.

For open models, two arrival possibilities exist: (1) either there is a single Poisson arrival stream with rate $\lambda(k)$, where $k$ is the total actual population of the queueing network. A fraction $r_{0;i,r}$ of the arrivals goes as a class $r$ job to station $i$; or (2) every routing chain has its own Poisson arrival stream with a rate only dependent on the population of that chain (denoted $\lambda_c(k_c)$ with $c \in C$; see below). A fraction $r_{0;i,c}$ of these arrivals arrive at queue $i$.

For every routing chain $c \in C$ ($C$ is the set of all routing chains, $N_C = |C|$), the following traffic equation can be established:

$$\lambda_{i,r} = \lambda_{i,r}^* + \sum_{(j,s)} \lambda_{j,s} r_{i,r;j,s}, \tag{13.1}$$

where $\lambda_{i,r}^*$ is determined by the external arrivals of class $r$ to node $i$ (in the case of closed networks this term equals 0; for open networks it equals $\lambda r_{0;i,c}$ (one arrival process) or

$\lambda_r r_{0;i,r}$ (arrivals per chain/class)). As a result of this, one obtains the throughputs $\lambda_{i,r}$ for open chains and the visit ratios $V_{i,r}$ for closed chains (both per node and per class). In many cases, however, the visit counts $V_{i,r}$ are directly given as part of the QN specification.

To conclude this section, let us list the most striking characteristics of BCMP QNs in comparison to the JQNs and GNQNs we discussed before:

- queueing stations can be of four different types, instead of just two (IS and FCFS);

- all station types may have load-dependent service rates;

- customers may belong to different classes, each following their own route through the QN and requesting class-specific service;

- the service time distributions are all of Coxian type, except for the FCFS stations, where we still have to adhere to negative exponentially distributed service times;

- BCMP QNs allow for closed and open routes;

- arrivals at the QN (for the open classes) may depend on the QN population.

## 13.1.2   Steady-state customer probability distribution

Without going into derivations, we simply present the BCMP theorem below. Before doing so, we need to know how to represent the states of a BCMP QN. Let $\underline{N}_i = (N_{i,1}, N_{i,2}, \cdots, N_{i,R})$ be the state of node $i$ where $N_{i,r}$ presents the number of class $r$ customers present in queue $i$ and let $N_i = \sum_{r=1}^{R} N_{i,r}$ be the total number of jobs in queue $i$. The overall state is given by the vector $\underline{N} = (\underline{N}_1, \underline{N}_2, \cdots, \underline{N}_M)$ and the overall number of customers in the QN is given by $K = \sum_{i=1}^{M} N_i$.

**Theorem 13.1. BCMP.**
The steady-state probability distribution in a BCMP QN has the following form:

$$\Pr\{\underline{N} = \underline{n}\} = \frac{1}{G} A(\underline{n}) \prod_{i=1}^{M} p_i(\underline{n}_i), \qquad (13.2)$$

where $G$ is a normalising constant, $A(\underline{n})$ is a function of the arrival process and the functions $p_i(\underline{n}_i)$ are the "per-node" steady-state distributions, to be specified below. We refer to the next section for the definition and computation of the normalising constant $G$.

When node $i$ is of type FCFS, we have in the load-independent case

$$p_i(\underline{n_i}) = n_i! \left( \prod_{r=1}^{R} \frac{1}{n_{i,r}!} V_{i,r}^{n_{i,r}} \right) \left( \frac{1}{\mu_i} \right)^{n_i}, \tag{13.3}$$

and in the load-dependent case

$$p_i(\underline{n_i}) = n_i! \left( \prod_{r=1}^{R} \frac{1}{n_{i,r}!} V_{i,r}^{n_{i,r}} \right) \prod_{j=1}^{n_i} \left( \frac{1}{\mu_i(j)} \right). \tag{13.4}$$

When node $i$ is of type PS or LCFSPR, we have in the load-independent case

$$p_i(\underline{n_i}) = n_i! \prod_{r=1}^{R} \frac{1}{n_{i,r}!} \left( \frac{V_{i,r}}{\mu_{i,r}} \right)^{n_{i,r}}, \tag{13.5}$$

and in the load-dependent case

$$p_i(\underline{n_i}) = n_i! \prod_{r=1}^{R} \frac{1}{n_{i,r}!} V_{i,r}^{n_{i,r}} \prod_{j=1}^{n_i} \frac{1}{\mu_{i,r}(j)}. \tag{13.6}$$

When node $i$ is of type IS, we have in the load-independent case

$$p_i(\underline{n_i}) = \prod_{r=1}^{R} \frac{1}{n_{i,r}!} \left( \frac{V_{i,r}}{\mu_{i,r}} \right)^{n_{i,r}}, \tag{13.7}$$

and in the load-dependent case

$$p_i(\underline{n_i}) = \prod_{r=1}^{R} \frac{1}{n_{i,r}!} V_{i,r}^{n_{i,r}} \prod_{j=1}^{n_i} \frac{1}{\mu_{i,r}(j)}. \tag{13.8}$$

Notice that the load-dependent cases we have addressed here refer to the case where the service rate for a customer of a particular class depends on the *total* number of customers in the queueing station ($n_i$). In the BCMP paper, other forms of load-dependency are also discussed, e.g., the case where the service rate of a class $r$ customer at queue $i$ depends on the number of customers of that class at that station ($n_{i,r}$); we do not address these cases here.

The term $A(\underline{n})$ is determined by the arrival processes. If all chains are closed $A(\underline{n}) = 1$. If the arrivals depend on the total QN population, its value equals $A(\underline{n}) = \prod_{j=0}^{k-1} \lambda(j)$, where $k$ is the actual network population. If the arrivals are per chain, its value equals $A(\underline{n}) = \prod_{c=1}^{N_C} \prod_{j=0}^{k_c-1} \lambda_c(j)$, where $k_c$ is the actual population in routing chain $c$. □

Important to note is that although the service time distribution in PS, IS and LCFSPR nodes is of Coxian type, only its mean value is of importance in the expressions for the steady-state distributions. This is also known as the *insensitivity property* (with respect to higher moments) of BCMP queueing networks.

### Example 13.1. Single-class, load-independent open networks.

A simplification of the BCMP theorem is obtained when only open networks are addressed in which there is only a single, load-independent Poisson arrival process with rate $\lambda$ and where the service rates are fixed as well. In that case, the steady-state distribution

$$\Pr\{\underline{\mathbf{N}} = \underline{\mathbf{n}}\} = \prod_{i=1}^{M} p_i(n_i), \tag{13.9}$$

with

$$p_i(n_i) = \begin{cases} (1 - \rho_i)\rho_i^{n_i}, & \text{FCFS, PS, LCFSPR type,} \\ e^{-\rho_i}\frac{\rho_i^{n_i}}{n_i!}, & \text{IS type,} \end{cases} \tag{13.10}$$

where $\rho_i$ is defined as

$$\rho_i = \begin{cases} \sum_{r \in R_i} \frac{\lambda V_{i,r}}{\mu_i}, & \text{FCFS type,} \\ \sum_{r \in R_i} \frac{\lambda V_{i,r}}{\mu_{i,r}}, & \text{PS, IS, LCFSPR type,} \end{cases} \tag{13.11}$$

with $R_i$ the set of classes asking service at station $i$. Notice that the value $A(\underline{\mathbf{n}}) = \lambda^k$ is not explicitly used in the expression for $\Pr\{\underline{\mathbf{N}} = \underline{\mathbf{n}}\}$; it is hidden in the product of the $\rho_i$-terms. Furthermore, realize that in this simplified case, nodes of FCFS, PS and LCFSPR type operate as if they are M|M|1 queues studied in isolation (see also Chapter 6 where we found a similar result for the M|G|1 queue with processor sharing scheduling). To conclude, this special case of the BCMP theorem leads to a slight generalisation of the JQNs we have studied in Chapter 10. □

### Example 13.2. Closed, multi-class, load-independent BCMP networks.

A class of BCMP networks that is of particular interest encompasses load-independent servers, multiple customer classes (without class changes) and fixed populations per class. For such QNs, the steady-state distribution equals

$$\Pr\{\underline{\mathbf{N}} = \underline{\mathbf{n}}\} = \frac{1}{G} \prod_{i=1}^{M} p_i(\underline{n}_i), \tag{13.12}$$

with

$$
p_i(\underline{n}_i) = \begin{cases} n_i! \left(\frac{1}{\mu_i}\right)^{n_i} \prod_{r=1}^{R} \frac{1}{n_{i,r}!} V_{i,r}, & \text{FCFS type,} \\[3mm] n_i! \prod_{r=1}^{R} \frac{1}{n_{i,r}!} \left(\frac{V_{i,r}}{\mu_{i,r}}\right)^{n_{i,r}}, & \text{PS, LCFSPR type,} \\[3mm] \prod_{r=1}^{R} \frac{1}{n_{i,r}!} \left(\frac{V_{i,r}}{\mu_{i,r}}\right)^{n_{i,r}}, & \text{IS type.} \end{cases}
\tag{13.13}
$$

Note that $n_i = \sum_{r=1}^{R} n_{i,r}$. $\qquad\qquad\qquad\qquad\qquad\qquad\qquad\qquad\qquad\qquad$ $\square$

## 13.2  Computational algorithms

Specifying BCMP QNs is one thing, evaluating them is a completely different story. Generalisations of the convolution and MVA algorithms we have discussed do exist, but they are notationally not so convenient anymore, and they do have a high time and space complexity.

We will start with a brief treatment of the extension of the convolution method in Section 13.2.1. We then present MVA algorithms for a number of special cases of BCMP QNs in Section 13.2.2.

### 13.2.1  The convolution algorithm

We address the case of a closed queueing network with $R$ classes of customers, no class changes and $M$ load-independent nodes. The fixed population is given by the vector $\underline{K} = (K_1, K_2, \cdots, K_R)$ and $K = \sum_{i=1}^{R} K_i$. The state space $\mathcal{I}(M, \underline{K})$ is now specified as follows:

$$
\mathcal{I}(M,\underline{K}) = \{(\underline{n}_1, \cdots, \underline{n}_M) \in \mathbb{N}^{M \cdot R} | \underline{n}_i = (n_{i,1}, \cdots, n_{i,R}), \sum_{i=1}^{M} n_{i,j} = K_j, i = 1, \cdots, R\}.
\tag{13.14}
$$

The normalising constant is now dependent on both the number of nodes $M$ and the population vector $\underline{K}$, and is defined as

$$
G(M,\underline{K}) = \sum_{n \in \mathcal{I}(M,\underline{K})} \prod_{i=1}^{M} p_i(\underline{n}_i),
\tag{13.15}
$$

where the terms $p_i(\underline{n}_i)$ are dependent on the node type and defined in (13.3)–(13.8). A direct computation of the normalising constant would involve

$$
\prod_{j=1}^{R} \binom{K_j + M - 1}{M - 1}
$$

computational steps (one for each state) where each step consists of multiple multiplications. This is clearly not a practical approach to use. Therefore, an extension of the convolution approach has been proposed. Without derivation, we state that the following recursive relation holds:

$$G(M, \underline{K}) = \sum_{k_1=0}^{K_1} \sum_{k_2=0}^{K_2} \cdots \sum_{k_R=0}^{K_R} p_M(k_1, k_2, \cdots, k_R) G(M-1, \underline{K} - (k_1, k_2, \cdots, k_R)). \quad (13.16)$$

We observe that the recursion is multi-dimensional along all the routing chains. As initial values, we have $G(1, \underline{K}) = p_1(\underline{K})$, and $G(M, \underline{K}) = 0$, as soon as one of the components of $\underline{K}$ is negative.

The above expression can be simplified in case we exclusively deal with load-independent nodes of types FCFS, PS or LCFSPR, in which case we have:

$$G(M, \underline{K}) = G(M-1, \underline{K}) + \sum_{r=1}^{R} \frac{V_{i,r}}{\mu_{i,r}} G(M, \underline{K} - \underline{1}_r), \quad (13.17)$$

where $\underline{1}_r$ is a unit-vector with a 1 on the $r$-th position. Here, we see that the recurrence is again over the classes: the normalising constant $G(M, \underline{K})$ is the weighted sum of normalising constants with one node less, and with one customer less in each of the classes. Note that for a node $i$ of FCFS type, the value $\mu_{i,r} = \mu_i$, for all classes $r$.

The throughput of customers of class $r$ at node $i$ can again be expressed as a quotient of normalising constants:

$$X_{i,r} = V_{i,r} \frac{G(M, \underline{K} - \underline{1}_r)}{G(M, \underline{K})}. \quad (13.18)$$

Other measures of interest can be computed in a similar way as we have seen before.

The computational time complexity of this convolution algorithm is $O(MR \prod_{r=1}^{R}(K_r + 1))$ and the space complexity is $O(M \prod_{r=1}^{R}(K_r + 1))$. Hence, the inclusion of more customer classes, even if the number of customers remains the same, increases the number of operations to be performed significantly.

## 13.2.2  Mean-value analysis

The MVA algorithm can be extended to the multi-class case in a straightforward way. We adhere to the same class of QNs as in the previous section. If we define the average service demand for class $r$ at node $i$ as $D_{i,r} = V_{i,r}/\mu_{i,r}$, the arrival theorem states that the response time (per passage) for a class $r$ customer at node $i$ is given as follows

$$E[\hat{R}_{i,r}(\underline{K})] = \begin{cases} D_{i,r} \left( \sum_{j=1}^{R} E[N_{i,j}(\underline{K} - \underline{1}_j)] + 1 \right), & \text{FCFS, PS, LCFSPR nodes,} \\ D_{i,r}, & \text{IS nodes.} \end{cases}$$

$$(13.19)$$

The throughput for class $r$ customers (through the node with $V_{i,r} = 1$) is given as:

$$X_r(\underline{K}) = \frac{K_r}{\sum_{i=1}^{M} E[\hat{R}_{i,r}(\underline{K})]},$$  (13.20)

and the expected number of class $r$ customers in node $i$ is, according to Little's law, given as

$$E[N_{i,r}(\underline{K})] = X_r(\underline{K})E[\hat{R}_{i,r}(\underline{K})].$$  (13.21)

Of course, $E[N_{i,r}(\underline{K})] = 0$ if $K_r = 0$.

The time and space complexity of this MVA algorithm are similar to those of the multi-class convolution algorithm. Especially when dealing with many classes and with many customers, a direct computation along this scheme therefore becomes prohibitive. To avoid such direct computations, approximation schemes have been devised. For the multi-class MVA algorithm, one can use the following variant of the Bard-Schweitzer approximation to break the recursion.

Instead of using $E[N_{i,j}(\underline{K}-\underline{1}_j)]$ for the number of class $j$ customers present upon arrival at node $i$, one can estimate this value as

$$\frac{K_j - 1}{K_j}E[N_{i,j}(\underline{K})] + \sum_{l \neq j} E[N_{i,l}(\underline{K})].$$

In this approximation, it is assumed that removing a class $j$ customer does not affect the performance of other classes (which is not true!) and affects all class $j$ queue lengths in the same way. An advantage of this approach is that the system of recursive MVA equations is transformed in a system of non-linear equations independent of the value of the population vector $\underline{K}$ that can be solved using a fixed-point iteration technique. Especially for larger populations this is an advantage. As initial estimates one might take $E[N_{i,r}(\underline{K})] \approx K_r/M$ (per class, the customers are uniformly spread over all queues). In practice, good results have been obtained with this approximation scheme; errors typically stay within 10%, and a few dozen iterations are needed at most.

The MVA presented here can also be extended to QNs with load-dependent service rates. We do not discuss these here but refer to the appropriate literature.

## 13.3   Further reading

BCMP queueing networks have been introduced in [14] as extension of the work on Jackson networks by Buzen [37]. Around the same time, Denning and Buzen published their so-called operational analysis method which also addresses QNs with a variety of characteristics [72]. Their paper also includes some computational algorithms. The MVA schemes have been developed by Reiser and Lavenberg [245, 243]. Reiser also presented approximation schemes to break the recursion [242]. The MVA algorithms, as well as bounds and a few approximations, are also discussed in [177]. In the books by King [156], Harrison and Patel [117] and Kant [152] some more computational techniques for BCMP queueing networks are discussed (e.g., LBANC [45] and RECAL [64]). Lam discusses the relation between various algorithms [170] as well as ways to deal with large normalising constants [169]. The books by Bruell and Balbo [30] and by Conway and Georganas [65] deal exclusively with computational algorithms for BCMP networks. Conway also discusses the applicability of queueing network models for the analysis of layered communication systems [63]. Onvural discusses closed-form solutions and algorithms for queueing network with blocking [224].

## 13.4   Exercises

### 13.1. The GNQN-special case of BCMP queueing networks.
Show that the BCMP theorem reduces to the product-form result for GNQN when we deal with single-class, load-independent servers of FCFS type in a closed network.

### 13.2. Use of BCMP queueing networks.
List examples of computer or communication system components that can best be modelled by BCMP nodes of types 1 through 4 (FCFS, PS, IS or LCFSPR).

# Part IV

# Stochastic Petri net models

# Chapter 14

# Stochastic Petri nets

IN this chapter we present the basic theory concerning stochastic Petri nets (SPNs). SPNs grew out of the general theory of (non-timed) Petri nets developed by Petri in the early 1960s, through the introduction of stochastic timing in these models. The first papers in the field of stochastic Petri nets appeared in the late 1970s and early 1980s; refer to the end of the chapter for an overview.

SPNs are, like queueing networks, a graph-based modelling formalism allowing for the easy specification of finite-state machine models. Under suitable assumptions regarding the involved stochastic timing, a large class of SPN models can be mapped (automatically) to an underlying CTMC with finite state space. Such a CTMC can then be analysed numerically, thus yielding information about the SPN.

In this chapter we present a fairly general class of SPNs in which the involved distributions are all of negative exponential type so that an underlying CTMC can be readily computed. Notation and terminology is introduced in Section 14.1. Structural properties of these Petri net models are discussed in Section 14.2. We present important SPN-related performance measures in Section 14.3. The actual mapping of SPNs to the underlying CTMCs is then discussed in Section 14.4.

Note that the discussion of the numerical solution of the CTMCs generated from the SPNs is postponed until Chapter 15. Chapter 16 is devoted to various applications of SPN modelling.

## 14.1 Definition

In this section we introduce a class of SPN models. In Section 14.1.1 we present the static structure of SPNs, after which we discuss the dynamic properties of SPNs in Section 14.1.2.

We finally comment on a number of wide-spread model extensions in Section 14.1.3.

## 14.1.1  Static SPN properties

Stochastic Petri net models are graph models. More precisely, SPNs are directed bipartite graphs where the set of vertices is formed by the union of a set of *places* $P$ and a set of *transitions* $T$. The edges are a subset of the union of a set of *input arcs* (pointing from places to transitions), a set of *output arcs* (pointing from transitions to places) and a set of *inhibitor arcs* (pointing from places to transitions; actually, inhibitor arcs were first introduced in *generalised* SPNs, but we will consider them here as well). Places are depicted as circles, transitions as bars. Input and output arcs are depicted as arrows and inhibitor arcs as arrows with a small circle as arrow head (see also Figure 14.1).

Transitions can be one of two types: *immediate* or *timed*. Immediate transitions do not take any time at all to complete, whereas timed transitions require a negative exponential time to fire, after they have become enabled. Immediate transitions are normally drawn as thin bars and used to model system aspects that do not have physical time associated with them, or system aspects that take only very little time when compared to the time consuming activities in a system. Timed transitions are depicted as thick bars.

Finally, places may contain one or more *tokens*, depicted as small black circles. A distribution of tokens over places is called a *marking*.

Before we elaborate more on the operation of SPNs, let us first define them formally. An SPN is given as:

$$SPN = (P, T, Pr, I, O, H, W, \underline{m}_0), \tag{14.1}$$

where $P = \{P_1, P_2, \cdots, P_{n_p}\}$ is a set of places ($|P| = n_p$), $T = \{t_1, t_2, \cdots, t_{n_t}\}$ is a set of transitions ($|T| = n_t$), $Pr : T \to I\!N$ is a function which associates priorities with transitions, where timed transitions have lowest priority (coded as 0 here) and immediate transitions have higher priorities $(1, 2, \cdots)$. $I : P \times T \to I\!N$ is a function which associates a multiplicity with each input arc. $O : T \times P \to I\!N$ is a function which associates a multiplicity with each output arc, and $H : P \times T \to I\!N$ is a function which associates a multiplicity with each inhibitor arc. $W : T \to I\!R^+$ is a function which associates with every transition $t$, either (i) a firing rate $W(t)$ whenever $t$ is a timed transition $(Pr(t) = 0)$, or (ii) a weight $W(t)$ whenever $t$ is an immediate transition $(Pr(t) > 0)$. Finally, $\underline{m}_0 \in I\!N^{n_p}$ is the initial marking, that is, the initial distribution of tokens over the $n_p$ places; we assume that $\underline{m}_0$ is finite. Based on this definition, we can define the following sets:

- the input places of transition $t$: $I_p(t) = \{p \in P | I(p, t) > 0\}$;

- the output places of transition $t$: $O_p(t) = \{p \in P | O(t,p) > 0\}$;

- the inhibiting places of transition $t$: $H_p(t) = \{p \in P | H(p,t) > 0\}$.

We will use these sets in the description of the dynamic properties of SPNs below.

## 14.1.2  Dynamic SPN properties

The dynamic properties of SPNs describe the possible movements of tokens from place to place. The following so-called *firing rules* describe the dynamic properties:

- A transition $t$ is said to be *enabled* in a marking $\underline{m}$ when all its input places $I_p(t)$ contain at least $I(p,t)$ tokens and when no inhibiting place in $H_p(t)$ contains more than $H(p,t)$ tokens.

- When there are immediate transitions enabled in marking $\underline{m}$, this marking is said to be *vanishing*. Then, the following rules apply:

    - The set $E_i(\underline{m}) \subseteq T$ of enabled transitions of highest priority is determined. Let $W$ be the sum of the weights of the transition in $E_i(\underline{m})$, i.e., $W = \sum_{t \in E_i(\underline{m})} W(t)$.
    - Transition $t$ is selected to fire with probability $W(t)/W$.
    - Upon firing, transition $t$ removes $I(p,t)$ tokens from input place $p \in I_p(t)$ (for all $p \in I_p(t)$) and adds $O(t,p)$ tokens to output place $p \in O_p(t)$. Thus, the firing of transition $t$ in marking $\underline{m}$ yields a new marking $\underline{m}'$. Firing is an atomic action, it either takes place completely, or not at all.

- When there are no immediate transitions enabled, the marking $\underline{m}$ is said to be *tangible*. Then, the following rules apply:

    - An enabled transition $t$ fires after an exponentially distributed time with rate $W(t)$.
    - Upon firing, a transition $t$ removes $I(p,t)$ tokens from input place $p \in I_p(t)$ and adds $O(t,p)$ tokens to output place $p \in O_p(t)$. Thus, the firing of transition $t$ in marking $\underline{m}$ yields a new marking $\underline{m}'$.
    - When in a particular marking $\underline{m}$ more than one timed transition is enabled, one of them is selected probabilistically as follows:

        * Let $E_t(\underline{m}) \subseteq T$ denote the set of transitions enabled in marking $\underline{m}$.

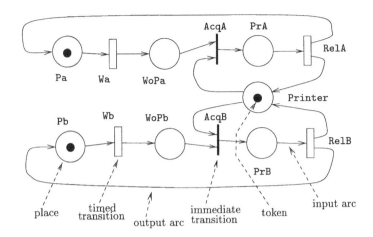

Figure 14.1: SPN model of simultaneous resource possessing

* All the enabled transitions $t \in E_t(\underline{m})$ take a sample from their corresponding exponential distribution with rate $W(t)$. The transition with the minimum sample time fires first, and a new marking arises according to the token flow along the input and output arcs of that transition. Alternatively, one can define $W = \sum_{t \in E_t(\underline{m})} W(t)$ as the total outgoing rate of marking $\underline{m}$. The delay in marking $\underline{m}$ is then exponentially distributed with rate $W$; after that delay, transition $t$ will fire (without further timing delay) with probability $W(t)/W$. This interpretation is equivalent to the former one by the memoryless property of the negative exponential distribution.

## Example 14.1. Simultaneous resource possessing (I).

Consider two computer system users $A$ and $B$ that want to make use of a single, scarce resource such as a printer, every once in a while. The behaviour of both users can be described by an infinite repetition of the following activities: do normal work—acquire printer—use printer—release printer—$\cdots$. We can model this by a SPN as depicted in Figure 14.1. Formally, we have:

$$P = \quad \{\texttt{Pa}, \texttt{Pb}, \texttt{WoPa}, \texttt{WoPb}, \texttt{PrA}, \texttt{PrB}, \texttt{Printer}\}$$

$$T = \quad \{\texttt{Wa}, \texttt{Wb}, \texttt{AcqA}, \texttt{AcqB}, \texttt{RelA}, \texttt{RelB}\};$$

$$Pr = \quad \{(\texttt{Wa}, 0), (\texttt{Wb}, 0), (\texttt{AcqA}, 1), (\texttt{AcqB}, 1), (\texttt{RelA}, 0), (\texttt{RelB}, 0)\};$$

$$I = \quad \{(\texttt{Pa}, \texttt{Wa}, 1), (\texttt{Pb}, \texttt{Wb}, 1), (\texttt{WoPa}, \texttt{AcqA}, 1), (\texttt{WoPb}, \texttt{AcqB}, 1), (\texttt{Printer}, \texttt{AcqA}, 1),$$
$$\quad (\texttt{Printer}, \texttt{AcqB}, 1), (\texttt{PrA}, \texttt{RelA}, 1), (\texttt{PrB}, \texttt{RelB}, 1)\};$$

$$O = \quad \{(\texttt{Wa}, \texttt{WoPa}, 1), (\texttt{Wb}, \texttt{WoPb}, 1), (\texttt{AcqA}, \texttt{PrA}, 1), (\texttt{AcqB}, \texttt{PrB}, 1), (\texttt{RelA}, \texttt{Pa}, 1),$$
$$\quad (\texttt{RelB}, \texttt{Pb}, 1), (\texttt{RelA}, \texttt{Printer}, 1), (\texttt{RelB}, \texttt{Printer}, 1)\};$$

$$m_0 = \quad (1, 1, 0, 0, 0, 0, 1);$$

$$H = \quad \emptyset;$$

$$W = \quad \{(\texttt{Wa}, \lambda_a), (\texttt{Wb}, \lambda_b), (\texttt{AcqA}, 1), (\texttt{AcqB}, 1), (\texttt{RelA}, \mu_a), (\texttt{RelB}, \mu_b)\}.$$

An informal description of the above SPN is as follows. There are two users, represented by the tokens in places $\texttt{Pa}$ and $\texttt{Pb}$. They do an amount of work, represented by the timed transitions $\texttt{Wa}$ and $\texttt{Wb}$ respectively. After that, they try to acquire access to the single printer (represented by the single token in place $\texttt{Printer}$) via the immediate transitions $\texttt{AcqA}$ and $\texttt{AcqB}$ respectively, while remaining in the places ("in state") $\texttt{WoPa}$ and $\texttt{WoPb}$ (Wait on Printer). Note that when one of the users already has access to the printer, the other user is "blocked" since its corresponding acquire-transition cannot fire due to the fact that the place $\texttt{Printer}$ is already empty. After acquiring access to the printer, the printer is used for some time and released afterwards via the transitions $\texttt{RelA}$ and $\texttt{RelB}$. By the firing of these transitions, the printer becomes available again for other users, and the user who just used the printer resumes normal work. □

## Example 14.2. Priority systems (I).

Reconsider the SPN of Figure 14.1 and assume that the initial number of tokens in places $\texttt{Pa}$ and $\texttt{Pb}$ is much larger. We can then interpret this model as a two-class model, where customers of class A (and B) arrive at the system in their own buffers, and which require exclusive service from the system (the printer) with durations specified by the transitions $\texttt{RelA}$ and $\texttt{RelB}$. If both $\texttt{WoPa}$ and $\texttt{WoPb}$ contain tokens, the next customer taken into service is chosen probabilistically, using the weights of the transitions $\texttt{AcqA}$ and $\texttt{AcqB}$.

We can adapt this model to address the case where class A customers have non-preemptive priority over class B customers, by simply adding an inhibitor arc from $\texttt{WoPa}$ to $\texttt{Acqb}$; as long as there are class A customers waiting, no work on a class B customer may be started. Alternatively, we can set the priority of transition $\texttt{AcqA}$ higher than that of $\texttt{AcqB}$. □

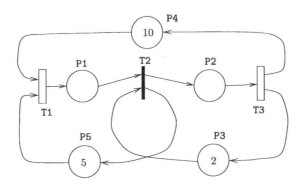

Figure 14.2: SPN representation of the M|M|2|5|10 queue

## Example 14.3. The M|M|2|5|10 queue (I).

Consider an SPN representation of the M|M|2|5|10 queue as depicted in Figure 14.2. The
waiting room is represented by place P1. Idle servers are represented by tokens in place
P3 and busy servers are represented by tokens in place P2. Place P4 models the outside
world; it is the finite source and sink of tokens. Notice that a token in place P2 signifies
a *server-customer pair*. The tokens in place P5 represent free buffer places (free places in
the waiting room P1). Once the waiting room is fully occupied, place P5 is empty, so that
no more arrivals are allowed since T1 is disabled. In order to exactly describe the multi-
server behaviour, the marking of place P2 should determine the rate at which customers
are served by the timed transition T3: its rate should be proportional to the number of
customers in service, i.e., the number of tokens in place P2; we come back to these so-called
marking-dependent firing rates below. Notice that the movement of customers waiting for
service in place P1 to the service area (place P2), via the immediate transition T2 does not
take any time at all.                                                                    □

It is important to note that the employed terminology of SPNs is very general. It is left open
to the user what places, transitions, etc., represent in reality. In most of the SPN models
we interpret tokens as customers or packets and places as buffers or queues; however, they
are actually more than that. Their interpretation depends on the place they are in. As an
example of this, in Figure 14.1, a token in place Pa or WoPa indeed represents a customer.
On the other hand, the token in place Printer represents a resource. Moreover, a token
in place PrA represents a customer using a particular resource. Similarly, SPN transitions
model system activities such as packet transmissions or the processing of jobs. However, a
single transition might consume two (or more) tokens at the same time from different places

and "transform" them into a single token for yet another place (as AcqA does). On the other hand, a single token taken from a single place by a transition may be transformed to multiple tokens put in multiple places (as RelA does). The complex of enabling possibilities by the input and output arcs then represents the rules for using resources, the involved protocols, etc. In the literature, SPNs have also been used to model completely different dynamic phenomena, such as the flow of traffic through cities and paperwork through offices, but also chemical systems where the transitions model partial chemical reactions and the tokens molecules.

### 14.1.3   SPN extensions

Over the years many enhancements and extensions to the definition of SPNs have been published. Below, we discuss a number of widely-used extensions.

- We have assumed so far that the weights $W(t)$ are constants. This need not be the case. The weights, represented by the function $W : T \rightarrow \mathbb{R}^+$, can be made *marking dependent*. Denoting with $M$ the set of possible markings, i.e., $M \subset \mathbb{N}^{n_p}$, the function $W$ becomes: $W : T \times M \rightarrow \mathbb{R}^+$. Using marking dependent weights often results in models that are easier to understand and more compact. Graphically, the symbol "#" is placed near a transition with a marking dependent rate; a separate specification of this dependence then needs to be given. As an example using this notation, in Figure 14.2, the rate of T3 should equal $\#P2 \cdot \mu$.

- On top of the normal firing rules, the use of *enabling functions* (or *guards*) has become more widespread. An enabling function $E : T \times M \rightarrow \{0, 1\}$ specifies for every transition $t \in T$ in marking $m \in M$ whether it is enabled (1) or not (0). Given a particular marking, the choice of which transition will fire first is based on the normal firing rules; however, for the transitions having passed this first selection, the enabling functions are evaluated. Only if these also evaluate to 1 are the transitions said to be enabled. The use of enabling functions eases the specification of SPNs, especially when complex enabling conditions have to be expressed. A disadvantage of the use of enabling functions is that part of the net semantics is no longer graphically visible.

- Modelling features that are often very convenient are *marking dependent arc multiplicities*. We then have to specify functions $I : P \times T \times M \rightarrow \mathbb{N}$ (and similar extensions for output and inhibitor arcs) that specify the multiplicity of an arc, dependent on the current marking. As an example of this, consider the case where an input arc $I(p, t, m)$ equals the actual number of tokens in $p$. Firing of $t$ then empties place $p$ (given $O(t, p, m) = 0$). Marking dependent arc multiplicities should be used with great care; although they often help in keeping the SPN models simple, they also might obscure the semantics of the model. Arcs with marking dependent multiplicity are often marked with a "zig-zag" as follows: $\longrightarrow\!\!\!\!\!\!z\!\!\!\!\rightarrow$.

### Example 14.4. Priority systems (II).

Reconsider the SPN of Figure 14.1 and again assume that the initial number of tokens in places Pa and Pb is larger than 1. Instead of giving absolute priority to class A (over B) we can also increase the probability of a class A (or B) customer to be taken into service if there are more of them waiting (in comparison to those waiting of the other class). We can do so by making the weights of AcqA and AcqB proportional to the number of customers of that class waiting.

If the printer server is extended to include a second printer, we can simply add an extra (initial) token to place Printer. However, to correctly model the cases where the two printers are handling jobs of either class A or B, we should double the rate of the transitions RelA and RelB in those cases. This can be accomplished by making the rate of these transitions proportional to the number of tokens in their input places; if there is only one token there, the normal print rate is employed, but if there are two tokens in that place, both printers are active for that class, hence, the effective rate is twice the original one.                                                                                                                    □

## 14.2 Structural properties

Given an SPN as defined in Section 14.1, we can check a number of properties directly from its structure, i.e., its places, transitions, and arcs, which can be used to verify whether the model actually models what it should (the system) as well as to find bounds on the size of the underlying CTMC. For the time being, assume that we do not need to make a distinction between timed and immediate transitions to determine the properties listed below.

Given a marking $m$, we say that marking $m'$ is *immediately reachable* from $m$, if $m'$ can be obtained by the firing of an enabled transition $t$ in marking $m$; we write $m \xrightarrow{t} m'$.

A marking $m'$ is *reachable* from marking $m$, if $m'$ is immediately reachable from $m$, or if $m''$ is immediately reachable from $m$, and $m'$ is reachable from $m''$; we write $m \longrightarrow m'$.

Given the initial marking $m_0$, the set of all possible markings that are reachable from $m_0$ is called the *reachability set* $\mathcal{R}(m_0)$; notice that $\mathcal{R}(m_0) \subset \mathbb{N}^{n_p}$. The graph $(R(m_0), E)$ in which all possible markings are the vertices (nodes) and in which an edge labelled $t$ exists between two vertices $m$ and $m'$ whenever $m \xrightarrow{t} m'$, is called the *reachability graph*.

A marking $m$ from which no other marking $m'$ is reachable is called a *dead marking*. In terms of the SPN, this means that after a marking $m$ is reached, no transition can fire any more. Such markings therefore generally point to deadlock or absorption situations (either in the system being modelled or in the model).

An SPN is said to be *k-bounded* when in all $m \in \mathcal{R}(m_0)$ the number of tokens per place is at most $k$. In the special case of 1-boundedness, we speak of a *safe* SPN. A $k$-bounded Petri net, possibly with inhibitor and multiple arcs, is *always* finite and can therefore be represented as a finite state machine with at most $(k+1)^{n_p}$ states.

An SPN is said to be *strictly conservative* if the sum of the number of tokens in all places is the same for all markings. This implies that for each transition the number of input and output arcs, measured by their multiplicity, must be equal. A Petri net is said to be *conservative* if the number of tokens in all places, weighted by a per-place weighting factor is the same in all markings. A *place invariant* then is a vector of weighting factors such that for that vector, the Petri net is conservative; note that some of the weighting factors may be zero!

When using SPNs to represent real systems (in which the tokens represent physical resources) the notion of conservation is important. Since physical resources are normally constant in number, the corresponding SPN will have to exhibit conservation properties. We can compute place invariants in the following way. We define $c_{p,t} = O(t,p) - I(p,t)$ as the effect that the firing of transition $t$ has on the marking of place $p$ (it takes $I(p,t)$ tokens from $p$, but adds another $O(t,p)$ to $p$). The matrix $\mathbf{C} = (c_{p,t})$ specifies in each column how the firing of a certain transition affects all the places. Define the column vector $\underline{f} \in \mathbb{N}^{n_t}$. It can then be proven that for all $m \in \mathcal{R}(m_0)$, we can write:

$$m = m_0 + \mathbf{C}\underline{f}, \tag{14.2}$$

where the vector $\underline{f}$ denotes how often every transition in $T$ has been fired, starting from $m_0$ to reach $m$. Multiplying this equation with a row vector $\underline{v}$ gives us $\underline{v} \cdot m = \underline{v} \cdot m_0$, for all $m \in \mathcal{R}(m_0)$, provided $\underline{v}\mathbf{C} = \underline{0}$. Since we know $m_0$, the product $\underline{v} \cdot m_0$ can readily be computed. Thus, once we have computed vectors $\underline{v} \neq \underline{0}$ such that $\underline{v}\mathbf{C} = \underline{0}$, we know the value of the product $\underline{v} \cdot m$ for any reachable marking $m$. This gives us a means to decide whether a certain marking can be reached or not. We call a vector $\underline{v} \neq \underline{0}$ such that $\underline{v}\mathbf{C} = \underline{0}$

a place invariant. Sometimes place invariants are called $S$-invariants, where the "$S$" stands for "Stellen", the German word for place.

**Example 14.5. The M|M|2|5|10 queue (II).**
We readdress the queueing model we have seen before. The matrix $\mathbf{C}$ can easily be obtained from Figure 14.2 as:

$$\mathbf{C} = \begin{pmatrix} 1 & -1 & 0 \\ 0 & 1 & -1 \\ 0 & -1 & 1 \\ -1 & 0 & 1 \\ -1 & 1 & 0 \end{pmatrix}.$$

Computing $\underline{v}\mathbf{C} = \underline{0}$ leads to the following equations:

$$\begin{cases} v_1 - v_4 - v_5 = 0, \\ -v_1 + v_2 - v_3 + v_5 = 0, \\ -v_2 + v_3 + v_4 = 0, \end{cases}$$

from which we can conclude the following place invariants: $(v_4 + v_5, v_3 + v_4, v_3, v_4, v_5)$. Notice that these place invariants are not determined uniquely! Assuming values for $v_3$, $v_4$ and $v_5$, we come to the following place invariants: $\underline{i}_1 = (0, 1, 1, 0, 0)$, $\underline{i}_2 = (1, 1, 0, 1, 0)$ and $\underline{i}_3 = (1, 0, 0, 0, 1)$. Multiplying these invariants with the initial marking $\underline{m}_0$, we find that:

$$P2 + P3 = 2, \quad P1 + P2 + P4 = 10, \quad \text{and} \quad P1 + P5 = 5,$$

where we have (informally) used the place identifiers to indicate the number of tokens in the places. The first place invariant states that the number of servers active and passive always sums up to 2, as it should. The second place invariant states that the number of customers buffered, served, or outside of the system, equals 10. The last place invariant states that the number of used and unused buffer places must equal 5. All reachable markings $\underline{m}$ should obey these invariants; hence, a marking like $(1, 1, 1, 0, 4)$ cannot be reached.                                                                                              □

A place $P_i$ is said to be *covered* by a place invariant $\underline{v}$ if the entry corresponding to place $P_i$ is non-zero, i.e., if $v_i > 0$. If a place is covered by a place invariant, than this place is bounded. If all the places of the SPN are covered by place invariants, then the SPN is bounded.

A transition $t$ is said to be *live* if for all possible markings $m \in \mathcal{R}(\underline{m}_0)$ there is a marking $\underline{m}'$, reachable from $\underline{m}$, that enables $t$. If this property holds for all transitions, the Petri net is said to be live. Liveness is a property which is closely related to liveness in computer or communication systems. When a system model is live, the corresponding system is deadlock free. A live Petri net cannot contain dead markings.

A *transition invariant* is a series of transitions that, when starting from marking $\underline{m}$, after the successive firing of these transitions, will yield marking $\underline{m}$ again. Using $\underline{f}$ as defined before, $\underline{f}$ is a transition invariant if

$$\underline{m} = \underline{m} + \mathbf{C}\underline{f}.$$

Hence, to find transition invariants, we have to find those $\underline{f} \neq \underline{0}$ such that $\mathbf{C}\underline{f} = \underline{0}$. If an SPN is bounded and live, all of its transitions should be part of at least one transition invariant (all transitions should be covered by transition invariants).

**Example 14.6. Simultaneous resource possessing (II).**
The transition invariants for the simultaneous resource possessing example are easy to compute from $\mathbf{C}\underline{f} = \underline{0}$ with

$$\mathbf{C} = \begin{pmatrix} -1 & 0 & 0 & 0 & 1 & 0 \\ 0 & -1 & 0 & 0 & 0 & 1 \\ 1 & 0 & -1 & 0 & 0 & 0 \\ 0 & 1 & 0 & -1 & 0 & 0 \\ 0 & 0 & 1 & 0 & -1 & 0 \\ 0 & 0 & 0 & 1 & 0 & -1 \\ 0 & 0 & -1 & -1 & 1 & 1 \end{pmatrix}.$$

The first group of three equations from the system $\mathbf{C}\underline{f} = \underline{0}$ yields $f_1 = f_3 = f_5$, and the second group of three equations gives $f_2 = f_4 = f_6 = 1$. The last equation is dependent on the former six. Thus, we have as transition invariants both $(1, 0, 1, 0, 1, 0)$ and $(0, 1, 0, 1, 0, 1)$. These can also be easily interpreted; either user A or user B will use the printer. After usage, they both leave the system in the same state as that they entered it. Parallel usage is not possible.                                                                      □

**Example 14.7. The M|M|2|5|10 queue (III).**
From $\mathbf{C}\underline{f} = \underline{0}$ we immediately find that $\underline{f} = (1, 1, 1)$. This means that after having fired all transitions once, given starting marking $\underline{m}$, we are back in $\underline{m}$ again.                □

We finally comment on the applicability of the structural properties for timed Petri nets. Originally, these properties have been defined for non-timed Petri nets. However,

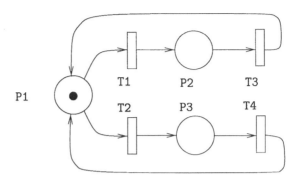

Figure 14.3: Structural properties in SPNs

as long as the timed transitions have delay distributions with support on $[0, \infty)$, and transition priorities and enabling functions are not used, nor are marking dependent arc multiplicities, the structural properties of the non-timed Petri nets are valid for their timed counterparts as well. For further details on invariants for SPNs with marking-dependent arc multiplicities, refer to [51].

**Example 14.8. Structural properties in SPNs.**
Consider the SPN as given in Figure 14.3. If all the transitions are non-timed, there will be two place invariants: $P1 + P2 = 1$ and $P1 + P3 = 1$. Furthermore, there will be two transition invariants: $(1, 0, 1, 0)$ and $(0, 1, 0, 1)$. When all the transitions have a negative exponential firing delay, these invariants still hold. However, if T1 has a deterministic delay of length 1 and T3 of length 2, then the second place and transition invariant will both not be valid any more. On the other hand, if T1 and T2 still exhibit negative exponential delays, but T3 and T4 have deterministic delays, then all the above invariants still hold.

Thus, it depends on the involved timing delays and their "position" in the SPN whether or not the invariants for the non-timed Petri net continue to hold.                             □

## 14.3 Measures to obtain from SPNs

Assuming that a given SPN is finite, that is $|\mathcal{R}(\underline{m}_0)| < \infty$, we can derive many interesting measures from the SPN. For the time being we focus on steady-state measures.

Let $\mathcal{R}(\underline{m}_0)$ denote the set of all possible markings, $\underline{m} \in \mathcal{R}(\underline{m}_0)$ and let $\#P(\underline{m})$ denote the number of tokens in place $P$ given marking $\underline{m}$ (one also often sees the notation $\#P$

leaving the "in marking $m$" implicit; when there is no confusion possible, we will do so as well). The following measures can easily be obtained:

- The probability $p_m$ of a particular marking $m$. This probability can be obtained from the CTMC underlying the SPN (see Section 14.4).

- The probability $\Pr\{\#P = k\}$, that is, the probability of having exactly $k$ tokens in place P. It is derived as follows:

$$\Pr\{\#P = k\} = \sum_{m \in \mathcal{R}(m_0), \#P(m)=k} p_m. \tag{14.3}$$

- More generally, the probability $\Pr\{A\}$ of an event $A$, where $A \subset \mathcal{R}(m_0)$ expresses some condition on the markings of interest, can be derived as

$$\Pr\{A\} = \sum_{m \in A} p_m. \tag{14.4}$$

Note that the condition $A$ can refer to multiple places so that complex conditions are allowed.

- The average number of tokens in a place P:

$$E[\#P] = \sum_{k=0}^{\infty} k \Pr\{\#P = k\}. \tag{14.5}$$

Note that the infinite summation does not occur in practice as the number of different markings is finite.

- The throughput $X_t$ of a timed transition $t$ can be computed as the weighted sum of the firing rate of $t$ over all markings in which $t$ is enabled:

$$X_t = \sum_{m \in \mathcal{R}(m), t \in E_t(m)} W(t, m) p_m, \tag{14.6}$$

where $W(t, m)$ is the rate at which transition $t$ fires, given marking $m$.

- The average delay $E[R]$ a token perceives when traversing a subnet of the SPN. It must be computed with Little's formula: $E[R] = E[N]/X$ where $E[N]$ is the average number of tokens in the subnet and $X$ is the throughput through the SPN subnet.

The measures expressed here all refer to steady-state. Of course, we can also study SPNs as a function of time. We then have to compute transient measures. Finally, we can also express interest in cumulative measures over time, e.g., to express the number of tokens having passed a certain place in a finite time interval. We will come back to such measures when we discuss the numerical analysis of the CTMC underlying the SPNs in Chapter 15. We will now first derive these CTMCs.

```
1.    input SPN = (P,T,Pr,I,O,H,W,m₀)
2.    NM := {m₀}; RS := {m₀}
3.    while NM ≠ ∅
4.    do
5.        let m ∈ NM
6.        NM := NM - {m}
7.        for all t ∈ Eₜ(m)
8.        do
9.            let m ──ᵗ──▸ m'
10.           store_Q(m, m', W(t,m))
11.           if m' ∉ RS
12.           then NM := NM ∪ {m'}
13.                RS := RS ∪ {m'}
14.       od
15.   od
16.   p(0) = (1,0,···,0)
```

Figure 14.4: Deriving a CTMC from a SPN

## 14.4  Mapping SPNs to CTMCs

As we have seen, $k$-bounded SPNs can be mapped on a finite state machine. Given that the state residence times are exponentially distributed, the underlying state machine can be interpreted as a CTMC. It is often referred to as the *underlying CTMC* of the SPN or the *embedded CTMC*. As a consequence of this, we can "solve" SPN models by successively constructing and solving the underlying CTMC. In this section we focus on the construction of the underlying CTMC from the SPN. We first address the case where the SPN does not contain immediate transitions. We then discuss the slightly more complicated case with immediate transitions.

Let us first recall how a CTMC is described (see Chapter 3): its generator matrix $\mathbf{Q}$ specifies the possible transitions and their rates; its initial probability vector $p(0)$ specifies the starting state. Since we are only interested in the non-null entries of $\mathbf{Q}$, we only need to know all triples $(i, j, q_{i,j})$ (where $i$ and $j$ are state identifiers) for which $q_{i,j} \neq 0$, and where $i \neq j$, since the diagonal entries of $\mathbf{Q}$ can be derived from the non-diagonal entries.

Let us now discuss the algorithm that derives a CTMC on state space $\mathcal{R}(\underline{m}_0)$, with generator matrix $\mathbf{Q}$ and initial probability vector $\underline{p}(0)$ from an SPN. For the time being we assume that there are only (exponentially) timed transitions.

The algorithm is given in Figure 14.4. First, the sets NM and RS (for new markings and reachability set, respectively) are initialised with the initial marking $\underline{m}_0$. As long as NM is not empty, an element $\underline{m}$ is taken from NM. Given this marking $\underline{m}$, all enabled (timed) transitions $t \in E_t(\underline{m})$ are generated. Then, one by one, the result of the firing of these transitions is determined. The firing of transition $t$ in marking $\underline{m}$ yields the marking $\underline{m}'$. The firing rate is $W(t, \underline{m})$. Therefore, the triple $(\underline{m}, \underline{m}', W(t, \underline{m}))$ is stored, representing an entry of the matrix $\mathbf{Q}$. When the newly derived marking $\underline{m}'$ has not been examined before, i.e., when it is not yet part of the reachability set, it is put in the reachability set as well as in the set of new markings for further examination. When all the markings have been examined, the set RS contains all possible markings (all states of the underlying CTMC) and all non-zero non-diagonal entries of the matrix $\mathbf{Q}$ have been stored. Assuming that the initial marking is the first one, the vector $\underline{p}$ is assigned its value.

When we allow for immediate transitions, we have to deal in a special way with the vanishing markings. In principle, we can apply a similar algorithm as before; however, we have to mark the entries in $\mathbf{Q}$ that correspond to the firing of immediate transitions. Instead of storing the corresponding rates, we have to store the firing probabilities. Since the obtained matrix is not really a generator matrix any more, we denote it as $\mathbf{Q}'$. Furthermore, note that the diagonal entries have not been given their value yet.

Suppose that we have used the above algorithm to derive a CTMC from an SPN and that we have marked those state transitions that correspond to the firing of immediate transitions. Note that these transitions come together in rows of which the corresponding starting state is a vanishing marking. We therefore can reorder the states in $\mathbf{Q}'$ in such a way that

$$\mathbf{Q}' = \mathbf{A} + \mathbf{B} = \begin{pmatrix} \mathbf{C} & \mathbf{D} \\ \mathbf{0} & \mathbf{0} \end{pmatrix} + \begin{pmatrix} \mathbf{0} & \mathbf{0} \\ \mathbf{E} & \mathbf{F} \end{pmatrix}, \tag{14.7}$$

where $\mathbf{C}$ is the matrix describing transitions between vanishing states, $\mathbf{D}$ the matrix describing transitions from vanishing to tangible states, $\mathbf{E}$ the matrix describing transitions from tangible to vanishing states, and $\mathbf{F}$ the matrix describing transitions between tangible states. The elements of the matrices $\mathbf{C}$, $\mathbf{D}$, and $\mathbf{E}$ are transition probabilities. Below, we will describe the derivation of the real generator matrix, denoted $\mathbf{Q}$ again, of the underlying CTMC.

A departure from the set of tangible markings, via a non-zero entry in the matrix $\mathbf{E}$, is followed by zero or more transitions between vanishing states, via non-zero entries in the matrix $\mathbf{C}$, and exactly one transition from a vanishing to a tangible state, via a non-zero entry in the matrix $\mathbf{D}$. We would like to reduce the matrix $\mathbf{Q}'$ in such a way that all the possible state transitions between tangible states via one or more vanishing states are accounted for. The thus obtained matrix $\mathbf{Q}$ (of the same size as $\mathbf{F}$) then describes the *reduced embedded Markov chain*.

To derive $\mathbf{Q}$ from $\mathbf{Q}'$, we let $i$ and $j$ denote tangible states and let $r$ and $s$ denote vanishing states. Going from one tangible state $i$ to another $j$ can either take place directly, with rate $f_{i,j}$, or indirectly with rate $\sum_r e_{i,r} \Pr\{r \to j\}$, where $e_{i,r}$ is the rate to leave a tangible marking $i$ to end up in a vanishing marking $r$, and where $\Pr\{r \to j\}$ is the probability of ending up in a tangible state $j$, starting from a vanishing state $r$, by one or more steps. Consequently, we set

$$q_{i,j} = \begin{cases} f_{i,j} + \sum_r e_{i,r} \Pr\{r \to j\}, & i \neq j, \\ 0, & i = j. \end{cases} \qquad (14.8)$$

From (14.7) we observe that the entries of the matrix $\mathbf{A}^l$ represent the probability of going from a vanishing state $r$ to any other state in exactly $l$ steps, under the condition that only vanishing intermediate states are visited. Since

$$\mathbf{A}^l = \begin{pmatrix} \mathbf{C}^l & \mathbf{C}^{l-1}\mathbf{D} \\ \mathbf{0} & \mathbf{0} \end{pmatrix}, \qquad (14.9)$$

the element $g_{r,i}^l$ of the matrix $\mathbf{G}^l = \sum_{h=1}^{l} \mathbf{C}^{h-1}\mathbf{D}$ signifies the probability of reaching tangible state $i$ from vanishing state $r$ in at most $l$ steps. Under mild regularity conditions (irreducibility) the matrix $\mathbf{G}^l$ exists and is finite, also for $l \to \infty$. Moreover, it can be shown that $\mathbf{G}^\infty = (\mathbf{I} - \mathbf{C})^{-1}\mathbf{D}$ (geometric series extended for matrices, see Appendix B.2). Using this result, we derive, for all $i \neq j$:

$$q_{i,j} = f_{i,j} + \sum_r e_{i,r} g_{r,j}^\infty, \qquad (14.10)$$

or, in matrix notation,

$$\mathbf{Q} = \mathbf{F} + \mathbf{E}\mathbf{G}^\infty = \mathbf{F} + \mathbf{E}(\mathbf{I} - \mathbf{C})^{-1}\mathbf{D}. \qquad (14.11)$$

This equation shows us how we can derive the generator matrix of the reduced embedded CTMC from elements of the matrix $\mathbf{Q}'$ of the embedded CTMC. The only thing still to be done is the computation of the diagonal entries. Notice that the reduced embedded CTMC is smaller than the embedded CTMC. The determination of this smaller matrix $\mathbf{Q}$, using (14.11), however, involves an expensive matrix inversion.

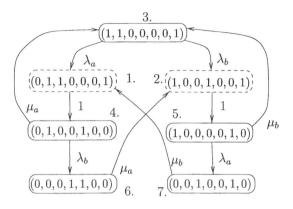

Figure 14.5: Generated (unreduced) reachability graph

Instead of removing the immediate transitions after the complete unreduced Markov chain has been generated, using (14.11), one can also remove the immediate transitions during the generation process itself ("on the fly") or by inspection of the matrix $\mathbf{Q}'$. Let $m_1$, $m_2$ and $m_3$ be tangible markings and let $m_v$ be a vanishing marking. After $\mathbf{Q}'$ has been constructed, it turns out that $m_1 \overset{\text{rate } \lambda}{\longrightarrow} m_v$, $m_v \overset{\text{prob. } \alpha}{\longrightarrow} m_2$ and $m_v \overset{\text{prob. } \beta}{\longrightarrow} m_2$. The vanishing marking is then removed and the following two transition (rates) are introduced: from $m_1$ to $m_2$ with rate $\alpha\lambda$ and from $m_1$ to $m_3$ with rate $\beta\lambda$. This approach can be followed for all vanishing markings encountered, and works well as long as there are no infinite sequences (loops) of immediate transitions possible. We think that the latter is no severe restriction; it might even be questioned whether using SPNs that allow for infinite loops of immediate transition firings are good modelling practice anyway. In software tools that allow for the construction of SPNs and for the automatic generation of the underlying CTMC, a typical restriction is set on the number of immediate transitions that might be enabled in sequence.

### Example 14.9. Simultaneous resource possessing (III).

We apply the state space generation algorithm of Figure 14.4 to the SPN given in Figure 14.1. The reachability graph generated is depicted in Figure 14.5 where the dashed ovals refer to vanishing markings and the other ovals to tangible markings. Numbering the states as indicated in this figure, we obtain the following matrix:

$$
Q' = \begin{pmatrix}
0 & 0 & 0 & 1 & 0 & 0 & 0 \\
0 & 0 & 0 & 0 & 1 & 0 & 0 \\
\lambda_a & \lambda_b & 0 & 0 & 0 & 0 & 0 \\
0 & 0 & \mu_a & 0 & 0 & \lambda_b & 0 \\
0 & 0 & \mu_b & 0 & 0 & 0 & \lambda_a \\
0 & \mu_a & 0 & 0 & 0 & 0 & 0 \\
\mu_b & 0 & 0 & 0 & 0 & 0 & 0
\end{pmatrix},
$$

in which we have indicated the partitioning in submatrices $C$ through $F$. The matrix $G^\infty = (I - C)^{-1}D = D$ so that

$$
EG^\infty = \begin{pmatrix}
0 & \lambda_a & \lambda_b & 0 & 0 \\
0 & 0 & 0 & 0 & 0 \\
0 & 0 & 0 & 0 & 0 \\
0 & 0 & \mu_a & 0 & 0 \\
0 & \mu_b & 0 & 0 & 0
\end{pmatrix},
$$

so that the (non-diagonal entries of) $Q$ can be computed:

$$
Q = F + EG^\infty = \begin{pmatrix}
\cdot & \lambda_a & \lambda_b & 0 & 0 \\
\mu_a & \cdot & 0 & \lambda_b & 0 \\
\mu_b & 0 & \cdot & 0 & \lambda_a \\
0 & 0 & \mu_a & \cdot & 0 \\
0 & \mu_b & 0 & 0 & \cdot
\end{pmatrix}.
$$

Notice that $Q$ could also have been derived by inspection of Figure 14.5. □

To conclude this chapter, we show in Figure 14.6, how SPNs are used in a model-based system evaluation. The system of interest is modelled as an SPN and the measures of interest are indicated as well. After the model has been checked on its correctness, e.g., by computing place invariants with the method discussed in Section 14.2, the actual solution can start. First, the underlying CTMC is generated with the algorithm discussed in Section 14.4. Then, from this CTMC the probabilities of interest are computed with the numerical methods to be discussed in Chapter 15. These probabilities are then used to compute the measures of interest, according to the rules of Section 14.3; we could say that the state probabilities are enhanced to yield system-oriented measures. Finally, these system-oriented measures are interpreted in terms of the system being studied (refer to Chapter 1 and the discussion of the GMTF, in particular to the example addressing tools for SPNs).

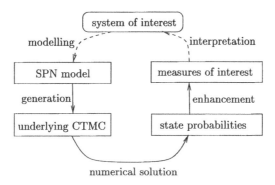

Figure 14.6: The model construction and solution trajectory in SPN-based system evaluation

## 14.5 Further reading

Petri published his Ph.D. thesis on non-timed Petri nets in the early 1960s [232]. He was awarded the Werner-von-Siemens-ring for his accomplishments in science and engineering early in 1998. The first stochastic extensions of Petri nets appeared in the late 1970s. Pioneering work has been accomplished by Natkin, Molloy, Ajmone Marsan *et al.* and Meyer *et al.*. Natkin published his Ph.D. thesis on stochastic petri nets in 1980 [214]. In the early 1980s Molloy published a paper on SPNs in which all the transitions had exponential timing [205]. At the same time, Ajmone Marsan *et al.* published the well-known paper on generalised SPNs (GSPNs) in which transitions could be either exponentially timed or immediate (as we used) [4]. At about the same time, Meyer *et al.* introduced stochastic activity networks (SANs) in which transitions are either of exponential type or immediate (instantaneous in their terminology) [210, 209, 199]. In the mid 1980s the amount of research on SPN formalisms and evaluation techniques increased sharply, also witnessed by the start of an bi-annual IEEE conference series on Petri nets and performance models in 1985 (published by the IEEE Computer Society Press as *Proceedings of the International Workshop on Petri Nets and Performance Models*).

A number of books have been devoted (almost) exclusively to the use of SPNs: we mention Ajmone Marsan *et al.* [1, 2] and Bause and Kritzinger [15]. The performance evaluation textbook by Kant [152] and the book on Sharpe by Sahner *et al.* [249] also address SPNs. Two surveys on the success of SPNs, including many references, have recently been published by Balbo [11, 10].

In the field of stochastic Petri nets, much research is still going on. Most of it addresses one of the following four issues: (i) modelling ease; (ii) largeness of the underlying CTMCs; (iii) timing distributions other than exponential; and (iv) alternative solution methods. We briefly touch upon these four issues below.

Over the years, a number of extensions to SPN models has been proposed. One of these extensions is the attribution of colours to tokens, leading to the so-called *coloured stochastic Petri nets* (CSPNs) [148, 149]. A marking then is not just an enumeration of the number of tokens in all places, but also includes the colours of the tokens. Correspondingly, transitions can be both marking and colour dependent. Coloured Petri nets can be transformed to "black-and-white" stochastic Petri nets as we have discussed here. They then generally become more complex to understand. For the solution, again the underlying CTMC is used.

A slightly different approach has been followed in the definition of *stochastic activity networks* (SANs) [253]. With SANs the enabling of transitions has been made more explicit by the use of *enabling functions* that must be specified with every transition. Furthermore, *input* and *output gates* are associated with transitions to indicate from which places tokens are taken and in which places tokens are stored upon firing of the transition. With SANs some nice hierarchical modelling constructs have been developed that decrease the size of the state space of the underlying CTMC by using results from the theory of lumping in CTMCs.

One of the largest problems in the application of SPNs is the growth of the state space of the underlying CTMC. Although CTMCs with hundreds of thousands of states can be handled with current-day workstations, there will always remain models that are just too big to be solved efficiently. Solutions that have been proposed are often based on (approximate) truncation techniques [121] or lumping [31, 32, 47, 253], thereby still performing the solution at the state space level. By employing the structure of the underlying CTMC, explicit generation of it can sometimes be avoided. This has led to alternative solution methods, e.g., via the use of product-forms results, leading to so-called product-form SPNs (PFSPNs) which allow for an efficient convolution or mean-value analysis style of solution [70, 75, 95], and the use of matrix-geometric methods (which will be discussed in Chapter 17).

Instead of using exponentially distributed firing times, deterministic and general timing distributions are also of interest. Apart from using phase-type expansion techniques, the state-of-the-art in generally-timed SPNs is such that only SPNs with at most one non-exponentially timed transition enabled in every marking can be handled at reasonable computational expense. These so-called deterministic and stochastic Petri nets (DSPNs) have been introduced by Ajmone Marsan and Chiola [3] and have been further developed by, among others, Lindemann and German [104, 103, 182, 183, 184], Ciardo *et al.* [52] and Choi *et al.* [49].

SPNs are not the only "high-level" formalisms to specify CTMCs. QN models can also be interpreted as specifications of CTMCs. However, since the queueing networks we have addressed allow for a specialised solution, using either MVA or convolution, it is not necessary to generate and solve the underlying CTMC; it is more efficient to use the special algorithms. When no special algorithms can be used, the underlying CTMC might be explicitly generated and solved. Next to QNs, other techniques, such as those based on production rule systems, process algebras and reliability block diagrams can be used. For an overview of high-level formalisms for the specification of CTMCs, we refer to [121].

## 14.6  Exercises

### 14.1. SPN model of a system with server vacations.
Consider an M|M|1 queue with finite population $K$ in which the server takes a vacation of exponentially distributed length after exactly $L$ customers have been served.

1. Construct an SPN for this queueing model when $L = 2$. Compute the place and transition invariants.

2. Derive the underlying CTMC when $K = 6$.

3. Generalise the model such that only the initial marking has to be changed when $L$ changes. Again compute the place invariants.

### 14.2. CTMC construction.
Consider the SPN as given in Figure 14.7.

1. Construct the embedded Markov chain, including both the vanishing and the tangible markings.

2. Construct the reduced embedded Markov chain, i.e., remove the vanishing markings

   - with the matrix method discussed in Section 14.4;
   - and by inspection of the matrix $\mathbf{Q}'$.

### 14.3. Preemptive priority systems.
Construct an SPN for a system in which two priority classes exist. There are $K_1$ (resp. $K_2$)

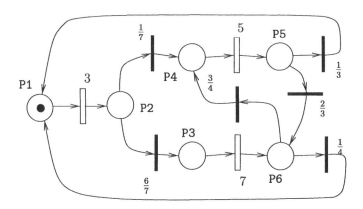

Figure 14.7: An example SPN for which the underlying CTMC is to be determined

customers in each class, and customers of class 1 have preemptive priority over customers of class 2. Assume that a class 2 customer is interrupted when a class 1 customer arrives and that the interrupted customer has to be reserved completely.

## 14.4. Polling systems.

In Chapter 9 we have discussed polling models and developed results for the mean waiting time in symmetric polling models. Let us now try to develop SPN-based polling models. Consider the case where we have three stations and where all the service times are exponentially distributed, possibly with different means. Likewise, we assume that the switch-over times are all exponentially distributed. Finally, assume that the arrival processes are Poisson processes, however, fed from a finite source, i.e., for every station there is a place that models the finite source (and sink) of jobs for that station.

1. Let there be at most one job at each station. Construct an SPN, modelling a three-station polling model, where every station has a 1-limited scheduling strategy.

2. Derive the underlying CTMC for such an SPN.

3. Now let there be more than one job at each station (we increase the number of jobs in the finite source). Construct an SPN, modelling a three-station polling model, where every station has an exhaustive scheduling strategy.

4. Is it still possible to derive the underlying CTMC by hand?

5. Construct a model for a polling system where some stations have 1-limited scheduling, and others have exhaustive scheduling. How is such a "mixed" model solved?

Does the asymmetry have any impact on the complexity of the numerical solution approach?

6. Construct a model of a station with a gated scheduling discipline.

7. Construct a model of a station with a time-based scheduling discipline, such as we have discussed for the IBM token ring.

In Chapter 16 we will present a number of SPN-based polling models.

## 14.5. Availability modelling.

Consider a system consisting of $n_A$ components of type $A$ and $n_B$ components of type $B$. The failure rate of components of type $A$ $(B)$ is $f_A$ $(f_B)$ and the repair rates are $r_A$ and $r_B$ respectively. We assume that the times to failure and the times to repair are exponentially distributed. There is a single repair unit available for repairing failed components; it can only repair one component at a time. Components that fail are immediately repaired, given the repair unit is free; otherwise they have to queue for repair.

1. Construct an SPN modelling the availability of the system.

2. What would be a reasonable initial marking?

3. How many states does the underlying CTMC have, given $n_A$ and $n_B$?

4. The system is considered operational (available) when at least one component of each class is non-failed. Express this condition in terms of required place occupancies. How would you compute this availability measure?

Haverkort discusses this model at length in [121]; we will also address it in Chapter 16.

# Chapter 15

# Numerical solution of Markov chains

$\mathbf{A}$ LTHOUGH a CTMC is completely described by its state space $\mathcal{I}$, its generator matrix $\mathbf{Q}$ and its initial probability vector $\underline{p}(0)$, in most cases we will not directly specify the CTMC at the state level. Instead, we use SPNs (or other high-level specification techniques) to specify the CTMCs.

In this chapter, we focus on the solution of CTMCs with a finite, but possibly large, state space, once they have been generated from a high-level specification. The solution of infinite-state CTMCs has been discussed in Chapter 4 (birth-death queueing models), Chapter 8 (quasi-birth-death queueing models) and Chapter 10 (open queueing network models) and will be discussed further in Chapter 17.

Finite CTMCs can be studied for their steady-state as well as for their transient behaviour. In the former case, systems of linear equations have to be solved. How to do this, using direct or iterative methods, is the topic of Section 15.1. In the latter case, linear systems of differential equations have to be solved, which is addressed in Section 15.2.

## 15.1 Computing steady-state probabilities

As presented in Chapter 3, for obtaining the steady-state probabilities of a finite CTMC with $N$ states (numbered 1 through $N$), we need to solve the following system of $N$ linear equations:

$$\underline{p}\mathbf{Q} = \underline{0}, \quad \sum_{i \in \mathcal{I}} p_i = 1, \tag{15.1}$$

where the right part is added to assure that the obtained solution is a probability vector. We assume here that the CTMC is irreducible and aperiodic such that $\underline{p}$ does exist and is independent of $\underline{p}(0)$. Notice that the left part of (15.1) in fact does not uniquely define the steady-state probabilities; however, together with the normalisation equation a unique solution is found. For the explanations that follow, we will transpose the matrix $\mathbf{Q}$ and denote it as $\mathbf{A}$. Hence, we basically have to solve the following system of linear equations:

$$\mathbf{A}\underline{p}^T = \underline{b}, \quad \text{with} \quad \mathbf{A} = \mathbf{Q}^T \quad \text{and} \quad \underline{b} = \underline{0}^T. \tag{15.2}$$

Starting from this system of equations, various solution approaches can be chosen:

1. Direct methods:

   - Gaussian elimination;

   - LU-decomposition;

2. Iterative methods:

   - Jacobi iteration;

   - Gauss-Seidel iteration;

   - Successive overrelaxation;

These methods will be discussed in more detail in the following sections.

## 15.1.1   Gaussian elimination

A characteristic of direct methods is that they aim at rewriting the system of equations in such a form that explicit expressions for the steady-state probabilities are obtained. Typically, this rewriting procedure takes place in an *a priori* known number of computations (given $N$). A very well-known and straightforward direct solution technique is *Gaussian elimination*. The Gaussian elimination procedure consists of two phases: a reduction phase and a substitution phase.

In the reduction phase repetitive subtractions of equations from one another are used to make the system of equations upper-triangular (see also Figure 15.1). To do so, let the $i$-th equation be $\sum_j a_{i,j} p_j = 0$ (this equals $\sum_j p_j q_{j,i} = 0$ in the non-transposed system). We now vary $i$ from 1 to $N$. The $j$-th equation, with $j = i+1, \cdots, N$, is now changed by subtracting the $i$-th equation $m_{j,i}$ times from it, where $m_{j,i} = a_{j,i}/a_{i,i}$, that is, we reassign the $a_{j,k}$ values as follows:

$$a_{j,k} := a_{j,k} - m_{j,i} a_{i,k}, \quad j, k > i. \tag{15.3}$$

Clearly, $a_{j,i} := a_{j,i} - m_{j,i} a_{i,i} = 0$, for all $j > i$. By repeating this procedure for increasing $i$, the linear system of equations is transformed, in $N - 1$ steps, to an upper-triangular

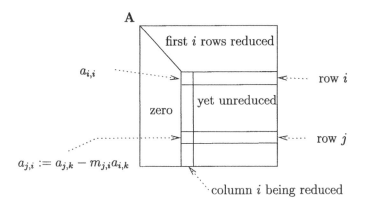

A

first $i$ rows reduced

$a_{i,i}$

row $i$

yet unreduced

zero

row $j$

$a_{j,i} := a_{j,k} - m_{j,i}a_{i,k}$

column $i$ being reduced

Figure 15.1: Schematic representation of the $i$-th reduction step in the Gaussian elimination procedure

system of equations. The element $a_{i,i}$ that acts as a divisor is called the *pivot*. If a pivot is encountered that equals 0, the algorithm would attempt to divide by 0. Such a failure indicates that the system of equations being solved does not have a solution. Since $\mathbf{Q}$ is a generator matrix of an irreducible ergodic CTMC, this problem will not occur. Moreover, since $\mathbf{A}$ is weakly diagonal dominant ($a_{i,i}$ is as large as the sum of all the values $a_{j,i}$ ($j \neq i$) in the same column) we have that $m_{j,i} < 1$ so that overflow problems are unlikely to occur.

At the end of the reduction phase, the $N$-th equation will always reduce to a trivial one ($0 = 0$). This is no surprise, since the system of equations without normalisation is not of full rank. We might even completely ignore the last equation. Since the right-hand side of the linear system of equations equals $\underline{0}$, we do not have to change anything there. When the right-hand side is a non-zero vector $\underline{b}$, we would have to set $b_j := b_j - m_{j,i}b_i$, for all $j > i$ in each step in the reduction process.

After the reduction has been performed, the substitution phase can start. The equation for $p_N$ does not help us any further; we therefore assume a value $\alpha > 0$ for $p_N$. This value for $p_N$ can be substituted in the first $N - 1$ equations, thus yielding a system of equations with one unknown less. We implement this by setting $b_j := b_j - a_{j,N}p_N$. Now, the $(N - 1)$-th equation will have only one unknown left which we can directly compute as $p_{N-1} = b_{N-1}/a_{N-1,N-1}$. This new value can be substituted in the $N - 2$ remaining equations, after which the $(N - 2)$-th equation has only one unknown. This procedure can be repeated until all probabilities have been computed explicitly in terms of $\alpha$. We then use the normalisation equation to compute $\alpha$ to obtain the true probability vector,

```
1. for i := 1 to N − 1
2. do for j := i + 1 to N
3.    do
4.        m_{j,i} := a_{j,i}/a_{i,i};  a_{j,i} := 0
5.        for k := i + 1 to N
6.        do a_{j,k} := a_{j,k} − m_{j,i}a_{i,k}
7.    od
8. od
7. p_N := α;  σ := α
8. for j := N downto 2
9. do
10.    for i := j − 1 downto 1
11.    do b_i := b_i − a_{i,j}p_j
12.    p_{j−1} := b_{j−1}/a_{j−1,j−1}
13.    σ := σ + p_{j−1}
14. od
15. for i := 1 to N do p_i := p_i/σ
```

Figure 15.2: The Gaussian elimination procedure

that is, we compute $\sigma = \sum_{i=1}^{N} p_i$ and set $p_i := p_i/\sigma$, for all $i$. We summarise the complete algorithm in Figure 15.2.

**Example 15.1. Gaussian elimination.**
As an example, consider a CTMC for which the matrix $\mathbf{Q}$ is given by

$$\mathbf{Q} = \begin{pmatrix} -4 & 2 & 2 \\ 1 & -2 & 1 \\ 6 & 0 & -6 \end{pmatrix}. \tag{15.4}$$

Writing $\underline{p}\mathbf{Q} = \underline{0}$, we obtain:

$$\begin{cases} -4p_1 & +p_2 & +6p_3 & = 0, \\ 2p_1 & -2p_2 & & = 0, \\ 2p_1 & +p_2 & -6p_3 & = 0. \end{cases} \tag{15.5}$$

Adding the first equation one-half times $(m_{2,1} = -\frac{1}{2})$ to the other equations, we obtain the following:

$$
\begin{cases}
-4p_1 & +p_2 & +6p_3 & = 0, \\
 & -1.5p_2 & +3p_3 & = 0, \\
 & 1.5p_2 & -3p_3 & = 0.
\end{cases}
\tag{15.6}
$$

We then add the second equation once to the third to obtain:

$$
\begin{cases}
-4p_1 & +p_2 & +6p_3 & = 0, \\
 & -1.5p_2 & +3p_3 & = 0,
\end{cases}
\tag{15.7}
$$

where the last equation has disappeared; we therefore assume $p_3 = \alpha$ and obtain the following system of equations by back-substitution:

$$
\begin{cases}
-4p_1 & +p_2 & = -6\alpha, \\
 & -1.5p_2 & = -3\alpha,
\end{cases}
\tag{15.8}
$$

from which we obtain that $p_2 = 2\alpha$. Substituting this result in the first equation, we obtain $p_1 = 2\alpha$. Thus, we find $\underline{p} = \alpha(2, 2, 1)$. Using the normalisation equation, we find $5\alpha = 1$ so that the final solution vector equals $\underline{p} = \left(\frac{2}{5}, \frac{2}{5}, \frac{1}{5}\right)$.  □

Instead of assuming the value $\alpha$ for $p_N$, we can also directly include the normalisation equation in the Gaussian elimination procedure. The best way to go then, is to replace the $N$-th equation with the equation $\sum_i p_i = 1$. In doing so, the last equation will directly give us $p_N$. The substitution phase can proceed as before.

Observing the algorithm in Figure 15.2 we see that the computational complexity is $O(N^3)$. By a more careful study of the algorithm, one will find that about $N^3/3 + N^2/2$ multiplications and additions have to be performed, as well as $N(N + 1)/2$ divisions. Clearly, these numbers increase rapidly with increasing $N$. The main problem with Gaussian elimination lies in the storage. Although $\mathbf{A}$ will initially be sparse for most models, the reduction procedure normally increases the number of non-zeros in $\mathbf{A}$. At the end of the reduction phase, most entries of the upper half of $\mathbf{A}$ will be non-zero. The non-zero elements generated during this phase are called *fill-ins*. They can only be inserted efficiently when direct storage structures (arrays) are used. To store the upper-triangular matrix $\mathbf{A}$, $N^2/2$ floats have to be stored, normally each taking 6 or 8 bytes. For moderately sized models generated from SPN specifications, $N$ can easily be as large as $10^4$ or even $10^5$. This then precludes the use of Gaussian elimination. Fortunately, there are methods to compute $\underline{p}$ that do not change $\mathbf{A}$ and that are very fast as well. We will discuss these methods after we have discussed one alternative direct method.

## 15.1.2 LU decomposition

A method known as LU decomposition is advantageous to use when multiple systems of equations have to be solved, all of the form $\mathbf{A}\underline{x} = \underline{b}$, for different values of $\underline{b}$. The method starts by decomposing $\mathbf{A}$ such that it can be written as the *product* of two matrices $\mathbf{L}$ and $\mathbf{U}$, where the former is lower-triangular, and the latter is upper-triangular. We have:

$$\mathbf{A}\underline{x} = \underline{b} \quad \Rightarrow \quad \mathbf{L}\underbrace{\mathbf{U}\underline{x}}_{\underline{z}} = \underline{b}. \tag{15.9}$$

After the decomposition has taken place, we have to solve $\mathbf{L}\underline{z} = \underline{b}$, after which we solve $\mathbf{U}\underline{x} = \underline{z}$. Since the last two systems of equations are triangular, their solution can be found by a simple forward- and back-substitution.

The main question then lies in the computation of suitable matrices $\mathbf{L}$ and $\mathbf{U}$. Since $\mathbf{A}$ is the product of these two matrices, we know that

$$a_{i,j} = \sum_{k=1}^{N} l_{i,k} u_{k,j}, \quad i,j = 1, \cdots, N. \tag{15.10}$$

Given the fact that $\mathbf{L}$ and $\mathbf{U}$ are lower- and upper-triangular, we have to find $N^2 + N$ unknowns:

$$\begin{cases} l_{i,j}, & i = 1, \cdots, N, \quad k = 1, \cdots, i, \\ u_{k,j}, & k = 1, \cdots, N, \quad j = k, \cdots, N. \end{cases} \tag{15.11}$$

Since (15.10) only consists of $N^2$ equations, we have to assume $N$ values to determine a unique solution. Two well-known schemes in this context are [268]:

- the Doolittle decomposition where one assumes $l_{i,i} = 1$, $i = 1, \cdots, N$;

- the Crout decomposition where one assumes $u_{i,i} = 1$, $i = 1, \cdots, N$.

In the sequel, we consider the Doolittle variant. First notice that in (15.10) many of the terms in the summation are zero, since one of the numbers being multiplied is zero. In fact, we can rewrite (15.10) in a more convenient form as follows:

$$\begin{cases} i \le j : & a_{i,j} = u_{i,j} + \sum_{k=1}^{i-1} l_{i,k} u_{k,j}, \\ i > j : & a_{i,j} = l_{i,j} u_{j,j} \sum_{k=1}^{j-1} l_{i,k} u_{k,j}. \end{cases} \tag{15.12}$$

From this system of equations, we can now iteratively compute the entries of $\mathbf{L}$ and $\mathbf{U}$ as follows:

$$\begin{cases} i \le j : & u_{i,j} = a_{i,j} - \sum_{k=1}^{i-1} l_{i,k} u_{k,j}, \\ i > j : & l_{i,j} = \frac{1}{u_{j,j}} \left( a_{i,j} - \sum_{k=1}^{j-1} l_{i,k} u_{k,j} \right), \end{cases} \tag{15.13}$$

by increasing $i$ from 1 until $N$ is reached.

**Example 15.2. LU decomposition (I).**
Suppose we want to decompose

$$\mathbf{A} = \begin{pmatrix} 3 & 2 & 5 \\ -6 & 1 & 8 \\ -7 & 2 & -3 \end{pmatrix},$$

using a Doolittle LU decomposition. We then know that

$$\mathbf{L} = \begin{pmatrix} 1 & 0 & 0 \\ \cdot & 1 & 0 \\ \cdot & \cdot & 1 \end{pmatrix} \quad \text{and} \quad \mathbf{U} = \begin{pmatrix} \cdot & \cdot & \cdot \\ 0 & \cdot & \cdot \\ 0 & 0 & \cdot \end{pmatrix}.$$

We start to compute $u_{1,1} = a_{1,1} = 3$. We then can compute $l_{2,1} = a_{2,1}/u_{1,1} = -2$. Then, $u_{1,2} = a_{1,2} = 2$. From this, we find $u_{2,2} = a_{2,2} - l_{2,1}u_{1,2} = 5$. We then compute $l_{3,1} = -\frac{7}{3}$ and find $l_{3,2} = \frac{4}{3}$. Via $u_{1,3} = a_{1,3} = 5$ and $u_{2,3} = 18$ we find $u_{3,3} = a_{3,3} - \sum_{k=1}^{2} l_{3,k}u_{k,3} = -\frac{46}{3}$.
We thus find:

$$\mathbf{A} = \mathbf{LU}, \quad \text{with } \mathbf{L} = \begin{pmatrix} 1 & 0 & 0 \\ -2 & 1 & 0 \\ -2\frac{1}{3} & 1\frac{1}{3} & 1 \end{pmatrix} \quad \text{and} \quad \mathbf{U} = \begin{pmatrix} 3 & 2 & 5 \\ 0 & 5 & 18 \\ 0 & 0 & -15\frac{1}{3} \end{pmatrix}.$$

□

**Example 15.3. LU decomposition (II).**
The result of the LU decomposition is given by the matrices $\mathbf{L}$ and $\mathbf{U}$ in the previous example. To solve $\mathbf{A}\underline{x} = \underline{1}$, we now first solve for $\underline{z}$ in $\mathbf{L}\underline{z} = \underline{1}$. A simple substitution procedure yields $\underline{z} = (1, 3, -\frac{2}{3})$. We now continue to solve $\mathbf{U}\underline{x} = \underline{z}$; also here a substitution procedure suffices to find $\underline{x} = \frac{1}{115}(-4, 51, 5)$. It is easily verified that this value for $\underline{x}$ indeed satisfies $\mathbf{A}\underline{x} = \underline{1}$.

□

**Example 15.4. LU decomposition (III).**
We reconsider the CTMC for which the matrix $\mathbf{Q}$ is given by

$$\mathbf{Q} = \begin{pmatrix} -4 & 2 & 2 \\ 1 & -2 & 1 \\ 6 & 0 & -6 \end{pmatrix}. \tag{15.14}$$

We now form the matrix $\mathbf{A} = \mathbf{Q}^T$ and in addition directly include the normalisation equation. To find the steady-state probabilities we have to solve:

$$\begin{pmatrix} -4 & 1 & 6 \\ 2 & -2 & 0 \\ 1 & 1 & 1 \end{pmatrix} \cdot \begin{pmatrix} p_1 \\ p_2 \\ p_3 \end{pmatrix} = \begin{pmatrix} 0 \\ 0 \\ 1 \end{pmatrix}. \tag{15.15}$$

We now decompose $\mathbf{A}$ using the Doolittle decomposition as follows:

$$\mathbf{A} = \mathbf{LU} = \begin{pmatrix} 1 & 0 & 0 \\ -\frac{1}{2} & 1 & 0 \\ -\frac{1}{4} & -\frac{10}{12} & 1 \end{pmatrix} \begin{pmatrix} -4 & 1 & 6 \\ 0 & -\frac{3}{2} & 3 \\ 0 & 0 & 5 \end{pmatrix}. \tag{15.16}$$

The solution of $\mathbf{L}\underline{z} = (0,0,1)^T$ now reveals, via a simple substitution, that $\underline{z} = (0,0,1)$. We now have to find $\underline{p}$ from $\mathbf{U}\underline{p} = \underline{z}$, from which we, again via a substitution procedure, find $\underline{p} = (\frac{2}{5}, \frac{2}{5}, \frac{1}{5})$, as we have seen before.                                                                        □

In the above example, we took a specific way to deal with the normalisation equation: we replaced one equation from the "normal" system with the normalisation equation. In doing so, the vector $\underline{b}$ changes to $\underline{b} = (0,0,1)$ and after the solution of $\mathbf{L}\underline{z} = \underline{b}$, we found $\underline{z} = (0,0,1)^T$. This is not only true for the above example; if we replace the last equation, the vector $\underline{z}$ always has this value, and so we do not really have to solve the system $\mathbf{L}\underline{z} = (0,0,1)^T$. Hence, after the LU decomposition has been performed, we can always directly solve $\underline{p}$ from $\mathbf{U}\underline{p} = (0, \cdots, 0, 1)^T$.

Opposed to the above variant, we can also postpone the normalisation, as we have done in the Gaussian elimination case. We then decompose $\mathbf{A} = \mathbf{Q}^T = \mathbf{LU}$, for which we will find that the last row of $\mathbf{U}$ contains only 0's. The solution of $\mathbf{L}\underline{z} = \underline{0}$ will then always yield $\underline{z} = \underline{0}$, so that we can immediately solve $\mathbf{U}\underline{p} = \underline{0}$. This triangular system of equations can easily be solved via a back-substitution procedure; however, we have to assume $p_N = \alpha$ and compute the rest of $\underline{p}$ relative to $\alpha$ as well. A final normalisation will then yield the ultimate steady-state probability vector $\underline{p}$.

Postponing the normalisation is preferred in most cases for at least two reasons: (i) it provides an implicit numerical accuracy test in that the last row of $\mathbf{U}$ should equal 0; and (ii) it requires less computations than the implicit normalisation since the number of non-zeros in the matrices that need to be handled is smaller. Of course, these advantages will become more important for larger values of $N$.

The LU decomposition solution method has the same computational complexity of $O(N^3)$ as the Gaussian elimination procedure. The decomposition can be performed with only one data structure (typically an array). Initially, the matrix $\mathbf{A}$ is stored in it, but during the decomposition the elements of $\mathbf{L}$ (except for the diagonal elements from $\mathbf{L}$, but these are equal to 1 anyway) and the elements of $\mathbf{U}$ replace the original values.

We finally comment on the occurrence of over- and underflow during the computations. Underflow can be dealt with by setting intermediate values smaller than some threshold, say $10^{-24}$ equal to 0. Overflow is unlikely to occur during the reduction phase in the Gaussian elimination (the pivots are the largest (absolute) quantities in every column). If in other parts of the algorithms overflow tends to occur (observed if some of the values grow above a certain threshold, say $10^{10}$) then an intermediate normalisation of the solution vector is required. A final normalisation then completes the procedures.

### 15.1.3   Power, Jacobi, Gauss-Seidel and SOR iterative methods

Although direct methods are suitable to solve smaller instances of the system of equations (15.2), for reasons of computational and memory efficiency they cannot be used when the number of states $N$ grows beyond about a thousand. Instead, we use iterative methods in these cases. With iterative methods, the involved matrices do not change (fill-in is avoided), so that they can be stored efficiently using sparse matrix methods. Moreover, these methods can be implemented such that in the matrix-multiplications only the multiplications with *two* non-zero operands are taken into account. This of course speeds up the computations enormously.

Iterative procedures do not result in an explicit solution of the system of equations. A key characteristic of iterative methods is that it is not possible to state *a priori* how many computational steps are required. Instead, a simple numerical procedure (the iteration step) is performed repeatedly until a desired level of accuracy is reached.

#### The Power method

We have already seen the simplest iterative method to solve for the steady-state probabilities of a DTMC in Chapter 4: the *Power method*. The Power method performs successive multiplication of the steady-state probability vector $\underline{v}$ with $\mathbf{P}$ until convergence is reached. The Power method can also be applied for CTMCs. Given a CTMC with generator matrix $\mathbf{Q}$, we can compute the DTMC transition matrix $\mathbf{P} = \mathbf{I} + \mathbf{Q}/\lambda$. If we take $\lambda \geq \max_i\{|q_{i,i}|\}$, the matrix $\mathbf{P}$ is a stochastic matrix and describes the evolution of the CTMC in time-steps of mean length $1/\lambda$ (see Section 15.2 for a more precise formulation). Using $\mathbf{P}$ and setting $\underline{p}^{(0)} = \underline{p}(0)$ as initial estimate for the steady-state probability vector, we can compute $\underline{p}^{(k+1)} = \underline{p}^{(k)}\mathbf{P}$ and find that $\underline{p} = \lim_{k\to\infty} \underline{p}^{(k)}$.

The Power method solves $p$ as the left Eigenvector of $\mathbf{P}$, corresponding to an Eigenvalue 1. The employed matrix $\mathbf{P}$ is called the iteration matrix and denoted as $\mathbf{\Phi}_P$.

Note that the Power method as sketched above is also often called uniformisation (see Section 15.2). It is also allowed to use values of $\lambda < \max_i\{|q_{i,i}|\}$ to construct a matrix $\mathbf{P}$. However, in that case $\mathbf{P}$ is not a stochastic matrix and the DTMC-interpretation is not valid any more. Furthermore, it is also possible to apply the Power method with a matrix $\mathbf{P}'$, with $p'_{i,j} = q_{i,j}/|q_{i,i}|$, for $i \neq j$, and $p'_{i,i} = 0$. After convergence, the resulting probability vector $\underline{v}'$ then needs to be renormalised to account for the different mean residence times per state, as we have seen for SMCs in Chapter 3.

In practice, the Power method is not very efficient (see also Chapter 8 where we discussed the convergence of the Power method to compute the largest Eigenvalue of a matrix). Since more efficient methods do exist, we do not discuss the Power method any further.

**The Jacobi method**

Two of the best-known (and simple) iterative methods are the *Jacobi iterative method* and the *Gauss-Seidel iterative method*. These methods first rewrite the $i$-th equation of the linear system (15.2) into:

$$p_i = \frac{1}{|a_{i,i}|}\left(\sum_{j<i} p_j a_{i,j} + \sum_{j>i} p_j a_{i,j}\right). \tag{15.17}$$

We clearly need $a_{i,i} \neq 0$; when the linear system is used to solve for the steady-state probabilities of an irreducible aperiodic CTMC, this is guaranteed.

The iterative procedures now proceed with assuming a first guess for $p$, denoted $\underline{p}^{(0)}$. If one does know an approximate solution for $p$, it can be used as initial guess, e.g., when a similar model with slightly different parameters has been solved before, the solution vector for that model might be used as initial estimate, although the convergence gain in doing so is mostly small. In other cases, the uniform distribution is a reasonable choice, i.e., $p_i^{(0)} = 1/N$. The next estimate for $\underline{p}$ is then computed as follows:

$$p_i^{(k+1)} = \frac{1}{|a_{i,i}|}\left(\sum_{j<i} p_j^{(k)} a_{i,j} + \sum_{j>i} p_j^{(k)} a_{i,j}\right) = \frac{1}{|a_{i,i}|}\left(\sum_{j\neq i} p_j^{(k)} a_{i,j}\right). \tag{15.18}$$

This is the Jacobi iteration scheme. We continue to iterate until two successive estimates for $p$ differ less than some $\epsilon$ from one another, i.e., when $||\underline{p}^{(k+1)} - \underline{p}^{(k)}|| < \epsilon$ (difference criterion). Notice that when this difference is very small, this does *not always* imply that the solution vector has been found. Indeed, it might be the case that the convergence towards the solution is very slow. Therefore, it is good to check whether $||\mathbf{A}\underline{p}^{(k)}|| < \epsilon$ (residual criterion). Since this way of checking convergence is more expensive, often a combination of these two methods is used: use the difference criterion normally; once it is satisfied use the residual criterion. If the convergence is really slow, two successive iterates might be very close to one another, although the actual value for $\underline{p}$ is still "far away". To avoid the difference criterion to stop the iteration process too soon, one might instead check on the difference between non-successive iterates, i.e., $||\underline{p}^{(k+1)} - \underline{p}^{(k-d)}|| < \epsilon$, with $d \in I\!N^+$ (and $d \leq k$).

When we denote the diagonal matrix $\mathbf{D} = \text{diag}(a_{i,i})$ and $\mathbf{L}$ and $\mathbf{U}$ respectively as the lower and upper triangular half of $\mathbf{A}$ (these matrices should not be confused with the matrices $\mathbf{L}$ and $\mathbf{U}$ used in the LU-decomposition!), we can write $\mathbf{Q}^T = \mathbf{A} = \mathbf{D} - (\mathbf{L} + \mathbf{U})$, so that we can write the Jacobi iteration scheme in matrix-vector notation as:

$$\underline{p}^{(k+1)} = \mathbf{D}^{-1}(\mathbf{L} + \mathbf{U})\underline{p}^{(k)}. \tag{15.19}$$

We observe that the Jacobi method has iteration matrix $\mathbf{\Phi}_J = \mathbf{D}^{-1}(\mathbf{L} + \mathbf{U})$.

### The Gauss-Seidel method

The Jacobi method requires the storage of both $\underline{p}^{(k)}$ and $\underline{p}^{(k+1)}$ during an iteration step. If, instead, the computation is structured such that the $(k + 1)$-th estimates are already used as soon as they have been computed, we obtain the *Gauss-Seidel* scheme:

$$p_i^{(k+1)} = \frac{1}{|a_{i,i}|}\left(\sum_{j<i} p_j^{(k+1)}a_{i,j} + \sum_{j>i} p_j^{(k)}a_{i,j}\right), \tag{15.20}$$

where we assume that the order of computation is from $p_1$ to $p_N$. This scheme then requires only one probability vector to be stored, since the $(k + 1)$-th estimate for $p_i$ immediately replaces the $k$-th estimate in the single stored vector $\underline{p}$.

Employing the same matrix notation as above, we can write the Gauss-Seidel iteration scheme in matrix-vector notation as

$$\mathbf{D}\underline{p}^{(k+1)} = \mathbf{L}\underline{p}^{(k+1)} + \mathbf{U}\underline{p}^{(k)}, \tag{15.21}$$

from which we conclude

$$\underline{p}^{(k+1)} = (\mathbf{D} - \mathbf{L})^{-1}\mathbf{U}\underline{p}^{(k)}. \tag{15.22}$$

We observe that the Gauss-Seidel method has iteration matrix $\mathbf{\Phi}_{GS} = (\mathbf{D} - \mathbf{L})^{-1}\mathbf{U}$.

**The SOR method**

The last method we mention is the *successive over-relaxation method* (SOR). SOR is an extension of the Gauss-Seidel method, in which the vector $\underline{p}^{(k+1)}$ is computed as the weighted average of the vector $\underline{p}^{(k)}$ and the vector $\underline{p}^{(k+1)}$ that would have been used in the (pure) Gauss-Seidel iteration. That is, we have, for $i = 1, \cdots, N$:

$$p_i^{(k+1)} = (1 - \omega)p_i^{(k)} + \frac{\omega}{|a_{i,i}|} \left( \sum_{j<i} p_j^{(k+1)} a_{i,j} + \sum_{j>i} p_j^{(k)} a_{i,j} \right), \tag{15.23}$$

where $\omega \in (0, 2)$ is the relaxation factor. When $\omega = 1$, this method reduces to the Gauss-Seidel iteration scheme; however, when we take $\omega > 1$ (or $\omega < 1$) we speak over over-relaxation (under-relaxation). With a proper choice of $\omega$, the iterative solution process can be accelerated significantly. Unfortunately, the optimal choice of $\omega$ cannot be determined *a priori*. We can, however, estimate $\omega$ during the solution process itself, as will be pointed out below.

Employing the same matrix notation as before, we can write the SOR iteration scheme in matrix-vector notation as

$$\mathbf{D}\underline{p}^{(k+1)} = (1 - \omega)\underline{p}^{(k)} + \omega\mathbf{D}^{-1}(\mathbf{L}\underline{p}^{(k+1)} + \mathbf{U}\underline{p}^{(k)}), \tag{15.24}$$

from which we conclude

$$\underline{p}^{(k+1)} = (\mathbf{D} - \omega\mathbf{L})^{-1}(\omega\mathbf{U} + (1 - \omega)\mathbf{D})\underline{p}^{(k)}. \tag{15.25}$$

We observe that the SOR method has iteration matrix $\mathbf{\Phi}_{SOR} = (\mathbf{D} - \omega\mathbf{L})^{-1}(\omega\mathbf{U} + (1-\omega)\mathbf{D})$.

When using the SOR method, we start with $\omega = 1$ for about 10 iteration steps. In order to find a better value for $\omega$, we can use the method proposed by Hageman and Young [116]. We then have to compute an estimate for the second largest Eigenvalue of the iteration matrix $\mathbf{\Phi}_{SOR}$ as follows:

$$\tilde{\lambda}_2 = \frac{||p^{(k+1)} - p^{(k)}||}{||p^{(k)} - p^{(k-1)}||}. \tag{15.26}$$

A new estimate for $\omega$, denoted $\omega'$ can then be computed as

$$\omega' = \frac{2}{1 + \sqrt{1 - \nu^2}}, \quad \text{with } \nu = \frac{\tilde{\lambda}_2 + \omega - 1}{\omega\sqrt{\tilde{\lambda}_2}}. \tag{15.27}$$

This new estimate then replaces the old value of $\omega$, and should be used for another number of iterations, after which the estimation procedure is repeated. Whenever successive iteration vectors are becoming worse, or when the estimated sub-dominant Eigenvalue $\tilde{\lambda}_2 > 1$, then $\omega$ should be reduced towards 1.

From the discussion of the Power method in Chapter 8 (in the context of the computation of Eigenvalues), we recall that convergence is achieved faster when the second-largest (sub-dominant) Eigenvalue is smaller. In the iteration matrices given above, the largest Eigenvalue always equals 1, and the speed of convergence of the discussed methods then depends on the sub-dominant Eigenvalue. With the SOR method, with a proper choice of $\omega$ one can adapt the iteration matrix such that its second-largest Eigenvalue becomes smaller.

### Time and space complexity

The above iterative methods can be used to solve the linear systems arising in the solution of the steady-state probabilities for CTMCs, with or without the normalisation equation. Quite generally we can state that it is better *not* to include the normalisation equation. If the normalisation equation is included, the actual iteration matrices change in such a way that the sub-dominant Eigenvalue increases, hence reducing the speed of convergence. Therefore, one better performs an explicit normalisation after a number of iterations.

We finally comment on the time and space complexity of the discussed iterative methods. All methods require the storage of the matrix $\mathbf{A}$ in some form. For larger modelling problems, $\mathbf{A}$ has to be stored sparsely; it is then important that the sparse storage structure is structured such that row-wise access is very efficient since all methods require the product of a row of $\mathbf{A}$ with the iteration vector $\underline{p}^{(k)}$. The Power and the Jacobi method require two iteration vectors to be stored, each of length $N$. The Gauss-Seidel and the SOR method only require one such vector. In all the iteration schemes the divisions by $|a_{i,i}|$ (and for SOR the multiplication with $\omega$) need to be done only once, either before the actual iteration process starts or during the first iteration step, by changing the matrix $\mathbf{A}$ accordingly. This saves $N$ divisions (and $N$ multiplications for SOR) per iteration. A single iteration can then be interpreted as a single matrix-vector multiplication (MVM). In a non-sparse implementation, a single MVM costs $O(N^2)$ multiplications and additions. However, in a suitably chosen sparse storage structure only $O(\eta)$ multiplications and additions are required, where $\eta$ is the number of non-zero elements in $\mathbf{A}$. Typically, the number of nonzero elements per column in $\mathbf{A}$ is limited to a few dozen. For example, considering an SPN used to generate an underlying CTMC, the number of nonzero elements per row in $\mathbf{Q}$ equals the number of enabled transitions in a particular marking. This number is bounded by the number of transitions in the SPN, which is normally much smaller than $N$ (especially when $N$ is large). Hence, it is reasonable to assume that $\eta$ is of order $O(N)$, so that one iteration step then takes $O(N)$ operations.

An important difference between the presented iterative methods is the number of required iterations that are typically required. This number can be estimated as

$$NoI = \frac{\log \epsilon}{\log \lambda_2},\tag{15.28}$$

where $\epsilon$ is the required accuracy and $\lambda_2$ is the sub-dominant Eigenvalue of the iteration matrix. Since we do not have knowledge about $\lambda_2$, we cannot compute $NoI$ a priori but we observe that the closer $\lambda_2$ is to $\lambda_1 = 1$, the slower the convergence. Typically, the Power method converges slowest, and the Gauss-Seidel method typically outperforms the Jacobi method. With the SOR method, a proper choice of the relaxation factor $\omega$ results in a smaller value for $\lambda_2$, hence, accelerates the iteration process, so that it often is the fastest method. In practical modelling problems, arising from CTMCs generated from SPN specifications, $NoI$ can range from just a few to a few thousands.

**Example 15.5. Comparing the Power, Jacobi and Gauss-Seidel methods.**
We reconsider the CTMC for which the matrix $\mathbf{Q}$ is given by

$$\mathbf{Q} = \begin{pmatrix} -4 & 2 & 2 \\ 1 & -2 & 1 \\ 6 & 0 & -6 \end{pmatrix}.$$

For the Power method we obtain the iteration matrix $\mathbf{\Phi}_P^T = \mathbf{I} + \mathbf{Q}/\lambda$, with $\lambda = 6$, so that

$$\mathbf{\Phi}_P = \frac{1}{6} \begin{pmatrix} 2 & 1 & 6 \\ 2 & 4 & 0 \\ 2 & 1 & 0 \end{pmatrix}.$$

The matrix $\mathbf{A} = \mathbf{Q}^T$ can be decomposed as $\mathbf{D} - (\mathbf{L} + \mathbf{U})$, so that we find:

$$\mathbf{\Phi}_J = \mathbf{D}^{-1}(\mathbf{L} + \mathbf{U}) = \begin{pmatrix} 0 & \frac{1}{4} & \frac{3}{2} \\ 1 & 0 & 0 \\ \frac{1}{3} & \frac{1}{6} & 0 \end{pmatrix}.$$

and

$$\mathbf{\Phi}_{GS} = (\mathbf{D} - \mathbf{L})^{-1}\mathbf{U} = \begin{pmatrix} 0 & \frac{1}{4} & \frac{3}{2} \\ 0 & \frac{1}{4} & \frac{3}{2} \\ 0 & \frac{1}{8} & \frac{3}{4} \end{pmatrix}.$$

These iteration matrices have the following Eigenvalues:

| $\mathbf{\Phi}_P$ | | | $\mathbf{\Phi}_J$ | | | $\mathbf{\Phi}_{GS}$ | | |
|---|---|---|---|---|---|---|---|---|
| 1.000 | 0.408 | -0.408 | 1.000 | -0.500 | -0.500 | 1.000 | 0.000 | 0.000 |

| # | Power | Jacobi | Gauss-Seidel |
|---|-------|--------|--------------|
| 1 | ( 0.5000, 0.3333, 0.1667 ) | ( 0.5385, 0.3077, 0.1538 ) | ( 0.5833, 0.5833, 0.2917 ) |
| 2 | ( 0.3889, 0.3889, 0.2222 ) | ( 0.4902, 0.3137, 0.1961 ) | ( 0.4000, 0.4000, 0.2000 ) |
| 3 | ( 0.4167, 0.3889, 0.1944 ) | ( 0.3796, 0.4213, 0.1991 ) | ( 0.4000, 0.4000, 0.2000 ) |
| 4 | ( 0.3981, 0.3981, 0.2037 ) | ( 0.3979, 0.4023, 0.1998 ) | ⋮ |
| 5 | ( 0.4028, 0.3981, 0.1991 ) | ( 0.4001, 0.3999, 0.2000 ) | ⋮ |
| 6 | ( 0.3997, 0.3997, 0.2006 ) | ( 0.4000, 0.4000, 0.2000 ) | ⋮ |
| 7 | ( 0.4005, 0.3997, 0.1998 ) | ( 0.4000, 0.4000, 0.2000 ) | ⋮ |
| 8 | ( 0.3999, 0.3999, 0.2001 ) | ( 0.4000, 0.4000, 0.2000 ) | ⋮ |
| 9 | ( 0.4001, 0.3999, 0.2000 ) | ⋮ | ⋮ |
| 10 | ( 0.4000, 0.4000, 0.2000 ) | ⋮ | ⋮ |

Table 15.1: The first few iteration vectors for three iterative solution methods

As starting vector for the iterations we take $(\frac{1}{3}, \frac{1}{3}, \frac{1}{3})$. In the Jacobi and Gauss-Seidel method we renormalized the probability vector after every iteration. In Table 15.1 we show the first ten iteration vectors for these methods. As can be seen, the Power method convergest slowest, followed by the Jacobi and the Gauss-Seidel method. □

## 15.2   Transient behaviour

In this section we discuss the solution of the time-dependent behaviour of a CTMC. In Section 15.2.1 we explain why transient behaviour is of interest and which equations we need to solve for that purpose. We then continue with the discussion of a simple Runge-Kutta method in Section 15.2.2. In Section 15.2.3 we proceed with a very reliable method, known as uniformisation, to compute the time-dependent state probabilities. This method exploits the special probabilistic properties of the problem at hand. Finally, in Section 15.2.4, we comment on the use of uniformisation to compute cumulative measures.

### 15.2.1   Introduction

Up till now we have mainly addressed the use and computation of the steady-state probabilities of CTMCs. In general, steady-state measures do suffice for the evaluation of the performance of most systems. There are, however, exceptions to this rule, for instance

- when the system life-time is so short that steady-state is not reached;

- when the start-up period towards the steady-state situation itself is of interest;

- when temporary overload periods, for which no steady-state solution exists, are of interest;

- when reliability and availability properties are taken into account in the model, e.g., non-repairable systems that are failure-prone are of no interest in steady-state, since then they will have completely failed.

The time-dependent state probabilities of a CTMC are specified by a linear system of differential equations (see also (3.39)):

$$\underline{p}'(t) = \underline{p}(t)\mathbf{Q}, \quad \text{given } \underline{p}(0). \tag{15.29}$$

Measures that are specified in terms of $\underline{p}(t)$ are called *instant-of-time measures*. If we associate a reward $r_i$ with every state, the expected reward at time $t$ can be computed as

$$E[X(t)] = \sum_{i=1}^{N} r_i p_i(t). \tag{15.30}$$

The rewards express the amount of gain (or costs) that is accumulated per unit of time in state $i$; $E[X(t)]$ then expresses the overall gain accumulated per time-unit.

In many modelling applications, not only the values of the state probabilities at a time instance $t$ are of importance, but also the total time spent in any state up to some time $t$. That is, we are interested in so-called *cumulative measures*. We therefore define the cumulative state vector $\underline{l}(t)$ as

$$\underline{l}(t) = \int_0^t \underline{p}(s)ds. \tag{15.31}$$

Notice that the entries of $\underline{l}(t)$ are no longer probabilities; $l_i(t)$ denotes the overall time spent in state $i$ during the interval $[0, t)$. Integrating (15.29), we obtain

$$\int_0^t \underline{p}'(s)ds = \int_0^t \underline{p}(s)\mathbf{Q}ds, \tag{15.32}$$

which can be rewritten as

$$\underline{p}(t) - \underline{p}(0) = \underline{l}(t)\mathbf{Q}, \tag{15.33}$$

which equals, after having substituted $\underline{l}'(t) = \underline{p}(t)$:

$$\underline{l}'(t) = \underline{l}(t)\mathbf{Q} + \underline{p}(0). \tag{15.34}$$

We see that a similar differential equation can be used to obtain $\underline{l}(t)$ as to obtain $\underline{p}(t)$. If $r_i$ is the *reward* for staying one time-unit in state $i$, then

$$Y(t) = \sum_{i=1}^{N} r_i l_i(t) \tag{15.35}$$

expresses the total amount of reward gained over the period $[0, t)$. The distribution $F_Y(y, t) = \Pr\{Y(t) \leq y\}$ has been defined by Meyer as the *performability distribution* [196, 197]; it expresses the probability that a reward of at most $y$ is gained in the period $[0, t)$. Meyer developed his performability measure in order to express the effectiveness of use of computer systems in failure prone environments. After the next example we will present an expression to compute $E[Y(t)]$ efficiently and comment on the computation of the distribution of $Y(t)$.

**Example 15.6. Measure interpretation.**
Consider a three-state CTMC with generator matrix

$$\mathbf{Q} = \begin{pmatrix} -2f & 2f & 0 \\ r & -(f+r) & f \\ 0 & r & -r \end{pmatrix}.$$

This CTMC models the availability of a computer system with two processors. In state 1 both processors are operational but can fail with rate $2f$. In state 2 only one processor is operational (and can fail with rate $f$); the other one is repaired with rate $r$. In state 3 both processors have failed; one of them is being repaired. Note that we assume that both the processor life-times and the repair times are negative exponentially distributed. Since in state 1 both processors operate, we assign a reward $2\mu$ to state 1, where $\mu$ is the effective processing rate of a single processor. Similarly, we assign $r_2 = \mu$ and $r_3 = 0$. We assume that the system is initially fully operational, i.e., $\underline{p}(0) = (1, 0, 0)$. The following measures can now be computed:

- Steady-state reward rate ($\sum_i r_i p_i$): the expected processing rate of the system in steady-state, i.e., the long-term average processing rate of the system;

- Expected instant reward rate ($\sum_i r_i p_i(t)$): the expected processing rate at a particular time instance $t$;

- Expected accumulated reward ($\sum_i r_i l_i(t)$): the expected number of jobs (of fixed length 1) processed in the interval $[0, t)$;

- Finally, the accumulated reward distribution $F_Y(y, t)$ at time $t$ expresses what the probability is that at most $y$ jobs (of fixed length 1) have been processed in $[0, t)$.

$\square$

## 15.2.2   Runge-Kutta methods

The numerical solution of systems of differential equations has long been (and still is) an important topic in numerical mathematics. Many numerical procedures have been developed for this purpose, all with specific strengths and weaknesses. Below, we will present one such method in a concise way, thereby focusing on the computation of $\underline{p}(t)$.

The basic idea with *Runge-Kutta methods* (RK-methods) is to approximate the continuous vector function $\underline{p}(t)$ that follows from the differential equation $\underline{p}'(t) = \underline{p}(t)\mathbf{Q}$, given $\underline{p}(0)$, by a discrete function $\underline{\pi}_i$ ($i \in \mathbb{N}$), where $\underline{\pi}_i$ approximates $\underline{p}(ih)$, i.e., $h$ is the fixed step-size in the discretisation. Normally, $\underline{\pi}_0 = \underline{p}(0)$, and the smaller $h$, the better (but more expensive) the solution is.

With Runge-Kutta methods, the last computed value for any point $\underline{\pi}_i$ is used to compute $\underline{\pi}_{i+1}$. The values $\underline{\pi}_0$ through $\underline{\pi}_{i-1}$ are not used to compute $\underline{\pi}_{i+1}$. Therefore, Runge-Kutta methods are called *single-step methods*. They are always stable, provided the step-size $h$ is taken sufficiently small. Unlike Euler-methods (and variants), Runge-Kutta methods do not require the computation of derivatives of the function of interest. Since the latter is normally a costly operation, RK-methods are fairly efficient. There are many Runge-Kutta schemes; they are distinguished on the basis of their *order*. A Runge-Kutta method is of order $k$ if the exact Taylor series for $\underline{p}(t + h)$ and the solution of the RK-scheme for time instance $t + h$ coincide as far as the terms up to $h^k$ are concerned.

One of the most widely used RK-methods is the RK4 method (Runge-Kutta method of order 4). For a (vector) differential equation $\underline{p}'(t) = \underline{p}(t)\mathbf{Q}$, given $\underline{p}(0)$, successive estimates for $\underline{\pi}_i$ are computed as follows:

$$\underline{\pi}_{i+1} = \underline{\pi}_i + \frac{h}{6}(\underline{k}_1 + 2\underline{k}_2 + 2\underline{k}_3 + \underline{k}_4), \tag{15.36}$$

with

$$\begin{cases} \underline{k}_1 &= \underline{\pi}_i\mathbf{Q}, \\ \underline{k}_2 &= (\underline{\pi}_i + \frac{h}{2}\underline{k}_1)\mathbf{Q}, \\ \underline{k}_3 &= (\underline{\pi}_i + \frac{h}{2}\underline{k}_2)\mathbf{Q}, \\ \underline{k}_4 &= (\underline{\pi}_i + h\underline{k}_3)\mathbf{Q}. \end{cases} \tag{15.37}$$

Since the RK4 method provides an explicit solution to $\pi_i$, it is called an *explicit 4th-order method*. Per iteration step of length $h$, it requires 4 matrix-vector multiplications, 7 vector-vector additions and 4 scalar-vector multiplications. Furthermore, apart from $\mathbf{Q}$ and $\underline{\pi}$ also storage for at least two intermediate probability vectors is required.

In contrast, other RK-methods will yield a system of linear equations in which the vector of interest, i.e., $\pi_i$, appears implicitly. Such methods are normally more expensive to employ and can therefore only be justified in special situations, e.g., when the CTMC under study is stiff, meaning that the ratio of the largest and smallest rate appearing in $\mathbf{Q}$ is very large, say of the order of $10^4$ or higher.

There is much more to say about numerical methods to solve differential equations, however, we will not do so. Instead, we will focus on a class of methods especially developed for the solution of the transient behaviour of CTMCs in the next section.

## 15.2.3 Uniformisation

We first consider the scalar differential equation $p'(t) = pQ$, given $p(0)$. From elementary analysis we know that the solution to this differential equation is $p(t) = p(0)e^{Qt}$. When we deal with a linear system of differential equations, as appears when addressing CTMCs, the transient behaviour can still be computed from an exponential function, now in terms of vectors and matrices:

$$\underline{p}(t) = \underline{p}(0)e^{\mathbf{Q}t}. \tag{15.38}$$

Direct computation of this matrix exponential, e.g., via a Taylor series as $\sum_{i=0}^{\infty}(\mathbf{Q}t)^i/i!$, is in general not feasible because [204]: (i) the infinite summation that appears in the Taylor series cannot be truncated efficiently; (ii) severe round-off errors usually will occur due to the fact that $\mathbf{Q}$ contains positive as well as negative entries; and (iii) the matrices $(\mathbf{Q}t)^i$ become non-sparse, thus requiring too much storage capacity for practically relevant applications. Although the last drawback can be handled by using larger memories, the former two drawbacks are more profound. An analysis based on the Eigenvalues and Eigenvectors of $\mathbf{Q}$ is possible, but this is a very expensive way to go, especially if $\mathbf{Q}$ is large. Therefore, other algorithms have been developed of which uniformisation is currently the most popular.

*Uniformisation* is based on the more general concept of uniformisation [147] and is also known as Jensen's method [110] or randomisation [113]. To use uniformisation, we define the matrix

$$\mathbf{P} = \mathbf{I} + \frac{\mathbf{Q}}{\lambda} \quad \Rightarrow \quad \mathbf{Q} = \lambda(\mathbf{P} - \mathbf{I}). \tag{15.39}$$

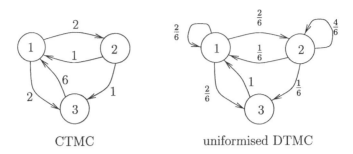

CTMC                                   uniformised DTMC

Figure 15.3: A small CTMC and the corresponding DTMC after uniformisation

If $\lambda$ is chosen such that $\lambda \geq \max_i\{|q_{i,i}|\}$, then the entries in $\mathbf{P}$ are all between 0 and 1, while the rows of $\mathbf{P}$ sum to 1. In other words, $\mathbf{P}$ is a stochastic matrix and describes a DTMC. The value of $\lambda$, the so-called *uniformisation rate*, can be derived from $\mathbf{Q}$ by inspection.

**Example 15.7. Uniformising a CTMC.**
Consider the CTMC given by

$$\mathbf{Q} = \begin{pmatrix} -4 & 2 & 2 \\ 1 & -2 & 1 \\ 6 & 0 & -6 \end{pmatrix}. \tag{15.40}$$

and initial probability vector $\underline{p}(0) = (1,0,0)$. For the uniformisation rate we find by inspection: $\lambda = 6$, so that the corresponding DTMC is given by:

$$\mathbf{P} = \frac{1}{6} \begin{pmatrix} 2 & 2 & 2 \\ 1 & 4 & 1 \\ 6 & 0 & 0 \end{pmatrix}. \tag{15.41}$$

The CTMC and the DTMC are given in Figure 15.3.                                   □

The uniformisation of a CTMC into a DTMC can be understood as follows. In the CTMC, the state residence times are exponentially distributed. The state with the shortest residence times provides us with the value $\lambda$. For that state, one epoch in the DTMC corresponds to one negative exponentially distributed delay with rate $\lambda$, after which one of the successor states is selected probabilistically. For the states in the CTMC that have total outgoing rate $\lambda$, the corresponding states in the DTMC will not have self-loops. For states in the CTMC having a state residence time distribution with a rate smaller than $\lambda$ (the states having on average a longer state residence time), one epoch in the DTMC might not be long enough; hence, in the next epoch these states might be revisited. This is made possible by the definition of $\mathbf{P}$, in which these states have self-loops, i.e., $p_{i,i} > 0$.

Using the matrix $\mathbf{P}$, we can write

$$\underline{p}(t) = \underline{p}(0)e^{\mathbf{Q}t} = \underline{p}(0)e^{\lambda(\mathbf{P}-\mathbf{I})t} = \underline{p}(0)e^{-\lambda\mathbf{I}t}e^{\lambda\mathbf{P}t} = \underline{p}(0)e^{-\lambda t}e^{\lambda\mathbf{P}t}. \tag{15.42}$$

We now employ a Taylor-series expansion for the last matrix exponential as follows

$$\underline{p}(t) = \underline{p}(0)e^{-\lambda t}\sum_{n=0}^{\infty}\frac{(\lambda t)^n\mathbf{P}^n}{n!} = \underline{p}(0)\sum_{n=0}^{\infty}\psi(\lambda t; n)\mathbf{P}^n, \tag{15.43}$$

where

$$\psi(\lambda t; n) = e^{-\lambda t}\frac{(\lambda t)^n}{n!}, \quad n \in \mathbb{N}, \tag{15.44}$$

are Poisson probabilities, i.e., $\psi(\lambda t; n)$ is the probability of $n$ events occurring in $[0, t)$ in a Poisson process with rate $\lambda$. Of course, we still deal with a Taylor series approach here; however, the involved $\mathbf{P}$-matrix is a probabilistic matrix with all its entries between 0 and 1, as are the Poisson probabilities. Hence, this Taylor series "behaves nicely", as we will discuss below.

Equation (15.43) can be understood as follows. At time $t$, the probability mass of the CTMC, initially distributed according to $\underline{p}(0)$ has been redistributed according to the DTMC with state-transition matrix $\mathbf{P}$. During the time interval $[0, t)$, with probability $\psi(\lambda t; n)$ exactly $n$ jumps have taken place. The effect of these $n$ jumps on the initial distribution $\underline{p}(0)$ is described by the vector-matrix product $\underline{p}(0)\mathbf{P}^n$. Weighting this vector with the associated Poisson probability $\psi(\lambda t; n)$, and summing over all possible numbers of jumps in $[0, t)$, we obtain, by the law of total probability, the probability vector $\underline{p}(t)$.

Uniformisation allows for an iterative solution algorithm in which no matrix-matrix multiplications take place, and thus no matrix fill-in occurs. Instead of directly computing (15.43) one considers the following sum of vectors:

$$\underline{p}(t) = \sum_{n=0}^{\infty}\psi(\lambda t; n)\left(\underline{p}(0)\mathbf{P}^n\right) = \sum_{n=0}^{\infty}\psi(\lambda t; n)\underline{\pi}_n, \tag{15.45}$$

where $\underline{\pi}_n$, being the state probability distribution vector after $n$ epochs in the DTMC with transition matrix $\mathbf{P}$, is derived recursively as

$$\underline{\pi}_0 = \underline{p}(0) \quad \text{and} \quad \underline{\pi}_n = \underline{\pi}_{n-1}\mathbf{P}, \quad n \in \mathbb{N}^+. \tag{15.46}$$

Clearly, the infinite sum in (15.45) has to be truncated, say after $k_\epsilon$ iterations or epochs in the DTMC. The actually computed state probability vector $\underline{\tilde{p}}(t)$ is then:

$$\underline{\tilde{p}}(t) = \sum_{n=0}^{k_\epsilon}\psi(\lambda t; n)\underline{\pi}_n. \tag{15.47}$$

|           |     |     |   | $\lambda t$ |    |    |    |
|-----------|-----|-----|---|---|----|----|----|
| $\epsilon$ | 0.1 | 0.2 | 1 | 2 | 4  | 8  | 16 |
| 0.0005    | 2   | 3   | 6 | 8 | 12 | 19 | 31 |
| 0.00005   | 3   | 3   | 7 | 10| 14 | 21 | 34 |
| 0.000005  | 3   | 4   | 8 | 11| 16 | 23 | 37 |

Table 15.2: The number of required steps $k_\epsilon$ as a function of $\epsilon$ and the product $\lambda t$

The number of terms that has to be added to reach a prespecified accuracy $\epsilon$ can now be computed *a priori* as follows. It can be shown that the difference between the computed and the exact value of the transient probability vector is bounded as follows:

$$||\underline{p}(t) - \tilde{\underline{p}}(t)|| \leq 1 - \sum_{n=0}^{k_\epsilon} e^{-\lambda t} \frac{(\lambda t)^n}{n!}. \qquad (15.48)$$

Thus, we have to find that value of $k_\epsilon$ such that $1 - \sum_{n=0}^{k_\epsilon} e^{-\lambda t}(\lambda t)^n/n! \leq \epsilon$. Stated differently, we need the smallest value of $k_\epsilon$ that satisfies

$$\sum_{n=0}^{k_\epsilon} \frac{(\lambda t)^n}{n!} \geq \frac{1 - \epsilon}{e^{-\lambda t}} = (1 - \epsilon)e^{\lambda t}. \qquad (15.49)$$

For reasons that will become clear below, $k_\epsilon$ is called the right truncation point.

**Example 15.8. How large should we take $k_\epsilon$.**
In Table 15.2 we show the number of required steps $k_\epsilon$ as a function of $\epsilon$ and the product $\lambda t$ in the uniformisation procedure. As can be observed, $k_\epsilon$ increases sharply with increasing $\lambda t$ and decreasing $\epsilon$. □

If the product $\lambda t$ is large, $k_\epsilon$ tends to be of order $O(\lambda t)$. On the other hand, if $\lambda t$ is large, the DTMC described by $\mathbf{P}$ might have reached steady-state along the way, so that the last matrix-vector multiplications do not need to be performed any more. Such a steady-state detection can be integrated in the computational procedure (see [213]).

**Example 15.9. Transient solution of the three-state CTMC.**
We consider the transient solution of the CTMC given in Figure 15.3; we already performed the uniformisation to form the matrix $\mathbf{P}$ with uniformisation rate $\lambda = 6$.
We first establish how many steps we have to take into account for increasing time values $t$. This number can be computed by checking the inequality (15.49) and taking $\epsilon = 10^{-4}$. We find:

| $t$ | 0.1 | 0.2 | 0.5 | 1 | 5 | 10 | 20 | 50 | 100 |
|---|---|---|---|---|---|---|---|---|---|
| $k_\epsilon$ | 5 | 7 | 11 | 17 | 52 | 91 | 163 | 367 | 693 |

We then continue to compute $\underline{p}(t)$ by adding the appropriate number of vectors $\underline{\pi}_n$, weighted by the Poisson probabilities according to (15.47), to find the curves for $p_i(t)$ as indicated in Figure 15.4. As can be observed, for $t \geq 2$ steady-state is reached. Hence, although for larger values of $t$ we require very many steps to be taken, the successive vectors $\underline{\pi}_n$ do not change any more after some time. This can be detected during the computations. To that end, denote with $k_{ss} < k_\epsilon$ the value after which $\underline{\pi}$ does not change any more. Instead of explicitly computing the sum (15.47) for all values of $n$, the last part of it can then be computed more efficiently as follows:

$$\underline{p}(t) = \sum_{n=0}^{k_\epsilon} \psi(\lambda t; n)\underline{\pi}_n = \sum_{n=0}^{k_{ss}} \psi(\lambda t; n)\underline{\pi}_n + \left( \sum_{n=k_{ss}+1}^{k_\epsilon} \psi(\lambda t; n) \right) \underline{\pi}_{k_{ss}}, \qquad (15.50)$$

thus saving the computation intensive matrix-vector multiplications in the last part of the sum. The point $k_{ss}$ is called the steady-state truncation point.

If the product $\lambda t$ is very large, the first group of Poisson probabilities is very small, often so small that the corresponding vectors $\underline{\pi}_n$ do (almost) cancel. We can exploit this by only starting to add the weighted vectors $\underline{\pi}_n$ after the Poisson weighting factors become reasonably large. Of course, we still have to compute the matrix-vector products (15.46). The point where we start to add the probability vectors is called the left truncation point and is denoted $k_0$. □

It should be noted that using the precomputed value of $k_\epsilon$, the truncation error is bounded by $\epsilon$; whether round-off introduces extra error is a separate issue. Finally, we note that the Poisson probabilities $\psi(\lambda t; n), n = 0, \cdots, N$, can be computed efficiently when taking into account the following recursive relations:

$$\psi(\lambda t; 0) = e^{-\lambda t}, \quad \text{and} \quad \psi(\lambda t; n+1) = \psi(\lambda t; n)\frac{\lambda t}{n+1}, \quad n \in I\!N. \qquad (15.51)$$

When $\lambda t$ is large, say larger than 25, overflow might easily occur. However, for these cases, the normal distribution can be used as an approximation. Fox and Glynn recently proposed a stable algorithm to compute Poisson probabilities [96].

To use uniformisation, the sparse matrix $P$ has to be stored, as well as two probability vectors. The main computational complexity lies in the $k_\epsilon$ matrix-vector multiplications that need to be performed (and the subsequent multiplication of these vectors with the appropriate Poisson probabilities; these are precomputed once). We finally remark that numerical instabilities do generally not occur when using uniformisation, since all computational elements are probabilities.

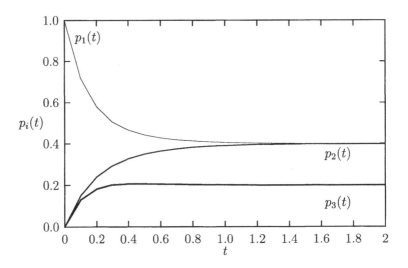

Figure 15.4: First two seconds in the evolution of the three-state CTMC computing via uniformisation

## 15.2.4   Cumulative measures

As we have seen, in many modelling applications, not only the value of the state probabilities at a time instance $t$ are of importance, but also the total time spent in any state up to some time $t$ is often of interest. We therefore defined the cumulative state vector $\underline{l}(t)$ and

$$Y(t) = \sum_{i=1}^{N} r_i l_i(t),\tag{15.52}$$

which expresses the total amount of reward gained over the period $[0, t)$. Below, we will present an expression to compute $E[Y(t)]$ efficiently and comment on the computation of the distribution of $Y(t)$.

In an interval $[0, t)$, the expected time between two jumps, when $k$ jumps have taken place according to a Poisson process with rate $\lambda$ equals $t/(k+1)$. The expected accumulated reward until time $t$, given $k$ jumps, then equals

$$\frac{t}{k+1} \sum_{i=1}^{N} r_i \sum_{m=0}^{k} \pi_i(m).$$

Summing this expression over all possible number of jumps during the interval $[0, t)$ and weighting these possibilities accordingly, we obtain:

$$
\begin{aligned}
E[Y(t)] &= \sum_{k=0}^{\infty} \psi(\lambda t; k) \frac{t}{k+1} \sum_{i=1}^{N} r_i \sum_{m=0}^{k} \pi_i(m) \\
&= \sum_{k=0}^{\infty} \sum_{i=1}^{N} \sum_{m=0}^{k} \pi_i(m) r_i e^{-\lambda t} \frac{\lambda^k t^{k+1}}{(k+1)!}.
\end{aligned}
\tag{15.53}
$$

Based on this expression, efficient numerical procedures can be devised [263, 264].

We finally comment on the solution of the performability distribution $F_Y(y, t) = \Pr\{Y(t) \le y\}$. Also here, uniformisation can be employed; however, a direct summation over all states does not suffice any more. Instead, we have to sum the accumulated reward over all paths of length $l$ (given a starting state) that can be taken through the DTMC, after which we have to compute a weighted sum over all these paths and their occurrence probabilities. De Souza e Silva and Gail have developed nice recursive solution procedures to efficiently compute $F_Y$ [263, 264]; these go beyond the scope of this book.

## 15.3   Further reading

For more details on the numerical solution of Markov chains (with a focus on steady-state probabilities) the recent books by Stewart [268] and Buchholz et al. [33] provide excellent material. The overview paper by Krieger et al. [165], and the comparisons by Stewart [266, 267] can also be recommended. General information on numerical methods for the solution of linear systems of (differential) equations can also be found in textbooks on numerical analysis [105, 116, 254].

Meyer introduced the concept of performability [195, 196, 200, 197, 198, 199], for which uniformisation turned out to be a very important computational method. Uniformisation for CTMCs has been presented by Gross and Miller [113], Grassmann [109, 108, 110], Van Dijk [73] and originally by Jensen [147]. Apart from the standard uniformisation procedure we have presented here, various variants do exist, most notably adaptive uniformisation [208], partial uniformisation, dynamic uniformisation, orthogonal uniformisation and layered uniformisation; the Ph.D. thesis of van Moorsel provides an excellent overview of uniformisation and its applications [206]. Van Moorsel and Haverkort discuss the use of partial uniformisation in the context of probabilistic validation [207]. De Souza e Silva and Gail as well as Qureshi and Sanders apply uniformisation for the computation of performability measures [236, 262, 263, 264].

For CTMCs with special properties, uniformisation might be second best. For instance, for CTMCs that are stiff, ordinary differential equation solution methods might be better;

Reibman *et al.* present comparisons in [239, 240, 238]. A procedure to handle the stiffness based on aggregation is proposed by Bobbio and Trivedi [23]. For acyclic CTMCs, a special algorithm known as ACE has been developed to compute the transient state probabilities efficiently, although this algorithm is not always numerically stable [190].

Trivedi *et al.* [281] and Haverkort and Trivedi [121] discuss the use of Markov-reward models for performance, reliability and performability evaluation. Haverkort and Niemegeers recently discussed software tools to support performability evaluation [125].

## 15.4   Exercises

### 15.1. Direct methods for steady-state.
A four-state CTMC is given by its generator matrix:

$$\mathbf{Q} = \begin{pmatrix} -3 & 2 & 0 & 1 \\ 0 & -4 & 1 & 3 \\ 1 & 0 & -1 & 0 \\ 0 & 2 & 0 & -2 \end{pmatrix}.$$

Compute the steady-state probability distribution for this CTMC, thereby handling the normalisation equation separately, using the following methods:

1. Gaussian elimination.

2. LU-decomposition in the Doolittle variant.

3. LU-decomposition in the Crout variant.

### 15.2. Iterative methods for steady-state.
Reuse the four-state CTMC of the previous exercise. Compute the steady-state probability distribution for this CTMC (again handling the normalisation equation separately) using the following methods:

1. The Power method (how large is $\lambda$?).

2. The Jacobi iterative method.

3. The Gauss-Seidel method.

### 15.3. Computing transient probabilities.

Reuse the four-state CTMC of the previous exercise and assume that $p(0) = (1, 0, 0, 0)$. Compute the transient probability distribution for $t = 1$ using the following methods:

1. The RK4-method (how large should $h$ be?).

2. The uniformisation method, thereby also addressing the following questions:

   (a) How large is the uniformisation rate $\lambda$?

   (b) How large is $k_\epsilon$ for $\epsilon = 10^{-n}$, $\quad n = 1, 2, 3, 4, 5$?

### 15.4. The RK4 method.

Show that the coefficients in the RK4 method have been chosen such that they yield the first four terms of the Taylor-series expansion of $p(t)$.

# Chapter 16

# Stochastic Petri net applications

IN this chapter we address a number of applications of the use of SPN models. All the addressed applications include aspects that are very difficult to capture by other performance evaluation techniques. The aim of this chapter is not to introduce new theory, but to make the reader more familiar with the use of SPNs.

We start with SPN models of a multiprogramming computer system in Section 16.1. We will show how to use exact SPN models for multiprogramming models including paging phenomena. Although the SPN-based solution approach is more expensive than one based on queueing networks, this study shows how to model system aspects that cannot be coped with by traditional queueing models. Then, in Section 16.2, we discuss SPN-based polling models for the analysis of token ring systems and traffic multiplexers. These models include aspects that could not be addressed with the techniques presented in Chapter 9. Since some of the models become very large, i.e., the underlying CTMC becomes very large, we also discuss a number of approximation procedures. We then present a simple SPN-based reliability model for which we will perform a transient analysis in Section 16.3. We finally present an SPN model of a very general resource reservation system in Section 16.4.

## 16.1  Multiprogramming systems

We briefly recall the most important system aspects to be modelled in Section 16.1.1. We then present the SPN model and perform invariant analysis in Section 16.1.2. We present some numerical results in Section 16.1.3

## 16.1.1   Multiprogramming computer systems

We consider a multiprogramming computer system at which $K$ system users work; they sit behind their terminals and issue requests after a negative exponentially distributed think time $E[Z]$. Requests are accepted by the system, but not necessarily put in operation immediately since there exists a multiprogramming limit $J$, such that at most $J$ customers are actively being processed. For its processing, the system uses its CPU and two disks, one of which is used exclusively for handling paging I/O. After having received a burst of CPU time, a customer either has to do a disk access (user I/O), or a new page has to be obtained from the paging device (page I/O), or a next CPU burst can be started, or an interaction with the terminal is necessary. In the latter case, the customer's code will be completely swapped out of main memory. We assume that every customer receives an equal share of the physical memory.

## 16.1.2   The SPN model

The SPN depicted in Figure 16.1 models the above sketched system. Place **terminal** models the users sitting behind their terminals; it initially contains $K$ tokens. The think time is modelled by transition **think**; its rate is **#terminals**$/E[Z]$, i.e., it is proportional to the number of users thinking. The place **swap** models the swap-in queue. Only if there are free pages available, modelled by available tokens in **free**, is a customer swapped in, via immediate transition **getmem**, to become active at the **cpu**. The place **used** is used to count the number of users being processed: it contains $J -$ **#free** tokens. After service at the **cpu**, a customer moves to place **decide**. There, it is decided what the next action the customer will undertake is: it might return to the terminals (via the immediate transition **freemem**), it might require an extra CPU burst (via the immediate transition **reserve**), or it might need I/O, either from the user-disk (via the immediate transition **user-io**) or from the paging disk (via the immediate transition **page-io**). The weight to be associated with transition **page-io** is made dependent on the number of customers being worked upon, i.e., on the number of tokens in place **used**, so as to model increased paging activity if there are more customers being processed simultaneously.

   We are interested in the throughput and (average) response time perceived at the terminals. Furthermore, to identify bottlenecks, we are interested in computing the utilisation of the servers and the expected number of customers active at the servers (note that we can not directly talk about queue lengths here, although a place like **cpu** might be seen as a queue that holds the customer in service as well and where **serve** is the corresponding

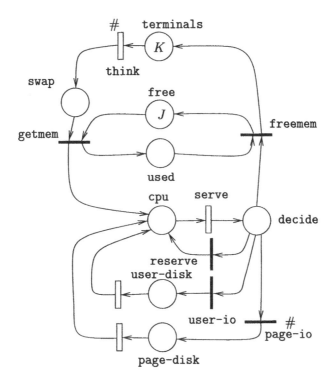

Figure 16.1: An SPN model of a multiprogramming computer system

server). The measures of interest can be defined and computed as follows:

- The component utilisations are defined as the probability that the corresponding places are non-empty. As an example, for the **cpu**, we find:

$$\rho_{\text{cpu}} = \sum_{\underline{m} \in \mathcal{R}(\underline{m}_0), \#\text{cpu}>0} \Pr\{\underline{m}\}. \tag{16.1}$$

- The expected number of tokens in a component is expressed as follows (as an example, we again consider the **cpu**):

$$E[N_{\text{cpu}}] = \sum_{\underline{m} \in \mathcal{R}(\underline{m}_0)} \#\text{cpu}(\underline{m}) \Pr\{\underline{m}\}. \tag{16.2}$$

- The total number of customers being operated upon and the number of customers waiting is denoted as the number in the system (**syst**):

$$E[N_{\text{syst}}] = \sum_{\underline{m} \in \mathcal{R}(\underline{m}_0)} (\#\text{used}(\underline{m}) + \#\text{swap}(\underline{m})) \Pr\{\underline{m}\}. \tag{16.3}$$

- The throughput perceived at the terminals:

$$X_t = \sum_{\underline{m} \in \mathcal{R}(\underline{m}_0)} \frac{\#\texttt{terminals}(\underline{m})}{E[Z]} \Pr\{\underline{m}\}. \tag{16.4}$$

- With Little's law, we finally can express the expected system response time as:

$$E[R] = E[N_{\text{syst}}]/X_t. \tag{16.5}$$

Before we proceed to the actual performance evaluation, we can compute the place invariants. In many cases, we can directly obtain them from the graphical representation of the SPN, as is the case here. Some care has to be taken regarding places that will only contain tokens in vanishing markings (as decide in this case). We thus find the following place invariants:

$$\texttt{free} + \texttt{used} = J, \quad \texttt{free} + \texttt{cpu} + \texttt{decide} + \texttt{user-disk} + \texttt{page-disk} = J,$$
$$\texttt{terminals} + \texttt{swap} + \texttt{cpu} + \texttt{decide} + \texttt{user-disk} + \texttt{page-disk} = K.$$

## 16.1.3   Some numerical results

To evaluate the model, we have assumed the following numerical parameters: the number of terminals $K = 30$, the think time at the terminals $E[Z] = 5$, the service time at the cpu $E[S_{\text{cpu}}] = 0.02$, the service time at the user disk $E[S_{\text{user-disk}}] = 0.1$, and the service time at the paging device $E[S_{\text{page-disk}}] = 0.0667$. The weights of the immediate transitions are, apart from one, all taken constant: $W(\texttt{getmem}) = 1$, $W(\texttt{freemem}) = 0.1$, $W(\texttt{reserve}) = 0.5$, and $W(\texttt{user-io}) = 0.2$. Finally, we have set $W(\texttt{page-io}, \underline{m}) = 0.2 + 0.04 \times \#\texttt{used}(\underline{m})$, i.e., the load on the paging device increases as the number of actually admitted customers increases. When we exclude paging effects, we simply set $W(\texttt{page-io}) = 0.2$. In the latter case, the five transitions that are enabled when decide contains a token form a probabilistic switch and the weights can be interpreted as fixed routing probabilities. In what follows, we will compare the performance of the multiprogrammed computer system for increasing multiprogramming degree $J$, when paging is taken into account, or not.

First of all, we study the throughput perceived at the terminals for increasing $J$ in Figure 16.2. When paging is not taken into account, we see an increase of the throughput for increasing $J$, until a certain maximum has been reached. When paging is included in the model, we observe that after an initial increase in throughput, a dramatic decrease in throughput takes place. By allowing more customers, the paging device will become more heavily loaded and the effective rate at which customers are completed decreases. Similar

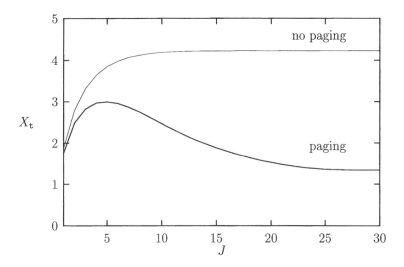

Figure 16.2: The terminal throughput $X_t$ as a function of the multiprogramming limit $J$ when paging effects are modelled and not modelled

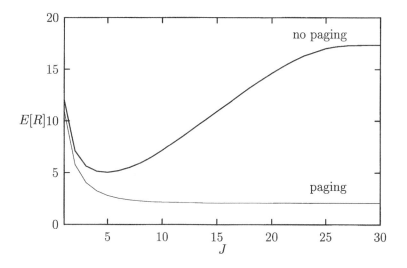

Figure 16.3: The expected response time $E[R]$ as a function of the multiprogramming limit $J$ when paging effects are modelled and not modelled

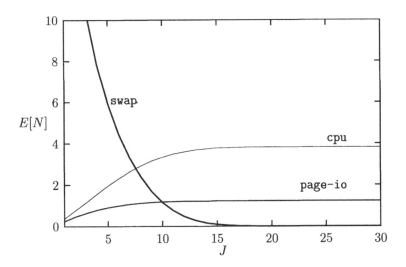

Figure 16.4: The mean number of customers in various components as a function of the multiprogramming limit $J$ when paging is not modelled

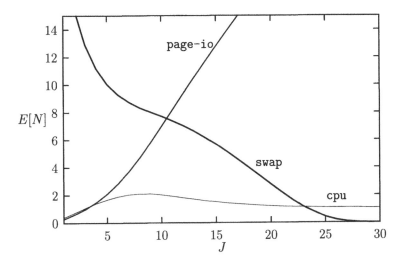

Figure 16.5: The mean number of customers in various components as a function of the multiprogramming limit $J$ when paging is modelled

observations can be made from Figure 16.3 where we compare, for the same scenarios, the expected response times. Allowing only a small number of customers leaves the system resources largely unused and only increases the expected number of tokens in place `swap`. Allowing too many customers, on the other hand, causes the extra paging activity which, in the end, overloads the paging device and causes thrashing to occur.

To obtain slightly more detailed insight into the system behaviour, we also show the expected number of customers in a number of queues, when paging is not taken into account (Figure 16.4) and when paging is taken into account (Figure 16.5). As can be observed, the monotonous behaviour of the expected place occupancies in the model without paging changes dramatically if paging is included in the model. First of all, by increasing the multiprogramming limit above a certain value (about 8 or 9) the number of customers queued at the CPU decreases, simply because more and more customers start to queue up at the paging device (the sharply increasing curve). The swap-in queue (place `swap`) does not decrease so fast in size any more when paging is modelled; it takes longer for customers to be completely served (including all their paging) before they return to the terminals; hence, the time they spend at the terminals becomes relatively smaller (in a complete cycle) so that they have to spend more time in the swap-in queue.

We finally comment on the size of the underlying reachability graph and CTMC of this SPN. We therefore show in Table 16.1 the number of tangible markings TM (which equals the number of states in the CTMC), the number of vanishing markings VM (which need to be removed during the CTMC construction process) and the number of nonzero entries ($\eta$) in the generator matrix of the CTMC, as a function of the multiprogramming limit $J$. Although the state space increases for increasing $J$, the models presented here can still be evaluated within reasonable time; for $J = 30$ the computation time remains below 60 seconds (Sun Sparc 20). Notice, however, that the human-readable reachability graph requires about 1.4 Mbyte of storage.

# 16.2   Polling models

In this section we discuss the use of SPNs to specify and solve polling models for the analysis of token ring systems. A class of cyclic polling models with count-based scheduling will be discussed in Section 16.2.1, whereas Section 16.2.2 is devoted to cyclic polling models with local time-based scheduling. We then comment on some computational aspects for large models in Section 16.2.3. We finally comment on the use of load-dependent visit-orderings in Section 16.2.4.

| J | TM | VM | $\eta$ | J | TM | VM | $\eta$ | J | TM | VM | $\eta$ |
|---|----|----|--------|---|----|----|--------|---|----|----|--------|
| 1 | 92 | 59 | 327 | 11 | 1846 | 3014 | 14022 | 21 | 4301 | 7469 | 34617 |
| 2 | 178 | 173 | 873 | 12 | 2093 | 3458 | 16068 | 22 | 4508 | 7843 | 36363 |
| 3 | 290 | 338 | 1650 | 13 | 2345 | 3913 | 18165 | 23 | 4700 | 8188 | 37980 |
| 4 | 425 | 550 | 2640 | 14 | 2600 | 4375 | 20295 | 24 | 4875 | 8500 | 39450 |
| 5 | 581 | 805 | 3825 | 15 | 2856 | 4840 | 22440 | 25 | 5031 | 8775 | 40755 |
| 6 | 756 | 1099 | 5187 | 16 | 3111 | 5304 | 24582 | 26 | 5166 | 9009 | 41877 |
| 7 | 948 | 1428 | 6708 | 17 | 3363 | 5763 | 26703 | 27 | 5278 | 9198 | 42798 |
| 8 | 1155 | 1788 | 8370 | 18 | 3610 | 6213 | 28785 | 28 | 5365 | 9338 | 43500 |
| 9 | 1375 | 2175 | 10155 | 19 | 3850 | 6650 | 30810 | 29 | 5425 | 9425 | 43965 |
| 10 | 1606 | 2585 | 12045 | 20 | 4081 | 7070 | 32760 | 30 | 5456 | 9920 | 44640 |

Table 16.1: The number of tangible and vanishing states and the number of nonzero entries in the CTMCs for increasing multiprogramming limit $J$

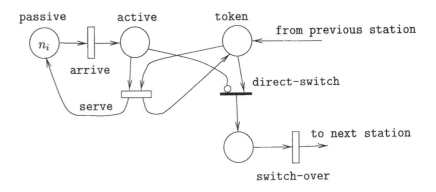

Figure 16.6: SPN model of a station with exhaustive scheduling strategy

## 16.2.1 Count-based, cyclic polling models

Using SPNs we can construct Markovian polling models of a wide variety. However, the choice for a numercial solution of a finite Markov chain implies that only finite-buffer (or finite-customer) systems can be modelled, and that all timing distributions are exponential or of phase-type. Both these restrictions do not imply fundamental problems; however, from a practical point of view, using phase-type distributions or large finite buffers results in large Markovian models which might be too costly to generate and solve. The recent developments in the use of so-called DSPNs [182, 183, 184] allow us to use deterministically timed transition as well, albeit in a restricted fashion.

Ibe and Trivedi discuss a number of SPN-based cyclic server models [142]. A few of them will be discussed here. First consider the exhaustive service model of which we depict a single station in Figure 16.6. The overall model consists of a cyclic composition of a number of station submodels. Tokens in place **passive** indicate potential customers; after an exponentially distributed time, they become active (they are moved to place **active** where they wait until they are served). When the server arrives at the station, indicated by a token in place **token**, two situations can arise. If there are customers waiting to be served, the service process starts, thereby using the server and transferring customers from place **active** to **passive** via transition **serve**. After each service completion, the server returns to place **token**. Transition **serve** models the customer service time. If there are no customers waiting (anymore) to be served (place **active** is empty), transition **serve** is disabled and the server is transferred via the immediate transition **direct-switch** to place **switch**. After the switch-over (transition **switch-over**), the server arrives at the place **token** of the next station.

Using the SPN model an underlying Markov chain can be constructed and solved. Suppose, for station $i$, the initial number of customers in place **passive** equals $n_i$ and the rate of customers arriving via transition **arrive** equals $\lambda_i$. Then, from the SPN analysis we can obtain $E[N_{\text{active}}]$, the expected number of customers in place **active**, and $\alpha_i$, the probability that place **passive** is empty. The effective arrival rate of customers to place **active** is $(1-\alpha_i)\lambda_i$ since only when **passive** is non-empty, is the arrival transition enabled. Using Little's law, the expected response time then equals

$$E[R_i] = \frac{E[N_{\text{active}}]}{(1-\alpha_i)\lambda_i}. \tag{16.6}$$

In Figure 16.7 we depict a similar model for the case when the scheduling strategy is $k$-limited. Notice that when $k = 1$, a simpler model can be used. If a token arrives at such a station, three situations can occur. Either there is nothing to send, so that

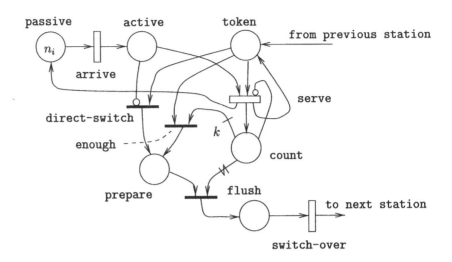

Figure 16.7: SPN model of a station with $k$-limited scheduling strategy

immediate transition **direct** fires and the token is forwarded to the next station. If there are customers waiting, at most $k$ of them can be served (transition **serve** is inhibited as soon as **count** contains $k$ tokens). Transition **enough** then fires, thus resetting place **count** to zero and taking the token into place **prepare**. Then, transition **flush** can fire, taking all tokens in place **count** (note the marking dependent arc multiplicity which is chosen to equal the number of tokens in place **count**; this number can also be zero, meaning that the arc is effectively not there), and preparing the token for the switch-over to the next station. When there are less than $k$ customers queued upon arrival of the token, these can all be served. After their service, only transition **direct** can fire, putting a token in **prepare**. Then, as before, transition **flush** fires and removes all tokens from **count**.

As can be observed here, the SPN approach towards the modelling of polling systems provides great flexibility. Not only can we model most "standard" polling mechanisms, we can also combine them as we like. Since the underlying CTMC is solved numerically, dealing with asymmetric models does not change the solution procedure. Notice that we have used Poisson arrival processes in the polling models of Chapter 9. In the models presented, we approximate these by using a place **passive** (per station submodel) as a finite source and sink of customers; by making the initial number of tokens in this place larger, we approximate the Poisson process better (and make the state space larger). Of course, we can use other arrival processes as well, i.e., we can use any phase-type renewal process, or even non-renewal processes.

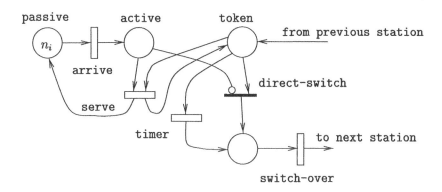

Figure 16.8: SPN-based station model with local, exponentially distributed THT

## 16.2.2 Local time-based, cyclic polling models

The SPN models presented so far all exhibit count-based scheduling. As we have seen before, time-based scheduling strategies are often closer to reality. We can easily model such time-based polling models using SPNs as well.

Consider the SPN as depicted in Figure 16.8. It represents a single station of a polling model. Once the token arrives at the station, i.e., a token is deposited in place **token**, two possibilities exist:

1. There are no customers buffered: the token is immediately released and passed to the next station in line, via the immediate transition **direct**;

2. There are customers buffered: these customers are served and simultaneously, the token holding timer (THT) is started. The service process can end in one of two ways:

   - The token holding timer expires by the firing of transition *timer*, in which case the token is passed to the next downstream station and the serving of customers stops;

   - All customers are served via transition **serve** before the token holding timer expires: the token is simply forwarded to the next downstream station.

Instead of using a single exponential transition to model the token holding timer, one can also use a more deterministic Erlang-*J* distributed token holding timer as depicted in Figure 16.9. The number *J* of exponential phases making up the overall Erlang distribution

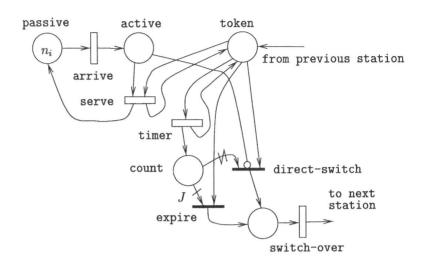

Figure 16.9: SPN-based station model with local, Erlang-$J$ distributed THT

is present in the model via the multiplicity of the arc from count to expire and the rate of transition timer which equals $J/tht$; place count now counts the number of phases in the Erlang-$J$ distributed timer that have been passed already. The operation of this SPN is similar to the one described before; the only difference is that transition timer now needs to fire $J$ times before the THT has expired (and transition expire becomes enabled). In case all customers have been served but the timer has not yet expired, transition direct will fire and move the token to the next station. Notice that one of its input arcs is marking dependent; its multiplicity equals the number of tokens in place count.

**Example 16.1. The influence of the THT in a symmetric model.**
Consider a 3-station cyclic polling model as depicted in Figure 16.9 with $J = 2$. The system is fully symmetric but for the THT values per station: we have $tht_1$ varying whereas $tht_{2,3} = 0.2$. The other system parameters are $\lambda = 3$, $E[S] = 0.1$ (exponentially distributed) and $\delta = 0.05$ (exponentially distributed).

In Figure 16.10 we depict the average waiting times perceived at station 1 and stations 2 and 3 (the latter two appear to be the same) when we vary $tht_1$ from 0.05 through 2.0 seconds. As can be observed, with increasing $tht_1$, the performance of station 1 improves at the cost of stations 2 and 3.                                                                    □

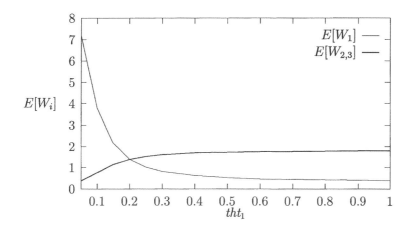

Figure 16.10: The influence of $tht_1$ on the average waiting times in a symmetric system

| $J$ | $K$ | $\eta$ | $E[W]$ | $E[N_q]$ | $J$ | $K$ | $\eta$ | $E[W]$ | $E[N_q]$ |
|---|---|---|---|---|---|---|---|---|---|
| 1 | 4488 | 20136 | 0.778 | 1.731 | 5 | 12648 | 58056 | 0.648 | 1.482 |
| 2 | 6528 | 29616 | 0.699 | 1.580 | 6 | 14688 | 67538 | 0.642 | 1.471 |
| 3 | 8568 | 39096 | 0.671 | 1.527 | 7 | 16728 | 77016 | 0.638 | 1.463 |
| 4 | 10608 | 48576 | 0.657 | 1.499 | 8 | 18768 | 86496 | 0.635 | 1.457 |

Table 16.2: The influence of the variability of the THT

**Example 16.2. Erlang-$J$ distributed THT.**
Consider a symmetric cyclic polling model consisting of $N = 3$ stations of the form as depicted in Figure 16.9. As system parameters we have $\lambda = 2$, $E[S] = 0.1$ (exponentially distributed) and $\delta = 0.05$ (exponentially distributed), and $tht = 0.2$ for all stations.

In Table 16.2 we show, for increasing $J$, the state space size $K$ and the number of non-zero entries $\eta$ in the Markov chain generator matrix $\mathbf{Q}$ which is a good measure for the required amount of computation, the expected waiting time, and the expected queue length. As can be observed, when the THT becomes more deterministic (when $J$ increases) the performance improves. This is due to the fact that variability is taken out of the model. □

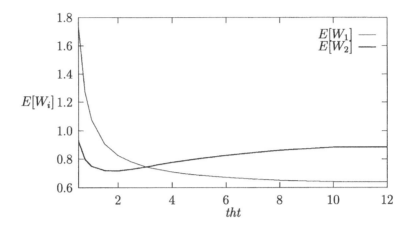

Figure 16.11: The influence of the THT on the average waiting times in an asymmetric system

**Example 16.3. The influence of the THT in an asymmetric model.**
Consider a 2-station polling model as depicted in Figure 16.9 with $J = 4$. Furthermore, we have $E[S_i] = 0.5$ (exponentially distributed) and $\delta_i = 0.1$ (exponentially distributed). The asymmetry exists in the arrival rates: $\lambda_1 = 0.8$ and $\lambda_2 = 0.2$. The system is moderately loaded: $\rho = 0.5$.

In Figure 16.11 we show $E[W_1]$ and $E[W_2]$ as a function of $tht$, which is the same in both stations. For small values of the THT, the system behaves approximately as a 1-limited system and in the higher loaded station (1) a higher average waiting time is perceived. When the THT becomes very large, the system behaves as an exhaustive service system in which station 1 dominates and station 2 suffers. Indeed, for $tht = 100$ (not in the figure), we find the limiting values $E[W_1] = 0.616$ and $E[W_2] = 0.947$ (see also Chapter 9). The performance perceived at station 2 is worse than at station 1, despite its lower load.

When increasing the THT, $E[W_1]$ monotonously decreases: the larger the THT the more station 1 profits. For station 2 this is not the case. When the THT increases, station 2 first profits from the increase in efficiency that is gained. However, when the THT grows beyond 1.5, station 2 starts to suffer from the dominance of station 1.                    □

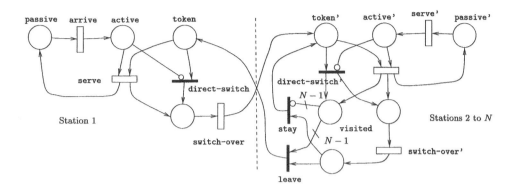

Figure 16.12: Folding an $N$-station model to an approximate 2-station model

## 16.2.3  Approximating large models

An advantage of the SPN approach is that asymmetric models are as easy to solve as symmetric models and that different scheduling strategies can be easily mixed. An inherent problem with this approach is that the state-space size increases rapidly with the number of stations and the maximum number of customers per station.

To cope with the problem of very large Markovian models, one can go at least two ways. One can try to exploit symmetries in the model in order to reduce the state space. This can sometimes be done in an exact way, in other circumstances only approximately. Another way to go is to decompose the model and to analyse the submodels in isolation (divide and conquer). Again, this can sometimes be done exactly, in other cases only approximately.

**Exploiting symmetries: folding.** When the model is highly symmetric it is possible to exploit this by folding together states which are statistically equivalent or near equivalent. As an example of this, consider the case where we model an $N$-station 1-limited polling model where stations $2, \cdots, N$ are statistically the same. About station 1 we do not make any assumptions. Instead of modelling stations 2 through $N$ separately, we can also fold them together, i.e., model them as one station with an increased arrival rate and which is visited $N - 1$ times after another, each time including a switch-over time, before a visit to station 1 occurs. This approach is illustrated in Figure 16.12 where basically two stations are depicted; however, the station on the right "models" stations 2 through $N$. The extra places in station 2 model a counter that takes care of visiting the folded model $N - 1$ times before visiting station 1 again; for details, see [50]. In this approach, the service of station 1 is interrupted every now and then. The interruption duration, i.e., the residence time

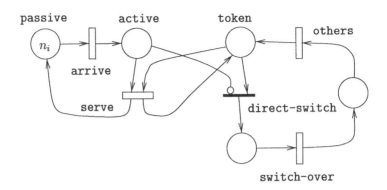

Figure 16.13: Approximate model $M_i$ for a single station in a polling model

of the server at stations 2 through $N$, is modelled fairly much in detail. A system aspect that is lost in this approach is the ordering of the stations. Suppose that, when $N = 8$, in the unfolded model the server is at station 4 and an arrival takes place at station 2. The server would not serve this job before going to station 1 first. In the folded model, however, it might be the case, dependent on other buffer conditions, that this customer is served before the server moves to station 1, simply because the station identity of the customer is lost. Choi and Trivedi report fairly accurate results with this approach even though the state-space size of the folded model is only a few percents of the unfolded model [50]. They have successfully applied this strategy in the analysis of client-server architectures with token ring and Ethernet communication infrastructures [140].

When the polling strategy itself would have been symmetric, i.e., when we would have dealt with a polling table with $p_{i,j} = 1/N$, the folding strategy would have yielded exact results. In such a case, the folding technique corresponds to the mathematically exact technique of state lumping in CTMCs. The software tool UltraSAN [68] supports this kind of lumping automatically.

**Model decomposition: fixed-point iteration.** When the models are asymmetric, a folding procedure cannot be followed. Instead, one can employ a procedure in which all the stations are analysed individually, thereby taking into account the "server unavailability" due to service granted at other stations. Since these latter quantities are unknown in advance, one can initially guess them. Using these guesses, a more exact approximation can be derived which can again be used to obtain a better approximation, etc.

Using such so-called fixed-point iteration techniques, Choi and Trivedi derive results for large asymmetric polling models with acceptable accuracy [50]. For every station (indexed

$i$), they solve a model (named $M_i$) similar to the one presented in Figure 16.13. In $M_i$, transition others models the time it takes to visit and serve all others stations $j \neq i$. Seen from station $i$, this time is just a vacation for the server; what the server actually does during this time is not important for station $i$. Initially, a reasonable guess is done for the rate of others, e.g., the reciprocal value of the sum of the switch-over times. From $M_i$ one can calculate the probability $p_i(k)$ of having $k \in \{0, \cdots, n_i\}$ customers queued in place buffer ($n_i$ is the initial number of tokens in place passive in station $i$). The expected delay the token perceives when passing through station $i$ then equals

$$d_i = \sum_{k=0}^{n_i} d_i(k) p_i(k),$$

where $d_i(k) = \delta_i + k/\mu_i$, $\delta_i$ is the switch-over time starting from station $i$, and $\mu_i$ is the service rate at station $i$. When all the values $d_i$ have been calculated, the mean server vacation time perceived at station $i$ equals $D_i = \sum_{j \neq i} d_j$. The reciprocal value $1/D_i$ can then be used as the new guess for the rate at which transition others completes in model $M_i$. This process is iterated until two successive values of $D_i$ do not differ by more than a prescribed error tolerance from one another.

An intrinsic assumption in this approach is that the server unavailability time perceived by a station is exponentially distributed. This is generally not the case in practice. Using phase-type distributions, this assumption might be relaxed.

From the analysis of $M_i$ with the converged value $1/D_i$ for the rate of others, various performance measures can easily be derived as before. Choi and Trivedi report relative errors on the mean response time per node of less then 1% for low utilisations (less than 50%) up to less than 10% for larger utilisations, when compared to the exact analysis of the complete models (when these complete models can still be solved). The solution time of the fixed-point iteration was reported to be only a few percent of the time required to solve the overall models. The fact that the sketched procedure indeed leads to a unique solution relies on the fixed-point theorem of Brouwer and is extensively discussed by Mainkar and Trivedi [189].

## 16.2.4   Polling with load-dependent visit ordering

In the polling models we have discussed so far, the visit-ordering of the stations has been fixed. We now address a two-station polling model where the visit-order is dependent on the length of the queues in the two stations. Of course, for such an ordering to be practically feasible, the server attending the queues must have knowledge of the status of all the queues, otherwise a proper decision cannot be taken. We therefore restrict ourselves to a simple case, with only two queues; we furthermore assume that the switch-over delays are equal to zero. Under these assumptions, this polling model can be seen as a model of a traffic multiplexer for two classes of traffic.

Lee and Sengupta recently proposed such a polling mechanism as a flexible priority mechanism to be used in high-speed networking switches [178]. They proposed their so-called threshold priority policy (TPP) as a priority mechanism that gives priority to one traffic class over another, only when really needed. In the following, we will assume that the two traffic classes are a video or real-time class (rt) and a data or nonreal-time class (nrt).

In the TPP, two buffers are used for the two traffic classes. A predetermined threshold $L$ is associated with the real-time buffer. When the queue length in the real-time buffer is less than or equal to $L$, the server alternates between the two buffers transmitting one cell from each buffer (as long as a queue is not empty). On the other hand, when the queue length in the real-time buffer exceeds $L$, the server continues to serve the real-time buffer until its queue length is reduced to $L$. The value of the threshold $L$ gives the degree of preferential treatment of the real-time traffic. When $L = 0$, real-time traffic is given an absolute non-preemptive priority. When $L = \infty$, both traffic classes are served alternatingly when not empty, i.e., the server acts as a 1-limited cyclic server. By selecting $L$ between these two extremes, one may provide an adequate quality of service to both real-time and nonreal-time traffic.

In Figure 16.14 we depict the SPN model of the multiplexer. On the left side, we see the arrival streams coming into the buffers for the two traffic classes; here appropriate arrival models should be added. The server is represented by the single token that alternates between places try-rt and try-nrt. After a cell of one class is served (via either transition serve-rt or serve-nrt) the server polls the other class. When nothing is buffered for a particular traffic class, the server also polls the other class, via the transitions empty-rt and empty-nrt. However, depending on whether there are more or less than $L$ cells buffered in place buff-rt, it can be decided that the server remains serving the real-time traffic class. This is enforced by the immediate transitions rt-rt, rt-nrt, nrt-nrt, nrt-rt1 and nrt-rt2. Apart from the normal enabling conditions for these transitions (at least a token in every input place and no tokens in places that are connected via an inhibitor arc to the transition) these transitions have enabling functions associated with them, as given in Table 16.3; they are taken such that the TPP is exactly enforced.

The TPP as proposed by Lee and Sengupta functions well when the arrival streams of the two traffic classes are Poisson streams. However, when one of the arrival streams is

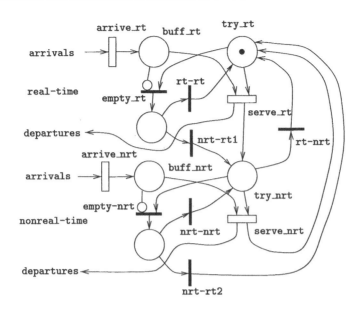

Figure 16.14: The TPP as an SPN model

| transition | enabling function |
|---|---|
| rt–rt | ($\#$buff_rt$> L$) or (($\#$buff_rt$> 0$) and ($\#$buff_nrt$= 0$)) |
| rt–nrt | ($\#$buff_rt$> 0$) and ($\#$buff_rt$\leq L$) |
| nrt–nrt | ($\#$buff_rt$= 0$) and ($\#$buff_nrt$> 0$) |
| nrt–rt1 | ($\#$buff_rt$> L$) |
| nrt–rt2 | ($\#$buff_rt$> 0$) |

Table 16.3: Enabling functions for the immediate transitions in the TPP model

more bursty, which can be the case for real-time video traffic, it does not function properly any more. We therefore recently introduced the *extended TPP* (ETPP) mechanism, which also works well in case of bursty real-time traffic [124]. In the ETPP, the server remains to serve the real-time queue until the burst of real-time traffic has been handled completely, instead of polling the nonreal-time queue already when there are less than $L$ real-time traffic jobs left.

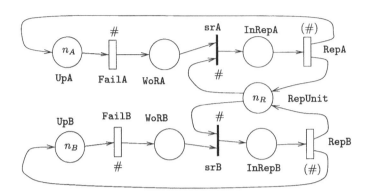

Figure 16.15: A simple availability model for a system consisting of multiple components of two classes and a single repair unit

## 16.3  An SPN availability model

We now consider a typical availability model for a multi-component system; we have already addressed this model in one of the exercises of Chapter 14.

Consider a system consisting of $n_A$ components of type $A$ and $n_B$ components of type $B$. The failure rate of components of type $A$ $(B)$ is $f_A$ $(f_B)$ and the repair rate is $r_A$ $(r_B)$. We assume that the times to failure and the times to repair are exponentially distributed. There is $n_R = 1$ repair unit available for repairing failed components; it can only repair one component at a time. Components that fail are immediately repaired, if the repair unit is free; otherwise they have to queue for repair.

The availability of such a system can be modelled using a fairly simple SPN, as given in Figure 16.15. The $n_A$ components in place UpA can fail, each with rate $f_A$, hence the rate of transition FailA is made marking dependent on the number of tokens in UpA. Once failed, these components have to wait on their repair in place WoRA. If the repair unit is free, i.e., if RepUnit is not empty, the immediate transition srA (start repair A) fires, thus bringing together the repair unit and the failed component. After an exponentially distributed time (with rate $r_A$) the repair is completed, bringing the component up again. For components of class B, the SPN operates similarly. The weights of the immediate transitions srA and srB have been made linearly dependent on the number of failed components waiting to be repaired in the places WoRA and WoRB. If multiple repair units are provided, i.e., $n_R > 1$, then the rate of the repair transitions RepA and RepB should be made dependent on the number of currently repaired components (per class); we only consider the case $n_R = 1$.

The number of tangible states in the underlying CTMC can be expressed as:

$$NoS = 1 + n_A + n_B + 2n_A n_B.$$

This can be understood as follows. There is one state with no components failed. Given that one or more components of class A have failed (and none of class B), one of them is being repaired; there are $n_A$ of such states. A similar reasoning is valid for the case when only one or more class B components have failed. There are $n_A n_B$ cases in which there are failed components of both classes A and B, in each of which either a class A component or a class B component is being repaired, which explains the factor 2.

Now consider the case in which the components of class A and B are used to process items of some sort. After an initial processing phase at a class A component, a class B component finishes the processing of the item. The $n_A$ components of class $A$ can each maintain a speed of item processing of $\mu_A$ items per minute. Similarly, the $n_B$ components of class B can each handle $\mu_B$ items per minute. Finally, items flow in at rate $\Lambda$ (items per minute). We assume that all times for item processing are deterministic. If some of the components have failed, their processing capacity is lost, leading to a smaller throughput of produced items. We assume that a measure of merit for the overall processing system, given "state" $(n_A, n_B)$, is given by $\min\{n_A \mu_A, n_B \mu_B\}$, i.e., the weakest link in the processing chain determines the reachable throughput $X$; this minimum value can be taken as reward to be associated with every state in the model.

To evaluate this model, we assume the following numerical parameters. We take as failure and repair characteristics for the components: $n_A = 20$, $n_B = 15$, $f_A = 0.0001$ failures per hour (fph), $f_B = 0.0005$ fph, and $r_A = 1$ repair per hour (rph) and $r_B = 0.5$ rph. Furthermore, the item production rates are $\mu_A = 7.5$ items per minute (ipm) and $\mu_B = 10$ ipm. We set $\Lambda = 150$, such that the overall item processing capacity of components of class A and B exactly matches the arrival rate of items to be processed. If one or more components fail, the production rate of items will fall. We now define the following measures for this system model:

- the probability that the system is fully operational at time $t$ (the availability $A(t)$);

- the probability that the system is not fully operational at time $t$ (the unavailability $U(t) = 1 - A(t)$); for these two measures, the limiting case for $t \to \infty$ is also of interest;

- the expected rate at which items are produced at time $t$, denoted $E[X(t)]$, measured in items per hour, using the rewards just defined;

| $t$ | $U(t)$ | $E[X(t)]$ | $E[Y_{\mathrm{loss}}(t)]$ | $k_0$ | $k_\epsilon$ | $k_{\mathrm{ss}}$ |
|---|---|---|---|---|---|---|
| 0.1 | 0.000921 | 8999.475 | 0.0265 | 0 | 7 | - |
| 0.2 | 0.001788 | 8998.980 | 0.1039 | 0 | 8 | - |
| 0.5 | 0.004097 | 8997.657 | 0.6140 | 0 | 9 | - |
| 1.0 | 0.007141 | 8995.891 | 2.2475 | 0 | 12 | - |
| 2.0 | 0.011154 | 8993.530 | 7.6420 | 0 | 15 | - |
| 5.0 | 0.015679 | 8990.796 | 32.153 | 0 | 23 | - |
| 10.0 | 0.016864 | 8990.056 | 80.700 | 0 | 33 | - |
| 20.0 | 0.016983 | 8989.978 | 180.757 | 2 | 52 | - |
| 50.0 | 0.016985 | 8989.978 | 481.430 | 19 | 98 | 55 |
| 100.0 | 0.016985 | 8989.978 | 982.555 | - | - | 55 |
| $\infty$ | 0.016985 | 8989.978 | - | - | - | - |

Table 16.4: Results for the transient analysis of a CTMC (636 states) of moderate size, using uniformisation

- the cumulative number of items not produced due to capacity loss due to failures, denoted $E[Y_{\mathrm{loss}}(t)]$, using the rewards just defined.

In Table 16.4 we show, for increasing values of $t$, some of the above measures. We also indicate the left-, right- and steady-state- truncation points in the summation of the uniformisation procedure taking $\epsilon = 10^{-7}$ (see Section 15.2). We observe that for increasing $t$, the unavailability steadily decreases towards its limiting value, as does the expected production throughput $E[X(t)]$. The column $E[Y_{\mathrm{loss}}(t)]$ shows that even a small unavailability can lead to a large loss in production. The column $k_0$ shows the left-truncation point in the uniformisation process. For small $t$, it equals 0; however, for increasing $t$, it shifts slightly higher. Similar remarks apply for the right-truncation point $k_\epsilon$. For $t \geq 50$, we see that steady-state is reached (column $k_{\mathrm{ss}}$), hence the tail of the summation can be performed more efficiently. For $t \geq 100$ we see that steady-state is reached before the actual addition of probability vectors starts, hence, for $t = 100$ the same results apply as for steady-state. Notice that $\lim_{t \to \infty} E[Y_{\mathrm{loss}}(t)] = \infty$.

## 16.4    Resource reservation systems

We finally present an SPN model for the analysis of reservation-based systems. A typical example of such a system can be found in circuit-switched telecommunication networks

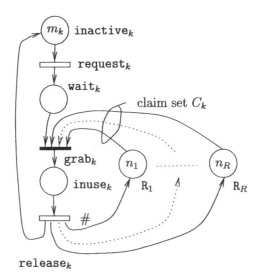

inactive$_k$

request$_k$

wait$_k$

claim set $C_k$

grab$_k$

$n_1$

$n_R$

$R_1$

$R_R$

inuse$_k$

#

release$_k$

Figure 16.16: A generic SPN model for a resource reservation system

where, before actual messages can be exchanged, a number of links (or part of their capacity) has to be reserved (connection reservation and set-up phase). After usage, these resources are then freed and can be used as part of other connections.

Let us consider the case in which there are $R$ resource types. Of each resource type, $n_r$ instances exist. Furthermore, we have $K$ types of resource users. We have $m_k$ instances of user type $k$, and a resource user of type $k$ is characterised by the following three quantities:

- its resource request rate $\lambda_k$;

- its resource usage rate $\mu_k$;

- its resource claim set $C_k \subseteq \{1, \cdots, R\}$.

Using these quantities, the typical operation of a user of class $k$ is as follows. First of all, the user remains inactive, i.e., it does not need any resources, for an exponentially distributed time with rate $\lambda_k$. This user then tries to claim all the resources it needs, i.e., it claims resources instances $r \in C_k$. After the user has acquired all its resources, it starts using them, for an exponentially distributed time with rate $\mu_k$. After that, the claimed resources are freed again, and the cycle restarts.

This type of behaviour can very well be described by the SPN (partially) given in Figure 16.16. For type $k$ of resource users, we have an arrival transition req$_k$. After such a user has made its request, an immediate transition $\mathtt{grab}_k$ takes all the required resources in the claim set $C_k$ and the usage of the resources starts. After an exponentially distributed time, modelled by transition $\mathtt{release}_k$, the resources are freed again, and the user of type $k$ remains $\mathtt{inactive}$ for some time. Notice that transition $\mathtt{release}_k$ should have infinite-server semantics; for every token in $\mathtt{inuse}_k$, an independent exponentially distributed time until resource release should be modelled. This implies that the rate of $\mathtt{release}_k$ should be made linearly dependent on the marking of place $\mathtt{inuse}_k$. Whether or not also transition $\mathtt{request}_k$ should have infinite-server semantics (with respect to place $\mathtt{inactive}_k$) depends on the actual behaviour of the users. Typical measures of interest for this type of model are the following:

- the number of outstanding requests for class $k$ that cannot be granted immediately, denoted $E[\#\mathtt{wait}_k]$, or the density of the number of tokens in place $\mathtt{wait}_k$;

- the throughput for customers of class $k$: $X_k = \frac{1}{\mu_k} \sum_{l=1}^{m_k} l \Pr\{\#\mathtt{inuse}_k = l\}$;

- the utilisation of resources of type $r$: $\rho_r = 1 - E[\#\mathtt{R}_r]/n_r$.

There are a number of possible extensions to the model sketched in Figure 16.16:

- the arrivals of requests could be made more general, e.g., by allowing more complex constellations of places and transitions instead of the single request-transition;

- the resource holding time could be made more deterministic or more variable, e.g., by allowing for more complex constellations of places and transitions instead of the single release-transition;

- the resource request could be made more general in the sense that some requests might require multiple instances of certain resources; the claim sets would then become multisets and the multiplicities of the arcs from the resource-places to the grab-transitions would have to be changed accordingly.

We finally comment on the solution of this type of SPN. Although a straightforward solution via the underlying CTMC is, in principle, always possible, in many practical cases the underlying CTMC becomes too large to be generated and evaluated, especially if $R$, $K$, and the values of $n_r$ and $m_k$ are not small. Therefore, various researchers have looked for approximations for this type of model. In particular, if the transitions $\mathtt{request}_k$ and $\mathtt{grab}_k$ are amalgamated (and place $\mathtt{wait}_k$ is removed, as in Figure 16.17) the SPN has a structure that allows for a product-form solution of a similar form to that seen for GNQNs

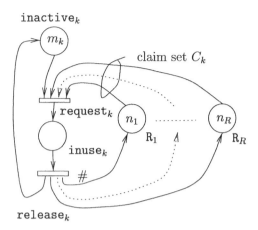

Figure 16.17: An approximate SPN model for a resource reservation system

[75, 134, 133]. The development of a mean-value analysis algorithm for a special case of such an SPN is demonstrated in [70]. It should be noted though, that the changed model might not accurately describe the real system operation anymore.

## 16.5  Further reading

Further application examples of SPNs can be found in a number of books on SPNs, e.g., by Ajmone Marsan *et al.* [1, 2] and by Bause and Kritzinger [15]. Also the book on Sharpe by Sahner *et al.* [249] provides application examples.

Regarding SPN-based polling models, we refer to papers from Ajmone Marsan *et al.* [5, 7, 6], Ibe *et al.* [141, 142, 140], Choi and Trivedi [50] and Haverkort *et al.* [124].

The model in Section 16.3 is elaborated in [121]. Sanders and Malhis also present SPN dependability models [252]. Ciardo *et al.* also present interesting SPN-based performance and dependability models in [54].

Finally, more application examples of SPNs can, among others, be found in the proceedings of the IEEE workshop series on Petri Nets and Performance Models. SPN-based dependability models can be found in the proceedings of the annual IEEE Fault-Tolerant Computer Systems Symposium and in the proceedings of the IEEE International Performance and Dependability Symposium.

## 16.6   Exercises

### 16.1. 1-limited polling.
Construct a simpler version of the SPN model of Figure 16.7 for a 1-limited scheduling strategy.

### 16.2. Globally-timed polling.
Construct an SPN-based polling model with global timing, as used in FDDI (see Chapter 9). Notice that in such a system, a timer is started when the token (the server) leaves a station. Upon return to the station, it is checked whether there is still time left to start transmission(s), i.e., whether the timer has yet expired or not.

### 16.3. ETPP polling.
In Section 16.2.4 we presented the threshold priority policy (TPP) as a polling model with load-dependent visit order. We are able to change this policy to an extended form (ETPP) in which the real-time buffer is completely emptied once its filling has reached the threshold $L$, before service is granted to the nonreal-time traffic. Starting from the SPN given in Figure 16.14, construct an SPN for the ETPP. For details on such models, we refer to [124].

### 16.4. Polling models with IPP workload.
Adapt the SPN-based polling models so that the arrival stream of jobs per station proceeds according to an IPP. How does this change affect the size of the underlying CTMC?

### 16.5. Polling models with PH-distributed services.
Adapt the SPN-based polling models so that job service times are PH-distributed. As possible PH-distributions, take an Erlang-$k$ distribution and a hyper-exponential distribution (with $k$ phases). How do these changes affect the size of the underlying CTMC?

### 16.6. The availability model.
Consider the following generalisation of the availability model of Section 16.3. We now deal with $C$ class of components. Component class $c \in \mathcal{C} = \{1, 2, \cdots, C\}$ has $n_c$ components. Show that the number of tangible states in the underlying CTMC can be expressed as:

$$\text{NoS} = 1 + \sum_{T \in \mathcal{T}, T \neq \emptyset} |T| \cdot \prod_{c \in T} n_c,$$

where $\mathcal{T}$ is the power set of $\{1, 2, \cdots, C\}$ and $|T|$ the cardinality of set $T$. Hint: try to generalise the reasoning for the case $C = 2$ as presented in Section 16.3. For more details on this model, and on the solution of this exercise, see [121].

# Chapter 17

# Infinite-state SPNs

T HE SPNs we have addressed in the previous chapters all have a possibly large, but finite state space. In this chapter we focus on a special class of stochastic Petri nets with unbounded state space, known as one-place unbounded SPNs or *infinite-state SPNs* (abbreviated as iSPNs). In particular, we focus on a class of SPNs of which the underlying CTMC has a QBD structure, for which efficient solution methods exist (see Chapter 8). The properties an SPN has to fulfill to belong to this class can be verified at the SPN level, without having to construct the reachability graph. The main advantage of iSPNs is that efficient matrix-geometric techniques for the solution are combined with the powerful description facilities of (general) SPNs. This not only allows non-specialists to use these methods, it also avoids the state-space explosion problem that is so common in traditional SPN analysis based on the complete (finite) underlying Markov chain.

We motivate the use of iSPNs in Section 17.1 and characterise the class of iSPNs by defining a number of constraints that have to be fulfilled in Section 17.2. We then discuss, in Section 17.3, how matrix-geometric methods can also be applied in this case. In Section 17.4 we comment on algorithms to detect the special iSPN structure and to compute reward-based measures efficiently. We finally discuss a number of application examples in Section 17.5.

## 17.1 Introduction

The general approach in solving SPNs is to translate them to an underlying finite CTMC which can be solved numerically. However, a problem that often arises when following this approach is the rapid growth of the state space. Various solutions have been proposed for this problem, e.g., the use of state space truncation techniques [121] or lumping techniques

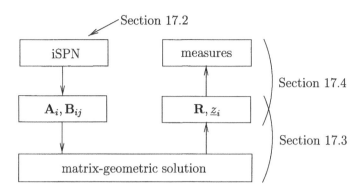

Figure 17.1: Overview of the modelling and solution approach for iSPNs

[31, 32, 47, 253]. For a restricted class of SPNs, product-form results apply, so that an efficient mean-value analysis style of solution becomes feasible [134, 75]. In all these cases, the "trick" lies in circumventing the generation of the large overall state space.

When studying queueing models, as we have done in Parts II and III, one observes that the analysis of models with an unbounded state space is often simpler than analysing similar models on a finite state space. This suggests the idea of studying SPNs that have an unbounded state space. Instead of generating and solving a very large but finite SPN model (as we have done so far) we solve infinitely large CTMCs derived from special SPN models. Of course, not all SPNs can be used for this purpose; we require them to exhibit a certain regular structure. Although this limits their applicability, it is surprising how many SPNs do fulfill the extra requirements.

A class of infinitely large Markovian models which allows for an efficient solution is the class of quasi-birth-death models, as described in Chapter 8. A state-level characterisation of such models is, however, cumbersome for practical applications. We therefore define a class of SPNs which has an underlying CTMC which is a QBD; these SPNs are denoted *iSPNs*.

In Figure 17.1 we present the GMTF (as introduced in Chapter 1) applied to iSPNs. The sections that follow are devoted to the specific parts indicated in this figure. Definitions and terminology for iSPNs are given in Section 17.2. The solution of the underlying QBD, starting from the block matrices $\mathbf{A}_i$ and $\mathbf{B}_{i,j}$ and yielding the matrix $\mathbf{R}$ and the probability vectors $\underline{z}_i$ is discussed in Section 17.3 (this section depends strongly on Chapter 8). The transformation process from the SPN description to the QBD structure and the enhancement of the steady-state probability vectors to reward-based performance measures is then discussed in Section 17.4.

## 17.2 Definitions

We discuss some preliminary notation and terminology in Section 17.2.1. The requirements for iSPNs are formally given in Section 17.2.2 and they are discussed in Section 17.2.3.

### 17.2.1 Preliminaries

The class of iSPNs is similar to the class of SPNs defined in Chapter 14. Without loss of generality we assume that the iSPN under study, denoted $iSPN$, has a set $P = \{P_0, P_1, \cdots, P_{n_p}\}$ of places of which $P_0$ may contain an infinitely large number of tokens. A distribution of tokens over the places is called a marking and denoted $\mathbf{m} = (m_0, \underline{m}) = (m_0, m_1, \cdots, m_n)$. With $m_0 \in \mathbb{N}$ and $\underline{m} \in \mathcal{R}'$, the set of all possible markings is denoted $\mathcal{R} = \mathbb{N} \times \mathcal{R}'$. Clearly, $|\mathbb{N}| = \infty$ and $|\mathcal{R}'| < \infty$. The set of transitions is denoted $T$.

We now define *level* $\mathcal{R}(k)$ to be the set of markings such that place $P_0$ contains $k$ tokens, i.e., $\mathcal{R}(k) = \{\mathbf{m} = (m_0, \underline{m}) \in \mathcal{R} | m_0 = k\}$. The levels $\mathcal{R}(k)$, $k \in \mathbb{N}$ constitute a partition of the overall state space: $\mathcal{R} = \bigcup_{k=0}^{\infty} \mathcal{R}(k)$ and $\mathcal{R}(k) \cap \mathcal{R}(l) = \emptyset, k \neq l$. For ease in notation, we also introduce $\mathcal{R}'(k) = \{\underline{m} | (k, \underline{m}) \in \mathcal{R}(k)\}$.

We furthermore define the following two *leads to* relations. We denote $\mathbf{m} \xrightarrow{t} \mathbf{m}'$ if transition $t$ is enabled in $\mathbf{m}$ and, upon firing, leads to marking $\mathbf{m}'$. The firing rate of $t$ is not important. We denote $\mathbf{m} \xrightarrow{t,\lambda} \mathbf{m}'$ if transition $t \in T$ is enabled in $\mathbf{m}$ and, upon firing, with rate $\lambda$, leads to marking $\mathbf{m}'$.

### 17.2.2 Requirements: formal definition

We now can define the class of iSPNs by imposing a number of requirements on the SPN structure and transition firing behaviour. It should be noted that these requirements are sufficient, rather than necessary.

**Requirement 1.** Given $iSPN$, there exists a $\kappa \in \mathbb{N}$ such that for all $k, l \geq \kappa$: $\mathcal{R}'(k) = \mathcal{R}'(l)$. We denote $L = |\mathcal{R}'(\kappa)|$.

**Requirement 2.** Given $iSPN$ and $\kappa$ as defined above, the following requirements should hold for the so-called repeating portion of the state space:

1. intra-level equivalence:
   $$\forall k, l \geq \kappa, \, t \in T, \, \lambda \in \mathbb{R}^+: \text{ if } (k, \underline{m}) \xrightarrow{t,\lambda} (k, \underline{m}') \text{ then } (l, \underline{m}) \xrightarrow{t,\lambda} (l, \underline{m}');$$

2. inter-level one-step increases only:

$\forall k \geq \kappa,\ \exists t \in T\colon (k, \underline{m}) \xrightarrow{\ t\ } (k+1, \underline{m}')$;

$\forall k \geq \kappa,\ t \in T,\ \lambda \in I\!\!R^+\colon$ if $(k, \underline{m}) \xrightarrow{t, \lambda} (k+1, \underline{m}')$ then $(k+1, \underline{m}) \xrightarrow{t, \lambda} (k+2, \underline{m}')$;

$\forall k \geq \kappa,\ \forall i \in I\!\!N, i \geq 2,\ \nexists t \in T\colon (k, \underline{m}) \xrightarrow{\ t\ } (k+i, \underline{m}')$;

3. inter-level one-step decreases only:

$\forall k > \kappa,\ \exists t \in T\colon (k+1, \underline{m}) \xrightarrow{\ t\ } (k, \underline{m}')$;

$\forall k > \kappa,\ t \in T,\ \lambda \in I\!\!R^+\colon$ if $(k+2, \underline{m}) \xrightarrow{t, \lambda} (k+1, \underline{m}')$ then $(k+1, \underline{m}) \xrightarrow{t, \lambda} (k, \underline{m}')$;

$\forall k > \kappa,\ \forall i \in I\!\!N, i \geq 2,\ \nexists t \in T\colon (k+i, \underline{m}) \xrightarrow{\ t\ } (k, \underline{m}')$;

**Requirement 3.** Given *iSPN* and $\kappa$ as defined above, for the so-called boundary portion of the state space the following requirements should hold:

1. no boundary jumping:

$\forall k < \kappa - 1, \forall l > \kappa,\ \nexists t_1 \in T\colon (k, \underline{m}) \xrightarrow{t_1} (l, \underline{m}')$;

$\forall k < \kappa - 1, \forall l > \kappa,\ \nexists t_2 \in T\colon (l, \underline{m}) \xrightarrow{t_2} (k, \underline{m}')$;

2. only boundary crossing:

$\exists t_1, t_2 \in T\colon (\kappa - 1, \underline{m}_1) \xrightarrow{t_1} (\kappa, \underline{m}_1'),\ (\kappa, \underline{m}_2) \xrightarrow{t_2} (\kappa - 1, \underline{m}_2')$;

## 17.2.3   Requirements: discussion

To ease the understanding, let us now discuss the formal requirements in a more informal way. We first address the state space and its partitioning in levels. The first requirement states that, starting from a certain level $\kappa$ upwards, all levels are the same as far as the non-infinite places (places $P_1$ through $P_n$) are concerned; they only differ in the number of tokens in place $P_0$. It is for this reason that the levels $k \geq \kappa$ are called the repeating portion (levels) of the state space. The levels $k < \kappa$ are called the boundary portion (levels) of the state space. In Figure 17.2 we depict the overall state space and its partitioning in levels. We have tried to visualise the fact that starting from level $\kappa$ upwards, the levels repeat one another. Levels 0 through $\kappa - 1$ can be totally different from one another. Between states from levels 0 through $\kappa - 1$ all kinds of transitions may occur. That is why we can also see these boundary levels as one aggregated boundary level (Requirement 1).

Transitions can occur within a level, and between levels. Since the repeating levels are always the same (apart from the level number itself) all internal transitions in one level must have similar equivalents in other repeating levels. There are no transitions possible between non-neighbouring levels. There have to exist up- and down-going transitions between

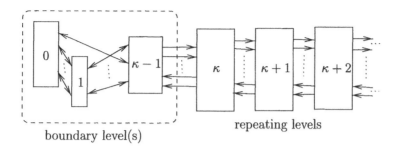

Figure 17.2: State space partitioning in levels

neighbouring levels. Also, for the repeating levels, their interaction with neighbouring levels is always the same (Requirement 2).

The transitions between the boundary levels and the repeating levels only take place in levels $\kappa - 1$ and $\kappa$; however, they may have any form (Requirement 3).

As a conclusion, due to the three requirements the CTMC underlying iSPNs obeys a quasi-birth-death structure. We will exploit this fact in the solution of this class of SPNs.

A final remark should be made regarding the necessity of the requirements. Indeed, the requirements are sufficient, however, not always necessary. One can imagine CTMCs which have a slightly different structure, especially in the boundary part of the state space, that still have a matrix-geometric solution. Stating necessary requirements, however, would make the requirements more cumbersome to validate.

## 17.3   Matrix-geometric solution

In this section we discuss the matrix-geometric solution of the class of iSPNs. Referring to Figure 17.2, it is easy to see that the generator matrix $\mathbf{Q}$ of the QBD has the following form:

$$Q = \begin{pmatrix}
\text{row}\backslash\text{col} & 0 & \cdots & \kappa-1 & \kappa & \kappa+1 & \kappa+2 & \cdots \\
\hline
0 & \mathbf{B}_{0,0} & \cdots & \mathbf{B}_{0,\kappa-1} & 0 & 0 & \cdots & \cdots \\
1 & \mathbf{B}_{1,0} & \cdots & \mathbf{B}_{1,\kappa-1} & 0 & 0 & \cdots & \cdots \\
\vdots & \vdots & \vdots & \vdots & \vdots & \vdots & \vdots & \vdots \\
\kappa-1 & \mathbf{B}_{\kappa-1,0} & \cdots & \mathbf{B}_{\kappa-1,\kappa-1} & \mathbf{B}_{\kappa-1,\kappa} & 0 & \cdots & \cdots \\
\kappa & 0 & \cdots & \mathbf{B}_{\kappa,\kappa-1} & \mathbf{B}_{\kappa,\kappa} & \mathbf{B}_{\kappa,\kappa+1} & 0 & \cdots \\
\kappa+1 & 0 & \cdots & 0 & \mathbf{B}_{\kappa+1,\kappa} & \mathbf{B}_{\kappa+1,\kappa+1} & \mathbf{B}_{\kappa+1,\kappa+2} & \cdots \\
\kappa+2 & 0 & \cdots & 0 & 0 & \mathbf{B}_{\kappa+2,\kappa+1} & \mathbf{B}_{\kappa+2,\kappa+2} & \cdots \\
\vdots & \vdots & \vdots & \vdots & \vdots & \vdots & \vdots & \ddots
\end{pmatrix}. \quad (17.1)$$

Now, by the requirements posed on the intra- and inter-level transitions, we have

$$\begin{cases}
\mathbf{B}_{k,k+1} = \mathbf{A}_0, & k = \kappa, \kappa+1\cdots, \\
\mathbf{B}_{k,k} = \mathbf{A}_1, & k = \kappa+1, \kappa+2\cdots, \\
\mathbf{B}_{k,k-1} = \mathbf{A}_2, & k = \kappa+1, \kappa+2\cdots.
\end{cases} \quad (17.2)$$

Using this notation, we may write $\mathbf{Q}$ as follows:

$$\mathbf{Q} = \begin{pmatrix}
\mathbf{B}_{0,0} & \cdots & \mathbf{B}_{0,\kappa-1} & 0 & \cdots & \cdots & \cdots \\
\vdots & \cdots & \vdots & 0 & \cdots & \cdots & \cdots \\
\mathbf{B}_{\kappa-1,0} & \cdots & \mathbf{B}_{\kappa-1,\kappa-1} & \mathbf{B}_{\kappa-1,\kappa} & 0 & \cdots & \cdots \\
0 & 0 & \mathbf{B}_{\kappa,\kappa-1} & \mathbf{B}_{\kappa,\kappa} & \mathbf{A}_0 & 0 & \cdots \\
0 & 0 & 0 & \mathbf{A}_2 & \mathbf{A}_1 & \mathbf{A}_0 & \cdots \\
0 & 0 & 0 & 0 & \mathbf{A}_2 & \mathbf{A}_1 & \cdots \\
\vdots & \vdots & \vdots & \vdots & \vdots & \vdots & \ddots
\end{pmatrix}. \quad (17.3)$$

From a CTMC with the above generator matrix, we can compute the steady-state probabilities $\underline{p}$ by solving the usual global balance equations (GBEs):

$$\underline{p}\mathbf{Q} = \underline{0}, \text{ and } \sum_i p_i = 1, \quad (17.4)$$

where the right part is a normalisation to make sure that all the probabilities sum to 1. First, we partition $\underline{p}$ according to the levels, i.e., $\underline{p} = (\underline{z}_0, \underline{z}_1, \cdots, \underline{z}_{\kappa-1}, \underline{z}_\kappa, \underline{z}_{\kappa+1}, \cdots)$. Substituting this in (17.4) we obtain the following system of linear equations:

$$\begin{cases}
i = 0, \cdots, \kappa-2 : & \sum_{j=0}^{\kappa-1} \underline{z}_j \mathbf{B}_{j,i} = \underline{0}, & \text{(a)} \\
i = \kappa-1 : & \sum_{j=0}^{\kappa} \underline{z}_j \mathbf{B}_{j,i} = \underline{0}, & \text{(b)} \\
i = \kappa : & \sum_{j=\kappa-1}^{\kappa+1} \underline{z}_j \mathbf{B}_{j,i} = \underline{0}, & \text{(c)} \\
i = \kappa+1, \cdots : & \sum_{j=0}^{2} \underline{z}_{i+j-1} \mathbf{A}_j = \underline{0}, & \text{(d)} \\
\text{normalisation} : & \sum_{i=0}^{\infty} \underline{z}_i \cdot \underline{1} = 1. & \text{(e)}
\end{cases} \quad (17.5)$$

We now exploit the regular structure of the state space in the solution process in a similar way to that in Chapter 8. In particular, looking at (17.5(d)), it seems reasonable to *assume* that for the state probabilities $\underline{z}_i$, $i = \kappa, \kappa + 1, \cdots$, only the neighbouring levels are of importance, so that they can be expressed as:

$$\underline{z}_{\kappa+1} = \underline{z}_\kappa \mathbf{R}, \ \underline{z}_{\kappa+2} = \underline{z}_{\kappa+1} \mathbf{R} = \underline{z}_\kappa \mathbf{R}^2, \cdots, \tag{17.6}$$

or, equivalently,

$$\underline{z}_{\kappa+i} = \underline{z}_\kappa \mathbf{R}^i, i \in I\!N, \tag{17.7}$$

where $\mathbf{R}$ is a square $L \times L$ matrix relating the steady-state probability vector at level $\kappa + i$ to the steady-state probability vector at level $\kappa + i - 1$ $(i = 1, 2, \cdots)$. As we have seen for QBDs in Chapter 8, we know that this is true when the matrix $\mathbf{R}$ satisfies the matrix polynomial:

$$\mathbf{A}_0 + \mathbf{R}\mathbf{A}_1 + \mathbf{R}^2 \mathbf{A}_2 = \mathbf{0}. \tag{17.8}$$

We have discussed means to solve this matrix polynomial in Section 8.3.

When $i = \kappa$, (17.5(c)) can be rewritten to incorporate the above assumption, because $\underline{z}_{\kappa+1}$ can be written in terms of $\underline{z}_\kappa$ and $\mathbf{B}_{\kappa+1,\kappa} = \mathbf{A}_2$:

$$
\begin{aligned}
\sum_{j=\kappa-1}^{\kappa+1} \underline{z}_j \mathbf{B}_{j,\kappa} &= \underline{z}_{\kappa-1} \mathbf{B}_{\kappa-1,\kappa} + \underline{z}_\kappa \mathbf{B}_{\kappa,\kappa} + \underline{z}_{\kappa+1} \mathbf{B}_{\kappa+1,\kappa}, \\
&= \underline{z}_{\kappa-1} \mathbf{B}_{\kappa-1,\kappa} + \underline{z}_\kappa (\mathbf{B}_{\kappa,\kappa} + \mathbf{R}\mathbf{A}_2) = \underline{0}.
\end{aligned} \tag{17.9}
$$

With this substitution, (17.5(a–c)) comprises a system of $\kappa+1$ linear vector equations with as many unknown vectors. However, as these vectors are still dependent, the normalisation (17.5(e)) has to be integrated in it, to yield a unique solution. This normalisation can be written as follows:

$$
\begin{aligned}
\sum_{i=0}^{\infty} \underline{z}_i \cdot \underline{1} &= \sum_{i=0}^{\kappa-1} \underline{z}_i \cdot \underline{1} + \sum_{i=\kappa}^{\infty} \underline{z}_i \cdot \underline{1} = \sum_{i=0}^{\kappa-1} \underline{z}_i \cdot \underline{1} + \sum_{i=\kappa}^{\infty} (\underline{z}_\kappa \mathbf{R}^i) \cdot \underline{1} \\
&= \sum_{i=0}^{\kappa-1} \underline{z}_i \cdot \underline{1} + \underline{z}_\kappa \mathbf{R}^\kappa (\mathbf{I} - \mathbf{R})^{-1} \cdot \underline{1} = 1.
\end{aligned} \tag{17.10}
$$

We have mentioned means to solve this system of linear equations in Section 8.3; details about these solution techniques can be found in Section 15.1.

Regarding the stability of the modelled system, similar remarks apply as given in Section 8.2.3 for PH|PH|1 queueing systems; condition (8.23) can be validated once the matrices $\mathbf{A}_i$ have been computed.

# 17.4   iSPN specification and measure computation

In Section 17.4.1 we reflect on an algorithm to translate iSPNs to the underlying QBD processes. In Section 17.4.2 we then present a number of techniques to evaluate reward-based measures for iSPNs in an efficient way.

## 17.4.1   From iSPN to the underlying QBD

The translation of an iSPNs to the underlying QBD can in principle be performed with well-known algorithms for state-space generation, as discussed in Chapter 14. It should be noted, however, that iSPNs have an unbounded number of states so that a "standard" algorithm will not terminate. Instead, a proper translation algorithm should end when it recognises that it is exploring the state space in the repeating part. One practical problem that one encounters is that the stated requirements are not easily verified in general. When inhibitor arcs and enabling functions are allowed in their most general setting, the verification problem is even undecidable (see also [18]). Therefore, the given requirements should be interpreted as being sufficient to allow for the matrix-geometric solution. However, we are free to pose extra requirements, in order to ease the decision task, albeit possibly at the cost of less modelling flexibility. Taking these considerations into account, we decided on the following practical restrictions on iSPNs:

- input and output arcs connected to place $P_0$ may only have multiplicity one;

- marking dependent rates and weights on the contents of place $P_0$ and enabling functions using the marking of place $P_0$ are not allowed.

Up till now, these restrictions did not bother us in performance evaluation studies.

In the above restrictions, as well as in Section 17.2, we assumed that the identity of the place that may contain an unbounded number of tokens is known in advance. Indeed, when using iSPNs it is normally easy for a modeller to indicate its identity; the whole model is normally built around this place. On the other hand, place $P_0$ can also be recognised automatically. Since only for $P_0$ is the marking unbounded, place $P_0$ will not appear in any place invariant. Thus, given an iSPN, an invariant analysis as discussed in Section 14.2 will reveal the identity of $P_0$.

A final problem in the translation algorithm is the determination of the level number $\kappa$ where the repetition starts, in order to stop the state-space generation process timely. Although this is easy for a human being, doing this for instance "by inspection" of the upper left part of the partially generated matrix $\mathbf{Q}$, it is less easy to grasp in an algorithm.

However, given the above restrictions, we have been able to prove that once two successive levels are the same, all levels beyond these will also be the same. The 3-page proof, based on finite induction, goes beyond the scope of this book [97].

## 17.4.2 Efficient computation of reward-based measures

Once the steady-state probabilities are known, reward-based performance measures can be computed easily. Let $r : \mathcal{R} \to \mathbb{R}$ denote a real-valued reward function defined on the state space of the model. The steady-state expected reward is then computed as

$$E[X] = \sum_{i=0}^{\infty} \sum_{\underline{m} \in \mathcal{R}'(i)} z_{i,\underline{m}} r(i, \underline{m}). \qquad (17.11)$$

Without any further restrictions on the form of $r(i, \underline{m})$ we cannot further reduce the above expression. Thus, to compute $E[X]$ in such cases, we start the infinite summation and continue to add more terms until the additional terms are smaller than a certain threshold. Assuming that all rewards are positive, we thus compute a lower bound on the actual expected reward.

There are, however, quite a number of reward-based measures that are of general interest and that can be computed more efficiently, without involving infinite summations. We discuss a number of these special cases below.

### Reward function only depending on the level

If the reward function only depends on the level number and not on the inter-level state, that is, if $r(i, \underline{m}) = r(i, \underline{m}')$, for all $i \in \mathbb{N}$ and for all $\underline{m}, \underline{m}' \in \mathcal{R}'(i)$, we may write $r(i, \underline{m}) = r(i)$. Note that this type of reward-based measure typically concerns the unbounded place $P_0$, when computing

- the probability that the number of tokens in $P_0$ is above a certain threshold $l$, we set $r(i) = \mathbf{1}\{P_0 > l\}$;

- the probability that $P_0$ contains exactly $l$ tokens, we set $r(i) = \mathbf{1}\{P_0 = l\}$;

- the expected number of tokens in $P_0$, we set $r(i) = i$.

For these cases, we can write:

$$E[X] = \sum_{i=0}^{\infty} r(i)(\underline{z_i} \cdot \underline{1})$$

$$
\begin{aligned}
&= \sum_{i=0}^{\kappa-1} r(i)(\underline{z}_i \cdot \underline{1}) + \sum_{i=\kappa}^{\infty} r(i)(\underline{z}_i \cdot \underline{1}) \\
&= \underbrace{\sum_{i=0}^{\kappa-1} r(i)(\underline{z}_i \cdot \underline{1})}_{LT} + \sum_{j=0}^{\infty} r(j)(\underline{z}_\kappa \mathbf{R}^{\kappa+j} \cdot \underline{1}).
\end{aligned} \tag{17.12}
$$

The first, finite, sum does not comprise a problem. We now concentrate on the second sum for each of the measures identified above:

- When $r(i) = \mathbf{1}\{P_0 = l\}$ the infinite summation contains at most one non-zero term, so that we have:

$$
E[X] = LT + \underline{z}_l \cdot \underline{1}. \tag{17.13}
$$

- If we want to compute the probability that $P_0$ contains more than $l$ tokens, this can be rewritten as 1 minus the probability that $P_0$ contains at most $l-1$ tokens. Thus, the infinite summation also reduces to a finite one.

- A more complex case arises when $r(i) = i$; however, here also a closed-form expression can be derived:

$$
\begin{aligned}
E[X] &= \sum_{i=0}^{\kappa-1} i(\underline{z}_i \cdot \underline{1}) + \sum_{j=0}^{\infty} (\kappa+j)(\underline{z}_\kappa \mathbf{R}^j \cdot \underline{1}) \\
&= \sum_{i=0}^{\kappa-1} i(\underline{z}_i \cdot \underline{1}) + \sum_{j=0}^{\infty} \kappa(\underline{z}_\kappa \mathbf{R}^j \cdot \underline{1}) + \sum_{j=0}^{\infty} j(\underline{z}_\kappa \mathbf{R}^j \cdot \underline{1}) \\
&= \sum_{i=0}^{\kappa-1} i(\underline{z}_i \cdot \underline{1}) + \kappa \underline{z}_\kappa \left( \sum_{j=0}^{\infty} \mathbf{R}^j \right) \underline{1} + \underline{z}_\kappa \mathbf{R} \left( \sum_{j=0}^{\infty} j \mathbf{R}^{j-1} \right) \underline{1} \\
&= \sum_{i=0}^{\kappa-1} i(\underline{z}_i \cdot \underline{1}) + \kappa \underline{z}_\kappa \left( \sum_{j=0}^{\infty} \mathbf{R}^j \right) \underline{1} + \underline{z}_\kappa \mathbf{R} \frac{d}{d\mathbf{R}} \left( (\mathbf{I} - \mathbf{R})^{-1} \right) \underline{1} \\
&= \sum_{i=0}^{\kappa-1} i(\underline{z}_i \cdot \underline{1}) + \left( \underline{z}_\kappa (\mathbf{I} - \mathbf{R})^{-1} (\kappa \mathbf{I} + \mathbf{R}(\mathbf{I} - \mathbf{R})^{-1}) \right) \cdot \underline{1}. \tag{17.14}
\end{aligned}
$$

**Reward function independent of level and $P_0$**

When computing mean place occupancies for places other than $P_0$, the rewards depend on $\underline{m}$ rather than on $i$: $r(i, \underline{m}) = r(\underline{m})$, irrespective of $i$. We start with the general reward-based expression:

$$
E[X] = \sum_{i=0}^{\infty} \sum_{\underline{m} \in \mathcal{R}'(i)} z_{i,\underline{m}} r(i, \underline{m})
$$

$$= \sum_{i=0}^{\kappa-1} \underbrace{\sum_{\underline{m} \in \mathcal{R}'(i)} z_{i,\underline{m}} r(i,\underline{m})}_{LT} + \sum_{i=\kappa}^{\infty} \sum_{\underline{m} \in \mathcal{R}'(i)} z_{i,\underline{m}} r(i,\underline{m}). \qquad (17.15)$$

The left additive term LT again does not cause problems. The right term can be reduced considerably by changing the summation order and using the fact that the rewards are level-independent as follows:

$$E[X] = LT + \sum_{\underline{m} \in \mathcal{R}'(\kappa)} r(\underline{m}) \sum_{i=\kappa}^{\infty} z_{i,\underline{m}}$$

$$= LT + \sum_{\underline{m} \in \mathcal{R}'(\kappa)} r(\underline{m}) \sum_{i=0}^{\infty} (\underline{z}_{\kappa} \mathbf{R}^i) \cdot \underline{e}_{\underline{m}}, \qquad (17.16)$$

where $\underline{e}_{\underline{m}}$ is a vector with a single one at its $\underline{m}$-th position. The right-most sum can be reduced, yielding:

$$E[X] = LT + \sum_{\underline{m} \in \mathcal{R}'(\kappa)} r(\underline{m}) \underline{z}_{\kappa} (\mathbf{I} - \mathbf{R})^{-1} \underline{e}_{\underline{m}}. \qquad (17.17)$$

Similar expressions are obtained when computing the probability that the number of tokens in a certain place (unequal $P_0$) is larger or smaller than a threshold $l$.

## 17.5  Application studies

To demonstrate the usability of iSPNs we present three small application examples. We present a queueing model with delayed service in Section 17.5.1; this model is so simple that we can solve it explicitly. We then continue with two more realistic models: a model of a connection management mechanism in Section 17.5.2 and a model of a queueing system with checkpointing and recovery in Section 17.5.3.

### 17.5.1  A queueing model with delayed service

Considers a single server queueing system (see Figure 17.3) at which customers arrive as a Poisson process with rate $\lambda$ via transition **arr** and are served with rate $\mu$ via transition **serve**. Before service, arriving customers are stored in a **buffer**. Service is not immediately granted to an arriving customer, even if the server is idle at that time (a token in place **sleep**). Only after there are at least $T$ (for threshold) customers queued does the server awake and start its duties. This is enforced by an enabling function associated with the immediate transition **wake-up**: $\#\text{buffer} \geq T$. The server subsequently remains awake until the buffer becomes empty, after which it resumes sleeping.

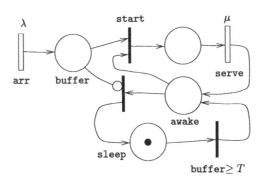

Figure 17.3: iSPN of a single server queueing system with delayed service

For a threshold $T = 3$, the corresponding CTMC is given in Figure 17.4. From the models, it can easily be seen that they fulfill requirements 1–3 with $\kappa = T = 3$. The generator matrix has the following form:

$$
Q = \begin{pmatrix}
-\Sigma & \lambda & 0 & 0 & 0 & 0 & 0 & \cdots \\
0 & -\Sigma & 0 & \lambda & 0 & 0 & 0 & \cdots \\
\mu & 0 & -\Sigma & 0 & \lambda & 0 & 0 & \cdots \\
0 & 0 & 0 & -\Sigma & 0 & \lambda & 0 & \cdots \\
0 & 0 & \mu & 0 & -\Sigma & \lambda & 0 & \cdots \\
0 & 0 & 0 & 0 & \mu & -\Sigma & \lambda & \cdots \\
0 & 0 & 0 & 0 & 0 & \mu & -\Sigma & \cdots \\
0 & 0 & 0 & 0 & 0 & 0 & \mu & \cdots \\
\vdots & \vdots & \vdots & \vdots & \vdots & \vdots & \vdots & \ddots
\end{pmatrix},
$$

where $\Sigma$ is chosen such that the row sums equal 0. From this matrix we observe that the A-matrices are in fact scalars or $1 \times 1$ matrices: $\mathbf{A}_0 = (\lambda)$, $\mathbf{A}_1 = (-(\lambda+\mu))$ and $\mathbf{A}_2 = (\mu)$. From these matrices we derive $\mu\mathbf{R}^2 - (\lambda + \mu)\mathbf{R} + \lambda = 0$ for which the only valid solution is $\mathbf{R} = (\lambda/\mu)$. From this, it once again becomes clear that $\mathbf{R}$ takes over the role of $\rho$ in simpler queueing analysis, such as in the M|M|1 queue.

Denoting $\underline{z}_i = z_i$, for $i = 0$ or $i = 3, 4, \cdots$, and $\underline{z}_i = (z_{i,S}, z_{i,A})$, for $i = 2, 3$, the boundary

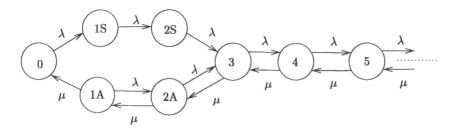

Figure 17.4: QBD of the single server queueing system with delayed service in case $T = 3$

equations, including the normalisation equation, become:

$$\begin{cases} -\lambda z_0 + \mu z_{1A} = 0, \\ \lambda z_0 - \lambda z_{1S} = 0, \\ -(\lambda + \mu)z_{1A} + \mu z_{2A} = 0, \\ \lambda z_{1S} - \lambda z_{2S} = 0, \\ \lambda z_{1A} - (\lambda + \mu)z_{2A} + \mu z_3 = 0, \\ \lambda z_{2S} + \lambda z_{2A} - (\lambda + \mu)z_3 + \mu z_4 = 0, \\ z_0 + z_{1S} + z_{1A} + z_{2S} + z_{2A} + z_3(1 - \rho)^{-1} = 1. \end{cases} \qquad (17.18)$$

As a numerical example, consider the case where $\lambda = 2$, $\mu = 3$, $T = 3$ and, consequently, $\rho = 2/3$. The matrix-geometric solution results in the following boundary steady-state probabilities:

$$\begin{cases} z_0 = 0.11111, \quad z_{1A} = 0.07407, \quad z_{1S} = 0.11111, \\ z_{2A} = 0.12346, \quad z_{2S} = 0.11111, \quad z_3 = 0.15638. \end{cases}$$

Using these probabilities, and $z_i = z_3 \rho^{i-3}$, $i = 4, 5, \cdots$, we obtain for the average number of customers in the system $E[N] = 3.00$.

## 17.5.2   Connection management in communication systems

An ATM/B-ISDN-based communication infrastructure offers a connection-oriented service. Via the ATM adaptation layers 3/4 and 5, connectionless services can also be provided [225, 251]. Packets arriving at the AAL service boundary to make use of such a service, suffer a possible delay from the connection establishment at the ATM service boundary, unless there already exists a connection when the packet arrives. Once the connection has been established, all buffered packets can be transmitted and the connection can be released. This can be done immediately, or with some delay. The former has the disadvantage that a connection is being maintained when it is not needed; however, it has the advantage

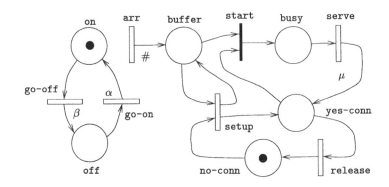

Figure 17.5: iSPN model of the OCDR mechanism

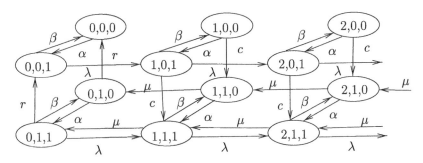

Figure 17.6: CTMC of the OCDR mechanism

that some packets might profit from the fact that there is still a connection when they arrive. Clearly, there is a trade-off between the release delay, the costs of maintaining an unused connection and the perceived performance (average delay). The above way of implementing connectionless services, has been proposed by Heijenk *et al.* [131] under the name "on-demand connection with delayed release" (OCDR).

An iSPN model for such a system is given in Figure 17.5. Packets arrive via transition **arr** and are placed in the **buffer**. The rate of transition **arr** is modulated by an independent on/off-model. A token in place **on** or **off** models the fact that the source is in a burst or not, respectively. When in a burst, packets are generated according to a Poisson process with rate $\lambda$ packets/second. When not in a burst, no packets are generated. The transitions **go-on** and **go-off**, with rates $\alpha$ and $\beta$ respectively, model the time durations the source remains in the off and on state. The service rate is $\mu$ Mbps and the average packet length is denoted $l$.

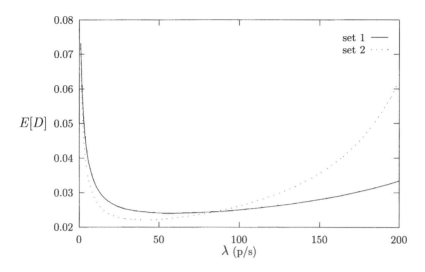

Figure 17.7: The expected delay $E[D]$ (in seconds) as a function of the arrival rate $\lambda$ in a burst

If the server is busy, there will be a token in place **busy** and arriving packets have to wait on their turn. If the server is idle, but there is no connection available, signified by a token in place **no-conn**, a connection will be established, causing a negative exponential delay with average length $1/c$ (transition **set-up**). Once there is a connection, normal packet transmissions can take place. Once the buffer is empty, the connection is released with a negative exponential delay with average length $1/r$ (transition **release**).

The corresponding CTMC is given in Figure 17.6. In this model, the states space $\mathcal{R} = \{(i, j, k) | i \in \mathbb{N}, j, k = 0, 1\}$. Parameter $i$ denotes the number of packets in the system, $j$ denotes whether there is a connection ($j = 1$) or not ($j = 0$), and $k$ denotes whether the arrival process is in a burst ($k = 1$) or not ($k = 0$). As can be seen from the CTMC, but as can also be verified using Requirements 1–3, this model has a structure that allows for a matrix-geometric solution. Every level consists of the $L = 4$ states with $i$ packets present, i.e., $\mathcal{R}(i) = \{(i, 0, 0), (i, 0, 1), (i, 1, 0), (i, 1, 1)\}$.

Clearly, $\kappa = 1$ and the boundary equations are given by the global balance equations for the first two levels, plus the normalisation equation, in total yielding a system of 8 linear equations. The $L \times L$ matrix $\mathbf{R}$ with $L = 4$ now has to be solved numerically.

Measures of interest we could address are: (i) the average node delay $E[D]$ (in seconds); (ii) the average reserved bandwidth $E[B_W]$ (in Mbps); and (ii) the expected number of connection establishments per second $E[C]$ (in per-second). All these quantities can be

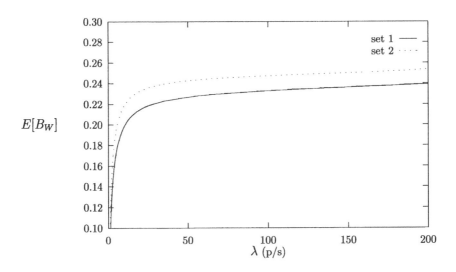

Figure 17.8: The expected bandwidth $E[B_W]$ (in Mbps) as a function of the arrival rate $\lambda$ in a burst

expressed in closed-form using $\mathbf{R}$ and the boundary vector $\underline{z}_0$ (for details, see [131]). Under the assumption that communication capacity can be claimed in various amounts, the service rate $\mu$ can be chosen freely. Given a certain workload, a higher requested transmission speed $\mu$ will yield smaller connection times, however, at higher costs per time unit. The parameter $\mu$ together with the connection release rate $r$ are therefore interesting quantities for controlling the system performance and cost.

Let us now turn to some numerical results. We assume that $\alpha = 1.0$, $\beta = 0.04$, $c = 10.0$, and $l = 10$ kbit. We address the following two combinations of transmission and release rates: $(\mu, r)_1 = (336.0, 1.0)$ and $(\mu, r)_2 = (236.0, 0.5)$. In the first case, the transmission speed is relatively high, but connections are rapidly released after usage. In the second case, a lower transmission speed is used, but a connection is maintained longer. Therefore, arriving packets have a smaller probability of experiencing an extra connection setup delay.

In Figure 17.7 we depict the expected delay $E[D]$ (in seconds) as a function of the arrival rate $\lambda$ in a burst. Although for $\lambda \approx 85$ the average delay values coincide ($E[D] \approx 0.0245$), for changing $\lambda$ this is certainly not the case. For the first parameter set, the average delay is less sensitive to changes in $\lambda$, especially towards higher values. For smaller values of $\lambda$, the average delay is smaller for parameter set 2. Surprisingly, the less sensitive solution requires a smaller average bandwidth as well, as illustrated in Figure 17.8. The number of connection establishments, however, is higher, as illustrated by Figure 17.9. Since the

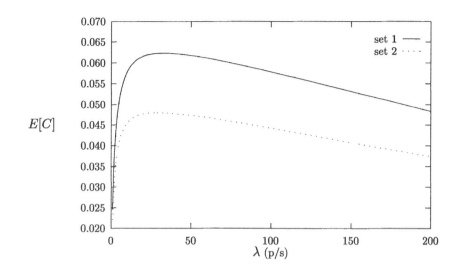

Figure 17.9: The expected connection setup rate $E[C]$ (in s$^{-1}$) as a function of the arrival rate $\lambda$ in a burst

latter can also be associated with costs in a B-ISDN context, the price for the less sensitive delay behaviour and for the smaller bandwidth consumption is paid here. Also observe, that for higher traffic, the number of connection establishments decreases, i.e., a connection that is once established, is used for a long time since the probability of having a connection and no packets present decreases with larger $\lambda$.

## 17.5.3   A queueing system with checkpointing and recovery

In this section we present an analysis of the time to complete tasks on systems that change their structure in the course of time (multi-mode systems). The task-completion time of jobs on multi-mode systems has been studied by several authors. Bobbio describes the completion-time problem as the time-to-absorption problem in a CTMC with an absorbing state [22]. Chimento and Trivedi consider different types of failures that can occur as well as different ways in which failed services might be resumed [46]. The above studies aim at the completion time distribution of single jobs; effects of queueing, due to congestion, are not taken into account. In [220] the performance of a queueing system in which the server is subject to breakdowns and repairs is studied, so that queueing *is* taken into account. Typically, variants of queues of M|G|1 type are studied, where, depending on the status of the server, jobs experience a delay in the queueing system. Related models occur when

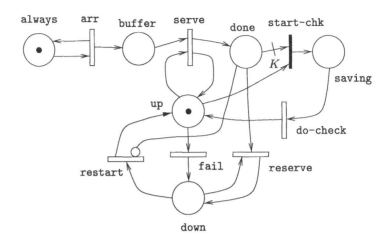

Figure 17.10: iSPN of the transaction processing system model with checkpointing and recovery

studying the effect of checkpointing strategies on the performance of computer systems that are subject to failures and repairs [40, 221, 237]. When increasing the checkpointing frequency, the amount of overhead increases; however, the amount of work to be done after a failure and subsequent rollback, i.e., the actual recovery time, decreases. This interesting trade-off has lead researchers to study the optimality of checkpointing strategies in various situations.

To illustrate the use of iSPNs we address a job completion-time problem taking into account queueing. We consider a simple model of a transaction processing system where jobs (transactions) arrive in a buffer. A single server is normally available to process these jobs. After $K$ jobs have been processed, a checkpoint is made. We refer to $K$ as the checkpointing interval. When making a checkpoint, the server is unable to serve other jobs. When the server is idle or processing ordinary jobs, it might fail. Once the server has failed, it requires a repair after which it needs to re-serve all the jobs that were processed since the last checkpoint. After that, the server becomes available for ordinary job processing. For simplicity, it is assumed that the server cannot fail when it is checkpointing or recovering. This assumption can be changed without altering the fundamental solution approach proposed here. Also, it is assumed that the service times, the checkpointing time and the repair time are exponentially distributed and that the arrivals form a Poisson process. The corresponding iSPN is depicted in Figure 17.10. In Table 17.1 we summarise the meaning of the places and transitions.

| place | meaning | init |
|---|---|---|
| buffer | input queue of jobs | 0 |
| up | server available | 1 |
| down | server down and recovering | 0 |
| done | number of jobs processed since last checkpoint | 0 |
| saving | server making a checkpoint | 0 |
| always | infinite source of jobs | 1 |
| transition | meaning | rate |
| arr | arrivals | $\lambda$ |
| serve | services | $\mu$ |
| reserve | recovery | $\mu$ |
| fail | failures | $\phi$ |
| do-check | checkpointing | $\sigma$ |
| restart | put into normal operation | $\beta$ |
| start-chk | start checkpointing | 1 |

Table 17.1: Places and transitions in the iSPN describing the job completion time problem including queueing aspects

Interesting reward-based performance measures are, among others, the average number of jobs queued, the average number of jobs that has not yet been checkpointed, the percentage of time that the processor is available for normal processing and the probability that the buffer is empty (or not), all as a function of the checkpointing interval $K$.

We have evaluated the above described model for three different scenarios (see Table 17.2) for varying checkpointing intervals $K$. First notice that the number of (tangible) states in the repeating levels equals $2K + 1$. This can be explained as follows. As long as the system is up, i.e., there is a token in place **up**, there can be 0 through $K - 1$ tokens in place **done**. When the $K$-th token arrives in place **done**, transition **start-chk** fires, yielding a single token in place **saving**, and none in **up**. This makes $K + 1$ different states already. Then, when the server is down, i.e., when there is a token in place **down**, there are up to $K - 1$ possible tokens in place **done**, thus making up another $K$ different situations. In total, this yields $2K + 1$ states per level. As a consequence of this, the matrices $\mathbf{A}_i$ and $\mathbf{R}$ have dimension $(2K+1) \times (2K+1)$. Since these matrices in principle remain transparent to the modeller, this is not a problem at all; however, the construction of these matrices

|   | 1 | 2 | 2 |
|---|------|------|------|
| $\lambda$ | 5.0 | 6.5 | 8.0 |
| $\mu$ | 10 | 10 | 10 |
| $\phi$ | 0.13 | 0.13 | 0.25 |
| $\sigma$ | 21.0 | 21.0 | 21.0 |
| $\beta$ | 11.0 | 11.0 | 11.0 |

Table 17.2: Parameters used in the three scenarios

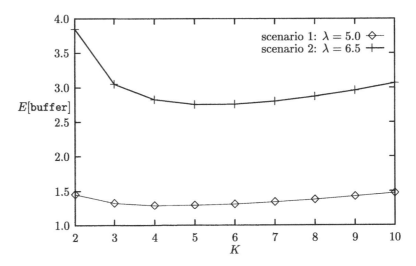

Figure 17.11: The expected buffer occupancy as a function of the checkpointing interval $K$

"by hand" would have been very impractical.

Studying the model reveals that the level number $\kappa$ at which the repeating structure begins is 1. This implies that the boundary equations comprise a system of $(4K + 2)$ linear equations. Consequently, the state probabilities for levels 0 and 1 are computed directly, including their normalisation, after which state probabilities for higher levels can be computed recursively.

In Figure 17.11 we present the expected buffer occupancy $E[\texttt{buffer}]$ as a function of the checkpointing interval $K$ for two values of the job arrival rate $\lambda$ (we compare scenarios 1 and 2 here). As can be observed, the buffer occupancy is higher for a more heavily loaded system, for all $K$. Interestingly, the curves show a pronounced minimum for $K = 4$

(scenario 1) or $K = 5$ (scenario 2); a choice of $K$ too small causes the system to make checkpoints too often (checkpoints take an amount of time that is independent of $K$), thus losing processing capacity. On the other hand, if only very few checkpoints are made, the recovery process, which requires the reprocessing of not-yet-checkpointed jobs plus the restart delay, will be longer. As such, this figure clearly illustrates the trade-off that exists in designing rollback/recovery schemes.

Then, in Figure 17.12, we present the percentage of time the server is making checkpoints ($E[\text{saving}]$), as well as the expected time the server is re-serving unchecked jobs after a failure has occurred plus the expected restart time ($E[\text{down}]$), again for scenarios 1 and 2. The latter quantity is almost the same for both scenarios and therefore drawn as a single line; since failures occur almost randomly, the number of unchecked jobs is almost the same in both cases, so that the percentage of time the server is actively recovering is also almost the same. The fact that the computed values for this probability are not exactly alike lies in the fact that the server can only fail when it is serving regular jobs or when it is idle. Since in scenario 2 the job arrival rate is larger than in scenario 1, the server is slightly more busy making checkpoints and therefore is slightly less failure prone. Therefore, in scenario 2 this probability is slightly smaller but the difference is at most $10^{-3}$. The other two curves show the decreasing percentage of time the server is busy making checkpoints when $K$ increases. As expected, in scenario 1 there is less load, so there is less checkpointing required.

We finally increase the job arrival rate to 8.0, as indicated in scenario 3. For this scenario we show two probabilities in Figure 17.13, again as a function of $K$. First notice that for $K = 2$ the system is not stable any more. This can be understood as follows. The percentage of time needed for normal processing equals $\lambda/\mu = 8/10 = 80\%$. On top of that comes, for $K = 2$, half a checkpointing time per job, requiring another $4/21 \approx 19.04\%$ capacity of the server. Taking into account the non-zero probability of failure, and the extra work required when failures occur, it becomes clear that the server cannot do all the work when $K = 2$.

Let us now address the cases where the system is stable. The upper curve shows the probability that the buffer is non-empty. As can be seen, this probability ranges around 95%. Here we see similar behaviour to that of the expected buffer occupancy. There is a pronounced minimum for $K = 6$. For $K < 6$, the server is making too many checkpoints. This extra work is not earned back by the shorter recovery time that results. On the other hand, for $K > 6$, the recovery times become larger so that the gain of less checkpointing overhead is lost. The lower curve shows the probability that the server is available for regular processing or for being idle, i.e., the probability that the server is not making

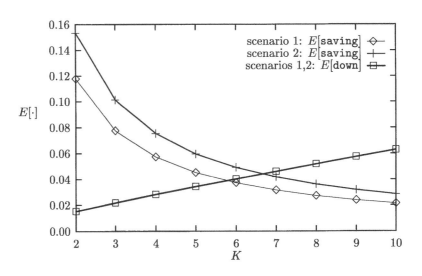

Figure 17.12: The percentage of time spent making checkpoints and the percentage of time recovering as a function of the checkpointing interval $K$

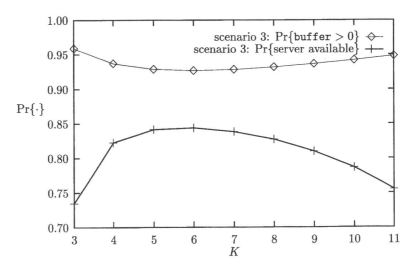

Figure 17.13: The probability of actual server availability and the probability of the buffer being non-empty as a function of the checkpointing interval $K$

checkpoints nor is recovering. Also here a choice of $K$ too small or too large yields a loss in performance.

## 17.6    Further reading

One-place unbounded SPNs were described in the mid-1980s by Florin and Natkin [92, 93, 94]. Haverkort proposed the more general class of iSPNs (not yet named as such) in [118], after which a software tool, named SPN2MGM, supporting the construction and evaluation of iSPNs was reported in [125]. The M.Sc. students Klein [158] and Frank [97] contributed to the development of SPN2MGM. Haverkort and Ost reported on the efficiency of the matrix-geometric solution method as compared to the spectral expansion method, using the model of Section 17.5.3 in [119]. In that paper, models with block sizes up to hundreds of states are addressed. The OCDR mechanism was introduced by Heijenk [131] and evaluated by Heijenk and Haverkort [132]. Recently, Ost *et al.* extended the OCDR model to include non-exponential connection-setup and -release times [226].

## 17.7    Exercises

### 17.1. OCDR model.
Extend the OCDR model of Figure 17.5 such that it includes:

- hyper-exponential or Erlangian connection-setup times;

- hyper-exponential or Erlangian connection-release times.

Discuss how the size of the levels changes due to the model changes. In the last case, be careful to reset the state of the connection-release places and transitions when a new job arrives before the connection-release time has completely expired. For details, see also [226].

Which of the two types of distributions do you think is more appropriate to model the setup- and release-times?

### 17.2. OCDR model with Poisson arrivals.
Consider the OCDR model of Figure 17.5 when the arrivals form a pure Poisson process.

1. Find the $2 \times 2$ matrices $\mathbf{A}_0$, $\mathbf{A}_1$ and $\mathbf{A}_2$ in symbolic form.

2. Explicitly solve the quadratic matrix equation and show that the matrix $\mathbf{R}$ has the following form:
$$\mathbf{R} = \begin{pmatrix} \frac{\lambda}{\lambda+c} & \frac{\lambda}{\mu} \\ 0 & \frac{\lambda}{\mu} \end{pmatrix}.$$

### 17.3. Checkpointing models.

Extend the model of Figure 17.10 such that:

- it includes system failures during the checkpointing process;

- checkpoints are made after $K$ jobs or after the expiration of a timer, whichever comes first. Model the timer as an Erlang-$l$ distribution.

### 17.4. Two queues in series.

Reconsider the two queues in series, as addressed in Exercise 8.4. Model this queueing system using iSPNs.

### 17.5. Polling models.

Consider a Markovian polling model with $N$ stations. Under which conditions can such a model be regarded as an iSPN (see also Exercise 8.5). Construct such an iSPN for $N = 3$ stations and 2-limited scheduling.

# Part V

# Simulation

# Chapter 18

# Simulation: methodology and statistics

In the previous chapters we have addressed models that can be solved by analytical or numerical means. Although the class of addressed models has been very wide, there are still models that cannot be solved adequately with the presented techniques. These models, however, can still be analysed using simulation. With simulation there are no fundamental restrictions towards what models can be solved. Practical restrictions do exist since the amount of computer time or memory required for running a simulation can be prohibitively large.

In this chapter we concentrate on the general set-up of simulations as well as on the statistical aspects of simulation studies. To compare the concept of simulation with analytical and numerical techniques we discuss the application of simulation for the computation of an integral in Section 18.1. Various forms of simulation are then classified in Section 18.2. Implementation aspects for so-called discrete event simulations are discussed in Section 18.3. In order to execute simulation programs, realisations of random variables have to be generated. This is an important task that deserves special attention since a wrong or biased number generation scheme can severely corrupt the outcome of a simulation. Random number generation is therefore considered in section 18.4. The gathering of measurements from the simulation and their processing is finally discussed in Section 18.5.

## 18.1  The idea of simulation

Consider the following mathematical problem. One has to obtain the (unknown) area $\alpha$ under the curve $y = f(x) = x^2$, from $x = 0$ to $x = 1$. Let $\tilde{a}$ denote the result of the calculation we perform to obtain this value. Since $f(x)$ is a simple quadratic term, this problem can easily be solved *analytically*:

$$\tilde{a} = \int_0^1 x^2 dx = \left(\frac{1}{3}x^3\right)_{x=0}^{x=1} = \frac{1}{3}. \tag{18.1}$$

Clearly, in this case, the calculated value $\tilde{a}$ is exactly the same as the real value $\alpha$.

Making the problem somewhat more complicated, we can pose the same question when $f(x) = x^{\sin x}$. Now, we cannot solve the problem analytically any more (as far as we have consulted integration tables). We can, however, resort to a numerical technique such as the trapezoid rule. We then have to split the interval $[0, 1]$ into $n$ consecutive intervals $[x_0, x_1], [x_1, x_2], \cdots, [x_{n-1}, x_n]$ so that the area under the curve can be approximated as:

$$\tilde{a} = \frac{1}{2}\sum_{i=1}^{n}(x_i - x_{i-1})(f(x_i) + f(x_{i-1})). \tag{18.2}$$

By making the intervals sufficiently small $\tilde{a}$ will approximate $a$ with any level of desired accuracy. This is an example of a *numerical* solution technique.

Surprisingly, we can also obtain a reasonable estimate $\tilde{a}$ for $\alpha$ by means of *stochastic simulation*. Studying $f(x) = x^{\sin x}$ on the interval $[0, 1]$, we see that $0 \le f(x) \le 1$. Taking two random samples $x_i$ and $y_i$ from the uniform distribution on $[0, 1]$, can be interpreted as picking a random point in the unit-square $\{(x, y)|0 \le x \le 1, \ 0 \le y \le 1\}$. Repeating this $N$ times, the variables $n_i = \mathbf{1}\{y_i \le f(x_i)\}$ indicate whether the $i$-point lies below $f(x)$, or not. Then, the value

$$\tilde{a} = \frac{1}{N}\sum_{i=1}^{N}n_i, \tag{18.3}$$

estimates the area $a$.

In trying to obtain $\alpha$ by means of a so-called *Monte Carlo simulation* we should keep track of the accuracy of the obtained results. Since $\tilde{a}$ is obtained as a function of a number of realisations of random variables, $\tilde{a}$ is itself a realisation of a random variable (which we denote as $\tilde{A}$). The random variable $\tilde{A}$ is often called the *estimator*, whereas the realisation $\tilde{a}$ is called the *estimate*. The random variable $\tilde{A}$ should be defined such that it obeys a number of properties, otherwise the estimate $\tilde{a}$ cannot be guaranteed to be accurate:

- $\tilde{A}$ should be *unbiased*, meaning that $E[\tilde{A}] = a$;

- $\tilde{A}$ should be *consistent*, meaning that the more samples we take, the more accurate the estimate $\tilde{a}$ becomes.

We will come back to these properties in Section 18.5. From the simulation we can compute an estimate for the variance of the estimator $\tilde{A}$ as follows:

$$\tilde{\sigma}^2 = \frac{1}{N(N-1)} \sum_{i=1}^{N} (n_i - \tilde{a})^2 . \tag{18.4}$$

Note that this estimator should not be confused with the esimator for the variance of a single sample, which is $N$ times larger; see also Section 18.5.2 and [231]. Now we can apply *Chebyshev's inequality*, which states that for any $\beta > 0$

$$\Pr\{|\tilde{A} - \tilde{a}| \geq \beta\} \leq \frac{\tilde{\sigma}^2}{\beta^2}. \tag{18.5}$$

In words, it states that the probability that $\tilde{A}$ deviates more than $\beta$ from the estimated value $\tilde{a}$, is at most equal to the quotient of $\tilde{\sigma}^2$ and $\beta$. The smaller the allowed deviation is, the weaker the bound on the probability. Rewriting (18.5) by setting $\delta = 1 - \tilde{\sigma}^2/\beta^2$ and $\tilde{\sigma} = \sqrt{\tilde{\sigma}^2}$, we obtain

$$\Pr\{|\tilde{A} - \tilde{a}| \leq \frac{\tilde{\sigma}}{\sqrt{1-\delta}}\} \geq \delta. \tag{18.6}$$

This equation tells us that $\tilde{A}$ deviates at most $\tilde{\sigma}/\sqrt{1-\delta}$ from $\tilde{a}$, with a probability of at least $\delta$. In this expression, we would like $\delta$ to be relatively large, e.g., 0.99. Then, $\sqrt{1-\delta} = 0.1$, so that $\Pr\{|\tilde{A} - \tilde{a}| \leq 10\tilde{\sigma}\} \geq 0.99$. In order to let this inequality have high significance, we must make sure that the term "$10\tilde{\sigma}$" is small. This can be accomplished by making many observations.

It is important to note that when there is an analytical solution available for a particular problem, this analytical solution typically gives far more insight than the numerical answers obtained from a simulation. Individual simulation results only give information about a particular solution to a problem, and not at all over the range of possible solutions, nor do they give insight into the sensitivity of the solution to changes in one or more of the model parameters.

## 18.2   Classifying simulations

In this section we will classify simulations according to two criteria: their state space and their time evolution. Note that we used the same classification criteria when discussing stochastic processes in Chapter 3.

In *continuous-event simulations*, systems are studied in which the state continuously changes with time. Typically, these systems are physical processes that can be described by

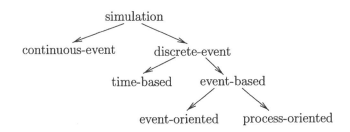

Figure 18.1: Classifying simulations

systems of differential equations with boundary conditions. The numerical solution of such a system of differential equations is sometimes called a simulation. In physical systems, time is a continuous parameter, although one can also observe systems at predefined time instances only, yielding a discrete time parameter. We do not further address continuous-state simulations, as we did not consider continuous-state stochastic processes.

More appropriate for our aims are *discrete-event simulations* (DES). In discrete-event simulations the state changes take place at discrete points in time. Again we can either take time as a continuous or as a discrete parameter. Depending on the application at hand, one of the two can be more or less suitable. In the discussions to follow we will assume that we deal with time as a continuous parameter.

In Figure 18.1 we show the discussed classification, together with some sub-classifications that follow below.

## 18.3   Implementation of discrete-event simulations

Before going into implementation details of discrete-event simulations, we first define some terminology in Section 18.3.1. We then present time-based simulations in Section 18.3.2 and event-based simulations in Section 18.3.3. We finally discuss implementation strategies for event-based discrete-event simulations in Section 18.3.4.

### 18.3.1   Terminology

The *simulation time* or *simulated time* of a simulation is the value of the parameter "time" that is used in the simulation program, which corresponds to the value of the time that would have been valid in the real system. The *run time* is the time it takes to execute a simulation program. Difference is often made between *wall-clock time* and *process time*;

the former includes any operating system overhead, whereas the latter includes only the required CPU, and possibly I/O time, for the simulation process.

In a discrete-event system, the state will change over time. The cause of a state variable change is called an *event*. Very often the state changes themselves are also called events. Since we consider simulations in which events take place one-by-one, that is, discrete in time, we speak of discrete-event simulations. In fact, it is because events in a discrete-event system happen one-by-one that discrete-event simulations are so much easier to handle than simulations of continuous-events systems. In discrete-event simulations we "jump" from event to event and it is the ordering of events and their relative timing we are interested in, because this exactly describes the performance of the simulated system. In a simulation program we will therefore mimic all the events. By keeping track of all these events and their timing, we are able to derive measures such as the average inter-event time or the average time between specific pairs of events. These then form the basis for the computation of performance estimates.

## 18.3.2   Time-based simulation

In a *time-based simulation* (also often called *synchronous simulation*) the main control loop of the simulation controls the time progress in constant steps. At the beginning of this control loop the time $t$ is increased by a step $\Delta t$ to $t + \Delta t$, with $\Delta t$ small. Then it is checked whether any events have happened in the time interval $[t, t + \Delta t]$. If so, these events will be executed, that is, the state will be changed according to these events, before the next cycle of the loop starts. It is assumed that the ordering of the events within the interval $[t, t + \Delta t]$ is not of importance and that these events are independent. The number of events that happened in the interval $[t, t + \Delta t]$ may change from time to time. When $t$ rises above some maximum, the simulation stops. In Figure 18.2 a diagram of the actions to be performed in a time-based simulation is given.

Time-based simulation is easy to implement. The implementation closely resembles the implementation of numerical methods for solving differential equations. However, there are some drawbacks associated with this method as well. Both the assumption that the ordering of events within an interval $[t, t + \Delta t]$ is not important and the assumption that these events are independent require that $\Delta t$ be sufficiently small, in order to minimize the probability of occurrence of mutually dependent events. For this reason, we normally have to take $\Delta t$ so small that the resulting simulation becomes very inefficient. Many very short time-steps will have to be performed without any event occurring at all. For these reasons time-based simulations are not often employed.

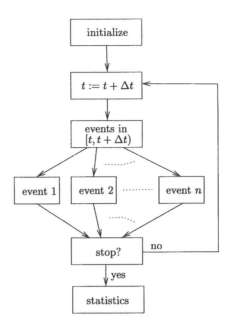

Figure 18.2: Diagram of the actions to be taken in a time-based simulation

## Example 18.1. A time-based M|M|1 simulation program.

As an example, we present the framework of a time-based simulation program for an M|M|1 queue with arrival rate $\lambda$ and service rate $\mu$. In this program, we use two state variables: $N_s \in \{0, 1\}$ denoting the number of jobs in service, and $N_q \in \mathbb{N}$ denoting the number of jobs queued. Notice that there is a slight redundancy in these two variables since $N_q > 0 \Rightarrow N_s = 1$. The aim of the simulation program is to generate a list of time-instances and the state variables at these instances. The variable $\Delta$ is assumed to be sufficiently small. Furthermore, we have to make use of a function $\mathtt{draw}(p)$, which evaluates to $\mathtt{true}$ with probability $p$ and to $\mathtt{false}$ with probability $1 - p$; see also Section 18.4.

The resulting program is presented in Figure 18.3. After the initialisation (lines 1–3), the main program loop starts. First, the time is updated (line 6). If during the period $[t, t + \Delta t)$ an arrival has taken place, which happens with probability $\lambda \cdot \Delta t$ in a Poisson process with rate $\lambda$, we have to increase the number of jobs in the queue (line 7). Then, we check whether there is a job in service. If not, the just arrived job enters the server (lines 13–14). If there is already a job in service, we verify whether its service has ended in the last interval (line 9). If so, the counter $N_s$ is set to 0 (line 12), unless there is another job waiting to be served (line 10); in that case a job is taken out of the queue and the server

```
1.   input (λ, μ, tₘₐₓ)
2.   t := 0
3.   Nₛ := 0;  N_q := 0
4.   while t < tₘₐₓ
5.   do
6.       t := t + Δt
7.       if draw(λ · Δt) then N_q := N_q + 1
8.       if Nₛ = 1
9.       then if draw(μ · Δt)
10.          then if N_q > 0
11.               then N_q := N_q − 1
12.               else Nₛ := 0
13.      if Nₛ = 0 and N_q > 0
14.      then Nₛ := 1;  N_q := N_q − 1
15.      writeln(t, N_q, Nₛ)
16.  od
```

Figure 18.3: Pseudo-code for a time-based M|M|1 simulation

remains occupied ($N_s$ does not need to be changed).                    □

## 18.3.3   Event-based simulation

In time-based simulations the time steps were of fixed length, but the number of events per time step varied. In *event-based simulations* (also often called *asynchronous simulation*) it is just the other way around. We then deal with time steps of varying length such that there is always exactly one event in every time step. So, the simulation is controlled by the occurrence of "next events". This is very efficient since the time steps are now just long enough to optimally proceed with the simulation and just short enough to exclude the possibility of having more than one event per time step, thus circumventing the problems of handling dependent events in one time step.

Whenever an event occurs this causes new events to occur in the future. Consider for instance the arrival of a job at a queue. This event causes the system state to change, but will also cause at least one event in the future, namely the event that the job is taken

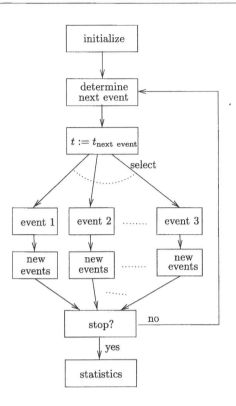

Figure 18.4: Diagram of the actions to be taken in a event-based simulation

into service. All future events are generally gathered in an *ordered event list*. The head of this list contains the next event to occur and its occurrence time. The tail of this list contains the future events, in their occurrence order. Whenever the first event is simulated (processed), it is taken from the list and the simulation time is updated accordingly. In the simulation of this event, new events may be created. These new events are inserted in the event list at the appropriate places. After that, the new head of the event list is processed. In Figure 18.4 we show a diagram of the actions to be performed in such a simulation.

Most of the discrete-event simulations performed in the field of computer and communication performance evaluation are of the event-based type. The only limitation to event-based simulation is that one must be able to compute the time instances at which future events take place. This is not always possible, e.g., if very complicated delay distributions are used, or if the system is a continuous-variable dynamic system. In those cases, time-based simulations may be preferred. Also when simulating at a very fine time-

```
 1.   input(λ, μ, t_max)
 2.   t := 0
 3.   N_s := 0;  N_q := 0
 4.   while t < t_max
 5.   do
 6.       if N_s = 1
 7.       then narr := negexp(λ)
 8.            ndep := negexp(μ)
 9.            if ndep < narr
10.            then t := t + ndep
11.               if N_q > 0
12.               then N_q := N_q − 1
13.               else N_s := 0
13.            else t := t + narr
14.                 N_q := N_q + 1
15.       else narr := negexp(λ)
16.            t := t + narr
17.            N_s := 1
18.       writeln( t, N_q, N_s)
19.   od
```

Figure 18.5: Pseudo-code for an event-based M|M|1 simulation

granularity, time-based simulations are often used, e.g., when simulating the execution of microprocessor instructions. In such cases, the time-steps will resemble the processor clock-cycles and the microprocessor should have been designed such that dependent events within a clock-cycle do not exist. We will only address event-based simulations from now on.

**Example 18.2. An event-based M|M|1 simulation program.**
We now present the framework of an event-based simulation program for the M|M|1 queue we addressed before. We again use two state variables: $N_s \in \{0, 1\}$ denoting the number of jobs in service, and $N_q \in \mathbb{N}$ denoting the number of jobs queued. We furthermore use two variables that represent the possible next events: **narr** denotes the time of the next arrival and **ndep** denotes the time of the next departure. Since there are at most two possible

next events, we can store them in just two variables (instead of in a list). The aim of the simulation program is to generate a list of events times, and the state variables at these instances. We have to make use of a function `negexp(`$\lambda$`)` which generates a realisation of a random variable with negative exponential distribution with rate $\lambda$; see also Section 18.4.

The resulting program is presented in Figure 18.5. After the initialisation (lines 1–3), the main program loop starts. Using the variable $N_s$, it is decided what the possible next events are (line 6). If there is no job being processed, the only possible next event is an arrival: the time until this next event is generated, the simulation time is updated accordingly and the state variable $N_s$ increased by 1 (lines 15–17). If there is a job being processed, then two possible next events exist. The times for these two events are computed (lines 7–8) and the one which occurs first is performed (decision in line 9). If the departure takes place first, the simulation time is adjusted accordingly, and if there are jobs queued, one of them is taken into service. Otherwise, the queue and server remain empty (lines 10–13). If the arrival takes place first, the time is updated accordingly and the queue is enlarged by 1 (lines 13–14).                                                                     □

## 18.3.4   Implementation strategies

Having chosen the event-based approach towards simulation, there exist different implementation forms. The implementation can either be *event-oriented* or *process-oriented*.

With the event-oriented implementation there is a procedure $P_i$ defined for every type of event $i$ that can occur. In the simulator an event list is defined. After initialisation of this event list the main control loop starts, consisting of the following steps. The first event to happen is taken from the list. The simulation time is incremented to the value at which this (current) event occurred. Then, if this event is of type $i$, the procedure $P_i$ is invoked. In this procedure the simulated system state is changed according to the occurrence of event $i$, and new events are generated and inserted in the event list at the appropriate places. After procedure $P_i$ terminates, some statistics may be collected, and the main control loop is continued. Typically employed stopping criteria include the simulated time, the number of processed events, the amount of used processing time, or the width of the confidence intervals that are computed for the measures of interest (see Section 18.5).

In an event-oriented implementation, the management of the events is explicitly visible. In a process-oriented implementation, on the other hand, a process is associated with every event-type. These processes exchange information to communicate state changes to one another, e.g., via explicit message passing or via shared variables. The simulated system operation can be seen as an execution path of the communicating event-processes. The scheduling of the events in the simulation is done implicitly in the scheduling of the event-processes. The latter can be done by the operating system or by the language run-time system. A prerequisite for this approach is that language elements for parallel programming are provided.

Both implementation strategies are used extensively. For the event-oriented implementation normal programming languages such as Pascal or C are used. For the process-oriented implementation, Simula'67 has been used widely for a long period; however, currently the use of C$^{++}$ in combination with public domain simulation classes is most common.

Instead of explicitly coding a simulation, there are many software packages available (both public domain and commercial) that serve to construct and execute simulations in an efficient way. Internally, these packages employ one of the two methods discussed above; however, to the user they represent themselves in a more application-oriented way, thus hiding most of the details of the actual simulation (see also Section 1.5 on the GMTF). A number of commercial software packages, using graphical interfaces, for the simulation of computer-communication systems have recently been discussed by Law and McComas [176]; with these tools, the simulations are described as block-diagrams representing the system components and their interactions. A different approach is taken with (graphical) simulation tools based on queueing networks and stochastic Petri nets. With such tools, the formalisms we have discussed for analytical and numerical performance evaluations are extended so that they can be interpreted as simulation specifications. The tools then automatically transform these specifications to executable simulation programs and present the results of these simulations in a tabular or graphical format. Of course, restrictions that apply for the analytic and numerical solutions of these models do not apply any more when the simulative solution is used. For more information, we refer to the literature, e.g., [125].

# 18.4   Random number generation

In order to simulate performance models of computer-communication systems using a computer program we have to be able to generate random numbers from certain probability distributions, as we have already seen in the examples in the previous section. Random number generation (RNG) is a difficult but important task; when the generated random numbers do not conform to the required distribution, the results obtained from the simulation should at least be regarded with suspicion.

To start with, *true* random numbers cannot be generated with a deterministic algorithm. This means that when using computers for RNG, we have to be satisfied with *pseudo-random numbers*. To generate pseudo-random numbers from a given distribution, we proceed in three steps. We first generate a series of pseudo-random numbers on a finite subset of $\mathbb{N}$, normally $\{0, \cdots, m-1\}$, $m \in \mathbb{N}$. This is discussed in Section 18.4.1. From this pseudo-random series, we compute (pseudo) uniformly distributed random numbers. To verify whether these pseudo-random numbers can be regarded as true random numbers we have to employ a number of statistical tests. These are discussed in Section 18.4.2. Using the uniform distributed random variables, various methods exist to compute non-uniform pseudo-random variables. These are discussed in Section 18.4.3.

### 18.4.1   Generating pseudo-random numbers

The generation of sequences of pseudo-random numbers is a challenging task. Although many methods exist for generating such sequences, we restrict ourselves here to the so-called *linear* and *additive congruential methods*, since these methods are relatively easy to implement and most commonly used. An RNG can be classified as good when:

- successive pseudo-random numbers can be computed with little cost;

- the generated sequence appears as truly random, i.e., successive pseudo-random numbers are independent from and uncorrelated with one another and conform to the desired distribution;

- its period (the time after which it repeats itself) is very long.

Below, we will present two RNGs and comment on the degree of fulfillment of these properties.

The basic idea of linear congruential RNGs is simple. Starting with a value $z_0$, the so-called *seed*, $z_{i+1}$ is computed from $z_i$ as follows:

$$z_{i+1} = (az_i + c) \text{ modulo } m. \tag{18.7}$$

With the right choice of parameters $a$, $c$, and $m$, this algorithm will generate $m$ different values, after which it starts anew. The number $m$ is called the *cycle length*. Since the next value of the series only depends on the current value, the cycle starts anew whenever a value reappears. The linear congruential RNG will generate a cycle of length $m$ if the following three conditions hold:

- the values $m$ and $c$ are relative primes, i.e., their greatest common divisor is 1;

- all prime factors of $m$ should divide $a - 1$;

- if 4 divides $m$, then 4 should also divide $a - 1$.

These conditions only state something about the cycle length; they do not imply that the resulting cycle appears as truly random.

**Example 18.3. Linear congruential method.**
Consider the case when $m = 16$, $c = 7$, and $a = 5$. We can easily check the conditions above. Starting with $z_0 = 0$, we obtain $z_1 = (5 \times 0 + 7)$ modulo $16 = 7$. Continuing in this way we obtain: $0, 7, 10, 9, 4, 11, 14, \cdots$. □

The main problem with linear congruential methods is that the cycles are relatively short, hence, there is too much repetition, too little randomness. This problem is avoided by using additive congruential methods. With these methods, the $i$-value $z_i$ is derived from the $k$ previous values $(z_{i-1}, \cdots, z_{i-k})$ in the following way:

$$z_i = \left( \sum_{j=1}^{k} a_j z_{i-j} \right) \text{ modulo } m. \tag{18.8}$$

The starting values $z_0$ through $z_{k-1}$ are generally derived by a linear congruential method, or by assuming $z_l = 0$, for $l < 0$. With an appropriate selection of the factors $a_j$ cycles of length $m^k - 1$ are obtained.

**Example 18.4. Additive congruential method.**
Choosing the value $k = 7$ and setting the coefficients $a_1 = a_7 = 1$ and $a_2 = \cdots = a_6 = 0$, we can extend the previous example. As starting sequence we take the first 7 terms computed before: $0, 7, 10, 9, 4, 11, 14$. The next value would then be $(14 + 0)$ modulo $16 = 14$. Continuing in this way we obtain: $0, 7, 10, 9, 4, 11, 14, 14, 5, 15, 8, 12, 7, 5, \cdots$. Observe that when a number reappears, this does not mean that the cycle restarts. For this example, the cycle length is limited by $16^7 - 1 = 268435455$. □

Finally, it is advisable to use a different RNG for each random number sequence to be used in the simulation, otherwise undesired dependencies between random variables can be introduced. Also, a proper choice of the seed is of importance. There are good RNGs that do not function properly, or not optimally, with wrongly chosen seeds. To be able to reproduce simulation experiments, it is necessary to control the seed selection process; taking a random number as seed is therefore not a good idea.

## 18.4.2   Testing pseudo-uniformly distributed random numbers

With the methods of Section 18.4.1 we are able to generate pseudo-random sequences. Since the largest number that is obtained is $m - 1$, we can simply divide the successive $z_i$ values by $m - 1$ to obtain a sequence of values $u_i = z_i/(m - 1)$. It is then assumed that these values are pseudo-uniformly distributed.

Before we proceed to compute random numbers obeying other distributions, it is now time to verify whether the generated sequence of pseudo-uniform random numbers can indeed be viewed as a realisation sequence of the uniform distribution.

### Testing the uniform distribution with the $\chi^2$-test

We apply the $\chi^2$-test to decide whether a sequence of $n$ random numbers $x_1, \cdots, x_n$ obeys the uniform distribution on $[0, 1]$. For this purpose, we divide the interval $[0, 1]$ in $k$ intervals $I_i = [(i - 1)/k, i/k]$, that is, $I_i$ is the $i$-th interval of length $1/k$ in $[0, 1]$ starting from the left, $i = 1, \cdots, k$. We now compute the number $n_i$ of generated random numbers in the $i$-th interval:

$$n_i = |\{x_j | x_j \in I_i, j = 1, \cdots, n\}|. \tag{18.9}$$

We would expect all values $n_i$ to be close to $n/k$. We now define as quality criterion for the RNG the relative squared difference of the values $n_i$ and their expectation [289]:

$$d = \frac{\sum_{i=1}^{k} \left( n_i - \frac{n}{k} \right)^2}{n/k}. \tag{18.10}$$

The value $d$ is a realisation of a stochastic variable $D$ which has approximately a $\chi^2$-distribution with $k - 1$ degrees of freedom. The hypothesis that the generated numbers do come from the uniform distribution on $[0, 1]$ cannot be rejected with probability $\alpha$, if $d$ is smaller than the critical value for $\chi^2_{\alpha, k-1}$, according to Table 18.1.

A few remarks are in order here. For the $\chi^2$-test to be valuable, we should have a large number of intervals $k$, and the number of random numbers in each interval should not be too small. Typically, one would require $k \geq 10$ and $n_i \geq 5$.

The $\chi^2$-test employs a discretisation to test the generated pseudo-random sequence. Alternatively, one could use the Kolmogorov-Smirnov test to directly test the real numbers generated. As quality measure, this test uses the maximum difference between the desired CDF and the observed CDF; for more details, see e.g., [137, 145].

| $k$ | $\alpha = 0.9$ | $\alpha = 0.95$ | $\alpha = 0.99$ |
|---|---|---|---|
| 2 | 4.605 | 5.991 | 9.210 |
| 3 | 6.253 | 7.817 | 11.356 |
| 4 | 7.779 | 9.488 | 13.277 |
| 5 | 9.236 | 11.071 | 15.086 |
| 6 | 10.645 | 12.592 | 16.812 |
| 7 | 12.017 | 14.067 | 18.475 |
| 8 | 13.362 | 15.507 | 20.090 |
| 9 | 14.684 | 16.919 | 21.666 |
| 10 | 15.987 | 18.307 | 23.209 |
| 15 | 22.307 | 24.996 | 30.578 |
| 20 | 28.412 | 31.410 | 37.566 |
| 25 | 34.382 | 37.653 | 44.314 |
| 30 | 40.256 | 43.773 | 50.892 |
| 40 | 51.805 | 55.759 | 63.691 |
| 50 | 63.17 | 67.505 | 76.154 |
| 60 | 74.40 | 79.082 | 88.379 |
| 70 | 85.53 | 90.531 | 100.425 |
| 80 | 96.58 | 101.879 | 112.329 |
| 90 | 107.6 | 113.145 | 124.116 |
| 100 | 118.5 | 124.342 | 135.807 |
| $k > 100$ | $\frac{1}{2}(h+1.28)^2$ | $\frac{1}{2}(h+1.64)^2$ | $\frac{1}{2}(h+2.33)^2$ |

Table 18.1: Critical values $x_{k,\alpha}$ for the $\chi^2$-distribution with $k$ degrees of freedom and confidence level $\alpha$ such that $\Pr\{D \leq x_{k,\alpha}\} = \alpha$ (with $h = \sqrt{2k-1}$)

### Testing the correlation structure

In order to test whether successive random numbers can be considered independent from one another, we have to study the correlation between the successive pseudo-random numbers. Let the random numbers $x_1, \cdots, x_n$ be generated uniform numbers on $[0,1]$. The *auto-correlation coefficient with lag $k \geq 1$* is then estimated by:

$$C_k = \frac{1}{n-k} \sum_{i=1}^{n-k} \left(X_i - \tfrac{1}{2}\right)\left(X_{i+k} - \tfrac{1}{2}\right). \tag{18.11}$$

Since $C_k$ is the sum of a large number of identically distributed random variables, it has a Normal distribution, here with mean 0 and variance $(144(n-k))^{-1}$. Therefore, the random

| $\alpha$ | 0.9 | 0.95 | 0.99 |
|---|---|---|---|
| $z$ | 1.645 | 1.960 | 2.576 |

Table 18.2: Critical values $z$ for the $N(0,1)$-distribution and confidence level $\alpha$ such that $\Pr\{|Z| \leq z\} = \alpha$

variable $A_k = 12C_k\sqrt{n-k}$ is $N(0,1)$-distributed. Hence, we can determine the value $z$ such that

$$\Pr\{C_k \leq z\} = \Pr\{|A_k| \leq z/12\sqrt{n-k}\} = \alpha, \tag{18.12}$$

by using Table 18.2. Thus, for a chosen confidence level $\alpha$, the autocorrelation coefficient at lag $k$ will lie in the interval $[c_k - z/12\sqrt{n-k}, c_k + z/12\sqrt{n-k}]$, where $c_k$ is a realisation of $C_k$. For a proper uniform RNG, the auto-correlation coefficients should be very close to 0, that is, the computed confidence intervals should contain 0.

### 18.4.3   Generation of non-uniformly distributed random numbers

There are various techniques to use uniform random numbers to obtain differently distributed random numbers that obey other distributions. We present some of these techniques below.

**The inversion method**

Consider the distribution function $F_Y(y)$ of some stochastic variable $Y$. Let $Z$ be a random variable defined as a function of the random variable $Y$, and let us choose as function a very special one, namely the distribution function of $Y$: i.e., $Z = F_Y(Y)$. The distribution function of $Z$, i.e., $F_Z(z)$, has the following form:

$$F_Z(z) = \Pr\{Z \leq z\} = \Pr\{F_Y(Y) \leq z\}. \tag{18.13}$$

Now, assuming that $F_Y$ can be inverted, we can equate the latter probability with $\Pr\{Y \leq F_Y^{-1}(z)\}$, for $0 \leq z \leq 1$. But, since $F_Y(y) = \Pr\{Y \leq y\}$ we find, after having substituted $F_Y^{-1}(z)$ for $y$:

$$F_Z(z) = F_Y(F_Y^{-1}(z)) = z, \quad \text{for } 0 \leq z \leq 1. \tag{18.14}$$

In conclusion, we find that $Z$ is distributed uniformly on $[0,1]$. To generate random numbers with a distribution $F_Y(y)$ we now proceed as follows. We generate a uniformly distributed random number $z$ and apply the inverse function to yield $y = F_Y^{-1}(z)$. The

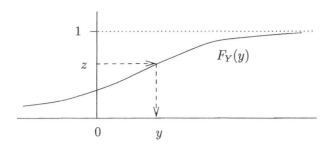

Figure 18.6: Deriving a continuous random variable from a uniformly distributed random variable

realisations $y$ are then distributed according to distribution function $F_Y$. In Figure 18.6 we visualise the inversion approach.

**Example 18.5. Negative exponential random numbers.**
To generate random numbers from the exponential distribution $F_Y(y) = 1 - e^{-\lambda y}$, $y > 0$, we proceed as follows. We solve $z = F_Y(y)$ for $y$ to find: $y = -\ln(1 - z)/\lambda$. Thus, we can generate uniformly distributed numbers $z$, and apply the just derived equation to obtain exponentially distributed random numbers $y$. To save one arithmetic operation, we can change the term $1 - z$ to $z$, since if $z$ is uniformly distributed, then $1 - z$ is so as well.  □

**Example 18.6. Erlang-$k$ random numbers.**
To generate random numbers from the Erlang-$k$ distribution, we generate $k$ random numbers, distributed according to a negative exponential distribution, and simply add these. In order to avoid having to take $k$ logarithms, we can consider the following. Let $u_1, \cdots, u_k$ be $k$ uniformly distributed random numbers, and let $x_i = -\ln(u_i)/\lambda$ be the corresponding $k$ negative exponential distributed random numbers ($\lambda$ is the rate per phase). We now compute the Erlang-$k$ distributed number $z$ as follows:

$$z = \sum_{i=1}^{k} x_i = -\frac{1}{\lambda} \sum_{i=1}^{k} \ln(u_i) = -\frac{1}{\lambda} \ln \left( \prod_{i=1}^{k} u_i \right). \qquad (18.15)$$

In conclusion, we simply have to multiply the $k$ terms, and have to take only one natural logarithm. Since RNGs are invoked very often during a simulation, such efficiency improvements are very important.  □

**Example 18.7. Hyper-exponential random numbers.**
The hyper-exponential distribution can be interpreted as a choice between $n$ negative expo-

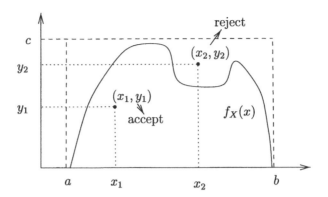

Figure 18.7: Rejection method for generating random variables with density $fX(x)$

nential distributions, each with rate $\lambda_i$. We therefore first generate a random integer $i$ from the set $\{1, \cdots, n\}$; this is the selection phase. We then generate a negative exponentially distributed random number with rate $\lambda_i$.                                                    $\square$

**The rejection method**

For obtaining random variables for which the inverse distribution function cannot be easily obtained, we can use the *rejection method*, provided we know the density function $f_X(x)$. Furthermore, the density function must have a finite domain, say $[a, b]$, as well as a finite image on $[a, b]$, say $[0, c]$. If there are values $x \notin [a, b]$ for which $f_X(x) > 0$, then the rejection method only provides approximate random numbers. In Figure 18.7 we show a density function fulfilling the requirements. We proceed as follows. We generate two uniformly distributed numbers $u_1$ and $u_2$ on $[0, 1]$ and derive the random numbers $x = a + (b - a)u_1$ and $y = cu_2$. The tuple $(x, y)$ is a randomly selected point in the rectangle $[a, b] \times [0, c]$. Now, whenever $y < f_X(x)$, that is, whenever the point $(x, y)$ lies below the density $f_X(x)$, we accept $x$. Successive values for $x$ then obey the density $f_X(x)$. Whenever $y \geq f_X(x)$ we repeat the procedure until we encounter a tuple for which the condition holds. This procedure is fairly efficient when the area under the density $f_X(x)$ is close to $c(b - a)$. In that case we have a relatively high probability that a sample point lies under the density, so that we do not need many sample points.

The proof of the rejection method is fairly simple. Consider two random variables: $X$ is distributed uniformly on $[a, b]$, and $Y$ is distributed uniformly on $[0, c]$. We then proceed to compute the following conditional probability, which exactly equals the probability distribution function for an accepted value $x$ according to the rejection scheme:

$$\Pr\{x \le X \le x + dx | Y \le f_X(X)\} = \frac{\Pr\{x \le X \le x + dx, Y \le f_X(x)\}}{\Pr\{Y \le f_X(X)\}}$$

$$= \left(\frac{dx}{b-a}\right)\left(\frac{f_X(x)}{c}\right)\left(\frac{1}{(b-a)c}\right)^{-1} = f_X(x)dx.$$

We see that the conditional probability reduces to the required probability density.

### Normally distributed random numbers

For some random variables, the distribution function cannot be explicitly computed or inverted, nor does the density function have a finite domain. For these cases we have to come up with even other methods to generate random numbers.

As a most interesting example of these, we address the normal distribution. We apply the central limit theorem to compute normally distributed random numbers as follows. We first generate $n$ independent and identically distributed random numbers $x_1, \cdots, x_n$, which can be seen as realisations of the random variables $X_1, \cdots, X_n$, which are all distributed as the random variable $X$ with mean $E[X]$ and variance $\text{var}[X]$. We can then define the random variable $S_n = X_1 + \cdots + X_n$. The central limit theorem then states that the random variable

$$N = \frac{S_n - nE[X]}{\sqrt{n\text{var}[X]}}$$

approaches a normally distributed random variable with mean 0 and variance 1, i.e., an $N(0,1)$ distribution.

Now, by choosing the uniform distribution on $[0,1]$ for $X$ ($X$ has mean $E[X] = 1/2$ and $\text{var}[X] = 1/12$) and taking $n = 12$ samples, $S_{12} = X_1 + \cdots + X_{12}$, so that

$$N = \frac{S_n - nE[X]}{\sqrt{n\text{var}[X]}} = \frac{S_n - 6}{\sqrt{12\frac{1}{12}}} = S_{12} - 6 \tag{18.16}$$

approaches a $N(0,1)$-distributed random variable. An advantage of using $N$ is that it is very efficient to compute. Of course, taking larger values for $n$ increases the accuracy of the generated random numbers.

## 18.5    Statistical evaluation of simulation results

A discrete-event simulation is performed to obtain quantitative insight into the operation of the modelled system. When executing a simulation (program), relevant events can be time-stamped. All the resulting samples (or observations) can be written to a *trace* or *log file*. In Section 18.5.1 we discuss how we can obtain single samples from a simulation execution. Although a complete log file contains all the available information, it is generally of little practical use. Therefore, the simulation log is "condensed" to a format that is more suitable for human interpretation. This step is performed using statistical techniques and is discussed in Section 18.5.2.

## 18.5.1 Obtaining measurements

We address the issues of obtaining individual samples and the removal of invalid samples (the initial transient) below.

### Sampling individual events

We distinguish two types of measures that can be obtained from a simulation: user-oriented measures and system-oriented measures. *User-oriented measures* are typically obtained by monitoring specific users of the system under study, i.e., by monitoring individual jobs. An example of a user-oriented measure is the job residence time in some part of the modelled system. When the $i$-th job enters that system part, a time-stamp $t_i^{(a)}$ ("a" for arrival) is taken. When the job leaves the system part a time-stamp $t_i^{(d)}$ ("d" for departure) is taken. The difference $t_i = t_i^{(d)} - t_i^{(a)}$ is an realisation of the job residence time. By summing over all simulated jobs, denoted as $n$, we finally obtain an estimate for the mean job residence time as:

$$\tilde{r} = \frac{1}{n} \sum_{i=1}^{n} (t_i^{(d)} - t_i^{(a)}) = \frac{1}{n} \left( \sum_{i=1}^{n} t_i^{(d)} - \sum_{i=1}^{n} t_i^{(a)} \right). \tag{18.17}$$

Notice that during the simulation, we do not have to store all the individual time-stamp values, since in the end we only need the difference of their sums.

For the derivation of *system-oriented measures* no individual jobs should be monitored, but the system state itself. A typical example is the case where the measure of interest is the long-run probability that a finite buffer is fully occupied. Upon every state change in the model the system state of interest is checked for this condition. If this condition becomes true, a time-stamp $t_i^{(f)}$ is taken ("f" for full). The next time-stamp, denoted $t_i^{(n)}$ ("n" for not full) is then taken when the buffer is not fully occupied anymore. The difference $t_i^{(n)} - t_i^{(f)}$ is a realisation of random variable that could be called the "buffer-full period". The sum of all these periods, divided by the total simulation time then estimates the long-run buffer full probability, i.e.,

$$\tilde{b} = \frac{1}{T}\sum_{i=1}^{n}(t_i^{(n)} - t_i^{(f)}) = \frac{1}{T}\left(\sum_{i=1}^{n} t_i^{(n)} - \sum_{i=1}^{n} t_i^{(f)}\right), \qquad (18.18)$$

where we assume that during the simulation of length $T$ we have experienced $n$ buffer full periods. Notice that the simulation time $T$ is predetermined for system-oriented measures, whereas the number of samples $n$ is prespecified for user-oriented measures, in order to obtain unbiased estimators.

### Initial transient removal

With most simulations, we try to obtain steady-state performance measures. However, when starting the simulation, the modelled system state will generally be very non-typical, e.g., in queueing network simulations one may choose all queues to be initially empty. Hence, the observations made during the first period of the simulation will be non-typical as well, thus influencing the simulation results in an inappropriate way. Therefore, we should ignore the measurements taken during this so-called *(initial) transient period*. The main question then is: how long should we ignore the measurements, or, in other words, how long should we take this initial transient? This question is not at all easy to answer; Pawlikowski discusses 11 "rules" to recognise the initial transient period [231]. Below, we briefly discuss a number of simple guidelines.

The first guideline is to simulate so long that the effect of the initial transient period becomes negligible. Of course, this is not an efficient method, nor does it provide any evidence. This method becomes slightly better when combined with a smart initial state in the simulation, e.g., based on an analytic queueing network model of a simplified version of the simulation model. In doing so, the period in which queues have to built up towards their mean occupation becomes smaller. But this method does not provide evidence for a particular choice.

The slightly better guideline is given by the *truncation method*, which removes the first $l < n$ samples from a sequence of samples $x_1, \cdots, x_n$, where $l$ is the smallest value such that:

$$\min\{x_{l+1}, \cdots, x_n\} \neq x_{l+1} \neq \max\{x_{l+1}, \cdots, x_n\}. \qquad (18.19)$$

In words: the samples $x_1, \cdots, x_l$ are removed when the $(l+1)$-th sample is no longer the maximum, nor the minimum of the remaining samples. This means that the samples that follow $x_{l+1}$ have values both smaller and larger than $x_{l+1}$, thus indicating that an oscillation around a stationary situation has started. This method corresponds to rule R1 in [231] and has been shown to overestimate the length of the initial transient period when simulating systems under low utilisation, and to underestimate it for high utilisation.

A better but still simple guideline is the following, based on an estimation of the variance. Consider a sequence of $n$ samples. The sample mean $m$ is computed as $(\sum_{i=1}^{n} x_i)/n$. Then, we split the $n$ observations into $k$ groups or batches, such that $k = \lfloor n/l \rfloor$. We start with batch size $l = 2$ and increase it stepwisely, thereby computing $k$ accordingly, until the sample variance starts to decrease, as follows. We compute the batch means as

$$m_i = \frac{1}{l} \sum_{j=1}^{l} x_{(i-1)l+j}, \quad i = 1, \cdots, k, \qquad (18.20)$$

and the sample variance as:

$$\sigma^2 = \frac{1}{k-1} \sum_{i=1}^{k} (m_i - m)^2. \qquad (18.21)$$

By increasing the batch size $l$, more and more samples of the initial transient period will become part of the first batch. If $l$ is small, many batches will contain samples from the initial transient period, thus making $\sigma^2$ larger, also for increasing $l$. However, if $l$ becomes so large that the first batch contains almost exclusively the samples that can be considered part of the initial transient period, only $m_1$ will significantly differ from $m$, thus making $\sigma^2$ smaller. The batch size $l$ for which $\sigma^2$ starts to decrease monotonously equals the number of samples that should not be considered any further (see also [145]).

## 18.5.2   Mean values and confidence intervals

Suppose we are executing a simulation to estimate the mean of the random variable $X$ with (unknown) $E[X] = a$. In doing so, a simulation is used to generate $n$ samples $x_i$, $i = 1, \cdots, n$, each of which can be seen as a realisation of a stochastic variable $X_i$. The simulation has been constructed such that the stochastic variables $X_i$ are all distributed as the random variable $X$. Furthermore, to compute confidence intervals, we require the $X_i$ to be independent of each other.

Below, we discuss how to estimate the mean value of $X$ and present means to compute confidence intervals for the obtained estimate. We also comment on ways to handle independence in the measurements.

**Mean values**

To estimate $E[X]$, we define a new stochastic variable, $\tilde{X}$, which is called *an estimator* of $X$. Whenever $E[\tilde{X}] = a$, the estimator $\tilde{X}$ is called *unbiased*. Whenever $\Pr\{|\tilde{X} - a| < \epsilon\} \to 0$

when $n \rightarrow \infty$, the estimator $\tilde{X}$ is called *consistent*. The latter condition translates itself to the requirement that $\text{var}[\tilde{X}] \rightarrow 0$, whenever the number of samples $n \rightarrow \infty$. Clearly, both unbiasedness and consistency are desirable properties of estimators. Whenever the observations $X_1, \cdots, X_n$ are independent, then

$$\tilde{X} = \frac{1}{n} \sum_{i=1}^{n} X_i \tag{18.22}$$

is an unbiased and consistent estimator for $E[X]$ since $E[\tilde{X}] = E[X]$ (unbiasedness) and $\text{var}[\tilde{X}] = \text{var}[X]/n$, so that $\text{var}[\tilde{X}] \rightarrow 0$, when $n \rightarrow \infty$ (consistence).

Although the estimator $\tilde{X}$ seems to be fine, the requirement that the random variables $X_i$ should be independent causes us problems (independence is required for consistency, not for unbiasedness). Indeed, successive samples taken from a simulation are generally not independent. For instance, suppose that the random variables $X_i$ signify samples of job response times in a particular queue. Whenever $X_i$ is large (or small), $X_{i+1}$ will most probably be large (or small) as well, so that successive samples are dependent. There are a number of ways to cope with the dependence between successive samples; these will be discussed below.

## Guaranteeing independence

There are a number of ways to obtain almost independent observations from simulations, as they are required to compute confidence intervals. We discuss the three most-widely used methods below.

With the method of *independent replicas* the simulation execution is replicated $n$ times, each time with a different seed for the RNG. In the $i$-th simulation run, the samples $x_{i,1}, \cdots, x_{i,m}$ are taken. Although these individual samples are not independent, the sample means $x_i = (\sum_{j=1}^{m} x_{i,j})/m$, $i = 1, \cdots, n$, are considered to be independent from one another. These $n$ mean values are therefore considered as the samples from which the overall mean value and confidence interval (see below) are estimated. The advantage of this method lies in the fact that the used samples are really independent, provided the RNGs deliver independent streams. A disadvantage is that the simulation has to be executed from start several times. This implies that also the transient behaviour at the beginning of every simulation has to performed and removed multiple times.

A method which circumvents the latter problem is the *batch means method*. It requires only a single simulation run from which the samples $x_1, \cdots, x_{n \cdot m}$ are split into $n$ batches of size $m$ each. Within every batch the samples are averaged as follows:

$$y_i = \frac{1}{m} \sum_{j=1}^{m} x_{(i-1)m+j}. \tag{18.23}$$

The samples $y_1, \cdots, y_n$ are assumed to be independent and used to compute the overall average and confidence intervals. The advantage of this method is that only a single simulation run is performed for which the initial transient has to be removed only once. A disadvantage of this method is the fact that the batches are not totally independent, hence, this method is only approximate. In practice, however, the batch-means method is most often used.

The fact that successive batches are not totally independent is overcome with the so-called *regenerative method*. With this method a single simulation execution is split into several batches as well; however, the splitting is done at so-called regeneration points in the simulation. Regeneration points are defined such that the behaviour before such a point is totally independent from the behaviour after it. A good example of a regeneration point is the moment the queue gets empty in the simulation of an M|G|1 queue. As before, the batch averages are taken as the samples to compute the overall mean and the confidence intervals; however, since the number of samples per batch is not constant, more complex, so-called ratio-estimators, must be used.

The advantage of the regeneration method is that the employed samples to compute the confidence intervals are really independent. The problems with it are the more complex estimators and the fact that regeneration points might occur only very rarely, thus yielding long simulation run times. True regeneration points that are visited frequently during a simulation are rare; the state in which the modelled system empties is often considered a regeneration point, but this is only correct when the times until the next events are drawn from memoryless distributions. To illustrate this, in an M|M|1 simulation, every arrival and departure point is a regeneration point. In an M|G|1 simulation, all departure instances and the first arrival instance are regeneration points. In contrast, in an G|G|1 simulation, only the first arrival instance is a regeneration point.

**Confidence intervals**

Since the random variables $X_i$ are assumed to be independent and identically distributed, the estimator $\tilde{X}$ as defined in (18.22) will, according to the central limit theorem, approximately have a Normal distribution with mean $a$ and variance $\sigma^2/n$ (we denote var$[X]$ as

$\sigma^2$). This implies that the random variable

$$Z' = \frac{\tilde{X} - a}{\sigma/\sqrt{n}} \qquad (18.24)$$

is $N(0,1)$-distributed. However, since we do not know the variance of the random variable $X$, we have to estimate it as well. An unbiased estimator for $\sigma^2$, known as the sample variance, is given as:

$$S^2 = \frac{1}{n-1} \sum_{i=1}^{n} \left( X_i - \tilde{X} \right)^2, \qquad (18.25)$$

The stochastic variable

$$Z = \frac{\tilde{X} - a}{\tilde{S}/\sqrt{n}} \qquad (18.26)$$

then has a Student- or $t$-distribution with $n-1$ degrees of freedom (a $t_{n-1}$-distribution). Notice that $a$ and $\tilde{\sigma}^2$ can easily be computed when $\sum_i x_i$ and $\sum_i x_i^2$ are known:

$$a = \frac{\sum_{i=1}^{n} x_i}{n}, \quad \text{and} \quad \tilde{\sigma}^2 = \frac{\sum_{i=1}^{n} x_i^2}{n-1} - \frac{\left(\sum_{i=1}^{n} x_i\right)}{n(n-1)}, \qquad (18.27)$$

so that during the simulation, only two real numbers have to be maintained per measure.

The Student distribution with three or more degrees of freedom is a symmetric bell-shaped distribution, similar in form to the Normal distribution (see Figure 18.8). For $n \to \infty$, the $t_n$-distribution approaches an $N(0,1)$ distribution. By using a standard table for it, such as given in Table 18.3, we can find the value $z > 0$ such that $\Pr\{|Z| \le z\} = \beta$; $z$ is called the *double-sided critical value* for the $t_n$-distribution, given $\beta$. The last row in Table 18.3 corresponds to the case of having an unbounded number of degrees of freedom, that is, these critical values follow from the $N(0,1)$ distribution. Using these double-sided critical values, we can write:

$$\Pr\{|Z| \le z\} = \Pr\left\{ \frac{|\tilde{X} - a|}{\sigma/\sqrt{n}} \le z \right\} = \Pr\{|\tilde{X} - a| \le z\sigma/\sqrt{n}\} = \beta, \qquad (18.28)$$

which states that the probability that the estimator $\tilde{X}$ deviates less than $z\sigma/\sqrt{n}$ from the mean $a$ is $\beta$. Stated differently, the probability that $X$ lies in the so-called *confidence interval* $[a - z\sigma/\sqrt{n}, a + z\sigma/\sqrt{n}]$ is $\beta$. The probability $\beta$ is called the confidence level. As can be observed, to make the confidence interval a factor $l$ smaller, $l^2$ times more observations are required, so that the simulation needs to be $l^2$ times as long.

Note that many statistical tables present *single-sided critical values*, i.e., those values $z'$ for which the probability $\Pr\{Z \le z'\} = \beta'$. Due to the symmetrical nature of the $t_n$-distribution, for $n \ge 3$, we have $z' = z$ if $\beta' = (1+\beta)/2$.

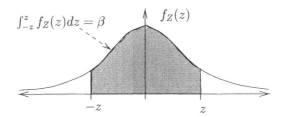

Figure 18.8: The bell-shaped Student-distribution with $n \geq 3$ degrees of freedom

We finally note that when using regenerative simulation, due to the use of ratio-estimators, the computation of confidence intervals becomes more complicated.

**Example 18.8. Confidence interval determination.**
From five mutually independent simulation runs we obtain the following five samples: $(x_1, \cdots, x_5) = (0.108, 0.112, 0.111, \ 0.115, 0.098)$. The sample mean $a = (\sum_{i=1}^{5} x_i)/5 = 0.1088$. The sample variance $\sigma^2 = \sum_{i=1}^{5}(x_i - a)^2/(5 - 1) = 0.0000427$. We assume a confidence level of $\beta = 0.9$. In Table 18.3, we find the corresponding double-sided critical value for the $t_4$-distribution with 90% confidence level $z = 2.132$. We thus obtain that:

$$\Pr\{|Z| \leq 2.132\} = \Pr\{|\tilde{X} - m| \leq 2.132\sigma/\sqrt{5}\},$$

from which we derive that $\Pr\{|\tilde{X} - m| \leq 0.00623\} = 0.90$. Thus, we know that:

$$\tilde{X} \in [0.1026, 0.1150] \ \text{ with 90\% confidence.}$$

Notice that in practical situations, we should always aim to have at least ten degrees of freedom, i.e., $n \geq 10$.                                                                   □

## 18.6 Further reading

More information on the statistical techniques to evaluate simulation results can be found in the performance evaluation textbooks by Jain [145], Mitrani [202], Trivedi [280] and in the survey by Pawlikowski [231]. The former two books also discuss the simulation setup and random number generation. More detailed information on the statistical techniques to be used in the evaluation of simulation results can be found in [90, 157, 175, 285] and statistics textbooks [137, 289]. Random number generation is treated extensively by Knuth

| $n$ | $\alpha = 90\%$ | $\alpha = 95\%$ | $\alpha = 99\%$ | $n$ | $\alpha = 90\%$ | $\alpha = 95\%$ | $\alpha = 99\%$ |
|-----|-----|-----|-----|-----|-----|-----|-----|
| 3 | 2.353 | 3.182 | 5.841 | 18 | 1.734 | 2.101 | 2.878 |
| 4 | 2.132 | 2.776 | 4.604 | 20 | 1.725 | 2.086 | 2.845 |
| 5 | 2.015 | 2.571 | 4.032 | 22 | 1.717 | 2.074 | 2.819 |
| 6 | 1.943 | 2.447 | 3.707 | 24 | 1.711 | 2.064 | 2.797 |
| 7 | 1.895 | 2.365 | 3.499 | 26 | 1.706 | 2.056 | 2.779 |
| 8 | 1.860 | 2.306 | 3.355 | 28 | 1.701 | 2.048 | 2.763 |
| 9 | 1.833 | 2.262 | 3.250 | 30 | 1.697 | 2.042 | 2.750 |
| 10 | 1.812 | 2.228 | 3.169 | 60 | 1.671 | 2.000 | 2.660 |
| 12 | 1.782 | 2.179 | 3.055 | 90 | 1.662 | 1.987 | 2.632 |
| 14 | 1.761 | 2.145 | 2.977 | 120 | 1.658 | 1.980 | 2.617 |
| 16 | 1.746 | 2.120 | 2.921 | $\infty$ | 1.645 | 1.960 | 2.576 |

Table 18.3: Double-sided critical values $z$ of the Student distribution for $n$ degrees of freedom and confidence level $\alpha$ such that $\Pr\{|Z| \le z\} = \alpha$

[162], l'Ecuyer [79, 80] and others [56, 229]. Some recent tests of random number generators can be found in [179].

Research in simulation techniques is still continuing. In particular, when the interest is in obtaining measures that are to be associated with events that occur rarely, e.g., packet loss probabilities in communication systems or complete system failures in fault-tolerant computer systems, simulations tend to be very long. Special techniques to deal with these so-called *rare-event simulations* are being developed, see [99, 130, 222]. Pawlikowski gives an overview of the problems (and solutions) of the simulation of queueing processes [231]. Also techniques to speed-up simulations using parallel and distributed computer systems are receiving increased attention; for an overview of these techniques see [102]. Chiola and Ferscha discuss the special case of parallel simulations of SPNs [48].

## 18.7 Exercises

### 18.1. Random number generation.
Use a linear congruential method with $m = 18$, $c = 17$, $a = 7$ and seed $z_0 = 3$ to generate random numbers in $[0, 17]$.

Now make use of an additive congruential method to generate random numbers, using $m = 18$ and $a_0 = \cdots = a_{17} = 1$, thereby using as seeds the values computed with the linear congruential method.

### 18.2. Uniform number generation.

Use the additive congruential method of the previous exercise to obtain 1000 uniformly-distributed random numbers on $[0, 1]$. Use the $\chi^2$-test to validate this RNG. Use the auto-correlation test to validate the independence of successive random numbers $k = 1, 2, 3, 4$ generated with this RNG.

### 18.3. Uniform number generation.

Validate the following two RNGs, recently proposed by Fishman and Moore [91]:

- $z_n = 48271 z_{n-1}$ modulo $2^{32} - 1$;

- $z_n = 696211 z_{n-1}$ modulo $2^{32} - 1$.

### 18.4. How fair is a coin.

We try to compute the probability $p$ with which the tossing of a coin yield "heads". We therefore toss the coin $n$ times. How large should we take $n$ such that with confidence level $\alpha = 0.9$ the width of the confidence interval is only 0.1 times the mean $np$. What happens (with $n$) if $p$ tends to 0, that is, when tossing "heads" becomes a rare event?

### 18.5. Confidence interval construction.

As a result of a batch-means simulation we have obtained following batch means:

$$2.45 \quad 2.55 \quad 2.39 \quad 2.41 \quad 2.49 \quad 2.67 \quad 2.38 \quad 2.44 \quad 2.47$$

Compute confidence intervals, with $\alpha = 0.9, 0.95, 0.99$. How does the width of the confidence intervals change when the confidence level gets closer to 1? How many batches do you expect to be necessary to decrease the width of the confidence interval by a factor $l$.

### 18.6. Simulating a G|M|1 and a G|G|1 queue.

We consider the event-based simulation of the M|M|1 queue, as sketched in Section 18.3. How should we adapt the given program to simulate queues of M|G|1 and of G|G|1 type. Hint: do not "redraw" random number for non-exponential distributions, unless the associated events have really been executed.

### 18.7. Simulating a CTMC.

We are given a finite CTMC on state space $\mathcal{I}$, with generator matrix $\mathbf{Q}$ and initial proba-bility distribution $p(0)$. We are interested in the long-run proportion of time that the state of the simulated CTMC is in some (given) subset $\mathcal{J}$ from $\mathcal{I}$. We start simulating at $t_s = 0$ until some value $t_e$; we only start collecting samples after the initial transient period of length $t_i$ is over.

1. What is a useful estimator for the measure of interest?

2. Outline a simulation program for CTMC simulation, thereby using properties of CTMCs.

**18.8. Simulating SPNs.**

Given is an SPN of the class we have discussed in Chapter 14, however, without any restrictions on the timings of the transitions. Furthermore, we assume that a transition which is disabled due to the firing of another transition will resume its activity once it becomes enabled again. Thus, the time until the firing of a transition is not resampled every time it becomes enabled, but only when it becomes first enabled (after having fired or after simulation starts). Present the outline of a simulation program for SPNs obeying the sketched sampling strategy. What are the advantages of simulating SPNs instead of numerically solving them? And what are the disadvantages?

# Part VI

# Appendices

# Appendix A

# Applied probability for performance analysts

IN this appendix we briefly discuss a number of elementary concepts of probability theory that are of use for performance evaluation purposes. By no means is this appendix intended to cover all of probability theory; it is included as a refresher for those having enrolled in a basic course on probability theory and statistics in the past. For further details, refer to the textbooks [87, 152, 280]

This appendix is further organised as follows. In Section A.1 we introduce the mathematical basis of probability theory and present some general laws and definitions. We introduce discrete random variables in Sections A.2 and A.3, and continuous random variables in Sections A.4 and A.5. Mean values and variances are discussed in Sections A.6 through A.8.

## A.1 Probability measures

The mathematical concept of *probability* can be defined as a triple $(S, E, \Pr)$ where $S$ is the *sample space* of all possible outcomes of an experiment, $E \subset 2^S$ (the power set of $S$) is a set of events, and $\Pr : E \to \mathbb{R}$ is a *probability mapping* from events to real numbers which satisfies the following three rules:

1. For all possible $e \in E$: $\Pr\{e\}$ exists and $0 \le \Pr\{e\} \le 1$, that is, any possible event occurs with a probability between 0 and 1;

2. $\Pr\{S\} = 1$, that is, the sum of probabilities of all possible events equals 1;

3. If $e, e' \in E$ are two mutually exclusive events then $\Pr\{e \cup e'\} = \Pr\{e\} + \Pr\{e'\}$.

**Example A.1. Rolling a dice (I).**
Consider a normal cubic dice with numbers 1 through 6. Rolling this dice will generate samples or events from the sample space $S = \{1, \cdots, 6\}$. $E$ is the set of all possible events: $E = \{\{1\}, \cdots, \{6\}\}$. The probability of rolling "6" is then most naturally set equal to $\Pr\{6\} = 1/6$ (for convenience we normally omit the double $\{\{\}\}$-notation from now on). The probability of rolling one of the numbers 1 through 6 equals $\Pr\{1, \cdots, 6\} = \Pr\{S\} = 1$. The probability of rolling "even" equals $\Pr\{\text{"even"}\} = \Pr\{2, 4, 6\} = \Pr\{2\} + \Pr\{4\} + \Pr\{6\} = 1/2$.                                                                                       □

When two events are not mutually exclusive the probability of occurrence of both events is *not* the sum of the probability of both events individually; one should account for the "overlapping" part of the events by subtracting the overlap. To be more concrete, if $e, e' \in E$, then

$$\Pr\{e \cup e'\} = \Pr\{e\} + \Pr\{e'\} - \Pr\{e \cap e'\}. \tag{A.1}$$

Two events $e, e' \in E$ that are disjoint, i.e., $e \cap e' = \emptyset$ are *mutually exclusive events*.

**Example A.2. Rolling a dice (II).**
Let event $e$ signify "even" rolls, i.e., $e = \{2, 4, 6\}$. Let $e'$ signify the event "at least three", i.e., $e' = \{3, 4, 5, 6\}$. We then have that $\Pr\{e \cup e'\} = \Pr\{e\} + \Pr\{e'\} - \Pr\{e \cap e'\} = \Pr\{2, 4, 6\} + \Pr\{3, 4, 5, 6\} - \Pr\{4, 6\} = 3/6 + 4/6 - 2/6 = 5/6$. The latter could also be derived directly, since $\Pr\{e \cup e'\} = \Pr\{2, 3, 4, 5, 6\} = 5/6$.                               □

The probability of *the complement* of an event $e$ equals 1 minus the probability of event $e$: $\Pr\{\neg e\} = 1 - \Pr\{e\}$.

**Example A.3. Rolling a dice (III).**
Let event $e$ signify the event "at least three", i.e., $e = \{3, 4, 5, 6\}$. We then have $\Pr\{e\} = 4/6$. Throwing less than three then has probability $\Pr\{\neg e\} = 1 - \Pr\{e\} = 2/6$.                  □

Let $\Pr\{e|e'\}$ denote the probability that $e$ happens, given that $e'$ already happens, and it is called *the conditional probability* of $e$, given $e'$. We have:

$$\Pr\{e, e'\} = \Pr\{e \cap e'\} = \Pr\{e|e'\} \Pr\{e'\} \Rightarrow \Pr\{e|e'\} = \frac{\Pr\{e \cap e'\}}{\Pr\{e'\}}. \tag{A.2}$$

Two events $e$ and $e'$ are said to be *independent* if $\Pr\{e, e'\} = \Pr\{e\} \Pr\{e'\}$. When $e$ and $e'$ are independent we of course have $\Pr\{e|e'\} = \Pr\{e\}$ and also $\Pr\{e'|e\} = \Pr\{e'\}$. In these cases, the occurrence of $e$ (or $e'$) does not say anything about the possible occurrence of $e'$

(or $e$). If $e$ and $e'$ are mutually exclusive events, then $\Pr\{e, e'\} = \Pr\{e \cap e'\} = 0$, and thus also $\Pr\{e|e'\} = \Pr\{e'|e\} = 0$.

Let $e_1, \cdots, e_n$ be mutually exclusive events such that $S = e_1 \cup \cdots \cup e_n$ and let $e \subseteq S$, then the *law of total probability* states:

$$\Pr\{e\} = \sum_{i=1}^{n} \Pr\{e|e_i\} \Pr\{e_i\}. \tag{A.3}$$

## A.2  Discrete random variables

Up till now we have only worked with probabilities. In the examples we only used the dice. This was convenient because the outcome of the experiment (the events) were numbers. In general this need not be the case. Consider the tossing of a coin. This can yield "heads" or "tails". What to do with these outcomes in a calculation? To encompass these problems, random variables have been introduced.

A *random variable* is a mapping from the sample space of a probability measure to, in the case of discrete random variables, the natural numbers or a subset thereof.

A discrete random variable $N$ can be characterised by its *probability distribution function* or *cumulative density function* (CDF) $F_N(n) = \Pr\{N \leq n\}$. The *probability density function* (PDF) or *probability mass function* (pmf) is defined as $f_N(n) = \Pr\{N = n\}$. The following relation exists between the CDF and PDF:

$$F_N(n) = \sum_{m=0}^{n} f_N(m). \tag{A.4}$$

As lower limit in the summation we have chosen 0. This will mostly be the case although this is not necessary. Since the sum of all probabilities of all events, or to be precise, of all images $n \in I\!N$ of events, must equal 1, we have

$$\sum_{\text{all } n} f_N(n) = 1. \tag{A.5}$$

Consequently, $F_N(n)$ is a monotonously increasing function with image in $[0, 1]$.

### Example A.4. Car counting.
The number of cars $C$ driving over a particular roundabout per minute can be regarded as a discrete random variable which can take values from 0 onwards. We say that the distribution of $C$ *has support on* $\{0, 1, \cdots\}$.  □

It is also possible to address two (or more) random variables simultaneously. Consider the case where $N$ and $K$ are random variables with *joint distribution function* $F_{N,K}(n, k) =$

$\Pr\{N \leq n, K \leq k\}$. Similarly, we have $f_{N,K}(n, k) = \Pr\{N = n, K = k\}$. Again, we have a simple relation between the joint CDF and the joint PDF:

$$F_{N,K}(n, k) = \sum_{i \leq n} \sum_{j \leq k} \Pr\{N = i, K = j\}. \tag{A.6}$$

The so-called *marginal probability density function* $f_N(n)$ is defined as follows:

$$f_N(n) = \sum_{k=0}^{\infty} f_{N,K}(n, k). \tag{A.7}$$

A similar definition can be given for the marginal PDF of $K$. The *conditional PDF* of $N$ with respect to $K$ is given as

$$f_{N|K}(n|k) = \Pr\{N = n|K = k\} = \frac{\Pr\{N = n, K = k\}}{\Pr\{K = k\}} = \frac{f_{N,K}(n, k)}{f_K(k)}, \tag{A.8}$$

by virtue of the definition of conditional probability.

If $N$ and $K$ are independent we have $F_{N|K}(n|k) = F_N(n)$, and consequently $f_{N,K}(n, k) = f_N(n)f_K(k)$. The latter two equalities also hold for the CDF's.

## A.3    Some important discrete distributions

**Bernoulli.** A discrete random variable $N$ has a Bernoulli distribution with parameter $p$ when it only takes two values, without loss of generality called "0" and "1", and for which $f_N(0) = \Pr\{N = 0\} = 1 - p$ and $f_N(1) = \Pr\{N = 1\} = p$.

The result of tossing a coin is generally assumed to generate a Bernoulli distribution (with $p = 0.5$). The event "0" is generally called a failure, the event "1" a success.

**Geometric.**   Consider again a series of Bernoulli experiments in which the success-probability is $p$. The number of trials $N$ until the first success, the success itself included, has a geometric distribution:

$$f_N(n) = \Pr\{N = n\} = (1 - p)^{n-1}p, \quad n = 1, 2, \cdots . \tag{A.9}$$

A geometrically distributed random variable has support on $1, 2, \cdots$.

The geometric distribution is the only discrete distribution that is *memoryless*. This means that the probability that a geometrically distributed random variable $N = n + m$, given that we know that $N > n$ (with $m \geq 1$), simply is equal to the probability that $N = m$:

$$\Pr\{N = n + m|N > n\} = \Pr\{N = m\}, \quad m \geq 1. \tag{A.10}$$

In words, this does mean that the fact that we have knowledge of the past (the fact that $N > n$) does not change the future behaviour.

**Modified geometric.** A slight variation occurs with the modified geometric distribution. Here the number of Bernoulli trials $M$ *before* the first success is of interest. A random variable $M$ distributed like this has support on $I\!N$:

$$f_M(m) = \Pr\{M = m\} = (1 - p)^m p, \quad m = 0, 1, \cdots. \tag{A.11}$$

**Binomial.** Consider again a Bernoulli experiment in which the success probability equals $p$. Now repeat this Bernoulli experiment $n$ times. The number of successes $N$ then has a binomial distribution with parameters $n$ and $p$:

$$f_N(k) = \Pr\{N = k\} = \binom{n}{k} p^k (1 - p)^{n-k}. \tag{A.12}$$

Note that $N$ has support over the range $0, \cdots, n$.

**Poisson.** When the number of trials $n$ in the binomial distribution becomes large, the calculation of the binomial probabilities might be cumbersome. Instead, one might approximate the binomial PDF by a Poisson PDF; however, this approximation is only good when $n \geq 20$ and $p \leq 0.05$. If this is the case, we can set $\alpha = np$ and use the following expression for the Poisson PDF:

$$f_N(n) = \Pr\{N = n\} = e^{-\alpha} \frac{\alpha^n}{n!}. \tag{A.13}$$

Note that a Poisson distributed number has support on $I\!N$.

**Uniform.** A discrete uniformly distributed random variable $N$ takes, with equal probability, one value out of a countable set. As an example, think of rolling a dice. If $N$ can take values in $S = \{n_1, \cdots, n_k\}$, we have $f_N(n_i) = 1/k$.

# A.4  Continuous random variables

In this section we address continuous random variables. Since a continuous random variable $X$ can assume values in a finite or infinite range of the real numbers there are always infinitely many possible values for $X$. Therefore, the probability of any particular value $x$ equals 0: $\Pr\{X = x\} = 0$. The *cumulative density function* or *distribution function* is defined as $F_X(x) = \Pr\{X \leq x\}$. The probability density function, if it exists, is defined as

$$f_X(x) = \lim_{\delta \to 0} \frac{F_X(x + \delta) - F_X(x)}{\delta} = \frac{dF_X(x)}{dx} = F_X'(x). \tag{A.14}$$

Stated differently, we see that $F_X(x)$ is the integral over an infinite range of $f_X(x)$ values, like $F_N(n)$ was the (discrete) sum over a finite countable set of $f_N(n)$ values:

$$F_X(x) = \int_{-\infty}^{x} f_X(u)du. \tag{A.15}$$

Consequently, $\Pr\{x \in [a,b]\} = \Pr\{a \le x \le b\} = \Pr\{x \le b\} - \Pr\{x \le a\} = F_X(b) - F_X(a)$. Because the probability of all outcomes must sum to one, we have

$$\int_{-\infty}^{\infty} f_X(x)dx = 1. \tag{A.16}$$

Consequently, under certain (technical) conditions, $F_X(x)$ is a monotonously increasing function with range $[0,1]$.

**Example A.5. Telephone calls.**
The duration of a telephone call is generally represented as a random variable with support on $[0, \infty)$, whereas the number of calls a particular exchange is handling at a particular time instance is a discrete random variable on $\{0, 1, \cdots\}$.                                    □

It is also possible to address two (or more) random variables simultaneously. Consider the case where $X$ and $Y$ are random variables with *joint distribution function* $F_{X,Y}(x,y) = \Pr\{X \le x, Y \le y\}$. We have a simple relation between the joint CDF and the joint PDF:

$$F_{X,Y}(x,y) = \int_{-\infty}^{x}\int_{-\infty}^{y} f_{X,Y}(u,v)dudv. \tag{A.17}$$

The so-called *marginal probability density function* $f_X(x)$ is defined as follows:

$$f_X(x) = \int_{-\infty}^{\infty} f_{X,Y}(x,y)dy. \tag{A.18}$$

A similar definition can be given for the marginal PDF of $Y$. The *conditional PDF* of $X$ with respect to $Y$ is given as:

$$f_{X|Y}(x|y) = \frac{f_{X,Y}(x,y)}{f_Y(y)}, \tag{A.19}$$

by virtue of the definition of conditional probability. If $X$ and $Y$ are independent we have $F_{X|Y}(x|y) = f_X(x)$, and consequently $f_{X,Y}(x,y) = f_X(x)f_Y(y)$. The latter two equalities also hold for the CDF's.

Now consider two independent random variables $X$ and $Y$, with distribution functions $F_X(x)$ and $F_Y(y)$, respectively. The sum $Z = X + Y$, is a random variable with as density the convolution of $f_X(x)$ and $f_Y(y)$ as follows:

$$f_Z(z) = \int_{-\infty}^{\infty} f_X(u)f_Y(z-u)du, \quad -\infty < z < \infty. \tag{A.20}$$

When $X$ and $Y$ are non-negative random variables, then this can be reduced to

$$f_Z(z) = \int_0^z f_X(u) f_Y(z-u) du, \quad 0 \le z < \infty. \tag{A.21}$$

## A.5   Some important continuous distributions

**Normal.** Let $X$ denote a random variable with support over the entire real axis and with mean $\mu$ and variance $\sigma^2$ ($\sigma$ is called the standard deviation; see also the next section). We say that $X$ has an $N(\mu, \sigma^2)$ distribution, if the associated PDF is:

$$f_X(x) = \frac{1}{\sqrt{2\pi\sigma^2}} e^{\frac{-(x-\mu)^2}{2\sigma^2}}. \tag{A.22}$$

No explicit expression exists for the CDF $F_X(x)$. There are a number of interesting properties associated with the normal distribution:

- When $X$ has an $N(\mu, \sigma^2)$ distribution, the random variable $(X-\mu)/\sigma$ has an $N(0,1)$ distribution.

- Let $X_1, \cdots, X_n$ be a set of mutually independent random variables with means $\mu_1, \cdots, \mu_n$ and standard deviations $\sigma_1, \cdots, \sigma_n$, such that, for all $i$, the values $\mu_i$, $\sigma_i$, and $\mu_i/\sigma_i$ are finite, then, as $n \to \infty$, the random variable

$$\frac{\sum_{i=1}^n X_i - \sum_{i=1}^n \mu_i}{\sqrt{\sum_{i=1}^n \sigma_i^2}} \to N(0, 1). \tag{A.23}$$

This is the *central limit theorem*. Note that although we did not assume anything about the distributions of the involved $X_i$, their arithmetic average tends to be normally distributed for large $n$. The normal distribution plays a role in the statistical evaluation of simulation results.

**Deterministic.** A deterministic random variable $X$ can only take one value, $d$, with probability 1. In fact, this random variable can be viewed as discrete as well as continuous:

$$f_X(x) = \text{Dirac}(d), \quad \text{and} \quad F_X(x) = \begin{cases} 0, & x < d, \\ 1, & x \ge d, \end{cases} \tag{A.24}$$

where $\text{Dirac}(d)$ is a Dirac impulse at $x = d$.

**Exponential.** A non-negative random variable $X$ has an exponential distribution with parameter $\lambda$ (sometimes also called a negative exponential distribution) when, for $\lambda, x > 0$, we have

$$f_X(x) = \lambda e^{-\lambda x} \quad \text{and} \quad F_X(x) = 1 - e^{-\lambda x}. \tag{A.25}$$

The exponential distribution has a very nice property: it is the only continuous *memoryless* distribution. The memoryless property states that

$$\Pr\{X \le x + y | X > y\} = \Pr\{X \le x\}. \tag{A.26}$$

This implies that the knowledge of $X$ being larger than $y$ does not matter at all for determining the probability that $X$ is larger than $x + y$. Somehow, the history of $X$ (its being larger than $y$) does not matter; it has no memory.

**Erlang.** Let $X_1, \cdots, X_n$ be identically and independently distributed random variables, all with the same exponential distribution. Then $X = \sum_{i=1}^{n} X_i$ has an $n$-stage Erlang distribution (an Erlang-$n$ distribution). An Erlang-$n$ distribution is a series of $n$ independent and identically distributed exponential distributions. We have, for $x, \lambda > 0$ and $n = 1, 2, \cdots$:

$$f_X(x) = \frac{\lambda(\lambda x)^{n-1}}{(n-1)!} e^{-\lambda x}, \tag{A.27}$$

and

$$F_X(x) = 1 - e^{-\lambda x} \sum_{j=0}^{n-1} \frac{(\lambda x)^j}{j!}. \tag{A.28}$$

Notice that the Erlang-$n$ density is the convolution of $n$ exponential densities (all with the same mean).

**Hypo-exponential.** This distribution is also called generalised Erlang distribution. It is similar to the Erlang distribution; however, the successive exponential stages need not have the same mean, that is, we have $X = \sum_{i=1}^{n} X_i$, where $X_i$ is an exponentially distributed random variable with parameter $\lambda_i$. When we have 2 stages and parameters $\lambda_1, \lambda_2 > 0$ and $x > 0$, we have:

$$\begin{aligned} f_X(x) &= \frac{\lambda_1 \lambda_2}{\lambda_2 - \lambda_1} (e^{-\lambda_1 x} - e^{-\lambda_2 x}), \quad \text{and} \\ F_X(x) &= 1 - \frac{\lambda_2}{\lambda_2 - \lambda_1} e^{-\lambda_1 x} + \frac{\lambda_1}{\lambda_2 - \lambda_1} e^{-\lambda_2 x}. \end{aligned} \tag{A.29}$$

Notice that the hypo-exponential density is the convolution of $n$ exponential densities.

**Hyperexponential.** Let $X_1$ and $X_2$ be two independent exponentially distributed random variables with parameters $\lambda_1$ and $\lambda_2$ respectively. Now, let $X$ be a random variable that with probability $p_1$ is distributed as $X_1$ and with probability $p_2$ as $X_2$. Note that $p_1+p_2 = 1$. We say that $X$ has a 2-stage hyperexponential distribution:

$$f_X(x) = p_1\lambda_1 e^{-\lambda_1 x} + p_2\lambda_2 e^{-\lambda_2 x}. \tag{A.30}$$

Generalisations to more than two stages are easy to imagine.

### Example A.6. Service times.

In the modelling of computer and communication systems, one often has to make assumptions about the involved job service times or the packet transmission times (the packet lengths). For these purposes often the exponential, Erlang, hypo- and hyper-exponential distribution are used. The exponential distribution is especially advantageous to use, due to its memoryless property.

Extensive monitoring of telephone exchanges has revealed that telephone call durations typically are exponentially distributed. Moreover, the average time between successive call arrivals obeys the exponential distribution. □

**Phase-type distributions.** The last three mentioned distributions are examples of the class of phase-type distributions, which are distributions that are formed by summing exponential distributions, or by probabilistically choosing among them. We discuss phase-type distributions in more detail in Chapter 3. A special type of phase-type distribution that is used often is the Coxian distribution. It is basically a hypo-exponential distribution; however, before every exponential phase, it is decided probabilistically whether a next phase is taken or not. Coxian distributions can be used to approximate any other distribution (with rational Laplace transform). They can also be seen as special cases of a phase-type distribution.

**Uniform.** A continuous random variable $X$ has a uniform distribution on $[a, b]$ when all the values in the interval $[a, b]$ have equal probability. The uniform PDF equals

$$f_X(x) = \begin{cases} \frac{1}{b-a}, & a < x < b, \\ 0, & \text{otherwise.} \end{cases} \tag{A.31}$$

The uniform CDF equals

$$f_X(x) = \begin{cases} 0, & x < a, \\ \frac{x-a}{b-a}, & a \le x < b, \\ 1, & x \ge b. \end{cases} \tag{A.32}$$

## A.6    Moments of random variables

In many situations we do not characterise a random variable by its complete distribution but rather by its *moments*. The most important moment of a random variable is the *mean* or the *expected value*. This first moment is calculated as

$$E[N] = \sum_{n=0}^{\infty} n f_N(n), \tag{A.33}$$

when $N$ is a discrete random variable, and as

$$E[X] = \int_{-\infty}^{\infty} x f_X(x) dx, \tag{A.34}$$

when $X$ is a continuous random variable. $E[\cdot]$ is called the expectation operator. This is generalised to the *k-th moment* $(k = 1, 2, \cdots)$ as follows:

$$E[N^k] = \sum_{n=0}^{\infty} n^k f_N(n), \tag{A.35}$$

when $N$ is a discrete random variable, and as

$$E[X^k] = \int_{-\infty}^{\infty} x^k f_X(x) dx, \tag{A.36}$$

when $X$ is a continuous random variable.

The quantity $E[(X - E[X])^k]$ is known as the *k-th central moment* $(k = 1, 2, \cdots)$. Note that the first central moment equals 0. The second central moment is known as the *variance*. It is denoted as $\text{var}[X]$ or as $\sigma_X^2$:

$$\sigma_X^2 = \text{var}[X] = E[(X - E[X])^2] = E[X^2] - E[X]^2. \tag{A.37}$$

A similar definition exists for the variance of discrete random variables (by just changing the $X$'s into $N$'s). We call $\text{var}[\cdot]$ the variance operator.

A measure that is often used in performance analysis is the *squared coefficient of variation*:

$$C_X^2 = \frac{\text{var}[X]}{E[X]^2}, \tag{A.38}$$

which expresses the variance of $X$ relative to its average value.

Note that we have assumed a number of properties of the expectation operator. First of all, that it is a linear operator. This means that whenever the random variable $Y = aX + b$, then $E[Y] = aE[X] + E[b] = aE[X] + b$, where $X$ is a random variable and where $a$ and $b$ are constant.

More generally, when $X_1, \cdots, X_n$ are random variables, we always have

$$E[\sum_{i=1}^{n} a_i X_i] = \sum_{i=1}^{n} a_i E[X_i]. \tag{A.39}$$

If the $X_i$ are mutually independent we have

$$E[\prod_{i=1}^{n} X_i] = \prod_{i=1}^{n} E[X_i]. \tag{A.40}$$

Also under the independence assumption, we have

$$\text{var}[\sum_{i=1}^{n} X_i] = \sum_{i=1}^{n} \text{var}[X_i], \tag{A.41}$$

and

$$\text{var}[\prod_{i=1}^{n} X_i] = \prod_{i=1}^{n} \text{var}[X_i]. \tag{A.42}$$

Important to note is the fact that the variance operator is *not* a linear operator: $\text{var}[aX + b] = a^2 \text{var}[X]$.

## A.7    Moments of discrete random variables

In Table A.1 we summarise the parameters and moments of the most important discrete random variables.

**Bernoulli.** Consider a Bernoulli distributed random variable $N$ with parameter $p$. $E[N] = 1 \times p + 0 \times (1-p) = p$. Similarly, we derive $E[N^2] = p$, so that $\text{var}[N] = p - p^2 = p(1-p)$. The squared coefficient of variation then equals: $C_N^2 = \text{var}[N]/E[N]^2 = (1-p)/p$.

**Binomial.** Consider a binomially distributed random variable $N$ with parameters $n$ and $p$. By the fact that a binomial distribution is derived from $n$ independent Bernoulli trials and the linearity of the expectation operator we immediately see that $E[N] = np$ and $\text{var}[N] = np(1-p)$. Consequently, $C_N^2 = (1-p)/np$.

**Poisson.** Consider a Poisson distributed random variable $N$ with parameter $\alpha$. The expectation then equals, analogously to the binomial distribution: $E[N] = \alpha$. We can also calculate that $\text{var}[N] = \alpha$. Consequently, we have $C_N^2 = 1/\alpha$.

**Geometric.** Consider a geometrically distributed random variable $N$ with parameter $p$. We can calculate $E[N] = 1/p$ and $\text{var}[N] = (1-p)/p^2$, so that $C_N^2 = 1 - p$.

**Modified geometric.** Consider a modified geometrically distributed random variable $N$ with parameter $p$. We now have $E[N] = (1-p)/p$, $\text{var}[N] = (1-p)/p^2$, and $C_N^2 = 1/(1-p)$

| distribution | parameters | $E[N]$ | var$[N]$ | $C_N^2$ |
|---|---|---|---|---|
| Bernoulli | $p$ | $p$ | $p(1-p)$ | $\dfrac{1-p}{p}$ |
| Geometric | $p$ | $\dfrac{1}{p}$ | $\dfrac{1-p}{p^2}$ | $1-p$ |
| Mod. Geo. | $p$ | $\dfrac{1-p}{p}$ | $\dfrac{1-p}{p^2}$ | $\dfrac{1}{1-p}$ |
| Binomial | $n,p$ | $np$ | $np(1-p)$ | $\dfrac{1-p}{np}$ |
| Poisson | $\alpha$ | $\alpha$ | $\alpha$ | $\dfrac{1}{\alpha}$ |
| Uniform | $n$ | $\dfrac{n+1}{2}$ | $\dfrac{n^2-1}{12}$ | $\dfrac{n-1}{3(n+1)}$ |

Table A.1: Moments of important discrete random variables

**Uniform.** Consider a discrete uniformly distributed random variable $N$ that can take values in $S = \{1, \cdots, n\}$. Its mean then equals $E[N] = (n+1)/2$ and its variance var$[N] = (n^2 - 1)/12$. Consequently, $C_N^2 = (n-1)/3(n+1)$.

## A.8 Moments of continuous random variables

In Table A.2 we summarise the parameters and moments of the most important continuous random variables.

**Normal.** A random variable $X$ with an $N(\mu, \sigma^2)$ distribution has, by definition, $E[X] = \mu$ and var$[X] = \sigma^2$. Consequently, $C_X^2 = (\sigma/\mu)^2$.

**Deterministic.** A deterministic random variable $X$ has as expectation its only possible value: $E[X] = d$. Since there is no randomness at all, var$[X] = 0$ ($E[X^2] = d^2$), so that $C_X^2 = 0$.

**Exponential.** An exponentially distributed random variable $X$ with parameter $\lambda$ has $E[X] = 1/\lambda$. This can be derived as follows:

$$E[X] \;=\; \int_{-\infty}^{\infty} x f_X(x)\,dx = \int_0^{\infty} \lambda x e^{-\lambda x}\,dx$$

| distribution | parameters | $E[X]$ | $E[X^2]$ | $\text{var}[X]$ | $C_X^2$ |
|---|---|---|---|---|---|
| Normal | $\mu, \sigma^2$ | $\mu$ | $\sigma^2 + \mu^2$ | $\sigma^2$ | $\dfrac{\sigma^2}{\mu^2}$ |
| Deterministic | $d$ | $d$ | $d^2$ | $0$ | $0$ |
| Exponential | $\lambda$ | $\dfrac{1}{\lambda}$ | $\dfrac{2}{\lambda^2}$ | $\dfrac{1}{\lambda^2}$ | $1$ |
| Erlang | $\lambda, n$ | $\dfrac{n}{\lambda}$ | $\dfrac{n(n+1)}{\lambda^2}$ | $\dfrac{n}{\lambda^2}$ | $\dfrac{1}{n}$ |
| Hypo-expo. | $\lambda_1, \cdots, \lambda_n$ | $\displaystyle\sum_{i=1}^{n} \dfrac{1}{\lambda_i}$ | $\displaystyle\sum_{i=1}^{n} \dfrac{2}{\lambda_i^2}$ | $\displaystyle\sum_{i=1}^{n} \dfrac{1}{\lambda_i^2}$ | $\leq 1$ |
| Hyper-expo. | $p_1, \cdots, p_n$ $\lambda_1, \cdots, \lambda_n$ | $\displaystyle\sum_{i=1}^{n} \dfrac{p_i}{\lambda_i}$ | $\displaystyle\sum_{i=1}^{n} \dfrac{2p_i}{\lambda_i^2}$ | def. | $> 1$ |
| Uniform | $a, b$ | $\dfrac{a+b}{2}$ | $\dfrac{b^3 - a^3}{3(b-a)}$ | $\dfrac{(b-a)^2}{12}$ | $\dfrac{(b-a)^2}{3(a+b)^2}$ |

Table A.2: Moments of important continuous random variables

$$= \left(\frac{\lambda x e^{-\lambda x}}{-\lambda}\right)_{x=0}^{x=\infty} + \frac{1}{\lambda}\int_0^\infty \lambda e^{-\lambda x}\,dx = \int_0^\infty e^{-\lambda x}\,dx = \frac{1}{\lambda}. \qquad (A.43)$$

By integrating by parts twice, it can be derived that $E[X^2] = 2/\lambda^2$, so that $\text{var}[X] = 1/\lambda^2$. Consequently, we have $C_X^2 = 1$.

**Erlang.** For the $n$-stage Erlang distribution we simply derive, by the linearity of the expectation operator, that $E[X] = n/\lambda$. We derive that $E[X^2] = n(n+1)/\lambda^2$, so that $\text{var}[X] = n/\lambda^2$. Consequently, we have $C_X^2 = 1/n$ which is always smaller than 1, for $n = 2, 3, \cdots$. An Erlang-$n$ distribution is "more deterministic" than an exponential distribution.

**Hypo-exponential.** Consider a hypo-exponentially distributed random variable $X$ with parameters $\lambda_1, \cdots, \lambda_n$, that is, $X$ is the sum of $n$ independent exponential stages $X_i$ with parameters $\lambda_i$ . By using the linearity of the expectation operator, we easily derive that $E[X] = \sum_{i=1}^n E[X_i] = \sum_{i=1}^n 1/\lambda_i$. Since the stages that constitute the hypo-exponential are independent, we also have linearity in the variance operator, so that $\text{var}[X] = \sum_{i=1}^n \text{var}[X_i] = \sum_{i=1}^n 1/\lambda_i^2$ For the coefficient of variation it can be derived that $C_X^2 \le 1$.

**Hyperexponential.** An $n$-stage hyperexponentially distributed random variable $X$ with parameters $p_1, \cdots, p_n$, and $\lambda_1, \cdots, \lambda_n$ has the following moments: $E[X] = \sum_{i=1}^n p_i/\lambda_i$ and $E[X^2] = \sum_{i=1}^n 2p_i/\lambda_i^2$. Consequently,

$$\text{var}[X] = 2\sum_{i=1}^n \frac{p_i}{\lambda_i^2} - \left(\sum_{i=1}^n \frac{p_i}{\lambda_i}\right)^2. \tag{A.44}$$

The coefficient of variation can then be derived as $C_X^2 = E[X^2]/E[X]^2 - 1$. It can be shown that $C_X^2 \ge 1$.

**Uniform.** A uniformly distributed random variable $X$ on $[a, b]$ has as average value $E[X] = (a+b)/2$. Its variance can be derived as $\text{var}[X] = (b-a)^2/12$. From these two, we derive the coefficient of variation as $C_X^2 = (b-a)^2/3(a+b)^2$.

# Appendix B

# Some useful techniques in applied probability

IN this appendix we present a brief introduction to Laplace transforms in Section B.1. We then present the geometric series in Section B.2, after which we introduce tensor operators in Section B.3.

## B.1  Laplace transforms

The Laplace transform is a useful tool in many stochastic models. In model-based performance evaluation, Laplace transforms of probability density functions play an important role. Let $f(x)$ be such a PDF (for $x > 0$). Then, whenever $|f(x)| < M e^{\alpha x}$, $M, \alpha > 0$, the Laplace transform of $f(x)$ can be computed as:

$$f^*(s) = \int_0^\infty f(x) e^{-sx} dx. \tag{B.1}$$

Using this definition, a number of "standard" Laplace transforms can easily be computed as given in Table B.1. There are a number of interesting properties associated with Laplace transforms. We list some of them below:

1. **Uniqueness.** If two Laplace transforms $f^*(s) = g^*(s)$, for all $s$, then $f(x) = g(x)$, for all $x$.

2. **Convolution.** Consider $n$ random variables $X_1$ through $X_n$, each distributed according to PDF $f_{X_i}(x)$. The PDF of the sum $Z = \sum_{i=1}^n X_i$ has Laplace transform:

$$f_Z^*(s) = \prod_{i=1}^n f_{X_i}^*(s). \tag{B.2}$$

| $f(x)$ | $f^*(s)$ | condition |
|:---:|:---:|:---:|
| $c$ | $\dfrac{c}{s}$ | |
| $x$ | $\dfrac{1}{s^2}$ | |
| $x^i$ | $\dfrac{i!}{s^{i+1}}$ | $i \in \mathbb{N}$ |
| $e^{-ax}$ | $\dfrac{1}{s+a}$ | $Re(s) > a$ |
| $x^i e^{-ax}$ | $\dfrac{i!}{(s+a)^{i+1}}$ | $i \in \mathbb{N}, Re(s) > a$ |

Table B.1: A number of standard Laplace transforms

We see that convolution in the $x$-domain transforms to a simple product in the Laplace domain (the $s$-domain).

3. **Linearity.** Let $f(x) = \sum_i c_i f_i(x)$, then $f^*(s) = \sum_i c_i f_i^*(s)$.

4. **Moment generation**. Let $X$ be a random variable distributed with PDF $f(x)$, and with Laplace transform $f^*(s)$, then the $k$-th moment of $X$ can be computed from the transform as follows:

$$E[X^k] = (-1)^k \left( \frac{d^k f^*(s)}{ds^k} \right)_{s=0}. \tag{B.3}$$

5. **Dirac impulse.** If $F(x) = 0$, for $x < d$, and $F(x) = 1$, for $x \geq d$, then $f(x)$ is a Dirac impulse at $x = d$. The corresponding Laplace transform is then given as $f^*(s) = e^{-sd}$.

More information on Laplace transforms can be found in textbooks on mathematical analysis, such as in Kwakernaak and Sivan [168], but also in some performance evaluation textbooks, e.g., [280].

## B.2  Geometric series

The geometric series is used extensively in model-based performance evaluation, most notably in the analysis of birth-death processes and their variants. Below, we will present some important results for this series.

Consider the sum $S_n(x) = \sum_{i=0}^n x^i$, with $n \in \mathbb{N}$, $x > 0$ and $x \neq 1$; $S_n(1) = n+1$. The sum $xS_n(x) = \sum_{i=0}^n x^{i+1}$. We now find:

$$S_n(x) - xS_n(x) = \sum_{i=0}^n x^i - \sum_{i=0}^n x^{i+1} = x^0 - x^{n+1} = 1 - x^{n+1},$$

which can be rewritten as:

$$(1-x)S_n(x) = 1 - x^{n+1} \quad \Rightarrow \quad S_n(x) = \frac{1 - x^{n+1}}{1 - x}. \tag{B.4}$$

This expression for $S_n(x)$ is valid for all $x > 0$ ($x \neq 1$) and for all $n \in \mathbb{N}$. If we now take $0 < x < 1$ and let $n \to \infty$, the term $x^{n+1}$ will vanish, so that we obtain:

$$S_\infty(x) = \sum_{i=0}^\infty x^i = \frac{1}{1-x}, \quad 0 < x < 1. \tag{B.5}$$

Related to $S_\infty(x)$, one often has to compute the series

$$T_\infty(x) = \sum_{i=0}^\infty i x^i,$$

e.g., in expectation computations. We can compute this expression explicitly by changing the order of summation and differentiating as follows:

$$\begin{aligned}
T_\infty(x) &= \sum_{i=0}^\infty i x^i = x \sum_{i=0}^\infty i x^{i-1} = x \sum_{i=0}^\infty \frac{d}{dx}\left(x^i\right) \\
&= x \frac{d}{dx}\left(\sum_{i=0}^\infty x^i\right) = x \frac{d}{dx}\left(\frac{1}{1-x}\right) = \frac{x}{(1-x)^2}.
\end{aligned} \tag{B.6}$$

The expressions for $S_\infty(x)$ and $T_\infty(x)$ extend to the case where $x$ is replaced by a square matrix $\mathbf{M}$ of which the largest Eigenvalue (the spectral radius) is smaller than 1 (in length):

$$S_\infty(\mathbf{M}) = \sum_{i=0}^\infty \mathbf{M}^i = (\mathbf{I} - \mathbf{M})^{-1}, \quad |\mathrm{sp}(\mathbf{M})| < 1, \tag{B.7}$$

and

$$T_\infty(\mathbf{M}) = \sum_{i=0}^\infty i \mathbf{M}^i = \mathbf{M}(\mathbf{I} - \mathbf{M})^{-2}, \quad |\mathrm{sp}(\mathbf{M})| < 1. \tag{B.8}$$

The matrix extensions are often used when evaluating performance models by means of matrix-geometric methods (Chapter 8 and 17).

## B.3  Tensor sums and products

Tensor sums and products (also often called Kronecker sums and products) can be used when composing large CTMCs out of smaller ones, as is done in Chapter 8.

Let $\mathcal{M}(d_1)$ and $\mathcal{M}(d_2)$ denote the sets of all matrices of sizes $d_1 \times d_1$ and $d_2 \times d_2$ respectively. Let $\mathbf{Q}_1 \in \mathcal{M}(d_1)$ and $\mathbf{Q}_2 \in \mathcal{M}(d_2)$ and let $\mathbf{I}_d$ be the identity matrix in $\mathcal{M}(d)$. The *tensor sum* $\mathbf{Q}_\oplus$ of the matrices $\mathbf{Q}_1$ and $\mathbf{Q}_2$ is defined as follows:

$$\mathbf{Q}_\oplus = \mathbf{Q}_1 \oplus \mathbf{Q}_2 = (\mathbf{Q}_1 \otimes \mathbf{I}_{d_2}) + (\mathbf{I}_{d_1} \otimes \mathbf{Q}_2), \tag{B.9}$$

where the $+$ operator is the normal element-to-element addition and $\otimes$ the tensor product. The *tensor product* $\mathbf{Q}_\otimes$ of two matrices $\mathbf{Q}_1 \in \mathcal{M}(d_1)$ and $\mathbf{Q}_2 \in \mathcal{M}(d_2)$ is a matrix in $\mathcal{M}(d_1 d_2)$, i.e., a matrix consisting of $d_1 \times d_1$ blocks, each of size $d_2 \times d_2$. Let $q_1(i_1, j_1)$ be an element of the matrix $\mathbf{Q}_1$ and let $q_2(i_2, j_2)$ be an element of the matrix $\mathbf{Q}_2$. Then, the element $q_\otimes(\bar{\imath}, \bar{\jmath})$ equals $q_1(i_1, j_1)q_2(i_2, j_2)$, where $\bar{\imath} = (i_1, i_2)$ and $\bar{\jmath} = (j_1, j_2)$. $(i_1, j_1)$ can be interpreted as the block coordinate of $q_\otimes(\bar{\imath}, \bar{\jmath})$, and $(i_2, j_2)$ as its position within this block. The tensor sum and product are associative.

Consider two independent CTMCs on state spaces $\mathcal{I}_1$ and $\mathcal{I}_2$ and with generator matrices $\mathbf{Q}_1$ and $\mathbf{Q}_2$ respectively. The state space of the combined CTMCs is given by the Cartesian product $\mathcal{I}_1 \times \mathcal{I}_2$, and the generator $\mathbf{Q}$ of the combined CTMC equals the tensor sum of the individual Markov generators, i.e., $\mathbf{Q} = \mathbf{Q}_1 \oplus \mathbf{Q}_2$.

**Example B.1. Tensor sum and product.**
Consider the following two matrices:

$$\mathbf{A} = \begin{pmatrix} a & b \\ c & d \end{pmatrix}, \quad \text{and} \quad \mathbf{B} = \begin{pmatrix} 1 & 2 \\ 3 & 4 \\ 5 & 6 \end{pmatrix}. \tag{B.10}$$

We then can compute

$$\mathbf{A} \otimes \mathbf{B} = \begin{pmatrix} a & 2a & b & 2b \\ 3a & 4a & 3b & 4b \\ 5a & 6a & 5b & 6b \\ c & 2c & d & 2d \\ 3c & 4c & 3d & 4d \\ 5c & 6c & 5d & 6d \end{pmatrix}, \tag{B.11}$$

and

$$
\mathbf{B} \otimes \mathbf{A} =
\begin{pmatrix}
a & b & 2a & 2b \\
c & d & 2c & 2d \\
3a & 3b & 4a & 4b \\
3c & 3d & 4c & 4d \\
5a & 5b & 6a & 6b \\
5c & 5d & 6c & 6d
\end{pmatrix}.
\tag{B.12}
$$

□

For further details on tensor algebra and its applications, see e.g., Massey [192] or Plateau *et al.* [234].

# Appendix C

# Abbreviations

| | |
|---|---|
| AAL | ATM adaptation layer |
| ACE | acyclic Markov chain evaluator |
| ACM | Association for Computing Machinery |
| ATM | asynchronous transfer mode |
| BASTA | Bernoulli arrivals see time averages |
| BCMP | Baskett, Chandy, Muntz, Palacios |
| CDF | cumulative density function |
| CHW | Chandy, Herzog, Woo (theorem) |
| CPU | central processing unit |
| CTMC | continuous-time Markov chain |
| CSPN | coloured stochastic Petri net |
| DES | discrete-event simulation |
| DSPN | deterministic and stochastic Petri net |
| DTMC | discrete-time Markov chain |
| EPT | elapsed processing time |
| ETPP | extended threshold priority policy |
| FCFS | first-come first-served |
| FDDI | fiber distributed data interface |
| FESC | flow-equivalent service center |
| FFQN | feed-forward queueing network |
| FIFO | first in, first out |
| GBE | global balance equations |
| GMTF | general modelling tool framework |

| | |
|---|---|
| GNQN | Gordon-Newell queueing network |
| GS | Gauss-Seidel |
| GSPN | generalised stochastic Petri net |
| HRN | highest response ratio next |
| IBM | International Business Machines |
| IEEE | Institute of Electrical and Electronics Engineers, Inc. |
| IO | input/output |
| IPP | interrupted Poisson process |
| IS | infinite server |
| iSPN | infinite-state stochastic Petri net |
| SDN | integrated services digital network |
| JQN | Jackson queueing network |
| KLB | Krämer and Langenbach-Belz |
| LAN | local-area network |
| LBE | local balance equations |
| LCFS | last-come first-served |
| LCFSPR | last-come first-served, with preemption |
| LDS | load-dependent server |
| LR | logarithmic reduction |
| LU | lower-upper (decomposition) |
| LWB | lower bound |
| MGM | matrix-geometric method |
| MMAP | Markov-modulated arrival process |
| MMPP | Markov-modulated Poisson process |
| MTTF | mean time to failure |
| MTTR | mean time to repair |
| MVA | mean-value analysis |
| MVM | matrix-vector multiplications |
| OCDR | on-demand connection with delayed release |
| PASTA | Poisson arrivals see time averages |
| PDF | probability density function |
| PFQN | product-form queueing network |
| PFSPN | product-form stochastic Petri net |
| PH | phase-type (distribution) |
| PK | Pollaczek-Khintchine (formula) |

| | |
|---|---|
| PRD | preemptive resume different |
| PRI | preemptive resume identical |
| PRIO | priority scheduling |
| PRS | preemptive resume |
| PS | processor sharing |
| QBD | quasi-birth-death process |
| QN | queueing network |
| QNA | queueing network analyzer |
| RNG | random number generator/generation |
| RK | Runge-Kutta |
| RR | round robin |
| SAN | stochastic activity network |
| SEPT | shortest elapsed processing time |
| SJN | shortest job next |
| SMC | semi-Markov chain |
| SOR | successive over-relaxation |
| SPN | stochastic Petri net |
| SRPT | shortest remaining processing time |
| SS | successive substitution |
| SU | standard uniformisation |
| THT | token holding timer |
| TMR | triple-modular redundancy |
| TPP | threshold priority policy |
| TTRT | target token rotation timer |
| UPB | upper bound |

# Bibliography

[1] M. Ajmone Marsan, G. Balbo and G. Conte. *Performance Models of Multiprocessor Systems*. The MIT Press, 1986.

[2] M. Ajmone Marsan, G. Balbo, G. Conte, S. Donatelli and G. Franceschinis. *Modelling with generalized stochastic Petri nets*. John Wiley & Sons, 1995.

[3] M. Ajmone Marsan and G. Chiola. On Petri nets with deterministic and exponentially distributed firing time. In: G. Rozenberg (editor), *Advances in Petri Nets*, pp.132–145. Springer-Verlag, 1987.

[4] M. Ajmone Marsan, G. Conte and G. Balbo. A class of generalized stochastic Petri nets for the performance evaluation of multiprocessor systems. *ACM Transactions on Computer Systems*, **2**(2):93–122, 1984.

[5] M. Ajmone Marsan, S. Donatelli and F. Neri. GSPN models of Markovian multiserver multiqueue systems. *Performance Evaluation*, **11**:227–240, 1990.

[6] M. Ajmone Marsan, S. Donatelli, F. Neri and U. Rubino. GSPN models of random, cyclic and optimal 1-limited multiserver multiqueue systems. *ACM Computer Communications Review*, **21**(4):69–80, 1991.

[7] M. Ajmone Marsan, S. Donatelli, F. Neri and U. Rubino. On the construction of abstract GSPNs: An exercise in modelling. In: *Proceedings of the 4th International Workshop on Petri Nets and Performance Models*, pp.2–17. IEEE Computer Society Press, 1991.

[8] G.M. Amdahl. Validity of the single-processor approach to achieving large scale computing capabilities. In: *Proceedings of the AFIPS Conference; Volume 30*, pp.483–485. AFIPS Press, 1967.

[9] B. Avi-Itzhak, W.L. Maxwell and L.W. Miller. Queueing with alternating priorities. *Operations Research*, **13**:306–318, 1965.

[10] G. Balbo. On the success of stochastic Petri nets. In: *Proceedings of the 5th International Workshop on Petri Nets and Performance Models*, pp.2–9. IEEE Computer Society Press, 1995.

[11] G. Balbo. Stochastic Petri nets: Accomplishments and open problems. In: *Proceedings of the 1st International Computer Performance and Dependability Symposium*, pp.51–60. IEEE Computer Society Press, 1995.

[12] Y. Bard. The VM/370 performance predictor. *ACM Computing Surveys*, **10**(3):333–342, 1978.

[13] Y. Bard. Some extensions to multiclass queueing network analysis. In: M. Arato, A. Butrimenko and E. Gelenbe (editors), *Performance of Computer Systems*, pp.51–61. North-Holland, 1979.

[14] F. Baskett, K.M. Chandy, R.R. Muntz and F. Palacios. Open, closed and mixed networks of queues with different classes of customers. *Journal of the ACM*, **22**(2):248–260, 1975.

[15] F. Bause and P.S. Kritzinger. *Stochastic Petri Nets: An Introduction to the Theory.* Vieweg Verlag, 1996.

[16] H. Beilner. Workload characterisation and performance modelling. In: *Proceedings of the International Workshop on Workload Characterisation of Computer Systems*, Pavia, Italy, 1985.

[17] S. Berson, E. de Souza e Silva and R.R. Muntz. *An object-oriented methodology for the specification of Markov models.* Technical report, University of California, Los Angeles, 1987.

[18] S.S. Berson and R.R. Muntz. *Detecting Block GI|M|1 and Block M|G|1 Matrices from Model Specifications.* Technical report, University of California, Los Angeles, 1994.

[19] G.A. Blaauw and F.P. Brooks. *Computer Architecture: Concepts and Evolution.* Addison Wesley, 1997.

[20] J.B.C. Blanc. An algorithmic solution of polling models with limited services disciplines. *IEEE Transactions on Communications*, **40**(7):1152–1155, 1992.

[21] J.B.C. Blanc. Performance evaluation of polling systems by means of the Power-series algorithm. *Annals of Operations Research*, **35**:155–186, 1992.

[22] A. Bobbio and L. Roberti. Distribution of the minimal completion time of parallel tasks in multi-reward semi-Markov models. *Performance Evaluation*, **14**:239–256, 1992.

[23] A. Bobbio and K.S. Trivedi. An aggregation technique for the transient analysis of stiff Markov chains. *IEEE Transactions on Computers*, **35**(9):803–814, 1986.

[24] P.P. Bocharov and V. Nauomov. Matrix-geometric stationary distribution for the PH|PH|1|r queue. *Elektronische Informationsverarbeitung und Kybernetik*, **22**(4):179–186, 1986.

[25] D.R. Boggs, J.C. Mogul and C.A. Kent. Measured capacity of an Ethernet: Myths and reality. *ACM Computer Communication Review*, **18**(4):222–234, 1988.

[26] G. Bolch, G. Fleischmann and R. Schreppel. Ein funktionales Konzept zur Analyse von Warteschlangennetzen und Optimierung von Leistungsgrössen. In: U. Herzog and M. Paterok (editors), *Messung, Modellierung und Bewertung von Rechensystemen*, Informatik Fachberichte 154, pp.327–342. Springer-Verlag, 1987.

[27] O.J. Boxma, W.P. Groenendijk and J.A. Weststrate. A pseudo-conservation law for service systems with a polling table. *IEEE Transactions on Communications*, **38**(10):1865–1870, 1993.

[28] O.J. Boxma and B. Meister. Waiting time approximations in multi-queue systems with cyclic service. *Performance Evaluation*, **7**(1):59–70, 1987.

[29] P. Brinch Hansen. *Operating System Principles*. Prentice-Hall, 1973.

[30] S.C. Bruell and G. Balbo. *Computational algorithms for closed queueing networks*. North-Holland, 1980.

[31] P. Buchholz. Hierarchical Markovian models: Symmetries and reduction. In: R. Pooley and J. Hillston (editors), *Computer Performance Evaluation '92: Modelling Techniques and Tools*, pp.305–319. Edinburgh University Press, 1992.

[32] P. Buchholz. Aggregation and reduction techniques for hierarchical GCSPNs. In: *Proceedings of the 5th International Workshop on Petri Nets and Performance Models*, pp.216–225. IEEE Computer Society Press, 1993.

[33] P. Buchholz, J. Dunkel, B. Müller-Clostermann, M. Sczittnick and S. Zäske. *Quantitative Systemanalyse mit Markovschen Ketten*. B.G. Teubner Verlag, 1994.

[34] P.J. Burke. The output of a queueing system. *Operations Research*, 4:699–704, 1956.

[35] W. Bux. Token-ring local-area networks and their performance. *Proceedings of the IEEE*, **77**(2):238–256, 1989.

[36] W. Bux and H.L. Truong. Mean-delay approximation for cyclic-server queueing systems. *Performance Evaluation*, **3**:187–196, 1983.

[37] J.P. Buzen. Computational algorithms for closed queueing networks with exponential servers. *Communications of the ACM*, **16**(9):527–531, 1973.

[38] J.P. Buzen. A queueing network model of MVS. *ACM Computing Surveys*, **10**(3):319–331, 1978.

[39] R. Chakka and I. Mitrani. Spectral expansion solution for a finite capacity multiserver system in a Markovian environment. In: D.D. Kouvatsos (editor), *Proceedings of the 3rd International Workshop on Queueing Networks with Finite Capacity*, pp.6.1–6.9, 1995.

[40] K.M. Chandy. A survey of analytic models of rollback and recovery strategies. *IEEE Computer*, **8**(5):40–47, 1975.

[41] K.M. Chandy, U. Herzog and L.S. Woo. Approximate analysis of general queueing networks. *IBM Journal of Research and Development*, **19**(1):43–49, 1975.

[42] K.M. Chandy, U. Herzog and L.S. Woo. Parametric analysis of queueing network models. *IBM Journal of Research and Development*, **19**(1):36–42, 1975.

[43] K.M. Chandy and D. Neuze. Linearizer: A heuristic algorithm for queueing network models of computing systems. *Communications of the ACM*, **25**(2):126–134, 1982.

[44] K.M. Chandy and C.H. Sauer. Approximate methods for analyzing queueing network models of computer systems. *ACM Computing Surveys*, **10**(3):281–317, 1978.

[45] K.M. Chandy and C.H. Sauer. Computational algorithms for product-form queueing networks. *Communications of the ACM*, **23**(10):573–583, 1980.

[46] P. Chimento and K.S. Trivedi. The completion time of programs on processors subject to failure and repair. *IEEE Transactions on Computers*, **42**(10):1184–1194, 1993.

[47] G. Chiola, C. Dutheillet, G. Franceschinis and S. Haddad. Stochastic well-formed coloured nets and symmetric modelling applications. *IEEE Transactions on Computers*, **42**(11):1343–1360, 1993.

[48] G. Chiola and A. Ferscha. Distributed simulation of Petri nets. *IEEE Parallel and Distributed Technology*, **1**(3):33–50, 1993.

[49] H. Choi, V.G. Kulkarni and K.S. Trivedi. Markov-regenerative stochastic Petri nets. In: G. Iazeolla and S.S. Lavenberg (editors), *Proceedings Performance '93*. North-Holland, 1993.

[50] H. Choi and K.S. Trivedi. Approximate performance models of polling systems using stochastic Petri nets. In: *Proceedings Infocom '92*, pp.2306–2314. IEEE Computer Society Press, 1992.

[51] G. Ciardo. Petri nets with marking-dependent arc cardinality: Properties and analysis. In: R. Valette (editor), *Application and Theory of Petri Nets 1994*, pp.179–198. Springer-Verlag, 1994.

[52] G. Ciardo, R. German and C. Lindemann. A characterization of the stochastic process underlying a stochastic Petri net. *IEEE Transactions on Software Engineering*, **20**(7):506–515, 1994.

[53] G. Ciardo, J. Muppala and K. S. Trivedi. SPNP: Stochastic Petri net package. In: *Proceedings of the 3rd International Workshop on Petri Nets and Performance Models*, pp.142–151. IEEE Computer Society Press, 1989.

[54] G. Ciardo, J.K. Muppala and K.S. Trivedi. Analyzing concurrent and fault-tolerant software using stochastic reward nets. *Journal of Parallel and Distributed Computing*, **15**:225–269, 1992.

[55] E. Çinlar. *Introduction to Stochastic Processes*. Prentice-Hall, 1975.

[56] R.F.W. Coates, G.J. Janacek and K.V. Leever. Monte Carlo simulation and random number generation. *IEEE Journal on Selected Areas in Communications*, **6**(1):58–65, 1988.

[57] A. Cobham. Priority assignments in waiting line problems. *Operations Research*, **2**:70–76, 1954.

[58] A. Cobham. Priority assignment—a correction. *Operations Research*, **3**:547, 1955.

[59] E.G. Coffman and P.J. Denning. *Operating Systems Theory*. Prentice-Hall, 1973.

[60] E.G. Coffman and L. Kleinrock. Feedback queueing models for time-shared systems. *Journal of the ACM*, **15**(4):549–576, 1968.

[61] E.G. Coffman, R.R. Muntz and H. Trotter. Waiting time distributions for processor-sharing systems. *Journal of the ACM*, **17**(1):123–130, 1970.

[62] J.W. Cohen. *The Single Server Queue*. North-Holland, 1969.

[63] A.E. Conway. A perspective on the analytical performance evaluation of multilayered communication protocol architectures. *IEEE Journal on Selected Areas in Communications*, **9**(1):4–14, 1991.

[64] A.E. Conway and N.D. Georganas. A new method for computing the normalisation constant of multiple-chain queueing networks. *INFOR*, **24**(3):184–198, 1986.

[65] A.E. Conway and N.D. Georganas. *Queueing Networks: Exact Computational Algorithms*. The MIT Press, 1989.

[66] R.B. Cooper. Queues served in cyclic order: Waiting times. *The Bell System technical Journal*, **49**:399–413, 1970.

[67] R.B. Cooper and G. Murray. Queues served in cyclic order. *The Bell System Technical Journal*, **48**:675–689, 1969.

[68] J.A. Couvillion, R. Freire, R. Johnson, W.D. Obal, A. Qureshi, M. Rai, W.H. Sanders and J.E. Tvedt. Performability modelling with UltraSAN. *IEEE Software*, **8**(5):69–80, 1991.

[69] D.R. Cox. A use of complex probabilities in the theory of stochastic processes. *Proceedings of the Cambridge Philosophical Society*, **51**:313–319, 1955.

[70] A.J. Coyle, B.R. Haverkort, W. Henderson and C.E.M. Pearce. A mean-value analysis of slotted-ring network models. *Telecommunication Systems*, **6**(2):203–227, 1996.

[71] J.N. Daigle and D.M. Lucantoni. Queueing systems having phase-dependent arrival and service rates. In: W.J. Stewart (editor), *Numerical Solution of Markov Chains*, pp.161–202. Marcel Dekker Inc., 1991.

[72] P.J. Denning and J.B. Buzen. The operational analysis of queueing network models. *ACM Computing Surveys*, **10**(3):225–261, 1978.

[73] N.M. van Dijk. On a simple proof of uniformization for continuous and discrete-state continuous-time Markov chains. *Advances in Applied Probability*, **22**:749–750, 1990.

[74] N.M. van Dijk. *Queueing Networks and Product Form: A Systems Approach*. John Wiley & Sons, 1993.

[75] S. Donatelli and M. Sereno. On the product-form solution for stochastic Petri nets. In: K. Jensen (editor), *Application and Theory of Petri Nets 1992*, pp.154–172. Springer-Verlag, 1992.

[76] B.T. Doshi. Queueing systems with vacations: A survey. *Queueing Systems*, **1**(1):29–66, 1986.

[77] D.L. Eager and K.C. Sevcik. Performance bound hierarchies for queueing networks. *ACM Transactions on Computer Systems*, **1**(2):99–116, 1983.

[78] D.L. Eager and K.C. Sevcik. Bound hierarchies for multiple-class queueing networks. *Journal of the ACM*, **33**(1):179–206, 1986.

[79] P. l'Ecuyer. Efficient and portable combined random number generators. *Communications of the ACM*, **31**(6):742–774, 1988.

[80] P. l'Ecuyer. Random numbers for simulation. *Communication of the ACM*, **33**(10):85–97, 1990.

[81] S. Eilon. A simpler proof of $L = \lambda W$. *Operations Research*, **17**(5):915–916, 1969.

[82] M. Eisenberg. Two queues with changeover times. *Operations Research*, **9**:386–401, 1971.

[83] M. Eisenberg. Queues with periodic service and changeover times. *Operations Research*, **20**:440–451, 1972.

[84] A.K. Erlang. Solution of some problems in the theory of probabilities of significance in automatic telephone exchanges. *The Post Office Electrical Engineer's Journal*, **10**:189–197, 1917.

[85] R.V. Evans. Geometric distribution in some two-dimensional queueing systems. *Operations Research*, **15**:830–846, 1967.

[86] D. Everitt. Simple approximations for token rings. *IEEE Transactions on Communications*, **34**(7):719–721, 1986.

[87] W. Feller. *An Introduction to Probability Theory and its Applications*. John Wiley & Sons, 1968.

[88] M.J. Ferguson and Y.J. Aminetzah. Exact results for nonsymmetric token ring systems. *IEEE Transactions on Communications*, **33**(3):223–331, 1985.

[89] W. Fischer and K.S. Meier-Hellstern. The Markov-modulated Poisson process (MMPP) cookbook. *Performance Evaluation*, **18**:149–171, 1992.

[90] G.S. Fishman. *Principles of Discrete Event Simulation*. John Wiley & Sons, 1978.

[91] G.S. Fishman and L.R. Moore. An exhaustive analysis of multiplicative congruential random number generators with modulus $2^{31} - 1$. *SIAM Journal on Scientific and Statistical Computing*, **7**:27–45, 1986.

[92] G. Florin and S. Natkin. On open synchronized queueing networks. In: *Proceedings of the 1st International Workshop on Timed Petri Nets*, pp.226–223. IEEE Computer Society Press, 1985.

[93] G. Florin and S. Natkin. One place unbounded stochastic Petri nets: Ergodicity criteria and steady-state solution. *Journal of Systems and Software*, **1**(2):103–115, 1986.

[94] G. Florin and S. Natkin. A necessary and sufficient saturation condition for open synchronized queueing networks. In: *Proceedings of the 2nd International Workshop on Petri Nets and Performance Models*, pp.4–13. IEEE Computer Society Press, 1987.

[95] G. Florin and S. Natkin. Generalizations of queueing network product-form solutions to stochastic Petri nets. *IEEE Transactions on Software Engineering*, **17**(2):99–107, 1991.

[96] B.L. Fox and P.W. Glynn. Computing Poisson probabilities. *Communications of the ACM*, **31**(4):440–445, 1988.

[97] C. Frank. *Bewertung von stochastischen Petrinetzen mit Hilfe der Matrix-geometrischen Methode*. Master's thesis, RWTH Aachen, 1997.

[98] K.A. Frenkel. Allan L. Scherr — Big Blue's time-sharing pioneer. *Communications of the ACM*, **30**(10):824–828, 1987.

[99] V.S. Frost, W.W. Laure and K.S. Shanmugan. Efficient techniques for the simulation of computer communication networks. *IEEE Journal on Selected Areas in Communications*, **6**(1):146–157, 1988.

[100] S.W. Fuhrmann and Y.T. Wang. Mean waiting time approximations of cyclic service systems with limited service. In: P.J. Courtois and G. Latouche (editors), *Proceedings Performance '87*, pp.253–265. North-Holland, 1987.

[101] S.W. Fuhrmann and Y.T. Wang. Analysis of cyclic service systems with limited service: Bounds and approximations. *Performance Evaluation*, **9**(1):35–54, 1988.

[102] M. Fujimoto. Parallel discrete-event simulation. *Communications of the ACM*, **33**(10):35–54, 1990.

[103] R. German. New results for the analysis of deterministic and stochastic Petri nets. In: *Proceedings of the 1st International Performance and Dependability Symposium*, pp.114–123. IEEE Computer Society Press, 1995.

[104] R. German and C. Lindemann. Analysis of stochastic Petri nets by the method of supplementary variables. *Performance Evaluation*, **20**:317–335, 1994.

[105] G.H. Golub and C.F. van Loan. *Matrix Computations*. Johns Hopkins University Press, 1989.

[106] W.J. Gordon and G.J. Newell. Closed queueing systems with exponential servers. *Operations Research*, **15**:254–265, 1967.

[107] G.S. Graham. Queueing network models of computer system performance. *ACM Computing Surveys*, **10**(3):219–224, 1978.

[108] W. Grassmann. Means and variances of time averages in Markovian environments. *European Journal of Operations Research*, **31**(1):132–139, 1987.

[109] W.K. Grassmann. Transient solutions in Markovian queueing systems. *Computers and Operations Research*, 4:47–53, 1977.

[110] W.K. Grassmann. Finding transient solutions in Markovian event systems through randomization. In: W.J. Stewart (editor), *Numerical Solution of Markov Chains*, pp.357–371. Marcel Dekker, 1991.

[111] W.P. Groenendijk. Waiting-time approximations for cyclic service systems with mixed service strategies. In: M. Bonatti (editor), *Teletraffic Science for New, Cost-Effective Systems, Networks and Services*, pp.1434–1441. North-Holland, 1989.

[112] W.P. Groenendijk. *Conservation Laws in Polling Systems*. PhD thesis, University of Utrecht, 1990.

[113] D. Gross and D.R. Miller. The randomization technique as a modeling tool and solution procedure for transient Markov processes. *Operations Research*, 32(2):343–361, 1984.

[114] L. Gün and A.M. Makowski. Matrix geometric solutions for finite capacity queues with phase-type distributions. In: P.J. Courtois and G. Latouche (editors), *Proceedings Performance '87*, pp.269–282, North-Holland, 1987.

[115] J.L. Gustafson. Reevaluating Amdahl's law. *Communications of the ACM*, 31(5):532–533, 1988.

[116] A.L. Hageman and D.M. Young. *Applied Iterative Methods*. Academic Press, 1981.

[117] P.G. Harrison and N.M. Patel. *Performance Modelling of Communication Networks and Computer Architectures*. Addison-Wesley, 1992.

[118] B.R. Haverkort. Matrix-geometric solution of infinite stochastic Petri nets. In: *Proceedings of the 1st International Computer Performance and Dependability Symposium*, pp.72–81. IEEE Computer Society Press, 1995.

[119] B.R. Haverkort and A. Ost. Steady-state analysis of infinite stochastic Petri nets: A comparison between the spectral expansion and the matrix-geometric method. In: *Proceedings of the 7th International Workshop on Petri Nets and Performance Models*, pp.36–45. IEEE Computer Society Press, 1997.

[120] B.R. Haverkort. *Performability Modelling Tools, Evaluation Techniques and Applications*. PhD thesis, University of Twente, 1990.

[121] B.R. Haverkort. Approximate performability and dependability modelling using generalized stochastic Petri nets. *Performance Evaluation*, **18**:61–78, 1993.

[122] B.R. Haverkort. Approximate analysis of networks of PH|PH|1|K queues: Theory & tool support. In: H. Beilner and F. Bause (editors), *Quantitative Evaluation of Computing and Communication Systems*, Lecture Notes in Computer Science 977, pp.239–253. Springer-Verlag, 1995.

[123] B.R. Haverkort. Approximate analysis of networks of PH|PH|1|K queues with customer losses: Test results. *Annals of Operations Research*, **79**:271–291, 1998.

[124] B.R. Haverkort, H. Idzenga and B.G. Kim. Performance evaluation of threshold-based ATM cell scheduling policies under Markov-modulated Poisson traffic using stochastic Petri nets. In: D.D. Kouvatsos (editor), *Performance Modelling and Evaluation of ATM Networks*, pp.553–572. Chapman and Hall, 1995.

[125] B.R. Haverkort and I.G. Niemegeers. Performability modelling tools and techniques. *Performance Evaluation*, **25**:17–40, 1996.

[126] B.R. Haverkort and K.S. Trivedi. Specification and generation of Markov reward models. *Discrete-Event Dynamic Systems: Theory and Applications*, **3**:219–247, 1993.

[127] B.R. Haverkort, A.P.A. van Moorsel and D.-J. Speelman. Xmgm: A performance analysis tool based on matrix geometric methods. In: *Proceedings of the 2nd International Workshop on Modelling, Analysis and Simulation of Computer and Telecommunication Systems*, pp.152–157. IEEE Computer Society Press, 1994.

[128] J.P. Hayes. *Computer Architecture and Organization*. McGraw-Hill, 1988.

[129] A. Heck. *Introduction to MAPLE*. Springer-Verlag, 1993.

[130] P. Heidelberger. Fast simulation of rare events in queueing and reliability models. *ACM Transactions on Modeling and Computer Simulation*, **5**(1):43–85, 1995.

[131] G.J. Heijenk. *Connectionless Communications using the Asynchronous Transfer Mode*. PhD thesis, University of Twente, 1995.

[132] G.J. Heijenk and B.R. Haverkort. Design and evaluation of a connection management mechanism for an ATM-based connectionless service. *Distributed System Engineering Journal*, **3**(1):53–67, 1996.

[133] W. Henderson and D. Lucic. Aggregation and disaggregation through insensitivity in stochastic Petri nets. *Performance Evaluation*, **17**:91–114, 1993.

[134] W. Henderson and P.G. Taylor. Embedded processes in stochastic Petri nets. *IEEE Transactions on Software Engineering*, **17**(2):108–116, 1991.

[135] R. Hofmann, R. Klar, B. Mohr, A. Quick and M. Siegle. Distributed performance monitoring: Methods, tools and applications. *IEEE Transactions on Parallel and Distributed Systems*, **5**(6):585–598, 1994.

[136] A.S. Hornby. *Oxford Advanced Learner's Dictionary of Current English*. Oxford University Press, 1974.

[137] R. Houterman. *Wiskundige Statistiek met Toepassingen*. Course Notes 153014, University of Twente, 1992.

[138] R.A. Howard. *Dynamic probabilistic systems; Volume I: Markov models*. John Wiley & Sons, 1971.

[139] R.A. Howard. *Dynamic Probabilistic Systems; Volume II: Semi-Markov and decision processes*. John Wiley & Sons, 1971.

[140] O.C. Ibe, H. Choi and K.S. Trivedi. Performance evaluation of client-server systems. *IEEE Transactions on Parallel and Distributed Systems*, **4**(11):1217–1229, 1993.

[141] O.C. Ibe, A. Sathaye, R.C. Howe and K.S. Trivedi. Stochastic Petri net modelling of VAXcluster system availability. In: *Proceedings of the 3rd International Workshop on Petri Nets and Performance Models*, pp.112–121. IEEE Computer Society Press, 1989.

[142] O.C. Ibe and K.S. Trivedi. Stochastic Petri net models of polling systems. *IEEE Journal on Selected Areas in Communications*, **8**(9):1649–1657, 1990.

[143] J.R. Jackson. Networks of waiting lines. *Operations Research*, **5**:518–521, 1957.

[144] J.R. Jackson. Jobshop-like queueing systems. *Management Sciences*, **10**:131–142, 1963.

[145] R. Jain. *The Art of Computer System Performance Evaluation*. John Wiley & Sons, 1991.

[146] R. Jain. Performance analysis of FDDI token ring networks: Effects of parameters and guidelines for setting TTRT. *IEEE Magazine of Lightwave Telecommunication Systems*, pp.16–22, 1991.

[147] A. Jensen. Markov chains as an aid in the study of Markov processes. *Skand. Aktuarietidskrift*, **3**:87–91, 1953.

[148] K. Jensen. *Coloured Petri Nets. Basic Concept, Analysis Methods and Practical Applications (Volume 1)*. EATCS Monographs on Theoretical Computer Science. Springer-Verlag, 1992.

[149] K. Jensen. *Coloured Petri Nets. Basic Concept, Analysis Methods and Practical Applications (Volume 2)*. EATCS Monographs on Theoretical Computer Science. Springer-Verlag, 1997.

[150] W.S. Jewell. A simple proof of $L = \lambda W$. *Operations Research*, **15**(6):1109–1116, 1967.

[151] M.J. Johnson. Proof that timing requirements of the FDDI token ring protocol are satisfied. *IEEE Transactions on Communications*, **35**(6):620–625, 1987.

[152] K. Kant. *Introduction to Computer System Performance Evaluation*. McGraw-Hill, 1992.

[153] F.P. Kelly. *Reversibility and Stochastic Networks*. John Wiley & Sons, 1979.

[154] J.G. Kemeny and J.L. Snell. *Finite Markov chains*. Van Nostrand, Princeton, 1960.

[155] D.G. Kendall. Some problems in the theory of queues. *Journal of the Royal Statistical Society, Ser. B*, **13**:151–185, 1951.

[156] P.J.B. King. *Computer and Communication Systems Performance Modelling*. Prentice-Hall, 1990.

[157] J.P.C. Kleijnen and W. van Groenendaal. *Simulation: A Statistical Perspective*. John Wiley & Sons, 1992.

[158] E.F.J. Klein. *SPN2MGM: a tool for solving a class of infinite GSPN models*. Master's thesis, University of Twente, 1995.

[159] L. Kleinrock. Time-shared systems: A theoretical treatment. *Journal of the ACM*, **14**(2):242–261, 1967.

[160] L. Kleinrock. *Queueing Systems; Volume 1: Theory.* John Wiley & Sons, 1975.

[161] L. Kleinrock. *Queueing Systems; Volume 2: Computer Applications.* John Wiley & Sons, 1976.

[162] D.E. Knuth. *The Art of Computer Programming; Volume 2: Seminumerical Algorithms.* Addison-Wesley, 1981.

[163] A.G. Konheim and B. Meister. Waiting lines and times in a system with polling. *Journal of the ACM,* **21**(7):470–490, 1974.

[164] W. Krämer and M. Langenbach-Belz. Approximate formulae for the delay in the queueing system GI|G|1. In: *Proceedings of the 8th International Teletraffic Congress,* pp.235–1/8, 1976.

[165] U. Krieger, B. Müller-Clostermann and M. Sczittnick. Modelling and analysis of communication systems based on computational methods for Markov chains. *IEEE Journal on Selected Areas in Communications,* **8**(9):1630–1648, 1990.

[166] P.J. Kühn. Approximate analysis of general queueing networks by decomposition. *IEEE Transactions on Communications,* **27**(1):113–126, 1979.

[167] P.J. Kühn. Multiqueue systems with non-exhaustive cyclic service. *The Bell System Technical Journal,* **58**(3):671–698, 1979.

[168] H. Kwakernaak and R. Sivan. *Modern Signals and Systems.* Prentice-Hall, 1991.

[169] S.S. Lam. Dynamic scaling and growth behaviour of queueing network normalization constants. *Journal of the ACM,* **29**(2):492–513, 1982.

[170] S.S. Lam. A simple derivation of the MVA and LBANC algorithms from the convolution algorithm. *IEEE Transactions on Computers,* **32**(11):1062–1064, 1983.

[171] F. Lange, R. Kroeger and M. Gergeleit. JEWEL: Design and implementation of a distributed measurement system. *IEEE Transactions on Parallel and Distributed Systems,* **3**(6):657–671, 1992.

[172] G. Latouche. Algorithms for infinite Markov chains with repeating columns. In: C.D. Meyer (editor), *Linear algebra, Markov chains and queueing models,* pp.231–265. Springer-Verlag, 1993.

[173] G. Latouche and V. Ramaswami. A logarithmic reduction algorithm for quasi birth and death processes. *Journal of Applied Probability*, **30**:650–674, 1993.

[174] S.S. Lavenberg and M. Reiser. Stationary state probabilities at arrival instants for closed queueing networks with multiple types of customers. *Journal of Applied Probability*, **17**(4):1048–1061, 1980.

[175] A.L. Law and W.D. Kelton. *Simulation Modeling and Analysis*. McGraw-Hill, 1991.

[176] A.M. Law and M.G. McComas. Simulation software for communications networks: The state of the art. *IEEE Communications Magazine*, **32**(3):44–50, 1994.

[177] E.D. Lazowska, J.L. Zahorjan, G.S. Graham and K.C. Sevcik. *Quantitative System Performance: Computer system analysis using queueing network models*. Prentice-Hall, 1982.

[178] D.S. Lee and B. Sengupta. Queueing analysis of a threshold based priority scheme for ATM networks. *IEEE/ACM Transactions on Networking*, **1**(6):709–717, 1993.

[179] H. Leeb and S. Wegenkittl. Inversive and linear congruential pseudorandom number generators in empirical tests. *ACM Transactions on Modeling and Computer Simulation*, **7**(2):272–286, 1997.

[180] R. Lepold. PENPET: A new approach to performability modelling using stochastic Petri nets. In: B.R. Haverkort, I.G. Niemegeers and N.M. van Dijk (editors), *Proceedings of the First International Workshop on Performability Modelling of Computer and Communication Systems*, pp.3–17. University of Twente, 1991.

[181] H. Levy and M. Sidi. Polling systems: Applications, modeling and optimization. *IEEE Transactions on Communications*, **38**(10):1750–1760, 1990.

[182] C. Lindemann. An improved numerical algorithm for calculating steady-state solutions of deterministic and stochastic Petri net models. In: *Proceedings of the 4th International Workshop on Petri Nets and Performance Models*, pp.176–185. IEEE Computer Society Press, 1991.

[183] C. Lindemann. An improved numerical algorithm for calculating steady-state solutions of deterministic and stochastic Petri nets. *Performance Evaluation*, **18**(1):79–95, 1993.

[184] C. Lindemann. *Performance Modeling with Deterministic and Stochastic Petri Nets.* John Wiley & Sons, 1998.

[185] D.V. Lindley. The theory of queues with a single server. *Proceedings of the Cambridge Philosophical Society,* **48**:277–289, 1952.

[186] J.D.C. Little. A proof of the queueing formula $L = \lambda W$. *Operations Research,* **9**(3):383–387, 1961.

[187] D.M. Lucantoni, K.S. Meier-Hellstern and M.F. Neuts. A single-server queue with server vacations and a class of non-renewal arrival processes. *Advances in Applied Probability,* **22**:676–705, 1990.

[188] D.M. Lucantoni and V. Ramaswami. Efficient algorithms for solving the non-linear matrix equations arising in phase-type queues. *Stochastic Models,* **1**(1):29–51, 1985.

[189] V. Mainkar and K.S. Trivedi. Sufficient conditions for existence of fixed-point in stochastic reward net-based iterative models. *IEEE Transactions on Software Engineering,* **22**(9):640–653, 1996.

[190] R.A. Marie, A.L. Reibman and K.S. Trivedi. Transient analysis of acyclic Markov chains. *Performance Evaluation,* **7**:175–194, 1987.

[191] K.T. Marshall. Some inequalities in queueing. *Operations Research,* **16**(3):651–665, 1981.

[192] W.A. Massey. Open networks of queues: their algebraic structure and estimating their transient behavior. *Advances in Applied Probability,* **16**:176–201, 1984.

[193] W.L. Maxwell. On the generality of the equation $L = \lambda W$. *Operations Research,* **18**(1):172–174, 1970.

[194] R.M. Metcalfe and D.R. Boggs. Ethernet: distributed packet switching for local computer networks. *Communications of the ACM,* **19**(7):395–404, 1976.

[195] J.F. Meyer. Computation-based reliability analysis. *IEEE Transactions on Computers,* **25**(6):578–584, 1976.

[196] J.F. Meyer. On evaluating the performability of degradable computing systems. *IEEE Transactions on Computers,* **29**(8):720–731, 1980.

[197] J.F. Meyer. Closed-form solutions of performability. *IEEE Transactions on Computers*, **31**(7):648–657, 1982.

[198] J.F. Meyer. Performability: A retrospective and some pointers to the future. *Performance Evaluation*, **14**(3):139–156, 1992.

[199] J.F. Meyer. Performability evaluation: Where it is and what lies ahead. In: *Proceedings of the 1st International Performance and Dependability Symposium*, pp.334–343. IEEE Computer Society Press, 1995.

[200] J.F. Meyer, D.G. Furchtgott and L.T. Wu. Performability evaluation of the SIFT computer. *IEEE Transactions on Computers*, **29**(6):501–506, 1980.

[201] L.W. Miller and L.E. Schrage. The queue M|G|1 with the shortest remaining processing time. *Operations Research*, **14**:670–683, 1966.

[202] I. Mitrani. *Simulation Techniques for Discrete-Event Systems*. Cambridge University Press, 1982.

[203] I. Mitrani and R. Chakka. Spectral expansion solution of a class of Markov models: Application and comparison with the matrix-geometric method. *Performance Evaluation*, **23**:241–260, 1995.

[204] C. Moler and C.F. van Loan. Nineteen dubious ways to compute the exponential of a matrix. *SIAM Review*, **20**(4):801–835, 1978.

[205] M.K. Molloy. Performance analysis using stochastic Petri nets. *IEEE Transactions on Computers*, **31**(9):913–917, 1982.

[206] A.P.A. van Moorsel. *Performability Evaluation Concepts and Techniques*. PhD thesis, University of Twente, 1993.

[207] A.P.A. van Moorsel and B.R. Haverkort. Probabilistic evaluation for the analytical solution of large Markov models: Algorithms and tool support. *Microelectronics and Reliability*, **36**(6):733–755, 1996.

[208] A.P.A. van Moorsel and W.H. Sanders. Adaptive uniformization. *Stochastic Models*, **10**(3):619–648, 1994.

[209] A. Movaghar. *Performability modeling with stochastic activity networks*. PhD thesis, The University of Michigan, 1985.

[210] A. Movaghar and J.F. Meyer. Performability modelling with stochastic activity networks. In: *Proceedings of the 1984 Real-Time Systems Symposium*, pp.215–224. IEEE Computer Society Press, 1984.

[211] M. Mulazzani and K.S. Trivedi. Dependability prediction: Comparison of tools and techniques. In: *Proceedings IFAC SAFECOMP*, pp.171–178, 1986.

[212] R.R. Muntz. Queueing networks: A critique of the state of the art and directions for the future. *ACM Computing Surveys*, **10**(3):353–359, 1978.

[213] J.K. Muppala and K.S. Trivedi. Numerical transient solution of finite Markovian queueing systems. In: U. Bhat (editor), *Queueing and Related Models*. Oxford University Press, 1992.

[214] S. Natkin. *Reseaux de Petri Stochastiques*. PhD thesis, CNAM, Paris, 1980.

[215] R. Nelson. *Matrix Geometric Solutions in Markov Models: A Mathematical Tutorial*. Technical report, IBM Research Report RC 16777, 1991.

[216] R. Nelson. *Probability, stochastic processes and queueing theory*. Springer-Verlag, 1995.

[217] M.F. Neuts. *Matrix Geometric Solutions in Stochastic Models: An Algorithmic Approach*. Johns Hopkins University Press, 1981.

[218] M.F. Neuts. The caudal characteristic curve of queues. *Advances in Applied Probability*, **18**:221–254, 1986.

[219] M.F. Neuts. *Structured Stochastic Matrices of* M|G|1 *Type and Their Applications*. Marcel Dekker, 1989.

[220] V.F. Nicola, V.G. Kulkarni and K.S. Trivedi. Queueing analysis of fault-tolerant computer systems. *IEEE Transactions on Software Engineering*, **13**(3):363–375, 1987.

[221] V.F. Nicola and J.M. van Spanje. Comparative analysis of different models of checkpointing and recovery. *IEEE Transactions on Software Engineering*, **16**(8):807–821, 1990.

[222] W.D. Obal and W.H. Sanders. Importance sampling simulation in UltraSAN. *Simulation*, **62**(2):98–111, 1994.

[223] W. Oberschelp and G. Vossen. *Rechneraufbau und Rechnerstrukturen*. Oldenbourg Verlag, 1997.

[224] R.O. Onvural. Survey of closed queueing networks with blocking. *ACM Computing Surveys*, **22**(2):83–121, 1990.

[225] R.O. Onvural. *Asynchronous Transfer Mode Networks: Performance Issues*. Artech House, 1994.

[226] A. Ost, C. Frank and B.R. Haverkort. Untersuchungen zum Verbindungsmanagement bei Videoverkehr mit Matrix-geometrischen stochastischen Petrinetzen. In: K. Irmscher (editor), *Proceedings of the 9th ITG/GI Workshop on Measurement, Modeling and Evaluation of Computer System Performance*, pp.71–85. VDE Verlag, 1997.

[227] T.W. Page, S.E. Berson, W.C. Cheng and R.R. Muntz. An object-oriented modelling environment. *ACM Sigplan Notices*, **24**(10):287–296, 1989.

[228] C. Palm. Intensitätsschwankungen im Fernsprechverkehr. *Ericsson Technics*, pp.1–189, 1943.

[229] S.K. Park and K.W. Miller. Random number generators: Good ones are hard to find. *Communications of the ACM*, **31**(10):1192–1201, 1988.

[230] M. Paterok, P. Dauphin and U. Herzog. The method of moments for higher moments and the usefulness of formula manipulation systems. In: H. Beilner and F. Bause (editors), *Quantitative Evaluation of Computing and Communication Systems*, Lecture Notes in Computer Science 977, pp.56–70. Springer-Verlag, 1995.

[231] K. Pawlikowski. Steady-state simulation of queueing processes: A survey of problems and solutions. *ACM Computing Surveys*, **22**(2):123–170, 1990.

[232] C.A. Petri. *Kommunikation mit Automaten*. PhD thesis, University of Bonn, 1962.

[233] T.E. Phipps. Machine repair as a priority waiting-line problem. *Operations Research*, **9**:732–742, 1961.

[234] B. Plateau, J.-M. Fourneau and K.-H. Lee. PEPS: A package for solving complex Markov models of parallel systems. In: R. Puigjaner and D. Potier (editors), *Modelling Techniques and Tools for Computer Performance Evaluation*, pp.291–305. Plenum Press, 1990.

[235] F. Pollaczek. Über eine Aufgabe der Wahrscheinlichkeitstheorie. *Mathematisches Zeitschrift*, **32**:729–750, 1930.

[236] M.A. Qureshi and W.H. Sanders. Reward model solution methods with impulse and rate rewards: An algorithm and numerical results. *Performance Evaluation*, **20**:413–436, 1994.

[237] A. Ranganathan and S.J. Upadhyaya. Performance evaluation of rollback-recovery techniques in computer programs. *IEEE Transactions on Reliability*, **42**(2):220–226, 1993.

[238] A.L. Reibman, R. Smith and K.S. Trivedi. Markov and Markov reward models transient analysis: An overview of numerical approaches. *European Journal of Operational Research*, **4**:257–267, 1989.

[239] A.L. Reibman and K.S. Trivedi. Numerical transient analysis of Markov models. *Computers and Operations Research*, **15**(1):19–36, 1988.

[240] A.L. Reibman and K.S. Trivedi. Transient analysis of cumulative measures of Markov model behavior. *Stochastic Models*, **5**(4):683–710, 1989.

[241] M. Reiser. Numerical methods in separable queueing networks. *Studies in the Management Sciences*, **7**:113–142, 1977.

[242] M. Reiser. A queueing network analysis of computer communication networks with window flow control. *IEEE Transactions on Communications*, **27**(8):1199–1209, 1979.

[243] M. Reiser. Mean value analysis and convolution method for queue dependent servers in closed queueing networks. *Performance Evaluation*, **1**(1):7–18, 1981.

[244] M. Reiser and H. Kobayashi. Queueing networks with multiple closed chains: Theory and computational algorithms. *IBM Journal of Research and Development*, **19**:285–294, 1975.

[245] M. Reiser and S.S. Lavenberg. Mean value analysis of closed multichain queueing networks. *Journal of the ACM*, **22**(4):313–322, 1980.

[246] F.E. Ross. An overview of FDDI: the fiber-distributed data interface. *IEEE Journal on Selected Areas in Communications*, **7**(7):1043–1051, 1989.

[247] S.M. Ross. *Stochastic Processes*. John Wiley & Sons, 1983.

[248] C. Ruemmler and J. Wilkes. An introduction to disk drive modelling. *IEEE Computer*, **27**(3):17–28, 1994.

[249] R. Sahner, K.S. Trivedi and A. Puliafito. *Performance and Reliability Analysis of Computer Systems: An Example-Based Approach using the SHARPE Software Package*. Kluwer Academic Publishers, 1996.

[250] R. A. Sahner and K. S. Trivedi. A software tool for learning about stochastic models. *IEEE Transactions on Education*, **36**(1):56–61, 1993.

[251] H. Saito. *Teletraffic Technologies in ATM Networks*. Artech House, 1994.

[252] W.H. Sanders and L.M. Malhis. Dependability evaluation using composed SAN-based reward models. *Journal on Parallel and Distributed Computing*, **15**:238–254, 1992.

[253] W.H. Sanders and J.F. Meyer. Reduced-base model construction for stochastic activity networks. *IEEE Journal on Selected Areas in Communications*, **9**(1):25–36, 1991.

[254] F. Scheid. *Theory and Problems of Numerical Analysis*. McGraw-Hill, 1983.

[255] A.L. Scherr. *An analysis of time-shared computer systems*. The MIT Press, 1966.

[256] L.E. Schrage. The queue M|G|1 with feedback to lower priority queues. *Management Science*, **13**:466–474, 1967.

[257] P. Schweitzer. Approximate analysis of multichain closed queueing networks. In: *Proceedings of the International Conference on Stochastic Control and Optimization*, 1979.

[258] M. Sczittnick and B. Müller-Clostermann. MACOM—a tool for the Markovian analysis of communication systems. In: R. Puigjaner (editor), *Partipants Proceedings of the 4th International Conference on Data Communication Systems and Their Performance*, pp.456–470, 1990.

[259] K.C. Sevcik and M.J. Johnson. Cycle time properties of the FDDI token ring protocol. *IEEE Transactions on Software Engineering*, **13**(3):376–385, 1987.

[260] K.C. Sevcik and I. Mitrani. The distribution of queueing network states at input and output instants. *Journal of the ACM*, **28**(2):358–371, 1981.

[261] A. Silberschatz and P.B. Galvin. *Operating System Concepts*. Addison Wesley, 1994.

[262] E. de Souza e Silva and H.R. Gail. Calculating cumulative operational time distributions of repairable computer systems. *IEEE Transactions on Computers*, **35**(4):322–332, 1986.

[263] E. de Souza e Silva and H.R. Gail. Calculating availability and performability measures of repairable computer systems using randomization. *Journal of the ACM*, **36**(1):171–193, 1989.

[264] E. de Souza e Silva and H.R. Gail. Performability analysis of computer systems: from model specification to solution. *Performance Evaluation*, **1**:157–196, 1992.

[265] J.D. Spragins, J.L. Hammond and K. Pawlikowski. *Telecommunication Protocols and Design*. Addison Wesley, 1991.

[266] W.J. Stewart. A comparison of numerical techniques in Markov modelling. *Communications of the ACM*, **21**(2):144–252, 1978.

[267] W.J. Stewart. On the use of numerical methods for ATM models. In: H. Perros, G. Pujolle and Y. Takahashi (editors), *Modelling and Performance Evaluation of ATM Technology*, pp.375–396. North-Holland, 1993.

[268] W.J. Stewart. *Introduction to the Numerical Solution of Markov Chains*. Princeton University Press, 1994.

[269] S. Stidham. $L = \lambda W$: A discounted analogue and a new proof. *Operations Research*, **20**(6):1115–1126, 1972.

[270] S. Stidham. A last word on $L = \lambda W$. *Operations Research*, **22**(2):417–421, 1974.

[271] H. Takagi. *Analysis of Polling Models*. The MIT Press, 1986.

[272] H. Takagi. Queueing analysis of polling models. *ACM Computing Surveys*, **20**(1):5–28, 1988.

[273] H. Takagi. Queueing analysis of polling models: An update. In: H. Takagi (editor), *Stochastic Analysis of Computer and Communication Systems*, pp.267–318, North-Holland, 1990.

[274] H. Takagi. *Queueing analysis: A foundation of performance evaluation; Volume 1: Vacation and Priority Models.* North-Holland, 1991.

[275] A.S. Tanenbaum. *Structured Computer Organization.* Prentice-Hall, 1990.

[276] A.S. Tanenbaum. *Distributed Operating Systems.* Prentice-Hall, 1995.

[277] A.S. Tanenbaum. *Computer Networks.* Prentice-Hall, 1996.

[278] A.S. Tanenbaum and A.S. Woodhull. *Operating Systems: Design and Implementation.* Prentice-Hall, 1997.

[279] M. Tangemann. Mean waiting time approximations for symmetric and asymmetric polling systems with time-limited service. In: B. Walke and O. Spaniol (editors), *Messung, Modellierung und Bewertung von Rechen- und Kommunikationssystemen*, pp.143–158. Springer-Verlag, 1993.

[280] K.S. Trivedi. *Probability and Statistics with Reliability, Queueing and Computer Science Applications.* Prentice-Hall, 1982.

[281] K.S. Trivedi, J.K. Muppala, S.P. Woolet and B.R. Haverkort. Composite performance and dependability analysis. *Performance Evaluation*, **14**:197–215, 1992.

[282] D. Wagner, V. Nauomov and U. Krieger. Analysis of a finite capacity multi-server delay-loss system with a general Markovian arrival process. In: S.S. Alfa and S. Chakravarthy (editors), *Matrix-Analytic Methods in Stochastic Models.* Marcel Dekker, 1995.

[283] J. Walrand. *An Introduction to Queueing Networks.* Prentice-Hall, 1988.

[284] J. Walrand. *Communication Networks.* Aksen Associates, 1991.

[285] P.D. Welch. The statistical analysis of simulation results. In: S.S. Lavenberg (editor), *Computer Performance Modelling Handbook*, pp.267–329. Academic Press, 1993.

[286] J.A. Weststrate. *Analysis and Optimization of Polling Models.* PhD thesis, Catholic University of Brabant, 1992.

[287] W. Whitt. Performance of the queueing network analyzer. *The Bell System Technical Journal*, **62**(9):2817–2843, 1983.

[288] W. Whitt. The queueing network analyzer. *The Bell System Technical Journal*, **62**(9):2779–2815, 1983.

[289] S.S. Wilks. *Mathematical Statistics*. John Wiley & Sons, 1962.

[290] R.A. Wolff. *Stochastic Modelling and Theory of Queues*. Prentice-Hall, 1989.

[291] R.W. Wolff. Poisson arrivals see time averages. *Operations Research*, **30**(2):223–231, 1982.

[292] J.W. Wong. Queueing network modelling of computer communication networks. *ACM Computing Surveys*, **10**(3):343–351, 1978.

[293] J. Ye and S. Li. Folding algorithm: A computational method for finite QBD processes with level-dependent transitions. *IEEE Transactions on Communications*, **42**(2):625–639, 1994.

[294] J.L. Zahorjan, K.C. Sevcik, D.L. Eager and B.I. Galler. Balanced job bound analysis of queueing networks. *Communications of the ACM*, **25**(2):134–141, 1982.

# Index

Printed and bound by CPI Group (UK) Ltd, Croydon, CR0 4YY

27/10/2024

14580294-0005